Lewis Carroll Among His Books

Lewis Carroll Among His Books

*A Descriptive Catalogue
of the Private Library
of Charles L. Dodgson*

CHARLIE LOVETT

McFarland & Company, Inc., Publishers
Jefferson, North Carolina, and London

All photographs, except where otherwise noted, are from
the Lovett Collection, Winston-Salem, N.C.

LIBRARY OF CONGRESS CATALOGUING-IN-PUBLICATION DATA

Lovett, Charles C.
Lewis Carroll among his books : a descriptive catalogue of the
private library of Charles L. Dodgson / Charlie Lovett.
p.   cm.
Includes bibliographical references and index.

ISBN 0-7864-2105-3 (softcover : 50# alkaline paper)

1. Carroll, Lewis, 1832–1898 — Books and reading.
2. Carroll, Lewis, 1832–1898 — Library — Catalogs.
3. Private libraries — England — Catalogs.
I. Carroll, Lewis, 1832–1898.   II. Title.
PR4612.L47   2005   828'.809 — dc22   2005007634

British Library cataloguing data are available

Cover art ©2005 Comstock Images;
portrait of Lewis Carroll ©2005 Clipart.com

Manufactured in the United States of America

*McFarland & Company, Inc., Publishers
Box 611, Jefferson, North Carolina 28640
www.mcfarlandpub.com*

For Mark and Catherine Richards,
with hopes you won't find this
a bit Ted-in-Bed

ACKNOWLEDGMENTS

First, I must express my indebtedness to Jeffrey Stern, whose pioneering work on Charles Dodgson's library both inspired the present study and served as a guide along the way. One has only to look at my dog-eared copy of *Lewis Carroll, Bibliophile* to know how much I depended on his work.

I am grateful to all those private collectors who answered queries, provided photocopies, wrote descriptions, and allowed me into their homes to examine books, especially Mark Burstein, Selwyn Goodacre, David Lansley, Jon Lindseth, Mark and Catherine Richards, Alan Tannenbaum, and Edward Wakeling. Thanks also to Justin Schiller for providing information on Dodgson's copy of *Notes and Queries*.

Other friends provided a variety of assistance, translating titles and answering often obscure queries, and to them I am most grateful — especially to August Imholtz, Bob Lovett, Stephanie Lovett, Elizabeth Reif, and Peter Terry.

Thanks are also due to the staffs of those libraries I visited to examine copies of Dodgson's books — especially the Firestone Library of Princeton University, the Berg Collection of the New York Public Library, and the Houghton Library of Harvard University. To the unnamed thousands of cataloguers who work at the British Library, the Bodleian Library, Harvard, Yale, the University of Texas, the University of Toronto, and scores of other libraries with searchable online catalogues I owe a great debt of gratitude. Without those catalogues, the present work would have been impossible.

Special thanks go to Mark Richards, who has been a supporter, research assistant, my London secretarial staff, and above all a friend throughout the years during which this project has been underway.

Lastly, to my wonderful wife, Janice, and my daughters, Jordan and Lucy, for their patience, support and understanding during the thousands of hours I spent sequestered in my study, I shall be eternally grateful.

CONTENTS

PREFACE

As a collector of items relating to the life and work of Charles Lutwidge Dodgson — better known by his pseudonym, Lewis Carroll — I have for some time had as my goal to build a library which may be of some use to Carroll scholars. But, a few years ago, I pondered the question: How is this possible? Were I to possess limitless funds and snap up every Dodgson item to appear at auction or in a bookseller's catalogue, I would still never be able to match the completeness of collections like those formed in the past century by Morris Parrish, Harcourt Amory, and Arthur Houghton — now housed at Princeton University, Harvard University, and the Pierpont Morgan Library respectively. There are no great uncollected caches of Carroll manuscripts or vast numbers of uncounted letters or photographs. What exactly can a present-day collector — more than 100 years after Dodgson's death — provide for scholars that has not already been provided?

The answer came to me as I read over the pages of Jeffrey Stern's 1997 monograph, *Lewis Carroll, Bibliophile* (the half-title page shows a comma between "*Carroll*" and "*Bibliophile*" while the title page does not: I am using the comma), which reproduces in facsimile several early auction and bookseller catalogues describing books in Dodgson's library and which is prefaced by an essay on Dodgson as a book collector and appended by a 58-page index of books he owned. Dodgson lived in a time when there was no television, film

or radio. His hundreds of trips to the theatre can be documented, but not reproduced in any real way; the sermons he listened to, if not published, are largely lost to the world. What remains then, outside his own writings, as the single most important window into his mind? His books. What if I could invite a scholar into a room and say, "You are now surrounded by the same books that surrounded Mr. Dodgson when he worked in his rooms at Christ Church, Oxford"? It seemed an intriguing possibility, and Stern's book might provide a roadmap to building such a collection.

Although it is impossible to overstate the contribution of Stern's work to the present study, the shortcomings of that work made it obvious, as I began slowly to accumulate copies of the same books that Dodgson had accumulated, that a more in-depth study was desperately needed. Stern describes himself, in his excellent prefatory essay, as a literary "archeologist" who has provided us with the relics of Dodgson's mind for further study. Careful analysis of his work makes an extension of this analogy possible. Stern has provided us with photographs of the excavation and a hodgepodge of bones, some labeled, some unlabeled, some incorrectly labeled. Others are missing altogether. The present study endeavors to correctly label and assemble these bones to give a clear and complete (to the extent possible) picture of the books that Dodgson read and owned, with some insight, or at least speculation, into their influence on him.

Stern's book provides facsimiles of six important early sources for recreating Dodgson's library (discussed individually below). Unlike his 1981 monograph *Lewis Carroll's Library*, which presented primary source material with no index, *Lewis Carroll, Bibliophile* adds a numbered list of 2231 items that Stern has identified in the primary sources. The list is alphabetized by author, and represents a great step forward. Unfortunately the index is plagued by errors, inconsistencies, omissions, and other problems. For instance, 373 items in the index (or about 17 percent) are listed as "Anonymous." The present study identifies authors for 255 (almost 70 percent) of these works. Stern's index includes over 50 entries that are duplicates of others and at least 15 entries that list more than one title. Some items are unnumbered; others split a book between two entries. Many author attributions are incorrect; many more are misspelled and still others are simply not listed in correct alphabetical order. Some items in the primary sources are not listed in the index at all.

Stern's index is also frustrating in the individual entries' lack of depth. In all but a few cases, only author and title are given — no edition, no description of the book's contents, no attempt to evaluate the importance of the book in its field or to place it in the context of Dodgson's life and work. Stern makes a strong argument that Dodgson was not just a book accumulator but a book collector, but that argument is strengthened when one looks not just at the titles he owned, but at the editions — his shelves contained first editions of important books in many fields.

So, though Stern's work was clearly valuable, it was as clearly flawed and incomplete. What was needed, I felt, was a true catalogue of Carroll's library that, to the extent possible, fully described each book, its edition, its contents, its importance, and any particular relevance it might have to Dodgson. Obviously this last category would be further developed by future scholars, but I longed to give them (and myself as a collector) the proper tools to delve into Dodgson's mind through his books. Thus the present study was born.

In spite of the fact that Dodgson's library was quickly dispersed after his death on 14 January 1898, primarily through an auction that took place in Oxford beginning on 10 May 1898, we are blessed with a wealth of primary source material in attempting to create a catalogue of the books he read and owned. That phrase "read and owned" is key here, for I have included in this catalogue any book which evidence indicates that Dodgson read, even if there is no evidence he owned a copy and even if we can only prove that he read part of it. In attempting to delve into the man's mind, the books that he read are key. He probably, after all, owned many books that he never read, and many of these are listed below; that he did *not* own some books he *did* read is no reason to exclude them. In fact, because of the practice of the auctioneer of lotting up groups of undescribed books at the May 10 auction, we can never know for sure that Dodgson did *not* own a particular book.

I have chosen to exclude one category of books included by Stern: books by Charles Dodgson himself. That he read and owned his own works is self-evident, and these works have been thoroughly catalogued and described elsewhere.

Sources

Stern's study uses six primary sources to identify books in Dodgson's library; the present study adds others. A detailed look at each source will provide an understanding of how this catalogue was built.

1. Dodgson's own writings, including his diaries and letters. This is an important source untapped by Stern. Especially in his early years of diary keeping, Dodgson made frequent mention of books he read, and many titles not listed in other sources are mentioned here and in his letters. Passing references to books which give no indication if he owned or read them are not included. Dodgson's published works, too, provide some clues. Books which Dodgson reviewed or from which he quoted at length in his published works are included here, even if they do not appear in any other source.

2. *Catalogue of the Personal Effects and ... Library of Books ... of the Late Rev. C. L. Dodgson ... More Widely Known as "Lewis Carroll," ... Which will be Sold at Auction by Mr. E. J. Brooks At the Holywell Music Room, Oxford, on Tuesday, May 10th and the following days....* (Hereinafter cited as *Brooks Catalogue*; referenced as 'A'.) The most important single source, as it includes so many of the books that were in Dodgson's library at the time of his death. Family members may have removed some books before the sale. Though no disbursements of books are listed in Wilfred Dodgson's reconciliation of expenses for his brother's estate — a reckoning that does include other items taken by family members— Dodgson did leave instructions that his nephew, Bertram Collingwood, be given any medical books he wanted. Of course, Dodgson probably owned and read many books during his life that were not on his shelves at the time of his death. Most of his books were sold on the second day of the sale (May 11), but more than 30 books, included with Dodgson's collection of artworks, were sold on the first day, and many of these are mysteriously absent from Stern's index. Excluding copies of Dodgson's own works (49 volumes) the *Brooks Catalogue* describes 1545 titles in 2711 volumes, and these titles form the core

of the present catalogue. Unfortunately, there are nearly as many items listed in the Brooks Catalogue as merely "others" or "bundle of books." If we guess that about ten books would equal a bundle, the Brooks sale might have included 1518 volumes not described in the sale catalogue. How many different titles these volumes represent is impossible to say. When Brooks writes "7 others," does he mean 7 other volumes or 7 other titles? We can only guess, then, at the total number of titles Dodgson owned at the time of his death, but a little over 4200 volumes representing about 2500 titles seems likely. The total number of titles could be over 3000, especially as Dodgson owned at least a few volumes that were bound collections of separately published sermons, pamphlets, etc.

3. *Catalogue of Miscellaneous Second-Hand Books, Chiefly in the various departments of Literature indexed below; to which is added by way of appendix a considerable number from the library of the late Rev. C. L. Dodgson ("Lewis Carroll"), M.A., of Christ Church, Oxon. On Sale by H. H. Blackwell ... Oxford.* (Hereinafter cited as *Blackwell Catalogue*; referenced as 'B'.) The *Blackwell Catalogue* was issued in June 1898, the month following the Brooks sale. Clearly Blackwell, a leading Oxford bookseller, bought heavily at the sale. The catalogue lists 359 items as "from the Library of the late Rev. C. L. Dodgson," and describes them much more fully than the Brooks Catalogue.

4. *Catalogue of Theological Books, English and Foreign ... Being Purchases from the Libraries of the late Dr. Sparrow Simpson, The Rev. R. J. Wilson, the Rev. C. L. Dodgson of Christ Church and Others* (James Parker, August 1898). (Hereinafter cited as *August Parker Catalogue*; referenced as 'C'.) Stern does not reproduce this catalogue in facsimile, but does list 10 items (3 of which are bound volumes of

pamphlets containing a total of 35 separate titles, most of which are not listed in Stern's index). I have retained Stern's numbering of these items. Stern lists only those items which, he says, do not appear in the *October Parker Catalogue* (see item 5 below).

5. *A Catalogue of Second-Hand Books and Books Reduced in Price Consisting of Part I.— A. Works by the late Rev. C. L. Dodgson (Lewis Carroll). Part I.— B. Purchases from the Library of the late Rev. C. L. Dodgson (many with his autograph) ... Offered at the Affixed Nett Prices for Cash, By Messrs. James Parker and Co., 27 Broad-Street, Oxford.* (Hereinafter cited as *October Parker Catalogue*; referenced as 'D'.) This catalogue was issued in October 1898 and includes 248 items listed as "Books from the Library of the late Rev. C. L. Dodgson." The books are well described, but unfortunately not numbered, making indexing more difficult. Stern assigns numbers "in sequence" in his index, but following his sequence has proved difficult. The present references do no correlate with Stern's, but do correlate with a careful sequential numbering of each separately priced item in this catalogue, beginning with Part I.— B.

6. *Catalogue of a Portion of the Unique Collection Formed by the late "Lewis Carroll" (The Rev. C. Lutwidge Dodgson, M.A., Student of Christ Church, Oxford).* (Oxford: The Art and Antique Agency, 1898.) (Hereinafter cited as *Art and Antique Catalogue*; referenced as 'E'.) This catalogue contains 429 numbered items (most of them books) plus another 46 lots, many of them books but some drawings, cards, photographs, etc. An additional 16 lots of "Fancy Dress Used by Lewis Carroll's Child Friends" is also included. The books are generally well described.

7. *Catalogue of Valuable Books and Manuscripts Ancient and Modern Including ... Books from the Library of "Lewis Car-* *roll." ... Which Will be Sold by Auction ... on Thursday 4th of December, 1902, and Five Following Days.* (London: Sotheby, Wilkinson, & Hodge.) (Hereinafter cited as *Sotheby's 1902 Catalogue*; referenced as 'F'.) This is the early source that has caused the most debate and misunderstanding among scholars. The catalogue was discovered by Selwyn Goodacre and printed in facsimile with an introductory note by him in *Jabberwocky— The Journal of the Lewis Carroll Society*, vol. 16, no. 2 (Winter/Spring, 1987). In a letter to the editor of *Jabberwocky*, vol. 17, nos. 3–4 (Summer/Autumn, 1988), Stern wrote of his suspicions about the *Sotheby's 1902 Catalogue*. Stern found a strong correlation between the Sotheby's list and the *Art and Antique Catalogue*, leading him to conclude that the Art and Antique Agency were probably the consignors. Stern's concern was with books only identified as Dodgson's by a "name stamp" and not appearing in any other source. He felt it likely that at least some of these items were not actually from Dodgson's library and that the stamp did not originate with Dodgson. Stern says in the introduction to his index that he will not list, with a separate number, books that appear only in the *Sotheby's 1902 Catalogue*; however, in several cases he does just this. He also lists, without a number, items from the *Sotheby's 1902 Catalogue* that contain evidence of ownership besides the stamp. For a full analysis of the stamp, and more on this source, see below. The present study includes all the items from the *Sotheby's 1902 Catalogue*; those identified only by the name stamp or with no identifying markings are designated "uncertain."

8. Later auction and booksellers catalogues. *Dodgson at Auction* (compiled by David Carlson and Jeffrey Eger, Somerville, NJ: D & D Galleries, 1999, cited as **DAA**) lists most relevant entries from twentieth century auction catalogues.

Auction and bookseller catalogues (and online listings) are otherwise cited individually. This is another source largely overlooked by Stern. One major source in this area is the 1930s manuscript listing of London bookseller Walter Spencer, described in more detail below.

9. Extant copies. Stern does describe some extant copies, but he personally examined only a few and completely neglects collections at Princeton University, the New York Public Library, the University of Texas at Austin, and the Pierpont Morgan Library. He also did not personally examine the major collection at Harvard University.

The Gothic Stamp and the Property Label

Many items extant from Dodgson's collections (not just books but some non–Dodgson photographs as well) are marked in one of two ways. The first is the "gothic stamp," already mentioned in connection with the *Sotheby's 1902 Catalogue* above. This is a name stamp measuring approximately 1.5 inches by .25 inches, almost always printed in purple ink and printed in gothic lettering reading "Charles L. Dodgson." The second is a white paper label of varying size (clearly the labels were printed on imperforated paper from which they were then cut) but with the text block occupying approximately 1 inch by .2 inches, printed in blue

and reading "This was the property / of LEWIS CARROLL." Both these marks present something of a mystery.

Stern is right to be suspicious of the gothic stamp in connection with the *Sotheby's 1902 Catalogue*— of the 72 lots, 60 make some mention of the name stamp, and 39 offer no evidence of ownership other than this stamp. Stern guesses that the name stamp was applied to make books more saleable, and notes that "in none of the other catalogues as reprinted in *Lewis Carroll's Library* is there any mention of a rubber stamp." Stern's proposed solution — that someone at Sotheby's or the Art and Antique Agency made up a rubber stamp and then applied it to books from Dodgson's library and, quite likely, some not from Dodgson's library — seems to fit the evidence he cites, but unfortunately the problem is not that easily disposed of.

First of all, Stern is wrong; a stamp is mentioned in another early catalogue. The *Art and Antique Catalogue* lists three books in three separate lots that note the presence of a name stamp. Lot 27 (*Der Schwarze Peter*, #2115) notes, "with the stamped name and initials of Lewis Carroll inside cover"; lot 66 (*Automatic Arithmetic*, #1769) notes, "with the stamp of Lewis Carroll inside cover"; and lot 132 (*Rational Medicine*, #2339) notes "with the stamp of Lewis Carroll's name." True, the Art and Antique Agency are among the suspects for creating a bogus stamp, but if it had been created by this time, why

Charles L. Dodgson

**Rev. E. H. Dodgson,
All Saints,
Shrewsbury.**

The gothic stamp bearing Charles Dodgson's name (left) and the matching stamp of his brother, E. H. Dodgson. (E. H. Dodgson stamp courtesy of Alan Tannenbaum.)

wouldn't they have applied it to all their stock, not just to three books out of several hundred?

New evidence indicates that the name stamp almost certainly originated in Dodgson's lifetime, but that he used it only rarely — as Stern points out, it was not his style. A copy of John James Blunt's *Undesigned Coincidences* (#187) in the collection of Alan Tannenbaum contains a vital clue about the gothic stamp. Charles Dodgson's ownership inscription is inside the front cover and below it a gothic stamp reading "Rev. E. H. Dodgson / All Saints / Shrewsbury." The stamp is identical in design to the "Charles L. Dodgson" gothic stamp — the same typeface and size, even the same purple ink. It is inconceivable that this could be a coincidence. Clearly the "Charles L. Dodgson" stamp and the "E. H. Dodgson" stamp originated from the same source. Edwin Heron Dodgson, Lewis Carroll's youngest brother, was a priest in the Church of England who served for much of his career as a missionary in places as far flung as Zanzibar and Tristan d'Acunha. According to parish records, he was a curate at All Saints Shrewsbury for only about six months in 1880, but Dodgson's diary indicates that he also worked in that parish in late 1878 prior to his departure for Zanzibar in March 1879.

So it does appear that the gothic stamp originated in Dodgson's lifetime, probably between 1878 and 1880. The stamp was placed in a few of Dodgson's books during his lifetime, probably around this same time (2 of the 3 books described as stamped in the *Arts and Antique Catalogue* were dated 1878 and the other was printed in 1870), though whether by him or by someone else one cannot say with certainty.

Another problem is presented by the Walter Spencer list, mentioned briefly above. Spencer was a London bookseller with premises at 27 New Oxford Street. He did not issue catalogues, but he did compile manuscript lists of items for sale to collectors. In the early to mid–1930s Walter Spencer sent a series of these descriptions of Carroll items for sale to American collector Warren Weaver. Weaver bought a number of items from Spencer, and those items, including some books from Dodgson's library, now reside in his collection at the University of Texas at Austin. Walter Spencer's manuscript lists are in the collection of the author and are cited in many cases below. The most interesting list, for the purposes of the present study, is one that begins with the following description:

> A wooden box height 18 inches Long 26 inches, wide 13 inches with 2 iron handles on each side and with his initials C. L. D. painted in white on each side. This was purchased, with the contents, by me at the sale of his effects at Oxford about 30 years ago.
>
> The following is a list of the contents. All the books etc., have a little printed ticket stuck on them as follows "This was the property of Lewis Carroll."

The list that follows includes 41 books plus several other items. What is remarkable about this document is that 27 of the books are described as having the "Charles L. Dodgson" name stamp. Yet these books, according to Spencer, came directly from the Brooks sale to this dealer's stock and did not pass through either the Art and Antique Agency or Sotheby's.

A closer look reveals what is probably a mistake in Spencer's memory (it had, after all, been over 30 years since the Brooks sale). Of the 41 books in Spencer's

This was the property
of LEWIS CARROLL

The Property Label.

Lewis Carroll Among His Books: A Descriptive Catalogue of the Private Library of Charles L. Dodgson

Charlie Lovett

383 pages $49.95 softcover (7 x 10)
Photographs, bibliography, indexes
ISBN 0-7864-2105-3 2005

Charles Lutwidge Dodgson—known better by his pseudonym, Lewis Carroll—was a 19th century English logician, mathematician, photographer, and novelist. He is especially remembered for his children's tale *Alice's Adventures in Wonderland* and its sequel, *Through the Looking Glass*. By the time of Dodgson's death in 1898, *Alice* (the integration of the two volumes) had become the most popular children's book in England. By the time of his centenary in 1932, it was perhaps the most famous in the world.

This book presents a complete catalogue of Dodgson's personal library, with attention to every book the author is known to have owned or read. Alphabetized entries fully describe each book, its edition, its contents, its importance, and any particular relevance it might have had to Dodgson. The library not only provides a plethora of fodder for further study on Dodgson, but also reflects the Victorian world of the second half of the 19th century, a time of unprecedented investigation, experimentation, invention, and imagination. Dodgson's volumes represent a vast array of academic interests from Victorian England and beyond, including homeopathic medicine, spiritualism, astrology, evolution, women's rights, children's literature, linguistics, theology, eugenics, and many others. The catalogue is designed for scholars seeking insight into the mind of Charles Dodgson through his books.

Charlie Lovett lives in Winston-Salem, North Carolina.

McFarland

Enclosed please find:

Lovett. **Lewis Carroll Among His Books**

Publication date: Available Now
Price: $49.95

This book is sent to you:

____ with the compliments of the author/publisher.

____ for examination.

____ as your desk copy, with our compliments.

 XX for review. We ask that you include our website
      address (**www.mcfarlandpub.com**) and our order
      line (**800-253-2187**) in any review. **Send one copy**
      of your published review, preferably via e-mail as
      a PDF file (or a link for online reviews), to
      bcox@mcfarlandpub.com. Alternately, publications
      and tear sheets can be mailed to Beth Cox,
      McFarland, Box 611, Jefferson NC 28640.

www.mcfarlandpub.com
orders 800-253-2187

list, 16 appeared previously in the *Art and Antique Catalogue*, 5 in the *Sotheby's 1902 Catalogue*, and 3 in both. Some of those 19 appear in earlier sources, but all passed through either the Art and Antique Agency or Sotheby's; hence Spencer could not have bought them at the Brooks sale.

	Extant Copies	Other Recorded Copies	All Copies
In *Sotheby's 1902*	13	71	84
In *Art and Antiques*	15	43	58
In Both	6	39	45
In Other Early Sources	18	21	39
Uncertain	9	36	45
TOTAL	38	81	119

Twenty-two are not listed in any source reprinted by Stern. Might Spencer be mixing up the two sales, Brooks and Sotheby's, in his memory? Perhaps Spencer actually bought these items at the Sotheby's 1902 sale where Stern suspects the Art and Antique Agency was the primary consignor. And what of the 22 items not listed in the *Sotheby's 1902 Catalogue*? These could simply be from the many lots that end in the designation "and others." This is a convenient solution, but surely not the only one, and it still leaves open the problem of whether to trust as authentic items identified only by the gothic stamp and not listed in any early source.

To get a fuller view of the gothic stamp a census of books with this stamp is helpful. The table below shows (for both extant copies and other recorded copies) the number of stamped items listed in the *Sotheby's 1902 Catalogue*, the number listed in the *Art and Antique Catalogue*, the number listed in other early sources or with other positive evidence of ownership, and the number for which ownership is claimed only by the presence of the gothic stamp without other evidence ("uncertain"). This table accounts only for books from Dodgson's library not by him, and does not include unnamed "other" items in the *Sotheby's 1902 Catalogue*. Copies of Dodgson's own books and even some photographs have been recorded with the stamp, but these can all be accounted for in the *Sotheby's 1902 Catalogue*.

Again we see a preponderance of ev-

idence to support Stern's claim that the gothic-stamped items all passed through either the Art and Antique Agency or Sotheby's. The majority of extant items (97 of 119) with the stamp are listed in one of those two catalogues; those which aren't could have been part of larger Sotheby's lots. However, if the Art and Antique Agency was the only consignor, why are there items with the gothic stamp, as well as items in the *Sotheby's 1902 Catalogue*, that are not listed in the *Art and Antique Catalogue* (more than half of the total)? Some of these items bear markings by Dodgson that clearly prove them authentic. It seems odd that, in a listing of over 400 items, the Art and Antique Agency would have left items uncatalogued. Might they have purchased them from other buyers (or from the unsold lots) after their initial catalogue was issued and included these lots in the Sotheby's consignment? Or did Sotheby's recruit other consignors to add items to the sale?

Whatever the answer, a majority of items with the stamp (both extant and otherwise) can be positively proved to have passed through the Art and Antique Agency, Sotheby's, or both; hence Stern is no doubt right in guessing that the large-scale stamping of books probably originated in one of these two places, or perhaps when the books moved from one location to the other. The stamp itself, as argued above, is clearly a relic from Dodgson himself. To what extent, however, can it be trusted as a mark of his books? Of 119 recorded stamped books, 74 have a provenance or other markings proving their authenticity. Certainly the stamp was applied to many books that were from Dodgson's library; whether it was applied to books not from Dodgson's library is entirely speculative. Might the plot have been not devious, as seen by Stern, but innocent? Might the Art and Antique Agency, faced with a large stock of books from Dodgson's library, have discovered a way to mark those books that bore no identifying mark — a way that even had the advantage of being somewhat authentic, since the stamp originated from Dodgson? Without further evidence, these questions must remain unanswered.

If the gothic stamp seems to come from the Art and Antique/Sotheby's transaction, the property label is even more closely linked to this partnership. Of the 17 extant books bearing the label, 9 are listed in the *Art and Antique Catalogue*, 5 in the *Sotheby's 1902 Catalogue*, and only 5 in neither. What is especially noteworthy about the property label is that it is present on every item in the Walter Spencer list. Barring an astonishing coincidence, this must indicate that the label originated wherever Spencer bought the books — which his memory to the contrary notwithstanding, was clearly at the 1902 Sotheby's sale. There are extant items from this sale without the label, but perhaps the labels were provided for buyers who wished to identify their purchases.

Dodgson's Book-Register

Stern writes, "It is virtually inconceivable that [Dodgson] had not prepared his own library catalogue." We know that Dodgson maintained a complex register of his correspondence — he describes it in his pamphlet *8 or 9 Wise Words About Letter-Writing*. No published source, however, gives any indication that he kept a similar record of his library. Unlike many Victorians, he did not place any kind of numbering or shelf marking on the books themselves (at least none has been seen on any extant books from his library), but did he keep some sort of book catalogue?

A previously unpublished letter, transcribed by Walter Spencer in one of the lists he sent to Warren Weaver, offers a tantalizing hint. The letter is to Wallace Hay Laverty (1847–1928), a fellow and mathematical lecturer at the Queen's College, Oxford, from 1869–1873 (see *Cohen* p. 303–4). Dated March 8, 1881, the letter reads, in part:

> Dear Laverty,
> Thanks for "Bledsoe." But for having a book-register I might have lost sight of it, but, as it was, I had my eye on you, & should have dunned you for it in the course of time.

Clearly Dodgson had loaned Laverty a copy of Albert Taylor Bledsoe's *The Philosophy of Mathematics* (#182) and Laverty returned it. So Dodgson did have a book register. What exactly was its nature? It may have been merely a log of books borrowed and loaned, or it could have been a complete listing of his library. Sadly, it seems to have perished along with the other personal papers that were burned en masse following his death.

The only document we have that gives a clue as to Dodgson's organization of his library is the *Brooks Catalogue* — there we see like books grouped together as might be expected if they were catalogued as they were pulled off the shelf. Not much can be read into the organizational scheme of Brooks, however, as there is no way of knowing if this is Brooks' own scheme or Dodgson's.

One thing should be mentioned about Stern's analysis of the number of titles in various categories. Stern writes, for instance, that he has identified 711 works of literature owned by Dodgson but only 305 works of theology. Did Dodgson own twice as much literature as theology? There is a problem in Stern's methodology, for he is basing his list only on identified titles. If we look, for instance, at four consecutive pages of the *Brooks Catalogue*, we begin to see the problem. Pages 38–39 contain mostly theological works; these pages contain 144 items listed as merely "others." Many of these probably remain unidentified. The next two pages, 40–41, list mostly literature and the number of "other" items is only 36. Throughout the *Brooks Catalogue*, literature is described in more detail than many other categories. Hence, it becomes difficult to put exact, or even approximate, numbers on any one genre of books.

Dodgson as Bookseller

It has been well documented that Dodgson was an enthusiastic buyer of books, but, in some cases at least, he sold books as well. He apparently had a relationship with the Oxford bookseller W. H. Gee that allowed trade to go both ways. According to an 1876 guide, W. H. Gee had premises at number 28 Amsterdam Court (a narrow passage just off the High Street, now demolished and part of Brasenose College). In his lists to Warren Weaver, Walter Spencer summarizes several letters from Dodgson to Gee over a period of nearly ten years. On 8 March 1881, Dodgson, writing in the third person, "sends a list of books with prices to Mr. Gee." On 8 Nov. 1889 he writes "asking Mr. Gee to examine a set of Punch for him." On 26 June 1890 Dodgson writes "about some books [he] wishes to sell." A letter of 26 June 1890 is mentioned only briefly, but Dodgson's letter of 15 July 1890 is "about some books [probably *Ingoldsby Legends*] which he wanted to buy back as he thought they may be 1st editions and which Mr.

Gee had already sold." Was Dodgson merely selling off duplicates that had accumulated in his library (as they do for all collectors), or was he raising money to feed his book buying habit by selling books that no longer interested him? And what of his attempt to re-purchase a book after he discovered it might be a first edition? Clearly Dodgson thought not just like a reader, but like a book collector.

The Library

What do we make of Dodgson's library? Certainly it reflects a multi-faceted mind and provides a plethora of fodder for further study. But this library reflects not just Dodgson, but the Victorian world. It can be viewed not only as the library of the man who wrote *Alice in Wonderland*, but as a representative sampling of the books owned by any educated Victorian. It is a glimpse into the remarkable world of the second half of the nineteenth century, a time of unprecedented investigation, experimentation, invention, and imagination.

It was a time when the world as it had been known for several centuries was called into question at every level, and those questions were posed in the pages of the books Dodgson read. New views of the church, education, science, women's rights, medicine, and scores of other issues crowded for attention. It was also an incredibly fertile time for creativity and a time in which literature was nearly as popular as television is now. In terms of the percentage of a nation who read a single author, Dickens and Tennyson still stand perhaps without rival. It was a changed world; it would have been unrecognizable to many who lived only two or three generations earlier. Set a man from the mid-eighteenth century down in 1875, and he might well have been forced to believe, like the White Queen, "six impossible things before breakfast." It was a smaller world, thanks to the combination of industrial revolution and the expansion of the empire. Stories from every corner of the earth rested on Dodgson's shelves, something that would have been far less likely in his grandfather's library. This Victorian world was reflected in all its aspects on the shelves of libraries like Dodgson's, and while a careful examination of his books can grant us new insights into the author of *Alice*, it can also shed light on his contemporaries and their world.

Even a generation before, it would have been difficult for a man of relatively modest means to build a significant private library. The private libraries of previous centuries resided in stately homes and were built by succeeding generations of aristocrats. But with revolutions in mass production and an increase in literacy rates, books became cheaper, and even those of more modest means could build libraries. Dodgson was in a slightly better position to buy books than some Oxford dons because of the income he received from his own publications. The present catalogue represents what is probably the first generation of a non-aristocratic college man's library.

Dodgson's library, not surprisingly, has a strong collection of books in his own field — mathematics and logic. His collection of children's books, too, might be considered as related to his profession. But together, these represent only a small part of the whole. The collection shows Dodgson as a man with an open mind, and in this sense he followed the prevailing winds — Victorian England in general seems to be an open mind, waiting for possibilities to become reality. He owned books dealing with the major controversies of his day, but, whatever his own opinion, he usually had at least some writings from every side of an issue.

The Oxford Movement, a movement within the Church of England that favored a more ritualistic approach to worship, is well represented. Dodgson owned some of his father's High Church writings, as well as many important works by leaders of the movement; he also owned many volumes that reflected his own somewhat broader views, as well as those that opposed the Tractarians with an Evangelical stance. The size and scope of his collection of books on religion and theology should force scholars to take a closer look at what was, for Dodgson, the most important aspect of his life — his faith. Another fact generally overlooked by scholars is that the religious books in Dodgson's library were by no means limited to Christianity. He owned works on comparative religion, a copy of the Koran, and books on Buddhism (including one on Esoteric Buddhism by an early Theosophist) and Mormonism. A deeply faithful Anglican, he nonetheless seems to have had a knowledge of other faiths as well.

The great clash between science and religion is well documented on Dodgson's shelves. Darwin and his supporters, along with many important works on animal intelligence, evolution, and related topics, appear alongside works challenging the new views Darwinism pressed onto the world and those which strove to reconcile the new science with the old religion. But Dodgson's interest in science does not end here; from amateurs' guides to natural history to important books on many aspects of science, Dodgson's scientific library reveals him as a man passionately interested in the world around him.

Dodgson's open-mindedness also led him into areas that, by today's standards, seem on the far fringes of what we would expect to occupy an educated man but, in Victorian England, were far more mainstream. Homœopathic medicine, spiritualism, magic, and astrology all find a place on his shelves. Much has previously been made of Dodgson as a collector of medical books, but with scant mention of the strong homœopathic slant of his collection. His collection of works related to spiritualism and supernatural phenomena was significant, and his interest in this area is certainly ripe for further investigation. He owned a number of works on women's rights by important early feminists and suffragettes. Certainly the image of Dodgson, which still turns up in the popular press, as a stodgy don stuck in the ways of old Oxford is belied by his library.

Some sections of the library add shadings to already well documented sides of his character. His manipulation of language in the *Alice* books, for instance, is legendary — and his collection of dictionaries, lexicons, and instruction books in several modern and ancient languages reveals a man who carefully studied linguistics. His taste in art, leaning to the Pre-Raphaelite, is well known, but his collection of illustrated books provides more depth of insight. The collection runs the gamut from volumes documenting exhibitions at the Royal Academy to books illustrated by Joseph Noël Paton, Frederick Leighton, Linley Sambourne, Richard Doyle, Arthur Hughes, and other important Victorian artists. He seems to have made a conscious effort to collect certain illustrators such as Alice Havers and Eleanor Vere Boyle. Many of the children's books on his shelves might have been as interesting to him for their illustrations as for their text.

Not surprisingly, Dodgson's library is strong in works of literature, especially by those giants of the Victorian world, Dickens and Tennyson. Other major Victorian figures, especially Ruskin, are, as expected, well represented. His passion for the theatre is represented by published editions of plays, biographies of actors, periodicals, and works on theatre history, the circus, and other aspects of performing. But some topics may seem more surprising to the casual student of Dodgson. Books on politics and the Irish question stood alongside books on true crime, sociology (including a landmark study of the London poor), gypsies, espionage, slavery and race in the American South, the law, and many other topics.

Then there are the books, and groups of books, that reinforce our view of Dodgson as a true book collector. His collection of miniature books published in the Pickering Diamond Classics series is a prime example, but there are many others; again and again, this catalogue describes books that would have been collectors' items when first acquired by Dodgson.

It is dangerous to draw too many conclusions from the presence of a particular book. All of us, after all, probably own many books that we have not read or that reflect a view radically different from our own. Books arrive as gifts or are left behind by visitors, and are subsumed into our own collections. Likewise, because many volumes remain unidentified, we cannot prove that any particular title was absent from the collection. But, when patterns emerge based on title after title, we are led to a better understanding of just how revolutionary Dodgson's thinking could be. Time and again we see important early books on various subjects on his shelves. Their importance is matched only by their variety; in addition to noteworthy works in the many fields mention above, Dodgson owned significant early works in fields as varied as science fiction, eugenics, philosophy, color theory, and education.

The Catalogue

The purpose of this catalogue is to present as full a picture as possible of the books Dodgson read and owned. As previously noted, any book he mentions having read is listed regardless of whether it is included in any of the early catalogues.

There are a few difficult categories of books to deal with.

First are those that are identified only by the "gothic stamp" and are not listed in any early catalogue, or those identified by the "gothic stamp" and listed only in the *Sotheby's 1902 Catalogue*. Are these legitimate? Stern thinks not, but it is impossible to say with any degree of certainty. The number of items in the *Sotheby's 1902 Catalogue* that are described as with the name stamp and which also do not appear in any other early source is only 33, against 85 items that either do appear in other early catalogues or that have other identifying marks such as signatures or presentations. Of course many items listed as "others" could be added to this total. Of these 33, 5 are sixteenth and seventeenth century books included in a small group of such volumes that includes 3 items making no mention of any markings. These seem far and away the most suspicious. All questionable books, including those identified only by the gothic stamp, are included here and designated "uncertain." One hopes that in the future the legitimacy of these books' presence on the list can be either confirmed or rejected.

Next, there are some books described in early catalogues but not sufficiently described to distinguish them from similar titles. In these cases, an entry has been made with the most likely candidates listed, in hopes that the appropriate title can someday be identified.

Finally, a few entries in the early catalogues are cryptic in the extreme and do not seem to correlate to any title traced. These items are listed in the section of "Mystery Books" at the end of the catalogue, in hopes that they may one day be properly identified.

Where Dodgson owned multiple copies of the same book, these copies are not generally listed in separate entries. The exception is if separate editions that are

significantly different have been identified or there is a change in the title. Books published in series by the same author and under the same title are generally listed in a single entry; in cases where there is a significant change in title, these books may be listed separately.

Not listed here are items that cannot be called reading materials. These include single maps (atlases *are* included) and some other small ephemera listed by Stern. Unpublished items (of which Stern lists a small number) are also not listed.

There are some items not included here that nonetheless rightly fall under the category of Dodgson's reading material. Copies of Dodgson's own publications are not listed, as it seems self-evident that he read his own works and they are thoroughly described elsewhere (see especially WMGC). Although copies of periodicals recorded in his library at the time of his death are listed, no attempt has been made at a thorough study of the periodicals Dodgson read. *Lewis Carroll and the Press* gives some insight into this, as it lists Dodgson's own contributions to periodicals, and we might guess that he read papers and magazines to which he contributed. Another source, in addition to mentions in his diaries, letters and published works, is the listing (in *Oxford*) of papers taken by the Christ Church Common Room, of which Dodgson was a member and sometime curator. Dodgson was a great writer of sqibs and short papers on various subjects which he circulated around Oxford. Doubtless he read many similar papers by other Oxford commentators, but little record of these has survived. Listed here are only those that we know, from evidence, that Dodgson read or owned. The Berg Collection, New York Public Library, has a collection of leaflets and broadsides on the proposed new examination statute of 1864 (on which Dodgson wrote two papers; see items 2 and

3 in *Oxford*). Although they are listed as "owned by Dodgson" in the Berg catalogue, there are no markings or evidence to support this assertion. Nonetheless, it seems likely that Dodgson read many of the papers in question. Still, without firm evidence, such papers are not listed here. Finally, no attempt has been made to list publications connected to Dodgson only through his parodying of them. This has been done fairly thoroughly elsewhere (see, for instance, *The Annotated Alice*), and proving that Dodgson owned (or even read) a book on the basis of his parodying a well-known poem or passage is problematic.

The entries in the catalogue list: the author, along with his or her dates; the full title; the city, publisher, and date of publication; number of volumes; number of pages (generally given as simply the last numbered page); illustrator, translator or other pertinent information; and series. This information is given in the first paragraph of each entry. Information that proved untraceable has been omitted without comment. When it has been possible to determine the precise edition Dodgson owned (as is often the case), that edition is described. Otherwise, the first or earliest traced edition is listed, except in cases where it seems highly unlikely that Dodgson would have owned a first. In some cases the edition described simply seems the most likely one for Dodgson to own,

and in these cases reasoning is given in the second paragraph.

The second paragraph of an entry includes the source(s) in which the item is found (the source that provides the most complete information is described in some detail, telling what information is listed there); the Stern number (if there is one); a description of markings on Dodgson's copy (if known); a brief note on the edition; a brief note on the author; a brief note on the contents of the book; and a brief note (where applicable) on any significant connection between Dodgson and the author, the book, or its contents. This last category could take up a large volume in itself, and not all connections are described in full. Information on the author and contents is not given in cases where the book is well known to most readers or in cases where such information proved unavailable. Contents are not described if they are self-evident from the title. Books of special interest are described in greater detail than more ordinary volumes.

Dodgson's world was a world of books. Those he wrote have been examined and analyzed by scholars for over a century. Those he read he would have viewed as equally important in shaping his character. To everyone fascinated by that character and the world it inhabited, this catalogue is presented.

ABBREVIATIONS FOR WORKS CITED

A–F See preface for details of these citations of auction and bookseller catalogues.

AAIW Carroll, Lewis. *Alice's Adventures in Wonderland*. London: Macmillan, 1865.

AAUG Carroll, Lewis. *Alice's Adventures Under Ground Being a Facsimile of the Original MS. Book Afterwards Developed into "Alice's Adventures in Wonderland."* London: Macmillan, 1886.

Alice on Stage Lovett, Charles C. *Alice on Stage: A History of the Early Theatrical Productions of Alice's Adventures in Wonderland*. Westport, CT: Meckler, 1990.

Allibone Allibone, Samuel. *A Critical Dictionary of English Literature and British and American Authors, Living and Deceased, etc.* Philadelphia: Lippincott, 1881. Plus supplement to same (1891).

Berg The Henry W. and Albert A. Berg Collection of English and American Literature, New York Public Library.

BL Online catalogue of the British Library, London.

BNF Online Catalogue of the Bibliothèque Nationale Française, Paris.

BOD OLIS, Online catalogue of holdings in the Bodleian and nearly 100 other Oxford libraries.

Brabant Moore, Alice, and Richard Landon. *All in the Golden Afternoon: The Inventions of Lewis Carroll. An Exhibition Selected from the Joseph Brabant Collection.* Toronto: Thomas Fisher Rare Book Library, University of Toronto, 1999.

CHEL Ousby, Ian, editor. *Cambridge History of English Literature*. Cambridge: Cambridge University Press, 1988.

CHEAL *Cambridge History of English and American Literature*, online edition. New York: bartleby.com, 2000.

Cohen Cohen, Morton. *Lewis Carroll: A Biography*. New York: Alfred A. Knopf. 1995.

Collingwood Collingwood, Stuart Dodgson. *The Life and Letters of Lewis Carroll*. London: Unwin, 1899.

DAA Carlson, David, and Jeffrey Eger. *Dodgson at Auction 1893–1999*. Somerville, NJ: D & D Galleries, 1999.

DEL Adams, William Davenport. *Dictionary of English Literature, Being a Comprehensive Guide to English Authors and Their Works*. London: Cassell, Petter & Galpin, [1878].

Diaries Green, Roger Lancelyn, editor. *The Diaries of Lewis Carroll*. London: Cassell, 1953.

***Diary 1,* etc.** Wakeling, Edward, editor. *Lewis Carroll's Diaries: The Private Journals of Charles Lutwidge Dodgson.* Vols. 1–7. London: Lewis Carroll Society, 1993–2003.

DNB *Dictionary of National Biography.* Oxford: Oxford University Press, 1920.

HAC Collection of Harcourt Amory, now housed at the Houghton Library, Harvard University.

Illustrators Cohen, Morton, and Edward Wakeling, editors. *Lewis Carroll and His Illustrators: Collaborations and Correspondence, 1865–1898.* Ithaca: Cornell University Press, 2003.

In Memoriam Imholtz, August, and Charlie Lovett. *In Memoriam: Charles Lutwidge Dodgson 1832–1898. Obituaries of Lewis Carroll and Related Pieces.* New York: Lewis Carroll Society of North America, 1998.

JS Stern, Jeffrey. *Lewis Carroll Bibliophile.* London: White Stone, 1997.

LC Online Catalogue of the Library of Congress, Washington, D.C.

LCA Lovett, Charles C., and Stephanie B. Lovett. *Lewis Carroll's Alice: An Annotated Checklist of the Lovett Collection.* Westport, CT: Meckler, 1990.

LCE Lovett, Charlie. *Lewis Carroll's England: An Illustrated Guide for the Literary Tourist.* London: White Stone, 1998.

LCP Lovett, Charlie. *Lewis Carroll and the Press: An Annotated Bibliography of Charles Dodgson's Contributions to Periodicals.* New Castle, DE: Oak Knoll Press, 1999.

Letters Cohen, Morton, editor. *The Letters of Lewis Carroll.* New York: Oxford University Press, 1979.

Livingston Livingston, Flora V. *The Harcourt Amory Collection of Lewis Carroll in the Harvard College Library.* Cambridge, MA: Privately printed, 1932.

Macmillan Cohen, Morton, and Anita Gandolfo, editors. *Lewis Carroll and the House of Macmillan.* Cambridge: Cambridge University Press, 1987.

Math Abeles, Francine, editor. *The Mathematical Pamphlets of Charles Lutwidge Dodgson and Related Pieces.* New York: Lewis Carroll Society of North America, 1994.

MBE *A Bibliographical Catalogue of Macmillan and Co.'s Publications from 1843 to 1889.* London: Macmillan and Co., 1891.

MOR Ward, Thomas Humphrey, editor. *Men of the Reign: A Biographical Dictionary of Eminent Persons of British and Colonial Birth Who Have Died During the Reign of Queen Victoria.* London: Routledge, 1885.

MOT Cooper, Thompson, editor. *Men of the Time: A Dictionary of Contemporaries, Containing Biographical Notices of Eminent Characters of Both Sexes.* 10th edition. London: Routledge, 1879.

NUC *National Union Catalogue, Pre-1956 Imprints.*

OCCL Carpenter, Humphrey, and Mari Prichard. *The Oxford Companion to Children's Literature.* Oxford: Oxford University Press, 1984.

OCEL Harvey, Paul. *The Oxford Companion to English Literature.* Oxford: 4th edition. Oxford University Press, 1969.

OCIL Welch, Robert. *Oxford Companion to Irish Literature.* Oxford: Clarendon Press, 1996.

ODCC Cross, F. L., and E. A. Livingstone. *The Oxford Dictionary of the Christian Church.* 3rd edition. Oxford: Oxford University Press, 1997.

Osborne   St. John, Judith. *The Osborne Collection of Early Children's Books 1566–1910: A Catalogue.* Toronto: Toronto Public Library, 1975.

Oxford   Wakeling, Edward, ed. *The Oxford Pamphlets, Leaflets and Circulars of Charles Lutwidge Dodgson.* Charlottesville VA: Lewis Carroll Society of North America, 1993.

Parrish   Collection of Morris Parrish, now housed at the Firestone Library, Princeton University.

PCL   *Penguin Companion to Literature.* Harmondsworth: Penguin, 1969–71.

Political   Abeles, Francine, editor. *The Political Pamphlets and Letters of Charles Lutwidge Dodgson and Related Pieces: A Mathematical Approach.* New York: Lewis Carroll Society of North America, 2001.

S & B   Spiller, Robert Ernest, and Philip Conklin Blackburn. *A Descriptive Bibliography of the Writings of James Fenimore Cooper.* New York: Franklin, 1968.

Snark   Carroll, Lewis. *The Hunting of the Snark.* London: Macmillan, 1876.

W & M   Williams, Sidney Herbert, and Falconer Madan. *A Handbook of the Literature of the Rev. C. L. Dodgson (Lewis Carroll).* Oxford: Oxford University Press, 1931.

WMGC   Williams, Sidney Herbert, Falconer Madan, Roger Lancelyn Green, and Denis Crutch. *The Lewis Carroll Handbook.* Hamden, CT: Archon Books, 1979.

WS   Manuscript listings of London bookseller Walter Smith (ca. 1930s) in the collection of the author.

WWC   Collection of Warren Weaver, now housed at the Harry Ransom Humanities Research Center, University of Texas at Austin.

THE CATALOGUE

1. [**Abbott**, Edwin Abbott] (1838–1926). *Flatland A Romance of Many Dimensions.* (London: Seeley & Co., 1884). 102pp. Illustrations by the author.

A574 (title), JS1. 1st edition. BL lists 2 editions in 1884 and no others before 1898. Abbott was a clergyman who wrote theological works, a Shakespearean grammar, and a biography of Bacon. He served as headmaster of the City of London School. A humorous tale of a two-dimensional land, *Flatland* was a highly influential early science fiction work. It includes social satire (especially with reference to the education of women), an imagination of a one-dimensional world (Lineland), and a glimpse into the three-dimensional world through the character of Sphere.

2. **Abbott**, Edwin A[bbott]. *Philomythus An Antidote Against Credulity, A Discussion of Cardinal Newman's Essay on Ecclesiastical Miracles.* (London: Macmillan, 1891). 259pp.

A792 (author, title misspelled), JS2 (repeats misspelling). 1st edition (BL lists a 2nd of the same date). A refutation of John Henry Newman's defense of miracles in *The Miracles of Ecclesiastical History Compared with those of Scripture, as Regards their Nature, Credibility and Evidence.*

3. [**Á Beckett**, Arthur William] (1844–1909), editor. *The Tomahawk: A Saturday Journal of Satire.* (London: 11 May 1867–27 August 1870). Nos. 1–173? Bound in 6 vols.

A729 (title, 6 vols.), JS217 (Anon./Periodicals). A729 does not specify numbers (1–173 were apparently all that were published). BL incorrectly gives the editor as Gilbert Arthur A'Beckett. MOT states, of Á Beckett, that at 23 he undertook "the editorship of the *Tomahawk*, a paper which he himself originated. At the outset the policy of this periodical was decided by the staff, and, during the first twelve numbers, two cartoons appeared which were considered disloyal, but as soon as Mr. Á Beckett had complete editorial control the tone of the paper became thoroughly loyal." The magazine was probably best known for its two-page cartoons by Matt Morgan. Printed in two colors, the cartoons were controversial enough to draw several libel suits, one of which put *The Tomahawk* out of business.

4. **A'Beckett**, Gilbert A[bbott] (1811–56). *Hop o' My Thumb.* (London: W.S. Orr & Co., 1844). Illustrated by [Alfred] Crowquill with 9 lithographic plates plus wood engravings. In the *Comic Nursery Tales* series.

A483 (series, title, publisher), JS53 (Anon./Children's). 1st edition. A'Beckett was a playwright whose best-known dramas were his adaptations (with Mark Lemon) of works by Dickens. He was also an early contributor to *Punch*. See 505 for a note on Crowquill. This work is a fairy story, originally found in Perrault, about seven brothers who are abandoned by their poor parents and eventually return home after tricking an ogre out of his wealth.

5. **Abney**, William de Wiveleslie (1843–1920). *Instruction in Photography.* (London: Piper & Carter, 1876). 196pp. 3rd edition.

E388 (author, title, date), JS3. Abney was editor, from 1881 to 1894, of the *Journal of the Photographic Society.* Dodgson was a keen amateur photographer who used the collodion wet-plate process. He gave up photography about 1880.

6. **Ackermann**, R[udolph] (1764–1834), publisher. *Ghost Stories Collected with a*

Particular View to Counteract the Vulgar Belief in Ghosts and Apparitions and to Promote a Rational Estimate of the Nature of Phenomena Commonly Considered as Super-natural. (London: Ackermann's Repository of Arts, 1823). 292pp. Illustrated with 6 coloured engravings.

A488, D76 (title, city, publisher, date), JS119 (Anon./Literature). Rudolph Ackermann was a German-born printer who published over 300 books through his "Repository of Arts." The artists here are uncredited, but Ackermann employed many leading painters of the day as illustrators. A collection of 18 ghost stories, only one of which is attributed to an author ("The Green Mantle of Venice" by H. Clauren). As the purpose of the book, stated in the preface, is to "counteract the belief in Ghosts and Spectres, and to prevent the pernicious consequences arising from the fear of them," each of the stories ends with a twist which provides a plausible explanation for seemingly supernatural events.

7. Acland, Henry W. (1815–1900). *The Plains of Troy.* (Oxford: J. Wyatt, 1839). Illustrated by a panoramic drawing taken on the spot, and by a map constructed after the latest survey.

Not in JS. Dodgson's copy is in Berg and has the gothic stamp on the front pastedown. Minor pencil notations and markings on 21 pages appear to be in Dodgson's hand. Acland was one of the most respected physicians of his era and Regius Professor of Medicine at Oxford. Largely through his effort the University [Natural History] Museum was established at Oxford. This was his first book, published when he was only 24. It is dedicated to Thomas Gaisford, Dean of Christ Church from 1831 to 1855. Most of his later works were related to medicine, science, and sanitation, a field close to Acland's heart. Dodgson met Acland in 1856, and mentions him several times in his diary.

8. Acton, William (1813–75). *Prostitution Considered in its Moral, Social, and Sanitary Aspects, in London and Other Large Cities. With Proposals for the Mitigation and Prevention of its Attendant Evils.* (London: John Churchill, 1857). 189pp.

A538 (author, title), JS4. Earliest edition in BL. Acton was a London doctor whose specialty was female venereal disease. The most in-depth study of prostitution at the time and a classic in its field. In 1885 Dodgson wrote an article, "Whoso Shall Offend one of These Little Ones—," for the *St. James's Gazette* in which he objected to the explicitness of another exposé of prostitution, the controversial series of articles by Thomas Stead published in the *Pall Mall Gazette* under the title "The Maiden Tribute of Modern Babylon" (see LCP, #243).

9. Adams, H[enry] G[ardiner] (1811?–81). *Nests and Eggs of Familiar Birds Described and Illustrated with an Account of the Haunts and Habits of the Feathered Architects, and Their Times and Modes of Building.* (London: Groombridge and Sons, 1854). 78pp. With plates.

A853 (author, title), JS6. Earliest edition in BL, but later editions may be more likely as they were much expanded. The 1871 edition of 238pp. with 16 color plates of eggs was reprinted in 1876 and 1880. The text in the 1871 edition makes it clear that this version, at least, was intended to include children in its audience. "To my young readers" begins the work, which then goes on to describe basic terms of ornithology.

10. Adams, W[illiam] (1814–48). *Sacred Allegories. The Shadow of the Cross. The Distant Hills. The Old Man's Home. The King's Messengers.* (London: F. & J. Rivington, 1844). 385pp.

A932 (author, title), JS7. Earliest edition traced. Adams was a fellow of Merton College, Oxford and held a small church living in Oxford. "Shadow of the Cross" and "The Distant Hills," which include explanatory dialogues after each section, are meant "to impress upon the minds of children of the Church, first, the blessedness of the position in which they are placed by holy baptism; secondly, the danger they incur, from their earliest years, of forfeiting that blessedness by giving way to temptation; and, thirdly, the fearful extent to which that danger may be increased by unrepented sin." "The Old Man's Home," "was written with the view of bringing out strongly the realities of the unseen world." "The King's Messengers" focuses on a single Christian duty, the need for sympathy for the poor, and "the allegorical meaning lies so completely on the surface, that the youngest child cannot fail to apprehend it."

11. Adams, W[illiam], and H[enry] C[adwallader] Adams (1817–99). *Tales of Charlton School; The Cherry Stones, The First of June.* (London: Routledge, Warne, and Routledge, 1862). In one volume. 143pp; 158pp. Illustrated by [John] Absolon. *The Cherry Stones*, by William Adams, is 7th edition. *The First of June*, by H. C. Adams, is 5th edition.

A932 (title "Tales of Charlton School"), JS80 (Anon./Children's). Earliest edition traced under this title. *The Cherry Stones* was first published separately (London: F. & J. Rivington, 1851). The earliest edition of *The First of June; or, Schoolboy Rivalry: A Second Tale of Charlton School* recorded in BL is also a separate edition (London: Rivingtons, 1856). The first title was published "partly from the manuscript of William Adams." H. C. Adams was William's younger brother. He received his B.A. from Magdalen College, Oxford and was vicar of Old Shoreham, Sussex. *The Cherry Stones* is a school story centering on Harry Mertoun, who steals cherries from the squire's grounds and later feels remorse and is haunted by the stones. *The First of June* is another story set at Charlton School.

12. Adams, William Davenport (1851–1904), editor. *The Comic Poets of the Nineteenth Century: Poems of Wit and Humour by Living Writers.* (London: George Routledge and Sons, Limited, [1876]). 400pp.

A843 (title), JS111 (Anon./Literature). Earliest edition in BL. Adams was the son of William Henry Davenport Adams (see 14). This book includes the following poems by Dodgson: "The Walrus and the Carpenter," "Jabberwocky," "Ye Carpette Knyghte," "The Whiting and the Snail," "Father William," and "Atalanta in Camden Town." On p. 379 a long note identifies the original appearances of the poems and the originals of which some of the poems are parodies. It also quotes Humpty Dumpty's explication of "Jabberwocky." An early reprinting of the poems and the excerpt from TTLG.

13. Adams, William Davenport. *Dictionary of English Literature, Being a Comprehensive Guide to English Authors and Their Works.* (London: Cassell, Petter & Galpin, [1878]). 708pp.

A579, D1 (author, title, city, n.d.), JS8. Earliest undated edition in BL. Encyclopedic listing of thousands of authors and works from English literature. The undated 3rd edition identifies Lewis Carroll as "C. Lutwidge Dodgson" and includes a separate entry for AAIW, which it calls "a fairy story for the young."

14. Adams, William Henry Davenport (1828–91). *Dwellers on the Threshold, or Magic and Magicians. With Some Illustrations of Human Error and Imposture.* (London: J. Maxwell & Co., 1864). 2 vols.

A903 (author, title), JS5. Only edition in BL. Adams was a journalist whose miscellaneous writings, translations, and adaptations number over 100. *Saturday Review* wrote of him, "He is by no means an unfavourable specimen of the average book-maker. He has read a good deal in his way, but digested little or nothing."

15. Adams, W[illiam] H[enry] D[avenport]. *Woman's Work and Worth in Girlhood, Maidenhood, and Wifehood. Illustrations of Woman's Character, Duties, Influence, &c. With Hints on Self-culture, and Chapters on the Higher Education and Employment of Women.* (London: John Hogg, 1880). 551pp.

D230 (author, title, city, date), JS9. Adams wrote several works on women. This volume includes chapters on woman as mother, as wife, as maiden, in the world of letters, in the world of art, as the heroine, as enthusiast and social reformer; the higher education of women; and employment for educated women. Quoting frequently from other sources the author has "sought to present a comprehensive view of the achievements, responsibilities, and influence of Woman."

16. Addison, Joseph (1672–1719), Richard Steele (1672–1729), and others. *The Spectator, with Sketches of the Lives of the Authors and Explanatory Notes.* (Edinburgh: Bell and Bradfute, 1816). 8 vols.

A325, B1241 (title, city, 8 vols., date), JS10. This it the only edition traced that matches the description in B1241. Originally issued from 1711 to 1712 and revived in 1714, *The Spectator* was a daily paper compiled principally by Addison and Steele. According to OCEL, "the papers are mainly concerned with manners, morals, and literature. Their object is 'to enliven morality with wit and to temper wit with morality'."

17. Adeler, Max [pseud. of Charles Heber Clarke] (1841–1915). *Out of the Hurly-Burly; or, Life in an Odd Corner.* (London: Routledge & Sons, 1874). 345pp. Illustrated by Arthur B. Frost and others.

Not in JS. In a letter of 7 February 1878 to Arthur Frost, who eventually illustrated Dodgson's *Rhyme and Reason?* and *A Tangled Tale*, Dodgson wrote, "I had quite forgotten your name in connection with *Out of the Hurly-Burly*. You will be surprised to hear that I know the book well, and examined the pictures carefully, more than a year ago, to see if the Artist would be likely to suit me." Dodgson concluded that the artist would not suit, and sent the book to Tenniel whose review of the pictures was not glowing (see *Illustrators*, 41–42). Earliest edition in BL, which also lists an undated edition of 1874 published by Ward, Lock & Tyler. Clarke was a reporter for the *Philadelphia Inquirer*. A comic novel about life in an American village. With upwards of 400 illustrations by Frost and others. The first book for both Clarke and Frost.

18. Adon [pseud. of Henry Frederick Traill] (1838–1905). *Through Storm and Sunshine.* (London: H. S. King & Co., 1875). 126pp. With illustrations by H. Paterson and the author.

A842 (title, pseudonym), JS11. Only edition in BL. Poems.

19. Aesop (ca. 6th century B.C.E.). *Some of Æsop's Fables, with Modern Instances.* (London: Macmillan, 1883). 79pp. Translated by Alfred Caldecott. "Shewn in Designs by Randolph Caldecott."

A532 (title, illustrator), J12. Alfred Caldecott (1850–1941) was the brother of the great illustrator Randolph Caldecott. See below for a note on Randolph.

20. Aikin, Anna Laetitia [afterwards Mrs. Barbauld] (1743–1825). *Poems.* (London: Joseph Johnson, 1777). 5th edition, corrected. 138pp.

D3 (author, title, edition, city, date), JS13. Anna Barbauld was a popular author of children's books, particularly moral tales. This was her first book, published under her maiden name, and went through 4 editions in a year. See 101–102 for more books by Aikin.

21. Aitken, M[ary] C[arlyle] (1848–95). *Scottish Song. A Selection of the Choicest Lyrics of Scotland, Compiled and Arranged, with Brief Notes by M. C. Aitken.* (London: Macmillan, 1874). 308pp. In the *Golden Treasury* series.

A844, E294 (title, author, date), F166, JS14, JS133 (Anon./Literature). F166 notes the gothic stamp. *The Spectator* wrote of this book, "Miss Aitken, it need scarcely be said, has retained nothing which is unfitted for general reading, and her book is one that should delight everybody." Dodgson ordered the book from Macmillan on 22 August 1886. On 15 January 1888, he wrote Macmillan to "point out a serious omission in your Book of Scottish Song. It provides no means for finding a song of which the *title* only is known."

22. [Alexander], C[ecil] F[rances] H[umphreys] (1818–95). *Hymns for Little Children.* (London: Joseph Masters, 1848). 72pp. With a prefatory note by J[ohn] K[eble].

E120 (title, date), JS507 (listed under Bibles, Prayer and Hymn Books). The work reached its 500th thousand in 1876. Cecil Frances Humphreys was born in Ireland about 1830 and married William Alexander, Bishop of Derry (see 25). She wrote and edited books of poetry (primarily moral and religious) for children.

23. Alexander, C[ecil] F[rances], [Humphreys], editor. *The Sunday Book of Poetry.* (London: Macmillan and Co., 1882). 314pp. In the *Golden Treasury* series.

A844, E51 (editor, title, date), JS15. E51 notes this has Dodgson's initials. Originally published in 1854. A collection of sacred poetry for children. On 21 March 1887, Dodgson wrote to Macmillan, "I have some corrections for your *Sunday Book of Poetry*, when you reprint it." Macmillan replied that they would appreciate his corrections as a new edition was about to be printed. He duly sent them on 23 March (see *Macmillan*, 223–24). Presumably, then, the 1887 edition includes corrections by Dodgson.

24. Alexander, E[dward] P[orter] (1835–1910). *Catterel Ratterel (Doggerel).* (New York and London: G. P. Putnam's Sons, 1890). 39pp. Illustrated by Bessie Alexander Ficklen.

E55 (author, illustrator), F182, JS1018 (listed

The hero of E. P. Alexander's *Catter Ratterel (Doggerel)* (item 24) reads Darwin and Herbert Spencer. Illustration by Bessie Alexander Ficklin.

under Ficklen). F182 notes the gothic stamp. A verse interpretation of Darwinism, told from the point of view of a rat. Alexander was an American graduate of West Point military academy who fought on the Confederate side during the Civil War.

25. Alexander, William (1824–1911). *Specimens, Poetical and Critical.* (London: Printed for Private Circulation, 1867). 207pp.

D4, E168 (title, author, "Printed for Private Circulation," date), JS16. Alexander was successively Bishop of Derry and Raphoe and Archbishop of Armagh.

26. Alford, Henry (1810–71), editor. *The Greek Testament: With a Critically Revised Text and a Critical and Exegetical Commentary.* (London, Cambridge: Deighton, Bell, & Co., 1859–71). 3rd edition. 4 vols.

A777 (title, editor, 5 vols.), mentioned in JS but not numbered. BL lists no 5-volume edition, but a copy of the 1859–71 edition has been catalogued by FineArt, Haywards Heath, UK, and described as 4 vols. bound in 5, thus this seems a likely choice. Alford was a churchman whose theological work was interspersed with

art, poetry, and magazine editing. He had parishes in Leicestershire and London and was made Dean of Canterbury in 1857. This is a monumental work and Alford's most important publication. For the first time English readers had access to a meticulous collation of all the important biblical manuscripts. Alford's emphasis was not theological, but philological in nature, and that fact made this book somewhat revolutionary.

27. Alford, Henry, editor. *The Greek Testament: With a Critically Revised Text and a Critical and Exegetical Commentary. Volume 1: The Four Gospels.* (1892).

A765, B942 (author, title, date), mentioned in JS but not numbered. Not in BL. See note above.

28. Alford, Henry. *The Queen's English: Stray Notes on Speaking and Spelling.* (London: Strahan & Co.; Cambridge: Deighton, Bell & Co., 1864 [1863]). 1st edition. 257pp.

A301, D5 (author, title, city, date), JS17. 2nd edition was also 1864, but the title changed to *A Plea for the Queen's English.* Wanders over a

Gertrude Thomson's illustration of fairies from William Allingham's poem (item 31).

wide array of topics relating to usage in English.

29. Alford, Henry. *The State of the Blessed Dead*. (London: Hodder & Stoughton, 1869). 100pp.

E249 (title, author, date), JS18. E249 notes this has Dodgson's initials. A series of sermons preached at Canterbury.

30. Alger, William R[ounceville] (1822–1905). *A Critical History of the Doctrines of a Future Life*. (Philadelphia: George W. Childs, 1864). 913pp.

A804 (author, title), JS19. Earliest edition traced. Alger was born in Freetown, MA, and attended Harvard and Cambridge Divinity School before becoming a Unitarian pastor. The book has particular interest for its bibliography of more than 5000 items.

31. Allingham, William (1824–89). *The Fairies. A Child's Song*. (London: Thos. De

la Rue & Co., [1883]). 24pp. Illustrated by Gertrude Thomson (including 6 full-page illustrations in color).

A542, E54 (author, title, illustrator), F183, F184, JS21, JS2070. F183 and F184 note the gothic stamp. 2 copies in HAC with gothic stamp. Allingham was an Irish-born poet and served as editor of *Fraser's Magazine* from 1874 to 79. He was a close friend of D. G. Rossetti, and an admirer of the Pre-Raphaelites. Thomson was a close friend of Dodgson. She provided the colored cover illustration for his *Nursery Alice* and illustrated his 1898 collection *Three Sunsets and Other Poems*. She also wrote a long reminiscence of Dodgson after his death (see *In Memoriam*). This illustrated poem is thought to be her first book. Her pictures are Pre-Raphaelite in style. Dodgson met Thomson in 1879 and visited her often in London. The two took excursions to the Royal Academy and the theatre (Dodgson's last trip to the theatre was with Miss Thomson). He was a great admirer of her artwork, particularly her fairy drawings, and once arranged for Ruskin to meet with her when he was preparing to lecture on illustrations of Fairyland. After he gave up photography in 1880, Dodgson would occasionally visit Thomson in her studio where the two would draw young girls together. In his diary for 16 November 1891, Dodgson wrote that he planned to send a copy of this book to Princess Alice, daughter of the Duchess of Albany, whom he saw that day at the Christ Church Deanery (see DAA3188), and he presented copies to other friends as well. See *Illustrators* for several mentions of this book in Dodgson's correspondence with Thomson (including his advice to her on keeping the title in print).

32. Allingham, William. *The Music Master, A Love Story; and Two Series of Day and Night Songs.* (London: G. Routledge & Co., 1855). 221pp. 9 woodcuts by Dante Gabriel Rossetti, John E. Millais, and Arthur Hughes.

A449 (author, title, illustrators, date), JS20. See 1708 and 1351 for notes on Rossetti and Millais. Arthur Hughes (1832–1915) was a Pre-Raphaelite painter and illustrator much admired by Dodgson who owned one of his paintings ("The Lady with the Lilacs"). Dodgson met Hughes at least as early as 21 July 1863 and on many occasions thereafter. He photographed both Hughes and his children. The present title was a tremendously influential illustrated book of poetry, credited with the revival of English book illustration and with introducing Edward Burne-Jones and William Morris (then undergraduates at Oxford) to D. G. Rossetti.

33. [Allyn, Avery]. *A Ritual and Illustrations of Free-masonry: and the Orange and Odd Fellows' Societies Accompanied by Numerous Engravings and a Key to the Phi Beta Kappa; also an Account of the Kidnapping and Murder of William Morgan.* (Devon: S. Thorne, 1851). 259pp. Abridged from American authors; by a traveler in the United States. With plates.

B1052 (title, date), JS90 (Anon./History). Avery wrote *A Ritual and Illustrations of Free-masonry Accompanied by Numerous Engravings and a Key to the Phi Beta Kappa* (published at least as early as 1805); other sections may be by other, anonymous, authors. The plates illustrate the rituals of freemasonry. William Morgan was the author of a book that revealed many secrets of freemasonry. He was abducted by masons on 12 September 1826, and never seen again. Presumably he was murdered by being thrown into the Niagara River, bound with weights.

34. Anacreon. *The Odes of Anacreon.* (London: J. C. Hotten, [1871]). 225pp. Translated by Thomas Moore. With 54 illustrations by [Anne Louis] Girodet de Roussy (called Girodet-Trison).

A539 (title, illustrator), JS22. Only English edition illustrated by Girodet in BL. Anacreon was a Greek lyric poet of the 6th–5th century B.C.E. who wrote of wine and women. See 1387 for a note on Thomas Moore. The introduction says of the illustrations, "Seldom indeed have chasteness of execution and voluptuousness of character been so curiously and indissolubly blended." A blend of ancient Greek and 19th-century European sensibilities, the illustrations, with their innocent depiction of the human figure, would certainly have appealed to Dodgson.

35. Andersen, Hans Christian (1805–75). *Little Thumb. A Fairy Story.* (London: Mansell & Co., [1883]). 10 double-page spreads. Translated by Miss [Caroline] Peachey, etc. Illustrated by Laura [Elizabeth Rachel] Troubridge.

A277, E72 (author, title, illustrator), JS23. Only Troubridge edition in BL. Troubridge was a great letter writer and diarist and her published journals and letters give marvelous insight into Victorian life. She illustrated several books, worked as a portrait painter, and married Adrian Hope (with whom she carried on a long, now published correspondence). The story of a girl the size of a human thumb. A lovely over-sized book. Troubridge's 10 full-page line drawings have a taste of the Pre-Raphaelite and are reminiscent of Gertrude Thomson's fairy drawings in Carroll's *Three Sunsets and Other Poems* and elsewhere. In September 1893, Dodgson gave Thomson a copy of this book (see *Illustrators*). A presentation copy of the book from Dodgson to his child friend Empsie Bowman, was offered at Maggs of London in 1930.

36. Andersen, Hans Christian. *The Story of the Mermaiden.* (London: Griffith, Far-

Illustration of Hans Christian Andersen's *Little Thumb* by Laura Troubridge (item 35).

ran & Co., 1888). 47pp. Adapted into verse from the German of Hans Andersen by E. Ashe. Illustrated by Laura Troubridge.

Not in JS. On 5 March 1894, Dodgson wrote to his publisher Macmillan extolling the virtues of Laura Troubridge, with whom he had lately become acquainted. After mentioning *Little Thumb* (see above) he writes, "Another is *The Little Mermaiden*: that does not give so good an idea of her skill, as she has drawn the pictures twice over, and the published book is not the best set. The best set appeared in some Magazine [*English Illustrated Magazine*]." In the same letter Dodgson recommended Troubridge's unpublished pictures for *The Queen of Hearts* (Macmillan agreed to look at the pictures but did not publish them).

37. Andersen, Hans Christian. *The White Swans and Other Tales*. (London: Hildesheimer & Faulkner, [1885]). 48pp. Translated by Mrs. H. B. Paull. Illustrated by Alice Havers.

Not in JS. In his diary for 11 December 1885, Dodgson writes, "Heard from Miss Alice Havers (to whom I had written about her lovely illustrations to *The White Swans*)." He apparently loaned the book to E. Gertrude Thomson, for he asked for its return in a letter of 21 January 1894. Only edition traced. See 880 for a note on Havers.

38. Andrews, William (1848–1908). *Curiosities of the Church: Studies of Curious Customs, Services, and Records*. (London: Methuen & Co., 1890). 202pp.

A795 (author, title), JS25. Earliest edition in BL. Andrews was a writer on historical subjects and produced a series of books on "Bygone" English counties. Reviewers wrote of this book, "Contains in popular and readable form much that is curious and instructive," and "Mr. Andrews is always chatty and expert in making a paper on a dry subject exceedingly readable."

39. Angus, Joseph (1816–1902). *The Bible Hand-book: An Introduction to the Study of*

Sacred Scripture. (London: 1856). 660pp. With a map.

A772, B944 (author, title, date [1856]), JS26. No 1856 traced, but all editions in BL are published by the Religious Tract Society. Dodgson's copy, according to B944, has a penciled inscription, "F. J. D. 1880, from him to C. L. D. 1883." Probably a gift from his sister, Frances Jane Dodgson (the "him" may be a misprint in B944, if not, it is cryptic as no other F. J. D. seems a likely candidate). Angus was Secretary of the Baptist Missionary Society and President of Stepney College. He was also on the committee that revised the New Testament for the American Bible Union.

40. *Animal Physiology.* Edition unknown.

Title only given in A563/JS157 (Anon./Medical). Many possibilities in BL, the most likely being Carpenter (the title is a perfect match and Dodgson owned at least 2 other books by the same author). One reason Dodgson might have owned a book on this subject is to help with his drawings of animals in AAUG (drawn between 1862 and 1864), in which case the date of the Carpenter volume would also favor it. Many of the 19th-century books by this title were published for use in schools, and leaving out those and various "Elementary Science Manuals" the most likely possibilities are:

Carpenter, William B[enjamin] (1813–1885). *Animal Physiology.* (London: Wm. S. Orr and Co., 1848). 579pp. A new edition, carefully revised. Earliest edition in BL.

Angell, John. *Buckmaster's Elements of Animal Physiology.* (London: Longman & Co.; Simpkin, Marshall & Co., 1866). 368pp. Later published as *Elements of Animal Physiology.*

Cleland, John. *Animal Physiology: The Structure and Functions of the Human Body, etc.* (London & Glasgow: Collins, 1874). 325pp.

41. Anstey, F. [i.e. Thomas Anstey Guthrie] (1856–1934). *Vice Versa: or A Lesson to Fathers.* (London: Smith, Elder & Co., 1883). 370pp. 2nd edition revised.

Not in JS. In his diary for 20 April 1885, Dodgson writes, "I have lately read *Vice Versa* (a clever idea, but done with too much padding)." First published in 1882, this is the edition closest to Dodgson's diary mention. The "clever idea" was a story about a father and son who switch ages and personalities. Anstey was a humorist and frequent contributor to *Punch.*

42. Anstey, F. [i.e. Thomas Anstey Guthrie]. *Voces Populi.* (London: Longmans & Co., 1890). 2 vols. 1st and 2nd series. Reprinted from *Punch.* Illustrated by J. Bernard Partridge.

A574 ("Anstey's Voces Populi, first and second series, illustrated"), (states author as Christopher Anstey). Earliest edition in BL. A collection of short, humorous dramatic sketches.

43. Anstie, Francis Edmund (1833–74). *On the Uses of Wines in Health and Disease.* (London: Macmillan & Co., 1877). 74pp. Reprinted from *The Practitioner.*

E266 (title, author, date), JS408. Dodgson's copy, with his initials, was offered for sale by Maggs of London in 1911. *The Practitioner* was "a monthly journal of therapeutics" started in 1868. Volumes 1–2 were edited by Anstie and H. Lawson. E266 states that this copy has the initials of Lewis Carroll on the title. Anstie was, in 1864, "Assistant Physician to Westminster Hospital, Lecturer on Materia Medica and Therapeutics to the School, and formerly Lecturer on Toxicology." He was also a member of the Royal College of Surgeons. Dodgson curated the Senior Common Room at Christ Church, Oxford for 12 years, and was responsible for ordering supplies of wine.

44. Anstie, Francis Edmund. *Stimulants and Narcotics, Their Mutual Relations: With Special Researches on the Action of Alcohol, Æther, and Choloroform, on the Vital Organism.* (London: Macmillan & Co., 1864). 489pp.

A923 (author, title), JS429. Only 19th-century edition in BL. Includes a chapter on "the origin of the doctrine of stimulus," followed by an investigation of stimulus and narcosis, supported by experiments. Anstie concluded that drugs could not be easily divided into stimulants and narcotics; that many substances long thought to be narcotics had many of the characteristics of stimulants. "To the philosophic student," he wrote, "who desires to arrange in orderly classification the weapons of his art, and thereby to multiply his resources, the accurate definition of these two classes of remedies offers a problem at once of great interest and of extreme difficulty." In his letter to the *St. James's Gazette* published on 10 April 1890 under the title "The Fasting Man" Dodgson quotes two passages from this book (see LCP, #266).

45. [**Anthony**, Charles] (1867–1885). *The Social and Political Dependence of Women.* (London: Longmans, Green, & Co., 1867). 75pp. 1st edition.

E259 (title, date), JS404 (Anon./Women). A 2nd edition, of 92pp., was also dated 1867. A work arguing for women's suffrage. "In enfranchising women, let us inaugurate a nobler era in the history of the human race. Let the strong no longer tyrranise over the weak; but let man and woman, united by identity of interest, by a common nature, and a tangible respect for honour and religion, fight out the battle of life, side by side."

46. Aristotle (384–22 B.C.E.). *Aristotelis De Poetica Liber. Textum Recensuit, Versionem Refinxit, et Animadversionibus Illustravit, Thomas Tyrwhitt.* (Oxford: Clarendon Press, 1806). 271pp. 3rd edition.

B947 (author, title, editor, city, date), JS412. Aristotle's *Poetics* in Latin. The *Poetics* was Aristotle's commentary and instruction on poetic drama. Tyrwhitt (1730–86) was a critic and editor.

47. Aristotle. *Aristotle's Poetics; or, Discourses Concerning Tragic and Epic Imitation. Translated from the Greek into English. (Extracts Concerning the Greek Theatre and Masks, Translated from the Greek of Julius Pollux.)* (London: J. Dodsley & Richardson & Urquhart, 1775). 2 pt. 107pp.

A926 ("Aristotle's Poetics, royal 8vo."), JS411. The edition described is conjecture based on the fact that it is the only pre-1898 British edition in BL to use the exact version of the title quoted in A926. BL describes the size of this edition as 8vo. The preceding item in A926 is a 1760 edition of Justinius, and it seems likely that 18th-century editions of classics were sold together.

48. *Arithmetical Aids to Responsions, Containing Concise Rules, with Examples Worked Out.* (Oxford: J. Thornton, 1883). 52pp.

E357 (title, city, date), JS144. Responsions were a set of examinations given by Oxford University in Latin, Greek, and Arithmetic.

49. *Arithmetical Tips for Responsions at Oxford.* (Oxford: A Thomas Shrimpton and Son; London: Simpkin, Marshall, and Co., 1884). 19pp.

E358 (title, city, date), JS145. Dodgson's copy is in HAC and includes corrections on p. 6, 7, 13, and 19. The markings, in brown ink, may not be by Dodgson, and are minor annotations. With the property label on front cover.

50. Armitage, Robert (1805–52?). *Doctor Hookwell: or, the Anglo-Catholic Family.* (London: R. Bentley, 1842). 3 vols.

A609 (title, 3 vols.), JS413. This is the only 3-volume edition in BL and the earliest edition listed. A novel.

51. Armstrong, John (1813–56). *Essays on Church Penitentiaries.* (London: J. H. & J. Parker, 1858). 132pp. Edited by T[homas] T[hellusson] Carter.

E210 (title, author, editor, date), JS414. Armstrong was first Bishop of Grahamstown (South Africa), arriving to take up his post in 1854. In 1855 he founded St. Andrews College.

52. Arnett, Braithwaite. *Rules and Formulæ in Elementary Mathematics. With Notes.* (Cambridge: William Tomlin, 1873). 104pp.

E219 (title, author, date), F139, JS415. F139 describes this as a presentation copy with the gothic stamp. Arnett was a mathematician who wrote texts on geometry and mathematics.

53. Arnold, Edwin (1832–1904). *Griselda, A Tragedy: And Other Poems.* (London: David Bogue, 1856). 308pp. 1st edition.

A436 (author, title, edition, date), E18, F166, JS416. F166 notes the gothic stamp. Arnold served as headmaster of a school in India for five years before joining the staff of the *Daily Telegraph* in 1861. In 1873 he became editor of that paper and guided its anti-Gladstone, pro-Disraeli policy. He is also known for his involvement in Eastern thought, including his translation of the Bhagavadgita.

54. Arnold, Edwin. *Poems, Narrative and Lyrical.* (Oxford: Francis Macpherson, 1853). 174pp. 1st edition.

A434, A435 (author, title, edition, city, date), JS417. Dodgson owned two copies.

55. Arnold, Edwin. *Potiphar's Wife, and Other Poems.* (London: Longmans, Green and Co., 1892). 136pp.

A829 (author, title), JS418. Only edition in BL or BOD. A book of poetry in three sections, "Egyptian Poems," "Japanese Poems," and "Other Poems." Among the Japanese pieces is "An Introduction (To O Yoshi San, with a Copy of 'Alice Through the Looking-Glass')," a poem exhorting Alice to befriend a Japanese maiden.

56. Arnold, Matthew (1822–88). *Poems.* (London: Longman, Brown, Green, Longmans and Roberts, 1857). 252pp. [First series], 3rd edition.

A828, D7 (author, title, edition, city, date), JS419. D7 notes Dodgson's initials. The son of Thomas Arnold (see below), Matthew Arnold was a fellow of Oriel College, Oxford, and Professor of Poetry at Oxford from 1857 to 1867. Dodgson sent some numbers of *The Train* (see 2322) to Arnold in 1856. The present volume is a reprint of the collection of *Poems* that first appeared in 1853, and which contained extracts from earlier collections by Arnold.

57. Arnold, Thomas (1795–1842). *Introductory Lectures on Modern History Delivered in Lent Term, MDCCCXLII, with the Inaugural Lecture.* (London: B. Fellowes, 1845). 315pp. 3rd edition.

A633, B948 (author, title, date), JS420. B948 describes Dodgson's copy: "Rugby School Prize, Christmas 1846, with Arms and inscription." Arnold was headmaster of Rugby School from 1827 to 1842. Dodgson attended Rugby from 1846 to 1849. Arnold was appointed Professor of History at Oxford in 1841, but delivered only these nine lectures before his sudden death in 1843.

58. Arnold, Thomas Kerchever (1800–53). *The First Hebrew Book.* (London: F. & J. Rivington, 1851). 234pp.

Not in JS. In his diary for 3 February 1866, Dodgson lists this among books he ordered at the suggestion of his friend H. P. Liddon in order to learn Hebrew (see *Diary 5*). Earliest edition in BL. Arnold was the rector of Lyndon, Rutland from 1830. He wrote several books on languages.

59. Arnold, Thomas Kerchever and Henry Browne. *The Second Hebrew Book: Containing the Book of Genesis; Together with a Hebrew Syntax, and a Vocabulary and Grammatical Commentary.* (London: F. & J. Rivington, 1853). 371pp.

Not in JS. In his diary for 3 February 1866, Dodgson lists this among books he ordered at the suggestion of his friend H. P. Liddon in order to learn Hebrew (see *Diary 5*). Only edition in BL.

60. Arnott, Neil (1788–1874). *Elements of Physics, or Natural Philosophy, General and Medical, Explained Independently of Technical Mathematics.* (London: Longman & Co., 1829). 2 vols. Vol. 1 is 4th edition; vol. 2, pt. 1 is 3rd edition. No more published.

A922, E350 (title, author, 2 vols., date), JS421. E350 describes this as having "extra pages at end for professional readers." Arnott was a Scottish physician who worked in London and in 1837 was made physician extraordinary to the queen. He was also an inventor with a strong interest in natural philosophy and a supporter of scientific education.

61. *The Art of Illumination*. Details unknown.

Title only given in A592/JS27. See 817 for more on Dodgson and illumination. BL has several possibilities (the Shaw seems most likely as it matches the title perfectly and was reprinted):

Shaw, Henry. *The Art of Illumination.* (London: 1870). 2nd edition, with colored illustrations, of the work published in 1866 as *A Handbook of the Art of Illumination as Practised During the Middle Ages. With a Description of the Metals, Pigments, and Processes Employed by the Artists at Different Periods.*

Wyatt, M. D. *The Art of Illumination.* (London: 1861).

Humphreys, Henry Noel. *The Art of Illumination and Missal Painting. Illustrated by Specimens.* (London: 1849). See index for works illustrated by Humphreys owned by Dodgson.

62. Ash, John (1724?–79). *The New and Complete Dictionary of the English Language: In which all the Words are Introduced, the Different Spellings Preserved, the Sounds of the Letters Occasionally Distinguished, the Obsolete and Uncommon Words Supported by Authorities, and the Different Construction and Uses Illustrated by Examples: To which is Prefixed, a Compendious*

Grammar. (London: Edward and Charles Dilly, etc., 1775). 2 vols. in 1. Ca. 1220pp.

A361, D8 (author, title, date [1875], issued 2 vols. in 1, 8vo), JS423. No edition of 1875 has been traced and as the edition of 1775 matches D73 in all particulars, the date 1875 may be a misprint. BL and BOD only list editions of 1775 and 1795. Ash was an English Baptist minister, lexicographer and grammarian probably best known for his often reprinted *Grammatical Institutes*, which styled itself "an easy introduction to Dr. Lowth's English grammar designed for the use of schools." Webster criticized Ash's dictionary for its large collection of "the lowest of all vulgar words."

63. Ashford, Constance M. *Latin Dialogues for School Representation*. (London: Swan Sonnenschein & Co., 1892). 71pp. Latin & English.

E326 (title, author, date), JS424. E326 described this as having "the initials of Lewis Carroll (and the usual correction of text)." A schoolbook.

64. Ashton, John (b. 1834). *Modern Street Ballads*. (London: Chatto & Windus, 1888). With 56 illustrations. 405pp.

A309, D9 (title, author, city, date), JS425. The introduction states, "Street Ballads ... held their own for many centuries, but have succumbed to a changed order of things, and a new generation has arisen, who will not stop in the streets to listen ... but prefer to have their music ... at Music Halls.... Rough though some of these Street Ballads may be, very few of them were coarse, and, on reading them, we must ever bear in mind the class for whom they were produced.... In this collection I have introduced nothing which can offend anybody except an absolute prude." The collection is divided into headings: Social, Humorous, Country, Sea, The Queen, Political, and Miscellaneous.

65. Association for the Improvement of Geometrical Teaching. *The Elements of Plane Geometry Part I*. (London: W. Swan Sonnenschein and Co., 1884 [1883]). Prepared by the Committee appointed by the Association.

E265 (title, group author), JS148 (Anon./Mathematics), JS426. Dodgson's copy is in HAC. It has the gothic stamp on the title-page and includes rows of numbers on the back end-

paper and annotations in Dodgson's hand on 33 pages. Part I corresponds to Euclid Books I–II. Part II was published in 1886 and covered Euclid through Book VI.

66. Association for the Improvement of Geometrical Teaching. *Syllabus of Plane Geometry (Corresponding to Euclid, Books I–VI)*. (London: Macmillan and Co., 1875). 58pp.

E301, JS155 (Anon./Mathematics). Dodgson's copy is in HAC. It has "C. L. D. Nov 26/76" on the front cover and notes in his hand on 32 pages. The notes are in purple ink, many are quite extensive, and some are critical of the work. Dodgson's published his own *Syllabus of Plane Algebraical Geometry* in 1860 (see WMGC, #24). This may be the work on which J. M. Wilson based the 1878 edition of his *Elementary Geometry* (see 2283). That work claims to be based on the "Syllabus prepared by the Geometrical Association." Dodgson refers to Wilson's work in his *Euclid and His Modern Rivals*.

67. Astle, Thomas (1735–1803). *The Origin and Progress of Writing, as Well Hieroglyphic as Elementary, Illustrated by Engravings Taken from Marbles, Manuscripts and Charters, Ancient and Modern: Also, Some Account of the Origin and Progress of Printing*. (London: The Author, 1784). 235pp. 31 plates.

A741, D10 (author, title, city, date), JS427. Astle was keeper of records at the Tower of London, an antiquary, and supervisor of printing for the Ancient Records of Parliament. This was the most complete work on the subject to date and argued that the art of printing had its roots in China.

68. A[tkinson], F[rancis] H[ome] (1840–1901). *Poems*. (1880).

E135 ("Poems, by F. H. A."), JS130 (Anon./Literature). Despite the cryptic description in E135, this no doubt refers to a book Dodgson received from his friend F. H. Atkinson in 1881. On 10 December of that year, he wrote to Atkinson, "Will you kindly write my name in the little book, and so add to it a tenfold value in my eyes. I return you many thanks for it." He demurs to send Atkinson a photo, writing "Possibly your book of poetry has not brought on you all the annoyances of one who, having been unlucky enough to perpetrate two small books for children …" These references clearly indicate that Atkinson had sent a book of poems. Dodgson's request was apparently fulfilled, for E15 notes that Dodgson's copy has "two inscriptions, to Lewis Carroll, who has marked an error in the text." No copy of this book has yet to come to light. In all likelihood it was privately printed in a small edition.

69. (Atlas). *Phillip's County Atlas.* Details unknown.

Title only given in A936/JS1645. No exact match found, but probably this is a volume from the series *Philip's County Geography of England and Wales* by J. P. Faunthorpe. The series, with individual atlases for numerous counties, was published primarily in 1871–73. As Dodgson often took long walks around Oxford, a likely candidate is: Faunthorpe, John Pincher. *The Geography of Oxfordshire and Buckinghamshire.* (London: G. Philip and Son, 1873).

70. Austen, Jane (1775–1817). *Jane Austen's Works.* (London: Richard Bentley & Son, 1882). 6 vols. Steventon Edition.

A666 ("J. Austen's Novels, 6 vols."), JS428. This is the only pre–1898 6-volume edition of Austen's novels listed in David Gilson's *A Bibliography of Jane Austen.* It was, according to Gilson, "the last complete edition of JA's works to be published by Bentley (it was however the first set issued by that firm in which the novels appear in the order of first publication)." Includes (in this order): *Sense and Sensibility, Pride and Prejudice, Mansfield Park, Emma, Northanger Abbey* and *Persuasion* (in one volume), and, in the final volume, a *Memoir* by J. E. Austen-Leigh (JA's nephew), *Lady Susan,* etc. In his diary for 26 July 1883, Dodgson lists several books he has been reading during a recent illness, including *Pride and Prejudice,* which he calls "a charming picture of bygone manners."

71. Austin, Alfred (1835–1913). *The Golden Age: A Satire.* (London: Chapman & Hall, 1871). 126pp. 1st edition.

A847 (author, title, edition), JS430. Alfred Austin was a journalist and poet. His second book, *The Season: A Satire* (1861), met with severe criticism, leading him to write *My Satire and its Censors* (1861). There followed many additional volumes of verse (including this one), largely satires and generally undistinguished. Austin was associated with the *Standard* from 1866 to 1896 and was, from 1883 to 1895, editor of the conservative *National Review.* In 1896, he succeeded Tennyson as Poet Laureate. CHEAL writes, "That [he] hardly deserved to be made poet laureate is a proposition which very few persons, whatever their personal or political attitude towards him, are likely to deny now, and which, in after times, nobody at all, except out of mere whim, is likely to dispute." Dodgson met Austin on a visit to Hatfield House between 17 May and 10 June 1889.

72. Austin, Alfred. *The Human Tragedy. A Poem.* (London: Robert Hardwicke, 1862). 219pp. 1st edition.

A846 (author, title, edition), JS431. PCL calls this work a "dreary narrative." This poem was published in an expanded version (as "a poem in four acts") in 1876. Dodgson's copy is described as "first edition," but that also could refer to the 1876 version (Edinburgh & London: W. Blackwood & Sons). 439pp.

73. Austin, Alfred. *Madonna's Child.* (Edinburgh & London: W. Blackwood & Sons, 1873). 80pp. 2nd edition.

A847 (author, title, edition), JS432. A poem professing to be an excerpt from the 2nd of 4 planned cantos together titled *Human Tragedy* (see also *Rome or Death!*). *The Spectator* wrote of *Madonna's Child,* "In his pictures of scenes and places, and in the more difficult task of portraying mental conflict, Mr. Austin is often very happy."

74. Austin, Alfred. *My Satire and Its Censors.* (London: George Manwaring, 1861). 52pp. 1st edition.

A847 (author, title, edition), B950, JS433. This is Austin's verse defense of his work *The Season* (see 77), which had suffered at the hands of the critics. He heaped much vitriol on William Hepworth Dixon, editor of *The Athenæum,* whose review had been especially harsh. Later in his career Austin suppressed this work, and it was never reprinted.

75. Austin, Alfred. *The Poetry of the Period.* (London: Richard Bentley, 1870). 294pp. 1st edition.

A485 (author, title, edition, date), JS434. Reprinted from *Temple Bar* magazine. In this survey of contemporary poetry, Austin says of Tennyson, "The stuff of a great poet was not in him"; of Browning that he is "grotesque … and

... indiscreet"; and of Arnold that he is "sick with a surfeit of analysis."

76. Austin, Alfred. *Rome or Death!* (Edinburgh & London: W. Blackwood & Sons, 1873). 184pp. 1st edition.

A836 (author, title), JS435. Although A836 does not specify 1st edition (as it does for the other two Austin titles there listed), this is the only edition listed in BL or BOD. A poem professing to be the 3rd of 4 planned cantos together titled *Human Tragedy* (see also *Madonna's Child*). This poem treats contemporary European events, particularly the campaign of Mentana in Italy. In his preface, the author suggests that the poem may answer the question, "Whether the political events and emotions of our own time admit of poetical treatment by a contemporary writer."

77. Austin, Alfred. *The Season: A Satire.* (London: J. C. Hotten, 1869). 77pp. New and revised edition. With frontispiece of "The Modern Muse," by T. G. Cooke.

A847 (author, title), JS436. A847 lists four books by Austin and specifies the other three as 1st editions. As this was Austin's second book and the earliest owned by Dodgson, it seems likely that A847 would have specified either the 1st or 2nd edition (both of which were published in 1861, the 1st by Hardwicke and the 2nd by Manwaring). Therefore, the new edition of 1869 seems the most likely candidate. The work is a satire on the social scene in London, featuring poetic profiles of real people. It met with critical disapproval, leading Austin to write *My Satire and its Censors* (see 74).

78. Austin, Alfred. *"Skeletons at the Feast." Or, The Radical Programme.* (London: W. H. Allen and Co., 1885). 32pp.

E345 (author, title, date), F171, JS437. E345 describes this as "a prose pamphlet." Originally published as an article in *National Review* VI (November 1885), 297–315.

79. Austin, Alfred. *The Tower of Babel. A Poetical Drama.* (Edinburgh & London: W. Blackwood & Sons, 1874). 256pp. 1st edition.

A846 (author, title, edition), JS438. Earliest edition in BL or BOD.

80. *The Autographic Mirror (L'Autographe Cosmopolite), Containing Facsimiles of Documents, Letters, etc., by Sovereigns, Statesmen, Warriors, Divines, Literary, Scientific, Artistic, and Theatrical Celebrities.* (London: 1864–66). 3 (of 4) vols. Lithographed by Vincent Brooks.

A284 ("The Autographic Mirror, 3 vols."), not in JS. A periodical publication published in 4 volumes of which Dodgson apparently owned only 3. BOD lists an edition of the first 3 volumes only. This described itself as "Autographic letters and sketches of illustrious and distinguished men of past and present times," and was filled with facsimile items. The title page was printed in French and English, but the text in English only.

81. Aveling, Stephen Thomas. *Carpentry and Joinery. A Useful Manual for the Many.* (London: F. Warne & Co., [1871]). 120pp. With illustrations.

D11 (author, title, city, date), JS439. As a young man, Dodgson made some wooden toys and a toy theatre for the amusement of his siblings, but the present work was published much later.

82. Aytoun, William Edmondstone (1813–65). *Lays of the Scottish Cavaliers and Other Poems.* (Edinburgh and London: William Blackwood & Sons, 1850). 351pp. 3rd edition.

A828 (author, title, edition, city, date), D12, JS440. Illustrated by Joseph Noël Paton and others. The author was a Scotsman who served as both Professor of Belle-Lettres at Edinburgh and Sheriff of Orkney. A collection of ballad-romances, on Scottish subjects. See 1507 for a note on Paton. See 763 for more work by Aytoun.

83. B., C. *The Story of a Nursery Rhyme.* (London: Field & Tuer, The Leadenhalle Presse, [1883]). 72pp. Illustrated by Edwin Ellis.

Not in JS. Dodgson's diary for 3 September 1891 lists a number of *Alice* imitations he has acquired and notes at the end of the entry, "One more book I have added, *The Story of a Nursery Rhyme*." Two editions of this story book were published by the Leadenhalle Presse in 1883, one illustrated by Margaret Hooper (35pp.) and another illustrated by Edwin J. Ellis; Dodgson certainly owned this version and may have owned both. In a letter to Harry Fur-

Edwin Ellis' illustration from *The Story of a Nursery Rhyme* (item 83) which Dodgson mentioned to Harry Furniss as an example of how to draw children.

niss about the dress of the fairy children in the illustrations for *Sylvie and Bruno* (27 November 1886), Dodgson writes, "The enclosed 11 pictures in light blue I cut out of a book called *A Tale of a Nursery Rhyme* in July 1883. They are by a Mr. Edwin Ellis. He has boldly solved the question by putting the 2 children (both girls, according to the book) into chemises, and those nearly transparent," (see *Illustrators*). The story is about Katie, who falls asleep after singing "Jack and Jill" to her doll. She meets Jill of the nursery rhyme who takes her inside a number of nursery rhymes. When she awakes, she says, "I don't think it *can* be all a dream — it did seem so very natural ..."

84. Baber, Henry Hervey (1775–1869), editor. *Vetus Testamentum Græcum, e Codice Ms. Alexandrino: qui Londini in Bibliotheca Musei Britannici Asservatur, Typis ad Similitudinem Ipsius Codicis Scriptura Fideliter Descriptum.* (London: Richard and Arthur Taylor, 1816–1828). 3 vols.

A952 (title, 3 vols.), JS497 (listed under Bible). Only edition listed of the only title in BL that matches the particulars in A952. A volume of prolegomena and notes was published in 1828. Baber was curator of printed books at the British Museum for 25 years. This is his chief work, a publication of the Old Testament portion of the Alexandrian manuscript. Housed in the British Museum, the manuscript is among the oldest Bible manuscript in the world.

85. Bacon, Francis (1561–1626). *Essays.* Edition unknown.

A369 (author, title), JS441. Bacon was a Renaissance author, courtier, and the father of deductive reasoning.

86. Bacon, Francis. *The Works of Francis Bacon.* (London: J. Johnson, etc., 1803). 10 vols.

A549 (author, title, 10 vols.), JS442. Earliest 10-volume edition in BL. 10-volume editions were also published by F. C. & J. Rivington, etc., in 1819 and W. Baynes & Son in 1824.

87. Bailey, N[athan] (d. 1742), editor. *Dictionarium Britannicum: or a More Compleat Universal Etymological English Dictionary than any Extant.* (London: T. Cox, 1736). 918pp. 2nd edition. Collected by several hands, the mathematical part by G[eorge] Gordon, the botanical by P[hilip] Miller. The whole revis'd and improv'd with many thousand additions, by N[athan] Bailey.

A740, B951 (author, title, edition, date), JS444. Originally published in 1730, this was an important precursor to Johnson's *Dictionary* (see 1079) and the most complete English dictionary to date.

88. Bailey, Philip James (1816–1902). *The Age; A Colloquial Satire.* (London: Chapman & Hall, 1858), 208pp. 1st edition.

A845, B953 (author, title, date), JS447. Bailey was a barrister before retiring to pursue a career as a poet. He is regarded as the father of the Spasmodic school of poetry. DEL gives the full subtitle of this collection of verse as *Politics, Poetry and Criticism: A Colloquial Satire.*

89. [**Bailey,** Philip James]. *Festus, a Poem.* (London: William Pickering, 1839). 360pp.

A829 (author, title), JS445. 1st edition of this oft reprinted and revised poem, written in its original form when the poet was 23 years old, and twice expanded. DEL calls *Festus* "a dramatic poem ... including, among the interlocutors, God, Christ, the Holy Ghost, Seraphim, Cherubim, Lucifer, Saints, Guardian Angel," etc. A reviewer for *The Times* called the poem, "the exhibition of a soul gifted, tried, buffeted, beguiled, stricken, purified, redeemed, pardoned, and triumphant." Not surprisingly, it has been compared to the Faust legend.

90. Bailey, Philip James. *The Mystic, and Other Poems.* (London: Chapman & Hall, 1855). 154pp. 1st edition.

A845, B952 (author, title, date), JS446. The 1st and 2nd editions were both published in 1855. The bulk of this volume was included in the final (1889) version of *Festus.*

91. Baillie, Joanna (1762–1851). *A Series of Plays: In Which It Is Attempted to Delineate the Stronger Passions of the Mind — Each Passion Being the Subject of a Tragedy and a Comedy.* (London: T. Cadell & W. Davies, 1798, 1802; Longman, Hurst, Rees, Orme, and Brown, 1812). 3 vols.

A677 ("Plays on the Passions by Baillie, 3 vols."), JS448. 1st editions. Each of the first 4 editions listed in BL contains 3 volumes. The first volume was published anonymously. Baillie's friend and fellow Scot, Walter Scott, called her a "female Shakespeare." Her "Introductory Discourse" to these plays is often cited as an example of early feminist literary criticism.

92. [**Baker,** H. W.] (1821–77), editor. *Hymns Ancient and Modern for Use in the Services of the Church, etc.* (London: Novello & Co., [1860]). 264pp.

E122 (title, 16mo), JS508. This is the 1st edition of what was then the standard hymnal for the Church of England. It went through many printings and revisions. The size listed in BL for this edition (14cm) roughly corresponds with the 16mo listed in E122. Dodgson may well have owned a later edition. Some later editions credited William Henry Monk (1823–89) as musical editor. A copy owned by Dodgson sold at Anderson Galleries, New York on 25–26 October 1922 (DAA987, described as "18mo, full brown morocco, gilt edges, brass clasp, London, n.d."), and resold at Parke-Bernet Galleries, New York on 29 November 1939. That copy had Dodgson's signature inside the front cover.

93. Balfour, Arthur James (1848–1930). *The Religion of Humanity. An Address Delivered at the Church Congress, Manchester, October, 1888.* (Edinburgh: David Douglas, 1888). 56pp.

D13 (author, title, city, date), JS449. BL also lists a 31pp. undated edition published in 1888; as D78 lists the date, the dated edition seems more likely. Balfour was the nephew of Dodgson's friend and the sometime prime minister Lord Salisbury. Balfour himself served as prime minister from 1902 to 1905. This work discusses Positivism, defined by the writer as "that general habit or scheme of thought which, on its negative side, refuses all belief in anything beyond phenomena and the laws connecting them, and on its positive side attempts to find in the 'worship of humanity,' … a form of religion unpolluted by any element of the supernatural.… What I have to say now relates solely to what may be called the religious elements of Positivism."

94. Balfour, Clara Lucas (1808–78). *Working Women of the Last Half Century: The Lesson of their Lives.* (London: W. & F. G. Cash, 1854). 384pp.

Uncertain. Not in JS. Listed in WS only and identified by gothic stamp and property label only. Dodgson's copy is in WWC and has the property label on the cover and the gothic stamp. Balfour was a lecturer and writer on issues related to women and to temperance.

95. Balfour, John Hutton (1808–84). *Botany and Religion, or Illustrations of the Works of God in the Structure, Functions, Arrangements, and General Distribution of Plants.* (Edinburgh: Oliphant, 1882). 436pp. 4th edition. With 200 illustrations.

A773, D14 (author, title, city, date), JS450. D14 notes Dodgson's initials. Balfour was Professor of Botany at Edinburgh University and also a physician who served as dean of the medical faculty. In his preface he calls the present book an "attempt to illustrate the works of God in the economy of vegetation."

96. Ball, Walter William Rouse (1850–1925). *Mathematical Recreations and Problems of Past and Present Times.* (London: Macmillan & Co., 1896). 276pp. 3rd edition.

B954 (author, title, date), JS451. A copy of this book inscribed "Edith Mary Rix, with an Uncle's love, from C. L. Dodgson, Aug. 27/97" was offered at Hodgson, London on 9 January 1924 (see DAA1014a). Dodgson acquired his copy from Macmillan, his publisher, in August 1897 (see *Macmillan*, 354–55). Ball was educated at Cambridge where he served as mathematical lecturer at Trinity College. He was called to the bar in 1876 and wrote a students' guide to the bar and a history of mathematics. The present book was brought out in new editions in the 20th century, and would naturally have appealed to Dodgson, who devised some of his own mathematical recreations and perpetuated others.

97. Ball, Wilfrid (1853–1917). *Sketches on the Cam.* ([1884]).

A237 (title, author), not in JS. Conjectural date from the library catalogue of Cambridge University. Ball was an artist who published several books of pictures of the English countryside.

98. Ball, Wilfrid. *Sketches on the Isis.*

A237 (author, title), not in JS. No copy traced.

99. [Bannerman, Anne] (d. 1829). *Tales of Superstition and Chivalry.* (London: Vernor & Hood, 1802). 144pp.

A842 (title), JS452. Only edition listed in BL. An illustrated book of Romantic poetry.

100. Banting, William (1797–1878). *Letter on Corpulence: Addressed to the Public. [With] The Treatment of Corpulence by the So-called Banting System, by Prof. [Felix von] Niemeyer.* (London: Harrison, 1869). 127pp. 4th edition.

E332 (author, title, date), JS453. Banting was an overweight London undertaker who sought assistance from a fellow of the Royal College of Surgeons, Dr. William Harvey, in reducing his weight. Harvey devised what many have called the first high-protein, low-carbohydrate diet, which was successful for Banting. To spread the word of this diet, Banting published *Letter on Corpulence* at his own expense. The first two editions (published in 1864) were given away by Banting, who saw the assistance of the corpulent as a way to serve mankind; the 3rd edition cost only 1 shilling; this 4th edition includes "remarks by the author, copious information from correspondents, and confirmatory evidence of the benefit of the dietary system which he recommended to public notice" as well as Dr. Niemeyer's explanation of why the diet worked, which helped in its acceptance by the medical profession. *Letter on Corpulence* is one of the most influential books on dieting and weight loss and led to the author's name becoming a verb—for many decades those on a diet were said to be "banting." There is no record that Dodgson was anything other than slim.

101. Barbauld, Mrs. [i.e. Anna Laetitia Aikin Barbauld] (1743–1825). *Hymns in Prose by Mrs. Barbauld for the Instruction of Young Children*. (London: Printed for the Booksellers by T. H. Keble, Margate, [ca. 1845]). 71pp. Frontis. + 9 wood engravings. 12mo. Pictorial glazed covers with cloth spine. A new and improved edition. The pages surrounded with texts of scripture and moral maxims.

E376 ("Hymns in Prose, by Mrs. Barbauld, for the Instruction of Young Children, with woodcuts, 16mo, picture boards, curious"), JS455. Not in BL or BOD which list many editions of Barbauld's popular work under its more usual title, *Hymns in Prose for Children*. This edition seems a likely match to E376 as it is the only one traced with a matching title and closely matching physical description. Anna Barbauld was a popular writer of books for children, especially moral tales. See 20 for an earlier work by Mrs. Barbauld. This collection was largely responsible for helping Barbauld achieve literary fame. The hymns were intended for memorization and were accompanied by some longer pieces of religious prose for children. The work remained in print until early in the 20th century.

102. Barbauld, Mrs. [i.e. Anna Laetitia Aikin Barbauld]. *A Legacy for Young Ladies, Consisting of Miscellaneous Pieces, in Prose and Verse*. (London: Longman & Co., 1826). 265pp. 1st edition. Edited by Lucy Aikin.

E323 (title, author, date), JS454. The editor was Barbauld's niece.

103. Baretti, Giuseppe (1719–89). *A Dictionary of the English and Italian Languages; Improved and Augmented with above Ten Thousand Words, Omitted in the Last Edition of Altieri; To which is Added an Italian and English Grammar*. (London: C. Hitch & L. Hawes, etc., 1760). 2 vols. The dedication composed by Samuel Johnson.

A949 (Baretti's Italian Dictionary, 2 vols.), JS456. 1st edition. BL lists 19th-century 2-volume editions as late as 1854. Baretti was an Italian writer who spent some years in England. His work is largely responsible for the popularity of Italian literature in 18th-century England. This was the standard work of its type until the 20th century. Johnson's dedication was to Don Felix, Marquis of Abren and Bertodano.

104. Baretti, Giuseppe. *A Dictionary, Spanish and English, and English Spanish, Containing the Signification of Words and their Different Uses; together with the Terms of Arts, Sciences, and Trades and the Spanish Words Accented and Spelled According to the Regulation of the Royal Spanish Academy of Madrid*. (London: Printed for F. Wingrave, etc., 1809). 2 vols. A new edition, corrected and greatly enlarged.

A949, E109 (author, title, date [1809], 2 vols.), JS253 (Anon./Reference) and JS457. NUC gives date as "1809, '07." No other edition of 1809 has been traced.

105. Baring-Gould, Sabine (1834–1924). *The Book of Werewolves: Being an Account of a Terrible Superstition*. (London: Smith Elder, 1865). 266pp. 1st edition.

A489 (author, title, edition, date), JS458. Baring-Gould was a prolific writer and folklorist whose courtship and marriage to a mill girl was said to have inspired his friend George Bernard Shaw to write *Pygmalion*. Perhaps his greatest fame came as the author of the words to the hymn "Onward Christian Soldiers." This is the first book in English devoted to lycanthropy. Dodgson also owned a 1st edition of the first book-length work on Vampires (see Polidori) and a scarce 2nd (1823) edition of *Frankenstein*.

106. Baring-Gould, S[abine]. *Curious Myths of the Middle Ages*. (Oxford and Cambridge: Rivingtons, 1881). 660pp. Illustrated

A894 (author, title), JS460. Earliest edition in BL. Contains: "The Wandering Jew," "Prester John," "The Divining Rod," "The Seven Sleepers of Ephesus," "William Tell," "The Dog Gellert," "Tailed Men," "Antichrist and Pope Joan," "The Man in the Moon," "The Mountain of Venus," "Fatality of Numbers," and "The Terrestrial Paradise." Baring-Gould traveled in Europe with his parents for 13 years, beginning at age 3, no doubt an experience that exposed him to many of these legends.

107. Baring-Gould, Sabine. *The Origin and Development of Religious Belief*. (London: Rivingtons, 1869–70). 2 vols.

A774 (author, title), JS459. Earliest edition traced. Though A774 does not specify 2 vols., no 1-volume edition has been traced. The volumes are *Heathenism and Mosaism* and *Christianity*. In later editions the first volume was titled *Polytheism and Monotheism*.

108. [Baring-Gould, Sabine and Charlotte Mary Yonge?] *Please Tell Me a Tale. A Collection of Short Stories for Children*. (London: Skeffington & Son, 1885). 142pp. 5th edition.

A640 (title), JS84 (Anon./Children). Earliest edition in BL. The speculation as to the editors is based on the description of a book published the following year: *Just One More Tale. A Second Collection of ... Stories ... Being a Companion Volume to "Please Tell Me a Tale."* By S. B. Gould, and C. M. Yonge. (London: Skeffington & Son, 1886). See 2323 for a note on Yonge.

109. Barker, T[homas] C[hilde] (1826–1910). *Aryan Civilization; Its Religious Origin, and Its Progress. With an Account of the Religion, Laws, and Institutions of Greece and Rome*. (London, Chipping Norton [printed]: 1871). Based on the work of [Numa Denis Fustel] De Coulanges [i.e. *La Cité Antique*].

B956 (author, title), JS462. The is the only edition in BL. According to B956, Dodgson's copy was a "Presentation copy to C. L. D. from the author, with inscription." Fustel De Coulanges (1830–89) was a French historian whose work *The Ancient City* examined the influence of primitive religion on Greece and Rome.

110. Barnes, Albert (1798–1870). *Notes, Explanatory and Practical, on the Gospels: Designed for Sunday School Teachers and Bible Classes*. (London: Religious Tract Society, [1835]). 2 vols. Condensed from the American edition (of 1833).

E175 ("Notes on the Gospels by Rev. A. Barnes"), JS463. Earliest edition traced. E175 describes Dodgson's copy as having "two autographs of Lewis Carroll in 1845." Although E175 does not specify 2 vols., no 1-volume edition before 1845 has been traced. The American edition referred to was published in New York by Jonathan Leavitt. The work was also published in 11 volumes (presumably including the entire New Testament) by Blackie & Son of Glasgow from 1841 to 1852. Barnes was pastor of First Church in Philadelphia, the mother church of American Presbyterianism. He wrote a popular series of books under similar names to the present title providing commentary on the books of the Bible.

111. Barnes, John. *Complete Triumph of Moral Good Over Evil*. (London: Longmans, Green, 1870). 505pp.

A587 ("Triumph of Good Over Evil"), JS334 (Anon./Theology). This is the only closely matching title traced.

112. Barrington, Daines (1727–1800). *Possibility of Approaching the North Pole Asserted*. (London: Printed for T. and J. Allman, W. H. Reid, and Baldwin, Cradock and Joy, 1818). 258pp. A new edition with an appendix, containing papers on the same subject, and on a north west passage, by Colonel Beaufroy

Uncertain. F175 (author, title, date), JS464. Identified as Dodgson's only by gothic stamp. Barrington was an Oxford trained lawyer and judge who retired to pursue the study of natural history and related fields. The evidence on which he based his claims was later refuted. Originally published in 1795; this new edition appends to the main account 2 appendices: "Queries Respecting the Probability of Reaching, from the Island of Spitsbergen, the North Pole, by Means of Rein Deer, During the Winter; and Answered by Persons who Wintered There" and "On the North West Passage, and the Insular Form of Greenland."

113. Barry, Alfred (1826–1910). *The Manifold Witness for Christ ... Being the Boyle Lectures for 1877 and 1878.* (London: John Murray, 1880). 400pp.

A790 ("Barry's Boyle Lectures 1877–78"), JS465. Only edition in BL or BOD. Barry was a churchman and educator. At the time of the Boyle lectures, he was canon of Worcester and in 1884 he was made Bishop of Sydney and primate of Australia. He returned five years later to hold a number of other ecclesiastical posts. This work was divided into two parts, "Christianity and Natural Theology," and "The Positive Evidences of Christianity."

114. Bartlett, John (1820–1905). *Dictionary of Americanisms. A Glossary of Words and Phrases, Usually Regarded as Peculiar to the United States.* (Boston: Little Brown & Co.; London: Trübner & Co., 1859). 524pp. 2nd edition.

A360 ("Butler's Dictionary of Americanisms"), JS640 (listed under Butler). Clearly an error in A360, as no work by this or any similar title by a Butler has been traced. Surely the Bartlett book, frequently reprinted and widely available, is the correct one. Earliest English edition in BL. The only other similar title published before 1898 and described in BL is John Stephen Farmer's 1888 work *Americanisms Old and New. A Dictionary of Words, Phrases and Colloquialisms,* but this title is not as close a match to A360 as Bartlett's.

115. Bartlett, John. *A Collection of Familiar Quotations, with Complete Indices of Authors and Subjects.* (London: G. Routledge & Sons, 1869). 524pp. New edition

A538 (author, title), JS466. Earliest English edition in BL.

116. Bartolini, Martio. *Insogni Pastorali di Martio Bartolini d'Arcidosso. Opera non men'vtile, che Diletteuole, e con vna Aggionta di Rime Diuerse, del Medesimo.* (Orvieto: A. Colaldi, 1596). 184pp.

Uncertain. F189 (author, title, city, date), JS467. F189 lists no identifying marks.

117. Baskerville, John (1706–75), printer. *Novum Testamentum. Juxta Exemplar Millianum.* (Oxford: John Baskerville/Clarendon Press, 1763). 676pp. 8vo.

B1155 (title, publisher, city, date, 8vo.), JS490. Baskerville was a renowned printer and is perhaps best known today as a designer of typefaces. This edition of the Greek New Testament was also issued in a 4to version the same year.

118. Bastin, Jean (1827–1909). *Guide du Voyageur à St. Pétersbourg, etc.* (St. Pétersbourg, Leipzig [printed]: 1867). 368pp.

E230 (title, author, date), JS469. Dodgson visited St. Petersburg from 22 July–2 August 1867 during his Russian journey with his friend H. P. Liddon. The title translates, "Guide for Travelers to St. Petersburg."

119. [Bath]. *The Historical and Local New Bath Guide Including Authentic Accounts of Bristol and the Hotwells, a Concise History of Cheltenham, etc.* (Bath: J. Barratt & Son, [1823]). 176pp. Embellished with eight original engravings, and a correct plan of the city.

E382 (title, "with map, copperplates and woodcuts [Bewick, etc.]"), JS356. Earliest edition in BL. The only other edition in BL (1835?) includes *With Observations on the Medicinal Virtues ... of the Bath Waters,* by Sir George Smith Gibbes.

120. [Baxter, Michael Paget] (1834–1910). *15 Predicted Events from 1892 until the End of this Age on April 11, 1901.* (London: Christian Herald, 1892).

E148 (title), JS238 (Anon./Reference). E148 describes this as "15 Predicted Events (from 1891 to 1901) with curious and other cuts; also marks of admiration, etc. pencilled by Lewis Carroll," but neither BL nor BOD list any such book. Either this refers to the present title and 1891 is merely a misprint, or an earlier edition of this same work is not catalogued by BL, BOD, or NUC. Baxter was a newspaper editor who wrote many books of dated "prophecy" from the 1860s onwards.

121. Baxter, W. G. *Studies from Shakspere and Dickens.* (Manchester: Cartwright & Rattray, [ca. 1885]). Unnumbered pages. 27 sketches.

A295 (title, author), not in JS. Baxter drew the Ally Sloper cartoons for the magazine *Judy* (which Dodgson sometimes read).

122. Bayley, Frederick W[illiam] N[aylor] (1807–52). *Blue Beard*. (London: Wm. S. Orr & Co., [1842]). 47pp. Illustrated. In the *Comic Nursery Tales* series.

A483 (series, title, publisher), JS50 (Anon./ Children). 1st edition. Bayley was the first editor of the *Illustrated London News*. He also wrote a number of popular songs. A children's picture book.

123. Bayley, F[rederick] W[illiam] N[aylor]. *Cinderella*. (London: Wm. S. Orr & Co., [1844]). 37pp. + plates. Illustrated by Cham (pseud. of Amédée de Noé). In the *Comic Nursery Tales* series.

A483 (series, title, publisher), JS47 (Anon./ Children's). Only edition in BL or BOD. A children's picture book. Amédée de Noé (1819–79) was a French caricaturist and lithographer.

124. Bayley, Jonathan (1810–86). *Great Truths on Great Subjects. Six Lectures*. (London: James Speirs, 1874). 216pp. 2nd edition.

Uncertain. Not in JS. Listed in WS (author, title, date) only and identified by gothic stamp and property label only. Bayley founded several schools and was a preacher in several free Church societies. This book included lectures on "The Christian Life," "Death and Resurrection," and "The Second Coming."

125. Beaumont, Francis (1584–1616) and John Fletcher (1579–1625). *The Works of Beaumont and Fletcher*. (London: George Routledge, 1866). 2 vols. New edition. With an introduction by George Darley. Part of *The Old Dramatists* series.

A736, B958 (authors, title, introduction details, 2 vols., date), JS471. Beaumont and Fletcher collaborated on a series of dramatic works from about 1606–1616. Darley (1795–1846) was a poet who also wrote several popular books on mathematics.

126. Beaumont, John (d. 1731). *An Historical, Physiological and Theological Treatise of Spirits, Apparitions, Witchcrafts, and Other Magical Practices. Containing an Account of the Genii or Familiar Spirits, both Good and Bad ... Also of Appearances of Spirits after Death; ... With a Refutation of Dr. Bekker's World Bewitch'd, and Other Authors That Have Opposed the Belief of Them*. (London: D. Browne, etc., 1705). 400pp.

B957 (author, title, date), JS472. B957 notes that this copy has "MSS notes in margins by a former owner." Beaumont was an English geologist and surgeon. The English edition of "Dr. Bekker's World" referred to in the title of the present work was: Bekker, Balthasar (1634–98). *The World Bewitched; or, an Examination of the Common Opinions Concerning Spirits*. (London: R. Baldwin, 1695). Bekker's book examined spiritual phenomena and discounted the idea of demonic possession. Beaumont's chatty volume reveals his strong belief in various spiritual phenomena and relates his personal experience of many.

127. Beaunis, H[enri Étienne] (1830–1921) and A[bel] Bouchard (1833–99). *Nouveaux Éléments d'Anatomie Descriptive et d'Embryologie*. (Paris: J. B. Baillière 1868). 1048pp.

A923 (authors, title), JS161 (Anon./Medical) and JS470. Earliest edition traced. Beaunis was a physiologist and later director of the Laboratory for Physiological Psychology at the Sorbonne (founded in 1889). The title translates, "New Elements of Descriptive Anatomy and Embryology." Includes chapters on organs of sense, the human body in general, and embryological development of the human.

128. Bechstein, Ludwig (1801–60). *As Pretty as Seven, and other Popular German Tales*. (London: J. C. Hotten, [1872]). 367pp. Illustrated by Richter, etc.

A645 (title), JS38 (Anon./Children). Only edition in BL. Bechstein was a collector of German folk stories. The stories in this collection are mostly from the *Deutches Märchenbuch*. Includes "Little One Eye" and other stories by the Brothers Grimm.

129. Bede, Cuthbert [pseud. of Edward Bradley] (1827–89). *The Adventures of Mr. Verdant Green, an Oxford Freshman*. (London: Nathaniel Cooke, 1853). 118pp. 1st edition. With numerous illustrations by the author. Part 1 (of 3) only.

A493 (author, title, date), JS473. Bradley was best known for this comic novel about Victo-

THE STARLING.

rian Oxford, but he also wrote a number of children's books, including a parody of Lear's *Book of Nonsense*. The Brooks catalogue does not list the latter two parts of this work. Perhaps Dodgson did not take to Bede's comic portrayal of Oxford undergraduate life, or maybe these volumes simply went missing or were not catalogued.

130. Bede, Cuthbert [pseud. of Edward Bradley]. *Nearer and Dearer: A Tale out of School. A Novelette.* (London: Richard Bentley, 1857). 182pp. 1st edition.

Uncertain. F174 (author, title, date, edition), not numbered in JS. Identified as Dodgson's only by gothic stamp. Humorous novelette.

131. Belcher, Thomas Waugh (1831–1910). *Our Lord's Miracles of Healing Considered in Relation to Some Modern Objections and to Medical Science, etc.* (Oxford & London: J. Parker & Co., 1872). 168pp.

A784 (author, title), JS475. Earliest edition in BOD or BL (BL incorrectly lists the 1890 2nd edition as 1800). Belcher was educated at Trinity College, Dublin and was rector of Frampton Cotterell in Somerset and a fellow of the Royal College of Physicians of Ireland. This work brings both his medical and theological training to bear.

132. Belcour, G. *A Selection of the Most Used French Proverbs with English Equivalents.* (London: Edward Stanford, 1882). 51pp.

E78 (title, author, date), JS476. E78 describes Dodgson's copy as having "many corrections in manuscript by Lewis Carroll."

133. Bell, Andrew [of Edinburgh]. *Mathematical Tables, Consisting of Logarithmic and Other Tables Required in the Various Branches of Practical Mathematics.* (Edinburgh: W. & R. Chambers?, 1851).

Top: Illustration of "The Starling" from Ludwig Bechstein's *As Pretty as Seven* (item 128). *Bottom:* Cuthbert Bede's title-page illustration of Mr. Verdant Green (item 129).

B959 (author, title, city, date), JS478. BL and BOD list only the 1844 edition (316 pp.) which was part of the *Chambers's Educational Course* series.

134. Bell, Arthur John. *Why Does Man Exist? The Continuation and Conclusion of Whence Comes Man?* (London: Wm. Isbister, 1890). 434pp.

A761 (title), JS337 (Anon./Theology). Only edition of the only matching title in BL. The prequel, *Whence Comes Man; from 'Nature' or from 'God'?* was published by Isbister in 1888.

135. Bell, Charles (1774–1842). *Essays on the Anatomy of Expression in Painting.* (London: Longman, Hurst, Rees, and Orme, 1806). 186pp.

A592 (author, title), JS477. Earliest edition in BL. The 3rd edition of 1844 was titled *The Anatomy and Philosophy of Expression, as Connected with the Fine Arts* and the work was frequently reprinted under that title. Bell was a Scottish surgeon and student of anatomy. He served as Professor of Anatomy and Surgery at the Royal College of Surgeons, London, and as Professor of Surgery at the University of Edinburgh. He was also an artist and this combination of talents made the present work an important treatise on the physiological basis of facial expressions.

136. Bell, Currer [pseud. of Charlotte Brontë] (1816–55). *Jane Eyre: An Autobiography.* (London: Smith, Elder & Co., 1848). 3 vols. 303, 304, 304pp. 3rd edition.

A664 (title, edition, 3 vols.), JS573. This edition includes not only the "Preface to the Second Edition," but also the "Note to the Third Edition," which reveals, for the first time, the true identity of the author (though her pseudonym is still used on the title page).

137. Bell, Currer [pseud. of Charlotte Brontë]. *The Professor. A Tale.* (London: Smith and Elder, 1857). 2 vols. 294, 258pp. 1st edition.

A664 (author, title, edition, 2 vols.), JS571. Novel of a young man working as a schoolteacher in Brussels.

138. Bell, Currer [pseud. of Charlotte Brontë]. *Shirley. A Tale.* (London: Smith, Elder & Co., 1849). 3 vols. 303, 308, 320pp. 1st edition.

A663 (author, title, 3 vols., edition), JS574. A novel set in Yorkshire during the Napoleonic wars in which a mill owner proposes marriage to Shirley, a wealthy young woman, but is rejected.

139. Bell, Currer [pseud. of Charlotte Brontë]. *Vilette.* (London: Smith, Elder & Co., 1853). 3 vols. 324, 319, 350pp. 1st edition.

A663 (author, title, 3 vols., edition), JS570. Novel about an English girl who pursues a career as a school teacher and her relationship with Professor Emanuel. Whether or not the two eventual marry is left for the reader to guess.

140. Bell, Currer, Ellis, and Acton [pseud. of Charlotte, Emily (1818–48), and Anne Brontë (1820–49)]. *Poems by Currer, Ellis, and Acton Bell.* (London: Smith, Elder and Co., 1846 [1848]). 165pp. 1st edition, 2nd issue in green cloth with the harp design.

A447 (author, title, date), JS569. Dodgson's copy is in Berg and has his monogram and last name in brown ink on the front pastedown. This was the first publication of any of the Brontë sisters.

141. *La Belle Assemblée, or Court and Fashionable Magazine; Containing Interesting and Original Literature, and Records of the Beau-Monde.* (London: J. Bell, etc., 1817?). Vol. XII only.

Not in JS. Listed in WS (title, vol. XII) only (not in WWC) and described there as having Dodgson's autograph initials. Publication of this annual began in 1806, thus volume 12 was likely published in 1817. A collection of colored plates from the annual was published in 1912 and represented "women's costume in England from 1807 to 1831."

142. Bennett, James Risdon (1809–91). *The Diseases of the Bible.* ([London]: Religious Tract Society, 1887). 143pp. No. 9 in the *By-Paths of Bible Knowledge* series.

B960 (author, title, date), JS479. Bennett was a British physician. In his introduction he notes how much has "been done in recent times to harmonise Scriptural records with the present state of natural science." He goes on to write, "In the following pages an attempt is made to investigate and illustrate the nature and course of some of the diseases particularly mentioned in the Bible, but not to give either a complete Biblical nosology or an account of Hebrew medicine." The text deals with leprosy, plague, blindness, diseases of the nervous system, and other conditions. The final chapter is titled, "Physical Cause of the Death of Christ."

143. Bennett, William Cox (1820–95). *Baby May, and Other Poems on Infants.* (London: Chapman & Hall, 1859). 32pp.

E362 (title, author, date), JS481. The title poem by this English poet had been first published privately ten years earlier and appeared in Jerrold's *Shilling Magazine* before going on to be popular in anthologies and recitations. In his introduction to this edition, Cox writes, "I hear of constant requests that this and other poems of mine, on kindred subjects, may be reprinted at a price which will enable the many who wish for them to obtain them." The title poem's subject was May Bennett, daughter of the poet. On 31 October 1883, Dodgson wrote to Bennett, "I presume I have the pleasure of addressing the writer who has given us dear little baby May. I thank you for the copy of The Lark, and will be very glad that you should make use of my verses on 'The Walrus and the Carpenter,' as you propose." The author has been unable to examine a copy of *The Lark* (see below) to see if it includes Dodgson's poem.

144. Bennett, William Cox, editor. *The Lark. Songs, Ballads, and Poems for the People.* (Greenwich, Birmingham: 1883–84). Issue unknown.

Not in JS. See above for the letter where Dodgson acknowledges receiving this. *The Lark* was a periodical published by Bennett for 6 issues. Presumably he sent Dodgson a single issue.

145. Bennett, William Cox. *The Worn Wedding-Ring, and Other Poems.* (London: Chapman & Hall, 1861). 192pp.

A851, B961 (author, title, date), JS480. This was Bennett's seventh book of poetry; his collected poems appeared in 1862. Includes 85 sonnets, apparently addressed to the volume's dedicatee H. M. Ticknor, referring to the literary and artistic world that Ticknor and Bennett shared, with allusions to many contemporary writers, and sonnets about Landor, the Brownings, Tennyson, Thackeray, Dickens, Leigh Hunt, and Ruskin.

146. [Benson, Edward White] (1829–96). *In the Court of the Archbishop of Canter-* *bury. Read and Others v. the Lord Bishop of Lincoln. Judgment. Nov. 21, 1890.* (London: Macmillan & Co, 1890). 122pp.

D104 (title, city, date), JS96 (Anon./Law). D104 notes Dodgson's initials. This is the judgment against Bishop Edward King (1829–1910) of Lincoln. King had been charged with Ritualism (using the sign of the cross, facing east, using candles on the altar, etc.) by the Church Association, led by Ernest de Lacy Read, a solicitor and churchwarden who witnessed the "offenses." Archbishop Benson, who began his career in the 1850s as a master at Rugby, re-established the Court of the Archbishop of Canterbury specifically for this case. The judgment was a mixed one, allowing some forbidden practices to continue while putting a stop to others. It was just one of many battles in the war between the High Church members of the Oxford Movement and anti-ritualistic powers within the Church.

147. Bernard, of Cluny (fl. 1150). *The Rhythm of Bernard de Morlaix, Monk of Cluny, on the Celestial Country.* (London: Hayes, [1858]). 48pp. Edited and Translated by John Mason Neale.

D151 (title, translator, city, n.d.), JS1577 (listed under Neale). D151 notes the inscription "C. L. D. from M. A. A. D." Earliest edition traced (dated from the preface). Bernard was a monk known as a poet and writer of hymns, his most famous work being the poem "On the Contempt of the World." John Mason Neale (1818–66) was a writer, translator and compiler of hymns. This work is a translation, by Neale, of the first portion of Bernard's famous poem which Neale calls "a description of the peace and glory of heaven, of such rare beauty, as not easily to be matched by any medieval composition on the same subject."

148. Besant, Walter (1836–1901). *All Sorts and Conditions of Men. An Impossible Story.* (London: Chatto & Windus, 1882). 3 vols. 313, 307, 284pp. With illustrations by Fred[erick] Barnard.

A605 (title, 3 vols.), JS99. Earliest edition in BL and the only to specify 3 vols. All items in A605 are by Besant (*Blind Love* is a Wilkie Collins novel completed by Besant). Besant was a novelist who began his career by collaborating on several works with James Rice (see 149). He wrote many historical novels and was an advocate for writers, helping found the Society of Authors. Here he writes of the miserable social conditions of East London. This work, together with his *Children of Gibeon* (1886) helped encourage the founding of The People's Palace, a center for "intellectual improvement and rational amusement" (OCEL). In a letter to Gertrude Thomson (15 December 1897) on the subject of the color of the cover for his book *Three Sunsets*, Dodgson writes, "Please look at a copy of Besant's book (any bookseller could show you one) and tell me if you would object to that colour for the cover" (see *Illustrators*, 317). Besant's most recently published book was *A Fountain Sealed* (London: Chatto & Windus, 1897), but whether Dodgson owned a copy or merely admired the color in a bookshop is not known.

149. Besant, Walter and James Rice (1853–82). *The Chaplain of the Fleet. A Novel.* (London: Chatto & Windus, 1881). 3 vols. 330, 276, 260 pp.

A605 (title, 3 vols.), JS377 (Anon./Unclassified). Only 19th-century edition in BL. All items in A605 are by Besant (*Blind Love* being a Wilkie Collins novel completed by Besant). Rice, a Cambridge man, collaborated on several novels with Besant. The two met when Rice purchased the periodical *Once a Week*. This is a novel of manners set in the mid–18th century.

150. Besant, William Henry (1828–1917). *Notes on Roulettes and Glissettes.* (Cambridge: Deighton, Bell & Co., 1870). 50 pp. With plates.

E68 (title, author, date), JS483. E68 notes that this is "perhaps the only unopened book in the Carroll collection." Besant was a fellow of St. John's College, Cambridge. A treatise on curves. The preface states, "The following pages contain the explanation of methods, and the investigation of formulae, which I have for some time past found useful in the discussion of the curves produced by the rolling or sliding of one curve on another.... I have ventured to introduce, and employ, the word Glissette as being co-expressive with Roulette, a word which has been in use amongst mathematicians for a considerable time."

151. [Bible]. Dodgson owned a number of English language Bibles which are not fully described in primary source materials.

A769/JS484 ("Bible, 2 vols., calf"); E178/JS484 ("Bible with two autographs of Lewis Carroll in 1844"); D16/JS484 ("Bible, Oxford, 1871. Brevier") (possibly published by Oxford University Press, no exact match traced), inscribed "C. L. Dodgson, Ch. Ch., May 1872"; D17/JS498 ("New Testament, Oxford, n.d. 32mo), inscribed with "name in full and initials." E430/JS487 may be the same book as D17 and is described as a "small, ordinary, cheap copy" of the New Testament. This copy is further described in E430: "Exceedingly interesting as being in Lewis Carroll's own use. It has remarks inside cover as to the purposes for which various portions of the New Testament are 'suitable.' The passages are marked in his purple ink, and three of the places are preserved by a curious three-fold book-marker of blue silk with tiny ivory pendants, and at top the crossed keys." DAA1988 lists a bible sold at Puttick & Simpson, London on 28 July 1938 with Dodgson's signature preceding the half-title and published in Cambridge in 1837 (BL lists 2 possibilities, published by Pitt Press and B. & F. B. S.). This copy was offered again at Sotheby's, London on 31 July–2 August 1939 (DAA2003).

152. [Bible]. *The Holy Bible, Containing the Old and New Testaments: Newly Translated Out of the Original Tongues; and with the Former Translations Diligently Compared and Revised. Bound together with The Book of Common Prayer, and Administration of the Sacraments, and other Rites and Ceremonies of the Church, According to the Use of the Church of England. Together with the Psalter or Psalms of David, Pointed as they are to be Sung or Said in Churches.* (Oxford: Printed by John Baskett, 1715). 1080pp. 185 plates. 4to.

B963 (title, publisher, date, 4to), JS486. Baskett published his Bible and prayer book in several formats; Dodgson owned the quarto edition. B963 states that his copy was inscribed "Charles Lutwidge Dodgson from L. L., April, 1873." Presumably a gift from his aunt Lucy Lutwidge.

153. [Bible]. *Novum Testamentum Græcum.* (London: Gulielmus Pickering, 1828). 511pp. In the *Pickering Diamond Classics* series.

A478 (title, publisher, series), JS488. This was one of at least 16 volumes of *Pickering's Diamond Classics* owned by Dodgson. This series of miniature books began in 1820, and was the first regular publishing venture to offer books bound in cloth. Most of the titles measured about 4.5 x 8 centimeters. Dodgson's other holdings in this series were: Catullus, Cicero (2 copies), Dante (2 copies), Homer, Horace, Horace & Virgil, Milton's *Paradise Lost*, Petrarch, Tasso, Terence, Walton's *Compleat Angler*, and Walton's *Lives*.

154. [Bible]. *The Prize Bible Told in Simple Words Chiefly from the Sacred Text.* (London: Wells Gardner, Darton, & Co., [1881–85]). 519pp. Illustrated with beautiful pictures, including color plates.

A751 (title), JS485. BL lists two possible titles, the other being *The Prize Bible; or, Covetousness*, published in Boston in 1863. Both the closer matching title and the London publication favor the present volume. Many of the illustrations are signed with a monogram that appears to read "A. R."

155. [Bible, Greek]. *Greek Testament.*

Dodgson owned at least 6 Greek Testaments. 3 are described elsewhere: 1) The edition edited by Alford (A777 and an odd volume of the same edition A765, see 26–27); 2) The edition edited by Scholefield (DAA2541, 1774); 3) A478/JS488 (The *Pickering Diamond Classics* edition, 153). 3 others are not sufficiently described in the primary source materials to identify: 4) A770/JS495 (described as "Greek Testament"); 5) A755/JS489 ("Greek and English Testament, 2 vols."); 6) E339/JS491 ("Novum Testamentum — Greek text, separated for study into 6 vols.").

156. [Bible, Hebrew]. *Bible, Hebrew and English.* Edition unknown.

A770 ("Bible, Hebrew and English"), JS493. A likely candidate is *The Holy Bible in Hebrew and English. With the Portions of the Prophets as Read in Synagogue. To which are Added the Explanatory, Critical, and Grammatical Notes of the Late David Levi.* (London: 1853). Genesis-Deuteronomy only.

157. [Bible, Polyglot]. *Biblia Polyglotta.* Edition unknown.

A770 ("Biblia Polyglotta"), JS494.

158. [Bible History] *The Gospels: Why are there Four? Why do they Differ? And Are they Fully Inspired?* (London: S. W. Partridge, [1867]). 32pp.

E258 (title, date), JS499. Dodgson's copy is in WWC. It is inscribed with his monogram. This tract answers the title questions thus: "Because God designed to set forth Christ in four different characters.... Because God had thus the better brought out those different characters....They are: God is the author."

159. [Bible Texts]. *Touching the Resurrection.* (London: Society for the Promotion of Christian Knowledge, [1890]).

E252 (title and description), JS333 (Anon./Theology). Only edition listed of the only matching title in BL and BOD. E252 describes this as "a booklet of texts with ornamental borders, richly printed in black and orange."

160. Bickersteth, Edward Henry (1825–1906). *The Reef, and Other Parables.* (London: Sampson Low & Co., 1874 [1873]). 172pp. With illustrations.

A932 (title), JS325 (Anon./Theology). Earliest edition of the only matching title in BL. Bickersteth was made Chaplain to the Bishop of Ripon in 1861, during the period when Dodgson stayed in Ripon while his father served as a canon at the cathedral. He became Bishop of Exeter in 1885. He was author of numerous books of theology and poetry and compiled *The Hymnal Companion to the Book of Common Prayer.* This work is a collection of parables for children.

161. Birks, T[homas] R[awson] (1810–83). *The Bible and Modern Thought.* (London: Religious Tract Society, [1861]). 417pp.

Uncertain. A761 (title), JS302 (Anon./Theology). This is the most likely of 3 possibilities in BL. George Emerson's book by the same title was published in Boston, not England; Robert Richard Rodgers' book (1890) is titled *The Bible and Modern Thought. Four Lectures* and is published in four parts. Dodgson owned other books by Birks, but no other titles by Rodgers or Emerson. The Birks book was reprinted at least once. The version listed in BL is in two parts (with appendix) totaling 515pp. A copy in the author's collection is in one part with no appendix and has 417pp. There is no mention of multiple parts in A761. Birks was Professor of Moral Theology, Divinity, and Moral Philosophy at Cambridge (appointed in 1872 in succession to Dodgson's friend F. D. Maurice, an appointment that caused some controversy as Birks was far mare conservative than the liberal Maurice). He was the son-in-law of Edward Bickersteth (see 160) and wrote books on many subjects as well as hymns. He served as honorary secretary to the Evangelical Alliance. According to his preface, Birks wrote this work at the behest of the Religious Tract Society "in order to supply some antidote, in a popular form, to that dangerous school of thought, which denies the miracles of the Bible, explains away its prophecies, and sets aside its Divine authority."

162. Birks, Thomas Rawson. *The Difficulties of Belief in Connexion with the Creation and the Fall.* (Cambridge: Macmillan & Co., 1855). 188pp.

A789 ("Burke's Difficulty of Belief"), JS619. Earliest edition in BL. Clearly a typographical error in A789 ("Burke's" for "Birks"). This homophonic error leads one to wonder if one cataloguer read titles off the shelf while another wrote them down (see also *Modern Physical Fatalism*, 164). In his diary for 24 July 1881 Dodgson writes, "I hope to read Birks' *Difficulties of Belief* again."

163. Birks, T[homas] R[awson]. *Justification and Imputed Righteousness. Being a Review of 'Ten Sermons on the Nature and Effects of Faith,' by James Thomas O'Brien D.D. Late Bishop of Ossory, Ferns, and Leighlin.* (London: Macmillan & Co., 1887). 230pp. Edited by H[erbert] A[lfred] Birks. With a preface by [Edward Harold Brown] the Lord Bishop of Winchester.

A791, B964 (gives H. A. Birks as author, title, attributes Preface to Bp. of Winchester, date), JS510 (attributed to H. A. Birks). See MBC for correct authorial attribution.

164. Birks, Thomas Rawson. *Modern Physical Fatalism and the Doctrine of Evolution, Including an Examination of Mr. H. Spencer's First Principles.* (London: Macmillan & Co., 1876). 311pp.

A773 ("Burke's Modern Physical Fatalism"), D20 (author, title, city, date), JS511, JS618. Clearly a typographical error in A789 ("Burke's" for "Birks," see also 162). The book mentioned in the title is Herbert Spencer's philosophical work, *First Principles*, published in 6 parts (1860–1862). Dodgson also owned a copy of this book (see 1919). Birks found Spencer's ideas, "radically unsound, full of logical inconsistency and contradiction, and flatly

opposed to the fundamental doctrines of Christianity and even the very existence of moral science." In October 1878, in a letter to Macmillan about the page size of his forthcoming *Euclid and His Modern Rivals* (1879), Dodgson wrote, "As the text is the same width as Birks' *Physical Fatalism*, I suppose the book had better be that size." (See *Macmillan*, 148).

165. Birks, Thomas Rawson. *On Matter and Ether; or, The Secret Laws of Physical Change.* (Cambridge & London: Macmillan & Co., 1862). 216pp.

D21 (author, title, city, date), JS512.

166. Birrell, Augustine (1850–1933). *Obiter Dicta.* (London: Elliot Stock, 1884). 234pp.

A561 (title), JS513. There were three volumes of these essays published (*Obiter Dicta, Obiter Dicta Second Series*, and *More Obiter Dicta*) and all were reprinted several times. As A561 does not specify a series and does not mention multiple volumes, it seems most likely to refer to this, the 1st edition of the 1st series. Called to the bar in 1875, Birrell went on to serve in Parliament and as Minister of Education and Secretary to Ireland. In addition to his work as a wit and essayist he wrote biographies of Charlotte Brontë, Hazlitt, and Marvell. The present volume includes essays on Carlyle, Browning, Falstaff, and Actors.

167. Bishop, John (1797–1873). *On Articulate Sounds; and On the Causes and Cure of Impediments of Speech.* (London: Samuel Highley, 1851). 79pp.

E233 (title, author, date), JS514. Bishop was a fellow of the Royal College of Physicians known for his successful work with speech impediments from which Dodgson and several members of his family suffered. In his preface the author states his disagreement with the idea of surgery as a cure for speech impediments.

168. [**Black**, Adam and Charles], publishers. *Black's Guide to Edinburgh and Environs. Including Hawthornden and Roslin.* (Edinburgh: Adam and Charles Black [R. Clark], 1871). 88pp.

E125 ("Edinburgh — Black's Guide, 1871"), JS345 (Anon./Topography). Dodgson probably purchased this for his 1871 trip to Scotland.

169. [**Black**, Adam and Charles], publishers. *Black's Picturesque Guide to the*

Trosachs, Loch Catrine, Loch Lomond, and Central Touring District of Scotland, etc. (Edinburgh: A. & C. Black, 1853). 212pp. 1st edition.

E370 ("The Trossachs [sic]—Black's Picturesque Guide, 1st edition, 1853"), JS346 (Anon./Topography). Dodgson probably purchased this for his 1857 trip to Scotland.

170. [**Black**, Adam and Charles], publishers. *Black's Picturesque Tourist of Scotland.* (Edinburgh: A. & C. Black, 1871). 616pp. 19th edition.

E419 (title), JS344. No edition specified, but Dodgson made two trips to Scotland, one in 1857 and one in 1871. His *Black's Guide to Edinburgh* is dated 1871. The 1857 13th edition is another possibility.

171. Black, William (1841–98). *Green Pastures and Piccadilly.* (London: Macmillan and Co., 1877). 3 vols. 290, 280, 284pp.

Not in JS. Dodgson's diary for 12 August 1880 reads, in part, "Just now I am reading William Black's [novel] *Green Pastures and Piccadilly*— it has a weary lot of 'padding'." This is the 1st edition. A 1-volume edition was printed later in 1877 and reprinted in 1878. Black was a Scottish journalist turned novelist who lived in Brighton and traveled widely, often taking inspiration for his works from the places he visited. His many novels proved popular from the early 1870s until his death.

172. Black, William. *The Handsome Humes.* (London: Sampson Low & Co., 1893). 3 vols. [240], [224], [232]pp. 1st edition.

A630, B967 (author, title, edition, 3 vols., date), JS520. Novel.

173. Black, William. *Judith Shakespeare: A Romance.* (London: Macmillan & Co., 1884). 3 vols. 246, 278, 256pp. 1st edition.

A630, B966 (author, title, edition, 3 vols., date), JS519. A novel about William Shakespeare's cousin.

174. Black, William. *Macleod of Dare. A Novel.* (London: Macmillan & Co., 1878). 3 vols. 286, 307, 320pp. 1st edition.

A629 (author, title, edition, 3 vols.), JS517. Set in Black's native Scotland. Shortly before his own assassination, President Garfield sent a message to Black that he ought not to have let *Macleod of Dare* end tragically.

175. Black, William. *Sunrise, A Story of These Times.* ([London]: Sampson Low & Co., 1880). 3 vols. 1st edition.

A627 (author, title, 3 vols., edition), JS515. Novel.

176. Black, William. *Three Feathers. A Novel.* (London: Sampson Low & Co., 1875). 3 vols. 1st edition.

A630, B965 (author, title, edition, 3 vols., date), JS518. A novel set in Cornwall.

177. Black, William. *Wolfenberg.* (London: Sampson Low & Co., 1892). 3 vols. [248], 268, 252pp. 1st edition.

A628 (author, title, edition, 3 vols.), JS516. Novel.

178. Blackie, John Stuart (1809–95), et al. *Edinburgh Essays by Members of the University. 1856.* (Edinburgh: Adam and Charles Black, 1857). 350pp.

A335, D138 (author, title with date), JS114 (Anon./Literature). Includes: "Plato," by John Stuart Blackie; "Early English Life in the Drama," by John Skelton; "Homœopathy," by William Gairdner; "Infanti Perduti," by Andrew Wilson; "Progress of Britain in the Mechanical Arts," by James Sime; "Scottish Ballads," by Alexander Smith; "Sir William Hamilton," by Thomas Spencer Baynes; and "Chemical Final Causes," by George Wilson.

179. Blake, William (1757–1827). *Poetical Sketches. Now First Reprinted from the Original Edition of 1783.* (London: B. M. Pickering, 1868). 96pp. Edited and prefaced by Richard Herne Shepherd.

A829 (author, title), JS523. 1st public edition. The private edition of 1783 survives in only 21 copies, and it is unlikely that Dodgson would have owned one (also A829 contains several items and surely a great rarity such as the private edition would have been listed separately). See 1833 for a note on Shepherd.

180. Blake, William. *Songs of Innocence.* Edition unknown.

A357 (author, title), JS522. Probably an edition of *Songs of Innocence and Experience*, as the former was rarely published separately. The most likely candidate is one of the many Pickering editions edited by Richard Herne Shepherd that were published during the 19th century.

181. Bland, Miles (1786–1867). *Algebraical Problems, Producing Simple and Quadratic Equations, with Their Solutions. Designed as an Introduction to the Higher Branches of Analytics.* (Cambridge: Printed by J. Smith; sold by J. Deighton, etc., 1812). 345pp.

A957 (author, title), JS524. Earliest of many editions in BL. Bland was a fellow and tutor of St. John's College, and also wrote on Hydrostatics and various branches of mathematics.

182. Bledsoe, Albert Taylor (1809–77). *The Philosophy of Mathematics, with Special Reference to the Elements of Geometry and the Infinitesimal Method.* (Philadelphia: J. B. Lippincott & Co., 1868). 248pp.

E328 (title, author, city, date), F149, JS525. E328 describes Dodgson's copy as having "initials of and corrective notes by Lewis Carroll." Bledsoe taught Mathematics at the University of Mississippi and the University of Virginia. He served as Assistant Secretary of War for the Confederacy and wrote several works of philosophy, including one in support of slavery. As founder and editor of the *Southern Review*, he continued to defend the Old South after the Civil War.

183. Bligh, William (1754–1817). *A Narrative of the Mutiny, on Board His Majesty's Ship Bounty: and the Subsequent Voyage of Part of the Crew, in the Ship's Boat, from Tofoa, One of the Friendly Islands, to Timor, a Dutch Settlement in the East Indies.* (London: Printed for G. Nicol, 1790). 88pp. Illustrated with charts, folding map.

A728 (Bligh's Narrative), JS526. This is the 1st edition, though Dodgson may certainly have owned a later reprint.

184. Blunt, John Henry (1823–84). *The Annotated Bible, Being a Household Commentary Upon the Holy Scriptures, Comprehending the Results of Modern Discovery and Criticism.* (London: Rivingtons, 1879–82). 3 vols. 1088, 212, 822pp. With the text (King James Version with the Apocrypha).

A745 (author, title, 3 vols.), JS500. Only edition in BL. Blunt was educated at Durham and ordained in 1852. He was vicar of Kennington, near Oxford from 1868 to 1873 and following that held the living of Beverston in Glouces-

tershire. He wrote a number of reference books relating to the church. A publisher's advertisement reads, "This book has been written with the object of providing for educated readers a compact intellectual exposition of the Holy Bible, in which they may find such explanations and illustrations of the Sacred Books as will meet the necessities of the ordinary inquirer of the present day."

185. Blunt, John Henry, editor. *The Annotated Book of Common Prayer. Being an Historical, Ritual, and Theological Commentary on the Devotional System of the Church of England.* (London: Rivingtons, 1866). 610pp.

A748 (editor, title), JS505. Earliest edition in BL. BL also lists this book under the heading William Bright (see 237). The *Guardian* wrote, "Whether as, historically, shewing how the Prayer Book came to be what it is, or, ritually, how it designs itself to be rendered from word into act, or, theologically, as exhibiting the relation between doctrine and worship on which it is framed, the book amasses a world of information, carefully digested."

186. Blunt, J[ohn] H[enry], editor. *Dictionary of Doctrinal and Historical Theology.* (London: Rivingtons, 1870). 850pp.

A748 (title; Blunt is author of previous book listed), JS311 (Anon./Theology). Earliest edition in BL. *The Standard* wrote, "It will be found of admirable service to all students of theology, as advancing and maintaining the Church's views on all subjects as fall within the range of fair argument and inquiry. It is not often that a work of so comprehensive and so profound a nature is marked to the very end by so many signs of wide and careful research, sound criticism, and well-founded and expressed belief."

187. Blunt, John James (1794–1855). *Undesigned Coincidences in the Old Testament and New Testament, an Argument of their Veracity: With an Appendix Containing Undesigned Coincidences between the Gospels and Acts, and Josephus.* (London: John Murray, 1853). 368pp.

WS, not in JS. Spencer describes this as "Dodgson's copy with the following on the inside of the front cover in his autograph, 'C. L. Dodgson Ch. Ch. Oxford 1862,' then underneath is a rubber stamp with 'Rev. C. L. Dodgson Shrewsbury.'" (See preface for a discussion of this stamp.) This copy sold at Sotheby's London on 10 November 1998 (DAA3148) and is now in the collection of Alan Tannenbaum, Austin TX. On the inside front cover are Dodgson's ownership inscription and the purple ownership stamp of his brother Edwin ("Rev. E. H. Dodgson All Saints Shrewsbury"). Clearly Spencer was confused about whose stamp this was. It also bears the ownership inscription "Coleridge Grove, 1854." Blunt was Lady Margaret Professor of Divinity at Cambridge and shortly before his death he declined the see of Salisbury. The work, which sets out to prove the truth of scripture, is an elaboration of a book on St. Paul's Epistles by William Paley (see 1483).

188. Blunt, Walter and Winthrop Mackworth Praed (1802–39). *The Etonian.* (Windsor: Knight & Dredge; London: John Warren, 1820–21). 2 vols.

A577 (title, 2 vols.), JS118 (Anon./Literature). Published from October 1820–August 1821. 1st edition. A 2nd edition was also 2 volumes; the 3rd and 4th editions were 3 volumes. A publication of Eton College containing essays, poems, letters, and stories. Praed was the son of the poet William Mackworth Praed. The younger Praed achieved distinction as a poet and also served in Parliament.

189. Boase, Charles William (1828–95). *Oxford.* (London: Longmans & Co., 1887). 230pp. In the *Historic Towns* series.

Uncertain. A318 ("Historic Towns"), JS355 (Anon./Topography). No book with this specific title published before 1898 has been traced, but this almost certainly refers to an item in Longmans' *Historic Towns* series (in all likelihood the entry was taken from the series title). Since all the other items in A318 relate to Oxford, it seems reasonable to conclude that the "Historic Towns" entry refers to the above described title. The series title "Historic Towns" is stamped prominently on both the spine and the front cover. Boase was a Fellow at Exeter College, Oxford, where he lectured in modern history and served as librarian.

190. Böckh, August (1785–1867). *The Public Economy of Athens.* (London: J. W. Parker, 1842). 688pp. 2nd edition, revised. Translated by George Cornewall Lewis.

Not in JS. In a letter to his sister Elizabeth on 24 June 1852, Dodgson writes, "I got just before

leaving Boeckh's *Public Economy of Athens,* which Mr. Gordon recommends me to read, and Papa had desired me to get last term" (see *Letters*). First published in 1828, this is the edition in BL closest to Dodgson's acquisition. Böckh was a German historian.

191. Bohn, Henry George (1796–1884), compiler. *A Handbook of Proverbs. Comprising an Entire Republication of Ray's Collection of English Proverbs with His Additions from Foreign Languages. And a Complete Alphabetical Index in Which are Introduced Large Additions, as Well of Proverbs as of Sayings.* (London: H. G. Bohn, 1860). 583pp. In *Bohn's Antiquarian Library* series.

A327, B969 (author, title, date), JS527. Bohn was an English bookseller, bibliographer, and publisher. John Ray (1628–1705) was a botanist and writer who published *A Collection of English Proverbs* in 1670.

192. Bolton, George Bucklet. "Statement of the Principle Circumstances Respecting the United Siamese Twins Now Exhibiting in London." (London: 1830). 5pp. + plate. An article excerpted from the *Philosophical Transactions.*

E126 (title ["On the United Siamese Twins"], author, full description and date), JS528. E126 describes Dodgson's copy as containing a "presentation to Dr. Hodgkin from the author." Bolton was a member of the Royal College of Surgeons and of the Medical and Chirurgical Society of London. The article describes something of the history of the twins Chang and Eng as well as several experiments conducted on them by Dr. Bolton. Dodgson's circular *Secondhand Books* (see JS p. x–xi) includes listed among his wants "Pamphlet on the Siamese Twins," but it impossible to know if this refers to the present item.

193. Bonney, Thomas George (1833–1923). *Old Truths in Modern Lights. The Boyle Lectures for 1890 with Other Sermons.* (London: Percival & Co., 1891). 286pp.

A792 (author, title), JS529. Only edition in BL. Bonney was an English clergyman and geologist with a special interest in the Alpine region. From 1868 he served for several years as tutor at St. John's College, Cambridge. A collection of sermons and lectures including "The

Present Conflict of Science and Theology" (in 8 lectures), "The Inspiration of Scripture," "The Origin of Evil," and others. In his preface, Bonney points that similarities between his own work and *Lux Mundi* (see 799) are "fortuitous," as he had not read that book prior to composing the present pieces.

194. Booker, John (1819–95). *A Scripture & Prayer Book Glossary; Being an Explanation of Obsolete Words and Phrases.* (Dublin: Hodges, Smith & Co., 1856). 101pp. 2nd edition, revised and enlarged, of *Obsolete Words and Phrases in the Bible and Apocrypha.*

E268 (title ["Obsolete Words and Phrases in the Apocrypha and Prayer Book,"] author, date), JS530. This is the only 1856 edition listed in BL; the exact title listed in E268 is not listed in BL at all, thus this would seem the correct edition. Booker's other works include histories of several ancient chapels.

195. Boole, George (1815–64). *A Treatise on the Calculus of Finite Differences.* (Cambridge & London: Macmillan & Co., 1860). 248pp.

D23 (author, title, city, date), JS531. According to D23, Dodgson's copy was signed by him. One of the leading mathematicians of his time, Boole pioneered the science of the logic of algebra, and Boolean algebra is today an important element in computers. He taught mathematics at the University of Cork. Dodgson may have owned a copy of Boole's *Investigation of the Laws of Thought* (A505/JS532); see 2076 for a note on this title; see 1020 and 1075 for responses to Boole.

196. Borrow, George [Henry] (1803–81). *The Bible in Spain; or, the Journeys, Adventures and Imprisonments of an Englishman in an Attempt to Circulate the Scriptures in the Peninsula.* (London: John Murray, 1843) 3 vols. 370, 398, 391pp. 4th edition.

A597 (title, edition), JS534. Borrow studied to be a solicitor before giving up the law for literature. He traveled extensively in Europe, and many of his novels are based on his own experiences. DEL describes this work as "remarkable for its 'graphic pictures of life, high, middle, and low, in the byways as well as the highways of the land of Gil Blas'."

197. Borrow, George Henry. *Lavengro; The Scholar, The Gypsy, The Priest.* (London: John Murray, 1851). 3 vols. 360, 366, 426pp. 1st edition. With a portrait.

A597 (author, title, edition, 3 vols.), JS533. DEL describes this work as "'a half-authentic, half-fanciful' account of the author's wanderings through England as tinker, gipsy, postilion, and ostler, 'after his desertion of London and literature.' The description of his adventures, which were far from being of an agreeable character, is continued in *The Romany Rye*, published in 1857."

198. Borrow, George Henry. *The Zincali; or, an Account of the Gypsies of Spain. With an Original Collection of Their Songs and Poetry, and a Copious Dictionary of Their Language.* (London: John Murray, 1841). 2 vols. 362; 156, 135pp. 1st edition.

A597 (title, edition, 2 vols.), JS535.

199. Bosanquet, Bernard (1848–1923). *Logic, or the Morphology of Knowledge.* (Oxford: Clarendon Press, 1888). 2 vols. 398, 240pp.

A508, D105 (author, title, 2 vols., city, date), JS536. Bosanquet was an important English philosopher. A fellow and tutor at University College in Oxford until his move to London in 1881, Bosanquet wrote, in this book and elsewhere, of the importance of logical thought in dealing with philosophical issues.

200. Bosanquet, George William (1845–69). *Essays and Stories by the Late G. W. Bosanquet.* (London: Sampson Low & Co., 1870). 289pp. With an Introductory Chapter by Capt. C. B. Brackenbury.

A562 ("Essays and Stories"), JS117 (Anon./ Literature). Only edition of the only pre–1898 matching title listed in BL. Bosanquet served for a time in the army and then took a post with the Exchequer. As a young man he delighted in writing stories and drawing; he died of a fever at the age of 24. His stories, some inspired by the cathedrals of France, are here collected, as are essays such as "Promotion in the Army," "Religion in the Army," and "The Rise and Progress of Combinations Among Workmen."

201. Boswell, James (1740–95). *The Life of Samuel Johnson, LL.D. Comprehending an Account of His Studies and Numerous*

Works, in Chronological Order; A Series of His Epistolary Correspondence and Conversations with Many Eminent Persons; and Various Original Pieces of his Composition, Never Before Published, etc. (London: Charles Dilly, 1791). 2 vols. 516, 588pp. 1st edition. With a portrait and facsimiles.

A519 (author, title, edition, 2 vols.), JS537.

202. Bosworth, J[oseph] (1789–1876). *A Dictionary of the Anglo-Saxon Language.* (London: Longman, Rees, Orme, Brown, Green and Longmans, 1838). 721pp.

A388 (author, title), JS538. Earliest edition in BL. Bosworth was an English vicar who served as a chaplain in Holland for a time and whose avocation was Anglo-Saxon studies. In 1857 he became Professor of Anglo-Saxon at Oxford. This is his chief work; he also wrote *Elements of Anglo-Saxon Grammar* (1823).

203. Bourne, Vincent (1695–1747). *The Poetical Works, Latin and English, of Vincent Bourne.* (Cambridge: Printed for W. P. Grant, and sold by H. Washbourne; London: Printed by Metcalfe and Palmer, 1838). 320pp. Text in Latin and English on facing pages.

A828, D24 (author, title, city [London], date), JS539. Bourne was a schoolmaster of Cowper at Westminster School.

204. Bowers, Georgina (b. 1836). *A Month in the Midlands.* (London: Bradbury, Evans & Co., 1868). 24 plates with captions.

Uncertain. F176 (author, title, n.d.), JS542. Identified as Dodgson's only by the gothic stamp. Bowers was a cartoonist for *Punch*, the *London Graphic*, and other papers. Though F176 states "n.d.," this is the only edition in BL. The title page is, in fact, undated, the date appearing only on the cover. A collection of mostly sporting prints. One includes a scene of a man and woman playing croquet.

205. Bowes, George Seaton. *Conversation: Why Don't We Do More Good By It?* (London: J. Nisbet & Co., 1886). 201pp.

B971 (author, title, date), JS543. Bowes was a rector and miscellaneous writer, educated at Cambridge.

206. Bowles, Thomas Gibson (1842–1922). *The Defence of Paris; Narrated as It Was Seen.* (London: Sampson Low & Co., 1871). 405pp. With illustrations, and a map of Paris.

A918 (author, title), JS544. Only edition in BL. Bowles was the founder and editor of *Vanity Fair*, to which Dodgson contributed his ongoing word game "Doublets." In 1884 he founded *The Lady*, and Dodgson contributed a similar word game "Syzzygies" to that publication. Dodgson met Bowles on several occasions, and Bowles was actively involved in administering (and commenting on in print) Dodgson's word games. In 1887 Bowles left publishing (eventually selling *Vanity Fair*) to pursue a career in politics. He served as an MP for 18 years. (See LCP, #70 for more on Bowles and Dodgson.) An account of the 1870–71 defence of Paris during the Franco-Prussian war which he wrote with the aid of the French artist James Tissot (1836–1902) who fought in Paris and fled to London in 1871. Tissot drew caricatures for *Vanity Fair.*

207. Bowles, Thomas Gibson. *The Log of the 'Nereid.'* (London: Simpkin, Marshall & Co., 1889). 229pp. Illustrated by Lockhart Bogle.

A918 ("The Log of the Neread [sic]"), JS545. Only edition in BL of the only possible match. A narrative of Bowles's voyage on a schooner with his four children to the Holy Land and the Nile.

208. [Bowles, Thomas Gibson]. *The Vanity Fair Album: A Show of Sovereigns, Statesmen, Judges, and Men of the Day; with Biographical and Critical Notices by Jehu Junior.* Vols. 11–13? (London: Vanity Fair, ?1879–81). 3 vols.

A528 (title, 3 vols.), JS218 (Anon./Periodicals). *The Vanity Fair Album*, a collection of the full-page color caricatures of "Men of the Day" which appeared in the weekly magazine, was published annually from 1869 to 1912. Dodgson contributed his word-game "Doublets" to *Vanity Fair* weekly from 1879 to 1881, thus it seems that those years are the most likely for him to have purchased (or perhaps received as a gift from the editor Thomas Gibson Bowles) the albums. A Christ Church Common Room agenda paper for February 1884 (see *Oxford*, 177) lists "Vanity Fair Albums from commencement in 1869 to end of 1881" as a gift to the Common Room from Dodgson. Bowles wrote the descriptive text accompanying the

"Warm Enough for Croquet" (from item 204).

cartoons under the pseudonym Jehu Junior. E424/JS219 describes a collection of 27 individual Vanity Fair prints, all from 1879: Bret Harte, Sir G. Boywer, Lord Bateman, Gounod, A. J. Otway, Verdi, Renan, Sir Geo. Jessel, Maj.-Gen. Crealock, Alma Tadema, Maj.-Gen. Havelock, Lord G. Hamilton, Ed. Stanhope, Michell Henry, Herbert Spencer, Lord Suffield, Justice Straight, G. O. Morgan, Col. Stanley, Sir P. J. W. Miles, Viscount Castlereagh, The Earl of Lonsdale, J. F. Leath, C. W. Williams-Wynn, Jules Grévy, Holman Hunt, Peter Rylands.

209. Bowling, Tom [i.e. Paul Rapsey Hodge]. *The Book of Knots: Being a Complete Treatise on the Art of Cordage Showing the Manner of Making Every Knot, Tie and Splice*. (London: Robert Hardwicke, 1866). 21pp. 1st edition. Illustrated with 472 diagrams (3 fold-out plates).

E130 (title, author, date), JS546.

210. Bowring, J[ohn] (1792–1872), translator and editor. *Servian Popular Poetry*. (London: Printed for the Author, 1827). 235pp.

A865 ("Servian Popular Poems"), JS135 (Anon./Literature). Only edition in BL of the only possible match there. Bowring was an English author, politician, and diplomat who learned many languages when traveling for business. He published a series of collections of translated literature from countries in eastern Europe and from Spain and Holland.

211. Bowring, John, editor. *Wybor Poezyi Polskiey. Specimens of the Polish Poets. With Notes and Observations on the Literature of Poland*. (London: Printed for the Author, 1827). 227pp.

A842 (author, title), JS547. Only edition in BL.

212. Boyce, John Cox (ca. 1826–89). *Nigh Unto the End; or, a Passage in Sacred Prophecy, (Rev. XVI. 12–15.) Now in Course of Translation into History, Considered*. (London: R. Bentley & Son, 1880). 256pp.

D25 (author, title, city, date), JS548. Boyce was an Oxfordshire rector and poet educated at Magdalen Hall, Oxford. He matriculated in 1848 and received his B.A. in 1854, and so could have known Dodgson as an undergraduate. The passage considered concerns the sixth angel and the vision of three foul spirits issuing from the mouths of the dragon, the beast, and the false prophet.

213. Boyd, A[ndrew] K[ennedy] H[utchinson] (1825–99). *The Commonplace Philosopher In Town and Country*. (London: Longman, Green, Longman, Roberts & Green, 1864). New edition.

Uncertain. Not in JS. Listed in WS (title, date) only and identified by gothic stamp and property label only. Boyd was a Scottish preacher and church leader whose popular essays carried much of the charm which is remembered in his own conversation.

214. Boyd, A[ndrew] K[ennedy] H[utchinson]. *Our Little Life. Essays Consolatory and Domestic, with Some Others*. (London: Longmans & Co., 1882). 329pp.

A342, B1157 (title, author, date), JS550.

215. Boyd, A[ndrew] K[ennedy] H[utchison]. *The Recreations of a Country Parson*. (London: J. W. Parker, 1859). 373pp.

B972 (author, title, "original edition, 1856"), JS549. Apparently a misprint in B972, as the 1st edition of this, the 1st of three series of this title, was published in 1859. A collection of popular essays including "Concerning the Country Parson's Life," "Concerning Work and Play," "Concerning Hurry and Leisure," and others.

216. Boyes, John Frederick (1811–79). *Lacon in Council*. (London: Bell & Daldy, 1865). 259pp.

D26 (author, title, date), JS552. D26 describes this as "From the Author." Boyes was educated at Lincoln and St. John's Colleges, Oxford and served as headmaster of Walthamstow Proprietary School. He was known for the breadth of his reading. A book of famous quotes on various subjects, each followed by Boyes' commentary. Subjects include Education, Dress, Manners and Courtesy, the Fair Sex, Argument, Politics and Religion. Dodgson was apparently acquainted with the Boyes family (see *Letters*, 462–63).

217. Boyes, John Frederick. *Life and Books; or, Records of Thought and Reading*. (London: Bell & Daldy, 1859). 256pp.

B973 (author, title), JS551. Only edition in BL. A collection of thoughts from the author's experience and reading, the latter supported with quotes from books.

218. Boyesen, H[jalmar] H[jorth]. *Gunnar. Eine Erzählung aus dem Norwegischen*. (Breslau, 1880).

D27 (author, title, city, date), JS553. This edition not traced; description taken from D27. German translation of the work published in English (at least as early as 1875) as *Gunnar A Tale of Norse Life*. Boyesen was a Norwegian-born American writer. In a flattering review of the American edition of this tale (written in English by Boyesen) *The Atlantic Monthly* (November 1874) wrote, "The plot is the love of a houseman's son for the daughter of a rich peasant landowner and relates to Gunnar's growth from a dreamy boyhood to the manhood of a young painter."

219. B[oyle], E[leanor] V[ere] [i.e. Mrs. Richard Cavendish Boyle] (1825–1916). *A Children's Summer.* (London: Addey & Co., 1853). 16 leaves. 11 etchings on steel by E. V. B. Illustrated in prose and rhyme by M. L. B. and W. M. C.

A289 (title), not in JS. Only matching title in BL, and Dodgson owned several other works by Boyle. Boyle exhibited at Grosvenor Gallery in the period from 1878 to 1881. She produced many books for children under the initials E. V. B. Later in life she wrote and illustrated books on gardening. The present title is the second listed in BL (her earliest is *Child's Play*, published in 1852). An illustrated book for children.

220. B[oyle], E[leanor] V[ere] [i.e. Mrs. Richard Cavendish Boyle]. *A Dream Book.* (London: Sampson Low & Co., 1870). 12 plates with accompanying letterpress.

A274 (title), not in JS. This is the only edition of the only matching title in BL; also, the other item in A274 is by E. V. Boyle. An illustrated book for children. The plates were created by a photographic process and then mounted.

221. B[oyle], E[leanor] V[ere] [i.e. Mrs. Richard Cavendish Boyle]. *A New Child's-Play.* (London: Sampson Low & Co., 1877). 16 Drawings.

A533 (title), JS554. Only separate edition of the only matching title in BL. Sequel to E. V. B.'s *Child's Play* (London: Sampson Low & Co., 1881 [1880]). An illustrated book for children.

222. B[oyle], E[leanor] V[ere] [i.e. Mrs. Richard Cavendish Boyle]. *Waifs and Strays from a Scrap Book.* (London: Cundall, Downes & Co., 1862). 2nd edition.

A274 (title, edition, date), not in JS. An illustrated book for children.

223. Boyle, Patrick (originator). *Boyle's New Fashionable Court and Country Guide and Town Visiting Directory (Boyle's Court Guide) for the year 1888.* (London: 1888).

E36 (title, date), JS231 (Anon./Reference). Begun in 1792 as *The Fashionable Court Guide,*

or the Town Visit Directory, Boyle's Court Guide was published through 1925.

224. [Braby, F.] *Fallen Angels. A Disquisition Upon Human Existence: An Attempt to Elucidate Some of its Mysteries, Especially those of Evil and Suffering. By One of Them.* (London: Gay & Bird, 1894). 230pp.

D68 (title), JS315 (Anon./Theology). Earliest edition in BL or BOD. An exploration of theological questions, especially the "why" of existence, evil, pain, etc. "The How, Why, and Wherefore," writes the author, "have not received the full amount of profound and reverent study that the ineffably intrinsic importance of the subject to ourselves warrants."

225. Brachet, Auguste (1846?–98). *An Etymological Dictionary of the French Language.* Translated by G[eorge] W[illiam] Kitchin (1827–1912). (Oxford: Clarendon Press, 1878). 407pp. 2nd edition.

A327, B974 (author, title, city, date), JS555. According to an article in the July 1870 *North American Review*, Brachet "belongs to a small circle of young French scholars who are laboring to introduce among their own countrymen the historical method of grammatical study which has accomplished such brilliant results in Germany." Kitchin was a Student of Christ Church, a mathematical examiner, Dean of Winchester and eventually Dean of Durham. Dodgson was friends with the Kitchin family, and the daughter "Xie" was one of his favorite photographic models.

226. Brachet, Auguste. *Historical Grammar of the French Tongue.* (Oxford: Clarendon Press, 1869). 211pp. Translated by G. W. Kitchin.

E133 (author, title, translator, date), JS556. A work in three parts: "Phonetics," "Inflection," and "The Formation of Words." The July 1870 *North American Review* called this book, "the best handbook of this science [i.e. teaching French to university students] we have yet met with."

227. Brackett, A[nna] C[allender] (1836–1911), editor. *The Education of American Girls. Considered in a Series of Essays.* (New York: G. P. Putnam's Sons, 1874). 401pp.

A588 (title), JS401 (Anon./Women). Only edition of the only matching title in BL or BOD. Brackett was an American poet and writer on education. Essays by A. C. Brackett, E. D. Cheney and others.

228. Bradley, Francis Herbert (1846–1924). *The Principles of Logic.* (London: Kegan Paul & Co., 1883). 534pp.

A515 (author, title), JS557. Only 19th-century edition in BL. Bradley was a fellow of Merton College, Oxford, and an influential philosopher. He was an early Neo-Idealist, and the present work was a groundbreaking treatise exposing the defects of empirical logic. He refused to allow it to be reprinted until he prepared a completely revised edition in 1922. CHEAL calls this work "A triumph for the idealist theory of knowledge." One reaction to this work was Bernard Bosanquet's *Knowledge and Reality. A Criticism of Mr. F. H. Bradley's "Principles of Logic"* (1885). Dodgson owned Bosanquet's *Logic* (see 199).

229. Brande, W[illiam] T[homas] (1788–1866) and George W. Cox (1827–1902), editors. *A Dictionary of Science, Literature, and Art.* (London: Longmans & Co., 1865–67). 3 vols.

A386 (editors, title, 3 vols.), JS558. Earliest edition of the Brande and Cox version in BL. Originally published as: *A Dictionary of Science, Literature, and Art. Comprising the History, Description & Scientific Principles of Every Branch of Human Knowledge; With the Derivation and Definition of All the Terms in General Use.* Edited by W. T. Brande assisted by Joseph Cauvin, etc. (London: Longmans & Co., 1842). Brande was a Professor of Chemistry in the Royal Institution.

230. [Brathwaite, Richard] (1588–1673). *Drunken Barnaby's Four Journeys to the North of England. In Latin and English Metre. Wittily and Merrily (Tho' an Hundred Years Ago) Compos'd; Found Among some Old Musty Books That Had Lain a Long Time By in a Corner, and Now at Last Made Public. Together with Bessy Bell. To Which Is Now Added, (Never Before Published) The Ancient Ballad of Chevy Chase. In Latin and English Verse.* (London: Printed for W. Stuart, 1778). 175pp. 4th edition. Illustrated with several neat copper-plates.

B1044 (title, date), JS559. Brathwaite was an English poet, educated at Oxford. This work

(first published in 1638) is a record (in Latin verse and English doggerel) of his pilgrimages through England. It includes the story of John Bartendale of York who was buried after being hanged. Some time later, observing the earth move, passersby dug him up and found him still alive.

231. Bray, Charles (1811–84). *The Philosophy of Necessity; or, The Law of Consequences; as Applicable to Mental, Moral, and Social Science.* (London: Longman and Co., 1841). 2 vols. 663pp.

A317 (title, 2 vols.), JS224 (Anon./Philosophy). Earliest edition in BL and the only in 2 vols. Includes an appendix by Mary Hennell subsequently published separately as *An Outline of the Various Social Systems & Communities which have been Founded on the Principle of Co-operation.* Bray was a philosopher who spent most of his life in Coventry. There he advocated all types of social reform, including public schools and workers' associations that resembled later labor unions.

232. Bree, Charles Robert (1811?–86). *An Exposition of Fallacies in the Hypothesis of Mr. Darwin.* (London: Longmans & Co., 1872). 418pp.

A910 (author, title), JS560. Only edition in BL. Bree was a physician and naturalist who wrote a multi-volume work on the birds of Europe. His was one of many voices raised in opposition to Darwin's theory of natural selection. He was also the author of *Species not Transmutable, nor the Result of Secondary Causes* (1860), published a year after Darwin's *On the Origin of Species.*

233. Brewer, Ebenezer Cobham (1810–97). *Dictionary of Phrase and Fable, Giving the Derivation, Source, or Origin of Common Phrases, Allusions, and Words That Have a Tale to Tell.* (London: Cassell & Co., [1872, 73]). 983pp. 3rd edition.

B975 (author, title, edition, n.d.), JS561. Brewer was an English author and lexicographer who wrote a number of reference works, of which this is the most famous.

234. Brewer, Ebenezer Cobham. *The Reader's Handbook of Allusions, References, Plots and Stories, etc.* (London: Chatto & Windus, 1880). 1170pp.

A358 (title), JS249 (Anon./Reference). Earliest edition in BL and the only pre–1898 title matching the short title in A358.

235. Brewer, George (b. 1766). *The Juvenile Lavater or a Familiar Explanation of the Passions of Le Brun. Calculated for the Instruction & Entertainment of Young Persons: Interspersed with Moral and Amusing Tales.* (London: Newman and Co., n.d.) 171pp. Illustrated with 19 plates.

B976 (author, title, 19 plates), JS562. See 1193 for a note on Lavater. This early 19th-century work includes illustrations of and lectures about both positive and negative human passions and attempts to make Lavater's theories of physiognomy (i.e. the analysis of human character through facial characteristics) accessible to the young. The introduction states, "The deformed Passions, disagreeable in their appearance, and dangerous in their consequences, are of a character that may be easily understood, and the features of ugliness so faithfully described to the pupil, as to cause him to avoid vice, since it has such frightful representations as would make him hateful to himself and to others, and in consequence prefer those passions which bestow on the countenance the beautiful and placid features of a good and quiet mind."

236. Brewster, David (1781–1868). *More Worlds Than One. The Creed of the Philosopher and the Hope of the Christian.* (London: John Murray, 1854). 259pp.

D28 (author, title, city, date), JS563. BL lists two 1854 editions, this and the "Fourth thousand, corrected and greatly enlarged." A copy of the 6th thousand in the author's collection is also dated 1854. Brewster made a number of important discoveries and inventions in the science of optics. He helped found the British Association for the Advancement of Science, was knighted in 1832, and elected president of the British Association in 1850. This work is "in reply" to William Whewell's *Of the Plurality of Worlds. An Essay* (London: 1853). Whewell argued that Earth was "the oasis in the desert of our system ... the largest sold opaque globe in it [and] ... really the largest planetary body in the Solar System, — its domestic hearth, and the only world in the Universe." Using "modern discoveries," Brewster defends the doctrine of "Plurality of Worlds" arguing that other planets are inhabited.

237. Bright, William (1824–1901). *Hymns and Other Poems.* (London: Rivingtons, 1866). 183pp.

A869 (author, title), JS564. This is the earlier of 2 editions in BL. Bright was a canon of Christ Church, Oxford, and an acquaintance of Dodgson.

238. Bright, William. *Waymarks in Church History.* (London: Longmans & Co., 1894). 436pp.

A786 (author, title), JS565. Only edition in BL. Collection of 12 papers on the history of the Christian Church including works on saints such as Basil and Cyril, movements such as Pelagianism and Gnosticism, and important figures in the English Church from the Venerable Bede to Archbishop William Laud.

239. Brightwell, D[aniel] B[arron] (1834–99). *A Concordance to the Entire Works of Alfred Tennyson.* (London: E. Moxon, Son & Co., 1869). 477pp.

A361, D208 (author, title, city, date), JS566. D208 notes Dodgson's initials. In 1862, the same publisher (Moxon) brought out *An Index to In Memoriam* (WMGC, #31), which was suggested by Dodgson and compiled chiefly by his sisters. No mention of this earlier index to a Tennyson poem is made in Brightwell's preface.

240. Brimley, George (1819–57). *Essays.* (Cambridge: Macmillan & Co., 1858). 336pp. 1st edition. Edited by William George Clark.

D29 (author, title, editor, city, date, edition), JS567. Brimley was an essayist and critic who wrote for *The Spectator* and *Fraser's Magazine.* DEL praises his criticisms of Tennyson and Wordsworth.

241. Brodie, Benjamin C[ollins] (1817–1880). *Psychological Inquiries: In a Series of Essays, Intended to Illustrate the Mutual Relations of the Physical Organization and the Mental Faculties.* (London: Longman, Brown, Green, and Longmans, 1856). 3rd edition. 276pp.

E284 (title, author, date), JS568. The work is divided into six dialogues and includes reference to stammering (Dodgson suffered from a slight hesitation of speech). It also includes a debunking of phrenology. Brodie was Professor of Chemistry at Oxford and both he and his children were acquaintances of Dodgson. In 1865 Dodgson took three of the Brodie children on a rowing trip to Nuneham.

242. Brontë, Emily (1818–48) and Anne (1820–49). *Wuthering Heights. Agnes Grey.* (London: Smith, Elder and Co., 1860). 2 vols. New edition.

A651, JS572. Dodgson's copy was offered at Sotheby's, London on 14 Dec. 1992 and is in the collection of Jon Lindseth, Cleveland, OH. The first volume is inscribed with his initials, the second with his signature. The new edition was 1st published in 1850. T. J. Wise notes, "The new edition of *Wuthering Heights and Agnes Grey* is a book of very considerable literary importance. Not only does it contain Charlotte's 'Biographical Notice' of her two sisters, together with a Preface to *Wuthering Heights*; it also includes a series of poems by both Emily and Anne which appeared in its pages for the first time" (*A Bibliography of the Writings in Prose and Verse of the Members of the Brontë Family*, London: Privately printed, 1917). For other works by the Brontës, see 136–40. In his diary for 21 May 1856, Dodgson writes, "Finished that extraordinary book *Wuthering Heights*; It is of all the novels I ever read the one I should least like to be a character in myself. All the 'dramatis personae' are so unusual and unpleasant. The only failure in the book is the writing it in the person of a gentleman. Heathcliff and Catherine are original and most powerfully drawn idealities: one cannot believe that such human beings ever existed: they have far more of the fiend in them. The vision at the beginning is I think the finest piece of writing in the book."

243. Brooke, Stopford Augustus (1832–1916). *Life and Letters of Frederick W. Robertson, Incumbent of Trinity Chapel, Brighton, 1847–53.* (London: Smith Elder, 1865). 356, 369pp. 2 vols.

A881 (title, 2 vols.), JS1747 (listed under Robertson). Earliest 2-volume edition in BL. Born in Ireland, Brooke became a clergyman in the Church of England, serving at one time as chaplain in ordinary to the Queen. He left the church over issues of dogma and became a Unitarian minister. A man of independent means, he achieved a reputation for writing works on literature and art. Frederick William Robertson (1816–53) was an Anglican preacher who moved from an Evangelical to a Broad Church stance in the 1840s. In Brighton he preached and lectured largely to the working classes. ODCC states that "The opposition he had to face throughout his time at Brighton, largely through his support of the revolutionary ideas of 1848, hastened his early death."

244. Brooke, Stopford Augustus. *Poems.* (London: Macmillan & Co., 1888). 284pp.

A829 (author, title), JS575. Only edition in BL.

245. Brooks, [Charles] Shirley (1815–74). *The Gordian Knot: A Story of Good and of Evil.* (London: Richard Bentley, 1860). 376pp. With illustrations by John Tenniel.

A665 (author, title, illustrator, date), JS576. Brooks contributed poems to *Punch* (where Tenniel was a cartoonist) from 1852 until his death in 1874, and was editor of that magazine from 1870 to 1874. A few years after the publication of this volume, Tenniel illustrated AAIW and TTLG (see 2022 for more). On 11 May 1867, Dodgson attended an amateur theatrical performance featuring several *Punch* contributors, including Brooks and Tenniel.

246. Brough, William (1826–70). *House out of Windows A Farce in One Act.* (London: T. H. Lacy, [1852]). 16pp. Volume 8 in *Lacy's Acting Edition of Plays* series.

Not in JS. In his diary for 24 March 1856, Dodgson, then at Ripon, notes that he got this play from London along with Morton's *Away with Melancholy*. He read the latter play to a party that afternoon. Only edition in BL. Brough was a journalist and dramatist.

247. Brown, J. H. *Spectropia; or, Surprising Spectral Illusions. Showing Ghosts Everywhere, and of Any Colour.* (London: Griffith and Farran, 1864). 11pp. + 16 hand-colored plates.

E309 (title, author, date), JS577. At least three editions were published in 1864. The plates are designed to create a optical illusions which, according to the introduction, "are founded on two well-known facts; namely the persistency of impressions, and the production of complementary colours, on the retina." The book includes a "Popular and Scientific Description" of the effect. The figures are in the shape of various "ghostly" spectres.

248. Brown, John (1810–82). *Horae Subsecivae.* (Edinburgh: Edmonston & Doug-

las, 1861). 2 vols. 456, 486pp. 1st and 2nd
Series.

A340, B978 (author, title, 1st and 2nd series,
date), JS579. Brown was a Scottish physician
and essayist. Essays and stories. A third series
was published in 1882. Brown wrote in the introduction to the first series that his purpose
was, in part "To give my vote for going back to
the old manly intellectual and literary culture
… when a physician fed, enlarged, and quick-
ened his entire nature; when he lived in the
world of letters as a freeholder, and reverenced
the ancients." Essays include "Locke and
Sydenham," "Henry Vaughan," "Letter to John
Cairns, D. D." and "Education through the
Senses." The 2nd series includes "Rab and His
Friends" (see 250).

249. Brown, John. *Marjorie Fleming, A
Sketch. Being the Paper Entitled "Pet Marjorie: A Story of Child Life Fifty Years Ago."*
(Edinburgh: Edmonston & Douglas, 1863).
32pp. Reprinted from the *North British Review.*

A544 (title, author, illustrated), JS578. Earliest edition in BL. Marjorie Fleming (1803–11)
wrote, in her short life, a diary and several
poems, including one on Mary Queen of Scots.
Brown includes an account of a friendship between Fleming and Walter Scott now thought
to be apocryphal.

250. Brown, John. *Rab and His Friends.*
(Edinburgh: T. Constable & Co., 1859).
31pp.

A533 (title), JS74 (Anon./Children). Earliest edition in BL. This work is a sentimental
dog story, frequently reprinted. "Rab is a dog,
whose fidelity to, and affection for his master
and mistress are painted with graphic power"
(DEL).

251. B[rown], J[ohn], of Bridport (1827–
63). *Chess Strategy. A Collection of the Most
Beautiful Chess Problems Composed by "J.
B., of Bridport" and Contributed by him to
the Chief Chess Periodicals during the Last
Fifteen Years.* (London: Trübner & Co.,
1865). 118pp. Illustrated by diagrams, and
accompanied by solutions.

B1004, JS284 (Anon./Sport). Dodgson's copy
is in HAC. On the front end-paper are "C. L.
Dodgson" in purple ink, and "C. L. D. Ch. Ch.
Oxford" in pencil. Problems 7, 9, 36 and 87 are
marked with pencil. The book consists of 174
illustrated chess problems (2 per page) with the
solutions in the back. AAIW was published in
1865 (like this book), and Dodgson may have
been thinking towards TTLG, a book based on
chess, when he saw this book.

252. Browne, Felicia Dorothea [later He-
mans] (1793–1835). *Poems.* (Liverpool: T.
Cadell and W. Davies, London, 1808).
111pp. 1st edition.

A733 ("Heman's Poems, 1808"), JS1189
(listed under Heman). Hemans was an English
poet who spent much of her life in Wales. This
work was one of two books published by
Browne in 1808. The Advertisement notes that
the poems "are the genuine productions of a
young lady, written between the age of eight
and thirteen years." Their youthful Romantic
exuberance would have appealed to Dodgson.
Under the name Hemans, the author published
a substantial volume of poetry including the
poem "Casabianca," known for its first line,
"The boy stood on the burning deck."

253. Browne, Maggie [pseud. of Margaret
Hamer, afterwards Andrewes]. *Wanted —
A King; or How Merle Set the Nursery
Rhymes to Rights.* (London: Cassell &
Company, 1890). 183pp. Illustrated by
Harry Furniss.

A646 (title, illustrator), JS24. Dodgson's
diary for 11 September 1891 lists this among the
"books of the *Alice* type" he had collected. This
was a book Dodgson enjoyed giving to child-
friends. The author's collection includes 2
copies inscribed by Dodgson to children, the
5th thousand and the 6th thousand. In a letter
to Maggie Bowman presenting the book to her,
Dodgson writes, "This book looks to me a *little* like *Alice*: but I hope that won't make you
dislike it." W & M describe this as "an imitation, sometimes rather close, usually far off and
not first-rate, of *Alice's Adventures* and *Through
the Looking-Glass*, in 14 chapters. Bo-peep finds
her sheep, the Boy Blue his horn, and so on."
Furniss was the illustrator of Dodgson's *Sylvie
and Bruno* novels (see 742).

254. Browne, Matthew [pseud. of Wil-
liam Brighty Rands] (1823–82). *Views and
Opinions.* (London & New York: Alexander
Strahan, 1866). 294pp.

B979 (author, title, date), JS582. See 1622 for
a note on Rands.

255. Browne, Thomas (1605–82). *Pseudodoxia Epidemica: or, Enquiries into Very Many Received Tenents, and Commonly Presumed Truths.* (London: Edward Dod, 1646). 386pp.

A741 (Browne's Vulgar Errors, 1646), JS583. This is the 1st edition of the book which became known as "Vulgar Errors." Browne was an English physician whose works introduced a wide range of words into the English language (electricity, hallucination, pathology, computer, etc.). This work is an attempt to dispel a wide array of errors and superstitions. It went through several editions in the 17th century.

256. Browning, Elizabeth Barrett (1806–61). *Aurora Leigh.* (London: Chapman & Hall, 1859). 403pp. 4th edition, revised.

A828, D31 (author, title, city, edition, date), JS589. Blank verse poem in which the title character, raised an orphan in her aunt's house, rejects the suit of her wealthy but arrogant cousin Romney. When Romney falls on misfortune and loses his fortune, he and Aurora are reunited. Browning weaves her social opinions throughout the text. In his diary for 5 January 1858, Dodgson writes "Received *Aurora Leigh* from Mudie [a London bookseller]. (I got it second-hand for seven shillings)." This implies that Dodgson also owned an earlier copy of *Aurora Leigh*, as the 4th edition described in D31 was not published until a year later. The 1st–3rd editions were published in 1856–57. On 7 January 1858 Dodgson noted that he had begun reading the book.

257. Browning, Elizabeth Barrett. *Casa Guidi Windows. A Poem.* (London: Chapman & Hall, 1851). 140pp. 1st edition.

A445, D30 (author, title, city, date, edition), JS587. D95 describes Dodgson's copy as "With autograph 'To Anne Jameson from her ever affectionate E. B. B.'" This work related to current political events in Italy and Mrs. Browning's support for Italian liberty.

258. Browning, Elizabeth Barrett. *Last Poems.* (London: Chapman & Hall, 1862). 142pp. 1st edition. Edited by Robert Browning.

A446 (author, title, edition, date), JS588. A posthumous collection of poems.

259. Browning, Elizabeth Barrett. *The Letters of Elizabeth Barrett Browning.* (London: Smith, Elder & Co., 1897). 2 vols. Edited with biographical additions by Frederic George Kenyon.

Uncertain. A354 ("Letters of E. B. Browning, 2 vols."), JS585. Only edition listed in BL of what seems the most likely title. Kenyon (1863–1952) became director of the British Museum in 1909. Another possibility is: *Letters of Elizabeth Barrett Browning addressed to R. H. Horne.* (London: R. Bentley & Son, 1877). With a connecting narrative by Richard Hengist Horne (see 999). Edited by S. R. T. Mayer.

260. Browning, Elizabeth Barrett. *Poems.* (London: Chapman & Hall, 1853). 2 vols. 3rd edition.

A444 (author, title, 2 vols., date), JS586.

261. Browning, Elizabeth Barrett. *A Selection from the Poetry of Elizabeth Barrett Browning.* (London: Smith, Elder & Co., 1841–42). 2 vols. First and second series.

A354 ("Selections from the Poetry of E. B. Browning, 2 vols."), JS584. This is the earliest 2-volume edition traced of the only closely matching title traced.

262. Browning, Robert (1812–89). *Asolando: Fancies and Facts.* (London: Smith Elder and Co, 1890). 157pp. 2nd edition.

A831, B981 (author, title, edition, date), JS596. The author's last volume of poetry.

263. Browning, Robert. *Christmas-Eve and Easter-Day. A Poem.* (London: Chapman & Hall, 1850). 142pp. 1st edition.

A441 (author, title, edition, date), B980, JS593. Two poems. The first compares experiences at a dissenting chapel, the Vatican, and a lecture by a German professor with the conclusion that the first is best for the heart. The second is a dispute between a Christian and a sceptic.

264. Browning, Robert. *Dramatis Personæ.* (London: Chapman & Hall, 1864). 250pp. 1st edition.

A443 (author, title, edition, date), JS595. A collection of poems.

265. Browning, Robert. *Fifine at the Fair.* (London: Smith, Elder & Co., 1872). 171pp. 1st edition.

A862 (author, title, edition), JS598. Poem about a man who becomes infatuated with a rope-dancer at the fair and leaves his wife to join her, suffering punishment in the epilogue.

266. Browning, Robert. *Jocoseria*. (London: Smith, Elder & Co., 1883). 143pp. 1st edition.

A862 (author, title, edition), JS599. Contains the dramatic monologue "Cristina and Monaldeschi."

267. Browning, Robert. *Men and Women*. (London: Chapman & Hall, 1855). 2 vols. 260, 244pp. 1st edition.

A442 (author, title, edition, 2 vols., date), JS594. A collection of poems including dramatic monologues and love poems.

268. Browning, Robert. *Parleyings with Certain People of Importance in their Day: To Wit: Bernard de Mandeville, Daniel Bartoli, Christopher Smart, George Bubb Dodington, Francis Furini, Gerard de Lairesse, and Charles Avison. Introduced by a Dialogue between Apollo and the Fates; Concluded by another between John Fust and his Friends*. (London: Smith, Elder & Co., 1887). 268pp. 1st edition.

A862 (author, title, edition), JS597. Poetry.

269. Browning, Robert. *The Pied Piper of Hamelin*. (London: George Routledge, [1888]). 64pp. With 35 Illustrations by Kate Greenaway. Engraved and printed in colours by Edmund Evans.

A530 (title, illustrated), JS72 (Anon./Children's Books). This is the first edition of Greenaway's version (see 1819 for a note on her), the only pre–1898 illustrated edition of this title in BL. There was a privately published edition of this title with illustrations by Jane E. Cook (London: 1880), but this seems a much less likely match. The story was printed in many works, as early as 1450, but Browning's poem was by far the most popular telling. The poem was first published in his *Dramatic Lyrics* (1842).

270. Browning, Robert. *Poems*. (London: Chapman & Hall, 1849). 2 vols. 385, 416pp. Edited by the author.

A439 (author, title, 2 vols., date), JS591. Only edition in BL matching the particulars in A439. A "new" edition of "Paracelsus" and the poems originally published under the title *Bells and Pomegranates* (in fact the first collected edition).

271. Browning, Robert. *Selections from the Poetical Works of Robert Browning*. (London: Smith, Elder & Co., 1872, 1880). 2 series. 348, 371pp. Edited by the author.

A355 (author, title, 2 vols.), JS590. Earliest edition in BL.

272. Browning, Robert. *Sordello*. (London: Edward Moxon, 1840). 253pp. 1st edition.

A440 (author, title, edition, date), JS592. Poem set in medieval Italy. The son of a powerful man is raised as a page. He becomes enamored of the poetic life but when his identity is revealed must choose between a life of action and power and one of high spiritual ideals. He dies trying to choose.

273. Browning, Robert and Elizabeth Barrett Browning. *The Brownings for the Young. Selections from the Poems of Robert and Elizabeth Barrett Browning*. (London: Smith, Elder & Co., 1896). 203pp. Edited by Frederic George Kenyon.

E278 (editor, title, date), JS1350. See 259 for a note on Kenyon.

274. [Brown's Handbooks]. *The Illustrated Guide to the City of Salisbury*. (Salisbury: Brown & Co.; London: Simpkin & Co., n.d.). 68pp. With 30 engravings. *Brown's Series of Strangers' Handbooks* no. 2.

E243 ("Salisbury — Illustrated Guide to the City of, with 30 engravings"), JS353. Only edition of the only book matching this description in BL.

275. Bruce, Alexander Balmain (1831–99). *The Training of the Twelve; or, Passages out of the Gospels Exhibiting the Twelve Disciples of Jesus Under Discipline for the Apostleship*. (Edinburgh: T. & T. Clark, 1871). 548pp.

A799 (title, author), JS600. Earliest edition in BL. Bruce was a Scottish divine in the Free Church remembered for his involvement with kenotic theory (theories about the reduction of divinity in Christ supposed to have been made necessary by the Incarnation). This work discusses Christ's relationship to his Apostles as teacher.

276. Brunton, Thomas Lauder (1844–1916). *The Bible and Science*. (London:

Macmillan & Co., 1881). 415pp. With illustrations.

A910 (author, title), JS601 (listed under
Alexander Brunton). Only edition in BL. Brunton was a Scottish physician and pioneer of
pharmacology. This work presents a popular
overview of evolution and attempts to reconcile that theory with Biblical accounts of creation.

277. Bruyssel, E[rnest Jean] van (1827–
1914). *The Population of an Old Pear-Tree;
or, Stories of Insect Life.* (London: Macmillan & Co., 1870). 221pp. From the French.
Edited by Charlotte M. Yonge. With numerous illustrations by Becker.

D218 (author, title, editor, city, date), JS602.
D218 notes Dodgson's initials. See 2323 for a
note on Charlotte Yonge. Like AAIW and
TTLG, this is a dream narrative. In it, the nar-
rator falls asleep under an old pear-tree and
finds himself shrunk to the scale of its insect inhabitants, whose interactions he observes in
detail before waking.

Illustration by Becker for *The Population of
an Old Pear-Tree* (item 277).

278. Bryant, William Cullen (1794–
1878). *The Fountain, and Other Poems.*
(New York & London: Wiley & Putnam,
1842). 100pp.

A470 (author, title, city, date), JS603. Bryant
was an American poet.

279. Bryant, William Cullen. *Poems.*
(London: Kent & Richards, 1849). 355pp.
With illustrations by E. Leutze.

A856, A873 ("Bryant's Poems, illustrated"),
JS604. Description based on the copy in HAC
which bears the gothic stamp. Misdated (1859)
in Livingston, who notes that the following five
poems are checked in the index: "To a Water-
Fowl," "Thanatopsis," "The Death of the Flowers," "Innocent Child and Snow-White
Flower," and "A Dream." Dodgson owned 2
copies of Bryant's poems, and they may have
been different editions. If so, a likely candidate
is: *Poems.* (London: Sampson Low & Co., 1858
[1857]). 343pp. Illustrated with 71 engravings
by the Brothers Dalziel, etc.

280. Buchanan, Robert Williams (1841–
1901). *The Fleshly School of Poetry and
Other Phenomena of the Day.* (London:
Strahan & Co., 1872). 97pp.

E173 (title, author, date), F152, JS605. Buchanan was a poet and playwright with an
affinity for Scottish subjects. F152 notes the
gothic stamp. A copy in HAC is catalogued as
Dodgson's, but is not marked as his in any way.
Algernon Charles Swinburne replied to this
work in *Under the Microscope [A Reply to the
Charges Made against Swinburne and Others in
"The Fleshly School of Poetry" by Robert W.
Buchanan.]* (London: D. White, 1872). In the
Houghton copy, Swinburne's reply is bound together with Buchanan's work, but neither of the
early catalogue entries refer to this pairing.
Pasted into the rear of the Houghton volume is
an article on Buchanan by Edmund Yates
(whom Carroll knew, see LCP) from *The World*
(26 September 1877), "A Scrofulous Scotch
Poet." In the front of the volume is tipped-in a
carte-de-visite of Swinburne. The Buchanan
title was originally published under a pseudonym in the *Contemporary Review.* In it,
Buchanan criticizes Baudelaire, Swinburne,
Rossetti, and others, especially the Pre-
Raphaelites. In his opening chapter he bemoans
that, among other frightening signs of the
times, "photographs of nude, indecent, and
hideous harlots, in every possible attitude that
vice can devise, flaunt from the shop windows." Rossetti also rebutted the pamphlet in
his own "The Stealthy School of Criticism."

Title illustration by H. G. Hine from Buckley's *Natural History of Tuft Hunters and Toadies* (item 283).

281. Buckland, A[nna] (b. 1827). *A Record of Ellen Watson*. (London: Macmillan, 1884). 279pp. Arranged and edited by A. Buckland. With a portrait.

A901, E348 (title, author, date), JS115 (Anon./Literature), JS607 (incorrect title). Buckland was a writer with a special interest in education. Ellen Watson (1856–80), a distinguished student at University College, London, traveled to South Africa due to frail health and became a beloved schoolteacher before her death of consumption at age 24.

282. Buckland, Francis Trevelyan (1826–80). *Curiosities of Natural History*. (London: Richard Bentley and Son, 1879). 4 vols. Popular Edition. 1st–4th series. Illustrated.

A551 (author, title, 4 vols.), JS606. Earliest 4-volume edition traced. Dodgson may have owned a set such as this (the Popular Edition was reprinted several times) or merely a collection of editions of the 4 series. Son of the eccentric geologist and natural scientist William Buckland, Francis Buckland was perhaps the most distinguished naturalist of his day. He took his M.A. at Christ Church, Oxford in 1846 and pursued a varied career with especial attention to fish, fisheries, and related topics. The present collection was among his most popular works. The first volume alone ranges from works on rats to fish to Buckland's own monkey, "Jacko."

283. [Buckley, Theodore William Alois] (1825–56). *The Natural History of Tuft-Hunters and Toadies*. (London: D. Bogue, 1848). 121pp. Illustrated by H. G. Hine.

A472 (title, date), JS1902 (listed with 2 other titles under Smith). Dodgson's copy was bound together with two other titles from the same series, the natural histories of *The Flirt* (by Albert Richard Smith, see 1872) and of *Humbugs* (by Angus Bethune Reach, see 1627). A humorous look at those who "hunt after noblemen" especially at University but also elsewhere. The attitude of the author to his subject is not kind.

284. Bucknill, John Charles (1817–97). *The Psychology of Shakespeare*. (London: Longman & Co., 1859). 264pp.

A871 (title), JS132 (Anon./Literature). Earliest edition in BL. Bucknill was an English psychologist who pioneered the use of electrical stimulation of the skin to treat depression. He wrote a number of works on insanity and various legal matters and at least three works relating psychology and medicine to Shakespeare.

285. Buckton, Mrs. Catherine M. *Health in the House; Twenty-Five Lectures on Elementary Physiology in its Application to the Daily Wants of Man and Animals Delivered to the Wives and Children of Working-men in Leeds and Saltaire*. (London: Longmans, Green, and Co., 1880). 207pp. 11th edition, revised throughout.

B983 (author, title, date), JS608. Buckton was a member of the Leeds School Board. This work covers such topics as impure air and ventilation, digestion, milk and mineral foods, the nerves and sense of hearing, sight and sunshine, the voice, treatment of animals, etc.

286. [Bulwer-Lytton, Edward George] (1803–73). *The Last Days of Pompeii*. (London: Richard Bentley, 1834). 3 vols. 315, 296, 315pp. 1st edition.

A615 (title, edition, 3 vols.), JS609. A love story set just before and after the eruption of Vesuvius in 79 B.C.E.

287. [Bunce, Oliver Bell] (1828–90). *Don't: A Manual of Mistakes and Improprieties More or Less Prevalent in Conduct and Speech. By Censor*. (London: Ward, Lock, and Co., [1884]?). 64pp.

E425 ("Don't"), JS610. This is the only pre–1898 matching title in BOD. Also published by Routledge in 1884 (these are the earliest editions traced). E425 notes this is "corrected by

Lewis Carroll." "It so happens," writes the author, "that most of the rules of society are prohibitory in character." This is a book of such rules. The section on correspondence has some overlap with Dodgson's 1890 work *8 or 9 Wise Words About Letter Writing* (WMGC, 223).

288. Bunner, Henry Cuyler (1855–96). *Airs from Arcady and Elsewhere*. (London: C. Hutt, 1885). 109pp.

A830, B985 (author, title, date), JS611. Bunner was an American journalist and poet known for his verse descriptions of New York City. This was his first book of poetry.

289. Bunyan, John (1628–88). *The Pilgrim's Progress: as Originally Published by John Bunyan: Being a Facsimile Reproduction of the First Edition*. (London: Elliot Stock, [1876?]). 232pp.

B986 (author, title, n.d.), JS612. Earliest undated printing of this work in BL. A dated edition of 1895 more closely matches the title given in B986 as it includes the addition, "published in 1678." That edition also adds an introduction by "Dr. John Brown" (see 248).

290. Bunyan, John. *The Pilgrim's Progress, From this World to that Which is to Come; Delivered under the Similitude of a Dream; wherein is Discovered, the Manner of his Setting Out; his Dangerous Journey; and his Arrival at the Desired Country*. (London: Houlston and Son, etc., 1838). 270pp. A new edition. Illustrated.

A767, C1 (author, title, date, crown 8vo.), JS612. This is the more likely match for C1 of two British 1838 editions which have been traced. The present title at 20cm. is better described as "crown 8vo" (as in C1) than another edition published by the Religious Tract Society and measuring 11 cm.

291. Burckhardt, Johann Carl (1773–1825). *Table des Diviseurs pour Tous les Nombres du Deuxième Million, ou plus Exactement, Depuis 1020000 à 2028000, Avec les Nombres Premiers qui s'y Trouvent*. (Paris: Mme Ve Courcier, 1814). 112pp.

A939 ("Table des Diviseurs Burckhardt"), JS620. Earliest edition in BL. "Table of Divisors for all the Numbers to Two Million, or More Exactly between 1,020,000 and 2,028,000, with the Prime Numbers Found There."

292. Burgon, John William (1813–88). *A Century of Verses, in Memory of the Reverend, the President of Magdalen College.* (Oxford: J. H. Parker, 1855).

Not in JS. In his diary for 23 January 1855, Dodgson writes, "Bought ... Burgon's Poems on Routh." Burgon was a High Churchman who remained within the Anglican Church, serving as vicar of St. Mary's, Oxford beginning in 1873 and becoming Dean of Chichester in 1876. He opposed Irish disestablishment and other reforms, and was a staunch defender of traditional scripture texts, writing against the Revised Version (1881–85). This volume was an elegy on the death of Martin Joseph Routh (1756–1854). Routh matriculated at Oxford in 1770 and served as President of Magdalen College from 1791 to 1854. On 10 March 1867, Dodgson assisted Burgon at a communion service at St. Mary's and Burgon asked Dodgson to preach that afternoon, which he did.

293. Burgon, John William. *Letters from Rome to Friends in England.* (London: John Murray, 1862). 420pp.

A525, A773 (author, title), JS614. Dodgson owned 2 copies. Only edition in BL. Written when Anglican clergy were still defecting to Rome following the Oxford Movement, these letters cover topics from the Catacombs to the Codex Vaticanus to the author's first-hand experience of Romanism as a system. Despite his High Church tendencies, Burgon had no wish for the Anglican Church to become overrun with Romanizing tendencies.

294. Burgon, John William. *Lives of Twelve Good Men: Martin Joseph Routh; Hugh James Rose; Charles Marriott; Edward Hawkins; Samuel Wilberforce; Richard Lynch Cotton; Richard Greswell; Henry Octavius Coxe; Henry Longueville Mansel; William Jacobson; Charles Page Eden; Charles Longuet Higgins.* (London: John Murray, 1888). 504, 428pp. 2 vols.

A902 (author, title, 2 vols.), JS617. Earliest edition in BL. A popular book containing brief lives of High Churchmen of the 19th century.

295. Burgon, John William. *The Oxford Diocesan Conference; and Romanizing within the Church of England: Two Sermons, Preached at St. Mary-the-Virgin's*

Oxford Oct. 12th and 19th 1873. (Oxford: J. Parker & Co., 1873). 40pp.

C4 (author, title), not in JS. Only edition in BL. C4 adds "with replies," indicating that one or more additional pamphlets in reply to this one may have been present (C4 is a bound volume of 12 pamphlets of which 9 are described). The most likely candidate is: *Another Phase of the Ritualistic Conspiracy; A Letter to the Protestants of Oxford by an Alarmed Undergraduate* (1873), which, according to BOD, was occasioned by Burgon's pamphlet.

296. Burgon, John William. *Petra, a Prize Poem.* (Oxford: Francis Macpherson, 1846). 62pp. 2nd edition. To which a few short poems are now added.

A400, E308 (title, author, date), F150, JS613. E308 describes Dodgson's copy as "Presentation copy to Eliz. F. Webb with remark and initials in Lewis Carroll's hand as to other verse inserted at end." F150 notes Dodgson's initials and the gothic stamp. Burgon's poem won the 1845 Newdigate Prize for English verse in Oxford University.

297. Burgon, John William. *A Plain Commentary on the Four Holy Gospels: Intended Chiefly for Devotional Reading.* (London: J. H. Parker, 1855). 4 vols. in 7.

A785, A787, B987 (author, title, 7 vols.), JS615. Dodgson owned 2 sets. Only edition in BL.

298. Burgon, John William. *Protests of the Bishops Against the Consecration of Dr. Temple to the See of Exeter: Preceded by a Letter to John Jackson, D.D., Bishop of London.* (Oxford & London: J. Parker & Co., 1870). 31pp.

C5 (title), not in JS. Only edition in BL. Frederick Temple was successively Bishop of Exeter and London, and Archbishop of Canterbury. The objections to his installation as Bishop of Exeter were over his contribution to the controversial 1860 collection *Essays and Reviews* (see 2075). Though Temple's essay was innocuous, it was thought he was keeping heretical company. He agreed to withdraw the essay from future editions. See 2021 for more on Temple.

299. Burnand, F[rancis] C[owley] (1836–1917). *Happy Thoughts.* (London: Bradbury, Evans, & Co., 1868). 303pp. *Handy-Volume Series* no 4.

A653, D32 (author, title, city, date), JS621. D32 notes Dodgson's signature. BL also lists the 10th thousand as dated 1868. Cohen notes (in *Letters*, 556) that a copy with Dodgson's signature is in the Ernest Mayhew collection, London. Burnand produced numerous burlesques for the theatre and began contributing to *Punch* in 1863. This series, first published in *Punch* in 1866, was quite popular. He assumed the editorship of *Punch* in 1880. *The Athenæum* wrote of this work, "Utterly ludicrous as his characters are, they are neither monstrosities nor abortions. They are exaggerations of what is perfectly real."

300. Burnand, Francis Cowley. *Mokeanna! A Treble Temptation*. (London: Bradbury, Agnew & Co., 1873). 270pp. With 4 double-page illustrations.

D33 (author, title, city, date), JS622. D33 notes Dodgson's signature. Another comic

work which first appeared in the pages of *Punch* in 1863, the year Burnand joined the staff. One of the pictures is by J. E. Millais and another by George DuMaurier. DuMaurier (1834–96) was a frequent contributor to *Punch* and the author of the novel *Trilby*. In 1867, Dodgson suggested a caption for a humorous illustration that DuMaurier subsequently drew for *Punch* (see LCP frontispiece). See 1351 for a note on Millais.

301. Burnand, Francis Cowley. *The New History of Sandford and Merton*. (London: Bradbury, Evans, & Co., 1872). With 76 illustrations by Linley Sambourne.

A933, JS67 (Anon./Children). Earliest edition in BL. Sambourne drew for *Punch* magazine. A parody of Thomas Day's popular and moralistic children's book *The History of Sandford and Merton*, which Dodgson also owned (see 542).

"The Torture Chamber." Linley Sambourne's frontispiece for F. C. Burnand's *The New History of Sandford and Merton* (item 301).

302. Burnet, Gilbert (1643–1715). *Some Passages of the Life and Death of the Right Honourable John Earl of Rochester, Who Died the 26th of July, 1680*. (London: Richard Chiswell, 1680). 182pp. Engraved frontispiece portrait by R. White.

A885 (author, title), JS625 (listed under Francis Hodgson Burnett). 1st edition. Burnet was Bishop of Salisbury and a prolific writer. Supposedly dictated to Burnet from Rochester's death-bed. John Wilmot (1647–80), Second Earl of Rochester, sometimes known as "The Rake of Rochester," was a poet and libertine. Confessing on his deathbed, Wilmot supposedly asked Burnet "not to spare him in anything which [he] thought might be of use to the Living." Though he mentioned Wilmot's shortcomings, Burnet claimed that he "touched them as tenderly as the occasion would bear: and I am sure with much more softness than he desired."

303. Burnett, Frances Hodgson (1849–1924). *Dolly. A Love Story*. (London: G. Routledge & Sons, [1877]). 219pp.

A655 (Burncot's Dolly — A Love Story), JS623 (listed under Burncot). A655, reads in part "Burncot's Dolly — a Love Story — Sarah Crewe." *Sarah Crewe* is by Burnett and BL lists no other work by the title "Dolly. A Love Story," so clearly this refers to Burnett's book. Earliest edition in BL. Burnett was an English-born writer of stories and novels (primarily for children) who lived most of her adult life in America. This story for children was later published as *Vagabondia: A Love Story*.

304. Burnett, Francis Hodgson. *Haworth's. A Novel*. (London: Macmillan and Co., 1887).

Not in JS. In a letter to Macmillan on 6 July 1887, Dodgson, then considering the design of his own inexpensive edition of the *Alice* books (released later that year as the People's Editions) wrote, "I bought your 2s. edition of *Haworth's* yesterday, and like the look of the book very much, and think the type much more readable than the one proposed for the cheap *Alice*. What would you think of bringing it out as one of that Series?" (See *Macmillan*, 232). *Haworth's* was originally published in 2 vols. in 1879 (at 21s.); this was a reprint of the 1-volume edition of 1880, but in smaller format, priced at 2s. In the end, the cheap *Alice* books did not appear as part of any other series.

305. Burnett, Francis Hodgson. *Little Lord Fauntleroy*. (London: Frederick Warne and Co., 1886). 269pp. 26 illustrations after Reginald B. Birch.

A518 (title), JS624. Dodgson's copy is in the Dodgson family collection. 1st English edition. The story of an American boy who inherits a British title. Burnett's first novel for children. Dodgson saw Burnett's stage adaptation of her famous novel at least twice in the 1888–89 season.

306. Burnett, Francis Hodgson. *Sara Crewe; or, What Happened at Miss Minchin's: and Editha's Burglar*. (London: F. Warne & Co., 1888). 159pp. 16 Engraved Plates By Reginald B. Birch.

A655 (title), JS626. This is the 1st English edition. Though A655 does not specify that the book includes *Editha's Burglar*, all British editions listed in BL include this second story. The 1st American edition was published, without *Edith's Burglar*, in New York by Charles Scribner's Sons (1888). The story of a girl whose fortunes at school change when she is kind to a beggar-girl.

307. Burnett, Frances Hodgson. *Through One Administration*. (London: F. Warne & Co., [1885]).

A655 ("Thro' One Administration"), JS392 (Anon./Unclassified). The only matching title in BL and A655 includes other works by Burnett. The 1st edition was published in 3 volumes by Warne in 1883. Since multiple volume works are usually so noted in A, the earliest London 1-volume edition in BL is described here. A novel about corruption in Washington, D.C.

308. [Burney, Fanny] (1752–1840). *Camilla: or, A Picture of Youth*. (London: T. Payne and Son … and T. Cadell Jun. and W. Davies, 1796). 5 vols. 390, 432, 468, 432, 556 pp. 1st edition.

A827 (author, title, edition, 5 vols.), JS627. A novel about the romantic pursuits of Camilla Tyrold and her sisters.

309. [Burney, Fanny]. *Cecilia, or Memoirs of An Heiress*. (London: T. Payne and Son … and T. Cadell, 1782). 5 vols. 293, 263, 365, 328, 398pp. 1st edition.

A827 (author, title, edition, 5 vols., date), JS628. Comedy of manners in which a rich heiress is left in the charge of three guardians who attempt to protect her from fortune-hunters.

310. Burney, Fanny. *Evelina or, A Young Lady's Entrance into the World*. (London: Printed for T. Lowndes, 1778). 3 vols.

A855 (author, title, 3 vols.), JS629. 1st edition. The only other 3-volume British editions listed in BL are the 2nd–4th, all published by Lowndes in 1779. Novel of the strange fates of Evelina, raised by a guardian and introduced into London society before eventually having her true identity revealed.

311. Burney, Fanny. *The Wanderer; or, Female Difficulties*. (London: Longman, Hurst, Rees, Orme, and Brown, 1814). 5 vols. 423, 458, 438, 359, 395pp.

A855 (author, title, 5 vols.), JS630. 1st edition. The only other 5-volume edition listed in BL is the 2nd, published by the same publisher in the same year. Romantic novel in which a poor émigré from revolutionary France with secrets to keep tries to earn a living in England.

312. Burney, Sarah Harriet (1772–1844). *Traits of Nature.* (London: Henry Colburn, 1812). 2nd edition. 4 vols.

A820 (title, 4 vols.), JS394 (Anon./Unclassified). Only 4-volume edition of the only work by this title listed in BL. Burney was a novelist and the half-sister of Fanny Burney (see above). "'This lady,' says one of her critics, 'has copied the style of her relative, but has not her raciness of humour or power of painting the varieties of the human species'" (DEL). Novel.

313. Burnley, James (1842–1919). *Idonia, and other Poems.* (London: Longmans & Co., 1869). 200pp.

A831, B989 (author, title, date), JS631. B989 states "Inscribed 'To Lewis Carroll, Esq., with the author's compliments, 13 April, 1869.'" It is unlikely that this was a personal presentation, as Dodgson would not have wanted to be addressed by his pseudonym; perhaps this copy was forwarded to Dodgson through his publishers. Burnley was a poet, dramatist, and journalist who spent much of his time in Bradford in the north of England. This was his first book of poems.

314. Burns, Robert (1759–96). *The Poetical Works of Robert Burns, Edited from the Best Printed and Manuscript Authorities with Glossarial Index and a Biographical Memoir by Alexander Smith.* (London: Macmillan & Co., 1883). 2 vols.

A830, B990 (author, title, editor, 2 vols., date), JS632. See 1879 for a note on Smith.

315. Bursill, Henry. *Hand Shadows to Be Thrown Upon the Wall: A Series of Novel and Amusing Figures Formed by the Hand, from Original Designs.* (London: Griffith and Farran, 1859). 18 plates.

E89 (title, author, date), JS633. Both the 1st and 2nd editions were published in 1859. This and the following book demonstrate patterns that can be made by placing the hands in front of a light source.

316. Bursill, Henry. *A Second Series of Hand Shadows to be Thrown Upon the Wall: Consisting of Novel and Amusing Figures Formed by the Hand.* (London: Griffith & Farran, 1860). 1st edition. 18 colored plates.

E90 (title, date), JS633.

317. Burton, Edward (1794–1836). *Lectures upon the Ecclesiastical History of the First Three Centuries: From the Crucifixion of Jesus Christ to the Year 313.* (Oxford: John Henry Parker, 1855). 680pp. 4th edition.

Not in JS. In his diary for 5 April 1855, Dodgson writes, "I began reading Burton's Lectures on Church History. I like his style; it is clear and concise, but his extreme caution, and continual use of such words as 'perhaps,' 'I think,' etc., etc., is very tedious." Nonetheless, on 23 April 1855, he writes, "Ordered Tasso and Burton's *Ecclesiastical History.*" Originally published by the author in 1831–33. This is the edition closest to Dodgson's date of purchase. Burton was educated at Christ Church, Oxford and was Regius Professor of Divinity at Oxford and a canon of Christ Church.

318. Burton, Richard Francis (1821–90), translator. *Vikram and Vampire; or, Tales of Hindu Devilry.* (London: Longmans & Co., 1870). 319pp. With 33 illustrations by Ernest Griset.

A885 (author, title), JS634. Earliest edition in BL. Burton was an explorer, linguist, soldier, anthropologist, and scholar, probably best known for discovering the source of the Nile and translating the Arabian Nights. Adapted from the *Baital Pachisi*, a Hindu text of vampire tales.

319. [Bury, Charlotte Susan Maria, née Campbell] (1775–1861). *Flirtation.* (London: H. Colburn, 1827). 3 vols. 304, 316, 380pp.

A609 (title, 3 vols.), JS635. Earliest 3-volume edition of the only matching title in BL or BOD. Novel.

320. Bushnell, Horace (1802–76). *Nature and the Supernatural, as Together Constituting the One System of God.* (Edinburgh: A. Strahan & Co., 1862). 373pp. 4th edition.

A883 (author, title), JS636. Earliest British edition in BL, which lists New York editions as early as 1858. Bushnell was a leading American theologian and pastor of a Congregational church in Hartford, Connecticut. He is also known as the creator of America's first public park. This work discusses miracles and attempts to "lift the natural into the supernatural," by pointing out the supernaturalness of man.

321. Butler, Arthur Gray (1831–1909). *Harold. A Drama in Four Acts; and Other Poems.* (London: Henry Frowde, 1892). 226pp.

A858, B991 (author [given as A. J. Butler], title, date), JS637. Dodgson's copy, with a presentation inscription to him from the author dated 27 June 1893, is in the collection of Selwyn Goodacre, Derbyshire, England. Butler was educated at Oxford and served as headmaster of Haileybury College from 1858 to 1868. He went on to be a poet and playwright. Dodgson met Butler on 3 November 1892 and became acquainted with his family (see *Letters*, 934).

322. Butler, Francis (1810–74). *Dogo-graphy: The Life and Adventures of the Celebrated Dog Tiger, Comprising a Variety of Amusing and Instructive Examples, Illustrative of the Happy Effects of the Appropriate Training and Education of Dogs.* (New York: Francis Butler, 1856). 111pp.

E402 (title, author, city, date), JS641. E402 calls this book "very scarce." The author is described on the title page as a "teacher and translator of languages." The preface to this dog story states, "Old Tiger's biographical object (it appears) in introducing us to so many of his most respectable canine acquaintances, is to demonstrate, by his own personal experience, the absolute necessity of a radical reform in the management, training, and education of dogs ... also, to induce his superiors to rescue his dishonored race from unmerited neglect and degradation."

323. Butler, Joseph (1692–1752). *The Works of the Right Reverend Father in God Joseph Butler, Late Lord Bishop of Durham to Which Is Prefixed a Preface Giving Some Account of the Character and Writings of the Author.* (Oxford: University Press, 1844). 2 vols. 344, 362pp. Edited and with additional material by Samuel Halifax.

Volume 1: *Analogy of Religion,* Volume 2: *Sermons.*

A779, D35 (author, title, 2 vols., city, date), JS639. D35 describes Dodgson's copy: "With inscription 'Charles Lutwidge Dodgson, from the Master of Rugby School [i.e. Archibald Campbell Tait], 2nd Divinity Prize, Oct. 1849'." Butler was born into a Presbyterian family but became an Anglican in 1714. He rose to the rank of Bishop of Durham and was renowned for his preaching. He is remembered as an exponent of natural theology and as a moral philosopher.

324. Butler, Josephine E. (1828–1906), editor. *Woman's Work and Woman's Culture. A Series of Essays.* (London: Macmillan & Co., 1869). 367pp.

D231, JS638. Dodgson's copy is in HAC and has the gothic stamp on the title page. Josephine Butler is commemorated in the Anglican Church calendar. She was a devout churchwoman who campaigned for women's rights, including the rights of prostitutes. The book includes a lengthy introduction by the editor and: "The Final Cause of Woman," by Frances Power Cobbe; "How to Provide for Superfluous Women," by Jessie Boucherett; "Education Considered as a Profession for Women," by Rev. G. Butler; "Medicine as a Profession for Women," by Sophia Jex-Blake; "The Teaching of Science," by James Stuart; "On Some Historical Aspects of Family Life," by Charles H. Pearson; "The Property Disabilities of a Married Woman, and Other Legal Effects of Marriage," by Herbert N. Mozley; "Female Suffrage, Considered Chiefly with Regard to its Indirect Results," by Julia Wedgwood; "The Education of Girls, Its Present and Its Future," by Elizabeth C. Wolstenholme; and "The Social Position of Women in the Present Age," by John Boyd-Kinnear.

325. Buttmann, Philipp Karl (1764–1829). *Dr. Buttmann's Intermediate or Larger Greek Grammar.* (London: Whitaker, 1841). 485pp. 2nd edition. Translated from German, edited by Charles Supf.

D34 (author, title, editor, city, date), JS643. D34 notes, "C. L. Dodgson, 2 early signatures." Buttmann was a German philologist whose writings had a great influence on the study of Greek. His Greek grammar was first published in German in 1792.

326. Buttmann, Philipp Karl. *Lexilogus; or A Critical Examination of the Meaning and Etymology of Numerous Greek Words and Passages, Intended Principally for Homer and Hesiod.* (London: J. Murray, 1846). 586pp. 3rd edition, revised. Translated and edited, with explanatory notes and copious indexes by J[ohn] R[oles] Fishlake.

B992 (author, title, translator, date), JS642. B992 notes that Dodgson's copy was a "Rugby Prize, Easter 1849, with inscription." Fishlake was educated at Wadham College, Oxford and served as rector of Little Cheverel, Wiltshire from 1823 until his death in 1868.

327. [Buxton, Henry John Wilmot] (b. ca. 1834). *Poems by an Oxonian.* (Oxford: Whittaker, 1865).

A842 (title), JS201 (Anon./Oxford). Only edition listed of the only matching title in BL or BOD. Buxton matriculated at Oxford in 1862 and attended Brasenose College. He was rector of Ifield, Kent from 1872 to 1878.

328. Byron, George Gordon Noël, Lord (1788–1824). *Childe Harold's Pilgrimage; A Romaunt.* (London: Murray, 1846?).

A322, D36 (author, title, city, date), JS647. No British edition of 1846 traced, but NUC lists Murray editions of 1845 (227pp.) and 1849 (331pp.). Byron writes that this was "written for the most part amid the scenes which it attempts to describe. It was begun in Albania; and the parts relative to Spain and Portugal were composed from the author's observations in those countries.... The scenes attempted to be sketched are in Spain, Portugal, Epirus, Acarnania, and Greece. A fictitious character is introduced for the sake of giving some connection to the piece."

329. Byron, George Gordon Noël, Lord. *Poetical Works.* No edition specified.

A328 ("Byron's Poetical Works"), JS644.

330. Byron, George Gordon Noël, Lord. *Poetry of Byron.* (London: Macmillan & Co., 1881). 276pp. Chosen and arranged by Matthew Arnold. In the *Golden Treasury Series.*

A339 ("Poetry of Byron"), JS646. In May 1883, Dodgson corresponded with Macmillan on the subject of books containing "selections" of work from the great poets (see *Macmillan*,

163). Macmillan specifically mentioned this edition of Byron and then sent Dodgson works of Wordsworth (which Dodgson acknowledged as being from this series, see 2310), Byron, and Shelley. The *Golden Treasury Series* are the only editions in which Macmillan published "selected" poetry from all three of these poets. This is the only edition described in MBC. See 56 for a note on Arnold.

331. Byron, George Gordon Noël, Lord. *The Works of Lord Byron: with his Letters and Journals, and His Life, by Thomas Moore.* (London: John Murray, 1832–33). 17 volumes. Edited by John Wright.

A362 ("Byron's Works, 17 vols."), JS645. This is the first printing of the only 17-volume edition of Byron's works traced. See 1387 for a note on Moore.

332. Caldecott, Randolph (1846–86). Picture Books. Including: *The Milkmaid, Hey Diddle Diddle and Baby Bunting, A Frog He Would A-wooing Go, The Fox Jumps over the Parson's Gate, Come Lasses and Lads, Ride a-Cock Horse and A Farmer Went Trotting, Mrs Mary Blaize An Elegy on the Glory of her Sex,* and *The Great Panjandrum Himself.* ([London]: George Routledge, n.d. [1882–85]). 8 of Caldecott's Picture Books bound in a single volume, all illustrated by Caldecott.

A370 ("Caldecott's Picture Books, bound in 2 vols."), JS648. The two volumes referred to in A370 were offered at auction by Christie's, South Kensington on 28 May 1999. The first volume was described as above, the second only as "another bound collection of works by Randolph Caldecott" (see DAA3173). The books listed in DAA3173 are the 2nd 8 of Caldecott's 16 picture books; it seems likely that the remaining volume included the 1st 8 picture books, published by Routledge from 1878 to 1881. The were: *The House that Jack Built, John Gilpin, Elegy on a Mad Dog, The Babes in the Woods, Sing a Song for Sixpence* (also listed separately as A542/E39/JS650), *The Three Jovial Huntsmen, The Farmer's Boy,* and *The Queen of Hearts.* HAC has a copy of *Mrs Mary Blaize An Elegy on the Glory of her Sex* (also listed separately as F183) which is identified as Dodgson's only by the gothic stamp. Caldecott was among the most popular book illustrators of the late 19th century. His collection of 16 picture books (issued two per year at Christmas) produced together with Edmund Evans, remains his most recognized achievement.

333. Caldecott, R[andolph]. *A Sketch-book of R. Caldecott's*. (London: George Routledge [1883]). 48pp. Sepia drawings and text on one side and colored drawings on the other.

A541, E24 (author, title, publisher), F150, JS649. 1st (and apparently only) edition. E24 and F150 describes this as having Dodgson's initials. OCCL describes this as "a random collection of pictures which shows Caldecott's versatility but which was not a commercial success."

334. Calmet, Augustin (1672–1757). *Calmet's Dictionary of the Holy Bible.* (London: Charles Taylor, 1823). 5 vols., 4th edition. Revised, corrected, and augmented, under the direction of Charles Taylor.

A941 (author, title, 5 vols.), JS651. Earliest 5-volume edition in BL. Calmet was a French Benedictine monk, a teacher of philosophy and theology, and a biblical scholar. His commentary on the Bible (1707–16) was published in 23 quarto volumes and, according to the *Catholic Encyclopedia,* "inaugurated a new method of Biblical exegesis." Originally published in French in 1820.

335. Calmet, Augustin. *The Phantom World; or, the Philosophy of Spirits, Apparitions, &c.* (London: Richard Bentley, 1850). 2 vols. 378, 362pp. 1st edition. Translated and edited, with an introduction and notes, by Henry Christmas.

A899, D178 (author, title, editor, date), JS652. D178 notes Dodgson's initials. Gives details of reports on vampires from Hungary, Moldavia, and Poland as well as a wide variety of other supernatural tales.

336. C[alverley], C[harles] S[tuart] (1831–84). *Fly Leaves.* (Cambridge: Deighton, Bell & Co, 1872). 120pp.

A453 (author, title, edition, date), JS654. Dodgson's copy, with his monogram on the title page, sold at Anderson Auction Co., New York, in December 1908 (DAA853). It is now in the collection of Jon Lindseth, Cleveland, OH. It also includes MS. notes by Dodgson on the contents pages concerning works parodied by Calverley. Calverley was educated at Oxford be-

fore being expelled for a prank and moving to Cambridge. He later became a barrister, but an injury prevented his pursuing that career after 1867. His two volumes of poetry (here and below) made him famous as a parodist of Browning, Macaulay, and others. Dodgson met Calverley in 1872 and corresponded with him on the subject of acrostics (see Collingwood, 152–6).

337. Calverley, Charles Stuart. *The Literary Remains of Charles Stuart Calverley. With a Memoir by Walter J. Sendall.* (London: G. Bell & Sons, 1885). 281pp. With portrait and illustrations.

A882, E21 (author, title, date), JS1842 (listed under Sendall). Sendall (1832–1904) was a colonial governor. His memoir covers 116pp.

338. C[alverley], C[harles] S[tuart]. *Verses and Translations.* (Cambridge: Deighton, Bell, 1862). 203pp. 1st edition.

A453 (author, title, edition, date), JS653. Dodgson's copy, with his autograph inside the front cover and monogram on the title page, sold at Anderson Auction Co., New York, in December 1908 (DAA850). Poems.

339. *Cambridge Essays, Contributed by Members of the University*. (London: J. W. Parker & Son, 1855–56). 2 vols.

A335, D138 (title, dates), JS106. Of this continuing series of essays, Dodgson owned the annual volumes for 1855 and 1856. 1855 volumes includes: "The Life and Genius of Moliere," by Christopher Knight Watson; "The English Language in America," by Charles Astor Bristed; "Notes on Modern Geography," by Francis Galton; "Limitations to Severity in War," by Charles Buxton; "On the Transmutation of Matter," by George Downing Living; "The Relation of Novels to Life," by Stephen Fitzjames; "Future Prospects of the British Navy," by Robert Edgar Hughes; "Alfred Tennyson's Poems," by George Brimley; and "General Education and Classical Studies," by William George Clark. 1856 volume includes: "Roman Law and Legal Education," by H. J. S. Maine; "On English Ethnography," by J. W. Donaldson; "Old Studies and New," by John Grote; "The Taste for the Picturesque among the Greeks," by E. M. Cope; "Apocryphal Gospels," by C. J. Ellicott; "The Protestant Church and Religious Freedom in France," by W. H. Waddington; "The Fly-fisher and his Library," by H. R. Francis; "The Text of Shakspeare," by

Charles Badham; and "Coleridge," by F. J. A. Hort.

340. *Cambridge Prize Poems. A Complete Collection of such English Poems as have Obtained the Annual Premium Instituted by the Rev. T. Seaton from the Year 1750 to the Year 1806. To which are Added Three Poems Likewise Written for the Prize.* (London: T. & J. Allman, 1818). 129pp.

A843 ("Cambridge Prize Poems"), JS107 (Anon./Literature). Earliest 1-volume edition under this title traced (A843 does not mention multiple volumes). The work was frequently reprinted and updated during the 19th century.

341. Cammann, Henry J[ulius] (d. 1920) and Hugh N. Camp. *The Charities of New York, Brooklyn, and Staten Island.* (New York: Hurd and Houghton, 1868). 596pp.

In January 1891, Dodgson, who wished to present copies of the rejected printing of *The Nursery Alice* to "American Hospitals and Homes where there are sick children," asked Macmillan if they could, "get me any statistics." Macmillan responded by sending him *Charities of New York* [this is the only matching title traced]. Dodgson wrote, "it has not proved much use, as it only names one, and gives no details: but it has told me all about the Charity Organization Society there, which appears to be in touch with Branches all over the States: so I am going to apply to them to put me in the way of getting the information I want." (See *Macmillan*, 286).

342. Campbell, Hugh. *Nervous Exhaustion and the Diseases Induced by it. With Observations on the Origin and Nature of Nervous Force.* (London: Longmans & Co., 1874). 184pp. 3rd edition.

E153 (title, author, date), JS655. E153 gives title as *Nervous Exhaustion and the Diseases Induced by it, Nervous Force, and Animal Electricity, etc.* Campbell was a physician and a member of the Royal College of Surgeons. His published works include treatises on deafness, consumption, and anatomy.

343. Campbell, Thomas (1777–1844). *The Poetical Works of Thomas Campbell.* (London: Edward Moxon, 1840). 343pp. Illus-trated by 37 wood-cuts, from designs by Harvey. With a portrait.

B994 (author, title, illustrator, date), JS656. Campbell was a Scottish poet best known for his war verse.

344. (Canterbury). *A Complete Handbook of the Antiquities of Canterbury.* (1869). Steel engravings.

E244 (title, date), JS342 (Anon./Topography). No copy traced; description taken from E244.

345. [Capes, John Moore] (1812–89). *Reasons for Returning to the Church of England.* (London: Strahan & Co., 1871). 233pp.

B1194 (title, date), JS324 (Anon./Theology). Capes was educated at Oxford, took Anglican orders, heavily endowed a new church, but gave up both his living and his fortune to convert to Roman Catholicism. He was not a follower of the Tractarians, but was seeking an infallible authority on matters of doctrine. He founded and for a time edited *The Rambler*, a periodical for recently converted English Catholics. He later recanted and returned to the English Church.

346. Capes, John Moore. *To Rome and Back.* (London: Smith, Elder & Co., 1873). 386pp.

A870, B996 (author, title, date), J657. Capes' autobiographical novel tells of leaving the English Church for Roman Catholicism and returning four years later. *The Spectator* wrote, "We confess that, after reading [these pages] with some care and much interest, we have not been able distinctly to ascertain what it was that led their author to Rome, or how he was brought back to England."

347. [Carew, Bampfylde Moore] (1693–1770?). *An Apology for the Life of Mr. Bampfylde-Moore Carew, Commonly Called the King of the Beggars; Being an Impartial Account of his Life, from his Leaving Tiverton School, at the Age of Fifteen, and Entering into a Society of Gypsies, to the Present Time, with his Travels Twice through Great Part of America. A Particular Account of the Original Government, Language, Laws and Customs of the Gypsies. And a Parallel Drawn after the Manner of Plutarch, between Mr. Bampfylde-Moore Carew* *and Mr. Thomas Jones.* (London: Printed for R. Goadby [etc.], 1768). 347pp. 8th edition.

B955 (title, date), JS658. The book has also been attributed to Robert Goadby and to Carew's wife. The book tells Carew's tale as one of England's most famous mendicants, his swindling, fraud, etc. Though he was transported to Maryland for vagrancy, Carew escaped and continued his career.

348. Carlyle, Thomas (1795–1881). *The French Revolution: A History.* (London: Chapman and Hall, 1842). 3 vols. 354, 375, 400pp. 2nd edition.

A631, B997 (author, title, edition, 3 vols., date), JS659. Carlyle was a Scottish-born historian and essayist and among the most influential scholars of the Victorian period.

349. Carlyle, Thomas. *Sartor Resartus the Life and Opinions of Herr Teufelsdrockh, In Three Books.* (London: Saunders and Otley, 1838). 310pp.

Not in JS. In a letter to Edith Rix (25 September 1885), Dodgson writes, "I have read very little of *Sartor Resartus.*" This is the 1st English trade edition of Carlyle's influential book which was especially admired by the Transcendentalists.

350. Carlyle, Thomas. *Shooting Niagara: And After?* (London: Chapman and Hall, 1867). 55pp. 1st edition.

D38 (author, title, city, date, edition), JS660. Reprinted from *Macmillan's Magazine* for August 1867, with some additions and corrections. Carlyle's response to the Second Reform Bill (which he opposed) and the brutal suppression of an uprising in Jamaica by Governor Eyre. In it he wishes for the emergence of political, economic, and religious aristocracies and foresees open civil war in England. Includes Carlyle's comments on the "Negro question."

351. Caron, Henry Le [pseud. of Thomas Miller Beach] (1841–94). *Twenty-Five Years in The Secret Service The Recollections of a Spy.* (London: William Heinemann, 1892). 311pp. Illustrated.

A917 (title), JS91 (Anon./History). Earliest edition in BL. 3rd and 6th editions are also recorded in 1892. Born in Colchester, Beach went to the United States where he served in the Union Army during the Civil War under the name of Henri Le Caron. From 1867–88 he served the British government as a spy in the United States. He was active in the Fenians and an organizer for the Irish Republican Army, but in 1889 gave testimony against the Irish before the Parnell Commission. Following that time he lived in seclusion, guarded by detectives round the clock. In his introduction, he writes that "There are many things, of course, to which I may not refer; but with respect to those upon which I feel at liberty to touch, one unalterable characteristic will apply all through, and that will be the absolute truthfulness of the record.... By my action lives have been saved, communities have been benefited, and right and justice allowed to triumph, to the confusion of law-breakers and would-be murderers."

352. Carové, Friedrich Wilhelm (1789–1852). *The Story without an End.* (London: Sampson Low & Co., 1868). 40pp. Translated from the German by Sarah Austin. With illustrations printed in colours after drawings by E. V. B. [i.e. Eleanor Vere Boyle] engraved by the Leighton Brothers.

A532 (title), JS661. There were many editions published in the 19th century; the present seems most likely because of Dodgson's interest in the illustrator (he had at least 4 other books by her in his library, see 219–22). Carové was a German critic and philosophical writer. Austin (1793–1867) translated from several languages and taught German to J. S. Mill. The illustrations were engraved from Boyle's detailed watercolors. A German Romantic fairy tale.

353. (Carpenter, Edward) (1844–1929). *Socialism and Religion; or Thoughts after Reading Mr. Carpenter's "Ideal England."* By an Onlooker. (London: Digby & Long, 1890). 29pp.

E229 (title), JS283. Only edition in BL. Carpenter was a social reformer and poet who argued for rights for both women and homosexuals. One of his homosexual relationships is said to have been the basis for E. M. Forster's novel *Maurice.* His tract *England's Ideal* was first printed in *To-Day* in May, 1884, and first printed separately by John Heywood, Manchester, 1885 in a 22pp. edition. A book of essays under the title *England's Ideal* was issued in 1887.

354. Carpenter, William Benjamin (1813–85). *Mesmerism, Spiritualism, &c., Histor-*

ically & Scientifically Considered. Being Two Lectures. (London: Longmans & Co., 1877). 158pp.

JS664. Dodgson's copy, with his monogram on the half title, is in the collection of Selwyn Goodacre, Derbyshire, England. Carpenter was a British physiologist and naturalist who was examiner in Physiology and Comparative Anatomy at the University of London before serving as registrar of that institution. He was involved in deep sea explorations beginning in 1868. *Saturday Review* wrote, "If Dr. Carpenter's treatment of these subjects has a fault, it is that he gives himself too much trouble to expose the feats of magnetizers, clairvoyants, and mediums in detail." In a letter of 4 December 1882, Dodgson seems to dismiss one of Carpenter's theories about false spiritualists (see *Letters*, 471–72).

355. Carpenter, William Benjamin. *Principles of Mental Physiology, with their Applications to the Training and Discipline of the Mind, and the Study of its Morbid Conditions.* (London: H. S. King & Co., 1874). 737pp.

B998 (author, title, date), F170, JS663. Earliest edition in BL. According to B998, Dodgson's copy was "bound in two vols." F170 notes the gothic stamp. *The Spectator* wrote "Dr. Carpenter has collected in this volume the researches and systematic thought of many years on the relations between the mind and its organism, and on the application of the conclusions arrived at to the best training of the mind for the purpose of the proper use of its organism, and of the best training of the organism to make it a suitable instrument for the mind."

356. Carpenter, William Boyd (1841–1918). *The Permanent Elements of Religion. Eight Lectures Preached Before the University of Oxford.* (London: Macmillan & Co., 1889). 423pp. The Bampton Lectures for 1887.

A802 ("Hessey's Bampton Lectures, Carpenter's ditto"), JS662. Earliest edition in BL. Carpenter was educated at Cambridge and held several ecclesiastical posts before being made Bishop of Ripon in 1884. Dodgson wrote a letter to Carpenter after one of the lectures chiding him for using humor in a sermon (see *Letters*, 677–78).

357. Carr, Alice Vansittart Strettel [Mrs. J. W. Comyns Carr] (b. 1850). *North Italian Folk. Sketches of Town and Country Life.* (London: Chatto & Windus, 1878). 282pp. Illustrated by Randolph Caldecott.

A482 (author, title, illustrator, date), JS665. One of two travel books illustrated by Caldecott (see 332).

358. Carr, G[eorge] S[hoobridge] (b. 1837). *A Synopsis of Elementary Results in Pure Mathematics, Containing Propositions, Formulæ, and Methods of Analysis with Abridged Demonstrations, Supplemented by an Index to the Papers on Pure Mathematics which are to be Found in the Principal Journals and Transactions of Learned Societies, both English and Foreign, of the Present Century.* (London: Francis Hodgson, 1886). 935pp.

A387, E100 (title, author, "vol. I," date), F147, JS666. E100 states "with the initials of Lewis Carroll on the title." F147 further notes the gothic stamp. An edition was also published in Cambridge in the same year by Macmillan and Bowes. BL lists only an 1880 London edition (described as "vol. 1"), and the Cambridge edition seems to be one volume only. The book consisted of thousands of problems in the various fields of mathematics.

359. Carrick, Alick [pseud.] *The Secret of the Circle, its Area Ascertained.* (London: H. Sotheran & Co., 1876). 2nd edition. 48pp. With a preface signed F. B. Playfair, F.R.C.S.

E365 (author, title, date), F162, JS667. Dodgson's copy, with the gothic stamp, is in the collection formed by Jeffrey Stern, now at Seitoku Gakuin College, Tokyo, Japan. A work on circle-squaring. Dodgson attacked circle-squarers in his own writings (see *Math*, 144).

360. Cartari, Vincenzo (b. ca. 1500). *Le Imagini, con la Spositione de i dei de gli Antichi.* (Venetia: Presso F. Zilletti, 1580). 566pp. Con molta diligenza reuiste e ricorrette.

Uncertain. F187 (author, title, city, date), JS669. F187 lists no identifying marks. Cartari was an Italian engraver. An important iconological sourcebook for Renaissance artists, first published in 1566.

361. Carter, Robert Brudenell (1828–1918). *Eyesight: Good & Bad. A Treatise on the Exercise and Preservation of Vision.* (London: Macmillan & Co., 1880). 265pp.

B1000 (author, title, date), JS668. Carter was a member of the Royal College of Surgeons and an ophthalmic surgeon to St. George's Hospital, London. He wrote works on vision, works on the nervous system, and *Our Homes and How to Make them Healthy*.

362. Carter, Thomas Thellusson (1808–1901). *The Doctrine of the Priesthood in the Church of England.* (London: Joseph Masters, 1863). 176pp. 2nd edition.

Uncertain. Not in JS. Listed in WS only and identified by the gothic stamp and property label only. Dodgson's copy is in WWC and bears the gothic stamp and the property label. It has manuscript notations in the text. Carter was educated at Christ Church, Oxford and served as rector of Clewer, near Windsor, from 1844 to 1880. There he was active in the High Church movement. He founded a number of charitable institutions, including one for the rescue of fallen women. In his introduction he writes, "Two different views are held of the meaning of the name, and of the character of the ministry, of a Priest. They may be distinguished as the Presbyter, and the Sacerdotal view. As one or other prevails, an entirely different idea of the Church system is the result."

363. Catlin, George (1796–1872). *The Breath of Life or Mal-Respiration and Its Effects Upon the Enjoyment & Life of Man.* (London: Trübner & Co., 1862). 75pp. 25 illustrations by the author.

E251, F146, JS670. Dodgson's copy is in HAC. Dodgson's signature is in brown ink inside the front cover. A pencil note on the front endpaper states "compare with 'Alice's Adventures Underground' H. A.," and in fact, the comparison is apt. Dodgson's copy is dated 1862, the year he began working on AAUG. The present book, like Dodgson's 1886 facsimile of AUG, is completely reproduced from the author's illustrated manuscript. Catlin was an American painter known for his depiction of native Americans. He claims here that he has discovered the reason for the relative health of the native people of the Americas, among whom he carried out his life's work, compared to "civilized communities," namely the difference in sanitary conditions. His concluding motto for healthy life: "Shut Your Mouth."

364. Catullus, [Gaius Valerius] (ca. 84–ca. 54 B.C.E.). *Tibullus et Propertius.* (London: G. Pickering, 1824). 3 vols. 61, 46, 93pp. In the *Pickering Diamond Classics* series.

A477 (series, author), JS671. This is the only edition of Catullus published by Pickering listed in BL. See 153 for more on this series. Catullus was a Roman poet.

365. Cayley, Charles Bagot (1823–83). *Psyche's Interludes.* (London: Longman & Co., 1857).

B1001 (author, title, date), JS672. Only edition in BL. Born in Russia and educated at King's College, London and Trinity College, Cambridge, Cayley was a scholar of Italian and was best known for his masterful translation of Dante, as well as other translations of the classics. The present volume comprises his original poetry.

366. Chaffers, William (1811–92). *Hall Marks on Gold and Silver Plate, with Tables of Annual Date Letters Employed in the Principal Assay Offices of England, Scotland, and Ireland, from the Earliest Period of their Use to the Present Day ... with Extracts from the Statutes ... Regulating the Manufacture and Stamping of the Precious Metals.* (London: J. Davy & Sons, 1863). 67pp.

A373 ("Chaffer's Hall-marks on Plate"), JS673. Earliest edition in BL. The work was frequently reprinted and updated under slightly varying titles.

367. Chaffers, William. *Marks and Monograms on Pottery and Porcelain, with Short Historical Notices of Each Manufactory, and an Introductory Essay on the Vasa Fictilia of England.* (London: J. Davy & Sons, 1863). 256pp. Illustrated.

A373 ("Chaffer's Pottery and Porcelain"), JS674. Earliest edition in BL. The work was frequently reprinted and updated under slightly varying titles.

368. [Chambers, John Charles] (1817–44). *The Priest in Absolution: A Manual for Such as are Called unto the Higher Ministries in the English Church.* (London: Privately Printed, 1866).

A570 (title), JS675. 1st edition. Dodgson may have owned the 1st public edition (London: Masters, 1869), 322pp. Chambers was an Anglican priest and writer, known for his work among poor children. This booklet was privately printed at the instigation of the Society of the Holy Cross, an Anglo-Catholic clergy society founded in 1855 of which Chambers was a member. A570 does not specify if Dodgson owned both parts, but he probably only owned the 1866 first part. The second part was supposed to be sold only to confessors and, according to ODCC, dealt with "certain sins which necessarily called for treatment in a technical manual." When a copy came to the attention of the House of Lords, it caused a protest against the High Church movement.

369. Chambers, R[obert] (1802–71), editor. *The Book of Days. A Miscellany of Popular Antiquities, in Connection with the Calendar.* (London: W. & R. Chambers, 1863–64). 2 vols.
   A737 (editor, title, 2 vols.), JS676. 1st edition. The work was reprinted several times. Chambers was co-founder (with his brother) of the Edinburgh publishing company W. & R. Chambers and wrote several books on Scottish history, biography, literature, etc. He founded *Chambers Journal* in 1832. This popular collection was an almanac of historical information related to dates of the calendar.

370. Chambers, Robert. *Popular Rhymes of Scotland. Original Poems.* (Edinburgh: W. & R. Chambers: Edinburgh, 1847). 357pp. 3rd edition, with additions. Volume 7 of *The Select Writings of Robert Chambers*.
   E19 (title, series, author, date), JS678. A collection of poetry.

371. Chambers, R[obert], editor. *The Songs of Scotland Prior to Burns. With the Tunes.* (Edinburgh & London: W. & R. Chambers, 1862). 462pp.
   B1239 (title, editor, date), JS677.

372. Champfleury [pseud. of Jules François Félix Husson] (1821–89). *Les Chats, Histoire, Mœurs, Observations, Anecdotes.* (Paris: J. Rothschild, 1870). 332pp. 4th edition.
   Uncertain. F182 (author, title, date), WS, not numbered in JS. Identified as Dodgson's only

by gothic stamp. WS also notes property label. This is the only 1870 edition in BL. F182 describes this as "edition de luxe" with colored and other illustrations. Champfleury was a French novelist and defender of Realism. This popular book about cats includes a specially commissioned etching by Manet as well as plates after Delacroix, Tissot, and other French artists.

373. [Chapman]. *Confessions of a Medium.* (London: Griffith, Farran, Okeben & Welsh, 1882). 232pp. With 5 illustrations.
   A900 (title), JS180 (Anon./Occult). Earliest edition in BL. A900 could also refer to the anonymous 1861 work *The Spiritualists at Home The Confessions of a Medium,* but the Chapman book seems much more likely as it matches the title precisely (no "The") and in the 1861 work *The Confessions of a Medium* is a subtitle. A full page advertisement for this book appears in another book Dodgson owned, Thomas Heaphy's *A Wonderful Ghost Story.* This book exposed tricks used by those claiming to be mediums. *Whitehall Review* wrote, "Will cause a flutter in the camp of the charlatans who have for years past been trading on human folly and credulity."

374. Chapman, George (1559?–1643?). *The Comedies and Tragedies of George Chapman. Now First Collected with Illustrative Notes and a Memoir of the Author* [by Richard Herne Shepherd]. (London: John Pearson, 1873). 3 vols.
   A672, B1002 (author, title, 3 vols., date), JS680. Chapman was an Elizabethan poet and dramatist. See 1833 for a note on Shepherd.

375. Charles I (1600–49). *King Charles the First's Declaration to his Subjects Concerning Lawful Sports to be Used on Sundays. 1633.* (London: Bernard Quaritch, 1862). 17 pp.
   D40 (title, city, date), JS681. Dodgson's was one of 100 copies reprinted by the Chiswick Press from the 1633 edition. It includes his signature. The king here chides Puritans for prohibiting recreations on Sundays and decrees sports legal following the Sunday service. He writes that this will enable men to be fit for war and that a prohibition might keep people from the church.

376. Chase, Drummond Percy (b. ca. 1831). *Endowment of the Greek Professorship.* (Oxford: 1861). Single sheet.

Not in JS. Dodgson responds to this broadside in his own broadside of the same title (See WMGC, #29). Both works concerned the controversy over whether or not the endowment should be raised for Professor Benjamin Jowett — a controversy complicated by Jowett's contribution to the controversial book *Essays and Reviews* (see 2075). Chase was principal of St. Mary's Hall, Oxford.

377. [Chatterton, Thomas] (1752–70). *Poems Supposed to have Been Written at Bristol, by Thomas Rowley, and Others, in the Fifteenth Century.* (Cambridge: Printed by B. Flower, for the Editor, 1794). 329pp. Engraved title and glossary.

B1003 (author, title, date), JS682. Chatterton wrote these poems as a teenager on bits of ancient parchment, claiming they were the work of a 15th-century monk. His forgeries were denounced by Horace Walpole and he turned to periodical writing before committing suicide at 17. The poems were first published in 1777 and it was another century before the controversy surrounding them died down and Chatterton was accepted as the author.

378. Chatwood, Arthur Brunel. *The New Photography.* (London: Downey & Co., 1896). 128pp. Frontispiece, plates and diagrams.

E387 (title, date), JS229 (Anon./Photography). E387 further describes the book thus: "X-Rays, Color, Retinal Impressions, Spirit Photography, and Anaglyphs."

379. Chaucer, Geoffrey (ca. 1343–1400). *The Poems of Geoffrey Chaucer, Modernized.* (London: Whittaker & Co., 1841). 331pp.

A856, D41 (author, title, date, partial list of contributors), JS683. The authors of the modern versions are: R. H. Horne, William Wordsworth, Thomas Powell, Leigh Hunt, Robert Bell, and Elizabeth Barrett.

380. Chauvenet, William (1820–70). *A Treatise on Elementary Geometry With Appendices Containing a Collection of Exercises for Students and an Introduction to Modern Geometry.* (Philadelphia: J. B. Lippincott & Co., 1876). 368pp.

D42 (author, title, city, date), JS684. Dodgson's copy is in HAC. It includes his monogram in purple ink on the title page and minor annotations in purple ink in the margins of pages 23–24. The author was Professor of Mathematics and chancellor at Washington University, St. Louis, Missouri. This was one of the books Dodgson examined in his *Euclid and His Modern Rivals* (134).

381. Cheadle, W[alter] B[utler] (1835–1910). *The Various Manifestations of the Rheumatic State as Exemplified in Childhood and Early Life. Lectures, etc.* (London: Smith, Elder & Co., 1889). 127pp. With colored frontispiece and other illustrations.

E324 ("The Rheumatic State in Childhood," author, date), JS685. Educated at Cambridge, Cheadle was an eminent physician with a specialty in treating children. In 1862 he participated in an expedition to explore the Rocky Mountains through Canada. He was a successful teacher of medicine, a political radical who favored the admission of women to the profession, and a pioneer in the treatment of childhood rheumatism.

382. Cheever, G[eorge] B[arrell] (1807–90). *Lectures on the Life, Genius, and Insanity of Cowper.* (London: J. Nisbet & Co., 1856). 339pp.

E14 (author, title, date), F175, JS686. 3 editions were published in 1856, according to BL, however one (New York: Carter & Bros.) was American and another (London: Knight & Son) not dated, so this seems the most likely. According to E14, Dodgson's copy has "the autograph of John Owen." F175 notes the gothic stamp. Cheever was pastor at the Church of the Puritans, which he founded, in New York, from 1846 to 1876. He was editor of the *Evangelist* and contributed to many religious periodicals. Cowper (1731–1800) was a British poet.

383. Chester, Norley [pseud. of Emily Underdown]. *Olga's Dream. A Nineteenth Century Fairy Tale.* (London: Skeffington & Son, 1892). 162pp. With original illustrations by Harry Furniss and Irving Montagu.

A638 (title, illustrator), JS1044 (listed under Furniss). Only edition in BL. Underdown wrote and adapted stories for children. Harry Furniss (see 742) illustrated Dodgson's *Sylvie and Bruno* books. A story very much in the spirit of Lewis Carroll in which Olga falls asleep while reading the dictionary and travels through fantastical versions of her various school subjects before waking up to discover it was all a dream.

384. Chevreul, M[ichel] E[ugène] (1786– 1889). *The Principles of Harmony and Contrast of Colours and their Application to the Arts, Including Painting, Decoration, Tapestry, Carpets, Mosaics, Coloured Glazing, Paper-staining, Calico-printing, Letterpress do., Map-colouring, Dress, Landscape and Flower Gardening, etc.* (London: Longman, Brown, Green and Longmans, 1854). 431pp. Translated by Charles Martel (pseud. of Thomas Delf).

A595, E22 (title, author, date), JS687. 1st English edition, translated from the 1st French edition of 1839. Later editions added chromolithographs, while the 1st was accompanied by an expensive atlas of plates (not mentioned in E22). Dodgson bought his copy on 9 January 1855 from the bookseller William Harrison in Ripon (see *Diary* 1). Among the most important 19th-century books on color, this work explored the idea that adjacent colors are partly responsible for the way we see a color. It was widely used by 19th-century painters.

385. Childs, G[eorge] B[orlase] (1816–88). *On the Improvement and Preservation of the Female Figure; With a New Mode of Treatment of Lateral Curvature of the Spine.* (London: Harvey & Darton, 1840). 188pp.

E84 (title, author, date), JS688. E84 states that Dodgson's copy has the "pencil autograph of C. Pusey."

386. Child, G[eorge] Chaplin [afterwards George C. Child Chaplin] *Benedicite: or the Song of the Three Children. Being Illustrations of the Power, Wisdom and Goodness of God, as Manifested in His Works.* (London: John Murray, 1869). 364pp. 3rd edition.

D39 (author, title, date, city), JS679. D39

Olga Meets the Giant Science. Illustration by Harry Furniss for Norley Chester's *Olga's Dream* (item 383).

notes Dodgson's signature. Child was a physician. A book illustrating the presence of God in nature, with chapters on aspects of the natural world from the stars to the weather to farm animals.

387. (Christ Church, Oxford). *General Recommendations of the Referees.* (Oxford: [1866]).

Not in JS. Dodgson writes in his diary on 8 January 1867, "Received a copy of the 'Recommendations' of the referees. The changes are pretty much what I expected, except the one to abolish the distinctions of noblemen and gentlemen-commoners, which is totally new to me, and in my opinion *very* bad" (see *Diary 5*). A list of 17 brief recommendations related to the reform of Dodgson's college. The document is reprinted in its entirety in E. G. W. Bill and J. F. A. Mason's *Christ Church and Reform 1850–1867* (238–40).

388. (Christ Church, Oxford). *Statutes Proposed to be Made by the University of Oxford Commissioners for Christ Church.* ([London]: 1881).

E314 ("Christ Church Statutes, interleaved, 1891"), JS195 (Anon./Oxford). No work by this title published in 1891 is listed in BOD, BL, or NUC. Probably an error in E314 ("1891" for "1881"). These new statutes were part of the movement to reform Christ Church and became law in 1882.

389. *Christ Church Ordinances. Ratified 12th August, 1867. Together with all Changes therein Sanctioned by the Queen in Council, up to Lady Day, 1872*. (Oxford: T. Combe, E. B. Gardner, and E. Pickard Hall, 1872). 32pp.

E272, JS194 (Anon./Oxford). Dodgson's copy is in HAC and has his monogram in brown ink and the property label both on the title page. It has been unbound, interleaved, and restitched. Several passages are marked in pencil on pp. 13, 15–21. Includes changes to the rules governing Christ Church mostly adopted from 1867 to 1869 as part of university reform.

390. *Christmas Stories*. Details unknown.

Title only listed in A659/JS109 (Anon./ Literature). Many possibilities in BL, but the most likely is that this is a collection of Dickens' Christmas stories. The earliest editions of these listed in BL, and another possibility are listed below:
Dickens, Charles. *Christmas Stories from the Household Words.* (London: Chapman & Hall; "All the Year Round" Office, [1859]). A collection of the extra Christmas numbers from 1851 to 1858. Dickens' Christmas stories from his magazine were published in several pre–1898 editions.
[E. Berens]. *Christmas Stories. Containing John Wildgoose the Poacher, The Smuggler, and Good-Nature, or Parish Matters.* (J. Parker: Oxford, 1823). Illustrated by George Cruikshank.

391. Church, R[ichard] W[illiam] (1815–90). *Human Life and its Conditions. Sermons Preached before the University of Oxford in 1876–1878, with Three Ordination Sermons.* (London: Macmillan & Co., 1878). 194pp.

C2 (author, title, date), JS690. C2 notes that Dodgson's copy has his initials on the title page. Church was a High Churchman, an active member of the Oxford Movement and, like Dodgson's father, participated in the project to create new translations of the early Church Fathers. He wrote a history of the Oxford Movement. He became Dean of St. Paul's in 1871. According to *Letters*, 250n, Dodgson "would certainly have become acquainted with Church in the 1850s, when they both were at Oxford." Dodgson corresponded with Church's daughter, who, in 1883, married Francis Paget, who succeeded H. G. Liddell as Dean of Christ Church in 1891.

392. Church, R[ichard] W[illiam]. *Village Sermons, Preached at Whatley.* (London: Macmillan, 1892). 316pp.

A756 (author, title), JS689. Church published three series of the Village Sermons, in 1892, 1894, and 1897. A756 does not indicate multiple volumes and it seems most likely that Dodgson would have bought the first series only. Church served as rector at Whatley from 1852 to 1871.

393. Church Association. *Tracts*, nos. 101–163 (1890).

E128 (title, numbers, date), JS305 (Anon./ Theology). The Church Association was an anti-ritualistic group opposed to the changes in worship supported by the Oxford Movement. The activities of the C. A. resulted in the jailing of several ritualistic priests.

394. *Church Services*. (Oxford: 1843).

D44 ("Church Services," city, date), JS306. No exact match traced. "Church Services" may be a description of the contents rather than the title (for instance, a Book of Common Prayer was published at the University Press in 1843). D44 notes that this has the inscription "C. L. Dodgson, Rugby School House."

395. Cicero, Marcus Tullius (106–45 B.C.E.). *De Senectute. With English Notes.* (Cambridge: 1840).

D45 (author, title, city, date), JS695. D45

notes, "C. L. Dodgson, early autograph." No copy traced; description taken from D45. A philosophical treatise on old age presented in dialogue form. Dodgson used a similar dialogue form in his squib *The Vision of the Three T's.*

396. (Cicero, Marcus Tullius). *The Life and Letters of Marcus Tullius Cicero. The Life of Cicero, by Dr. Middleton. Cicero's Letters to Several of his Friends, Translated by Wm. Melmoth. Cicero's Letters to Atticus, Translated by Dr. Heberden.* (London: E. Moxon, 1840). 828pp.

A925, B1006 (authors/translators, title, date), JS696. B1006 notes that Dodgson's copy was a "Rugby School Prize, to C. L. D., 1847, with Arms and inscription." This was awarded as 2nd Mathematical Prize in the general mathematical examination.

397. Cicero, M[arcus] T[ullius]. *M. T. Ciceronis Libri de Officiis, De Senectute, et De Amicitia.* (London: G. Pickering, 1821). 155pp. In the *Pickering Diamond Classics* series.

A477, A478 (series, author, title), JS692, JS693. Dodgson owned 2 copies of this item. For more on this series of miniature books, see 153.

398. Cicero, Marcus Tullius. *M. Tullii Ciceronis De Natura Deorum Libri Tres, cum Notis Integris Paullii Manutii, Petri Victorii, Joachimi Camerarii, Dionys. Lambini, Fulv. Ursini, et Joannis Walkeri. Recensuit, Suisque Animadversionibus illustravit ac Emaculavit Joannes Davisius.* (Oxford: Clarendon Press, 1807). New Edition.

B1005 (author, title, editor, city, date [1817]), JS694. No edition of 1817 has been traced; possibly 1817 in B1005 is a misprint for 1807. B1005 notes that Dodgson's copy is a prize to C. Dodgson (C.L.D.'s father) with an inscription dated May 1816—further evidence that the 1817 date is incorrect. Certainly this is the closest edition traced edited by John Davis (the earliest edition produced under his editorship traced is 1723). Essay on the nature of gods.

399. Cicero, Marcus Tullius. *Works.* 11 vols. Edition unknown.

A927 ("Cicero's Works, 11 vols., 4to), JS692.

No edition matching A927 has been traced. Editions of 11 volumes were published by Tauchnitz (Leipzig, 1860–69), and Wetstenios (Amsterdam, 1724), but neither records a 4to edition in BL, BOD, or NUC.

400. **Clark**, Mary Senior. *The Lost Legends of the Nursery Songs.* (London: Bell & Daldy, 1870). 248pp. Illustrated from the author's designs.

A641 (title), JS698. Earliest edition of the only matching title in BL. Fantastic re-tellings (featuring fairies, wizards, witches, etc.) of popular nursery rhymes.

401. **Clarke**, C[harles] H[enry Montague]. *The Sea-side Visitors' Guide, Showing at a Glance Where to Go — How to Get There — What to See, etc.* (London: The Proprietor, [1872]). 136pp.

E138 (title, author), JS699. Only edition in BL. According to E138, this work has a pictorial cover. Dodgson loved the seaside, and spent the last 20 summers of his life at Eastbourne. During younger days he often visited Whitby and other seaside towns.

402. **Clarke**, Henry Savile (1841–93). *Alice in Wonderland. A Dream Play for Children, in Two Acts. Founded Upon Mr. Lewis Carroll's 'Alice's Adventures in Wonderland,' and 'Through the Looking-Glass,' with the Express Sanc on [sic] of the Author.* (London: The Court Circular Office, 1886). 55pp.

D1 (full description), E12, JS700. D1 describes this copy as a "special copy evidently used by Mr. Dodgson during a performance of the Play, having the names of the Characters on p. 2 and 3 filled in with those of the Performers, in his handwriting ... and also notes in pencil by him criticising the performance." The first professionally staged dramatic adaptation of the *Alice* stories. For a full account of Savile Clarke's *Alice* drama, see *Alice on Stage.*

403. **Clarke**, M[ary] V[ictoria] Cowden (1809–98). *The Complete Concordance to Shakespere: Being a Verbal Index to All the Passages in the Dramatic Works of the Poet.* (London: C. Knight & Co., 1845). 860pp.

A375 (author, title), JS697 (listed as by Charles Cowden Clark). Earliest edition in BL. The cryptic entry at A375 is partly to blame for an incorrect listing in JS. Both seem to imply that this work is one with *Gleaning from Popular Authors* (the two are listed as one by JS). The original entry reads: "Cowden Clark's Concordance to Shakespeare and Gleanings from Popular Authors (2 vols.), half morocco." These are two separate works. *Gleanings from Popular Authors* is almost certainly the anonymous *Gleanings from Popular Authors Grave and Gay* (see 780) which includes "A Mad Tea-Party."

404. [**Clarke**, William] (1800–38). *The Boys Own Book A Complete Encyclopaedia of all the Diversions, Athletic, Scientific, and Recreative of Boyhood and Youth.* (1840). 462pp.

DAA2189 (title, date), not in JS. 1840 edition not traced. NUC lists the 16th (London: Whitehead, 1839) and 20th (London: Longman, 1842). Dodgson's copy was part of the Leicester Harmsworth collection and was offered for sale by Sotheby's, London on 26 March 1947. The sale catalogue described this item as "Inscribed at the head of the title 'Charles Lutwidge Dodgson, from his most Affte. Aunt and Godmother, Lucy Lutwidge, Jan. 27, 1841 [his 9th birthday].'"

405. Clarkson, Stanfield (1793–1867), illustrator. *The Continental Tourist, and Pictorial Companion. Illustrated with Sixty-Two Beautiful Engravings on Steel, of the Most Interesting European Scenery. Commencing at Antwerp, and proceeding through … the Netherlands; and by Way of Cologne to the Banks of that Beautiful River … Thence through the Baths of Nassau, and the Taunus Range of Mountains to Frankfort on the Main.* (London: Black and Armstrong, n.d.). 140pp.

Uncertain. F160 (title, "plates," n.d.), not numbered in JS (listed under Anon./Topography). Identified as Dodgson's only by gothic stamp. Also published in an undated edition by Parry & Co., London. Clarkson was an English sailor turned artist best known for his maritime paintings.

406. Claudianus, Claudius. *Cl. Claudiani Quae Exstant Varietate Lectionis et Perpetua Adnotatione Illustrata a Io. Matthia Gesnero Accedit Index Uberrimus.* (Lipsiae: In Officina Fritschia, 1759). 720pp.

A925, B1007 (author, title, illustrator, date), JS702. Claudianus was a Latin epic poet of the 4th–5th centuries.

407. *The Clergy List (With Which is Incorporated the Clerical Guide and Ecclesiastical Directory).* (London: Hall, 1883).

E276 (title, publisher, date), JS232 (Anon./Reference). This annual directory of British clergy was published from 1841 to 1917.

408. [**Clive**, Caroline, née Meysey-Wigley] (1801–73). *Paul Ferroll. A Tale.* (London: Saunders & Otley, 1855). 336pp.

Not in JS. In his diary for 10 July 1857, Dodgson writes, "Finished reading *Paul Ferroll* by the author of *IX Poems by V.*" Earliest edition in BL. Clive was a poet and novelist, and this novel of the sensational school was her best known work. Dodgson goes on to say, "It is a powerfully written and fascinating book, reminding one of *Jane Eyre* in some of its passages of description. There are so many novels describing the effects of sorrow and danger upon weak and common natures, that it is a relief to trace through similar scenes such a man as this— of iron will, strong powers of enjoyment, and the perfect self-command of a stoic or North American Indian. His ride by night, and the plunging of the horse through the Meer, is told in a strain of Wild German romance; and the account of the last night of the year and the broken lamp is worthy of Miss Brontë or Edgar Allan Poe. There is much pathos and much poetry in the book, (least shown perhaps in the actual stanzas introduced): and Janet is a beautiful picture throughout, though rather vague and unsubstantial." The novel is considered a seminal work in psychological fiction. Its hero murders his wife so that he can marry his true love but must decide, years later, whether to confess to save those who are wrongly accused.

409. [**Clive**, Caroline, née Meysey-Wigley]. *Poems by the Author of "Paul Ferroll". Including a New Edition of IX Poems by V, with Former and Recent Additions.* (London: Saunders & Otley, 1856). 229pp.

B1173 (title, date), JS703. First published in 1840.

410. Clodd, Edward (1840–1930). *Myths and Dreams.* (London: Chatto & Windus, 1885). 251pp.

A899 (author, title), JS704. Earliest edition in BL. The introduction states: "The object of this book is to present in compendious form the evidence which myths and dreams supply as to primitive man's interpretation of his own nature and of the external world, and more especially to indicate how such evidence carries within itself the history of the origin and growth of beliefs in the supernatural."

411. Clough, Arthur Hugh (1819–61). *The Bothie of Toper-na-Fuosich, a Long-Vacation Pastoral.* (Oxford: Francis Macpherson; London: Chapman & Hall, 1848). 55pp.

Uncertain. F167 (author, title, city, date), not numbered in JS. Identified as Dodgson's only by the gothic stamp. Clough was an English poet educated at Balliol College, Oxford, where he served as a tutor until 1848. He traveled on the continent, lectured at Harvard and pursued a career in the civil service. This poem in hexameter, written immediately after Clough left Oxford, is about an Oxford radical who falls in love with a farmer's daughter while on a reading party in Scotland.

412. Clough, Arthur Hugh. *Poems.* Edition unknown.

A832 (Clough's Poems), JS705. The following item listed in A832 is "Palgrave's Poems," making it possible that Dodgson owned this edition: *Poems, with a Memoir by F[rancis] T[urner] Palgrave.* (London: Macmillan & Co., 1862). 259pp.

413. Clowes, Sir William Laird (1856–1905). *Black America: A Study of the Exslave and his Late Master.* (London: Cassell & Co., 1891). 240pp. Reprinted, with large additions from *The Times.*

A342, B1008 (author, title, date), JS706. Clowes published several volumes of poetry. This work is a series of ten letters published in *The Times* from Clowes who traveled to America in 1890–91 to examine the "negro problem." His conclusion was that the best solution to this problem was to send all the free slaves back to Africa. See index under "Negro Problem" for similar works.

414. Cobbe, Frances Power (1822–1904). *The Hopes of the Human Race, Hereafter and Here.* (London & Edinburgh: Williams & Norgate, 1874). 218pp.

A552, JS708. Dodgson's copy is in the collection of Jon Lindseth, Cleveland, Ohio, and is signed with his initials in three places. Cobbe

was an anti-vivisectionist and feminist with whom Dodgson corresponded. She helped his article "Some Popular Fallacies About Vivisection" secure publication (see *Letters,* 223). In a letter to Lord Salisbury, Dodgson wrote, "I hope it is not an impertinence to call your attention to a most able letter and interesting essay in the last number of the *New Quarterly Review,* by Miss Frances Power Cobbe (who wrote a very powerful volume of essays, *The Hopes of the Human Race).*" (See *Letters* 237, *Diaries* 337 & 339.) The *Atlantic Monthly* (August 1876) wrote that Cobbe tries to, "show what are the arguments to incline a religious person to believe that the soul does exist after death.... She merely tries to show how unlikely it is that man is sent into the world to live for a time and then to perish utterly."

415. Cobbe, Frances Power. *Studies New and Old of Ethical and Social Subjects.* (London: Trübner & Co., 1865). 446pp.

A552 (author, title), JS707. Only edition of the only matching title in BL. Includes "The Philosophy of the Poor Laws" and "The Hierarchy of Art."

416. [Cockburn, Alexander James Edmund] (1802–80). *The Tichborne Trial: The Summing-up by the Lord Chief Justice of England. Together with the Addresses of the Judges, the Verdict, and the Sentence; The Whole Accompanied By A History of the Case and Copious Alphabetical Index.* (London: Ward, Lock, and Tyler, 1874). 302pp.

E180 (title, date), JS97. Cockburn was Lord Chief Justice from 1859 to 1880. The trial of Arthur Orton, who claimed to be a missing heir, Sir Roger Charles Doughty Tichborne, attracted great publicity and is often cited as a possible inspiration for Dodgson's *The Hunting of the Snark.*

417. Cockburn, Samuel. *The Laws of Nature and the Laws of God: A Reply to Prof. Drummond.* (London: Swan Sonnenschein, 1887?). 154pp.

D196 (title, city, date), D131 (Anon./Law). D131 notes Dodgson's initials. Only edition traced is 1886 (described here). The 1887 edition was probably published by Swan Sonnenschein also. Cockburn was a physician who wrote several works in support of Homœopathy. The book is a review of Henry Drummond's *Natural Law in the Spiritual World* (London: 1883). Dodgson owned a copy of Drummond's book (see 629).

418. Cockton, Henry (1807–53). *The Life and Adventures of Valentine Vox, the Ventriloquist.* (London: George Routledge, 1854). 620pp. New edition with 60 illustrations by T. Onwhyn.

Not is JS. In his diary for 16 January 1855, Dodgson wrote, "Read *Valentine Vox* in the morning." The earliest edition listed in BL is 1840, but the present edition is the closest in BL to the date of Dodgson's reading. Cockton was the author of humorous novels of which the present is the best known. The ventriloquist/magician hero of the book fights against injustice in the Victorian lunatic asylum system.

419. Cole, John William (d. 1870). *The Life and Theatrical Times of Charles Kean, F.S.A., Including a Summary of the English Stage for the Last Fifty Years and a Detailed Account of the Management of the Princess's Theatre from 1850 to 1859.* (London: Richard Bentley, 1859). 2 vols. 368, 391pp.

A880 ("Life of Charles Kean"), JS709. This is the earliest edition of the only life of Kean in BL. Earliest edition, but an 1860 reprint is also in 2 vols. A880 does not specify 2 vols., but it seems likely that either this was an oversight or Dodgson had his two volumes bound as one. *Saturday Review* called this "a most instructive chronicle of the stage in the present generation." Kean was an actor who managed the Princess's Theatre in the early years of Dodgson's theatregoing. Dodgson saw him in several productions, including *Henry VIII*, the first straight play he mentions seeing in his diary (22 June 1855). Dodgson owned several of Kean's editions of Shakespeare (see 1807–15).

420. Colenso, John William (1814–83). *Arithmetic, Designed for the Use of Schools.* (London: Longman & Co., 1855). 171pp. New edition.

E176 (author, title, date), JS710, WS. E176 describes Dodgson's copy as having two autographs and many markings by him. Colenso was a mathematics tutor at Cambridge who went on to a career in the church (see below). His manuals in mathematics and algebra were used in schools throughout England. The copy catalogued by Walter Spencer is dated 1859

(not in BL) and described as having "autograph initials and a line in [Dodgson's] hand also some groups of figures and other notes that may be in his hand." Thus, Dodgson probably owned two copies.

421. Colenso, John William, Robert Gray (1809–72), and Charles Thomas Longley (1794–1868). *Letters from the Archbishop of Canterbury, the Bishop of Capetown, and the Bishop of Natal, with Some Observations on the Archbishop of Canterbury's Reply to the Bishop of Natal.* (London: Trübner & Co., 1866).

C5 ("Correspondence of Archbishops with Colenso"), not in JS. This is the only closely matching title traced and the only edition listed in BL. Colenso was appointed as first Bishop of Natal in 1853 and soon began to elicit criticism for his unorthodox views. Following the publication of his controversial work on *The Pentateuch and the Book of Joshua* (see 1104), he was deposed by Robert Gray, Bishop of Capetown. He refused to recognize the Bishop's authority and through a series of judicial decisions in the Privy Council, managed to maintain his position, though Gray appointed a replacement. The schism in the diocese lasted until 1911. (see also 816, 1184). Longley, the Archbishop of Canterbury at the time of the controversy, was a friend of Dodgson. The two first met when Longley was Bishop of Ripon and Dodgson's father was a canon there.

422. Coleridge, Hartley (1796–1849). *Poems.* (London: Edward Moxon, 1851). 2 vols. 168, 367pp. With a memoir of his life by his brother [Derwent Coleridge]. With a portrait.

A832 (author, title, 2 vols.), JS711. Only 2-vol. edition in BL. Hartley and Derwent Coleridge were sons of Samuel Taylor Coleridge. Hartley's career was not highly distinguished, though he did write what OCEL calls "some lovely beautiful sonnets."

423. Coleridge, Samuel Taylor (1772–1834). *Aids to Reflection.* (London: W. Pickering, 1846?). 2 vols. 5th edition, enlarged. Edited by H. N. Coleridge

A767, B1011 (author, title, editor, 2 vols., date [1846]), JS716. No 1846 edition traced; possibly an error in B1101 ("1846" for "1848" or "1843"). The 5th edition was published by Pickering in 2 vols. in 1843 and the 6th in 1848. In his diary for 14 January 1855, Dodgson writes, "Read Coleridge's *Aids to Reflection* in the evening — it is one of those books that improve on a second reading: I find very little in it even obscure now." He later undertook an analysis of the book, which appeared to hold great meaning for him. Cohen, in his biography (357–60) takes a close look at Dodgson's relationship with this book which, Cohen writes, "offered inner light and conviction as the only evidence [for faith] worth seeking.... Coleridge insists that the essential source of moral knowledge is the intuition, not the intellect."

424. Coleridge, Samuel Taylor. *Confessions of an Inquiring Spirit*. (London: William Pickering, 1840). 95pp. Edited from the author's MS. by Henry Nelson Coleridge.

B1010 (author, title, editor, publisher, date), JS718. The editor was the author's nephew. A series of letters on the inspiration of the Bible.

425. Coleridge, Samuel Taylor. *The Friend. A Series of Essays to Aid in the Formation of Fixed Principles in Politics, Morals, and Religion with Literary Amusements Interspersed*. (London: William Pickering, 1837). 3 vols.

A357 (author, title, 3 vols., publisher), JS713. Earliest Pickering 3-volume edition in BL, which records a similar edition of 1844 and a 3-volume edition of the second series in 1850. Coleridge originally launched *The Friend* as a "literary, moral, and political weekly paper" in 1809; this work is a rewriting of the contents into book form.

426. Coleridge, Samuel Taylor. *On the Constitution of the Church and State, According to the Idea of Each*. (London: Edward Moxon, 1852). 224pp. 3rd edition. Edited by H. N. Coleridge.

A767, B1013 (author, title, editor, publisher, date), JS720. Coleridge's comments on the debate over Catholic Emancipation, which had become law in 1829.

427. Coleridge, Samuel Taylor. *The Poems of Samuel Taylor Coleridge*. (London: Edward Moxon, 1852). 388pp. Edited by Derwent and Sara Coleridge. A new edition.

B1012 (author, title, editors, publisher, date),

JS719. The editors were children of the author.

428. Coleridge, [Samuel Taylor]. *Rime of the Ancient Mariner*. (London: Art-Union of London, 1863). 12pp. of text plus 20 plates. Illustrated by Joseph Noël Paton.

A288, not in JS. Only edition in BL. See 1507 for a note on the illustrator, Paton.

429. Coleridge, Samuel Taylor. *The Rime of the Ancient Mariner*. (London: Doré Gallery, 1875). 39 plates. Illustrated by Gustave Doré.

A292 (title, illustrator), not in JS. Earliest edition traced. See 619 for a note on Doré.

430. Coleridge, Samuel Taylor. *Sibylline Leaves. A Collection of Poems*. (London: Rest Fenner, 1817). 303pp. 1st edition.

A416, B1009 (author, title, edition, date), JS717.

431. Coleridge, Samuel Taylor. *Specimens of the Table Talk of the Late Samuel Taylor Coleridge*. (London: John Murray, 1836). 326pp. 2nd edition. Edited by Henry Nelson Coleridge.

A357 (author, title), JS714. Earliest 1-volume edition (the 1st of 1835 was published in 2 vols.). Other items in A357 specify multiple volumes, so Dodgson probably did not own the 1st. A collection of anecdotes told at table by Coleridge.

432. Coleridge, Samuel Taylor. *Works*. Edition unknown, but possibly *The Poetical Works of Samuel Taylor Coleridge*. (London: G. Bell & Sons, 1885). 2 vols. Edited, with introduction and notes, by Thomas Ashe.

A359 ("Coleridge's Works, 2 vols."), JS715. This is the only 2-volume edition of Coleridge containing the word "Works" in the title in BL.

433. [**Coleridge**, Sara] (1802–52). *Phantasmion*. (London: W. Pickering, 1837). 387pp. 1st edition.

A653 (title, publisher, date), D141, JS129 (Anon./Literature), JS721. Only 250 copies of this edition were printed. Sara Coleridge was the only daughter of Samuel Taylor Coleridge. *Phantasmion*, modeled on Spenser's *Faerie Queene*, tells of a Prince in the land of Faerie.

Detail from an illustration of Coleridge's *Rime of the Ancient Mariner* by Joseph Noël Paton (item 428).

It is often considered the first fairy tale novel in English.

434. Coles, Elisha (1640?–1680). *Dictionary.*
A319/JS722 states only "Coles's Dictionary." No details known. Two possibilities in BL, the more likely being the first listed below (since A319 does not specify an English-Latin dictionary):

An English Dictionary; Explaining the Difficult Terms that are Used in Divinity, Husbandry, Physick, Phylosophy, Law, Navigation, Mathematicks, and Other Arts and Sciences, Containing Many Thousands of Hard Words, Together with the Etymological Derivation of Them from their Proper Fountains, etc. (London: Printed for Samuel Crouch, 1676). 1st edition.

Dictionary, English-Latin, and Latin-English, Containing All Things Necessary for the Translating of Either Language into the Other. (London: Printed by J. Richardson for P. Parker, etc., 1677). 1st edition.

435. Coles, Richard Edward (b. ca. 1841), initial editor. *College Rhymes.* Nos. 1–12, (1859–63). 4 vols. in 2.
A843 (title, 4 vols. in 2), not in JS. The numbers are speculative, but there is good

reason to suspect these. Dodgson edited this publication for two issues (nos. 10–11, October Term 1862–Lent Term 1863), and contributed poems to volumes 2, 3, and 4. The periodical was issued three times yearly from October Term 1859–Summer Term 1873, and an annual volume was issued each year. It seems likely that Dodgson owned the 1st 4 annual volumes (bound together in 2 vols.), 1859–63. This would cover all his own contributions, editorial and otherwise.

436. Collier, John Payne (1789–1883) and George Cruikshank (1792–1858). *Punch & Judy, Designed & Engraved by George Cruikshank. Accompanied by the Dialogue of the Puppet-Show, an Account of its Origin, & of Puppet-Plays in England.* (London: Printed for W. H. Reid, 1832). 141pp. 3rd edition. 24 plates by Cruikshank.
A459 (illustrator, title, date), JS773 (listed under Cruikshank, repeating a spelling error in A459). Cruikshank and Collier attended a Punch and Judy performance and together recorded it in this famous book, first published in 1828. It was the first printed version of the popular puppet play.

437. Collingwood, C[harles Edward] S[tuart] (1831–98). *Dr. Cowan and the Grange School, Sunderland With Recollections By Old Scholars etc.* (London: Simpkin, Marshall, Hamilton, Kent & Co.; Sunderland: Hills & Co., 1897). 235pp.

B1014 (author, title, date), JS723. B1014 describes Dodgson's copy as having a "presentation from the author, with inscription." The author was Dodgson's brother-in-law and father of Dodgson's godson and biographer Stuart Collingwood. Cowan was headmaster of the Grange School.

438. Collingwood, Charles Edward Stuart. *Memoirs of Bernard Gilpin, Parson of Houghton-le-Spring and Apostle of the North.* (London: Simpkin, Marshall & Co., 1884). 314pp.

A881 (Memoirs of Burnard [sic] Gilpin), JS482 (incorrectly listed under Benson), JS1070 (listed under Gilpin). Only edition in BL of the only matching title. Bernard Gilpin (1517–1583) became rector of Houghton le Spring in Northumbria, then one of the largest parishes in England, in 1557. He was renowned for his generosity, providing free meals at the rectory during his Sunday open houses between Michaelmas and Easter. He paid for the education of some of his parishioners, founded the Kepier Grammar School, and went on missionary journeys (like St. Aidan centuries before) into the wilds of Northumbria.

439. Collins, Charles Allston (1828–73). *The Bar Sinister. A Tale.* (London: Smith, Elder & Co., 1864). 2 vols.

A603 ("Collins' The Bar Spinster, 2 vols."), JS724 (corrects title). Clearly an error in A603, as there is no book by that illogical title in BL, but *The Bar Sinister* matches in all particulars and Dodgson read this during an illness in July 1883 (see *Diaries*) and again during an illness in 1895. Collins was the brother of Wilkie Collins. Charles was best known as a painter, who came under the influence of Millais and the Pre-Raphaelites. Collins married Kate Dickens, daughter of Charles Dickens. Troubled by his inability to finish paintings, he turned to writing but could not support his wife without help from his father-in-law and brother. *Saturday Review* wrote of this work, "There is no plot but of the weakest and flimsiest tenuity ... the personages, one and all, are absolutely uninteresting."

440. Collins, Charles Allston. *A Cruise upon Wheels: The Chronicle of Some Autumn Wanderings Among the Deserted Postroads of France.* (London, New York: Routledge, Warne and Routledge, 1862). 2 vols. 2nd edition.

A917 (title, author, 2 vols.), JS725. Earliest edition in either BL or BOD, though presumably the 1st might also have been in 2 vols. and is another candidate. Humorous stories of travels through France in the style of Jerome K. Jerome. Dodgson advertised for a copy of this book in his 1893 pamphlet *Second-Hand Books* (see JS, x–xi).

441. Collins, Charles Allston. *The Eye-Witness, and his Evidence about Many Wonderful Things.* (London: Sampson Low & Co., 1860). 341pp. Reprinted from *All the Year Round*.

Uncertain. Not in JS. In a letter to Edith Denman on 18 May 1878, Dodgson writes, "I'm afraid I had forgotten about *The Eye-Witness*, but I have now copied it out and enclose it." This is the only edition of the only matching title in BL, but Dodgson might also have been copying an excerpt from one of the articles as they originally appeared in *All the Year Round*. Cohen (see *Letters*, 309) describes this work as "24 essays, each a first-hand account, in a Swiftian vein, of a visit to a church, a theatre, or another landmark, or an examination of a strange phenomenon or a current issue.

442. Collins, Charles Allston. *A New Sentimental Journey.* (London: Chapman & Hall, 1859). 127pp. With a frontispiece by the author.

A492 (author, title, date), JS726. Originally serialized in *All the Year Round*, the publication edited by Collins' father-in-law, Charles Dickens.

443. Collins, [William] Wilkie (1824–89). *The Fallen Leaves: First Series.* (London: Chatto and Windus, 1879). 3 vols.

Not in JS. Dodgson's diary for 12 August 1880 reads, in part "I have been lately reading Wilkie Collins' *Fallen Leaves*." Earliest edition traced; a 1-volume edition was published by Chatto in 1880. Collins was an English novelist who collaborated with Dickens and whose book *The Woman in White* is considered the first detective novel in English. This novel was among his least successful. It focused on the lives of prostitutes and outcasts. Dodgson goes on to say, "it is clever and interesting, is not really improper, but, I think, moral in tone. Still it goes dangerously near the line, and in one respect most gratuitously so, in making the heroine (after twice, under exceptional circumstances, spending the night under the roof of 'Amelius'— with all possible propriety of motive) be afterwards allowed by him to take up her quarters there, when he could easily have arranged for her to board elsewhere. In real life this would have been a wanton sacrifice of her reputation."

444. **Collins**, [William] Wilkie. *Man and Wife*. (London: Smith, Elder & Co., 1871). 468pp. New edition.

Not in JS. In his diary for 14 February 1871, Dodgson writes, "I write at 2 a.m. having been sitting up reading *Man and Wife* by Wilkie Collins— a most interesting tale so far as I have gone." Originally published in a 3-volume edition in 1870, this is the edition closest to Dodgson's mention. Novel in which Collins attacks inequitable marriage laws.

445. **Collins**, William Wilkie and Walter Besant. *Blind Love*. (London: Chatto & Windus, 1890). 3 vols. 302, 303, 316pp. 1st edition.

A605 (title, 3 vols.), JS375 (Anon./Unclassified). The only 3-volume edition of a matching title in BL. This was Collins' final novel, which he left incomplete at his death in 1889. It was completed by Walter Besant (see 148) using Collins' detailed outline, notes, and fragments.

446. **Colton**, Charles Caleb (1780?–1832). *Lacon; or Many Things in Few Words; Addressed to Those who Think*. (London: Longman, Hurst, Rees, Orme & Brown; Budd & Calkin, 1820). 267pp.

A578 (author, title), JS727. 1st edition of this popular collection of aphorisms. By 1821, the book had already reached a 10th edition, and in 1822 a second volume was published. Dodgson probably owned one of the many later 1-volume editions, as A578 does not specify multiple volumes. Colton was an English clergyman. His sayings here recorded include "Men are born with two eyes, but with one tongue, in order that they should see twice as much as they say," and "Power will intoxicate the best hearts, as wine the strongest heads. No man is wise

enough, nor good enough to be trusted with unlimited power."

447. [**Colton**, Charles Caleb]. *Remarks, Critical and Moral, on the Talents of Lord Byron, and the Tendencies of Don Juan*. (London: Printed for the Author, 1819). 52pp.

Uncertain. F172 (title, date), not numbered in JS (listed under Byron). Identified as Dodgson's only by the gothic stamp.

448. [**Common Prayer**]. *The Book of Common Prayer*. (Oxford: University Press, 1840). Unpaginated.

A322 (possibly), E119 (title, city, date), JS503 (listed with other editions). A322 states only "Common Prayer," and Dodgson owned several copies of this, the official service book for the Church of England. E270 lists another copy without giving a publisher, city or date. This copy has "bookmarks as left in by Lewis Carroll," so it was most likely a mid–19th century edition used by Dodgson.

449. [**Common Prayer**]. *The Book of Common Prayer, and Administration of the Sacraments, and Other Rites and Ceremonies of the Church, According to the Use of the United Church of England and Ireland*. (London: Thomas Nelson & Sons, 1855). Unpaginated.

A322 (possibly), D46 (title, city, date, 32mo), JS504. Dodgson's copy, with his autograph inside the front cover, was offered for sale by Maggs of London in 1923. It sold at Parke-Bernet Galleries, New York on December 1, 1947 for $22 (DAA2224), where it was described as being from the Harmsworth Collection. At the sale of the Harmsworth Collection (Sotheby's, 26 March, 1947), the book was described as 12mo (DAA2188). Despite the mysterious change in size, it seems unlikely that this was a different volume, because of the stated provenance. It was sold again at Parke-Bernet Galleries, New York, on April 9–10, 1963, again described as 32mo (DAA2528).

450. [**Common Prayer in Latin**]. *Libri Precum Publicarum Ecclesiæ Anglicanæ Versio Latina, a Gulielmo Bright et Petro Goldsmith Medd*. (London: Rivington, 1865). 380pp. *The Book of Common Prayer* translated into Latin by William Bright and Peter Goldsmith Medd (1829–1908).

Uncertain. A771 ("Latin prayer book"), JS502. This seems the most likely of the many possibilities. Dodgson, a Broad Churchman, would not likely have owned a copy of the Roman Catholic service book in Latin. A771 could, of course, be merely a collection of prayers in Latin, but the phrase "prayer book" in the Anglican world, usually refers to *The Book of Common Prayer*. See 237 for a note on Bright. Medd was a High Church clergyman and a founder of Keble College.

451. Comte, Achille [Joseph] (1802–66). *Structure et Physiologie de l'Homme: Démontrées à l'Aide de Figures Coloriées, Découpées et Superposées.* (Paris: G. Masson, 1876). 11th edition. 244pp.

E85 (author, title, city, date), JS728. Comte was a French naturalist. The title translates, "Structure and Physiology of the Man: Shown with the Aid of Colored Figures, Cut Out and Superimposed." E85 notes, "The management of the numerous plates renders them as near models as possible and most useful."

452. Conybeare, William John (1815–57) and John Saul Howson (1816–85). *The Life and Epistles of St. Paul.* (London: Longman, Brown, Green and Longmans, 1851–52). 2 vols.

A781 (author, title), JS729. Earliest edition traced. A classic of biblical scholarship and a widely read study. Conybeare was the translator of the epistles and speeches of Paul, while Howson contributed the historical and geographical analysis.

453. Cook, Edward Dutton (1829–83). *A Book of the Play: Studies and Illustrations of Histrionic Story, Life, and Character.* (London: Sampson, Low, Marston, Searle, & Rivington, 1876). 2 vols.

A674 (author, title, 2 vols.), JS731. Only 2-volume edition in BL or BOD. Cook was dramatic critic to the *Pall Mall Gazette* (a paper to which Dodgson made many contributions, see LCP) from 1867 to 1875, edited *Cornhill Magazine*, and was dramatic critic to the *World*. Anecdotes from the history of the theatre. Cook attempts to pay special attention to previously neglected areas of theatre history, such as the development of the play-bill.

454. Cook, James (1728–79) and James King (1750–84). *A Voyage to the Pacific Ocean; Undertaken by Command of his Majesty, for Making Discoveries in the Northern Hemisphere ... Being a Copious, Comprehensive, and Satisfactory Abridgement of the Voyage.* (London: John Stockdale, 1784). 4 vols. Written by Captain James Cook, F.R.S. and Captain James King, etc. With plates, including a portrait and maps.

A915 ("Cook's Voyage, 4 vols."), JS730. BL lists only two British editions in 4 vols., the Stockdale and another published by Stockdale and others from 1784 to 1786. NUC includes other, later, 4-volume editions, all of which seem less likely. Cooke learned seafaring in the town of Whitby, where Dodgson took summer holidays in the 1850s.

455. Cooley, William Desborough (d. 1883). *The Elements of Geometry, Simplified and Explained, with Practical Geometry, and Supplement.* (London: Williams & Norgate, 1860). 94pp.

Not in JS. Dodgson examines this book is his *Euclid and His Modern Rivals* (59–62). An attempt to simplify Euclid (173 propositions become 36).

456. Coolidge, Susan [pseud. of Sarah Chauncey Woolsey] (1845–1905). *Nine Little Goslings.* (Boston: Roberts Bros., 1875). 289pp. With illustrations.

A642 (title), JS68 (Anon./Children). Only edition in BL or LC. Coolidge was an American author of books for children, the best known of which were *What Katy Did* and its sequels. She also published verse and edited correspondence of Fanny Burney and Jane Austen.

457. Cooper, J[ames] Fenimore (1789–1851). *Captain Spike; Or, The Islets of the Gulf.* (London: Richard Bentley, 1848). 3 vols. 302, 308, 316pp. 1st English edition.

A607 (author, title, edition, 3 vols.), JS734. Published in America under the title *Jack Tier; Or, The Florida Reef.* In all cases where Dodgson owned a "1st edition" of Cooper, it is assumed he owned the 1st English edition, the publication of which actually preceded the American editions in most cases (see S & B). A novel of the sea set during the time of the Mexican-American War.

458. Cooper, J[ames] Fenimore. *Eve Effingham; Or, Home.* (London: Richard Bentley, 1838). 3 vols. 300, 320, 292pp. 1st English edition.

A623 (author, title, edition, 3 vols.), JS735. Published in America under the title *Home as Found*. The story of a young woman who returns from a stay abroad provides an opportunity for Cooper to air his conservative political views in relation to contemporary American democracy.

459. [Cooper, James Fenimore]. *The Headsman; Or, The Abbaye des Vignerons. A Tale.* (London: Richard Bentley, 1833). 3 vols. 321, 317, 331pp.

A602 (title, 5 vols.), JS736. Possibly an error in A602 as no book by this title in 5 volumes is recorded in S & B, BL or NUC. This is the 1st English edition. The final novel in a trilogy about medieval Europe. The first two volumes, *The Bravo* (1831) and *The Heidenmauer* (1832) are not recorded as being in Dodgson's library. However, the "5 vols." description in A602 may include 1-volume editions of these works—such editions were published by Bentley in 1834 (*The Bravo*) and 1836 (*The Heidenmauer*).

460. [Cooper, James Fenimore]. *Lionel Lincoln; Or, The Leaguer of Boston.* (London: Printed for the Booksellers, n.d. [ca. 1830]). 3 vols. in 1.

A623 (author, title, 3 vols. in 1), JS737. S & B say only that this is "early." NUC gives the speculative date 1830. Only edition in either source that specifies 3 vols. in 1. A story set in Boston during the American Revolution. This was intended to be the first of a series of books set in each of the 13 original American states, but the rest of the novels were never written.

461. [Cooper, James Fenimore]. *Lucy Harding: A Second Series of Afloat and Ashore.* (London: Richard Bentley, 1844). 3 vols. 302, 294, 295pp. 1st English edition.

A623 (author, title, edition, 3 vols.), JS738. Published in America under the title *Afloat and Ashore; Or The Adventures of Miles Wallingford*. This is the second part of a two-part novel narrating the life of Miles Wallingford from his family estate on the Hudson River.

462. Cooper, J[ames] Fenimore. *Mercedes of Castile. A Romance of the Days of Columbus.* (London: Richard Bentley, 1841). 3 vols. 324, 338, 365pp. 1st English edition.

A607 (author, title, edition, 3 vols.), JS739. Published in America in 2 vols. under the title *Mercedes of Castile: Or, The Voyage to Cathay*. A novel of the sea set in late 15th-century Spain.

463. [Cooper, James Fenimore]. *The Monikins. A Tale.* (London: Richard Bentley, 1835). 3 vols. 300, 300, 318pp. 1st English edition

A608 (author, title, 3 vols., edition), JS740. Published in America under the title *The Monikins*. This was the only English edition published in Cooper's lifetime. This work of non-fiction was written after Cooper returned from abroad. It includes an attack on the American society he found on his return, in particular what he saw as abuses of democracy.

464. [Cooper, James Fenimore]. *The Pathfinder; Or, The Inland Sea.* (London: Richard Bentley, 1840). 3 vols. 320, 348, 339pp. 1st English edition.

A625 (author, title, edition, 3 vols.), JS741. The fourth in the series of "Leatherstocking Tales" (see below).

465. [Cooper, James Fenimore]. *The Prairie, A Tale.* (London: Henry Colburn, 1827). 3 vols. 340, 370, 366pp. 1st English edition.

A608 (author, title, 3 vols., edition), JS742. The third of five novels in the "Leatherstocking Tales." *Pioneers* (1823), *The Last of the Mohicans* (1826), *The Prairie, The Pathfinder* (see above), and *The Deerslayer* (1841) told of life among Native Americans in the wilderness and centered on the character of Natty Bumpo.

466. Cooper, J[ames] Fenimore. *Satanstoe; Or, The Family of Littlepage. A Tale of the Colony.* (London: Richard Bentley, 1845). 3 vols. 299, 300, 300pp. 1st English edition.

A607 (author, title, 3 vols., edition), JS743. Published in America under the title *Satanstoe; Or, The Littlepage Manuscripts. A Tale of the Colony*. Set in New York beginning in the colonial period, this novel of manners contrasts the worlds of the Yankees, the Middle Colonies, and the Dutch. It was the first of a trilogy

(*The Littlepage Manuscripts*) and dealt with issues of property rights extending into the 1840s.

467. [**Cooper,** James Fenimore]. *The Sea Lions; Or, The Lost Sealers.* (London: Richard Bentley, 1849). 3 vols. 304, 309, 304pp. 1st English edition.

A607 (author, title, 3 vols., edition), JS744. A novel of the sea, set partially in Antartica.

468. [**Cooper,** James Fenimore]. *The Spy; A Tale of the Neutral Ground; Referring to Some Particular Occurrences During the American War; Also Pourtraying American Scenery and Manners.* (London: G. and W. B. Whittaker, 1823). 3 vols. 2nd edition.

A608 (author, title, edition, 3 vols.), JS745. Published in America as *The Spy; A Tale of the Neutral Ground.* Cooper's 2nd novel, this tale of the American revolution brought him his first great success.

469. [**Cooper,** James Fenimore]. *The Water Witch; Or, The Skimmer of the Seas. A Tale.* (London: Henry Colburn and Richard Bentley, 1830). 3 vols. 321, 316, 308pp. 1st English edition.

A625 (author, title, edition, 3 vols.), JS746. One of Cooper's many novels set at sea.

470. Cooper, J[ames] Fenimore. *The Ways of the Hour.* (London: Richard Bentley, 1850). 3 vols. 319, 305, 311pp. 1st English edition.

A607 (author, title, 3 vols. edition), JS747. Published in America under the title *The Ways of the Hour; A Tale.* An 1840s murder trial provides the setting for Cooper's last novel in which he attacks many current social trends from the financial independence of women to the irresponsibility of the press.

471. Cooper, Thomas (1517?–1594). *Thesaurus Linguæ Romanæ & Britannicæ, tam Accurate Congestus, vt Nihil Penè in eo Desyderari Possit, quod vel Latinè Complectatur Amplissimus Stephani Thesaurus, vel Anglicè, Toties aucta Eliotæ Bibliotheca: Opera & Industria Thomæ Cooperi. Accessit Dictionarium Historicum et Poëticum Propria Vocabula Virorum, Mulierum Vr-*

bium & Cæterorum Locorum Complectens. (London: Henry Wykes, 1565). 1812pp.

A939 ("Cooper's Thesaurus"), JS733. Earliest edition of the only matching title in BL. Other editions listed in BL and BOD are dated no later than 1584. Cooper was successively Bishop of Lincoln and Winchester.

472. Cooper, Thomas (1805–1892). *The Purgatory of Suicides. A Prison-Rhyme in Ten Books.* (London: Jeremiah How, 1845). 344pp.

A858, B1015 (author, title), JS732. Earliest edition in BL. Cooper was a schoolmaster and provincial journalist who was jailed for two years for conspiracy in the aftermath of the Leicester riots of 1842. He later became a lecturer on politics and history in London and in 1855 embraced Christianity (he had been a sceptic) and preached throughout Britain on evidences of Christianity. The present poem was a result of his imprisonment.

473. Copland, James (1791–1870). *A Dictionary of Practical Medicine. Comprising General Pathology, the Nature and Treatment of Diseases …* (London: Longman, Brown, Green, Longmans, & Roberts, 1858). 3 vols.

A315 (author, title, 3 vols.), JS748. Only edition in BL in 3 vols. Originally published in 4 vols. from 1844 to 1858. Copland was a Scot, a physician and Fellow of the Royal Society and of the College of Physicians in London. The *London Medical and Surgical Journal* said of this book, "It is the product of a physician profoundly acquainted with the medical literature of all countries." In later years it was less highly thought of. Dodgson prints an extract from this book in his pamphlet *On Catching Cold* (WMGC, #148).

474. Copleston, Edward (1776–1849). *Remains of the Late Edward Copleston. With an Introduction, Containing some Reminiscences of his Life, by Richard Whately.* (London: John W. Parker & Sons, 1854). 327pp.

Uncertain. F163 (author, title, date), not numbered in JS. Identified as Dodgson's only by the gothic stamp. Copleston was dean and later provost of Oriel College, Oxford, vicar of St. Mary's, Oxford and Professor of Poetry. In 1827 he became Bishop of Llandaff. He also took an interest in politics. See 2231 for a note on Whately.

475. Copleston, Reginald Stephen (1845–1925). *Buddhism, Primitive and Present, in Magadha and in Ceylon.* (London: Longmans, Green & Co., 1892). 501pp.

A799 (author, title), JS749. This is the only pre–1898 edition in BL. Copleston, educated at Merton College, Oxford and a fellow of St. John's College, Oxford, was made Bishop of Colombo, Ceylon in 1875, and later Bishop of Calcutta.

476. [Copleston, Reginald Stephen, Edward Nolan and Thomas Humphry Ward]. *The Oxford Spectator.* (Oxford: 1867–68). Nos. 1–29.

A318 (title), JS200 (Anon./Oxford). Equally likely that Dodgson's copy was *The Oxford Spectator Reprinted* (London: Macmillan, 1869), which reprinted the contents of this short-lived periodical. Nolan matriculated at St. John's College in 1864, Ward at Brasenose in 1864, and Copleston at Merton in 1864. As undergraduates they edited this periodical which contained "features of Oxford life from an undergraduate's point of view" and "modern readings of books which undergraduates study." A largely comic collection of Oxford life. *The Oxford Spectator Reprinted* included a 52pp. catalogue of Macmillan's publications, including Dodgson's *Elementary Treatise on Determinants.* See 2195 for a note on Ward.

477. Cornwall, Barry [pseud. of Bryan Waller Procter] (1787–1874). *Dramatic Scenes. With other Poems, Now First Printed.* (London: Chapman & Hall, 1857). 403pp. Illustrated.

A848 (author, title, date), JS750. *Dramatic Scenes* first published in 1819. Proctor was an English writer, friend of Charles Lamb (whose biography he wrote) and father of poet Adelaide Proctor.

478. Cotton, George Edward Lynch (1813–66). *Instructions in the Doctrine and Practice of Christianity, Intended Chiefly as an Introduction to Confirmation.* (London: Hatchard, 1845). 143pp.

E209 (title, author, date), JS752. Cotton was an assistant at Rugby School during Dodgson's time there from 1846 to 1849 (he appears as the young master in Thomas Hughes' *Tom Brown's*

School Days). According to E209, this copy has "Dodgson, Sch. House" written inside the front cover. School House was Dodgson's house at Rugby. Cotton was later appointed Bishop of Calcutta.

479. Cotton, George Edward Lynch. *Short Prayers and Other Helps to Devotion, for the Use of the Scholars of Rugby School.* (1843).

E206 (title, date), JS261 (Anon./School Books). E206 notes this has Dodgson's autograph. No copy of this, the 1st edition, has been traced. The 2nd edition was published in 1843 in London by Hatchard & Son. The work was later published as: *Short Prayers and Other Helps to Devotion, for the Boys of a Public School.*

480. Cowper, William (1731–1800). *Poems.* Edition unknown.

A946 (author, title), JS753. Best known among Cowper's poems are "John Gilpin," "The Task," and "Verses Supposed to be Written by Alexander Selkirk." His style was more natural than many of the classical 18th-century poets, but Hazlitt wrote of him "With all his boasted simplicity and love of country, he seldom launches out into general descriptions of nature; he looks at her over his clipped hedges and from his well-swept garden-walks … Still he is a genuine poet and deserves his reputation."

481. Coxe, Arthur Cleveland (1818–96). *Christian Ballads, and Poems. With Corrections, and a Preface to the English Edition by the Author.* (Oxford: John Henry Parker, 1849). 244pp.

Not in JS. In a letter to his sister on 6 March 1851, Dodgson wrote, "The other day I borrowed a book called Coxe's *Christian Ballads*, thinking I might like to get a copy: however I found so many things in it I did not like, and so few I did, that I decided on not buying the book, but as some of the ballads are sold separate I got the 2 I like best, which I enclose." The book was originally published in America. The first English edition was published by Parker in 1848; this is the edition in BL dated closest to the mention in Dodgson's diary. Coxe was Bishop of Western New York.

482. Coxe, William (1747–1828). *History of the House of Austria. From the Foundation of the Monarchy by Rhodolph of Hapsburgh to the Death of Leopold the Second:*

1218 to 1792. (London: Henry G. Bohn, 1847). 3 vols. 528, 522, 592pp. 3rd edition.

A632 (author, title, 3 vols.), JS754. Earliest 3-volume edition in BL. Dodgson received this book as a prize at Rugby School in 1849. Coxe was an English clergyman who spent much of his time in literary pursuits. The *Encyclopedia Britannica* (11th edition) calls this work "dull."

483. Crabb, James (1774–1851). *The Gipsies' Advocate or, Observations on the Origin, Character, Manners and Habits of the English Gipsies: to Which are Added, Many Interesting Anecdotes, on the Success that has Attended the Plans of Several Benevolent Individuals, who Anxiously Desire their Conversion to God.* (London: Nisbet, 1832). 199pp. 3rd edition.

B1017 (author, date, title), JS755. Crabb was a Wesleyan Methodist preacher and schoolmaster near Southampton who took an interest in the welfare of the Gypsy population of the New Forest. He held gatherings at his home for Gypsies and the local gentry, and the profits from this book benefited the Southampton Committee for the Amelioration of the Condition of the Gipsies and the Lansdown and Kingland Infants' Schools of Southampton.

484. Crabbe, George (1754–1832). *The Life and Poetical Works of the Rev. George Crabbe.* (London: John Murray, 1847). 587pp. Edited by his son (George Crabbe). With portrait.

A825 ("Crabbe's Life and Works"), JS756. Earliest 1-volume edition of the most frequently reprinted *Life and Works of Crabbe*, and also the title in BL that most closely matches A825. It seems the most likely match. Crabbe was an English clergyman and poet with a gift for narrative verse and for depicting life in all its unpleasantness.

485. Craig, Isa [afterwards Knox] (1831–1903). *Duchess Agnes, A Drama and Other Poems.* (London: Alexander Strahan, 1865). 228pp. 2nd edition.

B1018 (author, title, date), JS757. Craig was a Scotch poet who contributed poems to newspapers before publishing books of verse. She won a prize in 1858 at the Crystal Palace for a poem on Robert Burns.

486. [Craig, Isa], editor. *Poems: An Offering to Lancashire.* (London: Emily Faithfull, 1863). 62pp. Printed and published for the Art Exhibition for the Relief of Distress in the Cotton Districts.

B1172 (title, date [1873]), JS131 (Anon./Literature). Dodgson's copy (dated 1863) was offered at Hodgson, London on 13 April 1921. It had his initials on the title and a note on p. 10. Though B1172 states 1873, 1863 is the only edition listed in BL, and it seems clear that 1873 is a misprint. Includes poems by Christina and D. G. Rossetti.

487. [Craik, Dinah Maria Mulock]. *Agatha's Husband; A Novel.* (London: Chapman and Hall, 1865). 302pp. 6th edition.

A602 (title), JS758. Earliest 1-volume English edition for which complete information has been traced (A602 does not mention multiple volumes, but does mention multiple volumes for another title). Originally published in 3 vols. (London: Chapman and Hall, 1853). A novel about failed communication between husband and wife.

488. [Craik, Dinah Maria Mulock]. *Children's Poetry.* (London: Macmillan & Co., 1881). 220pp.

A844, E295 (author, title, date), JS45 (Anon./Children), JS759. E295 notes this has Dodgson's initials twice.

489. [Craik, Dinah Maria Mulock]. *Christian's Mistake.* (London: Hurst & Blackett, 1865). 320pp.

A604 (title, 1 vol.), JS760. All other items in A604 are by Craik. Earliest edition in BL. A novel covering the stressful, but ultimately successful, first six months of the marriage of the heroine, Christian, to an older man.

490. [Craik, Dinah Maria Mulock]. *The Head of the Family. A Novel.* (London: Chapman and Hall, 1854). In the *Select Library of Fiction Series.*

A602 (title), JS761. Closest edition to Dodgson's diary mention (see below) and the earliest 1-volume edition traced (A602 does not mention multiple volumes but does for other items). Originally published in 3 vols. (London: Chapman and Hall, 1852). A family chronicle. Dodgson wrote a long review of this book, which he called "a really beautiful story" in his diary on 3 March 1855 (see *Diary 1*).

491. [Craik, Dinah Maria Mulock]. *John Halifax, Gentleman.* (London: Hurst and Blackett, 1856). 3 vols. 321, 331, 311pp. 1st edition.

A604 (title, edition, 3 vols.), JS762. A novel which follows the progress of its orphan hero from poverty to wealth and success in business. Dodgson writes a review of this book in his diary for 31 December 1857 (see *Diary 3*). He praises Craik's character development but is less kind about her plot management.

492. [Craik, Dinah Maria Mulock]. *A Life for a Life.* By the author of "John Halifax, Gentleman," (London: Hurst and Blackett, 1859). 3 vols. 303, 310, 316pp.

A604 (title, edition, 3 vols.), JS381 (Anon./Unclassified). This is the work in BL that best fits the description in A604, and several books by Craik are listed in A604. A novel in the form of overlapping diaries by a man who commits murder and a woman who has a child out of wedlock. Dodgson read this during an illness in February 1895 (see *Diaries*).

493. Craik, Dinah Maria [Mulock]. *The Little Lame Prince and His Travelling Cloak, A Parable for Young and Old.* (London: Daldy, Isbister, 1875). 169pp. With 24 illustrations by J. McL. Ralston.

A644 (title), JS763. 1st edition. Popular children's fantasy story of an exiled prince who receives a magic cloak from a fairy godmother. He travels the world through the magic of the cloak, eventually ruling his own kingdom. When he tires of the job, he disappears on the cloak.

494. Craik, Dinah Maria [Mulock]. *The Ogilvies.* (London: Chapman & Hall, 1855). Cheap edition, revised.

A602 (title), JS764. Edition closest to Dodgson's diary mention (see below); also appears to be a 1-volume edition (the description in BL is incomplete) and as such is the earliest 1-volume edition in BL (A602 does not mention multiple volumes, but does mention multiple volumes for another title). Originally published in 3 vols. (London: Chapman and Hall, 1849). Novel which follows three female cousins on their paths to marriage. This melodramatic work was the author's first novel and received critical praise, launching her successful career. Dodgson recorded reading this and wrote a long review of it in his diary on 1 May 1855 (see *Diary 1*).

495. Craik, Dinah Maria [Mulock]. *Olive, A Novel.* (London: Chapman & Hall, [1877?]). 431pp. New edition.

A602 (title), JS765. Earliest 1-volume English edition for which complete information can be found (A602 does not mention multiple volumes, but does mention multiple volumes for another title). Conjectural date from BL. Originally published in 3 vols. (London: Chapman and Hall, 1850). Novel in which an unattractive heroine tries to capture an uninterested lover.

496. Crane, Lucy (1842–82), editor and Walter Crane (1845–1915), illustrator. *The Baby's Opera. A Book of Old Rhymes with New Dresses by Walter Crane. The Music by the Earliest Masters.* (London: G. Routledge and Sons, [1876]). 56pp.

A531 ("Baby Opera"), JS766. This is the only pre–1898 edition listed in BL of the only possible match in BL. Walter Crane was a popular illustrator of books for children. His sister, Lucy, collected the music for this illustrated book. When Dodgson was looking, in 1877, for an artist to "succeed to Tenniel's place," his publisher wrote to him, "You should look at *Baby's Opera* by Walter Crane. I think for humour he is superior to Tenniel. I remember you did not admire some things I showed you of his, but this new book is unusually good." Dodgson did correspond with Crane about a collaboration, but it came to naught. (See *Macmillan*, 134).

497. Craven, Henry Thornton (1818–1905). *Done Brown A Vaudeville, in One Act.* (London: John Duncombe, [1850?]). 21pp.

Not in JS. In his diary for 11 July 1856, Dodgson writes, "The Tates came over to be photographed: afterwards I read aloud *Done Brown*." This is the edition traced closest to Dodgson's reading. Conjectural date from BL (Yale lists an undated edition of ca. 1845 published by T. H. Lacy). Craven was a dramatist and actor.

498. Croker, Thomas Crofton (1798–1854). *Fairy Legends and Traditions of the South of Ireland.* (London: John Murray, 1834). 344pp.

A885 ("Fairy Legends"), JS57 (Anon./Children's). As JS surmises, Croker's work is the most likely match for the cryptic entry in A885.

It was reprinted many times (the present entry is for what appears to be the earliest 1-volume edition, the 1st being published in 3 vols. from 1825 to 1828); it fits in well with Dodgson's interest in the folklore of the British isles; and it is certainly a more likely match than other possibilities: Hans Andersen's *Danish Fairy Legends and Tales* doesn't quite match the title in A885 and Jameson's *Fairy Legends of the French Provinces* is listed in BL only in an American edition (of 1887). Croker was inspired by the work of the brothers Grimm, and the Grimms later translated part of Croker's work into German.

499. Cromek, R[obert] H[artley] (1770–1812). *Remains of Nithsdale and Galloway Song: With Historical and Traditional Notices Relative to the Manners and Customs of the Peasantry.* (London: T. Cadell & W. Davies, 1810). 370pp.

A480 (author, title, date), D48, JS767. Cromek was an engraver who fell under suspicion when his book of reliques of Robert Burns was thought to contain some forgeries. This book was compiled during an 1809 tour of Scotland when Cromek met Allan Cunningham (see 508) who provided these "old songs," which in fact Cunningham wrote.

500. Croskery, Thomas (1830–86). *Plymouth-Brethrenism: A Refutation of its Principles and Doctrines.* (London & Belfast: William Mullan & Son, 1879). 168pp.

B1176 (title, author, date), JS768. Croskery was an Irishman who served as a Presbyterian minister from 1851 and as a professor of Logic and Belles-lettres at Magee College where in 1879 he was appointed to the Theology chair.

501. Crosland, Mrs. Newton [née Camilla Toulmin] (1812–95). *Light in the Valley: My Experiences of Spiritualism.* (London, New York: Published for the Author by G. Routledge, 1857). 228pp.

A889 (title), JS318 (Anon./Theology). Only 2 matching titles in BL. This, like all the other books listed in A889, relates to spiritualism. The other is: *Light in the Valley. A Memorial of Mary Elizabeth Stirling* (Philadelphia: 1852). The present title seems far more likely. Only edition in BL. Forced to support herself from an early age, Toulmin turned to journalism, writing articles on the condition of the poor and on spiritualism, in which she believed avidly.

502. Crowe, Catherine (1790–1876). *Ghosts and Family Legends. A Volume for Christmas.* (London: Thomas Cautley Newby, 1859). 339pp.

Uncertain. A898 (author, "Ghost Stories"), JS771 Only edition in BL. Though A898 does not explicitly state that Crowe is the author, the entry includes three books—the first is identified as by Crowe and the second is definitely by Crowe. The implication is that the word "Crowe's" at the beginning of the entry covers all the books that follow. This is the closest match among Crowe's works to the title "Ghost Stories." Crowe was a novelist of the supernatural following in the footsteps of Mary Shelley in her attempts to rationalize ghosts and other unexplained phenomena in her fiction.

503. Crowe, Catherine. *Light and Darkness; or, Mysteries of Life.* (London: Henry Colburn, 1850). 3 vols. 314, 320, 312pp.

A898 (author, title, 3 vols.), JS769. A collection of tales on dark and tragic sides of human existence.

504. Crowe, Catherine. *The Night Side of Nature: or, Ghosts and Ghost Seers.* (London: George Routledge & Sons, 1882). 155pp. *Routledge's Sixpenny Novels* series.

A898 (author, title), JS770. Earliest 1-volume edition in BL (A898 does not mention multiple volumes, but does mention multiple volumes for another title). The earliest edition in BL is 2 vols. (London, T. C. Newby, 1848). A collection of supposedly true tales exploring the "science" of ghosts.

505. Crowquill, Alfred [pseud. of Alfred Henry Forester] (1804–72), illustrator. *Sleeping Beauty of the Wood.* (London: Wm. S. Orr and Co., n.d. [between 1842–1849]). 49pp. + plates. With 24 illustrations. In the *Comic Nursery Tales* series.

A483 (title, series, publisher), JS49 (Anon./Children's). Only edition traced. Alfred Henry Forrester (1804–1872), a.k.a. Alfred Crowquill, was a founding member of *Punch*. He left the magazine in 1843 to concentrate on illustrating children's books. A retelling of the traditional fairy story.

506. Cruden, Alexander (1701–1770). *A Complete Concordance to the Holy Scrip-*

tures of the Old and New Testament: In Two Parts. Containing, I. The Appellative or Common Words II. The Proper Names in the Scriptures. To Which is Added a Concordance to the Books, called Apocrypha. (London: Printed for D. Midwinter, A. Bettesworth and C. Hitch [et al.], 1738). 1024pp.

A749, A751 (author, title), JS772. 1st edition of what became (and still is) a standard reference work. Dodgson owned at least 2 copies, though A749 and A751 give no indication of what edition of the many from the 18th and 19th centuries he owned. Cruden is best known for this work. He was a Scot who held a number of tutoring posts, and was bookseller to the Queen.

507. Cumming, John (1807–81). *Ritualism, the Highway to Rome. Twelve Lectures.* (London: Nisbet & Co., 1867).

B1019 (author, title, date), JS774. Cumming was the minister of the Scotch Church at Covent Garden, London, and a popular preacher and theologian. There were many who, at the time of this book's publication, argued that a move towards ritualism in the English Church would ultimately end in a return to Roman Catholicism.

508. Cunningham, Allan (1784–1842). *Poems and Songs.* (London: John Murray, 1847). 151pp. With an introduction, glossary, and notes by his son, Peter Cunningham.

A321, B1020 (author, title, date), JS775. In the introduction, the son says of his father, "It was the opinion of the author of the following Poems and Songs that his fame would rest hereafter chiefly, if not entirely, on the kindly criticisms of Sir Walter Scott and Southey, though he was willing to hope that a few of his Lyrics might find a place in some future Collection of Scottish Songs." The introduction quotes extensively from Cunningham's correspondence with R. H. Cromek (see 499). Allan Cunningham was a minor Scottish novelist and miscellaneous writer.

509. Cunningham, Allan. *Traditional Tales of the English and Scotish [sic] Peasantry.* (London: F. & W. Kerslake, 1874). 394pp. A new edition.

A882, E16 (title, author, date), JS776. The earliest edition in BL was published by Taylor & Hessey, London, 1822.

510. [**Cunningham**, Peter] (1816–69). *Handbook to London as it Is.* (London: John Murray, [1866]). New edition revised (of the work originally written by Peter Cunningham).

E327 (title, publisher), JS360 (Anon./Topography). Earliest edition under this title in BL; the work was first published by Murray in 1851 (about the time Dodgson first came to London) under the title *Murray's Handbook for Modern London. Modern London; or, London as it Is.* According to E327, this has Dodgson's autograph on the inside cover.

511. Curteis, George Herbert (1824–94). *Dissent in its Relation to the Church of England. Eight Lectures Preached before the University of Oxford in the Year 1871, on the Foundation of the Late Rev. John Bampton, Canon of Salisbury.* (London: Macmillan & Co., 1872). 448pp.

A802, D49 (author, title, "Original Edition"), JS777. D49 notes Dodgson's initials. Earliest edition in BL. Curteis was a fellow of Exeter College, Oxford and a canon of Litchfield Cathedral. He describes in the introduction his goal: "To strengthen her (i.e. the Church of England's) position in this country, to point out the true meaning of her connexion with the State, and (if possible) to conciliate by explanations those who are conscientiously — but, I think, under endless misapprehensions — endeavouring to subvert her influence and to destroy her vantage-ground for doing good." Curteis argues against what he calls the "Evangelical Alliance" that would "leave all Denominations free to exist and multiply" and in favor of "the Old-Catholic system" of unity in which "the one normal type, both of organization and of ritual, is loyally maintained."

512. Curzon, Robert (1810–73). *Visits to Monasteries in the Levant.* (London: John Murray, 1849). 449pp. With numerous woodcuts.

A589 (author, title), JS778. Earliest edition in BL. Terence Bowers of the College of Charleston summarizes Curzon's book: "Curzon narrates his journey toward the sacred destination of Jerusalem; but unlike many of those accounts, Curzon's gives up the fantasy of bringing the Holy Land back under Western (Christian) control. He does so largely because he discovers that the Holy Land is already too much under the dominance of Christian institutions and western commercial culture — to the point that it has become a degraded place, devoid of spirituality." (Abstract from a paper presented at A Conference on American and British Travel Writers and Writing, University of Minneapolis, 1997).

513. Cuthbertson, Francis. *Euclidian Geometry*. (London: Macmillan & Co., 1874). 266pp.

Not in JS. Dodgson examines this book is his *Euclid and His Modern Rivals* (63–69). Cuthbertson was a fellow of Corpus Christi College, Cambridge and later head mathematical master of the City of London School. Dodgson's copy was offered at American Art Association, New York on 15 April 1925 at the sale of the library of Rev. Paul F. McAlfnney (DAA1055), and again at Sotheby's London on 20–22 July 1936 (DAA1892). The latter entry describes this copy as "with his monogram C. L. D. inside cover, and autograph notes or corrections by him on about 15 leaves."

514. Dale, R[obert] W[illiam] (1829–95). *Christ and the Future Life*. (London: Hodder and Stoughton, 1895). 160pp. Part of the *Little Book on Religion* series.

E217 (author, title, "189?"), JS786. Only edition in BL. Dale was educated at Spring Hill College, Birmingham. In 1853 he became co-pastor of the Carr's Lane Congregationalist Chapel in that city. He later became pastor. Dale served as chairman of the Congregational Union of England and Wales and, in 1877, was the first Englishman appointed as Lyman Beecher Lecturer at Yale. He was a figure in nonconformist controversies and published volumes of sermons and lectures, many of which were first delivered to his Birmingham congregation, which consisted of working people. Dodgson wrote to him on at least one occasion (see 518).

515. Dale, R[obert] W[illiam]. *The Epistle to the Ephesians: Its Doctrine and Ethics*. (London: Hodder & Stoughton, 1882). 446pp.

A788 ("Dale's Lectures on the Ephesians"), JS782. Earliest edition in BOD or BL of the only work by Dale on the Ephesians (it is, indeed, a series of lectures).

516. Dale, R[obert] W[illiam]. *The Jewish Temple and the Christian Church; A Series of Discourses on the Epistle to the Hebrews*. (London: Jackson, Walford and Hodder, 1865). 421pp. 1st edition.

A772, B1021 (author, title, date), JS781.

517. Dale, R[obert] W[illiam]. *Laws of Christ for Common Life*. (London: Hodder & Stoughton, 1884). 304pp.

A799 (author, title), JS784. Earliest edition in BL. A series of 18 essays on how to incorporate the teachings of Christ into daily life. It includes essays such as "Every-Day Business a Divine Calling," "The Forgiveness of Injuries," "Courtesy and the Spirit of Service," "Family Life," and "Political and Municipal Duty."

518. Dale, R[obert] W[illiam]. *The Living Christ and the Four Gospels*. (London: Hodder & Stoughton, 1890). 299pp.

A804 (author, title), JS785. Earliest edition in BL is this, the 2nd. On 3 March 1892, Dodgson wrote to Dale that he was reading this book and suggesting that an edition be made available in which the quotations are taken from the Authorized version of the Bible instead of the Revised version. Dodgson describes the Revised version as having "wanton defacement of some of the loveliest passages in our dear old Bible."

519. Dale, R[obert] W[illiam]. *The Ten Commandments*. (London: Hodder & Stoughton, 1891). 245pp. 6th edition.

A765, B1022 (author, title, date), JS780. In his introduction Dale writes of this series of sermons: "It has always seemed to me a principal part of the work of a Christian Minister not only to insist on the duty of 'repentance towards God and faith in our Lord Jesus Christ,' but to illustrate in detail the obligations both of private and public morality; and I have felt it right to discuss in the pulpit on Sunday, the questions affecting the moral life of individuals or of nations, which I knew were being discussed in workshops and at dinner tables during the week."

520. Dale, R[obert] W[illiam]. *Week-day Sermons*. (London: Alexander Strahan & Co., 1867). 304pp.

A793 (author, title), JS783. Earliest edition in BL.

521. Daniel, [Charles] H[enry Olive] (1836–1919), editor. *Our Memories: Shad-*

ows of Old Oxford. (Oxford: Privately Printed by H. Daniel, 1888–1995). 1st series, nos. 1–20 (Dec. 1888–May 1893), 2nd series, nos. 1–2 (March–April 1895).

A415, B1023 ("Daniel Press," title, publisher, city, "1893"), D51 (title, 2nd series, dates), JS789. This periodical was published by Daniel, operator of a private press, the Daniel Press, in Oxford. D51 clearly indicates that Dodgson owned both issues of the second series. B1023 is more vague, giving only the date 1893 for a 4to bound volume. This could have contained all the issues of the 1st series (as described above), or only the issues for January–May 1893. Daniel's wife Emily produced an outdoor play of *Alice in Wonderland* at Worcester College, Oxford in 1895 (see *Alice on Stage* 101–2).

522. Daniel, Evan (1837–1904). *The Prayer-Book; Its History, Language and Contents.* (London: William Wells Gardner, 1877). 456pp.

A757 ("Daniel on the Prayer-book"), JS787. Earliest edition of the only matching title in BL. In his introduction the author writes, "Bearing in mind the large use we make of the Prayer-book, it must be highly important that every member of the Church should, as far as possible, be in possession of such knowledge as would enable him to fairly comprehend its scope, meaning, and authority. The history of the Prayer-book is in many cases absolutely necessary to a thorough comprehension of its formularies."

523. Daniel, Samuel (1562–1619). *The Collection of the History of England.* (London: Simon Waterson, 1634). 263pp. Revised, and by his last corrected copy printed.

Uncertain. F192 (author, title, date), not numbered in JS. Identified only by the gothic stamp. Daniel was a poet and historian.

524. [Daniel Press]. *The Garland of Rachel.* (Oxford: Press of H. Daniel, 1881). 67pp. "By Divers Kindly Hands.

A413 (full description), JS1090 (listed under Gosse). Limited to 36 copies, this book was published in honor of the first birthday of Rachel Anne Olive Daniel, daughter of Rev. Charles Henry Oliver Daniel, proprietor of the Daniel Press. Falconer Madan calls this "the most celebrated and valuable product of the Daniel Press" (*The Daniel Press*, Folkstone:

Dawsons, 1974). It consisted of a collection of eighteen poems by Dodgson, Austin Dobson, Andrew Lang, John Addington Symons, Robert Bridges, Edmund Gosse, Thomas Humphrey Ward, and others. See also WMGC. Rachel Daniel played the role of Alice in the 1895 outdoor play of *Alice in Wonderland* (see 521).

525. [Daniel Press]. *A New Sermon of the Newest Fashion.* (Oxford: Press of H. Daniel, 1876).

A412 (full description), JS790. A printing of a 17th-century manuscript found in the library of Worcester College. Madan describes the piece as "an anonymous satirical piece written by a Royalist in the guise of a discourse on I Cor. 4:10.... The principal objects of the attack are Bishops and Romanism." The original title was: *A New Sermon, of the Newest Fashion; That is to Say; A Longe Wasted One, without Stitch, Welt or Guard. Cutt out, & Made up by Ananias Snip a New Inspired Taylor.* Limited to 50 copies.

526. Daniell, John Frederic (1790–1845). *An Introduction to the Study of Chemical Philosophy.* (London: John W. Parker, 1839). 565pp.

A307 (author, title), A535, JS788. Earliest edition in BL. Dodgson owned 2 copies. A British meteorologist, chemist, and inventor, Daniell designed the Daniell-cell, a major improvement in battery technology that was adopted by British and American telegraph companies.

527. Dante Alighieri (1265–1321). *La Divina Commedia di Dante Alighieri.* (London: Pickering, 1823). 2 vols. (in 1). *Pickering Diamond Classics* series.

A476 (author, publisher, 2 vols. in 1), A478 (duplicate copy), JS791. See 153 for a note on this series. See 2004 for a note on Dodgson and Dante. In a letter to Edith Blakemore (31 March 1890) Dodgson writes, "I am sure the *Divina Commedia* is one of the grandest books in the world — though I am *not* sure whether the reading of it would *raise* one's life and give it a nobler purpose, or simply be a grand poetical treat" (see *Letters*).

528. Dante Alighieri. *The Divine Comedy of Dante Alighieri Translated by Henry Wadsworth Longfellow.* (London: G. Routledge, 1867). 3 vols.

A394 ("Longfellow's Translation of Dante"),

JS1442. Earliest British edition. A394 does not specify multiple volumes but no British 1-volume edition has been traced. The only pre–1898 1-volume edition traced was published in New York and Boston by Houghton Mifflin in 1895.

529. Darwin, Charles [Robert] (1809–82). *The Expression of the Emotions in Man and Animals.* (London: John Murray, 1872). 374pp. With 21 drawings & 7 folding Heliotype photographic reproductions.

A563 (author, title), JS792. 1st edition. Psychological study in which Darwin suggests that facial expressions as a mirror of emotions are innate. Dodgson recorded he was reading this book in December of 1872. He sent Darwin a photograph for possible use in the book (see *Diary 6*, 244).

530. Davenport, John (1789–1877) and [Guglielmo] Comelati. *A New Dictionary of the Italian and English Languages, Based Upon That of Baretti, and Containing, among other Additions and Improvements, Numerous Neologisms and a Copious List of Geographical and Proper Names.* (London: Longman & Co., 1854). 2 vols.

E75 (title, authors, 2 vols., date), JS793. Dodgson also owned a copy of Baretti's English-Italian dictionary, upon which the present work was based (see 103).

531. [Davenport, Richard Alfred] (1777?–1852). *Sketches of Imposture, Deception, and Credulity.* (London: Thomas Tegg & Son, 1837). 368pp. No. 63 in the *Family Library.*

E293 (title, series), JS136 (Anon./Literature). Dodgson's copy had the signature of Tom Taylor (playwright and editor of *Punch*) on the flyleaf. Davenport was a miscellaneous writer and editor whose works include a biographical dictionary and an edition of the Koran. The work exposes a wide variety of frauds. It includes chapters on religious and heathen superstitions, literary impostors, forged works of art, the South Sea Bubble, pantomime art, juggling, vampires, alchemy, horoscopes and medical frauds.

532. Davidge, William Pleater (1814–88). *Footlight Flashes.* (New York: American News Co., 1866). 274pp.

A670 (title), JS289 (Anon./Theatre). This is the only edition of the only matching title in BL or NUC. An autobiography of the British-born actor who spent much of his career in the United States. He was the first American Dick Deadeye in *H. M. S. Pinafore* and played over 1000 parts in his career.

533. Davidson, Ellis A. (?1828–78) *Pretty Arts for the Employment of Leisure Hours. A Book for Ladies.* (London: Chapman & Hall, 1879 [1878]). 169pp.

A593 (author, title), JS794. Only edition in BL. Includes "Wood Carving," "Fret Sawing," "Modelling in Clay and Casting Plaster," "Modelling in Wax," "Leather Work," "Drawing on Wood," "Wood Engraving," "Lithographic Drawing," "Etching on Copper," "Drawing from Objects," "Toys and How to Make Them," and "Cottages, etc. Modelled in Cardboard."

534. Davies, Charles Maurice (1828–1910). *Fun, Ancient and Modern.* (London: Tinsley Bros, 1878). 2 vols. 327, 308pp.

A911 (title, author, 2 vols.), JS795. Only edition in BL. Davies was a clergyman who wrote about spiritual life (occultism, religion, unorthodoxy) in London. A wide ranging survey of comic literature which is not base or sarcastic, but merely fun. Includes work from Roman satire to Chaucer and Shakespeare and much more.

535. Davies, Thomas Lewis Owen (b. 1833). *Bible English. Chapters on Old and Disused Expressions in the Authorized Version of the Scriptures and the Book of Common Prayer.* (London: George Bell & Sons, 1875). 292pp. With illustrations from contemporaneous literature.

B1025 (author, title, date), JS797. Davies was educated at Exeter College, Oxford, where he was an undergraduate in the early 1850s, at the same time as Dodgson. He later served as a vicar in Southampton.

536. Davis, Nathan (1812–82) and Benjamin Davidson (d. 1871). *Arabic Reading Lessons; Grammatically Analysed and Translated; Consisting of Extracts from the Koran, and Other Sources, with the Elements of Arabic Grammar.* (London: Samuel Bagster & Sons, [1854]). 134pp.

E253 (authors, title), JS798. Only edition in BL. Davis, a fellow of the Royal Geological Society and a non-conformist minister, spent many years in Northern Africa and worked at British Museum excavations at Carthage and Utica. Davidson was author of a Hebrew and Chaldee lexicon and other linguistic works.

537. Davy, Humphry (1778–1829). *Consolations in Travel, or the Last Days of a Philosopher.* (London: John Murray, 1831). 264pp. A new edition edited by John Davy.

B1026 (author, title, date), JS799. BL lists the 1831 edition variously as "3rd edition" and "New edition." Davy was a leading British scientist and inventor who was knighted by George III. He wrote this, his last book and the story of his travels, when he knew he was dying. John Davy was Humphry's brother.

538. Davy, Humphry. *Outlines of a Course of Lectures on Chemical Philosophy.* (London: Press of the Royal Institution, 1804). 54pp.

D50 (author, title, city, date), JS800. Dodgson's copy was bound together with John Sadler's *An Explanation of the Terms Used in Chemistry* (see 1753).

539. [Davy, Humphrey]. *Salmonia, or Days of Fly Fishing, in a Series of Conversations, With Some Accounts of the Fish Belonging to the Genus Salmo, by an Angler.* (London: John Murray, 1828). 273pp.

A562 (title), JS801. 1st edition of the only matching title in BL. A popular and important book on angling written near the end of Davy's career when his health drove him to seek fresh air.

540. Dawes, William (1671–1724). *The Duties of the Closet: Being an Earnest Exhortation to Private Devotion.* (London: Printed for J. Wilford, 1731). 226pp.

WS, not in JS. Dodgson's copy is in WWC, bears his autograph initials, and has the property label on the cover. It lacks the title-page and frontispiece. It has manuscript markings throughout. Dawes was Archbishop of York from 1714 to 1724.

541. Day, Henry N[oble] (1808–89). *The Science of Æsthetics; or, The Nature, Kinds, Laws, and Uses of Beauty.* (New Haven, CT: C. C. Chatfield & Co., 1872). 434pp. Plates.

E3 (author, title, city, date), JS802. Day was the president of Ohio Female College from 1858 to 1864. He wrote several works on logic, literature, ethics and philosophy. The frontispiece is a reproduction of The Madonna di San Sisto, by Raphael. Dodgson owned a print of this image as well. The book includes sections on the nature of beauty, kinds of beauty, laws of beauty, and relations of beauty and includes reference to architecture, landscape, sculpture, painting, poetry, and other fields of endeavor.

542. Day, Thomas (1748–1789). *The History of Sandford and Merton, a Work Intended for the Use of Children.* (London: J. Stockdale, 1783–89). 3 vols. 215, 306, 308pp.

A671 (title), JS803. 1st edition. Day was an English author who lived an austere life and reflected his own philosophy of simple living and hard labor in this, his most famous work. The book is a series of stories, mostly moral, linked together through the relationship of the wealthy and spoiled Tommy Merton and Harry Sandford, son of a farmer. The two boys are educated by Mr. Barlow, who spouts educational and political philosophy intended for adults. Tommy eventually becomes as likeable as Harry. Dodgson owned Burnand's parody of *Sandford and Merton* (see 301).

543. Day, William Henry (1830–1907). *Headaches: Their Nature, Causes, and Treatment.* (London: J. & A. Churchill, 1877). 312pp.

B1027 (author, title), JS804. Earliest edition in BL. Day was a physician to the Samaritan Hospital for Women and Children in London.

544. Deakin, Richard (1809–73). *Florigraphia Britannica; or Engravings and Descriptions of the Flowering Plants and Ferns of Britain.* (London: R. Groombridge and Sons, 1841–48). 4 vols. Illustrated.

A823, B1028 (author, title, 4 vols. date), JS805. Earliest edition traced.

545. [Defoe, Daniel] (1660?–1731). *Essay on the History and Reality of Apparitions. Being an Account of What They Are, and What They Are not ... As Also How we May Distinguish between the Apparitions of Good and Evil Spirits.* (London: J. Roberts, 1727). 395pp.

A884, B1029 (author, title, date), JS807. A

work that dismisses the reality of ghosts while leaving open the possibility of angelic communication through dreams.

546. [**Defoe**, Daniel]. *The Life and Strange Surprising Adventures of Robinson Crusoe of York, Mariner, as Related by Himself. Being a Facsimile Reprint of the First Edition Published in 1719.* (London: Elliot Stock, 1883). 364pp. With an introduction by Austin Dobson.

A661 ("Robinson Crusoe, facsimile reprint of first edition"), JS806. Only edition in Robert Lovett's *Robinson Crusoe A Bibliographical Checklist of English Language Editions 1719–1979* that matches the details in A661.The edition is not actually a facsimile. It has facsimiles of the title page, frontispiece, and preface of the 1st edition and reprints the text.

547. [**Defoe**, Daniel]. *Robinson Crusoe.* (London: William S. Orr and Co., 1844). 39pp. In the *Comic Nursery Tales* series.

A483 (series, title), not in JS.

548. [**Defoe**, Daniel]. *A System of Magick; or, a History of the Black Art. Being an Historical Account of Mankind's Most Early Dealing with the Devil; and how the Acquaintance on Both Sides First Began.* (London: J. Roberts, 1727). 403pp.

A884 (title, date), B1127, JS189 (Anon./Occult). Defoe wrote several works on the supernatural late in his life, general in a satirical vein. This work traces the history of the black arts in a satiric style.

549. [**Defoe**, Daniel]. *The Whole Life and Strange Surprising Adventures of Robinson Crusoe, of York, Mariner: Who Lived Eight and Twenty Years all Alone in an Uninhabited Island, on the Coast of America, near the Mouth of the Great River Oroonoque; And his Strange Surprizing Account of his Travels round Three Parts of the Globe.* (London: Printed at the Logographic Press and sold by J. Walter, T. Hookham, W. Richardson, and M. Wilson, 1785). 2 vols. 485, 452pp.

A661 (title, 2 vols., date), JS806. This is the only 2-volume edition of 1785 in Lovett (see 546). Lovett notes that "Logographic printing, a system whereby short words or groups of let-

ters could be set at once rather than one letter at a time, was invented by John Walter and Henry Johnson in 1780." One could imagine that this piece of printing history would have appealed to Dodgson, who took such interest in the printing of his own works.

550. De Lesseps, Ferdinand Marie (1805–94). *The Suez Canal. Letters and Documents Descriptive of its Rise and Progress in 1854–1856.* (London: H. S. King and Co., 1876). 311pp. Translated by N. D'Anvers [pseud. of Nancy R. E. Meugens, later Bell].

A639, D189 (title, author, translator, city, date), JS808. De Lesseps conceived of, raised much of the capital for, and supervised the construction of the Suez Canal.

551. De Morgan, Augustus (1806–71). *Arithmetical Books, From the Invention of Printing to the Present Time. Being Brief Notices of a Large Number of Works Drawn up from Actual Inspection.* (London: Taylor & Walton, 1847). 124pp.

E70 (title, author, date), JS809, WS. Dodgson's copy is in WWC. It has the gothic stamp and has the property label on the front cover. De Morgan was an important British mathematician and logician. He was the first Professor of Mathematics at the University of London and co-founder of the London Mathematical Society. Some of his most important contributions came in the field of logic (see 557). He also had a strong interest in the history of mathematics, and wrote biographies of Newton and Halley. The present volume covers works by over 1500 mathematicians and is considered by many to be the first scientific bibliography. In his diary for 23 February 1858, Dodgson lists this title among his recently purchased books.

552. De Morgan, Augustus. *The Book of Almanacs, With an Index of Reference, by Which the Almanac May be Found for Every Year ... Up to A.D. 2000. With Means of Finding the Day of any New or Full Moon from B.C. 2000 to A.D. 2000.* (London: Taylor, Walton, & Maberly, 1851). 89pp.

A540, B1030 (author, title, date), JS810. According to B1030, Dodgson also owned a copy of the 2nd edition (1871). He may have owned another edition as well, for A540 specifies "3 vols." Dodgson's interest in this volume may have been linked to his own work in trying to develop an algorithm "To Find the Day of the Week for Any Given Date" (LCP, #248). He was also interested in creating an algorithm to calculate the date of Easter for any year.

553. De Morgan, Augustus. *A Budget of Paradoxes*. (London: Longmans, Green, and Co., 1872). 511pp. Edited by Sophie De Morgan. Reprinted, with the Author's Additions, from *The Athenæum*.

A308 (author, title), JS811. Dodgson's copy is in Parrish and has the gothic stamp on the title page. It has several marginal notations by Dodgson, including his attempt to solve the problem "I was x years old in x^2" (one of Dodgson guesses is x=42). *Saturday Review* wrote, "Mr. De Morgan's 'paradoxes' are people who propound notions which deviate more or less widely from the accepted notions on any subject. The result is a book of which to say that it is full of the most curious oddities, most amusingly told, is to give a scant description of it."

554. De Morgan, Augustus. *Differential and Integral Calculus. Containing Differentiation Development Series Differential Equations, Differences, Summation Equations of Differences, Calculus of Variations, Definite Integrals, with Application to Algebra, Plane Geometry Solid Geometry and Mechanics also Elementary Illustrations of the Differential and Integral Calculus*. (London: Robert Baldwin, 1842). 785pp.

A582 (author, title), JS812. Earliest edition in BL.

555. De Morgan, Augustus. *The Elements of Arithmetic*. (London: 1848). 220pp.

E269 (title, author, date), JS813. Neither BL nor BOD list an 1848 edition, but both list a 5th edition of 1846, published by Taylor & Walton. Dodgson's copy was probably a reprint of that edition.

556. De Morgan, Augustus. *An Essay on Probabilities, and on Their Application to Life Contingencies and Insurance Offices*. (London: Longman, Orme, Brown, Green, & Longmans; John Taylor, 1838). 306pp.

A583 (author, title), JS815. Only edition

traced. According to Peter Heath, in *The Encyclopedia of Philosophy*, "De Morgan's conception of probability was largely derived from Laplace, whose ideas (and errors) he was thus instrumental in propagating among his nineteenth-century successors. His method of approach was to construe the theory as an extension of formal logic, that is, as an investigation of the rules whereby propositions not absolutely certain affect the certainty of other propositions with which they are connected." Dodgson bought this book on 23 February 1858 (see *Diary 3*).

557. De Morgan, Augustus. *Formal Logic: or, the Calculus of Inference, Necessary and Probable*. (London: Taylor & Walton, 1847). 336pp.

A508, D52 (author, title, city, date), JS814. D52 notes Dodgson's signature. An important work on logic in which De Morgan introduced the concept of quantification of the predicate, making it possible to solve problems unworkable by Aristotelian means.

558. De Morgan, Augustus. *Syllabus of a Proposed System of Logic*. (London: Walton & Maberly, 1860). 72pp.

D106 (author, title, city, date), JS817. D106 notes the following inscription: "Thomas Falconer — given me by Professor De Morgan."

559. De Morgan, Mary Augusta (1850–1907). *On a Pincushion, and Other Fairy Tales*. (London: Seeley, Jackson, & Halliday, 1877 [1876]). 228pp. With 32 illustrations, initials, and devices by William De Morgan.

A640 (title), JS818. Only 19th-century edition of the only matching title in BL. The "Other Tales" are "The Story of Vain Lamorna," "The Seeds of Love," "The Story of the Opal," "Siegfrid & Handa," "The Hair Tree," "A Toy Princess," and "Through the Fire." Mary, the author of several volumes of fairy stories, was the sister of William De Morgan (1839–1917), an arts and crafts designer, especially known for his work in tiles and other ceramics. Dodgson met William on several occasions, and, in 1883, purchased a set of De Morgan tiles for his fireplace. In 1887, Dodgson, then curator of the Senior Common Room at Christ Church, Oxford, had De Morgan tiles installed in the large fireplace in that room, where they remain to this day.

560. Demosthenes (384–322 B.C.E.). *Against Aphobus*. Edition unknown.

Not in JS. On 17 February 1858, Dodgson wrote of his reading plan in his diary and noted this among the books he was beginning with. BL does not list a separate edition of this work before 1858; Dodgson probably had a copy of the works of Demosthenes, of which there were many pre–1858 editions. Demosthenes was among the greatest of Greek orators; many of his orations were directed against King Philip of Macedon. Aphobus was a trustee of the estate of Demosthenes' father and the present orations were in conjunction with a lawsuit filed by Demosthenes accusing Aphobus of squandering the estate.

561. Denison, Edmund Beckett (1816–1905). *Astronomy Without Mathematics*. (London: Society for Promoting Christian Knowledge, 1867). 330pp. 3rd edition, much enlarged.

E197 (author, title, date), F169, JS821. Dodgson's copy is in Berg. It has the gothic stamp on the title page and the property label on the front cover. Dodgson's manuscript notations, corrections, and a diagram appear in purple ink on pages 4–9. An example of one of his marginal notations is: "i.e. if 2 points on the globe, 2 miles apart, be joined by a straight line, the ground rises 8 inches above the middle of that line." Denison was best known as a designer of clocks who brought a new level of accuracy to large public clocks. His best known work is seen daily throughout the world — the clock atop the tower of the Houses of Parliament, London.

562. Denison, George Anthony (1805–96). *Notes of my Life, 1805–1878*. (Oxford & London: James Parker & Co., 1878). 415pp.

A908 (author, title), JS819. Earliest edition in BL. Denison was Archdeacon of Taunton. A staunch High Churchman, he was charged by the acting Bishop of Bath and Wells with unsound policy in 1853. He responded with a series of sermons on the Real Presence of Christ in the Eucharist. This led to an unsuccessful prosecution against him by church courts. He was Chairman of the Committee in Oxford that condemned the controversial book *Essays and Reviews* (see 2075) as well as the writings of Dr. Colenso (see 421). This is his autobiography.

563. Dennis, George T. *The Cid: A Short Chronicle, Founded on the Early Poetry of Spain*. (London: C. Knight & Co., 1845). 220pp. Being [no.] 35 of *Knight's Weekly Volume for All Readers*.

E305 (author, title, series, date), JS820. Dodgson's copy, with the property label and his monogram, is in Berg. A prose retelling (with some poetry) of the Spanish chronicle of Rodrigue Diaz de Bivar, the 11th-century Spanish warrior and hero.

564. [De Quincey, Thomas] (1785–1859). *Klosterheim: or, the Masque*. (Edinburgh: William Blackwood; London: T. Cadell, 1832). 305pp.

A473 (author, title, edition, date), JS823. De Quincey was a prose writer and sometime friend of Wordsworth best known for his addiction to opium and his first book, *Confessions of an English Opium Eater* (1821). This brought him substantial notoriety and led to a successful writing career. A gothic novel.

565. De Quincey, Thomas. *Selections Grave and Gay, from Writings Published and Unpublished*. (Edinburgh: James Hogg; London: R. Groombridge & Sons, 1853–60). 14 vols. as follows: 1, 2: *Autobiographic Sketches*, 1853–54; 3, 4: *Miscellanies: Chiefly Narrative*, 1854; 5: *Confessions of an English Opium-Eater, etc.*, 1856; 6: *Sketches: Critical and Biographic*, 1857; 7: *Studies on Secret Records, Personal and Historic. With Other Papers*, 1858; 8: *Essays Sceptical and Anti-sceptical, on Problems Neglected or Misconceived*, 1858; 9: *Leaders in Literature with a Notice of Traditional Errors Affecting Them*, [1858]; 10: *Classic Records Reviewed or Deciphered*, [1859]; 11: *Critical Suggestions on Style and Rhetoric*, [1859]; 12, 13: *Speculations Literary and Philosophic*, [1859]; 14: *Letters to a Young Man Whose Education has Been Neglected*, 1860.

A350 (De Quincey's Works, 14 vols.), JS822. BL lists only two 14-volume editions of De Quincey's works, this and an edition of 1889–90 published by A. & C. Black of Edinburgh. Dodgson almost certainly owned this edition as he writes in his diary on 24 November 1857, "Finished the first volume of the De Quincey; it is perfectly delightful reading, and full of information of all kinds." On January 5, 1858, he wrote "Finished the second volume of De Quincey." This suggests that he purchased, during 1857, the first six volumes and then bought the others as they became available. On 7 January 1858, his diary notes that he "Finished the *Spanish Military Nun* by De Quincey." This described the adventures of a nun disguised as a soldier in South America.

566. De Vere, Aubrey (1788–1846). *A Song of Faith, Devout Exercises, and Sonnets.* (London: Pickering, 1842). 286pp.

D56 (author, title, city, publisher, date), JS830 (listed with the works of Aubrey Thomas De Vere). Sir Aubrey De Vere was the father of Aubrey Thomas De Vere (see below), and an Irish poet. A book of religious poetry.

567. De Vere, Aubrey Thomas (1814–1902). *May Carols.* (London: Longman, Brown, Green, Longmans, & Roberts, 1857). 126pp.

A859, B1035 (author, title, date), JS829. Aubrey Thomas De Vere was the son of Sir Aubrey De Vere (see above). He was an Irish poet who came to England and befriended Tennyson and Browning. He became a Roman Catholic in 1851 and returned to Dublin to serve as Professor of Social and Political Science at the Catholic University there. This work is a collection of hymns and poems. Dodgson photographed De Vere (see *Letters*, opposite p. 640).

568. De Vere, Aubrey Thomas. *Poems.* (London: Burns & Lambert, 1855). 319pp.
A859, B1034 (author, title, date), JS828.

569. De Vere, Aubrey Thomas. *The Search After Proserpine, Recollections of Greece, and Other Poems.* (Oxford: John Henry Parker; London: Rivingtons, 1843). 308pp.

A859, B1033 (author, title, date), JS827. According to his diary, Dodgson bought this book on 30 September 1863.

570. De Vere, Aubrey Thomas. *The Sisters, Inisfail, and Other Poems.* (London: Longman, Green, Longman & Roberts; Dublin: McGlashan & Gill, 1861). 342pp.

A859, B1036 (author, title, date), JS826.

571. Dicey, Albert Venn (1835–1922). *England's Case Against Home Rule.* (London: John Murray, 1886). 311pp.

A304 (author, title), JS831. Earliest edition in

BL. Dicey was Vinerian Professor of English Law at Oxford. In his preface, he writes, "My justification for publishing my thoughts on Home Rule is that the movement in favour of the Parliamentary independence of Ireland constitutes, whether its advocates recognise the fact or not, a demand for fundamental alterations in the whole Constitution of the United Kingdom ... I entertain the firmest conviction that any scheme for Home Rule in Ireland involves dangerous if not fatal innovations on the Constitution of Great Britain."

572. Dickens, Charles (1812–70). *The Adventures of Oliver Twist; or, The Parish Boy's Progress.* (London: Bradbury & Evans, 1846). 311pp. A new edition revised and corrected. With 24 illustrations by George Cruikshank.

A496, JS848, WS. Dodgson's copy is in Berg and has his monogram on the title-page in purple ink.

573. Dickens, Charles. *American Notes for General Circulation.* (London: Chapman & Hall, 1842). 2 vols. 2nd edition.

A667 (author, title, edition, 2 vols.), JS832. Published the same year as the 1st edition. Dickens' less than flattering account of Americans based on his journey to the U.S. For a reaction to this book see 2295.

574. Dickens, Charles. *Aventures de Monsieur Pickwick.* (Paris: 1859). 2 vols. [French translation of *Pickwick Papers*]. Traduit avec l'autorisation de l'auteur sous la direction de P[aul] Lorain, par P. Grolier.

A668 ("Pickwick Papers in French"), JS851. Dodgson owned 2 French translations of Dickens, both listed in A668. It seems most likely that he would have owned authorized translations and that he would have bought translations by the same translator. Only the works of Paul Lorain fit these requirements. He was associated with authorized translations of both *Nicholas Nickleby* (see 592) and *Pickwick Papers* and these translations were issued in 2-volume editions as described by A668. This translation was re-issued (also in 2 vols.) in 1880.

575. Dickens, Charles. *Bleak House.* (London: Bradbury and Evans, 1852). 624pp. 1st edition. With 40 illustrations by H. K. Browne.

A501 (author, title, date, edition), JS833. Dodgson owned many 1st editions of the works of Dickens. Whether he owned the 1st book editions or 1st editions bound from the original parts in which most of Dickens novels were published is not indicated. For the sake of clarity, the 1st book editions are described here. Browne (1815–82) was a prolific illustrator best known for his pictures in 10 of Dickens' novels. He frequently worked under the pseudonym "Phiz." Dickens and Browne were friends, though they eventually had a falling out.

576. Dickens, Charles. *A Child's History of England.* (London: Chapman & Hall, 1873). 431pp. New edition, in one volume. With illustrations by Marcus Stone.

A667 (author, title), JS835. The 1st edition of 1852–54 was published in 3 volumes. This is the first 1-volume edition. A667 does not mention multiple volumes.

577. Dickens, Charles. *A Christmas Carol in Prose, being a Ghost Story of Christmas.* (London: Chapman and Hall, [1873–74]). With colored illustrations by John Leech.

A669, E34 (title, author, illustrator, "reprint"), JS836. This copy, in the collection formed by Jeffrey Stern, now at Seitoku Gakuin College, Tokyo, Japan, is inscribed "C. L. Dodgson, Jan. 1874." John Leech (1817–64) was a prolific caricaturist and illustrator known for his comic work as well as for his many book illustrations.

578. Dickens, Charles. *The Christmas Carol. A Facsimile Reproduction of the Author's Original MS.* (London: Elliot Stock, 1890). 66pp. With an introduction by F. G. Kitton giving the history of the manuscript. One of 250 copies printed.

A280, D53 (author, title, city, date), JS836. D53 notes Dodgson's initials.

579. Dickens, Charles. *Dombey and Son.* (London: Bradbury and Evans, 1848). 624pp. 1st edition. With 40 illustrations by H. K. Browne.

A497 (author, title, edition, date), JS838. According to A497, Dodgson's copy contained extra illustrations.

580. Dickens, Charles. *The Lamplighter. A Farce.* (London: Printed by Ballantyne,

Hanson and Co., 1879). 45pp. With a plate by F. W. Pailthorpe. Now first printed from a manuscript in the Forster Collection at the South Kensington Museum. One of 250 copies printed.

B1037 (author, title, date, limitation), JS840. A play written for Charles Macready in 1838. Dickens read it to Macready, but it was never produced.

581. Dickens, Charles. *The Life and Adventures of Martin Chuzzlewit.* (London: Chapman and Hall, 1844). 624pp. 1st edition. With 40 illustrations by Phiz (Halbot K. Browne).

A499 (author, title, edition, illustrator, date), JS842.

582. Dickens, Charles. *The Life and Adventures of Nicholas Nickleby.* (London: Chapman and Hall, 1839). 624pp. 1st edition. With 40 illustrations by Phiz (H. K. Browne).

A498 (author, title, edition, illustrator, date), JS846.

583. Dickens, Charles. *Little Dorrit.* (London: Bradbury and Evans, 1857). 625pp. 1st edition. With 40 illustrations by H. K. Browne.

A501 (author, title, date, edition), JS841. In his diary for 8 February 1856, Dodgson writes, "Read third number of Little Dorrit," so he apparently purchased the monthly parts as they were published. The 4th part of this novel (March 1856) included an advertisement for *The Train* (see 2322) which listed "Lewis Carroll" as the contributor of the poem "Solitude." This may have been the first appearance of Dodgson's nom de plume in print.

584. Dickens, Charles. *Master Humphrey's Clock.* (London: Chapman & Hall, 1840–41). 3 vols. 306, 306, 426pp. With illustrations by George Cattermole and Halbot Browne.

A502 (author, title, 3 vols.), JS843. Dodgson's copy is described in A502 as "3 vols. in 2." By having the work thus bound, Dodgson would have ended up with volumes closer in thickness to Dickens' other volumes. This is the 1st book edition. A periodical containing the first appearance of two novels, *Barnaby Rudge* and *The Old Curiosity Shop.*

585. [Dickens, Charles]. "A Message from the Sea." In *All The Year Round*, "A Weekly Journal Conducted by Charles Dickens." Extra Christmas Number for volume IV (Christmas 1860). 48pp.

D54 (author, title, publication, date), JS844. A five-chapter story the authorship of which has caused controversy among scholars. Many believe that Dickens collaborated with Wilkie Collins and others on this work.

586. Dickens, Charles. *The Mystery of Edwin Drood.* (London: Chapman and Hall, 1870). 190pp. 1st edition. With 12 illustrations and a portrait by S. L. Fildes.

A503 (author, title), JS845. 1st book edition. This was Dickens' final novel, which was left incomplete at the time of his death. For a completion of the work, see 2144.

587. Dickens, Charles. *Our Mutual Friend.* (London: Chapman and Hall, 1865). 2 vols. 320, 309pp. 1st edition. With 40 illustrations by Marcus Stone.

A501 (author, title, edition), JS849. A501 describes Dodgson's copy as "2 vols. in 1" (see note for 584). In his diary for 16 January 1868, Dodgson writes, "One novel has been all my reading, *Our Mutual Friend*, one of the cleverest that Dickens has written."

588. Dickens, Charles. *The Personal History of David Copperfield.* (London: Bradbury & Evans, 1850). 624pp. 1st edition. With 40 illustrations by H. K. Browne.

A500 (author, title, edition, date), JS837. In a letter of 4 May 1849 Dodgson writes from Rugby School to his sister, "I have read the 1st number of Dickens' new tale Davy Copperfield. It purports to be his life & begins with his birth & childhood: it seems a poor plot, but some of the characters and scenes are very good. One of the persons that amused me, was a Mrs. Gummidge, a wretched melancholy person, who is always crying, happen what will."

589. Dickens, Charles. *The Posthumous Papers of the Pickwick Club.* (London: Chapman and Hall, 1837). 609pp. 1st edition. With 43 illustrations by R. Seymour and Phiz (H. K. Browne).

A495 (author, title, edition, illustrators, date), JS850. Dodgson's copy is in HAC. Livingston notes "on the fore-title is the following

note, "Bo't with the proceeds of a poem 'Faces in the Fire' contributed to *All the Year Round* [a publication edited by Dickens]." Dodgson's poem was published in the issue for February, 1860.

590. Dickens, Charles. *Sketches by "Boz," Illustrative of Every-Day Life, and Every-Day People.* (London: John Macrone, 1836). 2 vols. 348, 342pp. With 14 illustrations by George Cruikshank.

A503 (author, title), JS852. A503 does not specify the 1st edition (described here) and, since other nearby entries describing Dickens novels do mention firsts, it seems likely that Dodgson owned a reprint of this, Dickens' first novel.

591. Dickens, Charles. *A Tale of Two Cities.* (London: Chapman and Hall, 1859). 254pp. With 16 illustrations by H. K. Browne.

A503 (author, title), not in JS. A503 does not specify the first edition (described here) and, since other nearby entries describing Dickens novels do mention firsts, it seems likely that Dodgson owned a reprint.

592. Dickens, Charles. *Vie et Aventures de Nicolas Nickleby.* [French translation of *Nicholas Nickleby*]. Traduit avec l'autorisation de l'auteur par P[aul] Lorain. (Paris: [1857]). 2 vols.

A668 (Nicholas Nickleby in French, 2 vols.), JS847. This translation was re-issued (also in 2 volumes) in 1859. See 574 for why this translation is most likely the one Dodgson owned.

593. Dickens, Mary Angela. *Cross Currents. A Novel.* (London: Chapman & Hall, 1891). 3 vols.

A611 (author, title), JS854. Only edition in BL. M. A. Dickens was the granddaughter of Charles Dickens.

594. Dickens, Mary Angela. *A Mere Cypher. A Novel.* (London & New York: Macmillan & Co., 1893). 3 vols.

A611 (author, title), JS853. Only edition in BL.

595. Dickson, J[ames] A. R. (b. 1839). *Working for Jesus; or, Individual Effort for the Salvation of Precious Souls.* (London: Religious Tract Society, [1875]). 64pp.

E213 (title), JS341 (Anon./Theology). Only edition in BL. E213 records that Dodgson's copy was a "presentation to Lewis Carroll from a relative."

596. Diderot, Denis (1713–84). *The Paradox of Acting*. (London: Chatto & Windus, 1883). 108pp. Translated with annotations by Walter Herries Pollock. With a preface by Henry Irving.

A670 ("The Parody of Acting"), JS297 (Anon./Theatre). No work titled "The Parody of Acting" has been traced in any source, but surely this is an error in A570 ("Parody" for "Paradox") as no other conceivable match has been traced. This is the only pre–1898 edition in BL. Diderot was a French philosopher and writer who helped compile an important early encyclopedia. An important work on acting, influential in the French theatre. The paradox is that the actor, to move the audience, must himself remain unmoved.

597. [Diet]. *Manual of Diet*. Details unknown.

Title only given in A511/JS167 (Anon./Medical, not listed separately from other items). 3 possibilities in BL:

Chambers, Thomas King. *A Manual of Diet in Health and Disease*. (London: Smith, Elder & Co., 1875). 352pp.

Dobell, Horace Benge. *A Manual of Diet and Regimen for Physician and Patient*. (London: 1864). Went through at least 6 editions by 1875.

Turner, Duncan. *A Manual of Diet for the Invalid and Dyspeptic, with a Few Hints on Nursing*. (London: 1869). 2nd edition 1870.

598. Diprose, John (1814–79). *The Art of Talking and the Art of Pleasing in Conversation*. Frontispiece by Westall.

E136 (author, title, illustrator), JS856. Publication details unknown; description above taken from E136. The only copy traced is in BL and is described as "*The Art of Talking ... With Extracts from the Best Authors*. (6th edition.) London [1877]." Other books by Diprose (a book of epitaphs, a book of the stage and the players, an account of St. Clement Danes church, a book about life in London) were published in London by Diprose and Bateman.

599. Disraeli, Benjamin (1804–81). *Endymion*. (London: Longmans, Green, & Co., 1880). 3 vols. 331, 337, 346pp. 1st edition.

A809 (author, title, 3 vols., edition), JS857. Disraeli was among the most influential politicians of the 19th century, serving as prime minister and also pursuing a career as a novelist. This, his final novel, is filled with political references.

600. Disraeli, Benjamin. *Lothair*. (London: Longmans, Green, & Co., 1870). 3 vols. 328, 321, 333pp. 1st edition.

A809 (author, title, 3 vols., edition), JS858. Novel.

601. (Disraeli, Benjamin). A Biography. Specifics unknown.

A908 ("Disraeli A Biography"), JS113 (Anon./Literature), JS859. BL gives three possibilities:

Francis, George Henry. *The Rt. Hon. Benjamin Disraeli. A Critical Biography*. (London: 1852).

[O'Connor, T. P.] *Benjamin Disraeli, Earl of Beaconsfield. A Biography*. (London: S. O. Beeton, [1878]). A second volume of this work by Algernon Foggo was published in 1881, but A908 does not list multiple volumes.

MacKnight, Thomas. *The Right Honourable Benjamin Disraeli, M.P. A Literary and Political Biography. Addressed to the New Generation*. (London: 1854).

JS lists Froude, James Anthony. *Lord Beaconsfield*. (London: Sampson Low, Marston, Searle & Rivington, 1890) as a possibility, but the title is not as close a match as those listed above.

602. Dixon, Edward Travers. *The Foundations of Geometry*. (Cambridge: Deighton, Bell & Co., 1891). 143pp.

Not in JS. In a letter to the mathematical editor of the *Educational Times* (21 February 1891) Dodgson wrote, "I have carefully examined *The Foundations of Geometry* by E. T. Dixon, published by Deighton, Bell & Co., Cambridge, and would be glad to send you a short notice of it" (see *Letters*). The notice did not appear. Only edition in BL.

603. Dixon, Richard Watson (1833–1900). *The Story of Eudocia and her Brothers*. (Oxford: Printed by H. Daniel, 1888). 35pp.

A414 (full description), JS860. A product of the Daniel Press (see 521), limited to 50 copies. Dixon was an English poet who, as an undergraduate at Oxford, together with Edward Burne-Jones and William Morris, edited *The*

Oxford and Cambridge Magazine, a periodical devoted to the principals of the Pre-Raphaelite Brotherhood. He later held a number of church positions and was to stand for the Professorship of Poetry at Oxford in 1885, but he withdrew his name.

604. Dixon, William Hepworth (1821–79). *Spiritual Wives.* (London: Hurst and Blackett, 1868). 2 vols. 331, 344pp.

A893 (title, author, 2 vols.), JS861. Earliest edition in BL. The book had reached a 4th edition (also in 2 vols.) later in 1868. Dixon was editor of the *London Athenæum* from 1853 to 1869 and traveled widely. This work is an account of various religious sects and their attitudes about relationships between the sexes. When the *Pall Mall Gazette* accused the book of indecency, the author brought a suit against the paper and won damages of one farthing.

605. [Dobell, Sydney Thompson] (1824–74). *Balder.* (London: Smith, Elder & Co.; Bombay: 1854 [1853]). Part 1. 283pp.

B1038 (author, title, date), JS863. Only edition in BL, which does not list any subsequent parts. Romantic poem in which a poet lives with his wife (and later child) in an isolated tower. The child dies, the wife goes insane, and the poet eventually kills her. The most famous example of the Spasmodic school of poetry, of which Dobell was a leading member. This is the first part of the poem which was never completed, owing in part to the attack on it by Aytoun, who also wrote a parody of it.

606. Dobell, Sydney [Thompson]. *England in Time of War.* (London: Smith Elder & Co., 1856). 200pp.

A492 (author, title, date), JS862. War poems issued during the Crimean conflict.

607. [Dobell, Sydney Thompson]. *England's Day. A War-Saga.* (London: Strahan & Co., 1871). 15pp.

E226 (title, date), JS116 (Anon./Literature). Verse.

608. [Dobell, Sydney Thompson]. *Thoughts on Art, Philosophy, and Religion; Selected from the Unpublished Papers of S. D.* (London: Smith, Elder & Co., 1876). 339pp. With introductory note by J. Nichol. With a photograph.

A339 (author, title), JS864. Only edition in BL. Essays.

609. Dodgson, Charles (1800–1868). *The Controversy of Faith: Advice to Candidates for Holy Orders on the Case of Gorham v. the Bishop of Exeter: Containing an Analysis and Exposition of the Argument by which the Literal Interpretation of the Baptismal Services is to be Vindicated.* (London: John Murray, 1850). 102pp.

Not in JS. DAA2699 (Sotheby's, Los Angeles, 21 October 1973). Dodgson's copy is in the Berol Collection, New York University. It is inscribed on the half-title, "Charles Lutwidge Dodgson, from his affectionate Father." Dodgson was the father of Charles Lutwidge Dodgson and for 25 years rector of Croft, North Yorkshire. He also served as a canon of Ripon Cathedral. See 1534 for a description of the Gorham case. Dodgson, a High Churchman, opposed the Privy Council's decision to install Gorham.

610. Dodgson, Charles. *Do the First Works. A Sermon Addressed to the Newly-ordained Clergy at Ripon on Trinity Sunday 1851.* (London: G. Bell; Leeds: Richard Slocombe; Darlington: Coales and Farmer, 1851).

Not in JS. Dodgson's copy of this, his father's sermon, is in Berg. It is inscribed, "C. L. Dodgson with the author's most affectionate regards." The sermon was "Preached at the evening service in the Bishop's domestic chapel, and published at the request of his Lordship and of the clergy present." The elder Dodgson was, at the time, examining chaplain for Ripon and the newly-ordained clergy would have been partly his responsibility. The sermon, preached on Rev. 2:5, revealed Dodgson's High Church leanings, as an excerpt will show: "The strength of the Church of England, so far as God has vested it in human agents, lies not in any of the parties within her ... but it lies in a vast body of men, Lay as well as Clerical, who firmly attached to her system, as finally settled in the ages of the Reformation, and who are quietly opposed to all changes in that system, by whatever party they may be advocated. Let, then, this body be true to their own avowed principles: and when they contemplate the great and important deviations from the prescribed rule of the Church, which her practice in so many instances exhibits, let them strive, each as he may be enabled in his own sphere, to promote and encourage a gradual return to a system, towards which, as venerators of the Reformation, they implicitly profess their reverence and attachment."

611. Dodgson, Charles. *A Letter to the Lord Bishop of Ripon, on Some Objections Taken to the Author's Sermon, Lately Published under the Title of "Ritual Worship."* (Leeds: T. Harrison; London: F. and J. Rivington; Oxford: J. H. Parker, 1852). 23pp.

JS944. Dodgson's copy of this, his father's publication, is in HAC and is inscribed "From the Author." It is in an envelope labeled in purple ink in C.L.D.'s hand "Sermons &c. Rev. C. Dodgson," which also contains *Ritual Worship* and *Testimonial.* See below for the sermon Dodgson was defending. The sermon and this letter elicited another publication, *Examination of a Sermon "Ritual Worship," and of "a Letter" by C. Dodgson* (1852) by William Randall, Vicar of All Saints, Leeds. Dodgson states his pleasure that the bishop had praised the sermon in question, then goes on to express his surprise that a pamphlet by a clergyman of the diocese had accused him of unsound doctrine in the sermon and of Romish tendencies. Dodgson first objects to the idea that a sermon, praised by the bishop, can be condemned by a clergyman of the diocese. He goes on to discuss the history of the English Reformation and to address the specific questions of the relationship of Christ and his Church and of Eucharistic doctrine. He quotes such English theologians as Hooker, Andrewes, and Jeremy Taylor in his defense.

612. Dodgson, Charles. *Ritual Worship. A Sermon Preached at the Consecration of the Church of St. Thomas, in Leeds On the Feast of the Purification of St. Mary, 1852.* (Leeds: T. Harrison; London: F. and J. Rivington; Oxford, J. H. Parker: 1852). 28pp.

JS943. Dodgson's copy of this, his father's sermon, is in HAC and is inscribed "C. L. D. with the author's most affectionate regards." See also above Dodgson's letter to the Bishop concerning this sermon. The text for the sermon was Gen. 4:4–5. Dodgson defends High Church ritual worship, while at the same time decrying Romish doctrine such as Transubstantiation, writing, "There are many without these walls who are branding the Ritual Worship of the Church of England as heretical, because it is essentially different from that of Rome. There are many who are condemning it

as superstitious because it is essentially the same. The solution of this seeming paradox is, that we do indeed retain, and ever desire to retain, with Rome, every essential of Catholic worship: while we renounce, as vital corruptions, things which she retains as essential elements.... These very two principles, of rejecting what was Romish and of retaining what was Catholic, were the fundamental ones, on which our Reformers built their whole work."

613. Dodgson, Charles. "The Sabbath a Delight. (A Village Sermon)" In *Sermons by XXXIX Living Divines of the Church of England.* (London: J. Hatchard & Son; Manchester: Wareing Weld, 1840). Published under the superintendence of George Dugard and Alexander Watson.

Uncertain. Not in JS. In his diary for 21 May 1856, Dodgson writes, "Received from my father a copy of his *Sermons on the Christian Sabbath*" (see *Diary 2*). No work by this title by Dodgson's father is recorded; the present sermon, on Isaiah 58:13, is the only one traced in which he addresses the topic of the Sabbath. This diary entry could refer to an unpublished item. Only edition traced.

614. Dodgson, Charles. *The Sacraments of the Gospel, 2 Sermons. With a Full Account of the Proceedings of Dr. Goode Respecting Them; and the Correspondence Relative Thereto, between him and the Author.* (London: 1864).

Not in JS. In his diary for 21 May 1856, Dodgson notes that he received a copy of this book from his father. The sermons, on Rom. 4:11 and Deut. 29:29, were preached at Ripon on January 3 & 17, 1864. Dodgson was in Ripon with his family on 3 January, and probably heard his father preach the first of these sermons; by the 17th he had left for Oxford. A second edition was also published in 1864. In that same year, William Goode (1801–68) published *A Reply to Archdeacon Dodgson's Statement, Prefixed to his Sermons on the Sacraments; with Remarks on the Sermons.* Goode was Dean of Ripon and among the most learned of those who responded in print to the Tractarians (see 790). He took issue with Dodgson's High Church view of the sacraments.

615. (Dodgson, Charles). *Testimonial to the Rev. C. Dodgson, M. A., Rector of Croft, Examining Chaplain to the Lord Bishop of*

Ripon, from 185 Clergymen Who Have Received Ordination from the Bishop. (Np: 1852). 4pp.

J945. A request to the Lord Bishop of Ripon from clergymen who had studied under Charles Dodgson for permission to erect a window in Dodgson's honor. Also includes the Bishop's letter of permission, a letter from the clergymen informing Dodgson of their intention, a letter from Dodgson expressing his gratitude, and a description of the window. Dodgson's copy is in HAC. The 185 clergymen were all ordained by the Bishop of Ripon and studied under Charles Dodgson when he was the bishop's examining chaplain from 1836 to 1852. The window was installed and is still in the Bishop's Chapel, which was, in the 1990s, converted into a flat (see LCE, 20–21).

616. [**Dodsley**, Robert, editor] (1703–64). *A Collection of Poems in Six Volumes. By Several Hands.* (London: R. & J. Dodsley, 1758). 6 vols. 335, 336, 351, 361, 336, 336pp. 5th edition.

A896 (author, title, 6 vols.), JS947. This is earliest 6-volume edition. The first volumes were published in the 1740s, and the collection reached its final form with the publication of volumes 5–6 in 1758. This was a famous and popular 18th-century miscellany and included works by Johnson, Pope, Fielding, and many others.

617. Dolce, Lodovico (1508–68). *Delle Stanze di Diversi illvst. Poeti.* (Vinegia: 1580).

Uncertain. F190 (author, title, city, date), not numbered in JS. Identified only by the gothic stamp. Dolce was an Italian editor and author.

618. Domett, Alfred (1811–87). *Ranolf and Amohia: A South-Sea Day Dream.* (London: Smith, Elder & Co., 1872). 511pp. 1st edition.

A860 (author, title, edition), JS949. Educated at Cambridge, Domett served for a time as Prime Minister of New Zealand. After he returned to England in 1871, he published two books of verse about his experiences abroad, of which this was the first (the latter was *Flotsam and Jetsam* [1877]).

619. Doré, Louis Auguste Gustave (1832–83), illustrator. *The Legend of the Wander-ing Jew. With the Complainte and Béranger's Ballad Set to Music by Ernest Doré.* (London: Addey & Co., 1857). 83pp. 12 plates. Translated, with critical remarks by G. W. Thornbury.

A294 (title, illustrator), not in JS. Earliest English Doré edition in BL. Doré was perhaps the most successful French illustrator in the mid–19th century. Among his best known works are *Don Quixote* (1862), The Bible (1863), and *Inferno* (1861). His work is Romantic in style, with an infusion of the bizarre.

620. Douglas, Helen, ed. *The Silver Cross. A Collection of Poems and Hymns for the Sick and Suffering.* (London: Bell & Sons, 1897). 265pp.

A867 (title), JS388 (Anon./Unclassified). Only edition of the only pre–1898 match listed in BL or BOD.

621. Dowson, John, contributor. *Reed's Illustrated Guide to Whitby, and Visitor's Hand-book of the Town and Neighbourhood: Containing a History of the Abbey & Town, and a Full Description of the Rides and Walks in the Environs, with a Map of the Neighbourhood, and an Essay on Sea-bathing by John Dowson.* (S. Reed: Whitby, 1855). 101pp. 3rd edition.

E199 (author, title), JS950. Earliest edition traced. Dodgson spent time in Whitby during the summer of 1854 and for six of the following twelve summers.

622. Doyle, R[ichard] (1824–83), illustrator. *The Story of Jack and the Giants.* (London: Cundall & Addey, 1851). 35 drawings by Doyle.

A642 (title), JS79. Earliest edition in BL. Though the story of Jack the Giant Killer is a common one (see 1205), only the Doyle edition in BL uses this unusual wording in the title. Doyle was an important Victorian illustrator who worked for *Punch* and illustrated books by Ruskin, Dickens, Thackeray, and others.

623. [**Doyle**, Richard, John Leech and John Tenniel]. *Benjamin Disraeli, Earl of Beaconsfield, K.G. In upwards of 100 cartoons from the collection of "Mr Punch."* (London: Punch Office, 1878).

A533 (title), JS212 (Anon./Periodicals). 1st

edition. A new and enlarged edition was published in 1881 with 113 cartoons. See 577 for a note on Leech and 2022 for note on Tenniel.

624. Doyle, R[ichard] and Percival Leigh (1813–89). *Manners and Customs of ye Englyshe, Drawn from ye Quick by R. Doyle. To which be Added some Extracts from Mr. Pips hys Diary, Contributed by Percival Leigh*. (London: Bradbury & Agnew, 1876). 86pp.

A532 (title), JS64 (Anon./Children). Earliest 1-volume edition traced (A532 does not specify multiple volumes). First published in 2 vols. (London: Bradbury & Evans [1849–50]). A humorous take-off on Pepys diary with 40 cartoon drawings by Doyle. See 1204 for a note on Leigh.

625. Drelincourt, Charles [the elder] (1595–1669). *The Christian's Defence against the Fears of Death*. (London: D. Midwinter & A. Ward, etc., 1732). 502pp. Translated by Marius D'Assigny. 13th edition newly corrected. With an account of the author, etc. With "A True Relation of the Apparition of one Mrs Veal" (by Daniel Defoe).

A884, B1043 (author, title, translator, date), JS951. Drelincourt was a French Protestant divine and author of many devotional books. Defoe's fictional account of Mrs. Veal, who appears from another world to recommend Drelincourt's defense, was first added to the English translation in 1706.

626. Drew, W[illiam] H[enry] (1827?–82). *A Geometrical Treatise on Conic Sections, with a Copious Collection of Examples, Embodying Every Question which has been Proposed in the Senate House at Cambridge. For the Use of Schools and Students in the Universities*. (Cambridge: Macmillan, 1857). 122pp.

JS952. Dodgson's copy is in the collection formed by Jeffrey Stern, now at Seitoku Gakuin College, Tokyo, Japan. It includes Dodgson's signature on the front endpaper and, according to Stern, "numerous corrections, additions, and notes in his [i.e. Dodgson's] hand." Drew took his M.A. at St. John's College, Cambridge, and was second master at Blackheath Proprietary School.

627. Drew, W[illiam] H[enry]. *Solutions to the Problems Contained in A Geometrical Treatise on Conic Sections*. (London: Macmillan, 1862). 60pp.

Not in JS. Dodgson's copy, with his autograph inside the front cover, was offered for sale by Maggs of London in 1911. It was catalogued as dated 1852, but that is clearly a typographical error as 1862 was the 1st edition.

628. Driver, S[amuel] R[olles] (1846–1914). *An Introduction to the Literature of the Old Testament*. (Edinburgh: Clark, 1891). 522pp. Volume 1 of the *International Theological Library*, edited by S. D. F. Salmond, Stewart Dingwall Fordyce and Charles Augustus Briggs.

A763 (author, title), JS953. Earliest edition in BL. Driver was educated at Oxford and became Regius Professor of Hebrew (succeeding E. B. Pusey) and a canon of Christ Church in 1882. He was a member of the Old Testament Revision Company.

629. Drummond, Henry (1851–97). *Natural Law in the Spiritual World*. (London: Hodder and Stoughton, 1883). 414pp.

A306 (author, title), JS954. Earliest edition in BL. Drummond was a Scot and served as Professor of Natural History and Science at Free Church College, Glasgow. This book provoked a storm of responses. Drummond wrote there is "reason to believe that many of the Laws of the Spiritual World, hitherto regarded as occupying an entirely separate province, are simply the Laws of the Natural World." See also 417 and 1315.

630. (Drummond, Henry). *Nature and Law An Answer to Professor Drummond's Natural Law in the Spiritual World*. (London: George Redway, 1887). 86pp.

JS95 (Anon./Law), JS322 (Anon./Theology). Dodgson's copy, with his monogram on the endpaper, is in the collection of Selwyn Goodacre, Derbyshire, England. An anonymous reply to Drummond.

631. Drury, Henry (1812–63), editor. *Arundines Cami sive Musarum Cantabrigiensium Lusus Canori*. (Cambridge: J. G. Parker, 1843). 297pp.

A507, B949 (author, title, editor, city, date), JS422 (listed under Arundine), JS955. A507 misstates the title as "Arundine's Caine," leading to the mistake in JS422. No such book as "Arundine's Caine" has been traced, and this certainly refers to the present volume, described in B949. Drury was archdeacon of Wiltshire. A "Collection of Light-Hearted English and Latin Poetry from Cambridge Scholars."

632. Dryden, John (1631–1700). *The Poetical Works of John Dryden*. (London: F. C. & J. Rivington, 1811). 4 vols. Notes by Joseph Warton, John Warton, etc. Edited by Henry J. Todd.

A391 ("Dryden's Poetical Works, by Warton, 4 vols."), JS957. Only edition in BL matching the particulars in A391.

633. Dryden, John. *The Poetical Works of John Dryden*. (London: Macmillan & Co., 1870). 662pp. Edited with a memoir, revised text, and notes by W[illiam] D[ougal] Christie. The Globe Edition.

A368 ("Dryden's Work, Globe Edition"), JS956. This was the first printing of the Globe Edition.

634. Dubourg, Augustus W. (1830?–1910) *Four Original Plays, Unacted*. (London: R. Bentley & Son, 1883). 239pp.

A673 ("Four Original Plays"), JS290 (Anon./ Theatre). Only edition in BL of the only matching title. JS290 lists this as *Four Original Plays Apropos of Women in Theatres*. However, no such title exists in BL or BOD. A closer look at A673 shows that a line break occurs between "Four Original Plays" and "Apropos of Women and Theatres." Clearly a comma has been omitted, and these are two titles, both appearing in BL. See 1247 for *Apropos of Women and Theatres*, etc. Augustus Dubourg was a dramatist and an acquaintance of Dodgson with whom the latter discussed the possibility of staging *Alice* in 1873 (see *Alice on Stage*, p. 22ff).

635. Dufferin and Eva, Frederick Temple Hamilton-Temple-Blackwood, Marquis of (1826–1902). *Letters from High Latitudes; Being Some Account of a Voyage, in 1856, in the Schooner Yacht "Foam", to Iceland, Jan Mayen, and Spitzbergen*. (London: J. Murray, 1879). 248pp. 7th edition. Illustrated.

A599, D57 (author, title, city, date), JS521. Lord Dufferin was a diplomat, administrator, and politician who served as Governor General of Canada.

636. Duncan, Henry (1774–1846). *Sacred Philosophy of the Seasons; Illustrating the Perfections of God in the Phenomena of the Year. Summer*. (Edinburgh: W. Oliphant & Son, 1837).

B1045 (author, title, date), JS959. Part of a 4-volume set, one volume for each season. According to B1045, Dodgson's was a "presentation copy to 'Master Dodgson'." Duncan was a Scottish banker, editor, and religious writer. He was a clergyman, and part of the 1843 secession from the Church. Religious reflections on the natural world.

637. Dunlop, John Colin (1780–1842). *The History of Fiction: Being a Critical Account of the Most Celebrated Prose Works of Fiction, from the Earliest Greek Romances to the Novels of the Present Age*. (London: Longman, Hurst, Rees, Orme & Brown, 1814). 3 vols. 416, 409, 436pp.

A344 (author, title, 3 vols.), JS960. Earliest matching edition in BL. The introduction states, "In the following work I shall try to present a faithful analysis of those early and scarce productions which form, as it were, the landmarks of Fiction. Select passages will occasionally be added, and I shall endeavour by criticisms to give such a sketch as may enable the reader to form some idea of the nature and merit of the works themselves, and of the transmission of fable from one age and country to another."

638. Dutt, Shoshee Chunder (1824–85). *Historical Studies and Recreations*. (London: Trübner & Co., 1879). 2 vols.

A637, D58 (author, title, city, date, 2 vols.), JS961. Dutt was a native of Bengal who wrote about that region. Volume I contains: *The World's History Retold in Two Parts. I.— The Ancient World. II.— The Modern World.* Volume II contains: *I.— Bengal: An Account of the Country from Earliest Times. II.— The Great Wars of India. III.— The Ruins of the Old World, Read as Milestone of Civilisation*. *Saturday Review* wrote "His own country he knows thoroughly well."

639. Dykes, John Bacchus (1823–76). *Eucharistic Truth and Ritual. A Letter to the Lord Bishop of Durham Occasioned by his Reply to an Address from Certain Laymen in the Diocese*. (London: Masters; Durham:

Andrews, 1874?). 96pp. 2nd edition, with an appendix containing a reply to certain strictures on the Letter by the Archbishop of York.

C4 (author, title), not in JS. Only edition in BL, which lists no publisher; the publisher information is taken from the 3rd edition (1874) at Harvard University. Dykes was a hymn writer, precentor of Durham Cathedral (1849–62), and then vicar of St. Oswald's, Durham. His High Church ideals brought him into conflict (as here) with his bishop, Charles Thomas Baring. The letter in the appendix is by William Thomson.

640. Earle, Augustus (1793–1838). *A Narrative of a Nine Months' Residence in New Zealand, in 1827; Together with a Journal of a Residence in Tristan d'Acunha.* (London: Longman, Rees, Orme, Brown, Green, & Longman, 1832). 371pp. Engraved frontispiece plus 6 aquatints.

A918 (author, title), JS962. Earle was the draughtsman for the H.M.S. Beagle. Dodgson took a special interest in the remote south Atlantic island of Tristan d'Acunha as his brother, Edwin, was stationed there as a missionary. An important work which is among the first to record social customs of the Maori.

641. [Eberty, Felix] (1812–84). *The Stars and the Earth; or, Thoughts upon Space, Time, and Eternity.* (Boston: Noyes, Holmes and Company, 1874). 88pp. 4th American from the 3rd English edition. [Edited by Thomas Hill].

E403 (title, city, date), JS276 (Anon./Science). First published in 1846. E403 states "with the initials of Lewis Carroll." A book that shows the presence and wisdom of God the creator through science. In his Recommendatory Letter, Thomas Hill writes that the author makes "ingenious attempts to show that Space and Time are capable of indefinite contraction, therefore of annihilation, without the destruction of the phenomena manifested in them."

642. Edgeworth, Maria (1767–1849). *Comic Dramas, In Three Acts.* (London: R. Hunter, and Baldwin, Cradock and Joy, 1817). [384]pp. Introduction by R. L. Edgeworth.

A813 (author, title), JS963. 1st edition. Maria was the daughter of R. L. Edgeworth, who was passionately interested in childhood education. In 1791 she and her father began plans for a series of books for young children which would include an essay on education for parents and stories for emerging readers. She was a prolific writer of books for children, and in 1800 began to write novels for adults. The dramas in this collection are "Love and Law," "The Two Guardians," and "The Rose, Thistle, and Shamrock."

643. Edgeworth, Maria. *Early Lessons.* (London: Printed for R. Hunter, etc., 1824). 4 vols.

A818 (author, title, 4 vols.), JS964. Earliest 4-volume edition traced. Originally published in 1801, these stories were intended for beginning readers, and were published in large print with few words to the page. Includes tales of Harry and Lucy and of Rosamund (recurring characters in Edgeworth's stories).

644. Edgeworth, Maria. *Frank: A Sequel to Frank, in Early Lessons.* (London: Printed for R. Hunter; and Baldwin, Cradock and Joy, 1822). 3 vols. 324, 346, [300]pp.

A818 (author, title ["Frank"], 3 vols.), JS966. This is the only edition traced of this title first published in 3 vols. *Frank, Being the Sixth Part of Early Lessons* (1801) being published in 6 vols. and *Frank Part I, II, II, IV* (being the 7th–10th part of *Early Lessons*) being published in 4 vols. (1801). Stories.

645. Edgeworth, Maria. *Harrington, a Tale; and Ormond, a Tale.* (London: Printed for R. Hunter and Baldwin, Cradock, and Joy, 1817). 3 vols. [524], [424], [354]pp.

A817 (Edgeworth's Ormonde, 2 vols.... Harrington, 1 vol."), JS967, JS974. 1st edition. No 2-volume edition of *Ormond* has been traced, and no separate editions of *Harrington* have been traced (outside collected *Tales and Novels*). A817 describes 4 Edgeworth titles in 10 volumes, uniformly bound, so it is not surprising that the titles were mixed up. In all likelihood, Dodgson had this 3-volume edition bound with "Harrington" on the spine of one volume and "Ormond" printed on the spine of the other two. The cataloguer probably then copied titles from the spine as the books sat (mixed up) on the shelf. Harrington tells of a Christian hero who loves a Jewish woman and was apparently inspired by a letter Edgeworth received from an American Jewish reader complaining of the negative view of Judaism in some of Edgeworth's previous works.

646. Edgeworth, Maria. *Harry and Lucy, Being the First Part of Early Lessons.* (London: J. Johnson, 1801). 3 vols.

A648 (author, title ["Harry and Lucy"], 3 vols.), JS968. Earliest edition in BL or NUC of the only matching title traced in 3 vols. The Harry and Lucy stories began when Maria's father and his second wife Honora composed a story about two children by those names going through the simple tasks of the day — the intent being to provide easy and practical reading for early learners. Maria wrote many stories about these two children, including this work and the following.

647. Edgeworth, Maria. *Harry and Lucy Concluded. Being the Last Part of Early Lessons.* (London: R. Hunter; and Baldwin, Cradock and Joy, 1825). 4 vols. [288], 340, [320], 336pp.

A648 (author, title, 4 vols.), JS969. This is the 1st edition. More Harry and Lucy stories (see above).

648. Edgeworth, Maria. *Helen, A Tale.* (London: Richard Bentley, 1834). 3 vols. 336, 336, 322pp.

A817 (author, title, 3 vols.), JS970. 1st edition. Dodgson may also have owned a 2-volume edition (A820). The entry in A820 states only "Helen, 2 vols." This entry is near the entries for works by Edgeworth, but no other Edgeworth titles are listed in A820. Other novels by women, however, are listed there. "2 vols." could easily be a typographical error (for "3 vols."). If Dodgson did own a 2-volume edition of Edgeworth's *Helen*, it was likely the 1st American edition (Philadelphia: Carey, Lea & Blanchard; Boston: Allen & Ticknor, 1834). The only other possible match for the entry in A820 in BL is John Walter Sherer's 2-volume novel, *Helen, the Novelist.* (London: Chapman & Hall, 1888). OCIL calls Edgeworth's last novel, "a depressing view of the prospects for Irish society."

649. Edgeworth, Maria. *Lenora.* (London: J. Johnson, 1806). 2 vols. [292], [292]pp.

A813 (author, title, 2 vols.), JS972. 1st edition. A novel of contemporary English society.

650. Edgeworth, Maria. *Moral Tales for Young People.* (London: J. Johnson, 1801). 3 vols. [240], [198], 192pp.

A816 (author, title, 3 vols.), JS973. 1st edition. Following on the success of *The Parent's Assistant*, the present volume consisted of stories for older children.

651. Edgeworth, Maria. *The Parent's Assistant; or, Stories for Children, etc.* (London: J. Johnson, 1800). 6 vols. 3rd edition.

A813, A818 (author, title, 6 vols.), JS975. Dodgson owned 2 copies. Originally published in a 3-volume edition in 1796. Earliest 6-volume edition. This was Edgeworth's first book and consisted of moral tales and plays for children.

652. Edgeworth, Maria. *Patronage.* (London: J. Johnson, 1814). 4 vols. 418, [432], 402, [390]pp.

A817 (author, title, 4 vols.), JS976. 1st edition. A novel for adult readers.

653. Edgeworth, Maria. *Popular Tales.* (London: J. Johnson by C. Mercier, 1804). 3 vols. [386], [370], [396]pp.

A816 (author, title, 3 vols.), JS977. 1st edition. A collection of stories including "Lame Jervas," "The Contrast," "Murad the Unlucky," and many more.

654. Edgeworth, Maria. *Rosamund. A Sequel to Early Lessons.* (London: R. Hunter; and Baldwin, Cradock and Joy, 1821). 2 vols. 252, [274]pp.

A818 (author, title, 2 vols.), JS978. 1st edition. Moral stories of delinquent Rosamund.

655. Edgeworth, Maria. *Tales of Fashionable Life.* (London: J. Johnson, 1809–1812). 6 vols. [420], [392], 388, 460, 392, [468]pp. 2nd edition.

A816 (author, title, 6 vols.), JS965. The first three volumes originally published in 1809. This is the first complete 6-volume edition. Includes: "Ennui," "Almeria," "Madame de Fleury," "The Dun," "Manoeuvring," "Vivian," "Emilie de Coulanges," and "The Absentee." Moral stories based in high society.

656. Edgeworth, Maria and Richard Lovell Edgeworth. *Essay on Irish Bulls.* (London: J. Johnson, 1802). 316pp.

A813 (author, title), JS971. 1st edition. Collection of humorous essays on Irish matters, including "Irish Wit and Eloquence," "The Brogue," "The Irish Incognito," and "Irish Newspapers and The Bliss of Ignorance."

657. Edmonds, Charles, editor. *Poetry of the Anti-Jacobin: Comprising the Celebrated Political & Satirical Poems, Parodies, and Jeux-d'Esprits of the Right Hon. George Canning, the Earl of Carlisle, Marquis Wellesley, the Right Hon. J. H. Frere, W. Gifford, esq., the Rt. Hon. W. Pitt, G. Ellis, esq., and others.* (London: G. Willis, 1854). 248pp. 2nd edition, considerably enlarged. With 6 etchings by James Gillray.

A468 (author, title, illustrator, date [1254]), JS979. 1254 is clearly a typographical error for 1854. The poems are from *The Anti-Jacobin; or, Weekly Examiner*, edited by W. Gifford from 20 Nov. 1797–9 July 1798. A collection of political and satirical poems and parodies whose authors included two future prime ministers.

658. Edmunds, Albert Joseph (1857–1901). *English and American Poems.* (Philadelphia: Chambers Printing House, 1888). 1st series 42pp., 2nd series, 52pp.

B1047 (author, title, city, date), JS980. According to B1047, Dodgson's was a "presentation copy from the author." Poetry by a young American who went on to be a Buddhist scholar, librarian, and bibliographer. BL does not note that the 1st and 2nd series were published together in one volume, with separate title pages each dated 1888. As B1047 does not specify either 1st or 2nd series, it seems likely that Dodgson owned this combined volume. The title page of the 2nd series includes three poetic quotations, one a stanza from Dodgson's dedicatory poem in *The Hunting of the Snark* (1876). Includes "Seaside Idylls," which is prefaced by this line; "What the Heart of the Man said to the heart of the Child by the Summer Sea"—reminiscent of Dodgson's own attitude towards the children he met at the sea-side.

659. *The Educational Year Book*. (London: 1885?).

Not in JS. In April, 1887, Dodgson loaned a copy of "Educational Year Book" to his publisher, Macmillan. In it, Dodgson had marked the names of schoolmasters to whom he wished Macmillan to send copies of *The Game of Logic* (see *Macmillan*, 226). BL records five issues of this annual, 1879–82, 1885. The last issue would have been most useful as a directory when Dodgson used it in 1887.

660. Edwards, Lambart Campbell. *Formulæ in Pure and Mixed Mathematics, Designed for the Use of Students Intending to Compete at the Examinations for Admission to the Royal Military Academy, Woolwich.* (London: 1861).

E203 (title, date), JS149 (Anon./Mathematics).

661. Eliot, George [pseud. of Mary Anne Evans] (1819–80). *Scenes of Clerical Life.* (Edinburgh and London: William Blackwood and Sons, 1859). 2 vols. 309, 324pp. 2nd edition.

A810, E277, F142, JS981. Dodgson's copy is in the library of Princeton University. It has the gothic stamp on the title page of each volume and has his monogram in purple ink on the front endpaper of each volume. Eliot's first work of fiction, comprised of three stories first published in *Blackwood's Magazine*. In his diary for 29 January 1858, Dodgson writes, "Began reading *Scenes from Clerical Life* at the Union, beginning with 'Mr. Gilfil's love-story'."

662. *Ellen, or, The Naughty Girl Reclaimed: A Story Exemplified in a Series of Figures*. (London: Printed for S. and J. Fuller, 1811). 19pp.

A251 (title, date), not in JS. Osborne describes this as "A story in verse accompanied by 9 paper-doll figures and a movable head." A copy described as "once the property of C. L. Dodgson" sold at Sotheby's, London on 18–21 June 1928 (DAA1259).

663. Ellicott, C[harles] J[ohn] (1819–1905), explanatory paper by. *Modern Scepticism: A Course of Lectures Delivered at the Request of the Christian Evidence Society with an Explanatory Paper by the Right Reverend C. J. Ellicott.* (London: Hodder and Stoughton, 1871). 544pp. 3rd edition.

A768 ("Modern Scepticalism"), JS382 (Anon./Unclassified). No matching title in BL, BOD, or any other source traced. The present title seems the most likely—it is not only a close match, but also in the same series as *Credentials of Christianity* (see 1750), owned by Dodgson. The present edition is the only one traced. Ellicott was Bishop of Gloucester and Bristol. He also contributed to *Credentials of Christianity*. Includes: Archbishop of York, "Design in Nature"; Rigg, J. H., "Pantheism"; Jackson, W., "Positivism"; Payne Smith, R., "Science and Revelation"; Stoughton, John,

"The Nature and Value of the Miraculous Testimony to Christianity"; Bishop of Carlisle, "The Gradual Development of Revelation"; Rawlinson, George, "The Alleged Historical Difficulties of the Old And New Testaments, and the Light Thrown on Them by Modern Discoveries"; Row, Charles, "Mythical Theories of Christianity"; Leathes, Stanley, "The Evidential Value of St. Paul's Epistles"; Bishop of Ely, "Christ's Teaching and Influence on the World"; and Canon Cook, "The Completeness and Adequacy of the Evidences of Christianity."

664. [**Elliott**, Charlotte] (1789–1871). *Hours of Sorrow Cheered and Comforted.* (London: Haselden, 1849). 178pp. 4th edition.

D61 (author, title, city, date), JS982. According to D61, Dodgson wrote Charlotte Elliott's name on the title page. Elliott was best known as a hymn writer, author of "Just as I am without one Plea." She also edited *Religious Remembrancer* magazine. She was an invalid from about the age of 30, hence the current collection of religious verse. This was originally published in 1836 as *Hours of Sorrow; or, Thoughts in Verse, Chiefly Adapted to Seasons of Sickness.*

665. [**Elliott**, Charlotte]. *Morning and Evening Hymns for a Week.* (London: Charles Haselden, [1848]). 19th thousand.

E80 (author, title), JS983. E80 describes Dodgson's copy as having the author identified in Dodgson's handwriting and as being "presented to Lewis Carroll by his mother in 1849." The earliest edition in BL is published in Brighton by R. Sickelmore in 1836. The present edition is the closest to 1849, and it seems likely Mrs. Dodgson would have bought the book new.

666. Ellis, Alexander J[ohn] (1814–1890). *Algebra Identified with Geometry in a Series of Rough Notes, Forming Five Tracts: I. Euclid's Conception of Ratio and Proportion II. "Carnot's Principle" for Limits III. The Laws of Tensors; or, The Algebra of Proportion IV. The Laws of Clinants; or, The Algebra of Similar Triangles Lying upon the Same Plane V. Stigmatic Geometry; or, The Correspondence of Points in a Plane.* (London: C. F. Hodgson & Sons, 1874). 84pp.

E224 (title, author, date), JS984. E224 notes that Dodgson's copy has "initials and one correction of Lewis Carroll." Educated at Cambridge, Ellis was a philologist and mathematician. He served as both president and vice-president of the Philological Society and was a member of the Royal Society and the Society of Antiquaries.

667. Ellis, George James Welbore Agar, Lord Dover (1797–1833). *The Life of Frederic the Second, King of Prussia.* (London: Longman, Rees, Orme, Brown, and Green, 1832). 2 vols.

A905, B1042 (author, title, 2 vols. date), JS985. B1042 gives the author as Lord Dover. Ellis was the first Baron Dover and author of several works of history. He also edited correspondence of Walpole.

668. Emerson, Ralph Waldo (1803–82). *English Traits.* (London: G. Routledge & Co., 1856). 175pp.

E29 (author, title, date), JS986. 1st English edition. Emerson lectured in England in 1847 here records his impressions of the English character.

669. Emerson, Ralph Waldo. *Representative Men. Seven Lectures.* (London: G. Routledge & Co., 1850). 182pp. In the *Popular Library* series.

E32 (author, title, series, date), JS987. E32 describes this as having "Autograph [and 'Ch. Ch.'] of Lewis Carroll on title, and a few marks and notes by him." The lectures were delivered by Emerson in the United States in 1845–46 and in England in 1847. The first discusses the nature of great men, the other six are devoted to Plato, Swedenborg, Montaigne, Shakespeare, Napolean, and Goethe.

670. *Entomologists' Weekly Intelligencer*, vol. VIII and X, (1860–61).

Uncertain. F170 (title, volumes, date), not in JS. Identified as Dodgson's only by the gothic stamp. F170 list the dates, cryptically, as 1861–1. The above description seems more likely.

671. Erckmann, Émile (1822–99) and Chatrian, Pierre Alexandre (1826–90). *The Conscript. A Tale of the French War of 1813.* (London: Smith, Elder, & Co., 1870). Translated from the French work *Histoire d'un Conscrit de 1813.*

B1049 (author, French title, "with English translation in 1 vol.," date), JS988. This is the only 1870 edition of the book in either French or English listed in BL or BNF. Dodgson probably owned a made up volume which included this English edition together with an edition in French. Erckmann and Chatrian were joint authors of several novels which enjoyed success in English translations and many of which were, like the present novel, of a military nature.

672. Erskine, Thomas (1788–1870). *The Unconditional Freeness of the Gospel.* (Edinburgh: Edmonston, 1873). 159pp.

D63 (author, title, city, date), JS989. Erskine was a liberal Scottish theologian who exerted great influence through his correspondence. One of his correspondents was Dodgson's friend F. D. Maurice, the Christian Socialist. In the face of some of his Calvinist contemporaries, he declared in this work that "Christ died, not for believers, but for the world."

673. Eschwege, H. *The Knight's Tour in a Continuous and Uninterrupted Ride over 48 Boards or 3072 Squares.* (Shanklin: Silsbury Bros., 1896). [36]pp. Adapted from Byron's *Mazeppa.*

E223 (author, title, date), F140, JS990. F140 describes this as inscribed, "To the Rev. C. L. Dodgson. For auld lang syne, from his sincere friend, H. Eschwege." The author was apparently Hermann Eschwege, father of a young girl Dodgson befriended on a train journey in 1879 (see *Letters*, 350). Byron's *Mazeppa* was published in 1819. It was based on the true story of Mazeppa found in Voltaire's *The History of Charles XII, King of Sweden.* A bizarre combination of a chess puzzle (the Knight's Tour, this one provided by H. E. Dudeney) and poetry. Byron's poem is written over a series of 48 chessboards, following the path of the Knight's Tour. Dodgson's TTLG (1872) also merges chess and literature.

674. Esquirol, [Jean Étienne Dominique] (1772–1840), [and Liddell, William]. *Observations on the Illusions of the Insane, and on the Medico-legal Questions of Their Confinement.* (London: Renshaw and Rush, 1833). 89pp.

E222 (title, author [given as "M. Esquirol"], date), F170 (gives author as "Esquirol and Liddell"), JS991. F170 notes the gothic stamp. Not

in BL or BOD. LC lists the author as Esquirol, but gives William Liddell as a "related name." Perhaps he was the translator. Esquirol was a French psychiatrist and the first to combine clinical work with statistical analysis in the field of mental disorders.

675. (Eternal Punishment). *Declaration on the Inspiration of the Word of God, and the Eternity of Future Punishment, by Clergymen of the United Church of England and Ireland.* (Oxford: J. H. & J. Parker, 1864). 62pp.

C5 (title), not in JS. Only edition of the only matching title in BL. One of Dodgson's somewhat controversial theological stands was his refusal to accept the doctrine of Eternal Punishment.

676. Euclid (ca. 325–265 B.C.E.). *Elementa Geometriae [Elements of Geometry].* (Venice: Erhard Ratdolt, 25 May 1482). 137 (of 138 leaves). 1st edition, 2nd state. Translated by Adelard of Bath, edited and with commentary by Campanus of Novara. Illustrated with woodcut initials and diagrams.

Uncertain. Not in JS. Dodgson's copy was presented for auction at Bonham's on 23 February 1977 (not in DAA). In 2002, it was offered for sale by Heritage Book Shop of Los Angeles, CA, for $175,000. It has the bookplate of Henry Yates Tompson on the front pastedown and a note indicating he purchased the book at Tregaski's booksellers in London on 6 July 1898. He further notes that "This book belonged to the Revd. C. L. Dodgson/(Lewis Carroll) who besides Alice in Wonderland/etc. wrote 'Euclid & his Modern Rivals' London/1879 in which he no doubt refers to it." Arguably the most important book in the history of mathematics and one which has remained constantly in use since its origination. The fact that the book did not appear in the Brooks catalogue may mean that it was sold privately by Dodgson's executor, his brother Wilfrid, but it does not appear in Wilfrid's reckoning of income and expenses from the estate. While there is no particular reason to doubt the note on the pastedown, the absence of any other evidence placing this important volume in Dodgson's library must place it in the questionable category.

677. Euclid. *The Elements of Euclid for the Use of Schools and Colleges; Comprising the*

First Six Books and Portions of the Eleventh and Twelfth Books. (London: Macmillan & Co., 1862). 384pp. With notes by I[saac] Todhunter.

B1259.b (author, editor, date), JS995. There are 2 entries numbered 1259 in B. Dodgson owned 2 copies, the second being a reprint of 1887 (London: Macmillan and Co.), 400pp. with Notes, and Appendix and Exercises by Todhunter. This later edition is in the Houghton Library, Harvard University, a gift of Mrs. Flora V. Livingston. It has Dodgson's signature in brown ink on the front pastedown and the property label on the front cover. Additional notes on the rear endpaper do not appear to be in Dodgson's hand. See 2088 for a note on Todhunter.

678. Euclid. *Euclidis Quæ Supersunt Omnia.* Edited by David Gregory. (Oxford: At the Sheldonian Theatre, 1703). 685pp. Greek and Latin in parallel columns. With engraved frontispiece by Burghers and with numerous woodcut diagrams in the text.

D64 (author, title, editor, date), JS993. D64 notes Dodgson's signature. This may be the book referred to in A529/JS992, a handwritten entry which states simply, "Euclidis." D64 describes this as inscribed "C. L. Dodgson, 1861."

679. Euclid. *Euclid's Elements of Geometry [Books 1–6, 11–12], Chiefly from the Text of Dr. Simson, with Explanatory notes. Together with a Selection of Geometrical Exercises from the Senate-House and College Examination Papers; to which is Prefixed an Introduction, Containing a Brief Outline of the History of Geometry.* (Cambridge: University Press, 1845). 383pp. Edited by Robert Potts.

Not in JS. DAA849 (author, title, city, date). Dodgson's copy with his signature inside the front cover, was offered at Anderson Auction Co., New York on 26–27 March 1908. Robert Simson (1687–1768) was a Scottish mathematician who undertook a restoration of Euclid at the suggestion of Edmond Halley. See 1555 for a note on Potts.

680. Euclid. *Euclid's Elements of Geometry, The First Six Books, Chiefly from the Text of Dr. Simson, with Explanatory Notes; A Series of Questions on Each Book; and a Selection of Geometrical Exercises from the Senate-House and College Examination Papers; with Hints, &c.* (London: John W. Parker and Son, 1860). 361pp. The School Edition.

JS996. Dodgson's copy is in HAC. It is interleaved, with extensive commentary, corrections, solutions, etc. by him on the blank leaves (chiefly in purple ink, but some in brown ink). There are also numerous corrections in the text primarily in brown ink. Among the most highly annotated of books surviving from Dodgson's library. An earlier version of the title above.

681. Euclid. *Works.* Edition unknown.

A938 ("Euclidis Opera"), JS994.

682. (Euclid). *Schemata Geometrica ex Euclide et Aliis, Tabulis Æneis Expressa in Usum Tironum.* (Oxford: Clarendon Press, 1806). Engraved title (by Basire) + 48 geometric plates (no text).

E114 ("The Illustrations to Schemata Geometrica, in 28 copperplates, designed for the use of University students, with a fine picture engraving by Basire ... Clarendon Press, 1806."), JS468 (listed under Basire). Though E114 specifies 28 plates rather than the 48 described above, this is probably a typographical error, as the edition above matches E114 in all other respects.

683. Evans, Mark [pseud. of Paul Tidman]. *Theology for Children.* (London, 1872).

E257 (author, title, date), JS999. E257 states that Dodgson's copy has his initials on the half-title. Evans was the author of mostly religious books for children. The present title was reissued as *The Story of Our Father's Love.*

684. Evans, Sebastian (1830–1909). *Brother Fabian's Manuscript and Other Poems.* (London: Macmillan & Co., 1865). 270pp. 1st edition.

A860 (author, title [both with spelling errors], edition), JS997. Evans was educated at Cambridge and worked as a stained glass designer and artist, a poet, editor of the *Birmingham Daily Gazette,* and a lawyer. This was his first volume of verse. The title poem includes a section on Robin Hood.

685. Evans, Sebastian (1830–1909). *In the Studio. A Decade of Poems.* (London: Macmillan, 1875). 222pp. 1st edition. Includes translation from the Latin of J[ean] Charlier de Gerson (1363–1429).

A860 (author, title, edition), JS998. De Gerson was a French theologian and philosopher.

686. Evelyn, John (1620–1706). *The Life of Mrs. Godolphin.* (London: Pickering, 1848). 285pp. 3rd edition. Now first published and edited by Samuel [Wilberforce] Lord Bishop of Oxford, etc. Portrait frontispiece.

B1060 (author, title, editor, publisher, date), JS1000. B1060 states that Dodgson's copy contains presentation inscriptions to C. M. Lutwidge (1851) [Charlotte Menella Lutwidge (1807–57), Dodgson's maternal aunt] and to Dodgson (1857). Evelyn was educated at Oxford and served in public life in several capacities. On October 1672 the 20-year old Margaret Blagge (later Mrs. Godolphin) presented him with a signed declaration of "inviolable friendship." The two stayed close and he left this memoir as a manuscript at his death. When published in 1847, it received praise as a portrait of a beautiful soul. See 2252 for a note on Wilberforce.

687. Everett, J[oseph] D[avid] (1831–1904). *Units and Physical Constants.* (London: Macmillan, 1879). 175pp. 2nd edition.

E192 (title, author, date), JS1001. Everett was Professor of Mathematics at both Glasgow and King's College, Nova Scotia before becoming Professor of Natural Philosophy at Queen's College, Belfast. This work was originally published in 1875 as *Illustration to the Centimètre Gramme Second System of Units* [i.e. a metric system] (see also 1682).

688. *Every-Day Wonders; or Facts in Physiology which All Should Know*. (London: 1850). With woodcuts.

E218 (title, date), JS162 (Anon./Medical). Dodgson's copy, with his initials, was offered for sale by Maggs of London in 1911 and described as published in London in 1850. BL and other sources give no further information on this edition.

689. Ewald, Alexander Charles (1842–91). *The Life and Times of Prince Charles Stuart, Count of Albany, Commonly Called The Young Pretender. From the State Papers and Other Sources.* (London: Chapman & Hall, 1875). 2 vols. 377, 342pp.

A919 (author, title, 2 vols.), JS1002. Earliest edition and the only 2 vol. edition in BL. Charles Stuart was the grandson of King James II.

690. Ewing, Juliana Horatia (née Gatty) (1841–85). *The Brownies and Other Tales.* (London: Bell & Daldy, 1870). With 4 illustrations by George Cruikshank (the elder). 229pp.

A643 (author, title), JS1003. 1st edition. Ewing was a popular writer of stories for children, probably best known for her story *Jackanapes*. In addition to the title story, which is supposed to have suggested the name "Brownies" for the Junior Girl Guides, this collection includes "Christmas Crackers," "An Idyll of the Woods," and "The Land of Lost Toys," all originally published in *Aunt Judy's Magazine*, a publication to which Dodgson also contributed (see LCP), and which was edited by Ewing's mother, Margaret Gatty. Dodgson met Ewing on 15 March 1879.

691. (Exeter). *Pollard's Official Guide to Exeter. With an Account of the Ecclesiastical, Municipal and Commercial History of the City by Eminent Writers.* (Exeter: William Pollard & Co., 1894). 123pp. Folded plate, map.

E237 (title, date), JS1660 (listed under Pollard). E237 describes this as "in connection with Church Congress, [held in Exeter from Oct. 9–12] 1894." Dodgson's published diaries and letters do not mention his visiting Exeter.

692. F., W. B. *The Mormons. The Dream and the Reality: or, Leaves from the Sketchbook of Experience of One Who Left England to Join the Mormons in the City of Zion and Awoke to a Consciousness of its Heinous Wickedness and Abominations. Edited by a Clergyman.* (London: J. Masters, 1857). 92pp.

E342 (title, date), JS303 (Anon./Theology). JS303 lists this as "Book of Mormons" and refers not only to E342 but also to A783 ("Book of Mormons"). It is possible that these are the same book, equally possible that Dodgson owned a copy of *The Book of Mormon*, first published in 1830. See 1939–40 for other books by disenchanted English Mormons.

693. Fairlie, [Louisa] (d. 1843), editor. *Portraits of the Children of the Nobility: Engravings from Drawings by A[lfred] E[dward] Chalon and Other Artists…. With Illustrations in Verse by Distinguished Contributors.* (London: 1839). 2nd series. Engraved by Charles Heath. Includes engravings after Edwin Landseer.

A285, E60 (title, illustrators, editor, date), JS1004. Fairlie was a gentlelady whose editing of this and similar books was her only foray into public life.

694. Falconer, John (fl. 1685–92). *Cryptomenysis Patefacta: or The Art of Secret Information Disclosed Without a Key. Containing Plain and Demonstrative Rules for Decyphering All Manner of Secret Writing.* (London: Printed for Daniel Brown, 1685). 180pp. 1st edition.

B1050 (author, title, date), JS1005. An important early treatise on cryptography that includes a section on semeiology, defined by Falconer as "methods of secret information by signs and gestures." Dodgson was interested in cryptography, and invented at least two ciphers—the Alphabet Cipher and the Telegraph Cipher (see WMGC).

695. Faraday, Michael (1791–1867). *Faraday's Lectures.* Details unknown.

"Faraday's Lectures" listed in A303/JS1006. Faraday was a pioneering British chemist and physicist, especially known for his work on electricity and magnetism. BL lists 4 collections of lectures by Faraday published before 1898:
A Course of Six Lectures on the Various Forces of Matter and their Relations to Each Other. (London: Richard Griffin and Co., 1860). Edited by William Crookes.
A Course of Six Lectures on the Chemical History of a Candle; to Which is Added a Lecture on Platinum. (London: 1861). Edited by William Crookes.
The Subject Matter of a Course of Six Lectures on the Non-Metallic Elements. (London: 1853). Arranged by John Scoffern.
On the Various Forces of Nature and their Relations to Each Other. A Course of Lectures Delivered before a Juvenile Audience at the Royal Institution. (London: Chatto and Windus, [1874]). Edited by William Crookes.

696. Faraday, Michael and Henry Bence Jones (1814–73), editor. *The Life and Letters of [Michael] Faraday.* (London: Longmans, Green, and Co., 1870). 2 vols. 427, 499pp.

A905, B1051 (author, title, 2 vols. date), JS1007. Jones attended Trinity College, Cambridge and was a physician to St. George's Hospital, London. *Saturday Review* wrote, "Faraday's letters … his laboratory note-books, his Trinity House and other reports and memoranda, have furnished the materials for the biography before us. The connecting matter contributed by the editor is the slightest possible in quantity, and in quality seldom other than monotonous and dull."

697. Farrar, Frederic W[illiam] (1831–1903). *Eternal Hope. Five Sermons Preached in Westminster Abbey November and December, 1877.* (London: Macmillan, 1878). 226pp.

A789 (author, title), JS1008. 1st edition as described in MBC (Feb. 1878). Farrar was a canon of Westminster at the time he preached these sermons; he later rose to the post of Dean of Canterbury. He was educated at King's College, London, and influenced in his Broad Church views by Dodgson's friend the Christian Socialist F. D. Maurice. This book questioned the doctrine of Eternal Punishment, something Dodgson did in his own, unpublished, essay on the subject. *Eternal Hope* evoked a flurry of responses on the subject of Eternal Punishment (see 1602).

698. Farrar, [Frederic William], and others. *Inspiration, A Clerical Symposium on 'In What Sense, and Within What Limits, is the Bible the Word of God?'* (London: Nisbet, 1884). 242pp. Reprinted from *The Homiletic Magazine*.

D92 (title, author, city, date), JS1010.

699. Farrar, Frederic W[illiam]. *The Life of Christ.* (London: Cassell, Petter & Galpin, 1874). 2 vols.

A801 (author, title, 2 vols.), JS1009. Earliest edition in BL. This title went through many printings in 1874. As early as 1875 the two volumes each featured a frontispiece by the painter William Holman Hunt (see 700) which certainly would have appealed to Dodgson. This biography of Christ was written in a popular style, but nonetheless had great depth of scholarship.

HOLMAN HUNT, *Del.*

Interior of the carpenter's shop at Nazareth. Holman Hunt's frontispiece to vol. 1 of Farrar's *Life of Christ* (item 699).

700. Farrar, Frederic William and Mrs. Meynell [Alice C. Thompson]. *William Hunt. His Life & Work.* (London: The Art Journal, 1893). 32pp. Christmas number of *The Art Journal.*

A277, F150, not numbered in JS. Only edition in BL. F150 states that Dodgson's copy had his initials on the half-title. In addition to writing on art, Thompson was a writer of light plays. Holman Hunt (1827–1910) was a founding member of the Pre-Raphaelite Brotherhood. Dodgson met Hunt at Christ Church on 13 June 1857. His poem "After Three Days" (1860) was based on his viewing of Hunt's painting "The Finding of Christ in the Temple." Dodgson was a frequent visitor to Hunt's London studio, especially during the period 1863–65. In 1872 he photographed the artist and his son, Cyril.

701. Fasnacht, George Eugène. *Macmillan's Progressive French Course. II. Second Year.* (London: Macmillan & Co., 1884). 219pp. A new edition, enlarged, etc.

E77 (title, author, date), JS1011.

702. Faussett, Robert Godfrey (b. ca. 1827). *The Symmetry of Time: Being an Outline of Biblical Chronology Adapted to a Continuous Succession of Weeks of Years. From the Creation of Adam to the Exodus.* (Oxford: Parker & Co., 1881). 155pp.

E59 (title, author, date), F141, JS1012. According to E59, Dodgson's was a presentation copy from the author. Faussett was a colleague of Dodgson at Christ Church and served as mathematical lecturer until leaving for the Crimea in 1855. Dodgson often defended Faussett, and mentions him frequently in his diaries (see also *Letters*, 14).

703. Fergusson, William (1808–77). *Lectures on the Progress of Anatomy and Surgery during the Present Century.* (London: Churchill, 1867). 302pp.

A538, D69 (author, title, city, date), JS166 (Anon./Medical), JS1013. Fergusson was an influential Scottish physician who eventually worked in London and served as Professor of Surgery at King's College. He invented a number of surgical instruments, some of which continue in use today and he introduced the practice of "conservative surgery," in which joints were excised rather than limbs being amputated.

704. Fern, Fanny [pseud. of Sarah Payson Willis, later Eldredge, later Parton] (1811–72). *Fern Leaves from Fanny's Portfolio.* (London: Ingram, Cooke, and Co., 1853). 326pp. Illustrated by Birket Foster (engraved by Edmund Evans).

A640 (title, illustrator), JS1030 (listed under Foster). Earliest Foster edition in BL. "Fanny Fern" was the daughter of the founder of the American periodical *Youth's Companion* and wrote humorous essays for many New England publications. A number of these pieces were collected in *Fern Leaves*, which proved a bestseller. A second series was also published. In her book *Outlines of Men, Women, and Things*, Mary Clemmer Ames called "Fanny Fern" "one of the earliest to prove to American women that an honorable independence is within the reach of all who bring to bear upon any avocation to which they are adapted the industry, the faithfulness, the fearlessness, which characterized her." Foster (1825–99) was a friend of William Morris and Edward Burne-Jones but his rustic watercolors were not Pre-Raphaelite in style. In addition to his work as a painter he illustrated many books.

705. [**Ferrier**, Susan Edmonstone] (1782–1854). *Destiny; or, the Chief's Daughter.* (Edinburgh: Robert Cadell; London: Whittaker & Co., 1831). 3 vols. 337, 407, 399pp. 1st edition.

A812, D70 (author, title, 3 vols., city, date, edition), JS1014. Ferrier was the daughter of a Scottish lawyer who wrote three satirical novels about Edinburgh society. She stopped writing when she became an evangelical and member of the Free Church.

706. [**Ferrier**, Susan Edmonstone]. *The Inheritance.* (Edinburgh: Blackwood, 1824). 3 vols. 387, 415, 359pp. 1st edition.

A812, D70 (author, title, 3 vols., city, date, edition), JS1015. A story about a young woman who almost loses her inheritance because she chooses a husband of whom her lord disapproves.

707. [**Ferrier**, Susan Edmonstone]. *Marriage, A Novel.* (Edinburgh: William Blackwood; London: John Murray, 1818). 3 vols. [320], 314, [344]pp. 1st edition.

A812, D70 (author, title, 3 vols., city, date, edition), JS1016. The story of young Scottish women choosing their husbands and then living with the consequences of their choices.

708. Feuchtersleben, Ernst, Freiherr von (1806–49). *Hygiène de l'Âme.* (Paris: J. B. Baillière et Fils, 1870). 283pp. 3rd edition. Translated from the German of the 24th edition (of *Zur Diatetik der Seele*) by Schlesinger-Rahier.

E99 (author, title, date), JS1017. E99 states, "This work, if not already translated into English for the use of the medical profession, should be; it is a valuable study of the influence of the patient's mind upon his body." Dodgson's copy is WWC. It has the gothic stamp and has the property label on the front cover. Feuchtersleben was an Austrian physician, philosopher, and poet.

709. Field, Mrs. E. M. [Louise Frances Field, née Story] (1856–1940). *The Child and His Book. Some Account of the History and Progress of Children's Literature in England.* (London: Wells Gardner & Co., [1891]). 356pp. Illustrated.

A310, E279 (author, title), F173, JS1019. F173 notes "n.d." BL lists a 2nd edition, also undated but published in 1895 (this 2nd edition was originally published in a dated 1892 edition, not listed in BL). F173 notes the gothic stamp. The author wrote several stories for children. This book is a history of writings for children in England. It contains only a passing reference to Dodgson's works: AAIW is included in a list of "play-hour occupations of grave men."

710. Finden, William (1787–1852). *Finden's Gallery of the Graces: A Series of Portrait Illustrations of British Poets from Paintings Designed Expressly for this Work by the Most Eminent British Artists.* (London: C. Tilt, 1837). [80]pp. 36 plates.

Uncertain. F180 (author, title, date), not numbered in JS (listed under Anon./Art). Identified as Dodgson's only by the gothic stamp. Finden, along with his brother Edward Francis, was a successful engraver. This work is an illustrated anthology of poetry with excerpts from Byron, Thomas Campbell, Shakespeare,

Shelley, Wordsworth, and others. It was illustrated with engraved reproductions of works by W. Boxall, A. E. Chalon, Edwin Landseer, E. T. Parris, J. W. Wright, and others.

711. *Fisher's Drawing Room Scrapbook for 1844*. (London: Fisher, Son, and Jackson, 1844). Plates.

Uncertain. F180 (author, title, date), not numbered in JS (listed under Anon./Art). Identified as Dodgson's only by the gothic stamp. BL lists issues of this periodical from 1832 to 1851. The annual volume consisted of a collection of steel engravings with accompanying text in poetry or descriptive prose.

712. Fiske, N[athan] W[elby] (1798–1847). *Outlines of Mental Philosophy or Psychology in a System of Questions*. (Amherst [MA]: J. S. & C. Adams, 1842). 72pp.

A522 ("Outlines of Mental Philosophy"), JS273 (Anon./Science). No matching title in BL or BOD. This title from the catalogue of the Yale University Library is the only possible match traced. Fiske was a professor of languages at Amherst College and the father of Helen Hunt Jackson.

713. Fitzgerald, Percy (1834–1925). *Principles of Comedy and Dramatic Effect*. (London: Tinsley Brothers, 1870). 368pp.

A676 (title), JS296 (Anon./Theatre). Only edition of the only matching title in BL. Dodgson read this book in 1872 and wrote the author about the possibility of staging *Alice* (see *Letters*, 180; *Alice on Stage*, 21–22). Fitzgerald was an Irishman and prolific writer despite his work as a crown prosecutor. Many of his novels were first published in Dickens' journal *All the Year Round*. This work includes chapters on "The Dramatists," "Comedy," "Burlesque," "The French Stage," "Actors Past and Present," "The Actors of the Day," and "The Music Hall Question."

714. Fitzgerald, Percy. *The Romance of The English Stage*. (London: Richard Bentley and Son, 1874). 2 vols. 334, 328pp.

A676 (author, title, 2 vols.), JS1020. Only edition in BL. *Saturday Review* wrote of this work, "there is but meagre information about the stage, and the romance has to be supplied by the reader's imagination."

715. Fitzpatrick, William John (1830–95). *Who Wrote the Earlier Waverley Novels? An Essay Showing that Sir W. Scott's Relation to Waverley, Guy Mannering, Rob Roy, The Antiquary and the Tales of My Landlord was, at the Most, that of an Editor*. (London: Effingham Wilson, 1856). 120pp.

E33 (author, title, page count, date [1857]), JS1021. No 1857 edition traced, but NUC, BL and BOD all list this as the only edition matching all the particulars of E33. Fitzpatrick was an Irish Catholic historian and author of several biographies. First published as a series of letters to *Notes and Queries* and then earlier in 1856 in an 88-page edition as *Who wrote the Waverley Novels? Being an Investigation into Certain Mysterious Circumstances Attending their Production, and an Inquiry into the Literary Aid which Sir W. Scott may have Received from other Persons*, this book conjectures that the novels were, in fact, largely written by Thomas and Elizabeth Scott, the brother and sister-in-law of Walter Scott.

716. Fitzvictor, John [pseud. of Percy Bysshe Shelley and Thomas Jefferson Hogg (1792–1862)]. *Posthumous Fragments of Margaret Nicholson. Being Poems Found Amongst the Papers of that Noted Female who Attempted the Life of the King in 1786*. (Oxford: T. Munday, 1810). 29pp.

A548 (author [Shelley], title, city, date), JS1868 (listed under Shelley). Nicholson was an insane washerwoman who tried to assassinate King George III. Shelley's burlesque, written with the help of his friend and biographer Hogg, earned both men expulsion from Oxford. Nicholson was still living when the book was published. The 1810 1st edition is excessively rare (a 1924 census lists six copies), and if Dodgson did own a copy, as described in A548, he might rightly have treasured it (his copy brought £1 3s at auction). More likely is that his copy was of the exact facsimile published in London by Richard Herne Shepherd, ca. 1870, which is itself an uncommon book today.

717. Flint, Austin (the younger) (b. 1836). *The Physiology of Man; Designed to Represent the Existing State of Physiological Science as Applied to the Functions of the Human Body*. (New York: D. Appleton & Co., 1866–74). 5 vols. 502, 556, 526, 470, 517pp.

A512 (author, title, 5 vols.), JS1022. Only edition in BL. Flint was a Massachusetts-born physiologist who served as Professor of Physiology and Microscopic Anatomy at Bellevue Hospital Medical College and as surgeon general of New York State. *The Nation* said this book was "The best summary of human physiology in the English language."

718. Foote, Edward Bliss (1829–1906). *Plain Home Talk about the Human System ... Embracing Medical Common Sense.* (London: A. Lobell, 1873). 912pp.

A570 (author, "Plain Home Talk"), JS1023. Earliest British edition in BL. Foote was an early advocate of birth control and was convicted under the Comstock laws of distributing a birth control pamphlet through the mail. Originally published in 1870, this work was frequently reprinted, especially by Murray Hill Publishing Company of New York City. The 1896 revised edition carried this title: *Plain Home Talk about the Human System — The Habits of Men and Women — The Causes and Prevention of Disease — Our Sexual Relations and Social Natures. Embracing Medical Common Sense Applied to Causes, Prevention, and Cure of Chronic Diseases — The Natural Relations of Men and Women to Each Other — Society — Love — Marriage — Parentage, Etc.*

719. Forrester, Charles Robert (1803–50). *Tom Thumb.* (London: Wm. S. Orr & Co., [1844]). 55pp. + plates. Illustrations by Alfred Crowquill. In the *Comic Nursery Tales* series.

A483 (title, series, publisher), JS48 (Anon./Children's). Earliest edition traced. Forrester wrote light literature under the pseudonym Alfred Crowquill, the same name that his younger brother Alfred used to sign his illustrations (as in the present book). Charles Robert was a public notary but devoted much of his time to writing for periodicals. See 505 for a note on Crowquill the illustrator. Tom Thumb is a folk character who appears in the folklore of several countries including England. He is the size of a thumb.

720. Forster, Charles (1790–1871). *A Harmony of Primeval Alphabets.* (London: Day & Son, n.d. [ca. 1860]). Single sheet.

E154 (title), JS1031 (listed under Foster, A.). Dodgson's copy sold at Sotheby's, London on 29 June or 9 July 1984 and is in the collection formed by Jeffrey Stern, now at Seitoku Gakuin College, Tokyo, Japan. Forster was an Essex rector educated at Trinity College, Dublin. He was the author of several books on religion and the Holy Land, and a contributor to the volume *Essays and Reviews* (see 2075). Single lithographed sheet, folded, linen-backed, with reproductions of 45 alphabets, including Arabic, Hebrew, Sinai, and Rosetta.

721. Forster, John (1812–76). *The Life of Charles Dickens.* (London: Chapman & Hall, 1872–74). 3 vols. 398, 462, 552pp.

A908 (author, title, 3 vols.), JS1026. 1st edition. Forster served as commissioner of lunacy, but devoted much of his time to literary pursuits. He was a Dickens' closest friend and well suited to write this, the first major biography of the novelist. Dodgson appears to have met Forster, and wrote him at least one letter (see *Letters*, 699).

722. Foster, Joseph (1844–1905). *Alumni Oxonienses: The Members of the University of Oxford, 1715–1886: Their Parentage, Birthplace, and Year of Birth, with a Record of their Degrees. Being the Matriculation Register of the University, Alphabetically Arranged, Revised and Annotated.* (Oxford: Parker and Co., 1887–92). 4 vols. 1633pp. Illustrated with plates after Rudolph Ackermann and others.

A520, D71 (author, title, city, date, 8 vols.), JS1027. D71 notes Dodgson's initials. BL does not list an edition that precisely matches the description in D71. The book was published in 4 large volumes, but D71 states that Dodgson's was bound in "half brown morocco," so it seems he had his 4 volumes bound as 8 (and probably to match his *Oxford Men and Their Colleges,* see 724). Foster was the author of many genealogical works, biographical dictionaries, etc. Dodgson is listed on p. 375 of the 1888 edition. His father and other relatives are listed on pp. 375–76.

723. Foster, Joseph. *Index Ecclesiasticus; or, Alphabetical Lists of all Ecclesiastical Dignitaries in England and Wales Since the Reformation ... Including those Names which Appear in Le Neve's 'Fasti.' Volume for 1800–1840.* (Oxford: Parker & Co., 1890). 200pp.

A520, D72 (author, title, city, date), JS1029. D72 notes Dodgson's initials. Le Neve's Fasti is:

Le Neve, John. *Fasti Ecclesiæ Anglicanæ: or, An Essay Towards Deducing a Regular Succession of all the Principal Dignitaries in Each Cathedral, Collegiate Church or Chapel ... in ... England and Wales, from the First Erection thereof.... To which is Added, the Succession of the Prebendaries in each Prebendal Stall ... As also of the Heads ... of each College ... in Either of our Universities.* The earliest edition in BL is 1716. The present volume includes an entry for Dodgson's father, Charles Dodgson, listing him as perpetual curate of Daresbury.

724. Foster, Joseph. *Oxford Men and Their Colleges.* (Oxford and London: James Parker & Co., 1893). 663pp. Illustrated with portraits and views from Loggan, Hearne, Skelton, Ackermann and others.

A521 (author, title, 2 vols.), JS1028. Only edition in BL. The book was published in 1 large volume, but A521 states that Dodgson's was bound in "half brown morocco," so it seems likely he had his 1 volume bound as 2 (and probably to match his *Alumni Oxonienses*, see 722). Dodgson is listed on p. 407 under "Students of Christ Church."

725. Fothergill, J[ohn] Milner (1841–88). *The Maintenance of Health; A Medical Work for Lay Readers.* (London: Smith, Elder, 1874). 399pp.

Uncertain. A511 ("Maintenance of Health"), JS167 (Anon./Medical, not listed separately from other works). 1st edition of the closest match in BL. This seems a likely book for Dodgson to own. The only other possibility in BL is: *An Essay on the Maintenance of Health* by Henry Lowndes (London: Churchill, 1867). Fothergill was a physician practicing in London. He wrote medical books on diagnosis, diet, treatment, and other topics, as well as one novel, *Gaythorne Hall.*

726. Fowler, Thomas (1832–1904). *Elements of Deductive Logic: Designed Mainly for the Use of Junior Students in the Universities.* (Oxford: Clarendon Press, 1867). 174pp. 2nd edition.

Uncertain. Not in JS. Listed in WS only and identified by gothic stamp and property label only. Fowler was an undergraduate at Merton College, Oxford, and was a fellow of Lincoln College from 1855 to 1881 before becoming president of Corpus Christi College. He also served as Wykeham Professor of Logic. He was

a close friend of Dodgson and is mentioned often in the published diaries.

727. [Fraser, William] (1824–1877). *A Plain Commentary on the Book of Psalms (the Prayer-book Version,) Chiefly Founded on the Fathers.* (Oxford: J. H. & J. Parker, 1857). 2 vols.

A787 (title), B988 (title, author [attributed to J. W. Burgon], 2 vols., date), JS616 (listed under Burgon). The incorrect authorial attribution in B988 is probably due to the fact that the other item in lot A787 was *Burgon's Plain Commentary on the Four Holy Gospels* (see 297). Since this second item was published anonymously with a similar title, it was natural to assume Burgon was the author. William Fraser was educated at Worcester College, Oxford and served as vicar of Alton, Staffordshire. The Oxford Movement brought a resurgence of interest in the early church fathers, including a series of new translations of their writings (one volume translated by Dodgson's father).

728. Freeman, Edward Augustus (1823–1892). *Disestablishment and Disendowment, What Are They?* (London: Macmillan and Co., 1874). 76pp. Reprinted, with additions, from the *Pall Mall Gazette.*

Not in JS. In a letter to S. J. Owen on 8 March 1883, Dodgson writes, "I really think you would do a national service if you would persuade Mr. Freeman to publish, in a cheap popular form, the marrow of his excellent little book on *Disestablishment and Disendowment....* A 2*d.* pamphlet, containing its essence, would I think have a great sale and do great good." The 2nd edition of 1885 reduced the price from 2*s.* 6*d.* to 1*s.* Freeman was a fellow of Trinity College, Oxford. Cohen (in *Letters,* 487) quotes from this book, "Even if the notion of disestablishment ... should be pressed to the extremist point, all that it would demand in the way of confiscation or disendowment would be the surrender of such parts of the property of the Church as have come from direct parliamentary grants."

729. Freiligrath-Kroeker, Kate (1845–1904). *Alice and Other Fairy Plays for Children.* (London: W. Swan Sonnenschein and Allen, 1880 [1879]). 296pp. With 8 original plates (two illustrations of *Alice*), and 4 picture initials (one of *Alice*) by Mary Sibree.

A673 (title), not in JS. "Alice," appears on pp. [5]–64 and includes scenes from AAIW and TTLG plus musical settings for "Speak Roughly" and "Beautiful Soup." In the preface, the author writes, "I have to express my sincerest gratitude to Mr. Lewis Carroll for the permission to dramatise his charming story." Dodgson received his copy of this book from the author in November 1879. See *Alice on Stage*, 32–33 for more on this, the first printed dramatic adaptation of the *Alice* stories.

730. Freiligrath-Kroeker, Kate. *Alice thro' the Looking-Glass and Other Fairy Plays for Children*. (London: W. Swan Sonnenschein and Co., n.d. [ca. 1882]). 202pp. With an uncredited frontispiece of Alice and the Tweedles.

A726 (title), JS1032. The title play appears on pp. 9–50 and draws only from TTLG. In her preface the author writes, "sincerest thanks to Mr. Lewis Carroll, for his renewed kind permission to dramatise 'Through the Looking Glass'."

731. Frere, M[ary] (1845–1911). *Old Deccan Days; or, Hindoo Fairy Legends, Current in Southern India. Collected from Oral Tradition*. (London: John Murray, 1868). 331pp. With an introduction and notes by Sir Bartle Frere. Illustrations by C. F. Frere.

A647 (author, title), JS1033. Earliest edition in BL. Frere was the daughter of Sir Henry Bartle Edward Frere who served as governor of Bombay from 1862 to 1867, during which time the author doubtlessly collected these stories. *Saturday Review* wrote that, "For children the book is delightful, and will have a charm scarcely less than that of the Teutonic and Scandinavian tales with which they are daily growing more familiar."

732. Freund, John Christian (b. ca. 1849), editor. *The Dark Blue*. (London: S. Low, 1871–73). Only Vol. 1 no. 1–vol. 5 no. 1 were published.

Uncertain. F171 (title, contributors, issues not noted), not numbered in JS (listed under Anon./Periodicals). Identified as Dodgson's only by gothic stamp (though F171 leaves some doubt even as to that in its wording). Copies in HAC lack the gothic stamp. Freund was educated at Exeter College, Oxford, where he matriculated in 1868. Includes contributions by A.

C. Swinburne, Frederick Locker, Karl Blind, Andrew Lang, and W. M. Rossetti.

733. Frölich, L[orenz]. *The Little Darling at the Sea-side: A Series of Drawings by L[orenz] Frölich*. Text by her mamma. (London: Trübner & Co., [1863]). 20 leaves, printed one side only. Translated by Mrs. George Hooper [i.e. Jane Margaret Winnard].

A532 (title), JS62 (Anon./Children). Only edition of the only matching title in BL. Frölich was a Danish artist who illustrated works by Jules Verne, Hans Christian Andersen, and others (see index). Hooper was the wife of the journalist George Hooper (1824–90) and the author of several books for children. Illustrated children's book.

734. Frost, A[rthur] B[urdett] (1851–1928). *Stuff and Nonsense*. (New York: Charles Scribner's Sons, 1888). 92pp. With illustrations.

Not in JS. Frost presented this volume of comic drawings and nonsense verse to Dodgson in a letter dated 13 November 1884. As the letter was sent from Long Island, New York, the American edition seems likely. This was the first book written and illustrated by Frost, who later illustrated *Rhyme and Reason?* and *A Tangled Tale* for Dodgson (see *Illustrators*). He was perhaps best known for his illustrations to the *Uncle Remus* books. Dodgson wrote to Frost on 24 February 1885, "I think I would rather not criticise *Stuff and Nonsense*. The fun turns too exclusively on depicting brutal violence, terror, and physical pain, and even death, none of which are funny to me."

735. Frost, Percival (the elder) (1817–98). *An Elementary Treatise on Curve Tracing*. (London: Macmillan, 1872). 208pp.

A582 (author, title), JS1035. Only edition in BL or MBC. Frost was a mathematical lecturer at King's College, Cambridge.

736. Frost, Thomas (1821–1908). *Circus Life and Circus Celebrities*. (London: Tinsley Brothers, 1875). 328pp.

A657 (title only), JS286 (Anon./Theatre). Only matching title in BL and the earliest edition listed. A brief outline of the history of the circus in England is followed by descriptions of many circuses and circus acts.

737. Froude, James Anthony (1818–94). *Oceana, or England and Her Colonies.* (London: Longmans & Co., 1886). 341pp. Illustrated.

A918 (author, title), JS1038. Earliest edition in BL. Originally a follower of the High Church party, like his older brother Richard Hurrell Froude, James became disenchanted with that party and his repudiation of it led to the end of his career at Oxford. He spent most of his career working as a historian known for the literary quality (if not always the strict historical accuracy) of his works. This book is an early study of life in the British Empire with special attention to Australia and New Zealand, but also information on India, South Africa, and North America. See 2332 for another work by Froude.

738. Froude, James Anthony. *Short Studies on Great Subjects.* (London: Longmans, Green, and Co., 1867). 2 vols. [1st series].

A336 (author, title), D73 (author, title, "First Series," city, date), JS1036. D73 notes Dodgson's initials. This is the only 1867 edition listed in BL. Neither A336 nor D73 specify 2 vols. It is possible that Dodgson owned this edition but only one of the volumes. A336 states only "Froude's Short Studies," so it is also possible that this represents a later volume in the series (at least 4 series were published). A work of popular history.

739. [Fryer, Michael] (1774–1844). *The Trial and Life of Eugene Aram; Several of his Letters and Poems; and his Plan and Specimens of an Anglo-Celtic Lexicon.* (Richmond: M. Bell, 1842). 124pp. With copious notes and illustrations, and an engraved facsimile, etc.

D65 (title, city, date), JS410 (listed under Aram). The story of Eugene Aram was the subject of a poem by Hood (*The Dream of Eugene Aram The Murderer*) and a novel by Bulwer-Lytton (*Eugene Aram, A Tale*). Aram was a linguist who discovered the relationship between the Celtic languages and other European languages. He was arrested in 1758 for the 1745 murder of his friend Daniel Clark. Aram and his accomplice Richard Houseman had induced Clark to obtain a large number of valuables on credit. They lured him to a field where Aram killed and buried him. Aram was found guilty on Houseman's evidence and hanged at York on 6 August 1759.

740. Fuller, Samuel (d. 1736). *A Mathematical Miscellany, in Four Parts. I. An Essay Towards the Probable Solution of the Forty-five Surprizing Paradoxes in Gordon's Geography. II. Fifty-five New and Amazing Paradoxes.* (London: Printed for M. Cooper, 1751).

E386 ("Paradoxes—a Mathematical Miscellany, 1751), JS152 (Anon./Mathematics). Earliest edition traced. E386 implies that Dodgson owned only the sections relating to paradoxes, although all 4 parts were bound in a volume of 220pp. The other parts were: *III. An Algebraical Solution to the Problem Left Unanswered in Hill's Arithmetick, and Alexander's Algebra* and *IV. Miscellaneous Rules.*

741. Fullom, Stephen Watson (d. 1872). *The History of Woman, and Her Connexion with Religion, Civilization, and Domestic Manners, from the Earliest Period.* (London: G. Routledge & Co., 1855). 407pp. 3rd edition, revised.

A588, D235, JS1042. Dodgson's copy is in HAC. It is inscribed at the top of the title page "Margt. A. Lutwidge [Dodgson's Aunt] from Mrs. Mills." The initials "C. L. D." are to the left of the inscription in pencil (not the monogram). The inscription has been marked through in pencil. With a frontispiece of Florence Nightingale.

742. Furniss, Harry (1854–1925) and E. T. Milliken. *Holiday Romps.* (London: George

Comic illustration of a bathing machine by Harry Furniss from *Holiday Romps* (item 742).

Routledge, n.d.). 27pp. Illustrations by Furniss, with accompanying verses by Milliken.

F183, JS1046, see 743 note. Dodgson's copy is in HAC and is identified only by the gothic stamp. Harry Furniss was a cartoonist and illustrator. He drew for *Punch* and illustrated books, including Dodgson's *Sylvie and Bruno* books. The *Romps* series consisted of comic verses written to accompany comic illustrations by Furniss. The present title includes a comic depiction of a bathing-machine. See index for other items illustrated by Furniss.

743. Furniss, Harry and E. T. Milliken. *Romps all the Year Round.* (London: G. Routledge & Sons, [1886]). 27pp. Illustrations by Furniss, with accompanying verses by Milliken.

E40 (title, illustrator), JS1043 (title given only as "Romps"). Only edition in BL. This title and *Holiday Romps* were also issued together in a single volume under the cover title *More Romps*, which Dodgson also probably owned. In a letter to Harry Furniss on 13 December 1886, Dodgson writes, " I see *More Romps* is noticed in the *Observer*, and have ordered it, if it's a new one: I have 3 already (Seaside, Town, Holiday)" (see *Illustrators*, 135).

744. Furniss, Harry and Horace Lennard. *Romps at the Sea-side. Romps in Town.* (London: G. Routledge & Sons, 1855). 28, 27pp. Illustrations by Furniss, with accompanying verses by Lennard.

A541, E292, part of JS1043, JS1045. Dodgson's copy is in HAC. It has the gothic stamp on the title page. His copy of these two titles is bound together under the cover title *Romps*. F183 describes another copy of *Romps in Town* apparently issued separately (and with the gothic stamp). In a letter to Harry Furniss on 21 September 1889 Dodgson wrote of an illustration he wanted, "don't draw a podgy boy, a great eater of pudding, like the one on the left of p. 7 of *Romps by the Seaside*" (see *Illustrators*, 166).

745. Furniss, Harry. *Royal Academy Antics.* (London: Cassell & Co., 1890). 111pp. With more than 60 illustrations.

Not in JS. In a letter of 15 August 1890, Dodgson thanks Furniss for an inscribed copy of this book. Only edition in BL. An illustrated humorous look at the R. A. Furniss writes, "My object is to point out the necessity of a National Academy of Art in England … In doing this I may make the Royal Academy appear ridiculous." Only edition in BL.

746. G, W. A. [pseud. of John Lewis Roget] (1828–1908). *Familiar Illustrations of the Language of Mathematics, or, A New Picture-alphabet for Well-behaved Undergraduates Wherein a Ray to Illumine their Path is Transmitted through Nine Plates of a Rare Medium by Means of the Eccentrical Pencil of W. A. G.* (London: Ackerman & Co., 1850).

A279 (title), D67, (title, pseudonym, city, date, publisher), JS1756 (listed under Roget). Roget was a cartoonist and writer on art who also edited a new edition of the Thesaurus first compiled by Peter Mark Roget. A collection of humorous cartoons of Cambridge life.

747. Gairdner, James and James Spedding. *Studies in English History.* (Edinburgh: D. Douglas, 1881). 324pp.

A875, D74 (authors, title, city, date), JS1047. Gairdner worked in the Public Record Office and wrote a number of works on history, particularly on British royalty and on documents preserved in the Public Record Office. Spedding was educated at Cambridge where he traveled in literary circles. His primary work was on Francis Bacon.

748. G[albraith], J[oseph] A[llen] and S[amuel] H[aughton] (1821–97). *Manual of Tides and Tidal Currents.* (London: 1862). 2nd edition.

E143 (authors, title, date), JS1048.

749. Gall, James (the younger) (1808–95). *An Easy Guide to the Constellations, with a Miniature Atlas of the Stars and Key Maps.* (Edinburgh [printed], London: [1870]).

E79 (author, title), JS1049. E79 notes Dodgson's initials. An undated "new and enlarged edition" of 62pp. was published in London by Gall & Inglis. This copy may have appeared at auction on 6 February 1929 at Hodgson's, London (see DAA1387). That copy is described as inscribed from Dodgson to Winifred Schuster, but the date of the inscription is Oct. 22, 1898, several months after Dodgson's death. Perhaps that copy was inscribed by Schuster as being from his library. The Schuster copy was also sold at the Leicester Harmsworth sale at

Sotheby's, London, 26 March 1947. Gall was a Scottish born author of numerous religious works, including works claiming that dipping is not true baptism, and that Good Friday is a "chronological mistake."

750. Galton, Francis (1822–1911). *Hereditary Genius: An Enquiry into its Laws and Consequences.* (London: Macmillan and Co., 1869). 390pp.

A921 ("Gallows' Hereditary Genius"), JS1050. BL lists no work by this or any similar title under Gallows or Gallow. This work is almost certainly the one referred to (as JS conjectures). Earliest edition in BL. Galton was Charles Darwin's cousin who, after traveling in Africa, settled in London as a gentleman scientist. Galton worked in many scientific areas— he produced the first newspaper weather map and was an early proponent of fingerprint evidence. In this highly important work he studied the families of great men and concluded that scholarly, artistic, and athletic talents are hereditary. This book is seminal in the science of eugenics, a term coined by Galton.

751. Galton, Francis. *Inquiries into Human Faculty and its Development.* (London: Macmillan & Co., 1883). 390pp. 1st edition.

B1054 (author, title, date), JS1051. A continuation of Galton's work on heredity. It was in this book that he introduced his new word — eugenics.

752. Gardiner, Marguerite (née Margaret Power) (1789–1849). *The Governess.* (London: Longman, Orme, Brown, Green, and Longmans, 1839). 2 vols.

Uncertain. A609 ("The Governess, 2 vols."), not separately listed in JS (who lists A609 under *Book for Governesses* (see 1515) in Anon./Education). There are several possible titles in BL, but this is the only one listed in 2 vols. The only other multi-volume possibilities seem to be *The Governess: a Repertory of Female Education*, a periodical published in the 1850s (BL lists vols. 4–7, [1855]) or *The Governess. A Ladies' Literary Monthly*, Edited by J[oseph] Hughes begun in 1882 and continued in 1883 as *The Governess and Head-Mistress. A Weekly Journal for Certificated and High School Teachers*, 2 volumes. Sarah Fielding's 18th-century work *The Governess; or, Little Female Academy* and its 19th-century "recasting" by Mrs. Sherwood (née Mary Martha Butt) are listed in several editions

in BL, but none in 2 volumes. Gardiner was Countess of Blessington and a fixture in the London literary world of the early 19th century. She presided over fashionable salons, wrote poetry, novels, and travel books, and edited popular annuals and gift books. She had a long and scandalous relationship with Alfred, Count d'Orsay, twelve years her junior. The present volume is one of her novels of manners.

753. Gardner, James. *The Faiths of the World. An Account of All Religions and Religious Sects, their Doctrines, Rites, Ceremonies, and Customs.* (Edinburgh: A. Fullarton & Co., [1858–60]). 2 vols. 992, 930pp.

A753 ("Faiths of the World, 2 vols."), JS314 (Anon./Theology). This is the only matching title in BL that was published in 2 vols. and the only 2-volume edition in BL. Gardner was a clergyman whose works included several volumes of "memoirs" of Christians.

754. Gardner, John (1804–1880). *Household Medicine and Sick-room Guide: A Familiar Description of Diseases, Remedies and Methods of Treatment, Diet &c. Expressly Adapted for Family Use.* (London: 1878). 9th edition.

A536 ("Household Medicine and Sick Room Guide"), JS164 (Anon./Medical). Published in 1861 under the title *Household Medicine: Containing a Familiar Description of Diseases, Their Nature, Causes and Symptoms; the Most Approved Methods of Treatment, etc.* Earliest edition traced that adds "Sick-room Guide" to the title. Later London editions were published by Smith and Elder. Gardner was a London physician who help found the Royal College of Chemistry.

755. Garner, Richard Lynch (1848–1920). *The Speech of Monkeys.* (London: W. Heinemann, 1892). 260pp.

A852 (author, title), JS1052. Only edition in BL. Garner was a biologist with the American National Zoo. Part I is devoted to Garner's experiments and intense observation of primates in the African wild, Part II to his theory of speech among apes. A pioneering study of primate communication in which Garner identified about 25–30 "words" used by chimpanzees.

756. Garnett, Edward William (1868–1937). *The Paradox Club*. (London: T. F. Unwin, 1888). 208pp.

A657 (author [misspelled as Garnet], title), JS1053. This is the 1st edition of the novelist's first book. Novel about an unusual club.

757. Garratt, G. *Marvels and Mysteries of Instinct: or, Curiosities of Animal Life*. (London: Longman, Brown, Green, and Longmans, 1856). 248pp.

A853 (title), JS272 (Anon./Science). Earliest edition in BL of the only matching title there. Covers the divine method; nervous systems; instinct in man, apes, mammals, and birds; theory of sensation; animal intelligence; instinct in insects; and reason and instinct compared. The preface states, "If the Author's labours should prove instrumental in leading but one mind to the study of God's wonderful Creation, he would feel that his chief hopes had not been altogether disappointed."

758. [Gaskell, Elizabeth Cleghorn, née Stevenson] (1810–65). *Cranford*. (London: Chapman & Hall, 1855). 281pp. 2nd edition ("Cheap Edition").

Not in JS. In his diary for 29 March 1858, Dodgson notes that he began reading *Cranford*. First published in 1853; this is the closest edition in BL to Dodgson's diary entry. Mrs. Gaskell was a popular novelist who also wrote frequently for Dickens' publications *Household Words* (in which these pieces were first issued) and *All the Year Round*. *Cranford* is a novel, in vignettes, of life in a community of 19th-century women.

759. Gaskell, [Elizabeth Cleghorn, née Stevenson]. *The Life of Charlotte Brontë*. (London: Smith, Elder & Co., 1857). 2 vols. 352, 327pp.

A879 (title, 2 vols.), JS1054. Gaskell's was the only 2-volume biography of Brontë published in the 19th century. It was the definitive biography of its time. Some of the statements in the 1st edition (described here) were withdrawn in subsequent editions. According to his diary, Dodgson borrowed a copy of this book from Mrs. Longley (wife of Bishop Longley of Ripon) on 12 August 1857. On 31 August, he writes, "Finished a few days ago Mrs. Gaskell's *Life of Charlotte Brontë*. It seems to have been anything but a happy life. Her's was that peculiar talent which thrives best in solitude and de-

pression, the latter seems in her to have been almost morbid."

760. [Gaskell, Elizabeth Cleghorn, née Stevenson]. *North and South*. (London: Chapman and Hall, 1855). 2 vols. 320, [364]pp.

Not in JS. In his diary for 15 September 1855, Dodgson writes, "Finished reading *North and South* by the authoress of Mary Barton: It is well written and life-like, but the plot is exceedingly unconnected and unsatisfactory. I distrust the writer, after seeing her *Ruth* [1853], an utterly objectionable publication." This is the 1st edition. A novel of the industrial north of England contrasted with the life of leisure led by London society in the South.

761. [Gatty, Alfred] (1813–1903). *Fancies of a Rhymer*. (London: Printed by Davison, Simmons, and Co., 1833). 118pp.

A490 (author, title, date), JS1055. A490 notes that this item is "not published," though it is listed, with the information above, in both BL and BOD. NUC gives the printer, but also notes "Not published." Gatty was an undergraduate at Exeter College, Oxford, when he issued this volume of poems. He served for many years as vicar of Ecclesfield and was the husband of Margaret Gatty. He published works on religion, history, and literature.

762. Gatty, Mrs. Alfred [i.e. Margaret Scott Gatty] (1809–73). *British Sea-Weeds. Drawn from Professor Harvey's "Phycologia Britannica." With Descriptions, an Amateur's Synopsis, Rules for Laying out Seaweeds*. (London: Bell & Daldy, 1863). 166pp. 80 colored plates.

A389 ("British Sea Weed"), D75 (author, title, city, date), JS264 (Anon./Science) and JS1056. A389 and D75 are clearly the same book. BL contains no other exactly matching titles. Mrs. Gatty devoted much of her time to children's literature. She not only wrote books, but also edited the popular periodical for children *Aunt Judy's Magazine*, to which Lewis Carroll made several contributions, including "Bruno's Revenge" the genesis of the *Sylvie and Bruno* novels (see LCP for more on Dodgson and Gatty).

763. Gaultier, Bon [pseud. of Theodore Martin (1816–1909) and William Edmonstone Aytoun], editors. *The Book of Bal-*

lads. (Edinburgh and London: Blackwood, 1859). 256pp. 6th edition. Illustrated by Charles Altamont Doyle, John Leech and Alfred Crowquill.

A848 (editor, title, date), JS1057. See 82 for a note on Aytoun. Martin was a successful author and translator who wrote several biographies. See 505 for a note on Crowquill and 577 for a note on Leech. Includes "Spanish Ballads," "American Ballads," and "Miscellaneous Ballads." In his diary for 26 February 1856, Dodgson writes, "Borrowed Gaultier's *Ballads of Crewe,* they are very clever, but spoil the beautiful originals." This volume of parodies was originally published in 1845; Dodgson obviously acquired a copy subsequent to his borrowing a copy in 1856.

764. [**Gent,** L. C.]. *The Book of Familiar Quotations: Being a Collection of Popular Extracts and Aphorisms, Selected from the Works of the Best Authors.* (London: Whittaker & Co., 1852). 109pp.

A550 ("Book of Familiar Quotations"), JS230 (Anon./Reference). Earliest edition in BL. Only precisely matching 19th-century title in BL.

765. [**German**]. *German Dictionary.*

Title only given in A322/JS239 (Anon./ Reference). Dodgson also owned a German/ English Dictionary by Grieb (see 831).

766. Gervinus, G[eorge] G[ottfried] (1805– 71). *Shakespeare, Commentaries.* (London: Smith, Elder, 1863 [1862]). 2 vols. Translated under the author's superintendence by F[anny] E[lizabeth] Bunnett.

A871 (author, title, 2 vols.), JS1058. This is the only 2-volume edition in BL. Gervinus was a German historian, scholar and professor at Heidelberg. This work was originally published in German in 1849–50.

767. Gesenius, [Friedrich Heinrich] William [a.k.a. Wilhelm] (1786–1842). *Gesenius's Hebrew Grammar.* (London: Samuel Bagster & Sons, 1845). 276pp. Enlarged and improved by E[mil] Rödiger. Translated by Benjamin Davies. Re-edited after the 17th original edition by B. Davidson. With a *Hebrew Reading Book,* prepared by the translator.

A581, B1056 ("Gesenius's Hebrew Grammar improved by Rödiger, with a Hebrew Reading Book by B. Davies, sm. 4to, n.d."), JS1060. No undated edition traced; this is the earliest edition traced matching the other particulars in B1056. Gesenius was a German scholar whose works on ancient Hebrew and Chaldee were originally published in German. Dodgson ordered this and Gesenius' *Hebrew and Chaldee Lexicon* (see below) at the suggestion of his friend H. P. Liddon on 3 February 1866 (see *Diary 5*).

768. Gesenius, [Friedrich Heinrich] William [a.k.a. Wilhelm]. *Hebrew and Chaldee Lexicon to the Old Testament Scriptures.* (London: Samuel Bagster & Sons, 1859). 884pp. Translated with additions and corrections from the author's Thesaurus and other works by Samuel Prideaux Tregelles.

A581, B1055 (author, title, translator, date), JS1059. See above for a note on Dodgson's purchase of this book.

769. Gesenius, [Friedrich Heinrich] Wilhelm. *A Hebrew and English Lexicon Of The Old Testament, Including The Biblical Chaldee.* (London: James Duncan, 1832). 656pp. Edited with improvements from the German works of Gesenius by Josiah Willard Gibbs.

E107 (author, editor, title, date), JS1063 (listed under Gibbs). A771 states "Lexicon Hebraicum," and could refer to this item. Gibbs was Professor of Sacred Literature at Yale.

770. Ghosh, Kasiprasad. *The Shäïr and Other Poems.* (Calcutta: Scott, 1830). 201pp.

B1057 (author, title [misspelled as "She Shair," city, date), JS1062. In the preface, the author calls himself "the first Hindu who has ventured to publish a volume of English Poems."

771. Gift, Theo [pseud. of Dorothy Henrietta Havers, afterwards Boulger] (d. 1889). *Cape Town Dicky, or Colonel Jack's Boy.* (London: Hildesheimer & Faulkner, 1888). 64pp. Illustrated with color plates by Alice Havers and monotints by Ernest Wilson.

A543 (Capetown Dickey), JS541 (listed under Boulger). Only edition in BL. Dorothy Havers was born and spent her childhood on a small island in Oceania. She was an author of novels and books for children. See 880 for a note on Alice Havers. A children's story about a boy who comes to England from South Africa and is cured of his habit of cruelty to animals.

772. Gilbart, James William (1794–1863). *Logic for the Million. A Familiar Exposition of the Art of Reasoning. With an Appendix on the Philosophy of Language.* (London: Bell and Daldy, 1865). 388pp. With an appendix on the philosophy of language.

D107 (author, title, city, date), JS1064. The earliest edition listed in BL is 1851; the 6th edition was dated 1860. Gilbart was a banker who wrote widely on banking, including a book on logic and banking.

773. Gilbert, W[illiam] S[chwenck] (1836–1911). *The "Bab" Ballads. Much Sound and Little Sense.* (London: John Camden Hotten, 1869 [1868]). 222pp. 1st edition. With illustrations by the author.

A849 (author, title, edition, date), JS1065. Gilbert was a lawyer, though he practiced very little, and author of plays and poems. He is best known for his collaboration with Sir Arthur Sullivan on a series of comic operettas, most of which Dodgson saw in their original productions. His *Bab Ballads*, and their sequel, were a series of nonsense verses. Dodgson was acquainted with Gilbert (see for instance *Letters*, 479).

774. Gilbert, W[illiam] S[chwenck]. *More "Bab" Ballads. Much Sound and Little Sense.* (London: George Routledge & Sons, [1873]). 224pp. With illustrations by the author.

A849 (author, title), JS1066. Earliest edition in BL.

775. Gilchrist, Alexander (1828–61). *Life of William Blake, "Pictor Ignotus." With Selections from his Poems and Other Writings.* (London: Macmillan, 1863). 2 vols. 390, 268pp. Illustrated from Blake's own works.

A916 (author, title, 2 vols., date), JS1067. Gilchrist lived in Guildford for three years before moving to a home on Cheyne Row in Chelsea, near the Rossettis and next door to the Carlyles. This was his magnum opus, which he left unfinished. It was completed by his widow and W. M. Rossetti.

776. Gilfillan, George (1813–1878), editor. *British Poets; with Memoirs and Critical Dissertations.* (Edinburgh: Nicol, 1853–60). 48 vols.

A854 (notes 44 vols.), B977 (editor, title, 48 vols., date [1859]), JS1069. The date 1859 was undoubtedly taken from a single volume. Contains, according to B977, works by Addison and Gay, Akenside, Armstrong, Dyer, Green, Beattie, Blair, Falconer, Bowles, Burns, Butler, Chaucer, Churchill, Cowper, Crashaw and Quarles, Dryden, Goldsmith, Collins, Warton, Herbert, Johnson, Parnell, Gray, Milton, Percy, Pope, Prior, Scott, Shakespeare, Surrey, Shenstone, Spenser, Thomson, etc. DNB notes, "Gilfillan wrongly disdained the minute rectification of texts by a careful collation of the earliest editions or manuscripts, and his introductory essays and memoirs are not remarkable for accuracy." In his diary for 2 February 1856, Dodgson writes, "Ordered at Slatter's the rest of the *Gilfillan's Poets*: all for 1854 and 1855 (except Dryden) were sent over."

777. Gladstone, W[illiam] E[wart] (1809–98). *"Ecce Homo."* (London: Strahan & Co., 1868). 201pp. Reprinted from *Good Words*.

A783 (author, title), JS1071. Only edition in BL. Gladstone was a statesman, prime minister, and leader of the Liberal Party from 1868 to 1894. This book is a criticism of the anonymously published *Ecce Homo, A Survey of the Life and Work of Jesus Christ*, by J. R. Seeley (see 1790). Seeley's book presented a historic life of Christ, ignoring much Christian dogma, thus drawing accusations against the orthodoxy of the author from not only Gladstone (as here), but also John Henry Newman, Arthur Penrhyn Stanley, and others. Gladstone writes that "the chief objection which is thought to lie against this work from the side of the ancient Christian belief is, that it exhibits our Lord in His human nature, or on the human side of His person only." Gladstone admits however, that such teaching may serve a purpose, and "that which is not good as a resting-place may be excellent and most necessary as a stage in an onward journey."

778. Gladstone, William Ewart. *The State in Its Relations with the Church.* (London: John Murray, 1838). 324pp.

A795 (author, title), JS1072. Earliest edition in BL. Defends the idea of a single state religion, a position Gladstone later changed.

779. Glanvill, Joseph (1636–80). *Saducismus Triumphatus: or Full and Plain Evidence Concerning Witches and Apparitions. With a Letter of Dr H[enry] More on the Same Subject, and an Authentick Story of Certain Swedish Witches.* (London: For J. Collins, and S. Lownds, 1681). 328pp. Done into English by A[nthony] Horneck.

B1059 (author, title, date), JS1073. Glanvill was a believer in witches and other supernatural phenomena and here makes an attempt to factually prove the existence of such phenomena by cataloging stories of sightings, etc. The volume, published in the year following Glanvill's death, is a reworking of his book *Philosophical Considerations Touching Witches and Witchcraft* (1666) and the enlarged *A Blow at Modern Sadducism, in Some Philosophical Considerations about Witchcraft* (1668). Henry More was a Cambridge Platonist and close associate of Glanvill, the two forming what was essentially a society for psychical research.

780. *Gleanings from Popular Authors, Grave and Gay*. (London: Cassell & Co., 1882–83). 2 vols. Illustrated.

A375 (title, 2 vols.), JS697 (listed under Charles Cowden Clark). The rather cryptic entry at A375 is partly to blame for an incorrect listing in JS. Both seem to imply that this work is one with Clarke's *Concordance to Shakespeare* (403, the two are listed as one by JS). The original entry reads: "Cowden Clark's [sic] Concordance to Shakespeare and Gleanings from Popular Authors (2 vols.), half morocco." Certainly these are two separate works, as no such single work exists. This work matches the second half of the description (it is in 2 vols.) and is the only work in BL (excepting a shorthand version of the same work) that does so. The 1883 volume includes "A Mad Tea-Party" from AAIW.

781. Goethe, Johann Wolfgang von (1749–1832). *Faust*. Dodgson owned at least two editions, neither of which is sufficiently described in primary source material to be identified.

A394/JS1074 (Goethe's Faust in English), A678/JS1075 (Goethe's Faust). See also 878 and 1171.

782. Goethe, Johann Wolfgang von. *Poems and Ballads*. (Edinburgh: Blackwood and Sons, 1859). 240pp. Translated by William Edmondstone Aytoun and Theodore Martin.

A829 (author, title, translators), JS1076. 1st edition. See 82 for a note on Aytoun and 763 for a note on Martin.

783. Gogol, Nikolai Vasil'evich (1809–52). *Dead Souls*. (London: Vizetelly and Co., 1887). 372pp. In the *Vizetelly's Russian Novels* series.

A626 (title), JS1077. This is the only British pre–1898 edition in BL, but there was an 1893 edition published by T. Fisher Unwin which is often called the 1st English edition and may be a more likely candidate. Gogol was a Ukrainian born Russian novelist, dramatist and humorist. The present novel is his masterpiece, a comic story of Russian serfdom, and is considered by many as the foundation work of Russian literature.

784. Gogol, Nikolai Vasil'evich. *Nouvelles Choisies*. (Paris: L. Hachette, 1853). 162pp. Translated from the Russian by Louis Viardot.

B1061 (author, title, translator, city, date), JS1078. Includes "Diary of a Madman" and other stories in French.

785. [Goldsmith, Oliver?] (1730?–74). *Goody Two Shoes A Facsimile Reproduction of the Edition of 1766.* (London: Griffith & Farran, 1881). 156pp. With an introduction by Charles Welsh.

B1062 (title, introducer, date), JS59 (Anon./ Children's). This famous, but anonymous, children's book, first published by John Newbery in 1765, is thought by many to be the work of Goldsmith who was, at the time, living with and working for Newbery. The story tells of an orphan girl who grows up to become a teacher.

786. Goldsmith, Oliver. *The Miscellaneous Works of Oliver Goldsmith*. (London: Macmillan Co., 1869 [1868]). 695pp. The Globe Edition. With biographical introduction by Professor [David] Masson.

A368 ("Goldsmith's Works, Globe Edition"), JS1081. 1st printing of the Globe Edition.

787. Goldsmith, Oliver. *The Vicar of Wakefield*. Edition unknown.

A671 (title), JS1082.

788. [**Golightly**, Charles Portales] (1807–85). *The Position of the Right Rev. Samuel Wilberforce, D. D., Bishop of Oxford, in Reference to Ritualism, Together with a Prefatory Account of the Romeward Movement in the Church of England in the Days of Archbishop Laud.* (London: Hatchard; Oxford: Slatter and Rose, 1867). 97pp. By a Senior Resident Member of the University of Oxford.

C4 (title), not in JS. Earliest edition in BL. Golightly was educated at Oriel College, Oxford in the 1820s. He became a curate and wrote several anonymous pamphlets criticizing the Oxford Movement. He was the instigator of a drive to erect a memorial to the Oxford martyrs (the 16th-century bishops Cranmer, Latimer, and Ridley), a project designed to embarrass the Tractarians. Though Bishop Wilberforce (see 2252) tried to tread a *via media* between the Tractarians and the Evangelicals, he is here the object of Golightly's scorn.

789. Golightly, Charles Portales. *A Solemn Warning against Cuddesdon College.* (London: [1878]).

C4 (title), not in JS. Earliest edition in BOD or BL. Cuddesdon was a training college for Anglican clergy founded by Bishop of Oxford Samuel Wilberforce. Golightly accused it of sowing "broadcast the seeds of Romish perversion in the counties of Oxford Berks and Bucks." Wilberforce felt that Golightly's objections had more to do with the college's viceprincipal, H. P. Liddon, than with the college itself. See above for more on Golightly and Wilberforce. See 1168 for E. A. Knox's response to Golightly's "warning."

790. Goode, William (1801–68). *The Nature of Christ's Presence in the Eucharist: or, the Doctrine of the Real Presence Vindicated in Opposition to the Fictitious Real Presence Asserted by Archdeacon Denison, Mr. (late Archdeacon) Wilberforce, and Dr. Pusey.* (London: 1856). 2 vol.

A801 ("Goode on the Eucharist"), JS1083. Only edition in BL and the only work that closely matches A801. Goode was an Evangelical and one of the most learned and eloquent of those who responded in print to the Oxford Tractarians. He was Dean of Ripon from 1860 to 1868, after the period when Dodgson's father

was a canon residentiary there. This work was specifically in response to doctrines put forth by George Anthony Denison (see 562); Robert Isaac Wilberforce, brother of Oxford Bishop Samuel Wilberforce and one of many members of the Oxford Movement who converted to Rome; and Edward Bouverie Pusey (see 1591), in his sermon "The Presence of Christ in the Holy Eucharist" (see also 1594). Goode also responded to Dodgson's father, Archdeacon Charles Dodgson, another High Churchman, in *A Reply to Archdeacon Dodgson's Statement, Prefixed to his Sermons on the Sacraments; with Remarks on the Sermons* (see 614). Evangelicals saw the High Church doctrine of the Real Presence as dangerously close to the Roman doctrine of Transubstantiation.

791. [**Goodier**, Edith A. and Alice P. Wood, editors.] *The Sweep Papers.* (Manchester: Printed by J. & E. W. Jackson, March 1875–December 1879). 2 vols. Nos. 1–20 (all published).

A312, D191, JS1084. Dodgson's copy of this journal is in HAC. It is inscribed on the title page of volume 1 "With the Editor's compliments." Volume 1 has Dodgson's monogrammed signature in purple ink on the title page and the gothic stamp (touched up with purple ink) on the front pastedown. The gothic stamp (printed quite darkly) is also on the front pastedown of volume 2. Includes several minor corrections in purple ink in Dodgson's hand. Denis Crutch, in *A Day of Sea Air*, calls the editors, "two North Country ladies." The journal was published as being edited by "The Walrus and the Carpenter," and included on the title page of each number the first two stanzas of that poem. In a letter to the editors of 20 March 1875, Dodgson wrote, "I need hardly say that I regard it as a compliment that you have taken the idea of the title, and the motto, of your new magazine, from my little book … It may interest you to know that the verse you quote was written at first "The Walrus & the Carpenter / were walking hand-in-hand," but was altered [to "close at hand"] to suit the artist. The original reading seems more adapted to your editorship, & you are welcome to use it, if you care to do so, as an authorized 'varia lectio.' Subsequent numbers included this variation to the verse. (See Brabant, 38). The articles were largely on topics relating to art and literature.

792. Goodwin, Harvey (1818–91). *An Elementary Course of Mathematics: Designed*

Principally for Students of the University of Cambridge. (Cambridge: Simplain, Marshall and Co., 1849). 528pp. 3rd edition.

E347, F148, JS1086. Dodgson's copy is in the collection of Jon Lindseth, Cleveland, Ohio. It is inscribed in black ink "C. L. Dodgson, Ch. Ch." Goodwin was educated at Caius College, Cambridge where he became a fellow and mathematical lecturer. In 1858 he became Dean of Ely and in 1869 Bishop of Carlisle. His later writings were all of a religious nature.

793. Goodwin, Harvey. *Elementary Mechanics.* (Cambridge: 1851–53). 2 parts (Dodgson's copy bound in one volume).

E152 (author, title, 2 vols. in 1, date), F149, JS1085. According to E152 and F149 Dodgson's copy has his signature.

794. [Goodwyn, Henry of Blackheath]. *A Table of the Circles Arising from the Division of a Unit, or any other Whole Number, by all the Integers from 1 to 1024; Being all the Pure Decimal Quotients that can Arise from this Source.* (London: J. M. Richardson, 1823). 111pp.

E216 (title, date), JS156 (Anon./Mathematics).

795. (Gordon, George, 1751–93). *The Trial of Lord George Gordon, for High Treason, at the Bar of the Court of King's Bench, on Monday, February 5th, 1781. Published under the Inspection of his Lordship's Friends. To which are Subjoined, Several Original Papers Relating to the Subject.* (Edinburgh: Printed by J. Mennons and Co., [1781]). 200pp.

B1263 ("Trial of Lord George Gordon, for High Treason, 8vo, n.d."), JS98 (Anon./Law). There are two undated editions (both [1781]) listed in BL, but only this is 8vo, and thus seems the likely match. In July 1780, Gordon led a crowd of 50,000 in a march on Parliament, demanding the repeal of the 1778 Catholic Emancipation Act. The crowd erupted into five days of rioting, during which many Catholic homes and chapels were destroyed and nearly 300 rioters killed by the army. Gordon was tried for treason and found not guilty.

796. Gordon, Osborne (1813–83). *Oratio Censoria in Refectorio Ædis Christi Habita, Dec. 4, 1852.* (Oxford: Printed for Private Circulation, 1852). 15pp.

Not in JS. In a letter to his sister on 9 December 1852, Dodgson wrote, "Mr. Gordon has given me a copy of his Censor's speech (printed for private distribution) ... I think it is beautiful Latin; it is mostly about the Duke." The Duke of Wellington's funeral had been on 18 November (see 2039). Gordon matriculated at Christ Church, Oxford in 1832 and was a student there from 1834 to 1861, after which he was rector at Easthampstead, Berkshire.

797. Gore, Charles (1853–1932). *The Church and the Ministry. A Review of the Rev. E[dwin] Hatch's Bampton Lectures.* (London: Rivingtons, 1882). 69pp.

E131 (author, title, date), JS1089. Gore was a leader in the Anglo-Catholic movement. In 1884, at the recommendation of Dodgson's 1867 traveling companion to Russia, Henry Parry Liddon, Gore was made the first principal of Pusey House, an Oxford center for theological study and pastoral care in the Anglo-Catholic tradition. In 1911 Gore became Bishop of Oxford. He founded the Anglican Community of the Resurrection in 1892. See ODCC. Gore here reviews Edwin Hatch's book *The Organization of the Early Christian Churches,* of which Dodgson owned a copy (see 876).

798. Gore, Charles. *The Incarnation of the Son of God. Being the Bampton Lectures for the Year 1891.* (London: John Murray, 1891). 276pp.

A802 (author, Bampton Lectures), not in JS. Earliest edition in BL. Gore here argues, controversially, that Christ, in becoming incarnate, took on all human limitations and stripped himself of all divine qualities, including omniscience.

799. Gore, Charles, editor. *Lux Mundi. A Series of Studies in the Religion of the Incarnation.* Edited by Charles Gore. (London: John Murray, 1889) 525pp.

A796 (title), JS319 (Anon./Theology). Earliest edition in BL. Includes contributions by Henry Scott Holland, Aubrey Moore, J. R. Illingworth, Edward Stuart Talbot, Robert Campbell Moberly, Arthur Lyttelton, W. Lock, W. J. H. Campion, R. L. Ottley, and Francis Paget, who became Dean of Christ Church in 1892. An important book in the history of the Oxford Movement, *Lux Mundi* set out to "put the Catholic faith into its right relation to modern intellectual and moral problems." According to ODCC, Gore's own essay, on "The Holy Spirit and Inspiration" caused the greatest stir, by making a definitive break with E. B. Pusey and the Tractarians. ODCC mentions, among those High Churchmen who were distressed by *Lux Mundi*, Dodgson's old friend H. P. Liddon. A review quoted in a publisher's advertisement calls the essays "an attempt to show that between theology rightly interpreted and the best modes and results of modern philosophy there is no real discrepancy."

800. Gore, Charles. *The Roman Catholic Claims.* (London: Elliot Stock, [1886]). 108pp. Reprinted from *The Indian Churchman.*

A769 (author, title), JS1087. Earliest edition in BL. A defense of the Anglican Church against Romanist attacks.

801. Gore, Charles. *The Sermon on the Mount: A Practical Exposition.* (London: John Murray, 1896). 218pp.

A793 (author, title), JS1088. Earliest edition in BL. Gore also published, in 1892, a book titled *The Social Doctrine of the Sermon on the Mount*, but A793 states "The Sermon on the Mount," and the inclusion and capitalization of "The" leaves little doubt that this is the book listed.

802. Gosse, Philip Henry (1810–88). *Evenings at the Microscope: or, Researches among the Minuter Organs and Forms of Animal Life.* (London: Society for Promoting Christian Knowledge, 1859). 506pp. 113 text woodcuts.

A332 (author, title), JS1091. 1st edition. Gosse was a naturalist (less famous than his son Edmund) who rejected Darwinism and tried to reconcile the geological age of fossils with the biblical account of creation. The present study details his scientific observations with a microscope.

803. Gosse, Philip Henry. *A Year at the Shore.* (London, Edinburgh [printed]: Strahan, 1865). 330pp. With 36 illustrations by the author, printed in colours by Leighton Brothers.

A561 (author, "A Year at the Sea Side"), JS1092. This is the only book by any Gosse with a title remotely similar to that given in A561. Earliest edition in BL. This was Gosse's final book, a description of the shore arranged

chronologically by season of the year. In the final pages he reaffirms his belief in creationism.

804. Gough, John (1721–91). *A Discourse Concerning the Resurrection Bodies; Tending to Shew, from the Writings of Heathens, Jews and Christians, that There are Bodies, Called our Own, Which Will not be Raised from the Dead; That There are Bodies, Properly Called our Own, Which Will be Raised from the Dead; By What Means the Perfection and Immortality of the Resurrection Bodies are to be Obtained; and to What Effect.* (London: Printed by George Stafford, for L. Davis; J. Johnson, 1790). 70pp. 2nd edition.

E121 (author, title, date), JS1093. Originally published in 1788 under the pseudonym Philalethes. Gough was an 18th-century writer on religion and mathematics.

805. Goulburn, Edward Meyrick (1818–97). *Doctrine of the Resurrection of the Body as Taught in Holy Scripture. Eight Sermons Preached before the University of Oxford, in the year MDCCCL, at the Lecture Founded by the Late Canon Bampton.* (Oxford: J. Vincent, 1850). 377pp.

A802 ("Golburn's Bampton Lectures"), JS1080. 1st edition. Clearly a typographical error in A802, as Goulburn is the only Bampton Lecturer with a name similar to "Golburn." Only edition in BL. Goulburn was chaplain to Samuel Wilberforce, Bishop of Oxford. In 1849 he succeeded Archibald Campbell Tait as headmaster of Dodgson's school, Rugby. He eventually rose to the rank of Dean of Norwich. He was a conservative churchman with traditional orthodox views. His list of publications runs to over 30 items.

806. Goulburn, Edward Meyrick. *Thoughts on Personal Religion, Being a Treatise on the Christian Life, in its Two Chief Elements, Devotion and Practice.* (London: Rivingtons, 1865). 428pp. 8th edition.

A754 (Goldburn's Personal Religional), JS1079. Clearly a typographical error in A754. This is the only book remotely similar to A754 in BL. Originally published in 2 vols. in 1862, this is the earliest 1-volume edition in BL (A754

" It is Flossie and me, Sybil—don't you remember us?"

Carrots and Flossie meet Sybil. Illustration for Mrs. Molesworth's *Carrots* (item 808) by Walter Crane.

does not specify 2 vols.). A treatise on Christian living.

807. [**Graham**, Elizabeth Susanna Davenport] (1763–1844). *Voyage to Locuta: A Fragment, with Etchings and Notes of Illustration, Dedicated to Theresa Tidy by Lemuel Gulliver.* (London: Printed for J. Hatchard, 1818?). 47pp.

A474 (title, date [1848]), JS1094. Possibly a misprint in A474 ("1848" for "1818"). No 1848 edition traced. Only edition listed in BL, BOD, or NUC. BL describes this as "a grammatical tract." Graham wrote works on neatness (as Theresa Tidy) and a sequel to *Gulliver's Travels*.

808. Graham, Ennis [pseud. of Mrs. Mary Louisa Molesworth] (1839–1921). *"Carrots:" Just a Little Boy.* (London: Macmillan and Co., 1876). 242pp. Illustrated by Walter Crane.

A647 (title), JS1533 (listed under Molesworth). Listed in A647 just after Mrs. Molesworth's *Christmas Tree Land*, this entry clearly refers to the above title. This is the 1st edition. See 1369 for a note on Molesworth. This was her first children's novel, the story of a redhaired boy growing up as the youngest in his family. See 496 for more on Dodgson and Crane.

809. Graham, Ennis [pseud. of Mrs. Mary Louisa Molesworth]. *The Cuckoo-Clock.* (London: Macmillan and Co., 1877). 242pp. Illustrated by Walter Crane.

Not in JS. In a letter to his publisher Macmillan (26 November 1877), Dodgson writes, "*The Cuckoo-Clock* has converted me into an admirer of Mr. Walter Crane's drawings" (see *Macmillan*, 134). The 1st edition was printed in October 1877 and was followed by another printing in November. This was the author's best known novel. It is the story of a child (Griselda) who goes on adventures with the cuckoo who flies out of the clock in her aunts' house.

810. Grant, James (1822–87). *Frank Hilton, or the Queen's Own.* (London: 1855).

Not in JS. In his diary for 1 August 1855, Dodgson writes of this book which he had "read lately," that it was "a graphic well written story, though the incidents are wildly improbable." Earliest edition in BL, which lists no publisher (Routledge published an undated edition possibly as early as 1860). Grant served in the 62nd regiment and wrote military stories. A novel of military adventures in Aden and Arabia.

811. Grant, James (1840–85). *The Mysteries of All Nations: Rise and Progress of Superstition, Laws Against and Trial of Witches, Ancient and Modern Delusions, Together with Strange Customs, Fables and Tales Relating to Mythology.* (Leith, Edinburgh: Reid & Son, [1880]). 640pp.

A891 (title), JS246 (Anon./Reference). Dodgson's copy was offered by Chicago Book and Art Auctions on 22 January 1931 (DAA1523). It has the inscription, "C. L. D. bought in May/ 83." Grant was a Scottish antiquary and archeologist.

812. Grant, John Cameron (b. 1857). *Poems in Petroleum.* (London: E. W. Allen, 1892). 148pp.

E56 (title, author, date), JS1096. Grant is best known for his book *The Ethiopian: A Narrative of the Society of Human Leopards*, a fictional account of the African slave trade published in a small private edition in Paris in 1900. His books in Dodgson's library, including the present title, are minor verse collections.

813. Grant, John Cameron. *Songs from the Sunny South*. (London: Longmans & Co., 1882). 280pp.

A860 (author, title ["Songs for the Sunny South"]), JS1095. This is the closest matching title in BL and the only edition listed.

814. Grant, John Cameron. *Vauclin, and Other Verses*. (London: E. W. Allen, 1887). 50pp.

E166 (author, title, date), JS1097.

815. Gray, Henry (1825–1861). *Anatomy, Descriptive and Surgical*. (London: J. W. Parker, 1858). 750pp. The drawings by H. V. Carter. The dissections jointly by the author and Dr. Carter.

A922 (author, title), JS1098. 1st edition.

816. Gray, Robert (1809–72). *A Statement Relating to Facts which have been Misunderstood, and to Questions which have been Raised, in Connection with the Consecration, Trial, and Excommunication of Dr. Colenso*. (London: Rivingtons, 1867).

C5 ("Statement by Colenso"), not in JS. No work by Colenso containing the word "statement" or purporting to be a statement has been traced, but surely this is the work referred to in C5 — it is the only closely matching title traced. This is the earliest edition traced; a 2nd edition of 1867 had 92pp. Gray was Bishop of Capetown. See 421 and 1184 for a description of the controversy between Colenso and Gray.

817. Gray, Thomas (1716–71). *Gray's Elegy*. (London: Longman and Co., 1846). 36pp. Illuminated by Owen Jones in 34 color plates.

Not in JS. In his diary for 5 January 1855, Dodgson writes, "I borrowed [from the Bishop's Palace in Ripon] Gray's *Elegy*, illuminated by Owen Jones to copy out of." The book was reproduced in chromolithography from Jones's illuminated manuscript of Gray's famous poem. Dodgson's interest was in the art of the production. A few days later he wrote that, following two hours of morning work he

"did nothing but illumination and sketching." Only edition traced. Jones (1809–74) was an architect whose work included interior design for the Crystal Palace. He helped revive the art of illumination in the 19th century and wrote on art and decorative architecture.

818. Green, John Richard (1837–83). *A Short History of the English People*. (London: Macmillan, 1874). 847pp. With maps and tables. 1st edition.

A631, B1063 (author, title, date), JS1100. Green was an examiner in the School of Modern History, Oxford. A frequently reprinted work.

819. G[reenaway], K[ate] (1846–1901). *Under the Window. Pictures and Rhymes*. (London: G. Routledge & Sons, [1878]). 64pp. Engraved and printed in colors by E. Evans.

A533 (author, title), JS1101. 1st edition. Greenaway was one of the most popular artists for children in the latter half of the 19th century. In addition to illustrating children's books, she also wrote verse for children. This was her first book produced by the engraver Edmund Evans, with whom she had a close professional relationship thereafter. It was a book of nonsense verse with illustrations. 20,000 copies of the first edition were printed and the edition quickly sold out, despite the high price occasioned by the expensive color printing process.

820. G[reenfield], W[illiam] S[mith] (1846–1919). *Alcohol: Its Use and Abuse*. (London: Hardwicke & Bogue, 1878). 95pp. In the *Health Primers* series.

E151 (title, date), JS263 (Anon./Science). E151 notes that this "bears evidence of Lewis Carroll's critical examination." See 910–11 for other titles in this series. The author was a pathologist and member of the Royal College of Physicians. He also translated a book on alcoholism by the French doctor V. Magnan.

821. Greenwood, Frederick (1830–1910). *The Path of Roses*. (London: C. H. Clarke, [1859]). 225pp. Illustrated by Birket Foster, John Leech, Noel Humphreys, James Danby, Harrison Weir, etc.

A627, E37 (author, title, illustrators, [1885]), JS1104 (listed under James Greenwood). Only edition traced. The date is taken from BL, but as the item was not dated, it is not surprising that the conjectural date in E37 is incorrect. Frederick was the brother of James Greenwood (see 823) and the founder of the *Pall Mall Gazette* and the *St. James's Gazette*, to both of which Dodgson was a regular contributor (see LCP). This work is described by Allibone as "a tale."

822. [**Greenwood**, George] (1799–1875). *Hints on Horsemanship to a Nephew and Niece; or, Common Sense and Common Errors in Common Riding.* (London: E. Moxon, 1839). 105pp. With frontispiece and a second engraved title page plus other illustrations in line.

A897 (title), JS1102. Earliest edition in BL. Greenwood was an officer of the Household Brigade of Cavalry. A practical guide to horsemanship, including such chapters as "Holding and Handling the Reins," "Mounting and Dismounting," and "The Horse and His Stable."

823. Greenwood, James (1840s–1929). *Low-Life Deeps: An Account Of The Strange Fish To Be Found There.* (London: Chatto & Windus, 1876). 319pp. Illustrations by Alfred Concanen. 1st edition.

D78 (author, title, city, date), JS1106. James Greenwood was a journalist, the brother of Frederick Greenwood, and a frequent contributor to his brother's papers. He often wrote (as here) about the under classes in London.

824. Greenwood, James. *The Seven Curses of London.* (London: Stanley Rivers & Co, [1869]). 461pp. With a portrait of the author.

A309, D77 (author, title, n.d.), JS1103. Only edition in BL. Greenwood exposes thieves, beggars, prostitutes, drunks, gamblers, neglected children, and waste of charity.

825. [**Greenwood**, James]. *The Wren of the Curragh.* (London: Tinsley Bros., 1867). 52pp. Reprinted from the *Pall Mall Gazette.*

D200 (title, city, date), JS143 (Anon./Literature). D200 notes Dodgson's signature. An exposé about the Wrens of Curragh. The Wrens were a group of 19th-century Irish women living as outcasts on the plains of Kildare. The name "Curragh" comes from their shelters, hollowed out nests in the ground covered with furze. The community lived by what they called

"communistic principles," sharing everything. They were reviled by society — stoned, beaten, spat upon, denied basic care, even burnt out of their nests. They often died in ditches from exposure or disease.

826. Greg, Percy (1836–89). *The Devil's Advocate.* (London: Trübner and Co., 1878). 2 vols. 340, 352pp.

A306 (author [misspelled as "Gregg"], title, 2 vols.), JS1108. Only edition in BL. Greg was a journalist and miscellaneous writer whose book *Across the Zodiac* (1880) was an early inter-planetary novel. This work is a satirical look at modern ideas in the form of philosophical dialogues.

827. Greg, W[illiam] R[athbone] (1809–81). *Enigmas of Life.* (London: Trübner & Co., 1873). 308pp.

A305, D79 (author, title, city, date), JS1107. D79 notes Dodgson's initials. Several editions were published in 1873. Greg was a civil servant who wrote widely on political, economic, and theological matters. *The Spectator* wrote of this volume, "Mr. Greg has never written a more eloquent book than this, and never any so full of deep religious feeling, in spite of its deep underlying doubt." *The Athenæum* wrote "Mr. Greg has maintained a position which will be attacked on the one side by those theologians who practically regard the virtues of faith and hope as superfluities lacking a raison d'être, and, on the other side, by those men of science who think charity, in the large sense of the word, is a delusion." Includes: "Malthus Notwithstanding," and "Non-survival of the Fittest."

828. [**Gregory**, Robert (1819–1911) and Henry Parry Liddon (1829–90)]. *The Purchas Judgment. A Letter to the Bishop of London by the Two Senior Canons of St. Paul's Cathedral.* (London: 1871).

C4 (author, title), not in JS. Only edition in BL. Gregory was educated at Corpus Christi College, Oxford and served as a canon of St. Paul's with Liddon. See 1230 for a note on Dodgson's friend H. P. Liddon. The 1871 judgment of the Committee of the Privy Council against Rev. John Purchas (1823–72) was a major setback for ritualism in the Church of England, ruling that ritual practices such as Eucharistic vestments and the Eastward position were illegal and effectively making High Church ritualists law-breakers (see ODCC).

Liddon's High Church leanings are reflected here. See also 1575.

829. Grey, H. and J. *Practical Arithmetic; or Concise Calculator Adapted to the Commerce of Great Britain and Ireland.* (1838).

E264 (author, title, date), WS, JS1110. No copy of the 1838 edition has been traced. The closest edition for which complete publication information has been found is the 11th (London: Mills, Jowett, and Mills, 1832). WS describes this as having the gothic stamp and property label.

830. Grey, Maria Georgina [née Shirreff] (b. 1816). *Last Words to Girls on Life in School and After School.* (London: Rivingtons, 1889 [1888]). 357pp.

A513, A558, A560, E287 (author, title, date [1894]), JS61 (Anon./Children's), JS1099. Dodgson owned at least 3 copies of this work. No copy of the 1894 edition described in E287 has been traced; the 1889 edition is the only one traced. Grey was the founder, in 1872, of the National Union for the Education of Women of All Classes.

831. Grieb, Christoph Friedrich. *A Dictionary of the German and English Languages: Compiled from the Dictionaries of Heinsius, Adelung, Campe & Heyse, for the German: and Todd-Johnson, Richardson, Webster, Jamieson and Pickering, for the English.* (London: Williams and Norgate, 1847). 2 vols.

A349 (author, title, 2 vols.), JS1111. Earliest edition traced. Dodgson owned at least one other German dictionary (A322).

832. Griffith, Ralph Thomas Hotchkin (1826–1906). *Specimens of Old Indian Poetry, Translated from the Original Sanskrit into English Verse.* (London: A. Hall, Virtue & Co., 1852). 128pp.

D177 (author, title, city, date), JS1112. Griffith served in the Bengal civil service and was a director of public instruction.

833. Grimm, Carl Ludwig Wilibald (1807–91). *Lexicon Graeco-Latinum in Libros Novi Testamenti.* (Lipsiae: Libraria Arnold, 1868). 467pp.

A747 (author, title), JS1113. Earliest edition in BL. Dodgson presented a copy of the 2nd edition (Lipsiae, 1879) to George MacDonald on 15 January 1883. A Greek-English lexicon of the New Testament.

834. Grimm, [Jacob Ludwig Karl] (1785–1863) and [Wilhelm Karl] Grimm (1786–1859). *German Popular Stories, Translated from the Kinder und Haus Marchen, Collected by MM. G. from Oral Tradition.* (London: J. C. Hotten, [1869]). 335pp. Translated and edited by Edgar Taylor, with an introduction by John Ruskin and with illustrations after the original designs by George Cruikshank.

A643 (title, introducer, illustrator), JS1115. This is the only Ruskin/Cruikshank edition in BL. The Grimms' famous collection of fairy tales.

835. Grimm, Jakob Luwig Karl and W[ilhelm] K[arl] Grimm. *Kinder- und Hausmärchen, Gesammelt Durch die Brüder Grimm.* (Berlin: Duncker, 1864).

D80 (authors, title, city, date, Cr. 8vo), JS1114. Two editions listed in NUC: F. Duncker (311pp.) and J. J. Duncker (324pp.). The former at 16mo is not quite as close a match to the stated size (Crown 8vo) as the latter (17 cm.) Both state 11th edition. Grimms' fairy tales in the original German.

836. Grindon, Leopold Hartley (1818–1904). *Emblems: A Bird's-eye View of the Harmonies of Nature with Mankind.* (London: Pitman, 1869). 99pp.

E238 (author, title), F145 (author, title, date), JS1116. E238 and F145 note that Dodgson's copy has his initials inside the cover. Grindon was Lecturer on Botany at the Royal School of Medicine, Manchester. He wrote a number of works on Botany and several in which he shows the mark of the divine in nature (see below).

837. Grindon, Leopold Hartley. *The Little Things of Nature, Considered Especially in Relation to the Divine Benevolence.* (London: Fred. Pitman, 1865). 78pp.

E379 (author, title, date), JS1117. 1st edition; a 2nd edition was also published in 1865. E379 describes Dodgson's copy as having the "autograph of James Thompson, 1865 and the initials of Lewis Carroll."

838. Grocott, J[ohn] C[ooper] (1793–1874). *An Index To Familiar Quotations;*

Selected Principally From British Authors With Parallel Passages From Various Writers, Ancient and Modern. (Liverpool: Edward Howell, 1863). 531pp.

A358 ("Index of Quotations Ancient and Modern"), JS233 (Anon./Reference, not listed separately from *Dictionary of Poetical Quotations*). No precise matches traced; this is the only close match traced and seems a likely candidate. First published in 1854; this is the earliest edition traced under this title.

839. Grogan, [Mrs.] Mercy. *How Women May Earn a Living.* (London: Cassell, Petter, etc., [1880]). 124pp.

D236 (author, title), JS1118. D236 notes Dodgson's initials. Earliest edition in BL. Probably the first guide to employment for women, "This little book is written in the hope of directing their attention to some suitable and remunerative employments that are not universally known, and it is hoped it may prove useful to parents who are anxious to arm their daughters for the battle of life with a weapon no one can take from them ... a thorough knowledge of some remunerative employment would do more to make them independent of the 'slings and arrows of outrageous fortune' than the possession of any amount of money, especially in these days of bank failures and general depression of trade." Employments suggested include: china painting and art needlework; clerk based roles in the Post Office and law copying, telegraphy and bookkeeping; printing; the teaching of music and cookery; shop assistant work in linen draperies; becoming a school board visitor; the role of superintendent in laundries; concertina making; hairdressing; nursing and pharmacy work.

840. Guest, Edwin (1800–80). *A History of English Rhythms.* (London: W. Pickering, 1838). 2 vols. 318, 432pp.

A314, JS1119. Dodgson's copy is in the Robert Manning Strozier Library of Florida State University. "From Lewis Carroll's Library" is inscribed on the flyleaf. Guest was the Master of Caius College and Vice-Chancellor of Cambridge University. He was a founding member of the Philological Society. DNB writes, "A book the compilation of which entailed immense labour, many of the poems having to be consulted in manuscript."

841. Guinness, Henry Grattan (the elder) (1835–1910). *The Approaching End of the Age Viewed in the Light of History, Prophecy and Science.* (Frome and London: 1878). 615pp.

A805 (author, title), JS1120 (listed under Gordon Meyer Guinness). Earliest edition in BL or BOD. Guinness was a popular teacher who evangelized in Great Britain, Europe, and the United States, as well as starting a missionary school in London. He was also known for his extensive writings on prophecy. This work foretells the coming of Christ in the near future based on Biblical prophecy and includes a scientific approach to astronomy in its calculations.

842. Gunning, Peter (1614–84). *The Paschal or Lent-Fast Apostolical and Perpetual. At First Deliver'd in a Sermon [on Luke v. 35–38] Preached before His Majesty in Lent, and Since Enlarged. With an Appendix Containing an Answer to the Objections of the Presbyterians against the Fast of Lent.* (London: Garthwait, 1662). 542pp.

Uncertain. F186 (author, title, date), WS, JS1121. Both F186 and WS describe this as having the gothic stamp (WS notes property label), but describe no other markings. Gunning was successively Bishop of Chichester and of Ely.

843. Gurney, E[dmund] (1847–88), F[rederick] W[illiam] H[enry] Myers and F[rank] Podmore (1855–1910). *Phantasms of the Living.* (London: Society for Psychical Research, 1886). 2 vols.

A906 (title, 2 vols.), JS185 (Anon./Occult). Earliest edition in BL. Dodgson was a charter member of the Society for Psychical Research. This volume is a collection of over 700 case studies of telepathy. The cases are divided into categories, and one which may have been of special interest to Dodgson was "Borderland," described as "between sleeping and waking," similar to the "eerie" state Dodgson described in his two-part novel *Sylvie and Bruno.*

844. Haering, Georg Wilhelm Heinrich (1798–1871). *Walladmor: "Freely Translated into German from the English of Sir Walter Scott" and Now Freely Translated from the German of G. W. H. Haering into English.* (London: Taylor and Hessey, 1825). 2 vols. Translated by Thomas De Quincey.

A826, B1281 (author, title, 2 vols., date), JS1836 (listed under Scott). Haering was a German novelist. This curious book stems from a German production by Haering of a novel which purported to be by Scott. At a bookfair in Germany, Thomas De Quincey (see 564) saw this forgery for what it was, but nonetheless transformed it into an English novel. De Quincey's translation was so free, that the work is often attributed to him, and certainly he must be considered a major creative force in the shaping of this book — his role being far beyond that of translator.

845. Hain, James Friswell (1825–78). *Familiar Words: An Index Verborum or Quotation Handbook, with Parallel Passages, of Phrases which have Become Imbedded in our English Tongue.* (London: 1865 [1864]).

Uncertain. A550 ("Familiar Words"), JS237 (Anon./Reference). A550 matches only two books in BL, this and David Urquhart's *Familiar Words, as Affecting the Character of Englishmen and the Fate of England. (Second Series. Familiar Words as Affecting the Conduct of England in 1855)*, a work in two parts. There is no mention of parts in A550, and the present title seems more likely. Earliest edition traced; an 1866 edition was published by S. Low, Son, and Marston.

846. Hallam, Henry (1777–1859). *The Constitutional History of England from the Accession of Henry VII to the Death of George II.* (London: 1846). 2 vols. 719, 624pp. 5th edition.

A635, B1064 (author, title, 2 vols., date), JS85 (Anon./History), JS1122. According to B1064 these volumes are "Rugby Prize to C. L. D., Sept. 1849, with Arms and inscription." Hallam was an English historian who was educated at Christ Church, Oxford and who gave up practicing the law following the death of his father and lived on an inheritance, allowing him to pursue scholarly endeavors. He took a small part in politics, actively opposing the slave trade. The present book picks up the history of England after the essay in Hallam's book on the Middle Ages (see 848). Despite his effort to remain non-partisan by avoiding more recent events, Hallam was accused of showing his Whig colors in this work. The book became an important text for English politicians.

847. Hallam, Henry. *Introduction to the Literature of Europe.* (London: John Murray, 1847). 3 vols. 574, 589, 668pp.

A635, B1064 (author, title, date, 3 vols.), JS121 (Anon./Literature), JS1124. B1064 notes that Dodgson's copy is a "birthday gift from L. L. with inscription." L. L. is presumably Dodgson's aunt Lucy Lutwidge. Hallam traces the topic which he introduced in his work on the Middle Ages (see below). He defines literature broadly, including works on theology, philosophy, science, and law.

848. Hallam, Henry. *View of the State of Europe during the Middle Ages.* (London: John Murray, 1853). 3 vols. 504, 427, 517pp. 10th edition, with supplemental notes.

A635, B1064 (author, title, date, 3 vols.), JS1123. B1064 notes that Dodgson's copy is a "birthday gift from L. L. with inscription." L. L. is presumably Dodgson's aunt Lucy Lutwidge. A collection of nine essays, five being on the histories of France, Italy, Spain, Germany, and the Greek and Saracenic; the others being on the feudal system, the ecclesiastical system, the free political system, and the general state of society, commerce, manners, and literature.

849. Halliwell [later Halliwell-Phillipps], James Orchard (1820–89). *A Dictionary of Archaic and Provincial Words, Obsolete Phrases, Proverbs and Ancient Customs from the Fourteenth Century.* (London: J. R. Smith, 1847). 2 vols. 480, 480pp.

A360 (author, title, 2 vols.), JS1125. Earliest 2-volume edition of the only matching title in BL. Halliwell became a member of the Royal Society at the age of 18. He was an antiquary with a special interest in nursery rhymes (see below), and was the first to make a scholarly study of such verses. Later in his career he wrote a biography of Shakespeare and initiated the Shakespeare Museum in Stratford-upon-Avon.

850. Halliwell [later Halliwell-Phillipps], James Orchard, editor. *The Nursery Rhymes of England, Obtained Principally from Oral Tradition.* (London: Printed for the Percy Society by T. Richards, 1842). 192pp.

A842 (author, title), JS1126. Earliest edition in BL or BOD. Despite his claim about "oral tradition," Halliwell drew many of these rhymes from printed sources. He divided the rhymes into categories such as historical, jingles, riddles, proverbs, etc. He also gives notes describing the supposed origin of the rhymes. See below for the sequel.

851. Halliwell [later Halliwell-Phillipps], James Orchard, editor. *Popular Rhymes and Nursery Tales: A Sequel to the Nursery Rhymes of England.* (London: John Russell Smith, 1849). 276pp.

A874 (author, title), JS1127. Only edition in BL or BOD. Sequel to the above.

852. Halsted, George Bruce (1853–1922). *The Elements of Geometry.* (London: Macmillan and Co., 1886). 366pp.

A585 (author, title), JS1128 (listed under Halstead). Only edition in BL. Halsted was Professor of Mathematics at the University of Texas.

853. Hamerton, Philip Gilbert (1834–94). *Chapters on Animals.* (London: Seeley Jackson and Halliday, 1874). 252pp. With 20 etchings by J. Veyrassat and Karl Bodmer.

A824 (author, title), JS1129. Only edition in BL. Hamerton was an English author and artist who lived for a time in France and was briefly the art critic for *Saturday Review*. He launched *Portfolio*, an art review, in 1869 and contributed articles on art to many periodicals. The present book contains essays on dogs, cats, horses, bovines, asses, pigs, wild boars, wolves, kids, birds and animals in art. Bodmer (1809–93) was best known for his engravings of American Indians. Jules Jacques Veyrassat (1808–93) was a French painter of the Barbizon School.

854. Hamilton, Allan McLane (1848–1919). *Nervous Diseases: Their Description and Treatment.* (London: J. A. Churchill, 1878). 512pp.

A923 (author, title), JS1130 (listed as *Idiocy and Nervous Diseases*). While Hamilton did publish a work by the title listed in JS, BL describes this title only as being published "In Wood, George B. *Wood's Household Practice of Medicine*, 1881." The title listed here more closely matches the description in A923 ("Nervous Diseases by Hamilton"). A grandson of Alexander Hamilton, the author practiced medicine in New York City, specializing in nervous disorders.

855. Hamilton, James (1814–67). *The Mount of Olives, and Other Lectures on Prayer.* (London: J. Nisbet; Hamilton, Adams, 1846). 215pp. 20th thousand.

Uncertain. Not in JS. Listed in WS only and identified by property label only. Dodgson's copy is in WWC and has the property label on the cover. Hamilton was a minister of the National Scotch Church, Regent Square, London.

856. Hamilton, Robert George Crookshank (1836–95) and John Ball. *Book-keeping.* (Oxford: Clarendon Press, 1869). 92pp. 3rd edition.

E221 (authors, title, publisher, date), JS1131.

857. Hamilton, William (1704–54). *The Poetical Works of William Hamilton. Collated with the Best Editions by Thomas Park [1759–1854].* (London: John Sharpe, 1805). Vol. 1 (of 2). Part 23 of *Sharpe's Edition of the British Poets*.

Uncertain. Not in JS. Listed in WS only and identified by gothic stamp and property label only. WS makes no mention of 2 vols., but describes this edition in other particulars (date, editor). Dodgson's copy of volume 1 is in WWC. It is in its original wrappers and bears the gothic stamp and, on the cover, the property label. Hamilton, according to OCEL, made the "earliest Homeric translation into English blank verse."

858. Hamilton, William (1788–1856). *Lectures on Metaphysics and Logic.* (Edinburgh and London: Blackwood, 1861–66). 4 vols. 444, 568, 468, 520pp. 2nd edition, revised. Edited by Henry L. Mansel and John Veitch.

A509, B1065 (author, title, editors, 4 vols., 1861), JS1132. The 1st edition was published from 1859 to 1860. Dodgson's copy was likely this, the 2nd edition. Hamilton was a philosopher who attended Balliol College, Oxford. He held the chair in philosophy and metaphysics in Edinburgh from 1836. Hamilton introduced the logical doctrine of Quantification of the Predicate; his views as a philosopher were attacked by Mill (see 1349).

859. Hammond, Edward Payson (1831–1910). *The Conversion of Children.* (London: [1878]).

E354 (author, title), JS1133. Only 19th-century edition in BL. Hammond was an American evangelist who traveled throughout North America and Europe. He preached in London for six weeks in 1867 and helped establish the Children's Special Service Mission there. The full title of the 1st American edition (1878) was *The Conversion of Children: Can It Be Effected? How Young? Will They Remain Steadfast? Means to be Used, When Received and How Trained in the Church.*

860. *Hand-Book Guide for the University Galleries, Oxford. Containing Catalogues of the Works of Art in Sculpture and Painting.* (Oxford: J. Fischer, 1848). 57pp.

E76 (title, date), JS191 (Anon./Oxford). The University Galleries opened in 1845 and merged with the Ashmolean in 1908. This was an annual publication issued under various titles from 1846 until at least 1883.

861. Hardy, Thomas (1840–1928). *Tess of the D'Urbervilles.* (London: James R. Osgood, McIlvaine and Co., 1891). 3 vols. 264, 280, 280pp. 1st edition.

A624 (author, title, edition, 3 vols.), JS1134.

862. Harper, [William C.] (1790–1847), [James Henry] Hammond (1807–64), [William Gilmore] Simms (1806–70), [Thomas] Dew. *The Pro-Slavery Argument; as Maintained by the Most Distinguished Writers of the Southern States: Containing the Several Essays, on the Subject, of Chancellor Harper, Governor Hammond, Dr. Simms, and Professor Dew.* (Philadelphia: Lippincott, Grambo, & Co., 1853).

E341 (title, some contributors, city, date), JS282 (Anon./Sociology). First published in 1852 (400pp.). Harper was a South Carolina lawyer, judge, Speaker of the State House, and defender of states' rights. Hammond was editor of the *Southern Times*, served in Congress from 1835 to 1836, was governor of South Carolina from 1842 to 1844, and a senator from 1857 to 1860. Simms, a South Carolinian, felt that slavery was "an especially and wisely devised institution of heaven." Dew was an academic from Virginia who specialized in political science and economy. The book defends slavery on religious, moral, and economic grounds.

863. [Harris, Elizabeth Furlong Shipton] (1822–52). *From Oxford to Rome: and How it Fared with Some who Lately Made the Journey.* (London: Longman, Brown, Green & Longmans, 1847). 277pp.

A870, B1159 (title, author [given incorrectly as "Haries"], date), JS1135 (listed under Haries). Dodgson's copy is in the collection of Jon Lindseth, Cleveland, OH. It has Dodgson's monogram in pencil "in a juvenile hand" on the front pastedown and an advertisement for the Brooks sale pasted in. Harris encouraged John Henry Newman to write an account of his conversion to Rome, which became *Loss and Gain* (see 1435). A novelistic account of an Anglican parish priest and his conversion to Rome (and related topics). The hero finds Rome not quite what he had hoped. The author describes herself as "an actual convert."

864. [Harris, Elizabeth Furlong Shipton]. *Rest in the Church.* (London: Longman & Co., 1848). 348pp. "By the author of *From Oxford to Rome.*"

B1195 (title, "By the author of From Oxford to Rome"), JS1136. Only edition in BL. *The Athenæum* wrote, "Her present homily, if it mean anything, is put forward to recommend fidelity to conviction.... What childish, unworthy work this is ... crude and ill-digested theology." It further noted that the work was especially offensive as "it is shown, as in the case before us, that the neophyte would rather make up the mind of any other person than her own."

865. Harris, John (1667?–1719). *Navigantium Atque Itinerantium Bibliotheca, or, A Compleat Collection of Voyages and Travels. Consisting of Above Four Hundred of the most Authentick Writers, Beginning with Hackluit and Continued with Others of Note, Relating to any Part of Asia, Africa, America, Europe or the Islands thereof, to this Present Time. Also an Appendix of the Remarkable Accidents at Sea Together with the Invention and Use of the Magnet, and its Variation.* (London: Printed for Thomas Bennet, John Nicholson, and Daniel Midwinter, 1705). 2 vols.

A739 ("Harris's Voyages, 2 vols."), JS1137. Earliest edition in BL. Two other 2-volume editions are possibilities, one revised by J. Campbell (London: 1744–48), the other a republication of Campbell's version (London: T.

Osborne, 1764). Harris was an English writer best known for this collection of voyage writings and for editing one of the first English encyclopedias. Dodgson wrote an essay on Hakluyt which he read at "Gaudies" at Christ Church on 31 June 1856.

866. Harrison, Alexander James (b. 1839). *Problems of Christianity and Scepticism. Lessons from Twenty Years' Experience in the Field of Christian Evidence.* (London: Longmans & Co., 1891). 340pp.

A789 (author, title), JS1139. Earliest edition in BL. Harrison was a Master of Magdalene Hospital, Newcastle-on-Tyne, and a lecturer to the Christian Evidence Society. He wrote a number of works in the field of Christian evidence.

867. Harrison, Alexander James. *The Repose of Faith in View of Present-day Difficulties.* (London: Longmans, Green, 1894). 320pp.

A788 (author, title), JS1138. Only edition in BL. Defends Christianity in light of science and scepticism. The author writes of himself that he is "one of a large number who passed from Scepticism to Christianity, not only without ceasing to be free inquirers, but just because they were free inquirers."

868. Harrison, Mrs. Burton [Constance Cary Harrison] (1843–1920). *Alice in Wonderland. A Play for Children in Three Acts.* (New York: The deWitt Publishing House, 1890). 35pp.

A720, A721 ("Alice in Wonderland. A Play"), not in JS. This was one of only three plays of *Alice* published before Dodgson's death, and clearly the one referred to here as the others are listed under their proper titles elsewhere. In a letter of 11 March 1895 to Mrs. C. H. O. Daniel, Dodgson wrote "I have three dramatised versions of *Alice in Wonderland*, one by Mr. Savile Clarke, one by Mrs. Freiligrath-Kroeker, and one by Mrs. Burton Harrison." (See *Letters*, 1056).

869. Harrison, J. *The Etymological Enchiridion, or Practical Analyzer, Shewing the Etymon or Root of all the Words in the English Tongue, which are Derived from the Latin, Greek, Hebrew, French, Italian and Spanish Languages: Together with an Explication of the Proper Names Found in the Scriptures and in the Classics; as Well as the Meaning of Christian Names now Used among us, in French and English. The Whole Arranged Alphabetically, Synthetically, and Analytically.* (Preston, Lancashire: Printed for the author; sold in London by Harding, Mavor, and Lepard; Longman and Co., etc., 1823).

B1066 (author, title, date), JS1140. The author was the incumbent curate of Grimsargh, near Preston, Lancashire.

870. Harte, F[rancis] Bret (1836–1902). *That Heathen Chinee and Other Poems, Mostly Humorous.* (London: John Camden Hotten, [1871]). 140pp. Illustrated by Joseph Hull.

A252 (author, title, illustrator), not in JS. This is the 1st English edition, apparently quickly reprinted with the addition of music by Stephen Tucker. Harte was an American who lived his final years in England. The title poem was meant to be a satire on anti–Chinese sentiment. It was widely popular but frequently misinterpreted and used as a rallying cry against a low-paid Chinese labor force.

871. Harting, James Edmund (1841–1928). *The Ornithology of Shakespeare Critically Examined, Explained and Illustrated.* (London: J. Van Voorst, 1871). 321pp. Illustrated.

A871 (title), JS128 (Anon./Literature). Only 19th-century edition in BL. Harting wrote a number of books on birds. Twentieth-century reprints refer to this title as a "critical examination and explanation of bird life in Elizabethan times as reflected in the works of Shakespeare."

872. Hartland, Edwin Sidney (1848–1927). *The Science of Fairy Tales. An Inquiry into Fairy Mythology.* (London: Walter Scott, 1891 [1890]). 372pp. In *The Contemporary Science Series*, edited by Henry Havelock Ellis.

A903 (author, title), JS1141. Only 19th-century edition in BL or BOD. Hartland was a British folklorist. This work concentrates mainly on Celtic and Teutonic legends and examines the principles and methods used by those investigating popular superstitions.

873. H[artshorne], C[harles] H[enry] (1802–65), editor. *Ancient Metrical Tales;*

Printed Chiefly from Original Sources.
(London: W. Pickering, 1829). 344pp.

A888, B1067 (author, title, publisher, date),
JS1142. Hartshorne was educated at St. John's
College, Cambridge and served as rector of
Cogenhoe and of Holdenby, Northampton-
shire. This collection includes "King Aethel-
stone," "A Tale of King Edward and the
Shepard," "Piers of Fulham," "A Ladye that was
in Dyspeyre" "A Tale of the Unnatural Daughter," "The Mourning of the Hare," "A Tale of
Robin Hood," "The Cokwolds Daunce," and
others.

874. Harvey, William (1806–76). *The Ear
in Health and Disease, with Practical Remarks on the Prevention and Treatment of
Deafness.* (London: Renshaw, 1856). 235pp.
2nd edition, revised and improved.

E134 (title, author, date), JS1143. Harvey was
a fellow of the Royal College of Surgeons and
author of books on the ear, rheumatism, and
corpulence. Dodgson had hearing loss in one
ear as a result of a childhood illness. In a letter
recommending the service of Harvey to a
friend, Dodgson wrote, "I have formed a *very*
high opinion of his talents as an aurist." (See
Letters, 156).

875. Hatch, Edwin (1835–89). *The Influ-
ence of Greek Ideas and Usages upon the
Christian Church.* (London: Williams &
Norgate, 1890). 359pp. The Hibbert Lec-
tures for 1888. Edited by A[ndrew]
M[artin] Fairbairn.

A790 ("Hatch's Hibbert Lectures, 1888"),
JS1144. Earliest edition in BL or BOD. Hatch
was a controversial theologian and the vice-
principal of St. Mary's Hall, Oxford from 1867
to 1885. Though Dodgson makes scant mention of Hatch in his diary, he was quite well
acquainted with the Hatch family and kept up
close friendships with the children for many
years. This work was one of several in which
Hatch challenged the High Church party.

876. Hatch, Edwin. *The Organization of
the Early Christian Churches. Eight Lectures
Delivered before the University of Oxford,
in the Year 1880.* (London: Rivingtons,
1881). 216pp. Bampton Lectures.

B1068 (author, title, series, date), JS1145.
Lectures include "Bishops and Deacons,"
"Clergy and Laity," "The Clergy as a Separate

Class," "The Parish and the Cathedral," and
"Councils and the Unity of the Church." Again,
in this work, Hatch stands up against the High
Church movement. See 797 for a review of this
work.

877. [Hatch, Edwin], editor. *The Student's
Handbook to the University and Colleges of
Oxford.* (Oxford: Clarendon Press, 1881).
6th edition, revised.

E312 (title, publisher, date), JS205 (Anon./
Oxford). Dodgson also owned a copy of the
1889 10th edition, revised (E313/JS205). His
copy of the 6th edition included his autograph
inside the cover; the 10th edition included his
initials inside the cover.

878. Hatton, Joseph (1839–1907). *The Lyceum "Faust."* (London: J. S. Virtue and
Co., 1894). 30pp. New edition. With illustrations from drawings by W. Telbin,
Hawes Craven, W. H. Margetson, J. Bernard Partridge, and Helen H. Hatton.
Reprinted from *The Art Journal.*

E288, JS1146. Dodgson's copy is in HAC and
has the gothic stamp opposite the half-title.
Hatton was a newspaper man who edited many
publications and, among his many positions,
served as a dramatic critic for *The Observer.* This
is a souvenir of the production of W. G. Wills'
adaptation of Goethe's *Faust* starring Henry Irving and Ellen Terry first produced at the Lyceum
Theatre on 19 December 1885 and revived on
14 April 1894. Dodgson saw the original production on 14 May 1886 and wrote in his diary,
"It is magnificently put on the stage, and Irving as Mephistopheles is wonderfully good.
Ellen Terry is of course exquisite as 'Margaret,'
and Mrs. Stirling very clever as 'Martha'."

879. Haughton, Samuel (1821–97). *Principles of Animal Mechanics.* (London:
Longmans, Green and Co., 1873). 495pp.

A922 ("Haughton's Animal Mechanics"),
JS1257 (listed under Haughton). Clearly an
error in A922 as there is no book by that title
listed in BL under Haughton. This is the 1st
edition; a 2nd edition was also published in
1873. Haughton was Professor of Geology at
Trinity College, Dublin and author of many
books on science. The present study includes
chapters on the muscular anatomy of marsu-
pials, the emu, the rhea, the Irish terrier (compared with the Australian dingo), the badger,
the Virginia bear, the otter, and the rhinoceros.

880. Havers, Alice (illustrator) (d. 1890). *A Book of Old Ballads.* (London: Hildesheimer & Faulkner, [1892]). 44pp.

A277, F178 (illustrator, title), JS1148 (missing the A277 citation). Only edition in BL. Dodgson's copy was offered at auction at Sotheby's, London, on 18–21 June 1928 (DAA1226). Dodgson first met the artist Mary Alice Havers (Mrs. Frederick Morgan) on 30 December 1885 and "found her pleasant." Shortly thereafter he helped arrange for the publication of *Bumble-Bee Bogo's Budget* with illustrations by Havers (see 1992). In 1889, when Harry Furniss threatened to quit his work as illustrator of *Sylvie and Bruno*, Dodgson planned to engage Havers to complete the work. In the end, Furniss continued, but Havers did draw the picture of the locket in *Sylvie and Bruno*. Dodgson clearly liked Havers' work, as he owned several of her illustrated volumes (see index) as well as the original artwork for *Bumble-Bee Bogo's Budget* and a set of proofs of drawings by Havers (E117 and E459). Havers exhibited 18 pictures at the Royal Academy between 1873 and 1880. The present volume includes verse by Burns, Thomas Moore, Shakespeare and others.

881. Havet, Alfred G. (b. 1827). *The Complete French Class-Book; or, Grammatical and Idiomatical French Manual, for the Use of British Schools and Private Students, etc.* (London, Glasgow [printed]: 1853).

E411 (author, title), JS1150. Earliest edition listed in BL. Dodgson's also owned the companion volume, Havet's *Livre du Maître* (see 883). Havet was Professor of French at the Scottish Institution and director of the Foreign Language Institute in Edinburgh. The 1869 edition described itself thus: "Containing French reader with questions and notes, lists of words and phrases in daily use, a grammar exhibiting a comparison between the two languages, French lessons illustrative of all the principles and peculiarities, and English translation of all the French illustrative lessons, progressive exercises upon all the rules and remarks, a dictionary of 10,000 words and numerous idioms, forming a complete elementary course in one volume."

882. Havet, Alfred G. *Household French: Being a Practical Introduction to the French Language. With a Dictionary of the Words and Idioms.* (London: 1878). New edition.

E74 (author, title, date), JS1149. No publisher traced for this edition, but an 1874 edition was published by Simpkin, Marshall, & Co.

883. Havet, Alfred G. *Le Livre du Maître, ou Traduction Française de Tous les Thèmes, etc., du "Complete French Class-Book,"* etc. (London, Glasgow [printed]: [1858]).

E411 (author, title), not in JS. Only edition in BL. Dodgson's also owned the companion volume, Havet's *French Class–Book* (see 881). This book is "Adapted to the purposes of the teacher, and equally devised for self-instruction."

884. Haweis, Hugh Reginald (1838–1901). *Music and Morals.* (London: Strahan, 1873). 3rd edition. 566pp.

A330, D84 (author, title, city, date), JS1153, JS1261 (listed under Howeis). D84 notes Dodgson's initials. Haweis was educated at Cambridge and served in the war of Italian independence. Ordained in 1861, he was curate, in succession, of several churches in the greater London area. He was author of several hymns. The present work is in 4 books: "Philosophical: Music, Emotion, and Morals," "Biographical: From Ambrose to Handel," "Instrumental" (including sections on violins, piano-fortes, bells, and carillons), and "Critical: Music in England."

885. Haweis, Hugh Reginald. *The New Pet, or Pastimes and Penalties.* (London: 1875).

A557, A559, A644 (author, title), JS1151. BOD describes this as "A reissue of *Pet,* [see below] with chapter 10 rewritten and an extra chapter added at the end."

886. Haweis, Hugh Reginald. *Pet; or Pastimes and Penalties.* (London: 1874 [1873]). With fifty illustrations by M[ary] E[liza] Haweis.

A557, A559, A560, A644, E298 (author, title, date), JS1152. The 1874 New York edition had 314pp. An illustrated children's novel. Dodgson owned at least 7 copies (including those under the title *The New Pet,* see above). Dodgson saw the author preach on 12 May 1878 and wrote in his diary, "It was a very able and eloquent lecture on 'War', but not a Christian sermon, I thought." Dodgson apparently kept copies of *Pet* on hand to give to young friends. In a December 1873 letter to Caroline Erskine,

I shall never marry you now, Ben!

Ethel on her deathbed in the closing chapter of H. R. Haweis' *Pet*. Illustration by M. E. Haweis (item 886).

responding to her request for the names of new books for children he wrote, that *Pet*, "seems a very clever book, and has capital pictures by Mrs. Haweis. I have given one copy to a little girl of 9, who writes that she likes it 'very much indeed'." In an 1885 letter he writes of giving a copy to another child friend.

887. Hawthorne, Nathaniel (1804–64). *The Blithedale Romance*. (London: Chapman and Hall, 1854). 300pp. 2nd English edition. In the *Select Library of Fiction* series.

E15 (author, title, edition, date), JS1154. Hawthorne served as American Consul in Liverpool from 1853 to 1857. This work is a satire of the New England transcendentalists' experiment at Brook Farm.

888. Hawthorne, Nathaniel. *Dr. Grimshaw's Secret A Romance*. (London: Longmans, Green, and Co., 1883). 304pp.

A611 (author, title), JS1155. 1st English edition. The book was written in 1861 but published posthumously. It is said to contain much

that is autobiographical, especially the title character, said to represent Hawthorne's childhood guardian.

889. Hawthorne, Nathanial. *Our Old Home*. (London: Smith, Elder, 1864). 312pp. 2nd English edition.

A599, D85 (author, title, city, date), JS1156. D85 notes Dodgson's initials. One of two books (the other is *English Note Books*) in which Hawthorne records his life in England.

890. Hawthorne, Nathaniel. *Passages from the American Note-Books of Nathaniel Hawthorne*. (London: Smith Elder and Co., 1868). 309pp. 2nd edition.

DAA1258 (author, title, date), not in JS. This is the earliest 1-volume edition in BL (DAA does not specify multiple volumes). Dodgson's copy was offered at Sotheby's, London on 18–21 June 1928 and has his signature on the front end-paper. These notebooks were edited and published by his wife after Hawthorne's death.

891. Hawthorne, Nathaniel. *The Scarlet Letter*. Edition unknown.

A651 (author, title), JS1157. The early English editions were piracies, but the most likely of these are the second printing of the 1st edition (London: Henry G. Bohn, 1852) and the various printings of the 2nd English edition (London: G. Routledge, 1851–56).

892. Hawthorne, Nathaniel. *Transformation: or, The Romance of Monte Beni*. (London: Smith, Elder and Co., 1860). 3 vols. 273, 294, 285pp. 1st English edition.

A810, E299 (author, title, date, 3 vols.), JS1158. E299 notes that vol. 1 has the autograph of W. T. Dalby. Published in America in 1860 as *The Marble Faun*. Set in Rome, this novel is the story of how Count Donatello is transformed from an innocent into a remorseful killer.

893. Hawthorne, Nathaniel. *Twice Told Tales*. Edition unknown.

A651 (author, title), JS1159. The 1st English edition (a piracy) was published by Kent and Richards, [1849] and the pages reissued by William Tegg (1850). Other early English editions were published by Henry Bohn (1851) and G. Routledge (1852). Short stories.

894. Hawtrey, Stephen Thomas (1808–86). *An Introduction to the Elements of Eu-*

clid, *Being a Familiar Explanation of the First Twelve Propositions of the First Book.* (London: 1878). 2nd edition, [described as] Part 1.

E363 (author, title, date), JS1161. No publisher traced for the 1878 edition, but Longmans, Green, and Co. published the 3rd edition of 1880. Hawtrey was educated at Trinity College, Cambridge and was head mathematics master at Eton. He founded St. Mark's School in Windsor, and served as its Warden from 1851 to 1871.

895. Hawtrey, Stephen Thomas. *A Narrative-Essay on a Liberal Education, Chiefly Embodied in the Account of an Attempt to Give a Liberal Education to Children of the Working Classes.* (London: Hamilton, Adams, and Co., 1868). 102pp.

E322 (author, title, date), F140, JS1160. According to E322, Dodgson's was a presentation copy.

896. Hay, David Ramsay (1798–1866). *A Nomenclature of Colours, Hues, Tints and Shades, Applicable to the Arts and Natural Sciences, to Manufactures and Other Purposes of General Utility.* (Edinburgh [printed], and London: 1845). 72pp.

E275 (title, author, city, date), F159, JS1162. F159 notes the gothic stamp. Hay was a 19th-century Scottish house painter and color theorist who became influential in Victorian interior design. He and his company were decorative painters to Queen Victoria.

897. Haydn, Joseph (1786–1856). *Dictionary of Dates, and Universal Reference, Relating to all Ages and Nations ... With Copious Details of England, Scotland, and Ireland, etc.* (London: Edward Moxon, 1855). 724pp. 7th edition.

Not in JS. In his diary for 6 February 1856, Dodgson writes, "Got Haydn's *Dictionary of Dates*" (see *Diary 2*). First published in 1841; this is the edition closest to Dodgson's purchase.

898. Haydn, Joseph. *Haydn's Universal Index of Biography from The Creation to the Present Time, for the Use of The Statesman, the Historian, and the Journalist.* (London: E. Moxon, 1870). 586pp. Edited by J. Bertrand Payne.

A383, B1069 (author, title, date), JS1163. A biographical dictionary.

899. Haydon, Benjamin Robert (1786–1846). *Lectures on Painting and Design.* (London: Longman, Brown, Green and Longmans, 1844–46). 2 vols.

A593 (Haydon on Painting, 2 vols.), JS1164. Only edition in BL. Haydon was an English Romantic painter specializing in historical works on a grand scale. He painted portraits of Wordsworth and Keats.

900. Haydon, Benjamin Robert (1786–1846). *The Life of Benjamin Robert Haydon Historical Painter from his Autobiography and Journals.* (London: Longman, Brown, Green and Longmans, 1853). 3 vols. 386, 368, 358pp. Edited and compiled by Tom Taylor.

Not in JS. In his diary for 3 January 1855, Dodgson writes, "Read about half the first volume of Haydon's Life." He continued reading it in the following days. Only edition in BL. Taylor (1817–80) was a playwright, editor of *Punch*, and a friend of Dodgson.

901. Hazlehurst, George S. (b. 1850) *The Invisible Telegraph of the Future. Foretold in the Year of Her Majesty's Jubilee.* (London: Trübner & Co., 1887). 54pp.

D179 (author, title, city, date), JS1165. A book about communication by psychic force, which the author calls "mesmeric influence." Includes illustrations showing the results of communication between a sender and a blindfolded receiver, seated in separate rooms. "The time will come," Hazlehurst writes, "and probably during the lifetime of some now in the nursery, when our ocean cables will be reckoned among the crudities and lumber of a bygone age."

902. Hazlitt, William (1778–1830). *Characters in Shakespear's Plays.* (London: Printed by C. H. Reynell for R. Hunter, etc., 1817). 852pp.

A677 (author, title), JS1168. 1st edition. Another possibility is the edition edited by his son, William Carew Hazlitt (Dodgson owned at least 3 of his books); the earliest printing of this edition in was published in London by J. Templeman, 1838, (3rd ed.). A prolific essayist, Hazlitt wrote on art, drama, literature, and a variety of miscellaneous subjects. This was his first independent work on a literary topic.

903. Hazlitt, William. *Lectures on the English Poets. Delivered at the Surrey Institution.* (London: Printed for Taylor and Hessey, 1818). 331pp.

A578 (author, title), JS1167. 1st edition. Another possibility is the edition edited by Hazlitt's son, William Carew Hazlitt, first published in London by J. Templeman, 1841 (3rd ed.). Comprising eight lectures: "On Poetry in General," "On Chaucer and Spenser," "On Shakespeare and Milton," "On Dryden and Pope," "On Thomson and Cowper," "On Swift, Young, Gray, Collins, etc.," "On Burns, and the old English Ballads," and "On the Living Poets." The final essays includes some personal reminiscences of Coleridge and assessments of Wordsworth, Scott, and Southey.

904. Hazlitt, William Carew (1834–1913), editor. *English Proverbs and Proverbial Phrases, Collected from the Most Authentic Sources, Alphabetically Arranged and Annotated.* (London: Reeves and Turner, 1882). 532pp. 2nd edition, greatly enlarged and carefully revised.

A327, B1071 (editor, title, date), JS1166. William Carew Hazlitt was the son of the essayist William Hazlitt and edited editions of some of his father's works.

905. Hazlitt, William Carew. *The Present and the Future. A Little Book for Men and Women about Life and Death.* (London: Reeves & Turner, 1891). 136pp.

B1072 (author, title, date), JS1171.

906. Hazlitt, William Carew, editor. *Remains of the Early Popular Poetry of England.* (London: J. R. Smith, 1864–66). 4 vols. 288, 294, 321, 372pp. Collected, edited, and with an introduction and notes by William Carew Hazlitt.

A888, B1070 (editor, title, 4 vols., date [1864]), JS1170. A collection of medieval ballads and poems in Early English. Includes the adventures of Tom Thumb.

907. [Head, Francis Bond] (1793–1875). *Bubbles from the Brunnen of Nassau.* (London: John Murray, 1866). 282pp. 7th edition. "By an Old Man." Illustrated.

A914, B982 (author, title, date), JS1172. Head was a major in the Royal Army and the Lieutenant Governor of Upper Canada. *The Athenæum* described this book as "Just suited for the pocket and for Rhine travelers." It is a book of amusing anecdotes about the author's journeys in that region, after he was prescribed the waters from the "brunnen" of Nassau.

908. Headlam, A[rthur] W[illiam]. *In Memoriam of Thomas Dodgson, Esq. A Sermon Preached in Whorlton Church.* (1873).

E416 (author, title, date), JS1173. No copy traced; description taken from E416, which also notes "'The Reverend Charles Lutwidge Dodgson' inscribed." Thomas Dodgson was a distant relative of Charles L. Dodgson, but there is no mention of him in the published diaries or letters. Whorlton is in Country Durham near Castle Bernard. The author was the incumbent of that parish.

909. Headlam, Stewart Duckworth (1847–1924). *Priestcraft and Progress, Being Sermons and Lectures.* (London: J. Hodges, 1878). 116pp.

E227 (author, title, date), JS1174. Headlam was a controversial Anglican clergyman who fell, early in life, under the influence of Christian Socialist and Dodgson's friend F. D. Maurice. Some of Headlam's unorthodox opinions were shared by Dodgson, particularly his rejection of the doctrine of Eternal Punishment and his defense of the theatre as a harmless pastime.

910. [*Health Primers* series]. *Premature Death: Its Promotion or Prevention.* (London: Hardwicke & Bogue, 1878). 94pp.

E171 (title, series, date), JS171 (Anon./ Medical). E171 notes this has "Lewis Carroll's marking in two places." BL lists editors in the series as John Langdon Haydon Down, Joseph Mortimer Granville, Henry Power and John Tweedy. See 820 for another item in this series.

911. [*Health Primers* series]. *The Skin and its Troubles.* (London: Hardwicke & Bogue, 1878).

E364 (title), JS172 (Anon./Medical). Earliest edition traced. An 1896 D. Appleton edition was 94pp. E364 described this book as "including a section on the hair" and with the initial autograph of C. L. D. No publisher listed in BL, but other titles in this series published by Hardwicke & Bogue. See above for a note on this series.

Illustration of an image from the late second/
early third century for Thomas Heaphy's *The
Likeness of Christ* (item 912).

912. Heaphy, Thomas (1813–73). *The
Likeness of Christ, an Inquiry into the Veri-
similitude of the Received Likeness of our
Blessed Lord*. (London: D. Bogue, 1880).
78pp. With 12 mounted color lithographic
plates. Edited by Wyke Bayliss.

A543 (author, title), JS1175. A portion of this
work originally appeared in *The Art Journal*.
Dodgson's copy was sold at auction in 1938 (see
DAA1957). DAA describes this as dated 1881,
but neither BL nor BOD give editions other
than 1880 and 1886, nor has any 1881 edition
been discovered elsewhere. DAA describes
Dodgson's copy as "Signed on the end-paper,
'C. L. Dodgson, Ch. Ch. Oxford." Heaphy was
an artist admired by Dodgson, who commissioned him to do a painting called "Dreaming
of Fairyland." On 23 April 1867, Dodgson
called on Heaphy and wrote, "He showed me
also a most interesting collection of copies he
has made from the earliest and most authentic
portraits of Our saviour — he is going to publish a book on the subject." In a letter to his sister, Dodgson wrote of these portraits that
"They agree wonderfully in the character of the
face, and one, he says, there is no doubt was
done before the year 150." Dodgson may have
had some role in helping this book find publication. Following Heaphy's death in 1873
Dodgson had an advance version of this book
and he wrote in his diary in September 1873,

"Took Mr. Heaphy's book of sacred pictures to
show Macmillan," and in November 1873, "Mr.
and Mrs. Craik came to see Mr. Heaphy's
book," and "Ruskin came to see Mr. Heaphy's
book." The book compares early portraits of
Christ.

913. Heaphy, Thomas. *A Wonderful Ghost
Story, Being Mr. H.'s Own Narrative;
Reprinted from "All the Year Round," with
Letters, Hitherto Unpublished, of Charles
Dickens to the Author, Respecting It*. (Lon-
don: Griffith & Farran, 1882). 87pp. Edited
by Mrs. Heaphy.

B1073 (author, title, date), JS1176. *All the
Year Round* was edited by Charles Dickens.
B1073 describes this as a presentation copy
from the author. Dodgson wrote in his diary
on 23 April 1867, "Called and introduced myself to Heaphy the artist, with no further pre-
text than my admiration for his pictures and
the fact that Arthur Wilcox [Dodgson's cousin]
had corresponded with him about the ghost
story he wrote in *All the Year Round*.... We had
some talk about 'Mr. H's Story', and he told me
that the dinner party really consisted of five, as
the governess came down and sat on the same
side of the table as the ghost-lady."

914. Heather, John Fry (d. 1886). *A Treatise on Mathematical Instruments, Including Most of the Instruments Employed in
Drawing; for Assisting the Vision; in Sur-
veying and Levelling, in Practical Astronomy and for Measuring the Angles of Crys-
tals*. (London: John Weale, 1851). 170pp.
2nd edition.

E140 (author, title, date), JS1177. Heather was
the mathematics master at the Royal Military
Academy, Woolwich.

915. Heaton, James. *The Demon Expelled;
or, the Influence of Satan and the Power of
Christ Displayed in the Extraordinary
Affliction and Gracious Relief of a Boy about
Ten Years of Age, at Plymouth-Dock*. (Ply-
mouth Dock [England]: 1820). 156pp.

A885 ("Heaton's The Demon"), JS1178. Earliest traced edition of the only matching title in
BL. No publisher traced for this edition, but
the 2nd edition was published by Williams in
1822, the title beginning, "*The Extraordinary
Affliction*." The boy was John Evans.

916. Heber, Reginald (1783–1826). *Hymns, Written and Adapted to the Weekly Church Service of the Year.* (London: John Murray, 1827). 153pp. 1st edition. Edited by Amelia Heber, widow of the author.

A868 (author, title), JS1179. Earliest edition in BL. Heber became Bishop of Calcutta in 1823 and died in India. A preface to a later edition reads, in part, "The Hymns in this volume, which generally bear a relation to the Gospel of the Day, were arranged by the Bishop, and it was his intention to publish them soon after his arrival in India; but the arduous duties of his situation left little time, during the short life there allotted to him, for any employment not immediately connected with his diocese. The work is now given to the world in compliance with his wishes. Several of the Hymns are by [H. H. Milman, Walter Scott, Jeremy Taylor, &c.]; the remainder were composed by the Bishop at different intervals of leisure during his parochial ministry in Shropshire." Among Heber's best-known hymns are "Brightest and Best of the Sons of the Morning," and "Holy, Holy, Holy, Lord God Almighty."

917. Heber, Reginald. *Poems and Translations.* (London: Longman, Hurst, Rees, Orme, and Brown, 1812). 180pp.

A946 ("Heber's Poems"), JS1180. Earliest edition in BL of the closest matching title listed.

918. Helmore, Frederick. *Helmore's Singing Method. No. 1. The Little Ones' Book, etc.* (London: J. Masters & Co., [1881]).

E48 (author, title), JS1181. Only edition in BL. E48 states that this "contains the songs from *Alice in Wonderland*, those in *Through the Looking-Glass*, etc." Helmore was also author of a book called *Speakers, Singers, and Stammerers* (1874) which may have been of interest to Dodgson, who suffered from a hesitation of speech.

919. Helmuth, W[illia]m Tod (1833–1902). *A System of Surgery.* (New York: Carle & Grener, 1873). 1228pp. Adapted to Homœopathic practice. With over 400 woodcuts.

A538, D86 (author, title, city, date), JS175 (Anon./Medical), JS1182. Helmuth attended the Homœopathic Medical College of Pennsylvania before taking up his medical practice in Philadelphia. He helped found the Homœopathic Medical College of Missouri and served as President of the American Institute of Homœopathy. In 1870, he accepted the chair of Surgery in the New York Homœopathic Medical College. This work is his magnum opus.

920. Helps, Arthur (1817–75). *The Claims of Labour. An Essay on the Duties of the Employers to the Employed.* (London: William Pickering, 1844). 174pp.

A334 (author, title), JS1183. Earliest edition in BL. Arthur Helps was active in literary circles in Cambridge as an undergraduate before going on to a career in civil service. In 1859 he became Clerk of the Privy Council. Following Prince Albert's death, Helps revised, at the request of the Queen, the prince's speeches and also prepared Victoria's own *Leaves from the Journal of Our Life in the Highlands* for publication. He was the author of three novels and many other works, the most popular of which was *Friends in Council* (see 922). This work finds Helps writing on the relationship between masters and men, social government, and labour in factories. In his dedication he writes, "It appears to me that knowledge of the duties of an employer is every day becoming more important. The tendency of modern society is to draw the family circle within narrower and narrower limits. Those amusements which used to be shared by all classes are becoming less frequent … the master has less sympathy and social intercourse with his domestics."

921. Helps, Arthur. *Companions of My Solitude.* (London: William Pickering, 1851). 275pp.

A334 (author, title), JS1184. Earliest edition in BL. The companions are the same "characters" who appear as *Friends in Council* (see below). Though organized in chapters, instead of essays, this work is similar to *Friends in Council*. Helps shares his thoughts and allows his "companions" to comment on them as well.

922. Helps, Arthur. *Friends in Council: A Series of Readings and Discourse Thereon.* (London: William Pickering, 1847, 1849). 1st series, 2 vols. 228, 370pp.; and (London: John W. Parker and Son, 1859). New series, 2 vols. 274, 324pp.

A334, A341 (author, title, series), JS1185. 1st editions of the works which established Helps' reputation. A series of conversation between intellectual friends on topics including (in the first series) "Truth," "Greatness," "Living with Others," "Taking Criticism," "The Arts of Living Public Improvement," and "Conditions of the Rural Poor." In the second volume of the first series pieces on slavery occupy over half the book: "That Slavery is Cruel, Needless, Unauthorized, Mischievous," "That the Preceding Propositions Apply to All Races," and "That Slavery Can be Done Away." The new series includes essays on "Worry," "War," "Criticism," "Self Advancement," "On the Miseries of Human Life," "Life is not so Miserable After All," "Lovers' Quarrels," "Despotism," and "The Need for Tolerance." Despite the popularity of these conversations, CHEAL notes their "conspicuous lack of substance." In his diary for 16 March 1855, Dodgson wrote, "Finished this morning the first volume of *Friends in Council*, a book beautifully written, and I think well worth a second perusal. If the conversation has a fault, it is the too great similarity of style in the different speakers."

923. [**Helps**, Arthur]. *Realmah*. (London: Macmillan and Co., 1868). 2 vols. 299, 320pp.

A341 (author, title, 2 vols.), JS1186. 1st edition and the only 2-volume edition in either BL or BOD. Novel.

924. [**Helps**, Arthur]. *Social Pressure*. (London: Daldy Isbister & Co., 1875). 412pp. "By the author of Friends in Council."

A334 (author, title), JS1187. Only edition in BL or BOD. A final volume of the *Friends in Council* series (see 922).

925. Helps, Arthur. *Thoughts upon Government*. (London: Bell & Daldy, 1872). 245pp.

A341 (author, title), JS1188. Only edition in BL or BOD. A work divided into 21 chapters, including "The Fitness of the British People for Good Government," "The Relation between the Political and Permanent Officers of State," "On Attracting Able Men to the Service of Government," "On Improvement in Contrast with Reform," and "Government and the Press." In his dedication, Helps writes, "without ignoring the largest and deepest political questions, more of the social well-being of the people may be made to depend upon improvement, in the matters which I have alluded to, than even in what are called great reforms."

926. Henderson, William (1813–91) and S[abine] Baring-Gould. *Notes on the Folk-Lore of the Northern Counties of England and the Borders, by William Henderson, with an Appendix on Household Stories by S. Baring-Gould*. (London: Longmans, Green & Co., 1866). 344pp. Color frontispiece.

A882 ("Folklore of the Northern Counties of England"), E283 (title, authors, date), F173, JS351 (Anon./Topography), JS461, JS1190. 1st edition. E283 describes this as having "the initials of Lewis Carroll on the inside of cover." F173 notes the gothic stamp. See 105 for a note on Baring-Gould. *Saturday Review* wrote, "A pleasant collection of stories of various kinds, mainly from the bishopric of Durham and other parts of old Northumberland, but illustrated by kindred tales from other parts ... Mr. Henderson simply tells his stories; ... he makes no attempt to enter on the scientific side of his subject. This he leaves to Mr. Baring-Gould."

927. Henrici, Olaus [Magnus Friedrich Erdmann] (1840–1918). *Elementary Geometry: Congruent Figures*. (London: Longmans, Green, and Co., 1879). 188pp. In the *London Science Class-Books, Elementary Series*, edited by G. Carey Foster and Philip Magnus.

E162 (author, title, date), JS1191. Dodgson's copy is in HAC and has his monogram in purple ink on the front paste-down. Includes minor annotations in Dodgson's purple ink throughout. Henrici was a mathematician born in Germany who came to England in 1865. This work is a text intended for schools. Dodgson reviews this work at length in his *Supplement to Euclid and his Modern Rivals* (1885).

928. Herbert, George (1593–1633). *The Poetical Works of George Herbert, with Life, Critical Association, and Explanatory Notes by the Rev. George Gilfillan*. (Edinburgh: Nicol, 1853). 328pp.

A401 ("Herbert's Poems"), JS1192. Dodgson's copy is in the collection of Jon Lindseth, Cleveland, OH. It has "Herbert's Poems" on the spine, and so certainly corresponds to A401. It is signed "C. L. Dodgson Ch. Ch." in black ink on the front paste-down. Educated at Cambridge, Herbert served as public orator there from 1619 to 1627 before being appointed to the living at Bemerton. His poems are of a religious nature. According to his diary, on 26 January 1856 Dodgson sent a volume of Herbert to be bound. Herbert's poems and related material occupy pp. 1–214; pp. 215–328 include C. Hervey's *The Synagogue* (an imitation of Herbert) and *Jacule Pruveuture; or Outlandish Proverbs, Sentences, etc.,* (edited by Herbert). See 776 for more on Gilfillan.

929. Herbert, George and Francis Quarles. *Six Hymns with Alphabet.* (Brighton: Moon Printing Works). Printed in Dr. [William] Moon's Type for the Blind.

E113 (title, authors, type), JS1543. No copy traced, described from E113. William Moon (1818–94), who was blind by the time he was 20, invented a new method of embossed printing for the blind in the early 1840s. Moon's system soon became a great success and was the standard eventually displaced by Braille in the 1870s and 1880s. Publications in Moon type continued to be issued from his press in Brighton until 1960.

930. Herkomer, Hubert von (1849–1914). *An Idyl; A Pictorial-Music-Play, the Music Composed (and the Play Illustrated) by Hubert Herkomer. The Lyrics by Joseph Bennet.* (London: Novello, Ewer and Co. [1889]). 152pp. Illustrated with etchings. One of 500 signed copies printed on handmade paper with an illustrated title page.

D87 (authors, title, "etched title-page," "Signed"), JS1193. Herkomer was a German-born artist who trained in London and began his career as a book and magazine illustrator. He later turned to portraiture, which made him a wealthy man. He painted the posthumous portrait of Dodgson that hangs in the Great Hall at Christ Church, Oxford. Dodgson saw an amateur theatrical production by Herkomer on 13 June 1889, but it is not clear if that bore any relation to this publication.

931. Hermann, Charles Frederick. *A Manual of the Political Antiquities of Greece, Historically Considered.* (Oxford: D. A. Talboys, 1836). 423pp. Translated from the German.

B1075 (author, title, date), JS1195. B1075 notes that Dodgson's copy was a "Rugby School Prize, Christmas 1848, with arms and inscription." The preface states, "The author's object has been twofold; to give the philological public a comprehensive survey of the political institutions of ancient Greece ... and, at the same time, to supply the want of a satisfactory abstract of a study so generally interesting to scientific spirit of the age."

932. Herrick, Robert (1591–1674). *Chrysomela. A Selection from the Lyrical Poems of Robert Herrick.* (London: Macmillan & Co., 1877). 199pp. Arranged with Notes by Francis Turner Palgrave.

A831, B1076 (author, title, editor, date), JS1196. The 1st edition was published in May, 1877 and was reprinted in October of that same year. In his preface, Palgrave says of Herrick, "We have greater poets, not a few; none more faithful to nature as he saw her, none more perfect in his art; — none more companionable."

933. Hertz, Henrik (1798–1870). *King René's Daughter: A Danish Lyrical Drama.* (London: William S. Orr, 1850). 78pp.

A474 ("King Rene's Daughter, translated by Theodore Martin, scored for Miss Faircett [sic] in the character of Iolanthe, 1850"), JS1197. Hertz was a Danish poet and playwright. A note in the American edition of the same year explains, "This translation was prepared upwards of two years ago with the view of being produced on the English Stage. The part of Iolanthe, one of the most exquisite creations of modern poetry, seemed to be peculiarly adapted to the genius of Miss Helen Faucit [see 1304]. It was accepted and studied by that lady ... and the piece was on the point of being produced by her in Dublin last season, when circumstances occasioned its temporary postponement. The recent production of the piece at the Strand Theatre took place with Miss Faucit's permission." The actress Helen Faucit was the wife of the translator, Theodore Martin. Dodgson saw and admired her performance as Imogen in *Cymbeline* in 1864.

934. Hervey, Thomas Kibble (1799–1859). *Australia; With Other Poems.* (London: Hurst, Robinson & Co., 1825). 169pp. 2nd edition.

D225 (author, title, city, date), not in JS. Dodgson's copy was bound with Watts' *Poetical Sketches* (see 2213). Hervey was editor of *The Athenæum* from 1846 to 1854.

935. Hervey, Thomas Kibble. *The Poems of Thomas Kibble Hervey.* (Boston: Ticknor and Fields, 1866). 437pp.

Uncertain. A867 ("Hervey's Poems"), JS1198 (listed under James Hervey). James Hervey, according to both OCEL and DEL, was not a poet, nor do either BL or BOD list any poetic works by him. Thomas Kibble Hervey is the only Hervey listed as a poet in DEL. A867 could refer to the above volume [*Australia*], but that was bound together with another title not mentioned in A867. Still, the chance remains that Dodgson did not own the present book, but that A867 merely referred to *Australia* and the cataloguer did not notice the second title bound with it. This is the only collection of Hervey's poems listed in either BL or BOD.

936. Hessey, James Augustus (1814–92). *Moral Difficulties Connected with the Bible: Being the Boyle Lectures for 1871.* (London: Society for Promoting Christian Knowledge, 1871). 219pp. 1st (of 3) series only.

C3 (author, title, date), JS1200. C3 lists only one volume dated 1871, the three series were published in three volumes from 1871 to 1873. Educated at St. John's College, Oxford, Hessey went on to be headmaster of the Merchant Taylors' School from 1845 to 1870 and was made Archdeacon of Middlesex in 1875. Before their publication, the lectures were titled "The Moral Treatment of Unbelief."

937. Hessey, James Augustus. *Sunday, Its Origin, History, and Present Obligation, Considered in Eight Lectures Preached before the University of Oxford in the Year MDCCCLX.* (London: J. Murray, 1861). 544pp. 2nd edition. Bampton Lectures for 1860.

A802, D89 (author, title, date), JS1199. D89 notes this is signed "C. L. Dodgson, Ch. Ch." *Saturday Review* wrote, "No small praise is due to the author for his frankness in running counter to much of the popular and feeble religionism of the day." Writing of the early Church, Hessey says, "In no clearly genuine passage that I can discover in any writer of these two [the fourth and fifth] centuries, or in any public document, ecclesiastical or civil, is the fourth commandment referred to as the ground of the obligation to observe the Lord's Day."

938. Hessey, Robert Falkner (1827–1911). *Drifting into Unbelief. An Appeal to Think-*

ing Men. (London: Skeffington & Son, 1885). 80pp.

E246 (author, title, date), JS1201. Hessey was a fellow of Magdalen College and rector of Basing, Hampshire.

939. Hewlett, Henry G. (1832–97), editor. *The National Music of the World.* (London: Sampson Low & Co., 1880). 225pp.

A594 (title), JS178 (Anon./Music). Only 19th-century edition in BL. Hewlett was keeper of records of Inland Revenue.

940. Heygate, William Edward (b. ca. 1817). *Allegories and Tales.* (London: Rivingtons, 1873). 279pp.

A560, E420 (author, title, date), F173, JS1202. F173 notes the gothic stamp. Heygate attended St. John's College, Oxford and was ordained in 1840. In 1869 he became rector of Brightstone, Isle of Wight, and in 1887 a canon of Winchester. His oeuvre of over 25 titles comprises devotional works, religious works, novels and tales, poetry, and more. A collection of 63 short tales, chiefly moral.

941. Hime, Maurice Charles (b. 1841). *Morality. An Essay on Some Points Thereof, Addressed to Young Men.* (London: J. & A. Churchill, 1883). 175pp. 5th edition, enlarged.

D90 (author, title, date), JS1204. D90 notes Dodgson's initials. The 6th edition was also published in 1883. Hime, the headmaster of Foyle College in Londonderry, here makes an argument for chastity.

942. Hingeston, James Ansley. *Topics of the Day: Medical, Social and Scientific.* (London: John Churchill & Sons, 1863). 400pp.

E170 (author, title, date), JS1205.

943. Hinton, James (1822–75). *Life in Nature.* (London: Smith, Elder, 1862). 258pp.

E207 (author, title, date), JS1206. E207 notes this has the author's autograph. Hinton was a successful aural surgeon who gave up his post in 1874 to pursue his philosophical studies full time. The *Academy* wrote of him, "His thinking was a spiritual, not an intellectual, process; and the visions he saw revolved round the profoundest themes, — God, life, man, and above all, combining and concentrating them all, the great world-tragedy of woman." This work was originally published as a series of papers in

Cornhill Magazine under the title "Physiological Riddles," and showed his skill for making science popular.

944. [**Hinton**, James]. *Man and his Dwelling Place; An Essay Towards the Interpretation of Nature.* (London: John W. Parker and Son, 1859). 416pp.

A506 (title), JS1207. Earliest edition of the only matching title in BL. Published in the same year as *Origin of Species*, this represents Hinton's struggles to reconcile his Christianity with scientific advances.

945. Hinxman, Emmeline. *Poems.* (London: 1857). 2nd edition.

A834, B1077 (author, title, edition, date), JS1208. NUC and BL give no publisher for this edition; the 1st edition (1856) was published by Longman, Brown, Green, Longmans & Roberts (183pp.) *Saturday Review* wrote, "The simple and natural product of a thoughtful and earnest yet gentle mind."

946. [**Hodge**, John Barwick]. *West Somerset Ballads.* (London: J. Swain & Son, 1895). 32pp.

E260 (title), JS142 (Anon./Literature). Only edition in BL. Hodge matriculated at Christ Church, Oxford in 1882 and received his B.A. in 1886. E260 quotes the preface: "These poems have been translated into the London dialect for the convenience of readers, except where rhyme or rhythm demanded the retention of the original form."

947. Hoffmann, Louis [pseud. of Angelo John Lewis] (1839–1919). *Puzzles Old and New.* (London & New York: Frederick Warne & Co., 1893). 394pp.

A342, B1078 (author, title, date), JS1209. Lewis was a barrister and magician and an important writer on stage magic. This book includes hundreds of puzzles of many types— word puzzles, arithmetical puzzles, mechanical puzzles, puzzles with counters and many more. Dodgson was a great lover of puzzles and conundrums and invented many himself. On p. 241, under the title "Transformations," is essentially the same puzzle as Dodgson's "Doublets." Two of the examples are also used by Dodgson: Black into White (Dodgson does it in 7 moves to Hoffmann's 8) and Blue into Pink (4 moves for Hoffmann, who inexplicably cheats, 9 for Dodgson).

948. Hofmann, Johann Jakob (1635–1706). *Joh. Jacobi Hofmanni Lexicon Universale, Historiam Sacram et Profanam ... Chronologiam ad Haec Usque Tempora; Geographiam et Veteris et Novi Orbis ... Explanans.* (Lugduni Batavorum: Apud J. Hackium, C. Bovtesteyn, P. Vander Aa, & J. Lvchtmans, 1698). 4 vols. 1072, 900, 994, 762pp.

A744 ("Hofmann's Lexicon, 4 vols."), JS1210 Only 4-volume edition of the only matching title in BL. The title in JS1210 — *Hofmann's Lexicon der Chemisch-technischen und Pharmaceutischen Präparate ... Mit einem Vorworte und Sachregister von E. Winckler*— was published in 1 volume in 1861. Hofmann's encyclopedic work covered sacred and profane topics, history, mythology, etc.

949. Holbein, Hans (1497–1543). *Holbein's Dance of Death Exhibited in Elegant Engravings on Wood, with a Dissertation on the Several Representations of that Subject, by Francis Douce, Esq., F.A.S. Also, Holbein's Bible Cuts, Consisting of Ninety Illustrations on Wood, with Introduction by Thos. Frognall Dibdin.* (London: Henry G. Bohn, 1858). 475pp. In *Bohn's Illustrated Library.* Reprint of the 1833 edition.

E307 (author, title, date, publisher), JS1212. Holbein was a German artist who painted portraits of many of Henry VIII's court and was known for his precise drawings. *The Dance of Death* originated as a 14th-century morality poem or play. First published in Lyons in 1538, Holbein's collection of woodcuts titled *Dance of Death* quickly became one of the most popular early illustrated books. The cuts show the Peasant's War and Death as an equalizer of men. This was one of the finest 19th-century reproductions of Holbein's prints.

950. Hole, Charles. *A Brief Biographical Dictionary.* (London and Cambridge: Macmillan and Co., 1866). 485pp.

Not in JS. Dodgson wrote to his publisher, Macmillan, about this volume on 30 June 1878. First published in 1865, this edition is described as being closest to Dodgson's letter. Hole was educated at Trinity College, Cambridge and was a lecturer in Ecclesiastical History at King's College, London. Each entry includes name, occupation, year of birth and date of death,

"The Drunkards" from Hans Holbein's *Dance of Death* (item 949).

usually all on a single line. Dodgson's letter complained that dates of birth should be included also. Macmillan replied that it would have taken too much space, but Dodgson continued to press his argument replying with a way that the information could be abbreviated and remain in a single line.

951. Holland, Edward. *Mabel in Rhymeland; or, Little Mabel's Journey to Norwich and her Wonderful Adventures with the Man in the Moon, and Other Heroes and Heroines of Nursery Rhyme.* (London: 1885).

A638, not in JS. In his diary for 11 September 1891, Dodgson notes, "Got 'Mabel in Rhymeland' by Edward Holland, as part of the collection I intend making of books of the 'Alice' type." Only edition in BL.

952. Holland, Henry (1788–1873). *Chapters on Mental Physiology.* (London: Longmans, 1852). 301pp.

A922 ("Holland's Chapters on Mental Philosophy"), JS1213. There is no book in BL by the title given in A922; clearly "Philosophy" was a misprint for "Physiology." Earliest edition in BL. Holland was an influential physi-

cian who spent most of his career in London where he was well known in the highest circles of society. This work attempts to illustrate the relationship between the body and the mind. Darwin cites this book in his *Expression of the Emotions, etc.* (see 529).

953. Holman, Henry (1859?–1919). *Questions on Logic.* (London: 1891). Part 1. A companion to Welton's *Manual of Logic*.

E247 (author, title), JS1214. 1st edition. There was a 2nd edition of 1897. Dodgson owned Welton's *Manual of Logic* in 2 volumes (see 2227). As his volume 1 was dated 1891, this earlier edition of Part 1 of the companion seems likely.

954. Holmes, Oliver Wendell (1809–94). *The Autocrat of the Breakfast Table.* (Edinburgh: Alexander Strahan; London: Hamilton, Adams, and Co., 1859). 302pp.

Not in JS. In a letter of 18 August 1884, Dodgson writes, of Holmes, "I wonder if you know his *Autocrat of the Breakfast Table*? I delight in it." 1st English edition. Holmes was an American poet, novelist, essayist and Harvard Professor of Anatomy and Physiology, who also published on another subject of interest to Dodgson, Homœopathic Medicine (as a debunker). This book weaves essays and other material into the context of breakfast conversations. The first of a series (see 959, 961, and 962).

955. Holmes, Oliver Wendell. *Before the Curfew and Other Poems, Chiefly Occasional.* (London: Sampson Low, Marston, Searle & Rivington, [1888]). 110pp.

A834, B1079 (author, title, n.d.), JS1215. 1st English edition. Collection of poems, many of which were read to the Harvard graduating class of 1929 at their annual meeting.

956. Holmes, Oliver Wendell. *Elsie Venner; A Romance of Destiny.* (London: Routledge, Warne, and Routledge, 1861). 428pp.

A811 (author, title), JS1216. 1st English edition. First published as "The Professor's Story" in *Atlantic* (Jan. 1860–April 1861). A novel that explores the notion of original sin through the story of a young woman who exhibits snake-like qualities because her mother was bitten by a rattlesnake shortly before bearing her.

957. Holmes, Oliver Wendell. *The Guardian Angel.* (London: Sampson Low & Co., 1867). 2 vols.

A811 (author, title, date, 2 vols.), JS1217. Novel. In the preface, Holmes writes, "I have attempted to show the successive evolution of some inherited qualities in the character of Myrtle Hazard, not so obtrusively as to disturb the narrative, but plainly enough to be kept in sight by the small class of preface-readers." Dodgson records in his diary having read this book during a bout of influenza in February 1895.

958. Holmes, Oliver Wendell. *A Mortal Antipathy.* (London: Sampson Low, Marston, Searle & Rivington, 1886). 307pp.

A811 (author, title, date), JS1218. The third and least successful of Holmes' "medicated novels."

959. Holmes, Oliver Wendell. *Over the Teacups.* (London: Sampson Low, Marston, Searle & Rivington, 1890). 319pp.

A338 (author, title), JS1219. 1st English edition. A sequel to Holmes' popular *Breakfast Table* books (see 954). Now the imaginary conversations take place over tea. Also includes poetry.

960. Holmes, Oliver Wendell. *Poems.* (London: O. Rich and Sons, 1846). 175pp.

Not in JS. In a letter of 23 August 1854, Dodgson notes that he had recently "bought 3 other American poets in the cheap editions, Lowell, Willis, and Holmes." This is the only pre–1854 British edition listed in BL. The book was originally published in Boston in 1836, the year Holmes graduated from Harvard medical school.

961. Holmes, Oliver Wendell. *The Poet at the Breakfast-Table.* (London: G. Routledge and Sons, 1872). 370pp.

A338 (author, title), JS1220. 1st English edition. Another of the popular breakfast-table books (see 954).

962. Holmes, Oliver Wendell. *The Professor at the Breakfast-Table; with the Story of Iris.* (London: S. Low, Son & Co., 1860). 286pp.

A338 (author, title), JS1221. 1st English edition. A sequel to Holmes' *The Autocrat at the Breakfast Table* (see 954).

963. Holmes, Oliver Wendell. *Songs in Many Keys.* (London: Sampson Low, Son, and Co. 1863). 308pp.

A833 (author, title), JS1222. 1st English edition. Poetry.

964. Holmes, Oliver Wendell. *Soundings from the Atlantic.* (London: Sampson, Low, Son & Marston, 1864). 1st edition. 468 pp.

A338 (author, title), JS391 (Anon./Unclassified). 1st English edition. A collection of essays including "The Stereoscope and the Stereograph," and two other essays on photography. Holmes invented the American Stereoscope (a device for viewing images in 3-D) in 1860.

965. Holmes, Timothy (1825–1907), editor. *A System of Surgery, Theoretical and Practical, in Treatises by Various Authors.* (London: Longmans, Green, 1870–71). 5 vols. 2nd edition.

A534 (title, editor, 5 vols.), JS1223. Only 5-volume edition in BL. Holmes was a fellow of the Royal College of Surgeons and a consulting surgeon to St. George's Hospital, London. The five volumes comprise: "General Pathology," "Local Injuries," "Diseases of the Eye and Ear, the Organs of Circulation, Muscles, and Bones," "Diseases of the Organs of Locomotion, of Innervation, of Digestion, of Respiration, and the Urinary Organs," and "Diseases of the Genital Organs, of the Breast, Thyroid Gland, and Skin; Operative Surgery."

966. Holyoake, George Jacob (1817–1906). *Mathematics No Mystery: or the Beauties and Uses of Euclid.* (London: J. Watson, [1848]). 121pp. 2nd edition.

E94 (author, title), JS1224. Earliest edition in BL or BOD, but the piece was originally published in the *Athenæum* on 6 Nov. 1847, and that appearance may be the reason this is designated as 2nd edition. Holyoake was a leader of the free thought movement in England and was eventually convicted under English blasphemy laws, which he campaigned against. He campaigned for the education of the working classes, and taught mathematics at the Mechanics' Institution in Birmingham.

967. Home, Daniel Dunglas (1833–86). *Lights and Shadows of Spiritualism.* (London: Virtue & Co., 1877). 412pp.

A892, D180 (author, title, city, date), JS1225. Home was a Scottish spiritualist. He was adopted by an American aunt following the death of his mother and returned to England in 1855. He gave séances attended by many famous Victorians, including Robert Browning, who dismissed Home's abilities in the poem "Sludge the Medium." In 1866 he was adopted by a wealthy widow, who later sued for the return of her fortune, claiming Home had used "spiritual influence" to obtain her favor. Supposedly impartial scientists in both England and Russia tested Home's abilities, including his telekinesis, and concluded his claims were genuine. He was probably the most famous psychic of the Victorian age. He was always willing to perform or be tested in broad daylight. In this book he takes a strong stand against fraudulent mediums.

968. Homer (fl. 9th or 8th century B.C.E.). *Homeri Ilias et Odyssea.* (London: G. Pickering, 1831). 2 vols. 351, 272pp. *Pickering Diamond Classics* series.

A477 (author, series, 2 vols.), JS1226. *The Illiad* and *The Odyssey.* See 153 for a description of the *Pickering Diamond Classics.*

969. (Homœopathic Medicine). *British Homœopathic Medical Directory.* (1880).

So listed in E163/JS158, but no copy located. BOD lists editions from 1867 to 1874 of *The Homœopathic Medical Directory of Great Britain and Ireland,* and E163 probably represents the 1880 edition of that work.

970. (Homœopathic Medicine). *The Practical Test of Homœopathy: or, Cases of Cure by Homœopathic Remedies in the Practice of Various Physicians.* (London: Homœopathic Publishing Company, 1875). 2nd edition. 29pp. 4th of a series of *Homœopathic Missionary Tracts.*

Not listed separately in JS (see JS163). Dodgson's copy is in HAC in a small clothbound volume with 7 other tracts from this series and one additional Homœopathic pamphlet: *Ministers and Medicine* by Thomas Sims; *Principles, Practice, and Progress of Homœopathy* by E. H. Ruddock; *The Practical Test of Homœopathy; Measles; Homœopathy Explained* by John Wilde; *Constipation* by John Wilde; *Scarlet Fever* by John Maffey; and *Fallacies and Claims: Being a Word to the World on Homœopathy* by Peter Plain. The front pastedown bears the inscription "C. L. Dodgson, Ch. Ch. Oxford" in purple ink. Many of the pamphlets were reprinted from articles in *The Homœopathic World.* This pamphlet includes 12 cases by E. H. Ruddock, Adrian Stokes, J. C. Burnett, C. H. Marston, George Lade, J. H. Nankivell, A. C. Clifton and others. The pamphlet is trimmed closely on the bottom and Dodgson has written in the last line of text (a total of 5 words in purple ink) on pages 28–29.

971. Hone, William (1780–1842). *Ancient Mysteries Described: Especially the English Miracle Plays, Founded on Apocryphal New Testament Story, Extant among the Unpublished Manuscripts in The British Museum; Including Notices of Ecclesiastical Shows, The Festivals of Fools and Asses — The English Boy Bishop, The Descent Into Hell, The Lord Mayor's Show, The Guildhall Giants, Christmas Carols, with Glossary and Index.* (London: W. Hone, 1823). 298pp. Illustrated by George Cruikshank and others.

A676 (author, title), JS1230. Earliest edition in BL. Hone was a publisher, journalist and radical who challenged the powers that be in many areas. He lobbied for the extension of the franchise and the reform of insane asylums. After he was arrested for writing political satires in the form of parodies of the *Book of Common Prayer,* he won release and a major victory for freedom of the English press. One of the earliest works on the English miracle plays, this study is based on the collections of plays and notices at the British Museum.

972. Hone, William, editor. *The Apocryphal New Testament, Being all the Gospels, Epistles, and Other Pieces now Extant, Attributed in the First Four Centuries to Jesus Christ, His Apostles, and their Companions and not Included in the New Testament by its Compilers. Tr. from the Original Tongues, and Now First Collected into One Volume.* (London: W. Hone, 1820). 271pp.

A783 (title), JS496 (listed under Bible). Earliest edition traced of the only pre–1898 matching title in BL. Hone had been doing research in the British Museum for a planned, but never published, history of parody. This work and the preceding came as a result of that research. The book was highly controversial and condemned in the press. Hone seems to give

George Cruikshank illustrates *The Epping Hunt* (item 977).

equal weight to the gospels as to highly questionable writings such as Jeremiah Jones' (1693–1724) *New and Full Method of Settling the Canonical Authority of the New Testament* (London, 1726) and William Wake's *Genuine Epistles of the Apostolical Fathers* (London, 1693).

973. Hone, William. *Every-Day Book. Or The Guide To The Year: Relating the Popular Amusements, Sports, Ceremonies, Manners, Customs, and Events, Incident to The Three Hundred and Sixty-five Days in Past and Present Times: Being a Series of Five Thousand Anecdotes and Facts.* (London: Published for William Hone by Hunt & Clarke, 1826, 1827). 2 vols. 1719, 1711pp. Illustrated by George Cruikshank and others.

A397 (author, title, "original edition," date), JS1227. Each volume has an entry for every day of the year giving miscellaneous information in the style of an almanac. In spite of the popularity of the miscellany, Hone was driven into bankruptcy by the costs associated with its publication.

974. Hone, William. *The Table Book.* (London: Tegg and Co., 1827). 859pp.

A397 (author, title, "original edition," date), JS1229. On the same plan as *The Every-Day Book* (see above).

975. Hone, William. *The Year-Book of Daily Recreation and Information Concerning Remarkable Men and Manners, Times and Seasons … on the Plan of the Every-Day Book.* (London: Tegg and Co., 1832). 1643pp.

A397 (author, title, "original edition," date), JS1228. On the same plan as *The Every-Day Book* (see 973).

976. Hood, Thomas (1799–1845). *The Early Poems and Sketches of Thomas Hood Including "The Odes and Addresses to Great Men."* (London: E. Moxon, Son & Co., 1869). Edited by his daughter (Mrs. Frances Freeling Broderip).

B1081 (author, title, date), JS1231. Hood wrote comic and serious verse and edited several publications.

977. Hood, Thomas. *The Epping Hunt.* (London: Charles Tilt, 1829). 29pp. Illustrated with 6 engravings on wood after the designs of George Cruikshank.

A459 (author, title, illustrator, date), JS1232. A poem.

978. [Hood, Thomas]. *Memorials of Thomas Hood.* (London: E. Moxon, 1860). 2 vols. 343, 357pp. Collected, arranged, and edited by his daughter (Mrs. Frances Freeling Broderip). With a preface and notes by his son. Illustrated, with copies from his own sketches.

A879 (title, 2 vols.), JS1237. Only 2-volume edition in BL.

979. Hood, Thomas. *Miss Kilmansegg and Her Precious Leg: A Golden Legend.* (London: E. Moxon, 1870). 149pp. With 60 illustrations by Thomas Strong Seccombe.

A872 (author, title [given incorrectly as "Miss Vilmanseggs and Her Precious Leg"], illustrator), JS1236. Only 19th-century edition in BL. A serio-comic ballad poem about an heiress with an artificial leg made of gold.

980. Hood, Thomas. *Poems.* (London: Edward Moxon, 1846). 2 vols. 264, 273pp.

A945 ("Hood's Poems, 2 vols."), JS1233. See also A833 and A363. 1st edition. While there are other possibilities, this seems the most likely. It was the standard edition of Hood's works for many years, and was published in 2 vols. at least through the third edition of 1848. There are 3 editions of Hood's poems listed in the Brooks catalogue: A363 specifies 3 vols., yet there is no 3-volume edition listed in either BL or BOD; however, Dodgson might have had an edition specially bound in 3 volumes. A833 does not specify a number of volumes, and could be any of a number of editions, but if it were, for instance, that edited by Rossetti or that illustrated by Birket Foster, we might expect the Brooks catalogue to tell us so. A945 is probably the edition described above. In his diary for 28 February 1855, Dodgson writes, "young [Charles Sandford, a Christ Church graduate] presented me with *Hood's Poems*, as a sort of return for my coaching."

981. Hood, Thomas. *Whimsicalities: A Periodical Gathering. To Which are Added: 'York and Lancaster' and 'Lost and Found', the 'Epping Hunt' and 'Eugene Aram.'* (London: E. Moxon and Son, 1870). 605pp. Edited by his daughter (Mrs. Frances Freeling Broderip). With the original illustrations by the author, John Leech, George Cruikshank, and William Harvey.

A911 (author, title), JS1235. There was an 1844 edition, but it was published in 2 vols. As another item under A911 specifically mentions multiple volumes, it seems likely that this was a 1-volume edition. This is the earliest 1-volume edition in BL.

982. Hood, Thomas, the younger (1835–74). *From Nowhere to the North Pole A Noah's Ark-Æological Narrative.* (London: Chatto and Windus, 1875 [1874]). 232pp. Illustrated by W. Brunton and E. C. Barnes.

Not in JS. In his diary for 11 September 1891, Dodgson included this title in his list of "books of the 'Alice' type" he had collected. Hood was the son of the poet. He was editor of *Fun* and a prolific humorist. An article in *Nineteenth Century* in 1887 suggested that Dodgson may have taken the idea for AAIW from this book. Dodgson defended himself against the charge in a letter to the editor and in an advertisement that appeared in the back of many of his own books. When he discovered that *Nowhere* had been published nine years after *Alice*, he added this information to the advertisement. For a full account of this see Jan Susina "Imitations of Alice — Lewis Carroll and the Anxiety of Influence" (*Proceedings of the Second International Lewis Carroll Conference*). Susina calls *Nowhere* "a richly comic narrative." The story concerns a selfish boy named Frank whose experiences on a trip through fairyland cure him of his bad habits.

983. Hood, Tom [i.e. Thomas, the younger]. *Petsetilla's Posy: A Fairy Tale for Young and Old.* (London: George Routledge, [1870]). 156pp. 50 engravings by F. Barnard engraved by Dalziel brothers.

Not in JS. Dodgson's copy was in the collection of Denis Crutch and is now in the collection of David Lansley, Lincolnshire. It has Dodgson's monogram in purple ink on the front pastedown.

984. Hook, Walter Farquhar (1798–1875). *A Church Dictionary.* (London: J. Murray, 1854). 807pp. 7th edition.

A801 (author ["Hooke"], title), JS1240. Clearly a typographical error in A801. First published in 1842, but Dodgson probably owned this edition, as his copy was a gift from

Frank at the North Pole. Illustration from Tom Hood's *From Nowhere to the North Pole* (item 982).

his sisters for his 23rd birthday (27 January 1855, see *Diaries*, 40). Hook was educated at Christ Church, Oxford and became Dean of Chichester in 1859. A leader in the High Church party, he nonetheless shunned all things Romish. He worked for the improvement of education and to help the working classes. This work is a dictionary of terms relating to the Christian Church, many defined with essays of significant length. Dodgson heard Hook preach at St. Mary's, Oxford on 4 March 1857. "I was rather disappointed in my expectations of him," he wrote in his diary, "the sermon was very good, but not strikingly eloquent."

985. Hook, Walter Farquhar. *Short Meditations for Every Day in the Year*. (Leeds: Richard Slocombe, 1849–51). 4 vols.

A754 ("Hook's Meditations, 4 vols."), JS1239. Only 4-volume edition traced. Each meditation is based on a scripture verse.

986. Hooker, Richard (1554–1600). *The Works of that Learned and Judicious Divine, Mr. Robert Hooker; with an Account of his Life and Death, by Issac Walton. Arranged by John Keble*. (Oxford: University Press, 1841). 3 vols. 2nd edition.

A372 (author, title, editor [Keble], 3 vols.), JS1241. The 1st edition of the Keble version was published at the University Press in 1836 as 3 vols. in 4. The present is the earliest edition in NUC or BL recorded as 3 vols. only. Hooker was an Anglican divine, defender of the Elizabethan Church, and opponent of Puritanism. He posited the theory of natural law. See 1111 for a note on Keble.

987. Hoole, Charles Holland (1836?–1902). *Poems and Translations*. (London: Simpkin and Marshall, 1875). 120pp.

B1084 (author, title, city, date), JS1243. B1084 describes this as "From the author," and lists 2 copies. Hoole attended Magdalen College, Oxford as an undergraduate and became a senior Student of Christ Church, Oxford (and thus a colleague of Dodgson) in 1861.

988. Hoole, Charles Holland. *The Return of Ulysses. A Poem*. (London: M. Walbrook, 1879). 40pp.

B1085 (author, title, date [1876]), JS1244. Probably a misprint in B1085 ("1876" for "1879") as this is the earliest edition traced.

989. Hoole, Charles Holland. *A Voyage to Britain: A Poem.* (Oxford: Printed by Parker and Co., n.d.). 32pp.

B1083 (author, title, n.d.), JS1242. Only edition traced. B1083 describes this as printed for private circulation.

990. Hooper, William (fl. 1770). *Rational Recreations, in Which the Principles of Numbers and Natural Philosophy are Clearly and Copiously Elucidated, by a Series of Easy, Entertaining, Interesting Experiments. Among Which are all those Commonly Performed with the Cards.* (London: Printed for L. Davis, J. Robson, B. Law, and G. Robinson, 1774). 4 vols. 267, 280, 296, 367pp.

A958 (author, title, 4 vols.), JS1245. Earliest 4-volume edition in BL or BOD. A collection of scientific experiments for laypersons, many of which appear to have a magical aspect (optical toys, etc.). Some of the "recreations" are games, including the card "experiments" alluded to in the title.

991. Hooper, William Harcourt (1834–1912) and W. C. Phillips. *A Manual of Marks on Pottery and Porcelain; a Dictionary of Easy Reference.* (London: Macmillan and Co., 1876). 238pp.

A373 (author, title), JS1246. 1st edition as described in MBC.

992. Hope, Beryl. *The Shadow of a Life: A Girl's Story.* (London: W. H. Allen & Co., 1880). 3 vols. 304, 346, 342pp.

A610 (title, 3 vols.), JS1203 (listed under Hickson, *The Shadows of a Life*). Only matching title in BL in a 3-volume edition and the only edition listed there. A610 states "Shadow" not "Shadows," Hickson's book was published in only 1 volume, and it was not published until 1898 (Dodgson died in January of that year), so there is no argument for JS's conjecture. A love story that includes a libel trial.

993. Hopkins, G[eorge] Irving (b. 1849). *Manual of Plane Geometry, on the Heuristic Plan, with Numerous Extra Exercises, Both Thereoms and Problems, for Advanced Work.* (Boston: D. C. Heath & Company, 1891). 179pp. With an introduction by Truman Henry Safford of Williams College.

E390 (author, title, city, date), JS1247. Hopkins was instructor in Mathematics and Physics at the High School, Manchester, New Hampshire, USA. The book was published "primarily for the author's pupils, and secondarily for that constantly increasing number of teachers who are getting more and more dissatisfied with the old methods of teaching geometry."

994. Horace, [Quintus Horatius Flaccus] (65–8 B.C.E.). *The Odes and Carmen Sæculare of Horace.* (London: Bell and Daldy, 1863). 144pp. Translated into English verse by John Conington.

A837 (author, title, translator), JS1248. This is the only 19th-century edition listed in BL. Conington (1825–69) was Professor of Latin Literature at Oxford from 1854 until his death.

995. Horace, Quintus Horatius Flaccus. *Quinti Horatii Flacci Opera Omnia. The Works of Horace.* (Oxford: Clarendon Press, 1874, 1891). 2 vols. With commentary by Edward Charles Wickham.

A507 ("Wickham's Horace, 2 vols."), JS1250. Wickham also published a 2-volume set of the selected odes for school use, but the present edition seems a much more likely match for Dodgson, and is the only 19th-century 2-volume edition of Wickham's complete Horace in BL. Wickham (1834–1910) was a fellow and tutor of New College, Oxford from 1857, and became headmaster of Wellington College in 1873.

996. Horace, Quintus Horatius Flaccus. *Quintus Horatius Flaccus.* (London: Pickering, 1820). 185pp. In the *Pickering Diamond Classics* series.

A477, A478 (author, publisher, series), JS1249 (not listed separately from other editions of Horace's works). Dodgson apparently owned 2 copies as A477 and A478 both list Horace among the titles in the *Pickering Diamond Classics* series. One of Dodgson's copies is in the collection of Jon Lindseth, Cleveland, OH. See 153 for more information on the *Pickering Diamond Classics.*

997. Horace, [Quintus Horatius Flaccus]. *The Works of Horace.* (London: Bell, 1885). 325pp. Translated literally into English prose by Christopher Smart with a copious

selection of notes by Theodore Alois Buckley.

B1086 (author, title, translator, date), JS1249
(not listed separately from other editions of
Horace's works). Smart (1722–71) was an English poet.

998. Hornby, Thomas. *Gleanings in
Many Fields. Notes on the New Testament.*
(Liverpool: E. Howell, 1893). 2 vols. Edited
by Joseph Pulliblank.

A761, D91 (author, title, 2 vols.), JS1252.
Only edition in BL or BOD. A collection of
quotes from other works relating to a reading
of the New Testament.

999. Horne, Richard Henry [later Hen-
gist] (1803–84). *Ballad Romances.* (London: Charles Ollier, 1846). 248pp.

A834, B1087 (author, title, date), JS1255. The
same edition was published in the same year
with a cancel title page by John Russell Smith.
Horne's colorful life included shipwrecks, a
shark attack, friendship with Elizabeth Barrett
Browning and 17 years in Australia, where he
borrowed a middle name from a man he met
named Hengist.

1000. Horne, Richard Henry [later Hen-
gist]. *Judas Iscariot, A Miracle Play in Two
Acts, With other Poems.* (London: C.
Mitchell, 1848). 64pp.

A461 (author, title, date), JS1254. In poetry
and prose.

1001. Horne, Richard Henry, [later Hen-
gist]. *Orion: An Epic Poem. In Three Books.*
(London: J. Miller, 1843). 137pp.

A461 (author, title, date), JS1253. Dodgson's
copy was offered by Ritter-Hopson Galleries,
New York, at the sale of the Thomas Erwin Collection (15 December 1932) (DAA1668). It
was offered again by Anderson Galleries, New
York, on 14–15 January 1936 (DAA1844). It is
now in the collection formed by Jeffrey Stern,
now at Seitoku Gakuin College, Tokyo, Japan.
It has Dodgson's signature on the title page.
This was Horne's most famous and successful work, reaching at least 6 editions in the
first year. It was sold for a farthing, a pub-
licized bargain that no doubt helped its success.

1002. Horne, Thomas Hartwell (1780–
1862). *An Introduction to the Critical Study
and Knowledge of the Holy Scriptures.* (Lon-

don: T. Cadell, etc., 1821). 2nd edition, revised, corrected, and enlarged. 4 vols.
Illustrated with numerous maps and facsimiles of Biblical manuscripts.

A800 ("Horn's Introduction to the Bible, 4
vols."), JS1251. Earliest 4-volume edition of the
only possible match traced. At least the
2nd–10th editions (1822–1856) were published
in 4 volumes. Horn was the author of several
theological works, but it was the publication of
this work that lead to his being ordained by the
Bishop of London, though he had had no formal religious education. In 1833 he became a
rector in the City of London. He was also the
author of bibliographical works.

1003. Hosken, James Dryden (b. 1861).
Phaon and Sappho, and Nimrod. (London:
Macmillan and Co., 1892). 326pp.

A834, B1088 (author, title, date), JS1256.
Each is a drama in five acts, in verse and prose.

1004. Hovell, Dennis De Berdt (1811?–88).
"An Inquiry into The Real Nature Of Hys-
teria." In *British and Foreign Medico-
Chirugical Review* (1870).

E372 (title, author), JS1258. E372 gives no
publication information and no separately published edition has been traced, so Dodgson may
have owned a copy of the original article (published in 2 parts) excised from the journal. The
present description is taken from the catalogue
of the Freud Collection, Columbia University,
New York. Hovell was a fellow of the Royal College of Surgeons and surgeon at the London
Orphans' Asylum, Clapton.

1005. Howard, C. Frusher. *Howard's Cal-
ifornia Calculator: The Newest, Quickest
and Most Complete Instructor for All who
Desire to be Quick at Figures The Business
Man's Faithful Assistant, the School Boy's
Companion and Friend.* (San Francisco: C.
Frusher Howard, 1874). [96]pp.

E139 (author, title, date), JS1260. A self-pub-
lished book of methods for making speedy
mathematical calculations. Dodgson had an interest in mathematical short-cuts and published two methods for division in *Nature* (see
LCP).

1006. Howells, William Dean (1837–
1920). *A Chance Acquaintance.* (Boston:
Houghton Mifflin, 1873). 271pp. Illustrated by William L. Sheppard.

A822? Not in JS. In his diary for 23 Feb. 1895 Dodgson listed this among books read during a recent illness. This is the earliest Houghton Mifflin edition traced (see 1012 for why Dodgson owned an edition by this publisher). Howells was a prolific American writer and man of letters. He edited *Atlantic Monthly* and wrote about 40 novels. He is considered the father of American Realism and a strong influence on Mark Twain and Henry James. He also wrote works of literary criticism. Novel.

1007. Howells, William Dean. *An Imperative Duty: A Novel.* (New York: Harper Bros., 1892). 150pp.

A822? Not listed separately in JS (see 1012). A letter from Dodgson to his publisher, Macmillan (31 March 1896) reads in part, "Thanks for sending me *An Imperative Duty* [1891], by 'W. D. Howells.'" This is the earliest Harper Bros. edition traced (see 1012 for why Dodgson owned an edition by this publisher). Novel.

1008. Howells, William Dean. *Indian Summer.* (Boston: Houghton Mifflin, c. 1895). 395pp.

A822? Not listed separately in JS (see 1012). In his diary for 23 Feb. 1895 Dodgson listed this among books read during a recent illness. This is the earliest Houghton Mifflin edition traced (see 1012 for why Dodgson owned an edition by this publisher). Novel.

1009. Howells, William Dean. *The Lady of the Aroostook.* (Boston: Houghton Mifflin, 1879). 326pp.

A822? Not listed separately in JS (see 1012). In his diary for 26 July 1883, Dodgson listed this among book read during a recent illness and pronounced it "capitally written." This is the earliest Houghton Mifflin edition traced (see 1012 for why Dodgson owned an edition by this publisher). Novel.

1010. Howells, W[illiam] D[ean]. *A Little Girl Among the Old Masters.* (Boston: James R. Osgood, 1884). 65pp. + 54 plates.

A531 (title), JS35 (Anon./Children). Dodgson's copy is in the Dodgson family collection. Only edition in BL. A collection of drawings by Howells' ten-year-old daughter (including many drawings of angels) with an introduction and commentary by Howells.

1011. Howells, William Dean. *Poems.* (Boston: Ticknor and Company, 1886). 223pp.

A831, B1089 (author, title, city, date), JS1263. Mostly a reprint of an 1873 collection.

1012. Howells, William Dean. *Works.* (13 vols., Boston). No further details known.

A822 ("Howell's [sic] (W.D.) Works, 13 vols. (Boston)"), JS1262. No collected edition of Howells' works was published prior to 1898, so Dodgson must have owned Boston editions of 13 different Howells titles. We know from Dodgson's diaries and letters that he read or owned *The Lady of the Aroostook, Indian Summer, A Chance Acquaintance,* and *An Imperative Duty* (see above). We might guess that the other 10 volumes in Dodgson's collection included other novels by Howells: *A Foregone Conclusion* (1875), *The Undiscovered Country* (1880), *A Fearful Responsibility* (1881), *A Modern Instance* (1881), *The Rise of Silas Lapham* (1885) (the work on which his reputation rests), and *A Hazard of New Fortunes* (1890) are among Howells' pre–1898 novels. Dodgson may also have owned some of Howell's plays, for the letter to Macmillan goes on, "*The Lady of Aroostook,* with about 10 other novels, and several plays, are published by Houghton Mifflin & Co., Boston and New York. The name is given as 'W. D. Howells.' *An Imperative Duty,* with 5 other novels, and several plays, are published by Harper Bros., New York. The name is 'William Dean Howells.' The 2 lists of books *have nothing in common.* I strongly suspect that this second set of books are merely *imitations* of the first." Dodgson's suspicions were, of course, unfounded. Whether he owned, as is implied by this letter, 17 novels and a number of plays by Howells is not known.

1013. H[owitt], W[illiam] (1792–1879). *The Boy's Country-Book, Being the Real Life of a Country Boy Written by Himself. Exhibiting all the Amusements, Pleasures, and Pursuits of Children in the Country.* (London: Longman, Orme, Brown, Green, and Longmans, 1839). 308pp.

A932 ("Howith's Boys' Country Books"), JS1264 (listed under Howitt). Clearly an error in A932, as there is no such book. The present title is the only close match in BL. Earliest edition in BL. Neither BL nor BOD list a publisher for this edition, but an edition of 1841 was published by Longman, Orme, Brown, Green, and Longmans. Howitt was the husband of the writer Mary Howitt and the author of many popular books on a variety of subjects, some written in conjunction with his wife. The *London Monthly Chronicle* wrote of this work, "One of the most fascinating fictions for young and old that has ever graced our literature."

1014. Howitt, William. *The History of the Supernatural in all Ages and Nations, and in all Churches, Christian and Pagan, Demonstrating a Universal Faith.* (London: Longman, Green, Longman, Roberts and Green, 1863). 2 vols.

A883 (author, title, 2 vols.), JS1266. Only edition in BL. Howitt and his wife Mary spent time in Italy and became converts to Spiritualism. The preface states, "The author of this work intends by the Supernatural the operation of those higher and more recondite laws of God with which being yet but most imperfectly acquainted, we either denominate their effects miraculous, or, shutting our eyes firmly, deny their existence altogether." *Saturday Review* wrote, "A book about ghosts, magicians, and other supernatural events, which is as dull as a London directory."

1015. Howitt, William. *A Popular History of Priestcraft in all Ages and Nations.* (London: Effingham Wilson, 1833). 276pp.

B1090 (author, title, date), JS1265. Allibone notes that over 20,000 copies of this title sold by 1852.

1016. H[ows], J[ohn] W[illiam] S[tanhope] (1797–1871), editor. *Golden Leaves from the American Poets.* (London: Frederick Warne & Co., 1866). 384pp. With an introductory essay by Alexander Smith.

A843 (title), JS120. Only British edition in BL. Hows was born in London but moved to America where he worked as a drama critic and served as Professor of Oratory at Columbia College, New York. See 1879 for a note on Smith.

1017. Hoyle, Edmond (1672–1769). *Hoyle's Games Containing Laws on Chess, Draughts, etc.* (London, Woking [Printed]: 1854).

A897 (author, title), JS1267. Hoyle codified rules for Whist in *A Short Treatise on the Game of Whist* (1742), a book to which he later added rules of other games. Hoyle's *Games* went through many editions in the ensuing centuries. In his diary for 14 January 1858, Dodgson writes "Bought Hoyle's Games. I have taken to learning cards in the last few days, for the first time in my life." This is the edition in BL closest to Dodgson's diary entry, though he certainly may have owned a different one. Dodgson may have consulted Hoyle when he was devising rules for his own card game, "Court Circular" (see WMGC, #19, #30).

1018. H[ubbard], L[ouisa] M[aria] (1836–1906). *The Englishwoman's Year-book, a New Edition of the 'Year-book of Woman's Work' Together with a Directory to All Institutions Existing for the Benefit of Women and Children.* (London: Hatchards, 1886).

D233 (author, title, city, date), JS1268. D233 notes Dodgson's initials. This serial, under various titles, was first published in 1875. A new series in 1882 began an annual publication which lasted until 1916. Born in Russia, Hubbard moved to England where she became an active feminist. She campaigned in the movement to allow deaconesses in the Church of England and took a special interest in helping impoverished women find respectable employment. This work began as a series of articles in *Labour News* on employment opportunities for women.

1019. [Hudson, Marianne Spencer, née Stanhope]. *Almack's. A Novel.* (London: Saunders & Otley, 1826). 3 vols. 390, 346, 413pp.

A807 (title, date, 3 vols.), JS1946 (listed under Stanhope). A 2nd edition was also issued in 1826. The work was published anonymously, but BL and BOD both catalogue it under "Hudson" rather than "Stanhope." Novel of a great London club of the 18th and early 19th centuries.

1020. Hughlings, J[ohn] P[owell] (b. 1832?) *The Logic of Names: An Introduction to Boole's Laws of Thought.* (London: J. Walton, 1869). 88pp.

E235 (author, title, date), JS1269. Hughlings matriculated at Pembroke College, Oxford in 1853 and received his B.A. in 1856. E235 describes this as "Boole's theory put into non-mathematical language." The theory in question was that put forth by George Boole in his book *An Investigation of the Laws of Thought.* See also 2076 and 1075.

1021. Hullah, John (1812–84). *The Cultivation of the Speaking Voice.* (Oxford: Clarendon Press, 1870). 66pp. + fold out table.

B1091 (author, title, date), JS1270. Hullah was a popular teacher of singing who held many musical posts, including Professor of Vocal Music at King's College, London. He composed music for one of Dickens' theatrical productions. This work is adapted from two articles in *The Contemporary Review* (March and July 1869). In the preface the author states that his "frequent reference to the singing voice has been inseparable from the mode of treatment he has adopted. Any musical knowledge or skill the student who proposes to give these processes a fair trial may possess will of course increase the chance of turning them to good account. The trained voice and ear will assuredly prove more apt than the untrained.... At the same time, the musical preparation absolutely needed for this trial is the smallest conceivable — amounting to little more than the knowledge of the names and places, on some musical instrument, of three or four notes, and skill enough to imitate these (in pitch) with his voice."

1022. Hullah, John, editor. *The Song Book Words and Tunes from the Best Poets and Musicians.* (London: Macmillan, 1866). 368pp.

A844, E286 (title, editor, date), JS139 (Anon./Literature) and JS1271. Although A844 states only *The Song Book*, it is undoubtedly the same item as E286.

1023. Hume, David (1711–76). *The History of England.* Edition unknown.

A930 (author, title, 8 vols.), JS1272. BL lists 22 8-volume editions, many of which are late 18th/early 19th-century editions published by Cadell and including the author's last corrections. An 1826 edition published in Oxford as part of the *Oxford English Classics* is another possibility. Hume was an English philosopher and political writer. This, the first major history of England, was criticized for its Tory leanings and mistakes. Hume pays special attention to the development of the English system of government. The book was first published in 1754–61. In his diary for 8 April 1857, Dodgson writes, "Began Hume's *England,* and read the reign of William I. My present plan is to take about 20 pages a day ... I ought to have read (and *know*) Hume by about the end of the Long Vacation. More than a year later, on 17 February 1858 he records he is, as part of a plan of reading, beginning the Henry VIII section of Hume.

1024. Hunt, James Henry Leigh (1784–1859). *The Poetical Works of Leigh Hunt.* (London: Edward Moxon, 1832). 361pp.

A833 (author, title), JS1274. Earliest edition of the only possible matching title in BL. Hunt was a poet and journalist who edited *The Examiner* where he first published the works of Keats and Shelley. He later produced a series of periodicals.

1025. Hunt, James Henry Leigh. *Readings for Railways; or, Anecdotes and other Short Stories, Reflections, Maxims, Characteristics, Passages of Wit, Humor and Poetry; etc. Together with Points of Information on Matters of General Interest. Collected in the Course of His Own Reading.* (London: C. Gilpin, [1849]). 136pp.

A492 (author, title, date), JS1273.

1026. Hussey, Edward Law (1816–99). *Adversaria Coronatoria. Notes Made in Reading the Coroner's Act, and Sir John Jervis's Treatise on the Office and Duties of Coroners.* (Oxford: J. Parker & Co., 1896). 55pp.

E393 (author, title, date), F138, JS1275. F138 notes that this is a presentation copy to Dodgson and has the gothic stamp. Hussey became a surgeon of the Radcliffe Infirmary in 1850. In 1877 he was made coroner for the city of Oxford and when he refused to resign his post as surgeon (even though his first case as coroner found him examining one of his own patients) he was dismissed. He was, by most accounts, a difficult man to work with and wary of innovation. Although he did it through constant bickering with the Infirmary, Hussey worked to better define the role and responsibilities of coroner. According to *Letters,* 258n, Hussey "attended Dodgson during two illnesses at least, on July 14, 1881 and July 20, 1883." John Jervis's *A Practical Treatise on the Office and Duties of Coroners With an Appendix of Forms and Precedents* was first published in 1829. A 5th edition of 1888 included the Coroner's Act of 1887; another Coroner's Act was passed in 1892.

1027. Hussey, Robert (1801–56). *The Rise of Papal Power, Traced in Three Lectures.* (Oxford: Clarendon Press, 1863). New edition, with the author's last additions.

B1092 (author, title, city, date), JS1276. Hussey matriculated at Christ Church in 1821 and served as Regius Professor of Ecclesiastical History from 1842 until his death in 1856. He was probably acquainted with Dodgson (see *Letters*, 257).

1028. Hutchison, W[illiam] M[arshall] (b. 1854). *Song-Land: A Series of Ditties for Small Folks*. (London: [1882]). Selected, arranged and composed by W. M. Hutchison.

A530 (title), JS76 (Anon./Children). Only edition in BL of the only 19th-century title matching A530. Hutchison was a composer and music publisher.

1029. Huyshe, John (1802–80). *A Treatise on Logic, on the Basis of Aldrich; With Illustrative Notes*. (Oxford: J. Vincent, 1842). 164pp. 3rd edition.

Uncertain. Not in JS. Dodgson's copy is in the collection formed by Joseph Brabant, now at the University of Toronto. It includes the gothic stamp on the title page and the property label on the front cover. Huyshe was educated at Brasenose College, Oxford and served as rector of Clyston-Hydon from 1831 until his death. Henry Aldrich (1647–1710) of Christ Church, Oxford, was known as a controversialist, an opponent of popery, an architect, and a musician. The work referred to in the title is his *Artis Logicae Compendium*.

1030. Inchbald, Elizabeth (1753–1821). *A Simple Story, etc*. (London: G. G. & J. Rivington, 1791). 2nd edition. 4 vols. 233, 253, 209, 157pp.

A820 ("Simple Story, 4 vols."), JS389 (Anon./Unclassified). This is the only matching title in BL that has editions in 4 vols. There are 3 such editions listed in BL, all published by Rivington — 1791, 1793, and 1799. Inchbald was an actress who retired from a successful stage career in 1789 to concentrate on her efforts as a dramatist and novelist. Maria Edgeworth wrote of this novel, "I never read any novel that affected me so strongly, or that so completely possessed me with the belief in the real existence of all the persons it represents ... it is truly and deeply pathetic."

1031. Ingelow, Jean (1820–97). *Mopsa the Fairy*. (London: Longmans, Green & Co., 1869).

A933 (title), JS66 (Anon./Children). 1st edition. Ingelow was a poet who also wrote children's stories. This is the story of a boy who is borne off to fairyland by an albatross. It is generally included in the group of children's fantasies inspired or influenced by AAIW.

1032. Ingelow, Jean. *Poems*. (London: Longmans Green, 1867 [1866]). 318pp. With illustrations by A. B. Houghton, J. W. North, George John Pinwell, Edward John Poynter, etc., engraved by the Brothers Dalziel.

A872 (author, title, date, illustrated), JS1279.

1033. Ingelow, Jean. *A Story of Doom, and Other Poems*. (London: Longmans, Green and Company, 1867). 296pp.

A835, B1093 (author, title, date), JS1278. OCEL lists the title poem as among Ingelow's "most remarkable."

1034. Ingoldsby, Thomas [pseud. of R. H. Barham] (1788–1845). *The Ingoldsby Legends*. (London: Bentley, 1840–47). 3 vols. 338, 288, 364pp. Illustrated by George Cruikshank and John Leech.

Not in JS. In an undated manuscript list of letters offered for sale (collection of the author), bookseller Walter Spencer describes two letters which mention this book. The first, to Oxford bookseller Mr. Gee (see preface), is "about some books (probably *Ingoldsby Legends*) which [Dodgson] wanted to buy back as he thought they may be 1st editions and which Mr. Gee had already sold." The second is described as, "Autograph letter, 1 page, 8vo in the 3rd person to Mr. Gee '7 Lushington Road, Eastbourne July 10, 1890' respecting an *Ingoldsby Legends* he wishes to buy back again but to add whatever Mr. Gee thinks his reasonable profit." Barham was a clergyman. OCCL calls this famous collection, "a book of gruesomely comic stories in verse and prose."

1035. Ingram, James (1774–1850). *Memorials of Oxford*. (Oxford: John Henry Parker, 1834–1837). 3 vols. 100 engravings by John Le Keux, from drawings by Frederick MacKenzie.

A398, E13 (author, title, illustrators, publisher, 3 vols., city, date [given incorrectly as 1827]), JS1280. 1st edition and corresponds in every detail except date to E13 — clearly the date "1827" is an error. E13 adds that the book includes "wood engravings by Orlando Jewitt after De la Motte." Ingram was educated at Trinity College, Oxford, of which he later became president. He was Professor of Anglo-Saxon and keeper of the University Archives. MacKenzie (1789–1854) was a topographical and architectural draughtsman. A book on the buildings and monuments of Oxford.

1036. Ingram, John Henry (1849–1916). *Edgar Allan Poe, his Life, Letters, and Opinions, etc.* (London: W. H. Allen & Co., 1886). 488pp. New edition.

A881 ("Life and Letters of E. A. Poe"), JS1658 (listed under Poe). Only pre–1898 matching title in BL. First published by J. Hogg in London in 1880 in a 2-volume edition. Another item in A881 specifies multiple volumes, so this later, 1-volume edition seems more likely. Ingram was a civil servant who wrote for many periodicals in Europe and America. He wrote several biographies and edited the series *Eminent Women. Saturday Review* wrote, "In spite of all the faults of this Life — and they certainly are abundant enough, — there is nevertheless much ... that may be read with interest."

1037. Ingram, John Henry. *The Haunted Homes and Family Traditions of Great Britain.* (London: W. H. Allen & Co., 1884). 2 vols. (1st and 2nd series).

A900 (author, title, 2 vols.), JS1281. Only 2-volume edition in BL or BOD (also the earliest in BL or BOD).

1038. Inman, Thomas (1820–76). *On the Preservation of Health; or, Essays Explanatory of the Principles to be Adopted by those who Desire to Avoid Disease.* (London: H. K. Lewis, 1870). 207pp. 2nd edition.

Not in JS. Dodgson reprinted an extract from this edition of this book in his 1881 pamphlet *On Catching Cold* (WMGC, #148). He advertised for a copy in his 1893 pamphlet *Second-Hand Books* (see Stern, x–xi). Inman was physician to the Royal Infirmary, Liverpool and a lecturer on botany, medical jurisprudence, materia medica and therapeutics, and principals and practice of medicine. He attempted in this book (and the following) to write medical essays in a popular style. The *Edinburgh Medical Journal* wrote, "Viewed as a literary production, it is deserving of praise, but we cannot think the author wise in calling in the public as a fit judge and arbiter of so many disputed

points, where Dr. Inman takes one side, and the great majority of the profession another."

1039. Inman, Thomas. *Restoration of Health Being Essays on the Principles upon which the Treatment of Many Diseases is to be Conducted.* (London: H. K. Lewis, 1870). 288pp.

Not in JS. Dodgson reprinted an extract from this edition of this book in his 1881 pamphlet *On Catching Cold* (WMGC, #148).

1040. Inwood, William (1771?–1843). *Tables for the Purchasing of Estates, Freehold, Copyhold, or Leasehold; Annuities, Advowsons, etc.* (London: 1870).

B1094 (author, title, date [1870]), JS1282. No 1870 edition has been traced. The 1880 edition and editions from 1899 to 1930 published by Crosby and Lockwood. 1880 was the 21st edition; the 18th was 1866; thus the 1870 edition must be the 19th or 20th.

1041. Ion, M. *Ion's Helps to Memory, or Handy Billy, for the Local Marine Board Examinations.* (1880).

E241 (title, date), JS1283. E241 notes this has Dodgson's initials, "etc." Edition of 1880 not traced, but the 10th edition of 1887 was published in Liverpool by C. J. Ion.

1042. [Irving, Washington] (1783–1859). *Bracebridge Hall; or, The Humorists. By Geoffrey Canyon, Gent.* (London: John Murray, 1822). 2 vols.

A662 (author, title, 2 vols.), JS1285. 1st English edition. Irving was an American writer who lived in England for 17 years. This title is a sequel to Irving's *Sketchbook* (see 1044) and includes 49 stories and sketches.

1043. Irving, Washington. *Old Christmas, from the Sketchbook of Washington Irving.* (London: Macmillan, [1875]). 166pp. With illustrations by Randolph Caldecott. 1st edition.

A654 (author, title, illustrator, edition), JS1288. See 332 for a note on Caldecott.

1044. [Irving, Washington]. *The Sketch Book of Geoffrey Crayon, Gent.* (London: John Murray, 1820). 2 vols. New edition.

A662 (author, title, 2 vols.), JS1287. This seems the earliest likely edition. It was preceded by an 1820 edition published by John Miller, which firm failed shortly after publication. A collection of essays and tales, many about England, but also including his most famous American stories, "The Legend of Sleepy Hollow," and "Rip Van Winkle."

1045. [**Irving**, Washington]. *Tales of a Traveller, by Geoffrey Crayon, Gent.* (London: John Murray, 1824). 2 vols.

A662 (author, title, 2 vols.), JS1286. 1st English edition. Murray issued at least two subsequent 2-volume editions. Tales set in various countries including France and Italy.

1046. Irving, Washington, James Kirke Paulding (1778–1860) and William Irving. *Salmagundi; or, The Whim-Whams and Opinions of Launcelot Langstaff, Esq. and Others.* (London: Thomas Tegg, Rodwell and Martin; Edinburgh: R. Griffin, 1824). 389pp. 2nd English edition.

A650, D93 (author, title, city, date), JS1284. Published while Irving was living in England. Originally issued as a serial in collaboration with his brother William and with the American author Paulding. In the style of *The Spectator*, the authors assume various guises to weave this collection of essays on contemporary New York. The papers took a position in favor of aristocratic federalism rather than Jeffersonian democracy.

1047. [**Isle of Wight**]. *Guide to the Isle of Wight.* Details unknown.

E391 (title), JS354 (Anon./Topography). The guide published by Adam and Charles Black was perhaps the most frequently reprinted, but there were several others published in the 19th century. Dodgson owned at least one other guide to the Isle of Wight (see 1130).

1048. Jack, Richard (d. 1759). *Mathematical Principles of Theology, or, the Existence of God Geometrically Demonstrated. In Three Books. Wherein is Proved, the Existence of God from Eternity to Eternity; his Self-existence, Independency, and Unity. That God is Infinite in Wisdom, Power, Knowledge, &c. Also, that Matter is a Temporary Being; that God is the Cause of its Existence, and of the Existence of all Other Beings, that Ever Did, or Can Exist; and upon God the Continuation or Termination of their Existence Depends.* (London: Printed for G. Hawkins, 1747). 328pp.

E361 (author, title, date), JS1289. The author was a teacher of mathematics and an engineer.

1049. Jambon, Jean [pseud. of John Hay Athole Macdonald] (1836–1919). *Our Trip to Blunderland or Grand Excursion to Blunderland and Back.* (Edinburgh: William Blackwood and Sons, 1877). 231pp. With 60 illustrations by Charles Doyle.

Not in JS. In his diary for 11 September 1891, Dodgson included this title in his list of "books of the 'Alice' type" he had collected. Earliest edition in BL. Macdonald was the Lord Justice Clerk of Scotland and an early enthusiast for motorcars. A self-conscious imitation of AAIW beginning, "Three little boys … had been reading all about Alice, and the strange, funny things she saw and did when fast asleep." Alice appears in the first chapter, and the boys eventually fall asleep and have adventures. Charles Doyle (1832–93) was the brother of artist Richard Doyle and a successful artist.

Frontispiece by Charles Doyle for Jean Jambon's *Our Trip to Blunderland* (item 1049).

1050. James, George Payne Rainsford (1799–1860). *Richelieu, a Tale of France.* (London: Colburn, 1839). 2nd edition. Vol. 17 of *Colburn's Modern Standard Novelists.*

E17 (author, title, series), JS1290. James wrote primarily historical novels, of which this was the first, and some minor works of history. He served as Historiographer Royal to William IV, as British Consul in Massachusetts in 1850, and in an Austrian diplomatic post in 1856. Washington Irving, having seen some of James's contributions to the periodical press, encouraged him to write something more ambitious and the result was this successful novel.

1051. James, Henry (1843–1916). *The Portrait of a Lady.* (London: Macmillan and Co., 1882). 520pp. 2nd edition.

Not in JS. In a letter of 25 March 1886, Dodgson writes that he has read this book, though he had previously confused it with Burnett's *Through One Administration* (see 307). James's famous novel was originally published in 1881 in a 3-volume edition which was reprinted in 1882. This is the first 1-volume edition and the closest in date (excepting an edition that was part of James's collected works) to Dodgson's diary notation.

1052. James, M. E. *What Shall We Act? or, a Hundred Plays from Which to Choose. With Hints on Scene-painting, etc.* (London: Bell & Sons, 1882 [1881]). 127pp.

D94 (author, title, city, date), JS1291. D94 notes Dodgson's signature. A catalogue of 100 plays with descriptions of characters and scenes and a brief plot summary of each. Also includes hints on various aspects of producing amateur theatricals.

1053. Jameson, Anna Brownell [née Murphy] (1794–1860) and Elizabeth Rigby Eastlake (1809–93). *The History of our Lord as Exemplified in Works of Art: with that of his Types; St. John the Baptist; and Other Persons of the Old and New Testament.* (London: Longman, Green, Longman, Roberts, & Green, 1864). 2 vols. 398, 462pp.

A393 (author, title), JS1292. Earliest edition in BL or BOD. After working for a time as a governess, Anna Murphy married Robert Jameson, but the marriage was unhappy. Robert spent much of his time abroad, and

Anna pursued a career as a writer. Her travels in Europe spawned an interest in art, and her magnum opus was the series of *Sacred and Legendary Art* (see 1056) in which she discussed artistic representations of various aspects of Christianity and Christian history. Sir Charles Eastlake had originally intended to do this work himself, but he gave Jameson his preliminary notes and she undertook the monumental task. This final volume, in title not a part of the series but of similar intent, was completed by Lady Eastlake following Jameson's death.

1054. Jameson, Anna Brownell. *Legends of the Madonna, as Represented in the Fine Arts. Forming the Third Series of Sacred and Legendary Art.* (London: Longman, Brown, Green and Longmans, 1852). 369pp. Illustrated by drawings, etc.

A393 (author, title), JS1294. Earliest edition in BL or BOD. See 1056 for more on this series.

1055. Jameson, Anna Brownell. *Legends of the Monastic Orders: as Represented in the Fine Arts: Forming the Second Series of Sacred and Legendary Art.* (London: Longman, Brown, Green and Longmans, 1852). 462pp.

A393 (author, title), JS1293. Earliest edition in BL or BOD. See 1056 for more on this series.

1056. Jameson, Anna Brownell. *Sacred and Legendary Art.* (London: Printed for Longman, Brown, Green, and Longmans, 1848). 2 vols. 387, 439pp.

A393 (author, title, 2 vols.), JS1295. Earliest edition in BL or BOD. See above for the 2nd and 3rd series of this item. Volume I contains, "Legends of the Angels and Archangels, The Evangelists, The Apostles, The Doctors of the Church, and St. Mary Magdalene." Volume II contains, "The Patron Saints, The Martyrs, The Early Bishops, The Hermits, and The Warrior Saints of Christendom." Like all the volumes in the series, these are illustrated with reproductions of artwork in plates and in details printed in the text.

1057. Jamieson, John (1759–1838). *An Etymological Dictionary of the Scottish Language, Illustrating the Words in their Different Significations by Examples from Ancient*

and Modern Writers, Shewing their Affinity to those of Other Languages, and Especially the Northern; Explaining many Terms, which, though now Obsolete in England, were Formerly Common to both Countries, and Elucidating National Rites, Customs, and Institutions in their Analogy to those of Other Nations; To which is Prefixed a Dissertation on the Origin of the Scottish Language. (Edinburgh: Printed at the University Press for W. Creech, 1808). 2 vols.

A360 (author, title), JS1297. 1st edition. The first 1-volume edition was an abridgement (Edinburgh: A. Constable and Co. and A. Jameson, 1818). The most important work of the Scottish preacher and lexicographer.

1058. Janus [pseud. of Johann Joseph Ignaz von Döllinger] (1799–1853) and Johannes Huber (1830–79). *The Pope and the Council.* (London: Rivingtons, 1869). 425pp. Authorized translation from the German.

A870, B1175 (authors ["Janus (Huber)"], title, date), JS948 (listed under Dollinger). The original German edition (Leipzig, 1869), as described in BOD states that this work was written by Janus (a.k.a. Döllinger) "in collaboration with Johannes Huber." BL also lists a 2nd edition printed in 1869. B1175 records that Dodgson's copy contained a presentation from "R. to F. Lutwidge [probably his mother, Frances Lutwidge]." Döllinger was a German Roman Catholic historian and theologian. He was ordained priest, but worked as a university professor for many years. In 1870 he was excommunicated, and he went on to become president of the Royal Bavarian Academy of Sciences. Döllinger had a close friendship with the philosopher Johannes Huber. Döllinger's anonymous critique of the Vatican council was a contributing factor in his break with church.

1059. *Japanese Fairy Tales.* Thumb edition.

So listed in A568/JS83, but no exact match has been traced. The most widely available editions of Japanese fairy tales in Victorian England were those published individually as *Kobunsha's Japanese Fairy Tale Series*, though not all of the 20 titles in the series bore this heading. Some were published in Japan and others elsewhere, but all were illustrated English translations of traditional Japanese stories. These were all small volumes, folded in the traditional Japanese manner, so the designation "thumb edition" in A568 may refer to this format.

1060. Jaques, John. *Croquêt: The Laws and Regulations of the Game, with a Description of the Implements.* (London: Jaques and Son, 1865). 48pp. New edition. Illustrated with Diagrams and Engravings.

Uncertain. Not in JS. DAA2990 (author, title, date) (Christie's, South Kensington, 20 April 1990) describes a copy as inscribed, "Given to me Jany. 30 1900 by H. Downing, Esq., 'from the library of Lewis Carroll'." As Dodgson's own 1865 book, AAIW, is one of the first works of fiction to prominently mention the game of croquet, and given his interest in playing the game and his invention of a derivation of it (Croquet Castles, see WMGC, 23–4), it seems likely that Dodgson would have owned a copy of this frequently reprinted work. Jaques was (and his family business still is) the premiere purveyor of croquet equipment in England. The Dodgson and Jaques families were linked by marriage in the 20th century (Philip Dodgson Jaques was the great-nephew of Dodgson).

1061. Jelf, Richard William (1798–1871). *The Thirty-nine Articles of the Church of England Explained in a Series of Lectures.* (London: Rivingtons, 1873). 420pp. Edited by the Rev. John Richard King.

A801 ("Jelf on the Thirty-nine Articles"), JS1300. Only edition in BL. Jelf (brother of William Edward) was a canon of Christ Church and Principal of King's College, London. The 39 Articles are the articles of faith of the Anglican church.

1062. Jelf, William Edward (1811–75). *An Examination into the Doctrine and Practice of Confession.* (London: Longmans, Green, & Co., 1875). 240pp.

A794 ("Jelf on Confession"), JS1298 (listed under Richard William Jelf). Only edition of the only matching title in BL. Jelf (brother of Richard William) was educated at Christ Church, Oxford and became a tutor there (1836–49) and a university proctor. In 1849 he left Oxford to become vicar of Carleton, Yorkshire. He later served as preacher at Whitehall and founded a small church in Wales. Jelf was a strong opponent of Ritualism and all tendencies towards Rome in the English Church. Dodgson dined with Jelf in June of 1871.

1063. Jelf, William Edward. *Quousque? How Far? How Long?: Considerations on Ritualism, Suggested by a Late Funeral Ceremonial in the City of Oxford By a High Churchman of the Old School.* (London: Longmans, Green, and Co., 1873). 104pp.

C4 ("Quousque," subject), not in JS. Earliest edition in BL or BOD of the only matching title on the subject of Ritualism (C4 describes a bound volume of 12 pamphlets on that subject).

1064. Jelf, William Edward. *Ritualism, Romanism and the English Reformation.* (London: Longmans, Green, 1876). 178pp. Edited by M. K. J. (i.e. Mrs. Jelf.)

A794 ("Jelf on Ritualism"), JS1299 (listed under Richard William Jelf). Only edition of the only matching title in BL.

1065. Jenner, Stephen (d. 1880). *Quicksands: or, Prevalent Fallacies in Belief and Worship Pointed Out.* (London: 1875).

A783 (author, title), JS1301. Only edition of the only matching title in BL. Jenner was educated at St. John's College, Cambridge and served as vicar of Beaksbourne, near Canterbury.

1066. Jennings, Hargrave (1817?–1890). *The Childishness and Brutality of the Time: Some Plain Truths in Plain Language. Supplemented by Sundry Discursive Essays and Narratives.* (London: Vizetelly & Co., 1883). 339pp.

A575 ("Childishness and Brutality of the Times"), JS378 (Anon./Unclassified). Only edition of the only possible match in BL. Jennings was secretary to the operatic manager Col. Mapleson. He wrote widely on Eastern religions, spiritualism, and ancient mysteries, and claimed to have "anticipated the theories of psychical research and esoteric Buddhism" (Allibone). This book contains, "The Newspapers," "The Generally False, Affected and Pretentious Literature of the Present Day," "Life Assurance: Some Judicious Warnings Concerning the Abuse of It," "Modern Advertising, Its Emptiness, Its Falseness," "Our Governing Classes," "The Drama Generally, and the Theatre," "Before and Behind the Curtain at the Opera," "Law and Lawyers," "Society," "Silly Men," "Conceited Men," "A Droll Story," and "A Singular American."

1067. Jerrold, Douglas (1803–57). *Mrs. Caudle's Curtain Lectures, as Suffered by the Late Job Caudle.* (London: Published at the Punch Office, 1846). 142pp.

A671 (title), JS1303. 1st edition, but it seems equally likely that Dodgson would have owned the 1st illustrated edition (London: Bradbury, Evans & Co., 1866), with illustrations by Charles Keene. Jerrold was a journalist and playwright who had many dramatic success on London stages. He wrote for *Punch* from its early days, and this was first published there. This collection of essays comprise the humorous scoldings of the fictional Mrs. Caudle to her husband.

1068. Jerrold, William Blanchard (1826–84). *The Story of Madge and the Fairy Content.* (London: John Camden Hotten, [1870]).

A638 (author, title, illustrated), JS1302. Only edition in BL. Jerrold was the son of Douglas Jerrold. He trained as an artist, but soon turned to journalism. He was the author of four plays and a close friend of Gustave Doré. He wrote a wide variety of works, many offshoots of his journalistic work. A children's book about an unhappy child who is visited by a spirit who shows her all that goes into producing a Christmas pudding.

1069. Jesse, Edward (1780–1868). *Gleanings in Natural History; with Local Recollections. To which are Added Maxims and Hints for an Angler.* (London: John Murray 1832). 313pp.

A841, B1095 (author, title, date [1835], 3 vols.), JS1305. As is clear from the entry in B1095, Dodgson owned all three volumes in this series. The date 1835 may apply only to volume 3, or he may have owned reprints of the first two volumes (BL lists an 1835 reprint of this volume). Jesse was a civil servant who took an avid interest in natural history and produced a series of popular books on the subject. In addition to these, he also wrote guidebooks to historic sites such as Windsor and Hampton Court.

Illustration by Charles Keene from *Mrs. Caudle's Curtain Lectures* (item 1067).

1070. Jesse, Edward. *Gleanings in Natural History. Second Series. To which are added Some Extracts from the Unpublished Mss. of the Late Mr. White of Selborne.* (London: John Murray, 1834). 321pp.

A841, B1095 (author, title, date [1835], 3 vols.), JS1305. As is clear from the entry in B1095, Dodgson owned all three volumes in this series. The date 1835 may apply only to volume 3, or he may have owned reprints of the first two volumes (though neither BL nor BOD lists an 1835 reprint of this volume). Dodgson also owned a copy of Gilbert White's *The Natural History of Selborne* (see 2237).

1071. Jesse, Edward. *Gleanings in Natural History. Third and Last Series. To Which are Added Notices of Some of the Royal Parks and Residences.* (London: John Murray, 1835). 310pp.

A841, B1095 (author, title, date, 3 vols.), JS1305. As is clear from the entry in B1095, Dodgson owned all three volumes in this series.

1072. Jesse, John Heneage (1815–74). *Memoirs of the Court of England during the Reign of the Stuarts, Including the Protectorate.* (London: H. G. Bohn, Bell & Daldy, G. Bell & Sons, 1857). 3 vols. 478, 523,

539pp. In the Bohn's *Historical Library* series.

A631, B1096 (author, title, 3 vols., date), JS1304, JS1306 (listed under Edward Jesse). Originally published at least as early as 1840. John was the son of Edward Jesse (see above) and a clerk in the Department of the Admiralty. He wrote several historical works which, like the present volume, concentrated on the personalities of history rather than creating a complete narrative of historical events.

1073. Jessop, J. H. *The Concise Homœopathic Materia Medica for Domestic Use, Compiled from Standard Works*. (Oxford: J. H. Jessop, Homœopathic Chemist, n.d. [ca. 1875]). 13pp.

Not listed separately in JS (see JS163). Dodgson's copy is in HAC in a bound volume with 7 other tracts from this series and one additional Homœopathic pamphlet (see 970). Other items in this volume are dated 1875–77. The present tract includes information on the use of several Homœopathic remedies. Jessop is listed at 140 High Street in the 1887 *Oxford Post-Office Directory* owned by Dodgson, but not in his 1867 Oxford directory.

1074. Jevons, William Stanley (1835–82). *The Principles of Science: a Treatise on Logic and Scientific Method*. (London: Macmillan and Co., 1874). 2 vols. 463, 480pp.

A505 (author, title, 2 vols.), JS1307. 1st edition as described in MBC. Jevons had a successful academic career, holding chairs in Logic and Mental and Moral Philosophy at Owens College, Manchester and in Political Economy at University College, London, before giving up academics for literary pursuits. He wrote on logic, economics, politics, and other subjects. *The Spectator* wrote, "Whatever the shortcomings of this book, it is unquestionably the best treatise on scientific method in the English language, so far at least as regards physical science."

1075. Jevons, William Stanley. *Pure Logic; or, the Logic of Quality Apart from Quantity: with Remarks on Boole's System, and on the Relation of Logic and Mathematics*. (London: E. Stanford, 1864). 87pp.

E401 (author, title, date), JS1308. "Boole's System" refers to George Boole's *An Investigation of the Laws of Thought* (see also 2076 and 1020). Jevons was a supporter of Boole's ideas,

and elaborated on them in his own writings. In 1870 he exhibited his invention, "the logical piano," a machine for working logic problems that inspired elements of computer design.

1076. Jex-Blake, Sophia (1840–1912). *Medical Women. Two Essays. I. Medicine as a Profession for Women. II. Medical Education of Women*. (Edinburgh: W. Oliphant & Co., 1872). 162pp.

E156 (author, title, date), JS1309. E156 describes this as a presentation copy. Dodgson's copy is in the collection formed by Joseph Brabant, now at the University of Toronto. It has the gothic stamp and the property label and is a presentation copy from the author. Sophia Jex-Blake led the effort in Britain to open the medical profession to women. She entered medical school herself in Edinburgh in 1869, but had to wait for new legislation before she could qualify as a physician in 1877. She later became a campaigner for women's suffrage. The present study defends medicine as an appropriate field for women and advocates medical education for women.

1077. *The John Bull Magazine and Literary Recorder*. Vol. I, nos. i–vi. (London: 1824).

D95 (title, volume, issues), JS208 (Anon./ Periodicals). According to BOD only vol. I was ever published. Not to be confused with *John Bull*, a weekly newspaper started in 1820 by Theodore Hook.

1078. Johnson, C[harles] Pierpoint (d. 1893). *British Wild Flowers. Described with an Introduction and Key to the Natural Orders*. (Lambeth: John E. Sowerby, 1860). 168pp. 1st edition. Illustrated with hand-colored frontispiece and 80 color plates by John Edward Sowerby.

A823?, B1240 (author, title, illustrator, date), JS1934 (repeats mistake in A823), JS1935 (listed under Sowerby). A823 is a puzzling entry, but almost certainly refers to this book. In a list of books on flora, A823 concludes with "Sowerby's British Wild Birds." According to DNB, none of the noted Sowerby family of British naturalists wrote a book on British birds, nor is any book by this title written by any Sowerby listed in NUC or BL. Since all other items in A823 are books on flora, and since there is no other corresponding "A" entry for this item, surely the title was written incorrectly and should have read "Sowerby's British Wild Flowers," the book described in B1240. J. E. Sowerby (1825–70) was the grandson of James Sowerby (see 1913).

1079. Johnson, Samuel (1709–84). *A Dictionary of the English Language, in which the Words are Deduced from their Originals, and Illustrated in their Different Significations by Examples from the Best Writers. To which are Prefixed a History of the Language, and an English Grammar.* (London: Printed by W. Strahan for J. and P. Knapton, et al., 1755). 2 vols. Unpaginated. 1st edition.

A738 (author, title, edition, 2 vols., date), JS1313. Even in Dodgson's day, a first edition of Johnson's famous dictionary was a significant item for bibliophiles.

1080. Johnson, Samuel. *The History of Rasselas, Prince of Abyssinia.* (London: Charles Tilt, 1838). 168pp.

Not in JS. DAA877 (author, title, city, date). This is the only 1838 edition in BL. *Rasselas* is a long poem in which digressions on the choice life are hung onto the loose thread of a story.

1081. [Johnson, Samuel]. *A Journey to the Western Islands of Scotland.* (London: Printed for W. Strahan and T. Cadell, 1775). 268pp. 1st edition.

D96 (author, title, city, date, edition), JS1312. A record of the author's 1773 journey to the Scottish isles with James Boswell.

1082. Johnson, Samuel and John Langhorne (1735–79). *The History of Rasselas, Prince of Abyssinia; The Vanity of Human Wishes by Samuel Johnson. The History of Solyman and Almena by John Langhorne.* (London: C. Daly, 1841). 240pp.

D97 (author [Langhorne], titles, city, date), JS1314, JS1398. Langhorne was an English poet best known for his 1770 translation of Plutarch.

1083. Johnson, Samuel Jenkins. *Eclipses, Past and Future: With General Hints for Observing the Heavens.* (Oxford and London: J. Parker, 1874). 160pp.

E263 (author, title, date), JS1311. Jenkins was educated at St. John's College, Oxford, or-

dained in 1868 and served as vicar of Melpash. He was a fellow of the Royal Astronomy Society.

1084. J[ohnson], W[illiam] [afterwards W. J. Cory] (1823–92). *Ionica.* (London: Smith, Elder and Co., 1858). 116pp. 1st edition.

A462, B1016 (author, title, date), JS751 (listed under Cory). Johnson was an assistant master at Eton College. This was his first volume of poems. A second part was published in 1877. He also wrote several schoolbooks.

1085. Johnston, Alexander Keith (1804–1871). *A School Atlas of General and Descriptive Geography Exhibiting the Actual and Comparative Extent of all the Countries in the World, with their Present Political Divisions, Founded on the Most Recent Discoveries and Rectifications.* (Edinburgh: Keith Johnston, 1883). New Edition. 26 maps.

E71 (author ["A. K. and T. B. Johnston"], title, date [1889]), JS1315. Dodgson may have owned 2 copies. The edition described above is in the Dodgson family collection, Woking, and the maps are "numbered and lettered in Lewis Carroll's handwriting in blue ink." No 1889 edition traced. The citation of two Johnstons as authors in E71 may be a reference to the imprint. A. K. Johnston was Cartographer Royal of Scotland and founded a map publishing house which he later ran together with his son.

1086. Johnstone, Henry Alexander Munro Butler (1837–1902). *A Trip up the Volga to the Fair of Nijni-Novgorod.* (Oxford and London: James Parker and Co., 1876). 150pp. 2nd edition. With a fold-out map and 12 illustrations.

D130 (author, title, city, date), JS1573 (listed under Munro). Johnstone was educated at Christ Church, Oxford, finishing in 1861, and served from 1862 to 1878 as M.P. for Canterbury. "The greater part of this little book appeared in the form of letters addressed to the *Daily News* in 1874 … [and recounts where the author found] the pleasantest and most engaging people in the world." Includes substantial information on Russian commerce and goods.

1087. Johnstone, William Henry. *An Elementary Treatise on Logarithms.* (London: 1859).

E383 (author, title, date), JS1316. Johnstone was Chaplain of Addiscombe. A 2nd edition was published in 1868 by Longmans, Green and Co. (89pp.)

1088. Jones, Ebenezer (1820–60). *Studies of Sensation and Event: Poems.* (London: Charles Fox, 1843). 203pp.

A833 (author, title), JS1317. Earliest edition in BL. Jones was an English poet who worked for a tea merchant. The poor reception of the present volume caused him to burn his manuscripts and turn from literary pursuits until late in life when he wrote three poems for which is remembered. An edition published in London by Pickering in 1879, including revisions, additions, and an appreciation by D. G. Rossetti, an acquaintance of Dodgson, is also a candidate for ownership by Dodgson. Rossetti brought attention to Jones in 1870 with an appreciation in *Notes and Queries*.

1089. Jones, George. *Jones' Chemical Vade Mecum for Medical Students; Intended as a Refresher to the Memory upon the More Important Facts in Chemical Science.* (London: H. Kimpton, 1881). 87pp.

E187 (author, title, date), JS1318.

1090. Jones, George William (1837–1911). *Logarithmic Tables.* (London: Macmillan and Co., 1893). 160pp. 4th edition.

E380 (author, title, date), F162, JS1319. F162 notes the gothic stamp. Jones was Professor of Mathematics at Cornell University, Ithaca, New York.

1091. Jones, Joshua [later Joshua Hugh Games] (1831–1904). *On the Unsuitableness of Euclid as a Text-book of Geometry.* (London: Longmans, Green, Reader and Dyer, 1870). 46pp. Extracted from the *Transactions of the Liverpool Literary and Philosophical Society*.

E371 (author, title, date), F140, JS1320. E371 describes this as a "presentation copy, marked throughout by Lewis Carroll, the defender of Euclid." F140 further notes the presence of the gothic stamp. Games matriculated at Lincoln College, Oxford in 1848 and was a school principal and vicar on the Isle of Man. Dodgson's book *Euclid and his Modern Rivals* (1879) was a defense of Euclid against several modern detractors (but not Jones).

1092. Jones, Joshua [later Joshua Hugh Games]. *A Review of Mr. Todhunter's Essay on Elementary Geometry, in the Conflict of Studies and other Essays.* (London: 1875). Reprinted from the *Monthly Journal of Education.*

E385 (author, title, date), JS1321. The reference in the title is to Isaac Todhunter's *The Conflict of Studies, and Other Essays on Subjects Connected with Education*, of which Dodgson owned a copy (see 2088).

1093. Jones, Thomas Wharton (1808–91). *Evolution of the Human Race from Apes, and of Apes, from the Lower Animals a Doctrine Unsanctioned by Science.* (London: Smith, Elder & Co., 1876). 69pp.

D98 (author, title, city, date), JS1323. Jones was fellow of the Royal College of Surgeons. He practiced as an ophthalmic surgeon in London before retiring to Ventnor, Isle of Wight.

1094. *Jones' Views of the Seats, Mansions, Castles, &c. of Noblemen and Gentlemen in England, Wales, Scotland, and Ireland; and Other Picturesque Scenery Accompanied with Historical Description of the Mansions, Lists of Pictures, Statues, and Genealogical Sketches of the Families and their Possessors, Forming Part of the General Series of Jones' Great Britain Illustrated.* (London: Jones and Co., [1829]–30). 6 vols.

Uncertain. F181 (author, title, date [1829]), not numbered in JS. Identified as Dodgson's only by the gothic stamp. F181 makes no mention of multiple volumes; Dodgson may have owned a single volume. Single and multi-volume editions of 1829 advertised for sale in 2004 listed a wide range of number of plates. The images were printed two per page.

1095. Jonson, Ben (1572–1637). *The Works of Ben Jonson.* (London: E. Moxon, 1846). 819pp. With a biographical memoir by William Gifford. A new edition.

A736?, B1097 (author, title, "With a Memoir by W. Gifford"), JS1325. Earliest 1-volume edition of the Gifford edition in BL. As B1097 does not specify multiple volumes, it seems a likely candidate. A736 states merely "Ben Jonson."

1096. Jonson, Ben. *Works*. Edition unknown.

A656/JS1324 states "Ben Jonson's Dramatic Works, 3 vols." Two 3-volume editions of Jonson have been traced (neither titled "Dramatic Works.") The Gifford edition seems more likely as it was printed in several pre–1898 editions of 3 vols. Dodgson also owned a 1-volume edition of Gifford's version. The possibilities in BL and NUC are:

The Works of Ben Jonson. (London: Albert J. Crocker and Bros., 1870). 3 vols. With notes critical and explanatory and a biographical memoir by William Gifford.

Ben Jonson. (London: T. Fisher Unwin; New York: Scribner's, 1893–5). 3 vols. Edited by Brinsley Nicholson with an introduction by Charles Harold Herford.

1097. Jopling, Joseph. *The Practice of Isometrical Perspective*. (London: M. Taylor, 1842). 96pp. Illustrated. A new edition, improved.

E150 (author, title, date), F161, JS1310 (listed under Jobling). F161 notes the gothic stamp. Jopling was an architect and maker of drafting instruments. He invented Jopling's double cranks, which could be used to draw a variety of mathematical curves.

1098. Jukes, Andrew John (1815–1901). *The Characteristic Differences of the Four Gospels Considered as Revealing Various Relations of the Lord Jesus Christ*. (London: 1853).

B1098 (author, title, date), JS1326. A book presenting four views of Christ based on the four Gospels. The New York edition was published in the same year by Revell (167pp.)

1099. Junius [pseud.] *The Letters of Junius. Complete in One Volume. With Notes and Copious Index*. (London: Printed for the Assigns of John Wheble, the original publisher, 1814). 316pp.

A302, D99 (author, title, city, date, 12mo.), JS124. One of two editions in BL to match D99, the other being a 2-volume edition. As multi-volume works are specified in D, the one-volume edition is here described. Junius was the pseudonym of an unknown British author (various scholars have suggested nearly two dozen possibilities from Thomas Paine to Edmund Burke). These letters against George III were originally published in *The Public Advertiser* from 21 January 1769–21 January 1772.

1100. Justinus, Marcus Junianus. *Justini Historiae Philippicae cum Integris Commentariis J. Bongarsii, F. Modii, M. Berneceri, M. Z. Boxhornii, I. Vossii, I. F. Gronovii, J. G. Grævii, T. Fabri, J. Vorstii, J. Schefferi, et excerptis H. Loriti Glareani atque Editoris Oxoniensis, Curante A. Gronovio*. (Leiden: Luchtmans, 1760). 46, xliii, 1034, [171]pp. 2nd edition.

A926 (author, date), B1099 (author, title, editor), JS1327. B1097 notes that Dodgson's copy was a prize for Charles Dodgson (C. L. D.'s father), May, 1817. Justinus was a Roman historian who flourished in the 3rd century of the common era.

1101. Kavanagh, Julia (1824–77). *Daisy Burns, a Tale*. (London: R. Bentley, 1853). 3 vols. 1st edition.

A931 (author, title, 3 vols., edition), JS1329. Julia Kavanagh was daughter of the poet and philologist Morgan Kavanagh and an Irish novelist and biographer. In addition to many novels and the title below, she also wrote *Women of Christianity* (1852) and *French Women of Letters* (1861). She spent much of her early life in France before taking up a career as a writer in London. Most of her novels were infused with French life and character. *The Athenæum* wrote on her death that her writing "was quiet and simple in style, but pure and chaste, and characterized by the same high-toned thought and morality that was part of the author's own nature." This is one of her 20 or so novels.

1102. Kavanagh, Julia. *English Women of Letters. Biographical Sketches*. (London: Hurst and Blackett Publishers, 1863 [1862]). 2 vols. 331, 353pp.

A901 (author, title, 2 vols.), JS1328. This is the only 2-volume edition in BL or BOD. 22 sketches of women novelists including Aphra Behn, Lady Morgan, Sarah Fielding, Fanny Burney, Charlotte Smith, Maria Edgeworth, Ann Radcliffe, and Jane Austen.

1103. Kay, William (1820–86). *A Commentary on the Two Epistles of St. Paul to the Corinthians*. (London: Macmillan & Co., 1887). 145pp. Edited by John Slatter. With the text.

A797 (author, title), JS1330. Only edition in MBC. William Kay was rector of Great Leghs, Essex, a canon of St. Alban's, former Principal of Bishop's College, Calcutta, and a fellow and tutor of Lincoln College. See 1859 for a note on Slatter.

1104. Kay, William. *Crisis Hupfeldiana; Being an Examination of Hupfeld's Criticism on Genesis, as Recently set Forth in Bishop Colenso's Fifth Part.* (Oxford and London: John Henry and James Parker, 1865). 95pp.

C5 (author, title), not in JS. Only edition in BL. A response to John William Colenso's *The Pentateuch and Book of Joshua Critically Examined*, in which Colenso questioned both the accuracy and authorship of those books. For more on Colenso and the controversy surrounding him see 421 and 1184.

1105. Kayat, Assad Yakoob. *The Eastern Traveller's Interpreter; or, Arabic Without a Teacher.* (London: Printed by W. M'-Dowall for the Author, 1844). 172pp.

E144 (author, title, date), JS1331. A 2nd edition was also published (by both James Madden and the author) in 1844. A handbook for learning Arabic.

1106. Keary, A[nnie] (1825–79). *The Nations Around.* (London: Macmillan and Co., 1870). 332pp.

A772, B1100 (author, title, date), JS1332. Annie Keary was the daughter of an Irish clergyman and many of her writings address Irish issues. She wrote works of history, children's stories, and novels. The preface states, "The following sketch of the early history of the great Eastern Empires, whose territories surrounded, and sometimes included, Palestine, is entitled 'The Nations Around' because the writer's aim has been to dwell chiefly on the periods and circumstances which brought these people into connexion with the Hebrews, and to regard their history somewhat in the reflected light of the interest which attaches to all that concerns the heroes of the sacred narrative. This has been done in the double hope of making some points of the Bible history clearer to some readers, and of awakening a more lively interest in the history of 'The Nations Around the Jews,' than is usually felt when they are regarded quite independently."

1107. Keats, John (1795–1821). *Endymion: A Poetic Romance.* (London: Printed for

Taylor and Hessey, 1818). 207pp. 1st edition.

A422, B1101 (author, title, edition, date), JS1334. A poem in four parts, deeply rooted in Greek myth, telling the story of a shepherd prince and a moon goddess.

1108. Keats, John. *Lamia, Isabella, The Eve of St. Agnes, and Other Poems.* (London: Printed for Taylor and Hessey, 1820). 199pp. 1st edition.

A423, B1102 (author, title, edition, date), JS1335. The first poem tells of a witch masquerading as a beautiful woman; "The Eve of St. Agnes" is about a woman who has a vision of her lover.

1109. Keats, John. *Poems.* (London: Printed for C. & J. Ollier, 1817). 121pp. 1st edition.

A421 (author, title, edition, date), JS1333. Published with the help of Shelley, this collection of poems was not a financial success. The author's first book, rare even in 1898, it fetched £7 at the Brooks sale, one of the most expensive single volumes outside the 1865 *Alices*. A832 states simply "Keat's [sic] Poems" and is probably a later edition.

1110. [Keble College]. *An Account of the Proceedings at Keble College on the Occasion of the Opening of the Chapel and the Laying of the Foundation Stone of the Hall and Library on St. Mark's Day, 1876, with the Sermons and Speeches then Delivered and a Description of the Chapel.* (Oxford and London: J. Parker, 1876). 107pp.

E45 (title), JS197 (Anon./Oxford). Dodgson wrote in his diary on 25 April 1876, "Opening of Keble Chapel. Dined with Shaw Stewart in the hall there. Lord Salisbury etc. had been at the opening." Keble was conceived by those inspired by the Oxford Movement as a training college for High Church Anglican clergymen.

1111. Keble, John (1792–1866). *The Christian Year: Thoughts in Verse for the Sundays and Holydays Throughout the Year.* (Oxford: J. Parker, 1827). 2 vols. 201, 200pp. 1st edition.

A437 (author, title, edition, 2 vols., date), A568 (another copy, this of the "Thumb Edition"), JS304 (Anon./Theology), JS1336. Keble was a fellow at Oriel College and Professor of

Poetry at Oxford University. He was one of the leaders of the Oxford Movement, and John Henry Newman credits Keble with launching that movement with his sermon on "National Apostasy" in 1833. Keble's collection of verses was hugely popular during the Victorian era, reaching an 89th edition by 1865 and being constantly reprinted by many publishers.

1112. [**Keble**, John]. *A Concordance to "The Christian Year."* (Oxford & London: James Parker & Co., 1871). 524pp.

A550 (title), JS308 (Anon./Theology). Anonymous concordance of Keble's collection of religious verses (see above).

1113. Keble, John. *Miscellaneous Poems.* (Oxford and London: James Parker and Co., 1869). 309pp. With preface by G[eorge] M[oberly].

A836 ("Keble's Poems"), JS1338. 1st edition of the closest matching title (and the only real possibility) in BL.

1114. Keble, John. *The Original Draft of the "Christian Year," Being a Facsimile Reproduction of the First Form of Keble's Christian Year in the Author's Handwriting. With a Preface, and a Collation of the Variations Between the Original and the Published Editions.* (London: 1878 [1877]).

A438 (author, title, date), JS1337. In 1886 Dodgson published a facsimile of his own manuscript book, AAUG.

1115. Keightley, Thomas (1789–1872). *Tales and Popular Fictions; their Resemblance, and Transmission from Country to Country.* (London: Whittaker and Co., 1834). 354pp. 10 illustrations by W. H. Brooke, engraved by Baxter.

E291 (author, title, date, illustrator), JS1339. Thomas Keightley wrote a number of historical works, a life of Milton, and works on mythology. In his introduction, he writes, "When chance led me to think of writing the Fairy Mythology, I had to read a great quantity of poems, tales, romances, legends, and traditions of various countries and in various languages. I here met such a number of coincidences where there could hardly have been any communication, that I became convinced that the original sameness of the human mind revealed itself as plainly in fiction as in the me-

chanical arts, or in manners and customs, civil or religious."

1116. Keith, Alexander (1791–1880). *The Evidence of Prophecy; Partly Selected and Abridged, with Additional Reflections, from a Work by Alexander Keith Entitled Evidence of the Truth of the Christian Religion.* (London: Religious Tract Society, [1830?]). 162pp.

A795 ("Keith's Evidence of Prophecy"), JS1340. Earliest edition in BL under this title (the conjectural date is from BL). The work was frequently reprinted, later under the title: *The Evidence of Prophecy: Historical Testimony to the Truth of the Bible.* The original work of which this is an abridgement was titled: *Evidence of the Truth of the Christian Religion Derived from the Literal Fulfillment of Prophecy.* Keith was minister of St. Cyrus, Kincardineshire. Rev. Edward Bickersteth wrote of this volume, "A very useful work on the plan of Bishop Newton's Dissertations, with further proofs of the fulfillment of the Prophecies from modern and even infidel travellers."

1117. Kemble, Frances Anne [later F. A. Butler] (1809–93). *Poems.* (London: E. Moxon & Co., 1866 [1865]). 285pp.

B1104 (author, title, publisher, date), JS1342. It seems likely that A835/JS1347 ("Kendle's Poems") also refers to this item. No pre–1898 poet named Kendle has been traced. B also includes the other item listed in A835 (Ingelow's *Story of Doom*), so Blackwell's must have bought that lot. "Kendle" is therefore almost certainly a misprint for "Kemble." Kemble was an actress especially known for her Shakespearean performances. This was her sole literary output, though she did write a memoir. The poems were originally published in 1844. One of Dodgson's earliest theatrical experiences was hearing Fanny Kemble read *Henry V* at the Town Hall, Oxford on 19 February 1855.

1118. Kempe, Alfred Bray (1849–1922). *How to Draw a Straight Line. A Lecture on Linkages.* (London: Macmillan, 1877). 52pp. In the *Nature Series* series. Illustrated.

E200 (author, title, date), JS1343, WS. Dodgson's copy is in WWC. It has the gothic stamp and has the property label on the front cover. Educated at Trinity College, Cambridge,

Kempe had a great love of both music and mathematics, yet became a barrister. Through his career he served as legal advisor to a number of Anglican dioceses. The author writes in his preface, "But how do you draw a straight line? A circle is easy. In principle the method is perfect although in practice your pencil may be blunt. Creating a straight edge is as fraught with trial and error as making an engineer's surface table. How odd that Euclid didn't notice how different it is from a circle. Until 1874 no-one in England knew of a method for drawing a straight line that was, in principle, perfect."

1119. Kempis, Thomas À (1380–1471). *De Imitatione Christi libri quatuor.* (Oxonii: Johannes Henricus Parker, 1848). 256pp.

D101 (title, city, date), JS1344. Dodgson probably also owned an English translation, of which many were published in the 19th century. A568 lists "Imitation of Christ," and since listings of Latin books in A are usually rendered in Latin, it seems likely that this (listed also as JS317 Anon./Theology) is a separate item in English. There is no indication about which of the many English editions Dodgson might have owned. The author was an Augustinian monk. This, his most famous work, is a book of Christian mysticism which follows the progress of a soul to Christian perfection and then union with God.

1120. Kendal, Mrs. [Madge] [a.k.a. Dame Margaret Shafto Robertson] (1849–1935). "Dramatic Opinions." In *Murray's Magazine*, Vol. VI, nos. 33–36 (Sept. 1889–Dec. 1889). 4-part article extracted from *Murray's Magazine.*

JS209 (Anon./Periodicals). Dodgson's copy is in HAC and is in an envelope labeled in his hand, in purple ink, "Dramatic Opinions by Mrs. Kendall [sic]." An article about the current state of drama and the career of the author. Includes mention of some of Dodgson's favorite actors (such as Minnie Terry) and plays (such as *The Silver King*). Kendal was an actress-manager who, with her husband, William Hunter, helped bring respectability to her profession. Dodgson met Kendal on 16 January 1874 at the home of Henry Holiday. He saw her on stage on several occasions, praised her 1888 production of *The Real Little Lord Fauntleroy*, but wrote of her production of Pinero's *The Squire*, "It is the first distinctly objectionable piece I have known Mrs. Kendal to produce."

1121. Kendall, May (a.k.a. Emma Goldworth Kendall) (b. 1861). *Dreams to Sell.* (London: Longmans & Co., 1887). 145pp.

A831, B1106 (author, title, date), JS1345. The *Academy* wrote of this book of poetry, "In the present volume the cleverness and the wit have more justice done to them [than in her first book *That Very Mab*, see below], owing to the restraints of verse."

1122. Kendall, May (a.k.a. Emma Goldworth Kendall) and Andrew Lang (1844–1912). *That Very Mab.* (London: Longmans, Green & Co., 1885). 215pp.

A652 (title), JS1346. Only edition in BL of the only matching title. See 1186 for a note on Lang. The wryly humorous story of the Fairy Queen Mab and her return to England following a long stay in Samoa.

1123. Kenealy, Edward Vaughan [Hyde] (1819–80). *A New Pantomime.* (London: Reeves and Turner, 1863). 570pp.

A836 ["Kenealey (a new pantomime)"], JS292 (Anon./Theatre). Only edition in BL of the only possible match. Though the listing in A836 is somewhat cryptic (and interpreted by JS as a new pantomime titled *Kenealey*), this is clearly the proper item. Kenealy was the author of several books, but was best-known as the counsel for the defense in the Tichborne trial (see 416). It has been suggested (see Martin Gardner's *The Annotated Snark*) that he was the model for the barrister in *Snark*. This work was the author's final form of his verse pantomime, first published "in fragmentary form" as *Goethe: A New Pantomime.*

1124. Kenealy, Edward Vaughan. *Poems and Translations.* (London: Reeves and Turner, 1864). 460pp.

A845, B1105 (author, title, date), JS1348. Includes translations from Swedish, Danish, Magyar, Italian, German, Basque, and Persian into English and from English into Greek and other languages.

1125. Kennaway, Charles Edward (1800–75). *The War and the Newspapers: A Lecture.* (Ottery St. Mary: 1856).

E397 (author, title, date), JS1349. Kennaway was vicar of Chipping Camden, Gloucestershire from 1832 to 1873. The war in question was the Crimean War.

1126. Ker, John Bellenden (1765?–1842). *An Essay on the Archaiology of Popular English Phrases and Nursery Rhymes.* (Southampton: Fletcher and Son; London: Black, Young, & Young, 1834). 163pp.

A319 ("English Phrases and Nursery Rhymes"), JS235 (Anon./Reference). Earliest edition in BL of the only matching title listed there. Allibone quotes an uncited critic as saying of this book, "A work which has met with great abuse among the reviewers; but those who are fond of philological pursuits will read it… The author's attempt is to explain everything from the Dutch, which he believes was the same language as the Anglo-Saxon."

1127. Keynes, John Neville (1852–1949). *Studies and Exercises in Formal Logic, Including a Generalisation of Logical Processes in their Application to Complex Inferences.* (London: Macmillan & Co., 1887). 414pp. 3rd edition, re-written and enlarged.

A505, A508, D108 (author, title, date), JS1351. Dodgson owned two copies of this title — one listed in A505 as "Keyne's Formal Logic," and one listed as A508 as "Kynes' [sic] Formal Logic." One copy is identified in D108 as the 3rd edition of 1894 (476pp.) and is inscribed "Rev. C. L. Dodgson, with the Author's kind regards." The other (described above) is in the collection formed by Jeffrey Stern, now at Seitoku Gakuin College, Tokyo, Japan. This copy has a full page of notes in ink and pencil on the rear endpaper and marginalia on pp. 116 and 436. J. N. Keyes was an English economist, fellow of Pembroke College, Cambridge, and father of the renowned economist John Maynard Keynes. This work was successful because of its clear explanation of formal logic.

1128. Kidson, F[rank] (b. 1855), compiler and editor. *Traditional Tunes, a Collection of Ballad Airs, Chiefly Obtained in Yorkshire and the South of Scotland; together with their Appropriate Words.* (Oxford: C. Taphouse & Son, 1891). 174pp.

A594 (title), JS177 (Anon./Music). Only 19th-century edition in BL.

1129. [**King**, Edmund Fillingham], editor. *Ten Thousand Wonderful Things.* (London: Ward & Lock, [1859]). 332pp.

A894 (title), JS255 (Anon./Reference). A 2nd series was published in 1859, dated 1860. BL also lists a (presumably) combined edition: *Ten Thousand Wonderful Things. Comprising Whatever is Marvellous and Rare, Curious, Eccentric and Extraordinary in All Ages and Nations.* (London: G. Routledge and Sons, 1889). 684pp., an equally likely candidate for ownership by Dodgson. A compendium of interesting information.

1130. [**King**, Richard John] (1818–79). *A Handbook for Travellers in Surrey, Hampshire, and the Isle of Wight.* (London: John Murray, 1858). 322pp. With map.

E407 (title, publisher), JS363 (Anon./Topography). E407 notes that this has the pencil autograph of Dodgson. Earliest edition in BL. The 2nd edition was published in 1865, after Dodgson's first trips to the Isle of Wight, so he likely owned this edition.

1131. Kingsley, Charles (1819–75). *Alton Locke, Tailor and Poet, an Autobiography.* (London: Chapman and Hall, 1856 [1855]). 309pp. Cheap Edition. In the *Select Library of Fiction* series.

Not in JS. In his diary for 3 January 1856, Dodgson writes, "Went on with *Alton Locke*, a powerful, and grandly-written book." He finished the book on 7 January and wrote a long review in his diary that day (see *Diary 2*). Originally published in 1850 (Dodgson may have owned an earlier edition, as he might have avoided the "Cheap Edition," but this is the edition in BL that most closely matches the date of mention in the diary). Kingsley was a canon of Westminster, Professor of Modern History at Cambridge, an a campaigner (influenced by Dodgson's friend F. D. Maurice) for social reform. He was a novelist, poet, and essayist, writing on a wide variety of subjects. This novel, heavily influenced by Christian Socialism, tells of a tailor in a sweat shop who turns poet and, in his own way, revolutionary. Dodgson met Kingsley at the offices of their mutual publisher, Macmillan, on 7 January 1869.

1132. Kingsley, Charles. *Andromeda; and Other Poems.* (London: John W. Parker and Son, 1858). 169pp.

A448 (author, title), JS1352. Earliest edition in BL or BOD. DEL describes the title poem as "A poem in English hexameters, the subject of which is the well-known classical myth of Andromeda and Perseus."

1133. Kingsley, Charles. *Glaucus: or, the Wonders of the Shore.* (Cambridge: Macmillan & Co., 1855). 165pp. 2nd edition.

A302, D100 (author, title, edition, city, date), JS1353. The 1st edition was also published in 1855. DEL calls this "A book on the natural history of the beach." Dodgson also owned Sowerby's illustrated *Companion to Glaucus* (see 1912).

1134. Kingsley, Charles. *Hypatia, or New Foes with an Old Face.* (London: John W. Parker and Son, 1853). 2 vols.

Not in JS. According to his diaries, Dodgson began reading this book on 3 January 1857. This is the 1st edition and the only pre–1856 edition in 2 vols. (see reference below in this note to the 2nd volume). On 7 January 1857 he wrote, "Finished *Hypatia*: it is powerful, like all that Kingsley writes, outrageous to taste in some parts, which is a new fault (to me). I mean especially the sneers at Christianity which he puts into the mouths of some of the heathen characters, and the undisguised horrors of the gladiators' show in the theatre, and the death of Hypatia. It bears out the theory of the affinity between things dreadful and things beautiful, that he displays the most perfect sense of beauty, and some of his English reads like unmetrical poetry. One paragraph especially struck me, where the beauty of the *sound* seems to be as great as prose admits of, it is in the second volume, at the end of the theatre scene, and begins 'But Pelagia hid her face within her hands.' The book has interested me strongly in the history of Cyril, which I intend to read the next opportunity." The novel is set in 5th-century Alexandria and concerns conflict between Christians and neo-Platonists, especially in the person of the title character.

1135. Kingsley, Charles. *Madam How and Lady Why, or First Lessons in Earth Lore for Children.* (London: Bell and Daldy, 1870). 350pp.

A303 (author, title), JS1354. 1st edition. This was Kingsley's last children's book, a fanciful look at the science of geology. Madam How represents Nature, and Lady Why is her mistress, the mysterious and unknown reason for the occurrence of natural phenomena.

1136. Kingsley, Charles. *Sermons.* Details unknown.

A759/JS1355 states "2 vols. of Kingsley's Sermons." Kingsley published many volumes of sermons and the wording of the entry may indicate that Dodgson simply owned two of these volumes. There is one set of sermons that was originally published in 2 volumes, and thus seems the most likely candidate, but A759 is certainly not authoritative. The best possibility: *Sermons on National Subjects.* (London: R. Griffin & Co., 1852–54). 1st and 2nd series.

1137. Kingsley, Charles. *The Water-Babies: A Fairy Tale for a Land-baby.* (London: Macmillan and Co., 1864). 378pp. 2nd edition. With 2 illustrations by J. Noël Paton.

A654 (author, title, date), JS1356 (not listed separately from below). See 1507 for a note on Paton. Kingsley's most famous work, a children's book telling the story of a young chimney sweep who drowns in a river but awakes in a new form, that of a "water baby," in which form he explores the world beneath the surface. First published in 1863, two years before AAIW. Humphrey Carpenter (OCCL) calls this "one of the first classic fantasies by an English author," and it is frequently cited as a precursor to AAIW. Dodgson probably owned a copy prior to the publication of AAIW in 1865, as the cover deign for AAIW is closely based on that of *The Water-Babies.* He may also have owned a later printing as in a letter to Macmillan of 22 September 1868, Dodgson wrote, "Thanks for *The Water Babies.*"

Joseph Noël Paton's frontispiece for Charles Kingsley's *The Water-Babies* (item 1137).

1138. Kingsley, Charles. *The Water-Babies: A Fairy Tale for a Land-baby.* (London: Macmillan and Co., 1885). 372pp. 4th edition. With 100 illustrations by Linley Sambourne.

A675 (author, title, illustrator), JS1356 (not listed separately from above). 1st edition with Sambourne's illustrations. Sambourne (1844–1910) was an illustrator for *Punch*. Dodgson wrote to him in 1874 proposing that he illustrate *Phantasmagoria*. Dodgson met Sambourne in April of the following year. In February of 1876, Sambourne wrote to Dodgson that he could not, after all, provide illustrations for him. The following February Sambourne wrote to "re-open negotiations." Sambourne did, apparently, draw at least one illustration for Dodgson, but the collaboration never came to fruition.

1139. Kingsley, Henry (1830–76). *The Hillyars and Burtons: A Story of Two Families.* (London: Macmillan and Co., 1865). 3 vols. 288, 282, 318pp.

Not in JS. Dodgson read this book in the first fortnight of 1866 and called it (in his diary for 16 January) "clever, though quite inferior to *Ravenshoe.*" 1st edition and the only edition printed prior to Dodgson's diary mention. Kingsley was the younger brother of Charles. He left Oxford after some controversy and spent five years in Australia, an experience that had an influence on his novels. This novel is set in Australia. Dodgson met Kingsley on the Isle of Wight on 9 August 1864 (see *Diary 4*).

1140. Kingsley, Henry. *Ravenshoe.* (Cambridge: Macmillan, 1862). 3 vols. 310, 308, 302pp. 1st edition.

A808 (author, title, edition, 3 vols.), JS1357. Published in May, 1862 (the 2nd edition was published in August 1862). A novel about a disinherited heir who is eventually restored to his rightful position. See above for Dodgson's opinion of this book.

1141. Kingsley, Henry. *Recollections of Geoffry Hamlyn.* (Cambridge: Macmillan & Co., 1860). 2nd edition.

A808 (author, title), JS1358. Since A808 also lists *Ravenshoe* and specifies that it is 1st edition and 3 vols., it seems reasonable to suppose that this title, for which no edition or number of volumes is specified, is not a 1st and is a 1-volume edition. The edition described is the first published in a single volume and is preceded by the 3-volume 1st edition of 1859, also published by Macmillan. A story of settlers in Australia.

1142. Kingston, William Henry Giles (1814–80). *Infant Amusements; or, How to Make a Nursery Happy. With Practical Hints to Parents and Nurses on the Moral and Physical Training of Children.* (London: Griffith and Farran, 1867). 183pp. Frontispiece by Kate Greenaway.

B1107 (author, title, date), JS1359. Kingston was known primarily as a writer of novels and adventure stories for boys. This work is a collection of songs, hymns, and prayers for children. See 819 for a note on Greenaway.

1143. K[inloch], G[eorge] R[itchie] (1796?–1877), editor. *Ancient Scottish Ballads, Recovered from Tradition. With Notes Historical and Explanatory & an Appendix, Containing the Airs of Several of the Ballads.* (London and Edinburgh: Longman, Rees, Orme, Brown, & Green, 1827). 270pp.

A481, B943 (author, title, date), JS1360. A collection of folk songs and ballads. Allibone writes, "The collector of old poetry must secure this volume."

1144. Kipling, John Lockwood (1837–1911). *Beast and Man in India. A Popular Sketch of Indian Animals in their Relations with the People.* (London: Macmillan & Co., 1891). 401pp. 1st edition. With illustrations.

A614 (author, title, edition), JS1362 (listed under Rudyard Kipling, copying an error in A614). John Lockwood Kipling, father of Rudyard Kipling, was a potter who assisted with the decorations of what is now the Victoria and Albert Museum and was also curator of the Lahore Museum and principal of an art school in Lahore, India. This work is an account of various peoples of India and their relationships with animals including cows, oxen, etc.

1145. Kipling, Rudyard (1865–1936). *Barrack-Room Ballads and Other Verses.* (London: Methuen & Co., 1892). 208pp. 1st edition.

A861 (author, title, edition), JS1361. Born in India, Kipling was a prolific author of stories of adventure dealing with India, the jungle, the sea, etc., many of which were especially popular among boys. He also wrote verse and worked for a time as a journalist. He won the Nobel Prize in 1907. This collection is of poems originally published in the *Scots Observer* after Kipling's move to England in 1889.

1146. Kipling, Rudyard. *The City of Dreadful Night and Other Places.* (Allahabad: A. H. Wheeler & Co., 1891). 108pp. No. 14 of A. H. Wheeler & Co.'s *Indian Railway Library* series.

E42 (author, title, series), JS1363. See 1148 for more on this series. The city in question is Calcutta and Kipling gives a glimpse into such varied aspects of life as "The Police" and "The Opium Factory."

1147. Kipling, Rudyard. *Departmental Ditties and Other Verses.* (Calcutta: Thacker, Spink and Co., 1886). 63pp. 2nd edition.

A836 (author, title), JS1364. A836 does not specify 1st edition, as many other Kipling entries do, so there is no way to be certain what edition Dodgson owned. Thacker, Spink and Co. published the 1st edition in Calcutta in 1886 and many subsequent editions there. The 1st London edition does not seem to have been issued until 1899, following Dodgson's death, so he certainly would have owned one of the Thacker, Spink and Co. editions. This is the earliest non–1st in BL. A collection of verses (originally published in the *Civil and Military Gazette* of Lahore) reflecting the Anglo-Indian community in India.

1148. Kipling, Rudyard. *In Black & White.* (Allahabad: A. H. Wheeler & Co.; London: Sampson Low, Marston, & Co., [1891?]). 106pp. Number 3 in A. H. Wheeler & Co.'s *Indian Railway Library.* "Reprinted in chief from the *Week's News*"

A612 (author, title), JS1365. All of the items in A612 are titles originally published in this series. We know, from the entry for *City of Dreadful Night* in E42, that Dodgson owned at least one title from this series, and the listing of *Wee Willie Winkie* as a 1st edition in A612 indicates another. It seems likely that what the items in A612 have in common is that they are all part of Wheeler's *Indian Railway Library.* Together, the items in A612 and E42 compose all 7 of the Kipling titles listed in BL as being in this series. The series was originally published in Allahabad, India (this title in [1888]), but it seems more likely that Dodgson owned copies of the London editions. Earliest London edition in BL. Other Kipling items owned by Dodgson and known or conjectured to be in this series are: *City of Dreadful Night, Phantom Rickshaw, Soldiers Three, Stories of the Gadsbys, Under the Deodars,* and *Wee Willie Winkie.* Short stories.

1149. Kipling, Rudyard. *The Jungle Book.* (London: Macmillan, 1894). 212pp. With illustrations by J. L. Kipling, W. H. Drake and P. Frenzeny. 1st edition.

A614 (author, title, edition), JS1366. A collection of fanciful short stories about animals in India.

1150. Kipling, Rudyard. *Life's Handicap: Being Stories of Mine Own People.* (London: Macmillan, 1891). 352pp. 1st edition.

A613 (author, title, edition), JS1367. A collection of Indian pieces including all the stories from *Mine Own People* (1891) except "A Conference of the Powers," plus 16 additional stories and one poem.

1151. Kipling, Rudyard. *The Light that Failed.* (London: Macmillan, 1891). 339pp. 1st edition.

A613 (author, title, edition), JS1368. Dodgson's copy was offered for sale in 2002 by Bauman Rare Books of Philadelphia and described as having his monogram on the title page. F171 lists the first published edition of this work: "The Light that Failed," *Lippincott's Monthly Magazine* (Ward, Lock and Co.), January, 1891, 3–97. Since this is only listed in F, it has not been given a separate entry, but it is possible that Dodgson owned both this magazine appearance and the book edition. Kipling's first novel is the story of an artist attempting to finish his masterpiece before he goes blind. In the magazine version, the story had a happy ending, but in the book edition Kipling restored the unhappy ending he had originally planned.

1152. Kipling, Rudyard. *The Phantom 'Rickshaw and Other Tales.* (Allahabad: A. H. Wheeler & Co.; London: Sampson Low, Marston, & Co., [1890]). 104pp. Number 5 in A. H. Wheeler & Co.'s *Indian Railway Library.* "Reprinted in chief from the *Week's News.*"

A612 (author, title), JS1370. See 1148 for a detailed explanation of this series. BL lists no other separate British editions in Dodgson's lifetime. A collection of short stories originally published in the Allahabad *Pioneer* (under Kipling's editorship). Includes the story "The Man Who Would be King."

1153. Kipling, Rudyard. *Plain Tales from the Hills.* (Calcutta: Thacker, Spink; London: W. Thacker, 1888). 283pp.

A611 (author, title), JS1371. 1st edition. Kipling's first book of fiction, collecting 40 stories, 29 of which appeared previously in the *Civil and Military Gazette.* Many of these had to do with the Anglo-Indian community.

1154. Kipling, Rudyard, editor. *Soldiers Three, a Collection of Stories Setting Forth Certain Passages in the Lives and Adventures of Privates Terence Mulvaney, Stanley Ortheris, and John Learoyd.* (London: Sampson Low, Marston, Searle, & Rivington, Limited, 1890). 93pp. 6th edition. Number 1 in A. H. Wheeler & Co.'s *Indian Railway Library.* "Reprinted in chief from the *Week's News*"

A612 (author, title), JS1372. See 1148 for a detailed explanation of this series. BL lists no other separate British editions in Dodgson's lifetime except a 7th edition of the same date and publisher.

1155. Kipling, Rudyard. *The Story of the Gadsbys, A Tale without a Plot.* (London: Sampson, Low, Marston, Searle, & Rivington; Allahabad: A. H. Wheeler & Co., [1890]). 86pp. No. 2 of A. H. Wheeler & Co.'s *Indian Railway Library.* "Reprinted in chief from the *Week's News.*"

A612 (author, title), JS1373. 1st London printing. See 1148 for a detailed explanation of why this edition is most likely. Novel.

1156. Kipling, Rudyard. *Under the Deodars.* (London: Sampson Low, Marston, Searle, & Rivington; Allahabad: A. H. Wheeler & Co., [1890]). 96pp. No. 4 of A. H. Wheeler & Co.'s *Indian Railway Library.* "Reprinted in chief from the *Week's News.*"

A612 (author, title), JS1374. 1st London printing. See 1148 for a detailed explanation of why this edition is most likely. Fiction.

1157. Kipling, Rudyard. *Wee Willie Winkie and Other Stories.* (Allahabad: A. H. Wheeler & Co, n.d. [1888]). 104pp. Number 6 in A. H. Wheeler & Co.'s *Indian Railway Library.* "Reprinted in chief from the *Week's News.*" 1st edition.

A612 (author, title, edition), JS1375. It is equally likely that Dodgson owned the 1st London edition (see 1148 for a discussion of this issue). Dodgson owned 2 copies of this work, both listed in A612 but only one specified as 1st edition. The other, a copy of the 6th edition (Allahabad: A. H. Wheeler & Co.; London: Sampson Low, Marston & Company, [ca. 1890]) is now in the collection of Alan Tannenbaum, Austin, TX. It includes Dodgson's signature on the front paste-down. A collection of stories for children.

1158. Kipling, Rudyard and Wolcott Balestier. *The Naulahka: A Story of West and East.* (London: William Heinemann, 1892). 276pp. 1st edition.

A614 (author, title, edition), JS1369. Kipling's only real attempt at literary collaboration. Combining Kipling's writings about India and Balestier's about the American West, the story tells of a man from a boom-town in the American West who chases after a jewel in India.

1159. Kirby, Elizabeth (1823–73) and Mary Kirby [later Gregg] (1817–93). *Chapters on Trees. A Popular Account of Their Nature and Uses.* (London: Cassell, Petter, & Galpin, [1873]). 320pp.

A853 (author, title), JS1376. Only edition in BL. Elizabeth Kirby began story-telling at an early age and eventually settled with her sister, Mary, and brother-in-law. The two sisters wrote many books for children which the DNB called "homely and unpretentious little works." The present work includes chapters on nearly 40 varieties of trees, accompanied by illustrations of the same.

1160. Kirby, E[lizabeth] and Mary Kirby [later Gregg]. *The Talking Bird; or, The Little Girl who Knew What was Going to Happen.* (London: Grant and Griffith, 1856). 96pp. With illustrations by H. K. Browne.

A641 (title, illustrator), JS1109 (listed under Gregg). This is the earliest edition traced. A book for children.

1161. Kirkes, William Senhouse (1823–64) assisted by James Paget. *Hand-Book of Physiology*. (London: Walton & Maberly, 1856). 747pp. 3rd edition.

Not in JS. In his diary for 9 March 1858, Dodgson writes, "Got from Parker's ... Kirkes' Handbook on Physiology, and began reading it through. I find it *very* interesting." He again records reading it on 25 March 1858. First published in 1848; this is the closest edition traced to Dodgson's diary entry. See 1482 for a note on Paget. Kirkes was Demonstrator of Morbid Anatomy at St. Bartholomew's Hospital and a pioneer in cardiology and nephrology. *The Medical Gazette* wrote of this work, "We predict that this will take its place as a standard work on physiology in all our medical schools and colleges."

1162. Kirkpatrick, A[lexander] F[rancis] (1849–1940). *The Divine Library of the Old Testament. It's Origin, Preservation, Inspiration, and Permanent Value. Five Lectures.* (London: Macmillan and Co., 1892). 155pp.

B1108 (author, title, date), JS1377. Kirkpatrick was Regius Professor of Hebrew at Cambridge and a canon of Ely Cathedral. In the preface he writes, "The attempt to decry the critical study of the Old Testament on a priori grounds can only prove mischievous in the end. The intelligent Christian will not say, 'These views are contrary to my theory of inspiration,' or, 'They are incompatible with this or that dogma, and therefore they cannot be true'; but 'Are these views grounded upon facts? and if so how must I modify the theory, or qualify the inferences I have drawn from the dogma, and perhaps re-state it?'" Dodgson ordered this book from Macmillan on 19 April 1895 (see *Macmillan*, 315).

1163. Klose, Carl Ludwig (1791–1863). *Memoirs of Prince Charles Stuart, Count of Albany, Commonly Called the Young Pretender; with Notices of the Rebellion in 1745.* (London: Henry Colburn, 1845). 2 vols. 410, 383pp. Translated from the German.

A905, B1109 (author, title, date, 2 vols.), JS1378. See 689 for a note on Charles Stuart.

1164. Knatchbull-Hugessen, E[dward] H[ugessen] (1829–93). *Moonshine Fairy Stories*. (London and New York: Macmillan and Co., 1871). 338pp. Illustrated by William Brunton.

A646 (title, illustrated), JS1379. 1st edition, as described in MBC, of the only matching title in BL. BL and BOD list the author as Hugessen, but MBC lists it as above. Knatchbull-Hugessen was a great-nephew of Jane Austen and a junior minister in the government of Gladstone. He wrote several volumes of fairy stories, none of which is particularly distinguished.

1165. Knie, J[ohann] G. *A Guide to the Proper Management and Education of Blind Children During their Earlier Years. (Whether in their Own Family, in Public Schools, or under Private Teachers).* (London: Simpkin, 1876). 80pp. Translated by the Rev. William Taylor (d. 1869 or 70) who has added an introduction and an appendix.

E194 (author, title, date), JS1380, WS. Knie also wrote on education for the deaf.

1166. K[night], C[harles] (1791–1873). *The English Cyclopædia. A New Dictionary of Universal Knowledge.* (London: Bradbury & Evans, 1854–70). Conducted by C. K. [assisted by Alexander Ramsay and James Thorne]. 27 volumes bound in 16.

A379 (title, "27 vols. in 16"), JS236 (Anon./Reference). Only edition in BL. Charles Knight was a publisher of newspapers and magazines who wrote, compiled, or edited many books, including a popular edition of Shakespeare's works. This work was divided as follows: Arts and Sciences— 8 volumes plus supplement, Biography— 6 volumes plus supplement, Geography— 4 volumes plus supplement, Natural History — 4 volumes plus supplement, and a 1-volume Synoptical Index.

1167. K[night], C[harles], editor. *Half-hours with the Best Authors, Selected and Arranged, with Short Biographical and Critical Notices, by C. K.* (London: Charles Knight [vol. 1]; George Routledge and Co. [vols. 2–4], [1847–48]). 4 vols. 416, 416, 416, 426pp. Illustrated with portraits.

A330, D82 (author, title, city, 4 vols.), JS1381. Earliest edition in BL. Neither BL nor BOD lists the publishers for these volumes, but a set described as "pre-1855" was offered for sale in 2002 by Gatehouse Books of Morris, New York with the above publishers and seems to fit the description of the 1st BL edition. There were many subsequent reprints, most published by Routledge or Warne.

1168. Knox, Edmund Arbuthnott (1847–1937). *An Address Respecting Cuddesdon College, Intended to have been Delivered at the Oxford Diocesan Conference, October 10th, 1878*. (London: Simpkin, Marshall, [1878]).

C4 (author, title), not in JS. Only edition in BL. Knox matriculated at Corpus Christi College, Oxford in 1865 and was a fellow of Merton from 1868 to 1884. He served as vicar of St. John the Baptist, Oxford from 1874 to 1879 and after 1884 as rector of Kibworth Beauchamp in county Leicester. Among his published works was a history of the Oxford Movement. This was a response to Charles Golightly's *Warning Against Cuddesdon College* (see 789).

1169. Knox, Robert (1791–1862). *A Manual of Artistic Anatomy for the Use of Sculptors, Painters, and Amateurs*. (London: Henry Renshaw, 1852). 175pp. Illustrated.

E280 (author, title, date), JS1383. E280 notes this has Dodgson's initials. Knox was a physician of the Royal College of Surgeons in Edinburgh and wrote and translated several works on anatomy. In his diary for 25 March 1858, Dodgson writes, "In these last few days I have begun reading Physiology [including] … Knox's *Handbook of Anatomy*."

1170. Koch, Christophe Guillaume de (1737–1813). *History of the Revolutions in Europe, from the Subversion of the Roman Empire in the West, to the Congress of Vienna, from the French of Christopher William Koch; with a Continuation to the year 1815 by M. Schoell. To which is Added a Sketch of the Late Revolutions in Greece, Poland, Belgium, and France by J. Barrett, M. D. With a Comprehensive Account of the Revolutions in France, Italy, and the German States in 1848*. (Hartford: E. Hunt, 1849). 736pp. Translated by Andrew Crichton.

Not in JS. *Diary 1* (24) notes that a letter from Dodgson's mother lists "Koch's *History of Europe*" as a prize book won by Dodgson at Rugby, probably in 1849. This is the only 1849 edition traced, and it seems likely that Dodgson's prize would have been a current edition. Koch was a French historian and politician.

1171. Konewka, Paul (1841–71). *Falstaff und Seine Gesellen*. (Strassburg: M. Schauenburg, [1872]). 20 silhouettes with accompanying text from Goethe.

A273, F177, not listed separately in JS. Dodgson's copy is in the collection of Jon Lindseth, Cleveland, OH. Mr. Lindseth's catalogue describes it as "laid in original blue cloth portfolio." It has the gothic stamp. City and date taken from description in BL. Konewka was a German artist who studied under the sculptor Drake and the painter Menzel. He was primarily known for his silhouette illustrations, which were published not only in Germany but, after his death, in England and Sweden. See index for other works by Konewka. In a letter to Arthur Frost (7 May 1878) Dodgson writes, "*Many* thanks for the silhouette: I like it very much, but you are bold to take a style which so directly challenges comparison with Konewka. I quite think you may be his *equal* some day, but you will find it hard to *beat* him! To me, at least, his designs seem faultless."

1172. Konewka, Paul. *Silhouettes*. Details unknown.

A545/JS1384 states "Silhouettes by Konewka." Several possibilities in BL including *Album. 6 Silhouetten Erfunden und Geschnitten von P. K. Fünfte Auflage* (Berlin: 1872); *Silhouetter af P. K.* (editions listed as published in Copenhagen, 1875–77 and Stockholm, 1875–77); and *Konewka's Silhouetten-Bilderbuch. 12 Heitere Bilder aus dem Leben. Mit Hübschen Reimen von F[ranz] S[traessle]* (Stuttgart: 1872).

1173. Konstam, Gertrude A[ngela Mary] (d. 1937), Ella Casella and Nelia Casella. *Dreams, Dances and Disappointments*. (London: Thos. De la Rue, [1881]). 32pp. Illustrated with 12 full color scenes and other pictures in brown ink.

E41, JS1385. Dodgson's copy is in HAC and has the gothic stamp on the illustrated front cover. Konstam was an actress, writer, and painter. Verse.

1174. [Koran]. *Koran, Commonly Called the Alcoran of Mohammed, Translated into*

English Immediately from the Original Arabic; with Explanatory Notes, Taken from the Most Approved Commentators. To Which is Prefixed a Preliminary Discourse by George Sale. (London: Printed by C. Ackers for J. Wilcox, 1734 [1733]). 187, 508pp.

A796 (title, translator), JS1811. 1st edition of Sale's translation, but it is more likely that Dodgson owned one of the many 19th-century editions. Sale (1697–1736) was a lawyer and orientalist. His studies of Arabic led him to participate in the Arabic translation of the New Testament and to produce this paraphrastic translation of the Koran.

1175. Kuhff, Henry. *Elements of the Calculus of Finite Differences: with the Application of its Principles to the Summation and Interpolation of Series. A Selection of Geometrical Problems, Intended Chiefly as Illustrations of the Method of Geometrical Analysis.* (Cambridge: J. Hall, 1831). 77pp.

E86 (author, title, date), JS1386 (copies misspelling "Kunff" from E86). E86 states that Dodgson's copy has "the autograph of Lewis Carroll inside cover, and two calculations (14 lines) in his hand, dated." Dodgson also spells the author "Kunff" in his diary; Yale University gives the author as Henry Kuhff.

1176. Kynaston, Herbert (1809–78). *Miscellaneous Poetry.* (London: B. Fellowes, 1841).

A831, B1110 (author, title, date), JS1387. Kynaston was educated at Christ Church, Oxford and served as headmaster at St. Paul's School, London from 1838 to 1876.

1177. La Bruyère, Jean de (1645–1696). *Les Caractères de La Bruyère.* (Paris: 1818). 3 vols.

E384 (author, title, city, date, 3 vols.), JS376 (Anon./Unclassified). Exact edition untraced, though the BNF has many similar editions: (Paris: A. Egron, 1817, 3 vols.), (Paris: P. Didot L'aine, 1818, 2 vols.), (Paris: Lefevre, 1818, 2 vols.). La Bruyère was a French moralizer whose great work (the present one) is part translation of the ancient Greek philosopher Theophrastus, part collection of maxims and character sketches. It shows, in an ironic manner, his views on economy, poverty, and the idle life of the rich.

1178. [Lamb, Charles] (1775–1834). *The Essays of Elia.* (London: Edward Moxon, 1853). 436pp. A new edition.

A340, B1111 (author, title, publisher, date), JS1388. Lamb was an English essayist and poet who also wrote books for children (some of them adaptations of classics produced with his sister, Mary) and who entertained in literary circles. The essays on widely varying topics in this collection were originally contributed to *The London Magazine* from 1820 to 1823. Their light-heartedness made them popular and established Lamb as an essayist.

1179. Lamb, Charles. *Works.* Edition unknown.

A825 ("Charles Lamb's Works"), JS1392.

1180. [Lamb, Charles and Mary (1764–1847)]. *Mrs. Leicester's School.* (London: M. J. Godwin & Co., 1825). 172pp. 9th edition.

A527 (title, date), JS1389. A book for children comprising a series of stories in which different girls at the school tell the tales (which are moral) of their lives.

1181. Lamb, Charles and Mary. *Poetry for Children, To which are Added Prince Dorus and some Uncollected Poems by Charles Lamb.* (London: Chatto and Windus, 1878 [1877]). 94pp. Edited, prefaced and annotated by Richard Herne Shepherd.

A830, B1112 (author, title, editor), JS1390. An earlier (Pickering, 1872) edition is listed in BL, but this is the earliest to give the full title (*...To which are Added, etc.*) as listed in B1112. See below for a note on *Prince Dorus*. See 1833 for a note on Shepherd.

1182. Lamb, Charles and Mary. *Prince Dorus.* (London: Field & Tuer, 1889). 31pp. 9 illustrations in facsimile, hand-coloured. Reprinted from the edition of 1811, with an introduction by Andrew White Tuer.

A470 ("Lamb's Prince Dorus a reprint, Field and Tuer"), JS1391. The original title was *Prince Dorus: or, Flattery Put out of Countenance, a Poetical Version of an Ancient Tale.* In this verse story, Dorus can only marry his love when he learns how absurdly long his nose is, but his courtiers will not tell him.

1183. Lambert, N[icolas]. *Hamel's French Grammar and Exercises.* (London: Longman, Brown, Green, and Longmans, and

Whittaker and Co., 1844). 438pp. A new edition in one volume.

E98, JS1393. Dodgson's copy is in HAC. "C. L. Dodgson, School House, Rugby," is inscribed on the front endpaper in brown ink together with an algebra problem, apparently also in Dodgson's hand. The gothic stamp is at the bottom of the same page. Apparently one of Dodgson's schoolbooks.

1184. (Lambeth Conference). *Conference of Bishops of the Anglican Communion, Holden at Lambeth Palace, September 24–27, 1867. I. An Address Delivered at the Opening of the Conference, by Charles Thomas, Lord Archbishop of Canterbury. II. The Resolutions of the Conference. III. Address of the Bishops to the Faithful in Christ Jesus.* (London: Rivingtons, 1867). 16pp.

C5 ("Conference of Bishops"), not in JS. Though not specified in C5, this is clearly the conference in question (it was the first Lambeth Conference, a meeting of the leaders of the worldwide Anglican communion that takes place every ten years). This item is bound (in Dodgson's library) in a collection of church pamphlets and in the middle of three pamphlets on the controversy over the Bishop of Natal, J. W. Colenso (see 421). That controversy was discussed at the 1867 conference, and the following resolution (printed herein) was reached: "That, in the judgment of the bishops now assembled, the whole Anglican Communion is deeply injured by the present condition of the Church in Natal; and that a committee be now appointed at this general meeting to report on the best mode by which the Church may be delivered from the continuance of this scandal, and the true faith maintained. That such report be forwarded to His Grace the Lord Archbishop of Canterbury, with the request that he will be pleased to transmit the same to all the bishops of the Anglican Communion, and to ask for their judgment thereupon."

1185. Landor, Walter Savage (1775–1864). *Selections from the Writings of Walter Savage Landor.* (London: Macmillan and Co., 1882). 375pp. Arranged and edited by Sidney Colvin. In the *Golden Treasury* series.

A328 ("Selections from Landor"), JS1395. Only closely matching title in BL that was published in Britain prior to 1898. Landor was an English poet and essayist.

1186. Lang, Andrew (1844–1912). *The Library.* (London: Macmillan and Co., 1881). 184pp. With a chapter on modern illustrated books by Austin Dobson. Illustrated by Walter Crane, Kate Greenaway, Harry Furniss, George Du Maurier, John Tenniel and others. In the *Art at Home Series.*

A897 ("Laing's The Library"), JS1396. Although there are some catalogues of libraries by authors named Laing in BL, none bear the title "The Library." JS conjectures, probably correctly, that A897 is a typographical error for "Lang," and this seems a likely book for Dodgson to own. 1st edition as described in MBC. Lang was a Scottish scholar, folklorist, and man of letters probably best known for his series of "Fairy Books." A useful and instructive book about books and book collecting. Includes reproductions of two of Tenniel's illustrations for the *Alice* books and a discussion of Tenniel as illustrator. "What ... could be more delightful than the picture ... of the 'Mad Tea Party?' Observe the hopelessly distraught expression of the March hare, and the eager incoherence of the hatter!"

1187. Langbridge, Frederick (b. 1849). *Gaslight and Stars. A Book of Verse.* (London: M. Ward & Co., 1880). 174pp.

A836 (author, title), JS1397. Only edition in BL. Educated at Alban Hall, Oxford, Langbridge served as rector of St. John's Limerick and wrote over 20 books, including poetry and books (some of a religious nature) for children. Dodgson had some correspondence with Langbridge (see *Letters,* 1103, 1108).

1188. Langbridge, Frederick. *The Scales of Heaven: Poems, Narrative, Legendary, and Meditative, with a Few Sonnets.* (London: E. Stock, 1896). 193pp.

A868 (title), JS385 (Anon./Unclassified). Only edition of the only matching title listed in BL.

1189. [Lankester, Edwin] (1814–74). *Half-Hours with the Microscope; Being a Popular Guide to the Use of the Microscope.* (London: Robert Hardwicke, [1859]). 92pp. Illustrated from nature by T. West.

D83 (title, illustrator, city, n.d.), JS1394 (listed under Lancaster). Earliest of several undated editions in BL. Lankester was coroner for Middlesex from 1862. He delivered courses of popular lectures and published several books on food, health, and related topics. There was a microscope among Dodgson's effects at his death (see A195).

1190. Latham, Henry (1821–1902). *On the Action of Examinations Considered as a Means of Selection.* (Cambridge: Deighton, Bell and Co., 1877). 544pp.

A553, F169 (author, title, date), JS1399, WS. Dodgson's copy is in WWC. It has the gothic stamp and has the property label on the front cover. Latham was vice-master of Trinity Hall, Cambridge from 1850 to 1888 when he became master. Latham here discusses various matters relating to examinations, including what we might today call "grading on the curve." He also warned of the effects of examinations on teaching (i.e. the dangers of "teaching to the test"). Dodgson met Latham at St. Leonards on Sea in September 1897 (see *Diaries*).

1191. Latham, Henry. *Pastor Pastorum; or, The Schooling of the Apostles by Our Lord.* (Cambridge: Deighton, Bell; London: George Bell, 1890). 499pp.

A791, B1115 (author, title, city, date), JS1400. Dodgson wrote to Latham asking if quotes from scripture herein might be from the Authorised rather than the Revised version (he said he hated the latter). In a letter to his brother Skeffington (10 June 1891), Dodgson writes of this book that he "found it intensely interesting" (see *Letters*).

1192. Laurence, Richard (1760–1838), translator. *The Book of Enoch, the Prophet: An Apocryphal Production, Supposed for Ages to have been Lost; but Discovered at the Close of the Last Century in Abyssinia; now First Translated from an Ethiopic Ms. in the Bodleian Library.* (Oxford: J. H. Parker, 1838). 250pp. 3rd edition.

A795, D62 (author, translator, city, date), JS1401. D62 notes Dodgson's signature. Enoch was the grandfather of Noah, and his book, quoted in the Bible, was long thought to be lost. Manuscript copies were discovered by the explorer James Bruce who returned from Abyssinia with three copies in 1773. Laurence's translation (the first in English) was first published in 1821.

1193. Lavater, Johann Casper (1741–1801). *Physiognomy; or, The Corresponding Anal-*

ogy between the Conformation of the Features and the Ruling Passions of the Mind. (London: H. D. Symonds, [ca. 1791]). 280pp. Translated by Samuel Shaw.

A580 ("Lavater's Physiology"), JS1402. Clearly a misprint in A580 "Physiology" for "Physiognomy" as no work on Physiology by a Lavater is listed in NUC, BL or any other standard source, while Lavater's *Physiognomy* was a frequently reprinted work. This is the earliest English language edition traced. Lavater was a Swiss theologian and poet who first published essays on the science of physiognomy (i.e. the analysis of human character through facial characteristics). This work is part of his attempt to defend physiognomy. See 235 for an adaptation of Lavater for children.

1194. (Law). *The People's Own Law Book, Forming a Concise Compendium of the Common and Statute Law of England and Wales. Including Technical Terms, Historical Memoranda, Legal Points and Practical Suggestions.* (London: Ward, Lock and Co., [1887]). 487pp.

A325, B1117 (title), JS93 (Anon./Law). Only edition of the only closely matching title in BL. A325 describes this as "Law Dictionary," and B1117 calls this *Law Dictionary, Forming a Concise Compendium of the Common and Statute Law of England and Wales.*

1195. [Lawrence, George Alfred] (1827–76), editor. *A Bundle of Ballads.* (London: Tinsley, Brothers, 1864). 141pp.

A845, B984 (title, editor, date), JS105. Lawrence was educated at Rugby and Balliol College, Oxford. He was called to the bar in 1852, but spent most of his life in literary pursuits, writing a number of anonymous novels, the best known of which was *Guy Livingstone.* In his diary for 19 December 1863, Dodgson writes, "Walked with [Richard] Tyrwhitt [see 2131] in the afternoon: he showed me *A Bundle of Ballads,* which is just out, by him and Lawrence." Tyrwhitt's involvement with the book is not known, but perhaps he contributed some pieces anonymously.

1196. Leathes, E. Stanley, compiler. *Alice's Wonderland Birthday Book.* (London: Griffith and Farran, 1884). Unpaginated. Illustrated by JPM.

A720 (title, compiler), A720, E464, F134, JS882. Only edition. Dodgson owned at least two copies of this book which includes a quote from the *Alice* books for every day of the year. The copy described in A720 is inscribed "To Mr. Lewis Carrol [sic] from his grateful and devoted admirer E. Stanley Leathes, April 28, 1884." This book was produced with Dodgson's permission. The illustrations are among the earliest non–Tenniel illustrations for the *Alice* books.

1197. Lee, Frederick George (1832–1902), compiler. *A Glossary of Liturgical and Ecclesiastical Terms.* (London: Bernard Quaritch, 1877). 452pp. With numerous illustrations on wood.

A800 (author, title), JS1405. Only edition in BL. Lee was educated at St. Edmund Hall, Oxford and served as vicar of All Saints', Lambeth. He was a great supporter of unity between the English and Roman churches. He founded and edited the *Union Review* (1863–9) and was the honorary secretary of the Association for the Promotion of the Unity of Christendom. He wrote many works on the English Church and other religious and spiritual topics. *Saturday Review* wrote of the present book, "However imperfect and at times almost slovenly its execution may be, it may fairly be pronounced to be useful as a book of reference on subjects of increasing interest."

1198. Lee, Frederick George, editor. *More Glimpses of the World Unseen.* (London: Chatto & Windus, 1878). 248pp. Illustrated.

B1118 (author, title, date), JS1406. The sequel to *The Other World* (see note below). Andrew Lang wrote of this book, "The Rev. F. G. Lee has published a new volume of ghost-stories. He is not to be daunted, he says, by sceptical and anonymous writers who talk of his 'grovelling superstition' and 'debasing gullibility.' ... On the other hand, Dr. Lee's critics are not more anonymous than the witnesses who testify to his ghosts."

1199. Lee, Frederick George, editor. *The Other World; or, Glimpses of the Supernatural. Being Facts, Records, and Traditions Relating to Dreams, Omens, Miraculous Occurrences, Apparitions, Wraiths, Warnings, Second-sight, Witchcraft, Necromancy, etc.* (London: H. S. King and Co., 1875). 2 vols.

A889 (author, title, 2 vols.), JS1407. Only edition in BL. *More Glimpses of the World Unseen* (above) is the sequel. *Saturday Review* wrote, "[Lee] makes no secret of his own profound faith in the reality of the phenomena he is handling.... We are certainly not aware of any work which affords so copious or well arranged an assortment of materials bearing on the subject."

1200. Lee, Robert (1793–1877). *A Treatise on Hysteria.* (London: Churchill, 1871). 25pp.

D102 (author, title, date), JS1408. Lee was a fellow of the Royal College of Physicians. He was educated at Edinburgh and spent several years in Russia serving as physician to Prince Woronzow. He held, for 30 years, the chair of Midwifery at St. George's Hospital, London.

1201. Lee, Robert James (b. 1841). *Hooping-Cough. Remarks on its History, Prevalence, Symptoms, and Treatment.* (London: Smith, Elder, & Co., 1876). 14pp.

E245 (author, title, date), JS1409. Lee was a medical lecturer in London. He wrote several works including one on diseases of children and another on the effect of exercise on health.

1202. Legendre, Adrien Marie (1752–1833). *Éléments de Géométrie, Avec Additions et Modifications, par M. A. Blanchet.* (Paris: Firmin Didot, 1849). 2 vols. 293, 271pp. 2nd edition after the 15th edition, "donnée par A. M. Legendre."

A586 (author, title, 2 vols.), JS1410. Earliest 2 vol. edition in BNF of the work published as early as 1794. Legendre was a French mathematician known for this textbook on geometry and for work on elliptic functions and integrals. This is one of the books Dodgson examines in his *Euclid and His Modern Rivals* (54–58).

1203. Leigh, Henry Sambrooke (1837–83). *Carols of Cockayne.* (London: J. C. Hotten, 1869 [1868]). 207pp. With illustrations by A. Concanen and John Leech. Includes music. 1st edition.

A849 (author, title, date, edition, illustrated), JS1411. See 577 for a note on John Leech. Leigh was an English poet. A collection of light verse.

1204. [Leigh, Percival] (1813–89). *The Comic Latin Grammar; a New and Face-*

tious Introduction to the Latin Tongue. (London: C. Tilt, 1840). 163pp. With numerous illustrations [by John Leech].

A420, E49 (title, illustrator, date), F151, JS1412. Leigh was a poet and frequent contributor to *Punch.* F151 notes the gothic stamp.

1205. [Leigh, Percival]. *Jack the Giant Killer.* (London: W. S. Orr & Co., 1844). 59pp. Illustrated by [John] Leech with 12 tinted plates and 7 woodcuts. In the *Comic Nursery Tales* series.

A483 (title, series, publisher), JS51 (Anon./ Children). 1st edition. Leigh's telling of the English folk-tale about the son of a Cornish farmer who begins his career in giant slaying by disposing of a giant who lives in a cave on St. Michael's Mount and terrorizes Cornwall.

1206. Leighton, Alexander (1800–74). *Mysterious Legends of Edinburgh, Now for the First Time Told in Print with Illustrations.* (Edinburgh: W. P. Nimmo, 1864). 272pp.

E281 (title, date), JS89 (Anon./History). Leighton was a Scotsman known chiefly for his work on Wilson's *Tales of the Borders* (see 2284). In addition to tales written for this collection, he wrote several collections of sketches.

Illustration from *Jack the Giant Killer* by John Leech (item 1205).

1207. Leighton, Frederic (1830–96). *Twenty-five Illustrations by F. Leighton, Designed for "The Cornhill Magazine." With Extracts Descriptive of Each Picture.* (London: Smith, Elder and Co., 1867). 61pp.

A287, E116 (author, title, date), F178, JS1413. Dodgson's copy, with the gothic stamp, was offered at auction at Sotheby's, London, on 18–21 June 1928 (DAA1226). One of the most popular and praised artists of Victorian Britain, Leighton was the leader of the Victorian Classical school of painting, he trained in Europe and lived in Italy before returning to England, settling in London in 1860. Beginning in the 1860s he focused on classical subjects. He became president of the Royal Academy in 1878. Dodgson admired Leighton's paintings and on 4 July 1874 he wrote in his diary, "Called, by appointment, on Sir Frederick Leighton, whom I had never seen before and whom I was much taken with. He showed me some lovely unfinished paintings…" Dodgson called on Leighton again on 18 January 1881, when he visited the artist at Leighton House, today a gallery open to the public.

1208. Lemon, Don [pseud. of Eli Lemon Sheldon]. *Everybody's Illustrated Book of Puzzles. Seven Hundred and Ninety-Four Rebuses, Puzzles, Enigmas, Etc., with Answers.* (London: Saxon & Co., 1890). 125pp. Selected by Don Lemon.

E410 (author, title, date), JS1414. E410 notes this has Dodgson's initials. Apparently originally an American production, as many of the solutions are rendered in dollars or lists of American presidents or American geographical names. Versions of two of Dodgson's word puzzles are printed here, though it seems unlikely they were copied directly from his publications. Number 465, "Transformations," is the same as Dodgson's "Doublets." Only one of the six "transformations" posed is the same as one of Dodgson's "Doublets" (Change Blue to Pink). Dodgson accomplished the change in 8 steps; Lemon takes 10. Number 613 is a crude version of the game Dodgson called "Syzzygies." The book also includes many acrostics, anagrams, and other forms of word puzzles practiced by Dodgson.

1209. Lemon, Mark (1809–70). *Fairy Tales.* (London: Bradbury, Evans & Co., 1868). 189pp. With illustrations by Richard Doyle and Charles Henry Bennett.

A645 (author, title, illustrator), JS1416. Earliest edition in BL. Lemon was a novelist, prolific playwright, a founder of *Punch*, and its editor from 1841 to 1870. He was a friend of Dickens, often performing in the novelist's private theatricals. Dodgson saw one of his plays and also saw Lemon act in an amateur theatrical. Lemon accepted Dodgson's verse on "Atalanta in Camden Town" (see LCP, #50) for publication in *Punch* in 1867. The present collection includes "The Enchanted Doll" and "The Three Sisters," the latter being similar to "Beauty and the Beast."

1210. Lemon, Mark. *Tinykin's Transformations. A Child's Story*. (London: Evans & Co., 1869). 183pp. Illustrated by Charles Green.

A645 (author, title, illustrated), JS1415. Only edition in BL. Probably Lemon's best fairy tale, this story tells how Titania enchants the son of a forester into a series of animals.

1211. Lennox, William Pitt (1799–1881). *Plays, Players and Playhouses at Home and Abroad; with Anecdotes of the Drama and the Stage*. (London: Hurst & Blackett, 1881). 2 vols. 303, 271pp.

A674 (title, 2 vols.), JS295 (Anon./Theatre). This is the only matching pre–1898 title in BL and the only edition listed. The fourth son of a nobleman, Lord Lennox served for a time on the staff of the Duke of Wellington. He wrote for many magazines and newspapers and wrote a wide variety of books. A wide ranging anecdotal history of drama with a focus on England but including reference to other countries and substantial information on the French drama.

1212. Le Roux, H[ugues] (1860–1925). *Acrobats and Mountebanks*. (London: Chapman & Hall, 1890 [1889]). 336pp. Translated from the French by A. P. Morton. With 233 illustrations by Jules Garnier.

A850, B941 (author, title, illustrator, translator, date), JS1403. Le Roux was a French writer with a varied output, most of which was not translated into English. This is a history of acrobats and the circus.

1213. Le Vengeur-D'Orsan, A. *Our Satellite, A Selenography According to the Present State of Science*. (London: 1862).

A283, E62 (author, title, date), F179, JS779 (listed under D'Orsan). F179 notes the gothic stamp. A283 states "1st number"; F179 states "Part I." This was the first part of a planned book of highly detailed photographs and drawings of the moon with accompanying text. BL does not record that any other parts were issued. Dodgson's interest in it may have been in the photographs, which the author called "on a scale never before executed — probably never before attempted."

1214. Lever, Charles James (1806–72). *Charles O'Malley, the Irish Dragoon*. (Dublin: William Curry, jun. and Company; Edinburgh: Fraser and Crawford; London: W. S. Orr and Company, 1841– 42). 2 vols. 348, 336pp. "Edited by Harry Lorrequer" [pseud. of Lever]. Illustrations by Phiz [H. K. Browne].

A814 (author, title, 2 vols.), JS1417. Originally published in monthly parts from March 1840 to December 1841. 1st book edition. Lever was an Irish novelist who portrayed military life and Irish society. Novel.

1215. Lever, Charles James. *The Confessions of Con Cregan: The Irish Gil Blas*. (London: W. S. Orr, 1849). 2 vols. Illustrations by H. K. Browne.

A814 (author, title), JS1418. 1st edition. Though A814 does not specify multiple volumes, BL records no 1-volume edition of this novel prior to a mention in Dodgson's diary. In his diary for 9 July 1855, Dodgson writes, "Today I finished *Con Cregan*, an exceedingly clever novel, full of the most graphic incidents: the author is *obliged* by his own scheme to make his hero a consummate liar, and if not a thief, at least a perfectly unscrupulous appropriator of stray goods. It is something in the style of *Charles O'Malley*."

1216. Lewes, George Henry (1817–78). *On Actors and the Art of Acting*. (London: Smith, Elder & Co., 1875). 278pp.

A674 ("Actors and Acting"), JS285 (Anon./Theatre). 1st collected edition of these articles originally published in periodicals. This is the closest matching pre–1898 title in BL and seems likely, as Dodgson owned three other books by the same author. Lewes was the grandson of the actor Charles Lee Lewes, a writer on various subjects, and the partner of Mary Ann Evans (George Eliot). He was active in the press, especially as a drama critic, and founder of the *Fortnightly Review*. Includes essays on drama in Germany, Spain and France as well as descriptions of the acting of Charles and Edmund Kean, Charles Macready, Frederic Lemaitre, Charles Mathew, and others. Dodgson saw one of Lewes' plays on 13 June 1856.

1217. Lewes, George Henry. *The Physiology of Common Life.* (Edinburgh: W. Blackwood, 1859–60). 2 vols. 456, 486pp.

A573 (author, title, 2 vols.), JS1421. Earliest edition in BL or BOD. In the 1850s, Lewes began to turn his attention to scientific studies, and the present book was one of several that resulted from that work. Dodgson prints an extract from this book in his letter to the *St. James's Gazette* (10 April 1890) on the subject of "The Fasting Man" (LCP, #266).

1218. Lewes, George Henry. *Problems of Life and Mind. First Series. The Foundation of a Creed.* (London: Trübner, 1874–5). 2 vols.

A316, B1119 (author, series title, "the three series complete, 4 vols."), JS1419. The series consisted of 5 vols.— 2 in series 1, 1 in series 2, and 2 in series 3. This supposedly "complete" collection lacks one volume. The most likely candidate for the missing volume is the final volume (that is, volume 2 of the 3rd series, see note below). Early volumes in the series were reprinted as subsequent volumes were issued, so Dodgson may not have owned 1st editions of all volumes (the firsts are described here and below). OCEL calls this series "a philosophical work of considerable importance."

1219. Lewes, George Henry. *Problems of Life and Mind. Second Series. The Physical Basis of Mind.* (London: Trübner, 1877). 493pp.

A316, B1119 (author, series title, "the three series complete, 4 vols."), JS1419. See note above on this series.

1220. Lewes, George Henry. *Problems of Life and Mind. Third Series. Problem the First: The Study of Psychology, its Object, Scope and Method.* (London: Trübner & Co., 1879). 189pp.

A316, B1119 (author, series title, "the three series complete, 4 vols."), JS1419. As noted above, Dodgson lacked one of the five volumes in this series, most likely the second volume of

the 3rd series: *Mind as a Function of the Organism: The Sphere of Sense and Logic of Feeling: The Sphere of Intellect and Logic of Signs* (London: Trübner & Co, 1879), 189pp. This 3rd series was published posthumously as Lewes died in 1878. The total work was left unfinished.

1221. Lewes, George Henry. *Sea-side Studies at Ilfracombe, Tenby, the Scilly Isles, and Jersey.* (Edinburgh: W. Blackwood and Sons, 1858). 414pp. 6 plates.

A332 (author, title), JS1420. Earliest edition in BL.

1222. [Lewis, Matthew Gregory] (1775–1818). *Tales of Terror; with an Introductory Dialogue.* (London: Printed for R. Faulder, etc., 1808). 2nd edition. 155pp. 3 plates.

B1248 (title, date), JS140. Lewis was a novelist, poet, and dramatist. A collection of verse written, translated, and collected by Lewis.

1223. L[ewis], M[atthew] G[regory]. *Tales of Wonder.* (London: J. Bell, 1801). 252pp. 2nd edition.

A474 (author, title, date), JS1424. The 2nd edition seems more likely than the 1st of the same year, as the 1st was in 2 vols. and multiple volumes are not specified in A474. In addition to his own verse, Lewis includes here contributions by Walter Scott, Robert Southey, and others. Includes some of the earliest translations (by Lewis) of Goethe. Walter Scott's contributions include: "The Fire-King," "Glenfinlas, or Lord Ronald's Coronach," "The Eve of Saint John," "Frederick and Alice," and "The Wild Huntsmen." Southey's include: "The Old Woman of Berkeley," "Bishop Bruno," "Lord William," "The Painter of Florence," "Donica," "Cornelius Agrippa's Bloody Book," and "Rudiger."

1224. Lewis, Samuel (d. 1865). *Atlas to the Topographical Dictionaries of England and Wales, Comprising a General Map of England and Wales, a Plan of London, and Maps of the Counties, etc. Drawn and Engraved for Lewis' Topographical Dictionary.* (London: S. Lewis & Co., 1844). 1p. 57 maps.

A942 ("Lewis's Topographical Dictionary to England, 4 vols., and Atlas"), JS1423. This seems the most likely of several atlases attributed to Lewis in BL, as it is the only one linked by title to the *Topographical Dictionary of England*. This is the earliest edition traced.

1225. Lewis, Samuel. *A Topographical Dictionary of England, Comprising the Several Counties, Cities, Boroughs, Corporate and Market Towns, Parishes, and Townships, and the Islands of Guernsey, Jersey, and Man, with Historical and Statistical Descriptions.* (London: S. Lewis and Co., 1845). 4 vols. 5th edition.

A942, E438 (author, title, 4 vols., date), JS1422. A work of huge depth, giving details on even the smallest of villages. Lewis also created similar works on Ireland, Scotland, and Wales.

1226. *Lexicon Hebraicum*. Details unknown.

So listed in A771/JS243 (Anon./Reference). This could refer to Gesenius (see 767). If not, there are several possibilities in BL, the most likely of which are (earliest BL editions listed):

Buxtorfius, Joannes. *Lexicon Hebraicum et Chaldaicum acc. Lexicon Breve Rabbinico-philosophicum et Index Latinus.* (Glasquæ, 1824).

Leopold, Ernestus Fridericus. *Lexicon Hebraicum et Chaldaicum in Libros Veteris Testamenti.* (Lipsiæ, 1832).

Meinigius, Christian Gottlieb. *Lexicon Hebraicum in Compendium Redactum.* (Lipsiæ, 1712).

Rossi, Giovanni Bernardo de. *Lexicon Hebraicum Anthologiae Viri Clariss.* (Cremonae, 1822).

Solomon, ben Abraham ben Parchon. *Lexicon Hebraicum Selectum.* (Parmae, 1805).

1227. Lias, John James (1834–1923). *Are Miracles Credible?* (London: Hodder & Stoughton, 1883). 280pp. In the *Theological Library* series.

A784 (author, title), JS1425. Only edition listed in BL. Lias was the vicar of St. Edward's, Cambridge and the Hulsean Lecturer for 1884. The preface states, "This work does not profess to be an exhaustive statement for the cause of miracles. All that can be done within such limits as those to which this book is confined, is to give such an outline of the arguments as may serve to show on what considerations the defence of miracles rests. Great care has been taken to make the book of as popular a kind as the subject permits."

1228. Liddell, [Henry George] (1811–98) and [Robert] Scott (1811–87). *A Greek-English Lexicon, Based on the German Work of Francis Passow.* (Oxford: University Press, 1849). 1623pp. 3rd edition.

A313 (author, title), JS1426. Dodgson's copy is in the collection formed by Jeffrey Stern, now at Seitoku Gakuin College, Tokyo, Japan. Stern describes it thus: "signed on the title page: 'C. L. Dodgson ex CC de Christi,' with a pencilled note in his hand on inside back cover (identifying a double cross reference)." A522/JS240 (Anon./Reference) states merely "Greek and English Lexicon" and could refer to another copy of Liddell-Scott. Liddell was the Dean of Christ Church and father of Alice Liddell, the little girl who inspired Alice in AAIW. This work was his magnum opus and brought him a substantial income. In a revised version, it remains the standard Greek-English lexicon to this day. Dodgson's relationship with the Liddell family has been detailed in his various biographies. Scott was Master of Balliol College, Oxford before becoming Dean of Rochester in 1870. He wrote a comic piece for *Macmillan's Magazine* (Feb. 1872), suggesting "Jabberwocky" was a translation of a German original.

1229. Liddell, [Henry George] and [Robert] Scott. *A Lexicon Abridged from Liddell and Scott's Greek-English Lexicon.* (Oxford: Clarendon Press, Henry Frowde; London: Longmans, Green, and Co., 1892). 804pp. 25th edition, carefully revised throughout.

B1120 (author, title, abridged, date), JS1426. This abridgement was originally prepared in 1871, and was, according to the preliminary advertisement, "intended chiefly for use in Schools."

1230. Liddon, Henry Parry (1829–90). *The Divinity of our Lord and Saviour Jesus Christ; Eight Lectures Preached before the University of Oxford in 1866, on the Foundation of the late Rev. John Bampton.* (London, Oxford: Rivingtons, 1867). 776pp.

A803 ("Liddon's Bampton Lectures"), JS1427. Earliest edition in BL. Liddon was a friend of Dodgson and accompanied him on his only foreign journey, a trip to Russia in 1867. A member of the High Church party, he served as Vice Principal of Cuddesdon Theological College (a training college for priests started by Bishop of Oxford Samuel Wilberforce) and in 1870 became a canon of St. Paul's Cathedral in London, where his sermons were immensely popular — three to four thousand people gathering under the dome to hear him preach. In his preface, Liddon writes, "The present volume attempts only to notice, more or less directly, some of those assaults upon the doctrine of our Lord's Divinity which have been prominent or popular of late years, and which have, unhappily, had a certain weight among persons with whom the writer is acquainted." Dodgson, who looked over proof sheets of this book for Liddon, also owned Charles Voysey's anonymous response to these sermons (see 2165).

1231. Liddon, Henry Parry. *Easter in St. Paul's. Sermons Bearing Chiefly on the Resurrection of Our Lord.* (London: Rivingtons, 1885). 2 vols.

A756 (author, title, 2 vols.), JS1428. Earliest edition in BL.

1232. Liddon, Henry Parry. *Some Elements of Religion. Lent Lectures 1870.* (London: Rivingtons, 1872). 241pp.

A756 (author, title), JS1429. Earliest edition in BL. The lectures are "The Idea of Religion," "God, The Object of Religion," "The Subject of Religion — The Soul," "The Obstacle to Religion — Sin," "Prayer, the Characteristic Action of Religion," and "The Mediator, The Guarantee of Religious Life."

1233. Liddon, Henry Parry. *University Sermons.* Details unknown.

A764 ("Liddon's University Sermons"), JS1430. Liddon's University Sermons were first published as *Some Words for God: Being Sermons Preached Before the University of Oxford, Chiefly During the Years 1863–1865.* (London, Oxford, & Cambridge: J. H. & J. Parker, 1865). The 2nd edition of 1866, published by Rivington, bore the title *Sermons. Preached before the University of Oxford, Chiefly During the Years 1863–1865.* The 3rd edition (Rivingtons: London, 1869) contained sermons from 1859 to 1868. This collection was eventually designated as "First Series" and a "Second Series" of sermons from 1868 to 1879 was published in 1879, and was eventually expanded to contain sermons preached through 1882. In the preface to *Some Words for God*, Liddon writes that the sermons in the collection "have little in common with each other beyond a certain apologetic charac-

ter." In the "Second Series," Liddon, among other things, addresses himself to the recent "divorce" of the University of Oxford from the Church of England (a.k.a. University reform).

1234. Lilly, William (1602–81). *An Introduction to Astrology. With Numerous Emendations, Adapted to the Improved State of the Science in the Present Day; A Grammar of Astrology, and Tables for Calculating Nativities by Zadkiel* (London: Bell, 1878). 491pp.

D103 (author, title, city, date), JS1431. Lily was a 17th-century astrologer who also had an interest in magic and other forms of occultism. He became involved with political intrigue during the Civil War. He was known as the English Merlin to some, and during the protectorate sales of his annual almanac reached 30,000. Lily wrote this book to explain astrology to the educated men of his day (it was originally published in 1647). It includes definitions of astrological terms and presents the theories of astrology in everyday terms. Zadkiel was the pseudonym of Richard James Morrison (1795–1874), a 19th-century astrologer.

1235. Lindsay, William Lauder (1829–80). *Mind in the Lower Animals in Health and Disease.* (London: Kegan Paul & Trench & Co., 1879). 2 vols. 543, 571pp.

A824 (author, title, 2 vols.), JS1432. Only edition in BL or BOD. Lindsay was a Scottish physician and botanist. This work examines the animal mind in psychological, physiological, medical, veterinary, theological, metaphysical, and philosophical terms and looks at similarities in the minds of animals and of man. Includes chapters on instinct and reason, capacity for education, language, law and punishment, courtship and marriage, deception, insanity, dreams and delusions, suicide, crime and criminality, and curability and treatment of animal insanity.

1236. L[inklater], R[obert]. *Sunday and Recreation: A Symposium.* (London, Edinburgh [printed]: Griffith, Farran & Co., 1889). 219pp.

A774 ("Sunday and Recreation"), JS332 (Anon./Theology). Only edition of the only matching title in BL or BOD.

1237. Linton, Elizabeth Lynn (1822–98), compiler. *Witch Stories.* (London: Chapman & Hall, 1861). 428pp.

A887 (author, title), JS1459 (listed under Lynton, repeating the error in A887). Earliest edition in BL. Linton was a novelist and writer on various subjects. The present work is a collection of stories of alleged witchcraft incidents from early times to the 1751 mob murder of Ruth Osborne, the so-called "Witch of Tring."

1238. Linwood, William (1817–78), editor. *Anthologia Oxoniensis*. (London: Longman, Brown, Green, and Longman, 1846). 306pp.

A507, B945 (author, title, date), JS1433. Linwood was a classical scholar and a Student at Christ Church, Oxford from 1837 to 1851, leaving the college just after Dodgson arrived. This work is a collection of light hearted verse rendered into Latin and Greek by Oxford scholars.

1239. L[ipperheide], F[rieda von] (1840–96). *Muster Altitalienischer Leinenstickerei. Gesammelt und Herausgegeben von F. L.* (Berlin: Franz Lipperheide, 1883 and 1886). 36, 28pp.

Uncertain. F177 (title, date), not in JS. Identified as Dodgson's only by the gothic stamp. "Old Italian Patterns for Linen Embroidery, Collected and Analyzed by F. L." The author was a collector of embroidery. No reference has been found for the 1886 volume, but an 1883 volume is recorded in BL. F177 describes this as "numerous illustrations, in two portfolios."

1240. Lloyd, Charles (1784–1829), editor. *Novum Testamentum. Accedunt Parallela S. Scripturæ Loca, Necnon Vetus Capitulorum Notatis et Canones Eusebii.* (Oxford: University Press, 1851). 696pp.

E208 (title, date), JS491. This edition of the New Testament in Greek was first published in 1828. Lloyd was educated at Christ Church, Oxford, where he was a student, censor, and canon. In 1827 he became Bishop of Oxford. He was a High Churchman who influenced the leaders of the later Oxford Movement. Dodgson was a friend of Lloyd's daughter Catherine.

1241. Lloyd, J[ulius] (1830–92?). *An Analysis of the First Eleven Chapters of the Book of Genesis; with Reference to the Hebrew Grammar of Gesenius; and with Notes, Critical and Explanatory.* (London: Bagster, 1869). 157pp.

B1122 (author, title, date), JS1434. Dodgson owned a copy of the *Hebrew Grammar* referred to in the title of this item (see 767). Lloyd was a Manchester clergyman educated at Trinity College, Cambridge. BL attributes this work to him, but it is not listed among his works in DNB. NUC attributes the book to John Lloyd, rector of Llanvapley.

1242. Locke, John (1632–1704). *The Philosophical Works of John Locke.* (London: G. Virtue, 1843). 610pp. With a preliminary discourse and notes, by J. A. St. John.

A317 ("Locke's Philosophical Works"), JS1435. Earliest edition traced of the only matching title in BL. Includes "On the Conduct of the Understanding," "Essay Concerning Human Understanding," "Elements of Natural Philosophy," etc.

1243. Locker [afterwards Locker-Lampson], Frederick (1821–95). *London Lyrics.* (London: Chapman & Hall, 1857). 90pp. With an illustration by G[eorge] Cruikshank.

A863 (title), JS126 (Anon./Literature). Earliest edition in BL. Locker left government service and edited several anthologies of poetry and prose (see below). The present volume is a collection of his own poetry.

1244. Locker [afterwards Locker-Lampson], Frederick, editor. *Lyra Elegantiarum. A Collection of Some of the Best Specimens of Vers de Société and Vers d'Occasion in the English Language by Deceased Authors.* (London: Edward Moxon, 1867). 360pp. 1st edition.

A457 (author, title, edition, date), JS1436. The 1st edition of this collection included a group of poems by Walter Savage Landor to which Landor's executor, John Forster, objected and the edition was suppressed. Unlike Dodgson's own famously suppressed AAIW, quite a few copies of the book seem to have made it into circulation before Forster's objection, so Dodgson did not, in this case, own a great rarity. (See *Book Collector* VIII, 1959).

1245. Lockhart, John Gibson (1794–1854). *Theodore Hook. A Sketch.* (London: John Murray, 1852). 102pp. 3rd edition. From the *Murray's Reading for the Rail* series.

B1082 (author, title, date), JS1238 (listed under Hook). Lockhart was a novelist, biographer and critic who edited *The Quarterly Review*. Theodore Hook (1788–1841) was a popular English novelist (perhaps the most popular in the era immediately preceding Dickens). He is sometimes credited as father of modern political satire, and was editor of *John Bull* (from 1820) and of *New Monthly* (from 1836).

1246. Lockyer, Joseph Norman (1836–1920). *Astronomy*. (London: Macmillan and Co., 1874). 676pp. In the *Science Primers* series.

A583 ("Lockyer's Astronomy"), JS1437. 1st edition as described in MBC. Lockyer was also the author of the 1868 work *Elementary Lessons in Astronomy*, but as that title is a less accurate match with the entry in A583, it seems less likely. Lockyer was educated on the continent and in 1870 became secretary to the Royal Commission on Scientific Instruction and astronomical lecturer to the Normal School of Science in London. In 1871 he became Rede lecturer at Cambridge.

1247. Logan [afterwards Sikes], Olive (1839?–1909). *Apropos of Women and Theatres. With a Paper or Two on Parisian Topics, etc.* (New York: Carleton; London: S. Low, Son, & Co., 1869). 240pp.

A673 (title), JS290 (Anon./Theatre). Only edition in BL of the only matching title. JS290 lists this as *Four Original Plays Apropos of Women in Theatres*, and, at first glance, that appears to be the title in A673. However, no such title exists in BL or BOD. A closer look at A673 shows that a line break occurs between "Four Original Plays" and "Apropos of Women and Theatres." Clearly a comma has been omitted, and these are two titles, both appearing in BL. The one not described here (i.e. *Four Original Plays, Unacted*) is by Augustus Dubourg (see 634). Logan was an actress, dramatist, journalist and suffragette who argued that women should be able to support themselves by working outside the home. This collection of her essays on the theatre includes much on women in the 18th century.

1248. [London Dialectical Society]. *Report on Spiritualism, of the Committee of the London Dialectical Society, Together with the Evidence, Oral and Written, and a Selection from the Correspondence.* (London: Longmans, Green, Reader & Dyer, 1871). 412pp.

D182 (title, date), JS326 (Anon./Theology). D182 notes Dodgson's initials. In 1869 the *London Dialectical Society* charged a committee of 33 "to investigate the phenomena alleged to be spiritual manifestations, and to report thereon." The present report urges further study into spiritual phenomena, and states that "motion may be produced in solid bodies without material contact, by some hitherto unrecognized force operating within an undefined distance from the human organism, and beyond the range of muscular action." It was among the most favorable 19th-century views given of spiritualism by any investigating body.

1249. Longfellow, Henry Wadsworth (1807–82). *The Courtship of Miles Standish, and Other Poems.* (London: W. Kent & Co., 1858). 227pp.

A863 (author, title), JS1438. This is the 1st English edition.

1250. Longfellow, Henry Wadsworth. *New Poems*. Illustrated. Details unknown.

So described in A873/JS1439, but no copy of a book by this title has been traced. Probably a reference to a new edition of Longfellow's *Poems*. The most likely candidate is: *Poems*. (London: George Routledge & Co., 1856). 400pp. A new edition. Illustrated with upwards of one hundred engravings, designed by John Gilbert, engraved by Dalziel brothers. See below for other editions of Longfellow's *Poems*.

1251. Longfellow, Henry Wadsworth. *Poems*. (London: D. Bogue, 1854). 334pp. Illustrated with upwards of 100 engravings on wood, from designs by Jane E. Benham, Birket Foster, etc.

A848 (author, title, illustrators, date), JS1441. Dodgson owned another copy of Longfellow's *Poems* (A946/JS1440) but no publication details are known (the description being merely "Longfellow's Poems"). See above for another edition of Longfellow's *Poems*.

1252. Longfellow, Henry Wadsworth. *Tales of a Wayside Inn*. (London: Routledge, Warne, & Routledge, 1864). 140pp.

A863 (author, title), not in JS. Earliest English edition in NUC.

1253. Loomis, Elias (1811–89). *Elements of Geometry, Conic Sections and Plane Trigonometry*. (New York: Harper & Brothers, 1876). Revised edition.

D112 (author, title, city, date), JS1443. D112 notes Dodgson's initials. Loomis was an American professor of Mathematics and Natural Philosophy who taught at a number of schools including Western Reserve, New York University, and Yale (where he first worked writing mathematics textbooks). He did important work in astronomy and meteorology, and his various textbooks (of which this is one) sold over 600,000 copies. This was one of the books Dodgson examined in his *Euclid and His Modern Rivals* (136).

1254. Lotze, Rudolph Hermann (1817–81). *Logic in Three Books of Thought, of Investigation, and of Knowledge.* (Oxford: Clarendon Press, 1884). 538pp. English translation edited by Bernard Bosanquet. In the *Clarendon Press Series.* Comprising part 1 of the work *Lotze's System of Philosophy.*

D109 (author, title, editor, date), JS1444. Lotze was an influential German philosopher whose work was especially well accepted among theologians. He argued that logical laws were rooted in the demand for the good. See 199 for a note on Bosanquet.

1255. Lounger [pseud. of Jeremiah Whitaker Newman] (1759–1819). *Lounger.* Being volume XXV (only) of *The British Essayists; with Prefaces Biographical, Historical, and Critical.* (London, J. F. Dove, 1827). Series edited by Robert Lynam (1796–1845).

D113 (title, volume number, city, date), JS125 (Anon./Literature). Newman was an English essayist whose work was published in 1792 under the title *The Lounger's Common-place Book; or Alphabetical Anecdotes, Being a Biographic, Literary, Political, and Satirical Vademecum which he who Runs May Read.*

1256. Lovelace, Richard (1618–58). *Lucasta; Epodes, Odes, Sonnets, Songs, etc. To which is Added Aramantha, a Pastorall.* (London: Printed by T. Harper for T. Ewster, 1649). 164pp.

A426 (author, title, date), JS1445. Lovelace was a wealthy educator who took the royalist cause and was briefly imprisoned in 1642 (when he wrote his most famous lyric "To Althea") and again in 1648. During his second incarceration, he prepared this book of verse for the press.

1257. Lovelace, Richard. *Lucasta: Posthume Poems of Richard Lovelace, Esq.; Elegies Sacred to the Memory of the Author: By Several of his Friends.* (London: W. Godbid for C. Darby, 1659–60). 107pp. 2 parts. Edited by Dudley Posthumus Lovelace.

A426 (author, titles, date), JS1446, JS1447 (BL and BOD list this as a single item, BL notes two parts, but neither specifies separate volumes). Edited by the poet's brother after Lovelace's death.

1258. Lowe, Edward Joseph (1825–1900). *A Natural History of British Grasses.* (London: 1858). 245pp. With coloured illustrations.

A735 (author, title), JS1448. 1st edition. Lowe was a founder of the Meteorological Society and a member of many scientific societies. He made a series of daily weather observations for over 40 years and wrote on weather and flora.

1259. Lowe, Robert (1811–92). *Speeches and Letters on Reform; With a Preface.* (London: R. J. Bush, 1867). 212pp.

B1123 (author, title, date), JS1449. BL and BOD both also list a 2nd edition in 1867, but neither lists an earlier edition or a publisher. The present description is from LC, which does not specify an edition. Lowe was a statesman who served in Parliament and eventually as Chancellor of the Exchequer under Gladstone. In 1866 he lead the attack on his own government's reform bill, ultimately defeating it. This work is on the reform of the franchise.

1260. Lowell, James Russell (1819–91). *Poems.* (Boston: Ticknor, Reed, and Fields, 1849). 2 vols.

A863 ("Lowell's Poems, 2 vols."), JS1450 (listed under Robert Lowell). Robert Lowell was a 20th century poet; A863 makes clear that this refers to American poet James Russell Lowell — the entry reads "Lowell's Poems, 2 vols., and Under the Willow and Other Poems," and the latter title is by J. R. Lowell (see below). BL and BOD list no 2-volume English editions; this is the earliest 2-volume American edition traced.

1261. Lowell, James Russell. *Under the Willows and Other Poems.* (London: Macmillan, 1869, [1868]). 304pp.

A863 (title), JS141 (Anon./Literature). 1st British edition.

1262. Lubbock, John (1843–1913). *The Pleasures of Life.* (London: Macmillan and Co., 1887). 191pp.

A311 (author, title), JS1451. 1st edition as described in MBC. There was also a "Part 2" of this title, published in 1889. Lubbock was a writer who also served in parliament and founded the Proportional Representation Society. Dodgson's own writings on proportional representation make reference to Lubbock (see *Political*). The present volume is a book both spiritual and philosophical about happiness. Includes chapters such as "The Duty of Happiness," "A Song of Books," "The Blessing of Friends," "The Value of Time," "The Pleasure of Travel," and "The Pleasure of Home."

1263. [Lucas, Samuel] (1818–68). *Eminent Men and Popular Books. From "The Times."* (London, New York: Routledge, Warne & Routledge, 1859). 310pp. A series of reviews reprinted from *The Times.*

B1048 (title), JS213 (Anon./Periodicals). Only edition in BL. A second series of Lucas' reviews was issued by the same publisher in 1860 under the title *Biography & Criticism; Being a Second Series of "Eminent Men & Popular Books."* Founder and briefly editor of the Tory weekly, *The Press,* Lucas later held a Tory Party appointment and served as a critic for *The Times.* This work includes writings on: George Stephenson, Macaulay's *History of England,* Sydney Smith, Kingsley's *Westward Ho!,* Tom Moore, Thackeray's *Miscellanies,* Gainsborough, Charlotte Brontë, James Boswell, Herodotus, and others.

1264. Lucian of Samosata (c. 115–200). *Luciani Opera, Cum Nova Versione T. Hemsterhusii et J. M. Gesneri, Graecis Scholiis, ac Notis Omnium Proximae Editionis Commentatorum, Additis J. Brodaei, J. Jensii, L. Kusteri, B. Bosii, H. Vitringae, J. de la Faye, E. Leedes ac Praecipue M. Solani et J. M. Gesneri, Priorem Partem Curavit T. Hemsterhusius. Ceteras Partes Ordinavit, Notasque Suas Adjecit, J. F. Reitzius. (Index Verborum ac Phrasium Sive Lexicon ad Editiones Omnes, Maxime Westenianam Concinnatum a C. C. Reitzio).* (Amsterdam: Trajecti ad Rhenum, 1743–46). 4 vols. Large paper edition.

A928, B1124 (title, city, date), JS1452. B1124

describes Dodgson's copy as a "Ch. Ch. Prize, with arms on sides, inscribed Caroli Dodgson, &c., 1822." This was a prize presented to CLD's father, Charles Dodgson, who received his B.A. in 1822. Works of Lucian, the Greek writer of satire.

1265. Luckock, Herbert Mortimer (1833–1909). *After Death. An Examination of the Testimony of Primitive Times Respecting the State of the Faithful Dead and their Relationship to the Living.* (London: Rivingtons, 1879). 271pp.

A805 (author, title), JS1453. Earliest edition in BL. Dodgson also owned the sequel (see below). Luckock was a canon of Ely and a High Churchman. In this work on the state of the soul after death he defends the practice of offering prayers for the dead. See 2179 for a response to this book.

1266. Luckock, Herbert Mortimer. *The Intermediate State Between Death and Judgment, Being a Sequel to After Death.* (London: Longmans & Co., 1890). 258pp.

A805 (author, title), JS1454. Earliest edition in BL. Deals with questions raised in correspondence with readers of the author's *After Death* (see above). "Unlike the former book," Luckock writes, "the present is in part speculative."

1267. Lukin, James (fl. 1849–88). *Toy Making for Amateurs: Being Instructions for the Home Construction of Simple Wooden Toys, and of Others that are Moved or Driven by Weights, Clockwork, Steam, Electricity, &c.* (London: L. Upcott Gill, The "Bazaar" Office, 1882). 276pp. 125 text figures.

D114 (author, title, date), JS1455. Lukin wrote a number of books, primarily for amateurs, on various aspects of woodworking and mechanics. As a young man Dodgson constructed a toy theatre with which to entertain his siblings (long before the publication of this book).

1268. Lupton, Sydney (b. 1850). *Numerical Tables and Constants in Elementary Science.* (London: Macmillan and Co., 1884). 96pp. 1 folding table.

B1125 (author, title), JS1456. 1st edition as described in MBC. Lupton was a chemist who matriculated at Christ Church in 1868 and was a junior student there from 1870 to 1875. He studied mathematics with Dodgson and rates a single mention in Dodgson's diary, when Dodgson attended a dinner jointly hosted by Lupton on 1 March 1873.

1269. Luvini, Jean [a.k.a. Giovanni Luvini] (1818–92). *Tables of Logarithms, with Seven Places of Decimals.* (London: Trübner & Co., 1866). 368pp. The logarithmic differences calculated together with an index, by Julia and Clara Nicola.

E201 (author, title, date), JS1457. E201 describes Dodgson's as a "presentation copy with Lewis Carroll's autograph."

1270. Lyall, Edna [pseud. of Ada Ellen Bayly] (1857–1903). *The Autobiography of a Slander.* (London: Longmans & Co., 1887). 119pp.

A652 (author, title), JS1458. Earliest edition in BL. Bayly was a Unitarian, a supporter of women's suffrage, and an opposer of the Boer War. This story is about Mrs. O'Reilly, "who found a little bit of scandal now & then added a piquant flavour to the homely fare provided by the commonplace life," and how the slander she started destroyed a freedom-loving Russian Democrat whom she labeled "nihilist."

1271. MacAlpine, Neil (1786–1867). *A Pronouncing Gaelic Dictionary: to Which is Prefixed a Concise but Most Comprehensive Gaelic Grammar.* (Edinburgh: Stirling & Kenney, 1853). 549pp. 4th edition.

B1130 (author, title, date), JS1460.

1272. Macaulay, Thomas Babington (1800–59). *Critical and Historical Essays. Contributed to the Edinburgh Review.* (London: Longman Brown & Longmans, 1852). 836pp.

A336, D115 (author, title, city, date), JS1461. According to D115, Dodgson's copy was inscribed "Charles Lutwidge Dodgson. A Birthday Gift from his most affectionate Aunt, Lucy Lutwidge, January 27, 1853 [Dodgson's 21st birthday]." Macauley was an English historian and essayist who also served in Parliament, and was especially remembered for his support of the Reform Bill of 1831–32.

1273. Macaulay, Thomas Babington. *The History of England from the Accession of James the Second.* (London: Longman, Green, Longman, and Roberts: 1858–62). 8 vols.

A634, B1126 (author, title, 8 vols., date [1858]), JS1462. Only 8-volume 1858 edition in BL or NUC. Originally published in 1848, this work was a huge commercial success and established Macauley as an author of the first rank. Dodgson must have begun reading this work in an earlier edition, for he writes in a letter to his sister on 4 May 1849, "I have not yet been able to get the 2nd vol.: Macaulay's *England* to read: I have seen it however & one passage struck me when 7 bishops signed the invitation to the pretender…" Dodgson goes on to discuss the incident when one of the bishops was interviewed by King James.

1274. Macaulay, Thomas Babington. *Lays of Ancient Rome.* (London: Longman, 1842). 191pp.

A856 (author, title), JS1463. 1st edition. Written while Macauley was in India, this series of poems is on subjects from ancient Roman writers.

1275. MacCarthy, Denis Florence (1817–82). *Shelley's Early Life from Original Sources. With Curious Incidents, Letters, and Writings now First Published or Collected.* (London: J. C. Hotten, [1872]). 408pp.

A904 (author, title), JS1464. Only edition in BL. MacCarthy was an Irish poet.

1276. MacDonald, George (1824–1905). *Alec Forbes of Howglen.* (London: Hurst and Blackett, 1865). 3 vols. 304, 300, 300pp. 1st edition.

A821 (author, title, edition, 3 vols.), JS1465. MacDonald was a popular author of fairy stories and fantasies for children, as well as of other works. His friendship with Dodgson has been well documented (see, for instance, John Docherty's *The Literary Products of the Lewis Carroll — George MacDonald Friendship*). Dodgson showed MacDonald his manuscript AAUG and MacDonald encouraged Dodgson to have it published. The eventual product was AAIW. This work is an autobiographical novel. Dodgson read this book in the first fortnight of 1866 and in his diary for 16 January he called it "enjoyable, and the character of Annie Anderson one of the most delightful I have ever met with in fiction. The Scotch dialect, too, is pleasant enough when one gets a little used to it."

1277. MacDonald, George. *David Elgin-brod*. (London: Hurst and Blackett, 1863). 3 vols. 1st edition.

A821 (author, title, edition, 3 vols.), JS1467. OCCL describes this as "a long, didactic, and gothically romantic novel about a young man who has a career not dissimilar to MacDonald's own." It was this book that firmly established MacDonald's career as a writer. In his diary for 9 February 1863, Dodgson notes that he spent the evening at the MacDonald house. Of George MacDonald, he writes, "We had some talk about his new novel *David Elginbrod*, which I have just finished reading."

1278. MacDonald, George. *Dealings with the Fairies*. (London: Alexander Strahan, 1867). 308pp. Illustrated by Arthur Hughes.

A935 (author, title, illustrated), JS1468. 1st edition. A collection of fairy stories that included "The Light Princess," "The Giant's Heart," "The Shadows," "Cross Purposes," and "The Golden Key."

1279. MacDonald, George. *England's Antiphon*. (London: Macmillan & Co., [1868]). 332pp. 3 plates by Arthur Hughes. Part of the *Sunday Library for Household Reading*.

A869 ("England, Antiphon"), JS379 (Anon./Unclassified), JS409 (Antiphon, unidentified work). 1st book edition. The original citation in A869 is confusing, and led JS to assume that "Antiphon" was a work by the orator of that name. However, items in A are not listed by author only, and a printed citation as nebulous as "England" seems unlikely, especially when such an easy solution presents itself—a book by Dodgson's good friend George MacDonald (several of whose works he owned) on a topic that would have interested Dodgson (the history of religious poetry in England) and illustrated by an artist Dodgson admired. Dodgson offered to loan this book to Edith Rix in 1888 (see *Letters*, 695). This work was originally published in three monthly parts in Oct., Nov., and Dec. 1868.

1280. MacDonald, George. *Phantastes: A Faerie Romance for Men and Women*. (London: Smith, Elder and Co., 1858). 323pp. 1st edition.

A650, D116 (author, title, city, date, edition), JS1470. D116 notes Dodgson's signature. MacDonald's first book of prose, *Phantastes* is the story of a young man who enters fairyland and has a series of what OCCL calls "dream-like adventures." The book was not written for children, but nonetheless began MacDonald's career as a writer of fairy stories, and may well have influenced Dodgson's *Alice* stories.

1281. MacDonald, George. *Poetical Works*. (London: Chatto & Windus, 1893). 2 vols. 448, 424pp.

A858 ("MacDonald's Poems, 2 vols."), JS1469. Only pre–1898 edition in BL or NUC of the only 2-volume collection of MacDonald's poetry. DEL quotes American Edmund Clarence Stedman, author of the 1875 study *Victorian Poets*, saying of MacDonald's poetry that, "too often, when not common-place, [it] is vague, effeminate, or otherwise poor." Certainly MacDonald's poetry remains the least well-known part of his oeuvre.

1282. MacDonald, Louisa [Mrs. George MacDonald, née Powell] (1822–1902). *Chamber Dramas for Children*. (London: Strahan & Co., 1870). 291pp.

A559 ("Chamber Dramas by Mr. Geo. MacDonald"), JS1466 (listed under George MacDonald). Clearly a misprint "Mr." for "Mrs." in A559. There is no such volume by Mr. MacDonald. Only edition in BL. Dodgson was friends with Mrs. MacDonald. In his diary for 1 July 1871 he writes, "Went up to town, to the MacDonalds, where I arrived just after the play had begun. It was one of Mrs. MacDonald's dramas, *Snowdrop*, and was acted by the children, and two or three friends. The stage was out in the garden, with curtains next the audience (100 poor people from Marylebone—Ruskin's tenants; and a few friends), but no back-ground, which rather spoiled the effect. However, it was capitally done."

1283. [MacFarlane, Charles] (d. 1858). *The Book of Table-Talk*. (London: C. Cox, 1847). 2 vols. in 1. 242, 235pp. By several contributors. Illustrated with wood-cuts. New edition.

A321, B970 (title, "by several Contributors," 2 vols. in 1, date) JS104 (Anon./Literature). MacFarlane was a prolific author of works on many subjects including history, travel (especially Italy where he lived for some time) and biography. A collection of humorous anecdotes and conversation starters. The 1st edition was published in 1836 by Charles Knight as part of the *Library of Anecdote*.

1284. MacKay, Charles (1814–89). *Memoirs of Extraordinary Popular Delusions and the Madness of Crowds*. (London: Office of the National Illustrated Library, 1852). 2 vols. 303, 322pp.

A579, D117 (author, title, city, date, 2 vols.), JS1471. MacKay was a Scottish-born journalist and poet who worked for several papers over the years. Some of his poetry was set to music and became popular and he also wrote some lyrics specifically for songs. He was special correspondent for *The Times* during the American Civil War. This book might best be described as a history of obsessions. In his preface, Mackay writes, "In reading the history of nations, we find that, like individuals, they have their whims and their peculiarities; their seasons of excitement and recklessness, when they care not what they do. We find that whole communities suddenly fix their minds upon one object, and go mad in its pursuit; that millions of people become simultaneously impressed with one delusion, and run after it." As Martin Gardner points out in his *Annotated Alice*, one obsession covered in MacKay's pages is a brief infatuation, on the streets of London, with the phrase "Who are you?" Dodgson's caterpillar in AAIW repeats this phrase which MacKay writes, "like a mushroom, seems to have sprung up in a night." He goes on to describe a scene of chaos in a courtroom caused by the judge uttering this phrase. Since Dodgson's edition of MacKay's book was dated 1852, he could certainly have been referring to this fad when he put the words "Who are you?" into the mouth of his mushroom-perching caterpillar over a decade later.

1285. Mackenzie, Alexander Campbell (1847–1935) and Francis Heuffer. *Colomba: A Lyrical Drama in Four Acts Founded on Prosper Mérimée's Tale: Op. 28*. (London: Novello, Ewer & Co., [1883]). 229pp. By Francis Hueffer; the music composed by A. C. Mackenzie; the pianoforte arrangement by Edouard Silas.

E96 (composer, date, publisher), JS1473. Earliest edition in BL or BOD. Vocal score with libretto and piano accompaniment. Mackenzie was a Scottish composer who wrote operas, cantatas, chamber music, songs, and even a concerto. In August of 1883, Dodgson wrote to Mackenzie suggesting that the two collaborate on an *Alice* operetta, an idea that was eventu-

ally abandoned (see *Alice on Stage*). *Colomba* is one of his five operas.

1286. Mackenzie, Alexander Campbell and William Grist. *Jason. A Dramatic Cantata for Solo Voices, Chorus and Orchestra*. (London: Novello, Ewer & Co., [1882]). 156pp. The poem written by William Grist; the music composed by A. C. Mackenzie.

E95 (composer, date, publisher), JS1472. Earliest edition in BL or BOD. Vocal score with libretto and piano accompaniment.

1287. Mackenzie-Quin, Quin. *A Method to Multiply or Divide any Number of Figures by a Like or a Less Number, so Expeditely, that any Fifty Figures may Either be Multiplied or Divided by any Fifty Figures, all in One Line, in Five Minutes Time. Invented by Quin Mackenzie-Quin at the Eighth Year of his Age*. (London: Printed for the Author, 1750). 23pp. Plates.

B1129 (author, title, date), JS1474. Dodgson was fascinated by mathematical "short cuts" and invented some of his own (see for instance his contributions to *Nature*, LCP).

1288. Maffey, John. *Scarlet Fever; Being an Attempt to Point out How the Ravages of this Very Fatal Disease May be Limited*. (London: Homœopathic Publishing Company, 1875). 29pp. 8th of a series of *Homœopathic Missionary Tracts*.

Not listed separately in JS (see JS163). Dodgson's copy is in HAC in a bound volume with 7 other tracts from this series and one additional Homœopathic pamphlet (see 970). The author was a licentiate of both the Royal College of Physicians and the Royal College of Surgeons.

1289. Mahan, Asa (1799–1889). *Modern Mysteries, Explained And Exposed, In Four Parts: I. Clairvoyant Revelations of A. J. Davis. II. Phenomena of Spiritualism Explained and Exposed. III. Evidence That the Bible is Given by Inspiration. IV. Clairvoyant Revelations of Emmanuel Swedenborg*. (Boston: Jewett Cleveland, Jewett; New York: Sheldons; London: Trübner, 1855). 466pp.

A886, B1128 (author, title, date), JS1476. Mahan was the first president of Oberlin College, USA. This work is a defense of the divine authority of the Bible that takes a religious view of clairvoyance and spiritualism. Authors referred to in the title are: Andrew Jackson Davis, author of *The Principles of Nature, Her Divine Revelations, and a Voice to Mankind* (1847); and Emmanuel Swedenborg (1688–1772), Swedish scientist, philosopher and theologian.

1290. Maldonati, Joannis [a.k.a. Juan Maldonado] (1533–83). *Commentarii in Quatuor Evangelistas. Ad Optimorum Librorum Fidem Accuratissime Recudi Curavit Franciscus Sausen.* (Moguntiae: Sumptibus Kirchhemii, Schotti & Thielmanni, 1840). 5 vols. in 3.

A763, JS1477. Dodgson's copy, signed "C. L. Dodgson, Ch. Ch. Oxford," is in the collection of Selwyn Goodacre, Derbyshire, England. Maldonado was a Spanish theologian and member of the Society of Jesus. He served as a professor at the Jesuit College de Clement in Paris where his teaching was attacked by the Sorbonne in 1574. He was cleared of charges of heresy by the Bishop of Paris. ODCC writes of these, his commentaries on the four gospels, that they are "held in deservedly high repute."

1291. Mangnall, Richmal (1769–1820). *Historical and Miscellaneous Questions, for the Use of Young People: with a Selection of British and General Biography.* (London: Longman, Hurst, Rees, Orme, and Brown, 1812). 434pp. 9th edition.

E177 ("Magnall's [sic] Questions"), JS1475. Earliest edition in BL. The book went through dozens of editions in the 19th century. Answers questions on subjects from theology and scripture knowledge to classics, history, and astronomy.

1292. Manning, Henry Edward (1808–92). *Sermons.* (London: 1843–50). 4 vols. 403, 400, 451, 393pp. 2nd edition of vol. 1, 1st editions? of vols. 2–4.

A776, B1131 (author, title, dates, 4 vols.), JS1478. Volume 1 was 1st published in 1842 with a 2nd edition in 1843; vol. 2 had reached a 5th edition by 1849; vols. 3 and 4 were first published in 1850 but both had multiple editions that year — so Dodgson may have owned later editions of all volumes. Manning was an Anglican priest and strong adherent to the Oxford Movement. In 1851, shortly after the publica-

tion of these sermons, he converted to Roman Catholicism. He was made Catholic Archbishop of Westminster in 1865 and Cardinal in 1875.

1293. Mansel, Henry Longueville (1820–71). *The Demons of the Wind and Other Poems.* (London: J. W. Southgate, 1838). 120pp.

A469 (author, title, date), JS1479. Mansel published this book of poems when he was just 18. He was a fellow of St. John's College, Oxford and, in 1866, became Regius Professor of Ecclesiastical History at Oxford and a canon of Christ Church, thus would probably have known Dodgson. He became Dean of St. Paul's in 1868.

1294. Mansel, Henry Longueville. *Letters, Lectures, and Reviews: Including The Phrontisterion, or, Oxford in the 19th Century.* (London: John Murray, 1873). 408pp. Edited by Henry W. Chandler.

A337 (author, title), JS1480. This is the only 19th-century edition listed in BL or BOD. A posthumously published collection. MOR says of *The Phrontisterion* (a satire on the 1850 University Commission) that it is "still considered among the brightest of Oxford jeux d'esprit." Dodgson also wrote several Oxford satires around this time (see *Oxford*).

1295. Mansel, Henry Longueville. *The Limits of Religious Thought Examined in Eight Lectures: Preached before the University of Oxford, in the year M.DCCC.LVIII, on the Foundation of the late Rev. John Bampton.* (London: John Murray, 1858). 435pp.

B1132 (author, title, date), JS1481. Mansel's lectures applied William Hamilton's concept of "relativity of knowledge" to religion, and asserted that, since we cannot absolutely know anything of God, faith is necessary. MOR says of Mansel's Bampton Lectures that they "gave rise to an elaborate controversy between himself and Professor [F. D.] Maurice."

1296. Mansel, Henry Longueville. *Prolegomena Logica: An Inquiry into the Psychological Character of Logical Processes.* (Oxford: Henry Hammans; London: Whittaker, 1860). 359pp. A portion reprinted from the *North British Review*.

A510, B1133 (author, title, edition, date), JS1482. Again showing the influence of William Hamilton, Mansel here defines his formal view of science.

1297. [**Marcello**, Benedetto] (1686-1739). *Il Toscanismo e la Crusca, e sia il Cruscante Impazzito: Tragicommedia Giocosa e Novissima.* (Venezia: 1739).

Uncertain, F188 (title, city, date), not in JS. F188 lists no identifying marks. Some sources attribute this collection of plays to Francesco Azizzi.

1298. [**Marcet**, Jane] (1769–1858). *Bertha's Visit to her Uncle in England.* (London: John Murray, 1830). 3 vols. [324], [292], [256]pp.

A933 (title, 3 vols.), JS40 (Anon./Children's). Earliest edition in BL; only this and the edition of 1831 specify 3 vols. Marcet was the author of many books of instruction for young people, almost single-handedly inventing the form of the simple scientific textbook with her 1806 *Conversations on Chemistry, Intended More Especially for the Female Sex.* The present book is in the form of a journal kept for her mother by Bertha, a young girl visiting England from Rio di Janeiro. The entries, telling of all she learned from her uncle, cover topics from natural history, to religion, to history.

1299. Marlowe, Christopher (1564–93). *Works.* Edition unknown.

A656 ("Marlowe's Works"), JS1483.

1300. [**Marryat**, Frederick] (1792–1848). *Snarleyyow; or, the Dog Fiend.* (London: Henry Colburn, 1837). 3 vols. 307, 299, 307pp. 1st edition.

A615 (title, edition, 3 vols.), JS1484. Marryat went to sea at the age of 13 and worked his way up to captain his own ship before retiring from the sea to write (primarily) adventure tales. This novel opens with the sentence "It was in the month of January, 1699, that a one-masted vessel, with black sides, was running along the coast near Beachy Head, at the rate of about five miles per hour." Dodgson, who spent summers from 1877 to 1897 in nearby Eastbourne, was fond of walking on Beachy Head. OCEL calls the novel "the story of a mysterious and indestructable cur."

1301. [**Marshall**, Emily]. *Woman's Worth; or, Hints to Raise the Female Character.*

(London: Stevens & Co., 1847). 224pp. 2nd edition.

E228 (title, date), JS406 (Anon./Women). Author attribution is from the Harvard University Library catalogue. A work that describes the sources of virtue in a woman as coming from her role as mother and wife.

1302. [**Marshall**, Frederic]. *French Home Life.* (Edinburgh: Blackwood's, 1873). 349pp. Originally published in *Blackwood's Magazine.*

A914, B1053 (title, date), JS352 (Anon./Topography). Earliest edition in BL. "In republishing these Essays in a collected form, the writer hopes that they may serve to show what some of the springs of French Home Life at this moment are; or, more exactly, what they appear to be to an English looker-on, who has lived for a quarter of a century in France." The subjects of the essays are servants, children, furniture, food, manners, language, dress, and marriage.

1303. Marston, John Westland (1819–90). *The Heart and the World, A Play in Five Acts. As Represented at the Theatre Royal, Haymarket.* (London: C. Mitchell, 1847). 85pp.

Uncertain. F168 (author, title, date), not numbered in JS. Identified as Dodgson's only by the gothic stamp. Marston was the author of popular plays but is now better remembered for his literary criticism. Partly in verse.

1304. Martin, Lady Helena [a.k.a. Helena Faucit] (1817–98). *On Some of Shakespeare's Female Characters.* (Edinburgh: Blackwood & Sons, 1885). 443pp.

A871 (title), JS138. Earliest edition in BL. Helena Faucit acted with Macready from the mid–1830s until the mid–1840s. She was married in 1851, but continued to act on occasion. Dodgson saw her play Imogen in *Cymbeline* at the Drury Lane in 1864 and wrote "beautifully she looked and acted the part." Under the name Helena Martin, she had previously published separate booklets on Beatrice, Desdemona, Imogen, Juliet, Ophelia, Portia, and Rosalind (from articles in *Blackwood's Magazine*). This work includes essays on these heroines as well as Hermione.

1305. Marvell, Andrew (1621–78). *The Works of Andrew Marvell. To Which is*

Prefixed an Account of the Life and Writings of the Author. By Mr. [Thomas] Cooke. (London: E. Curll, 1726). 2 vols.

A484 (author, title, date, 2 vols.), JS1485. Marvell was a poet, politician, and friend of John Milton. His works included not only serious poetry, but also political pamphlets and satires.

1306. Marx, Carl Friedrich Heinrich (1796–1877). *On the Decrease of Disease Effected by the Progress of Civilization.* (London: Longman, Brown, Green, and Longmans, 1844). 102pp. Translated from the German by Robert Willis.

E335 (author, translator, title, date), JS1486. A German physician and professor, Marx wrote a thesis on "Medical Euthanasia," in which he advocated a palliative death for terminal patients similar to what is advocated by today's hospice groups.

1307. Masheder, Richard. *The Right Honourable W. E. Gladstone: A Political Review.* (London: Saunders, 1865). 228pp.

B1058 (author, title, date), not listed separately in JS, but mentioned under Gladstone. There was also a 2nd edition published in 1865. Among the earliest biographies of Gladstone. He had held a number of important political posts by 1865, but had not yet served as prime minister. See 777 for a note on Gladstone.

1308. Maskell, William (1814–1890). *A Letter to the Rev. Dr. Pusey on his Practice of Receiving Persons in Auricular Confession.* (London: W. Pickering, 1850). 51pp.

C7 (author, title), JS1694 (listed under Pusey and not listed separately). Only edition in BL. One of 11 items by or related to Pusey bound together in a volume and described in C7 as "Eleven Sermons and Pamphlets, 1843–1878." For a complete list of items enumerated in C7 see 1591. Maskell was an English clergyman active in the High Church movement. He was, as chaplain to the Bishop of Exeter, closely involved in the Gorham case (see 1534), and in 1850, the year of the present publication, converted to the Roman Catholic Church.

1309. Mason, James. *Old Fairy Tales.* (London: Cassell, Petter, & Galpin, [1873]). 564pp. Illustrated by John Moyr Smith.

A932 (title), JS70 (Anon./Children's). Only edition in BL of the only matching title in BL.

The next closest match is Laura Valentine (née Jewry), *The Old Old Fairy Tales* (London: F. Warne & Co., 1889). A collection of classic tales including "Snow-White and Rose-Red," "Little Red-Riding-Hood," "Cinderella," "Jack and the Beanstalk," "Beauty and the Beast," and others.

1310. Mason, Thomas Monck (1803–89). *New Lights upon Old Lines; or, Vexed Questions in Theological Controversy at the Present Day Critically and Exegetically Discussed.* (London, Edinburgh: James Nisbet, 1877). 303pp.

A793 (author, title), JS1487 (listed under William Tate Mason). Only edition listed in BL or BOD. A 2nd series was published in 1878, but as A793 makes no mention of series, it most likely refers to the 1877 volume. Mason was an Irishman and one of three men who traveled from London to Germany in 1836 via balloon. In his youth he studied music and was a distinguished flautist and composer. In later years he turned to a study of theology. Mason considers Biblical narratives in the light of recent scientific discoveries and re-interprets (but does not dismiss) the stories.

1311. Massey, Gerald (1828–1907). *A Tale of Eternity, and Other Poems.* (London: Strahan, 1879). 425pp.

A864 (author, title), JS1488. The 1st British edition was a large paper "Private edition dedicated to the Lady Marian Alford," published in 1870. A Boston edition was published in that same year. The present edition is the first public edition published in Britain, and seems the most likely match. Massey was a British poet who served as a secretary to the Christian Socialists (who were headed by Dodgson's friend F. D. Maurice).

1312. Masson, Gustave (1819–88). *La Lyre Française.* (London: Macmillan, 1867). 440pp. In the *Golden Treasury Series.*

E381 (author, title, date), F166, JS1489. E381 lists the date as 1876, but neither BL nor MBC list an edition of that date. F166 lists the date as 1867, the date of this the earliest edition in MBC. E381 clearly has a typographical error in which the last two digits of the date were reversed. F166 notes the gothic stamp. Masson was a master at Harrow School. This book has an English introduction followed by an account of the French chanson going back to the 11th century and a collection of French lyric poetry.

1313. (Mathematics). *The Quarterly Journal of Pure and Applied Mathematics.* Nos. 1–4 (April 1855–March 1856). (London: J. W. Parker, 1855–56).

E255 (title, numbers, dates), JS153 (Anon./Mathematics). Possibly edited by J. J. Sylvester.

1314. Mather, Cotton (1663–1728). *The Wonders of the Invisible World: Being an Account of the Tryals of Several Witches Lately Executed in New-England: and of Several Remarkable Curiosities Therein Occurring. Together with, I. Observations upon the Nature, the Number, and the Operations of the Devils: II. A Short Narrative of a Late Outrage Committed by a Knot of Witches in Swede-Land, very much Resembling, and so far Explaining, that under which New-England has Laboured: III. Some Councels Directing a Due Improvement of the Terrible Things Lately Done by the Unusual and Amazing Range of Evil-spirits in New-England: IV. A Brief Discourse upon those Temptations which are the More Ordinary Devices of Satan.* (London: J. Dunton, 1693). 98pp.

A883 (author, title), JS1490. 1st British edition. Dodgson probably owned a later edition; that published in London by J. R. Smith in 1862 (which adds *A Farther Account of the Tryals of the New-England Witches* by Increase Mather) seems likely. Mather was among the most famous of New England Puritan preachers, and is rarely today pictured in a sympathetic light. Though he officially disapproved of the Salem witch trials, he helped whip up the fear which led to them through his 1689 book *Memorable Providences Relating to Witchcraft and Possessions.* The present study is another work on satanic possession.

1315. Matheson, George (1842–1906). *Can the Old Faith Live with the New? Or, the Problem of Evolution and Revelation.* (Edinburgh: Blackwood & Sons, 1885). 391pp.

A788 (author, title), JS1491. Earliest edition in BL. Matheson was a liberal Scottish theologian who, though blind from the age of 20, earned a reputation as a preacher and author. The preface states, "Our object in this volume is to consider the relationship of the modern doctrine of Evolution to those doctrines of the Bible which bear on the development of the world; and as natural evolution is supposed to involve religious agnosticism, we have prefaced the inquiry by considering the scientific value of the religious sentiment in general.... There are two important books which have stimulated us to make this attempt — that of Mr. Joseph John Murphy on *The Scientific Bases of Faith*, and that of Professor H. Drummond on *Natural Law in the Spiritual World.*" Dodgson owned a copy of the latter work (see 629).

1316. *Mathiesons' Oxford Directory (Including Abingdon) For 1867.* (Oxford: Wheeler & Day; London: Adams & Francis, 1867). 210pp.

E417, JS196 (Anon./Oxford). The new edition of what had been called *The Oxford Directory, Court, Street, Trade, and Commercial* (then published by Wheeler & Day of Oxford). Dodgson's copy is in HAC and has "C. L. Dodgson" in ink on the front cover. Dodgson is included in a list on p. 138, his address given as Christ Church. The full cover illustrated advertisement on the rear cover is for "Nosotti's Looking Glasses." Dodgson would have begun work on TTLG about this time.

1317. Maudsley, Henry (1835–1916). *The Physiology and Pathology of the Mind.* (London: Macmillan and Co., 1867). 442pp.

A347 (author, title), JS1492. Earliest edition in BL. This work was preceded by Maudsley's *On the Method of the Study of Mind: An Introductory Chapter to a Physiology and Pathology of the Mind.* Maudsley was a London physician and formerly Resident Physician to the Manchester Royal Lunatic Hospital.

1318. Maunder, Samuel (1785–1849). *The Treasury of Knowledge, and Library of Reference.* (London: 1841).

B1134 (author, title, date), JS1493. No edition of 1841 traced, but the 12th edition of 1840 (2 parts in 1 volume) was published by Longman, Orme, Brown, Green, and Longmans and the 16th edition of 1845 was published by Longmans & Co. The 12th edition included: *English Dictionary and Grammar, New Universal Gazeteer, Classical Dictionary, Scripture Names, Analysis of General History, Dictionary of Law Terms, the Whole Surrounded by Maxims and Proverbs of all Nations.* By 1859 this general reference book had sold nearly 100,000 copies.

Maunder was the author of reference books and books of history.

1319. Maurice, F[rederick] D[enison] (1805–72). *The Conscience. Lectures on Casuistry*, Delivered in the University of Cambridge. (London and Cambridge: Macmillan and Co., 1872). 2nd edition.

Not in JS. In a letter of 2 March [1877?], Dodgson writes, "having just awakened from a long nap, which followed the perusal of some of Maurice's book on *The Conscience...*" First published in 1868, this is the edition closest to Dodgson's mention. Maurice was a co-founder, in 1848, of the Christian Socialist movement and among the most prolific and influential religious writers of the Victorian era. He was elected Knightsbridge Professor of Moral Philosophy at Cambridge in 1866. Dodgson was acquainted with Maurice and attended services in Maurice's chapel in Vere St., London, on many occasions (he wrote in his diary on one visit to London, "Maurice's church as usual.") He photographed Maurice in July of 1863.

1320. Maurice, F[rederick] D[enison]. *Social Morality. Twenty-one Lectures Delivered in the University of Cambridge.* (London and Cambridge: Macmillan, 1869). 483pp.

A337 (author, title), JS1494. 1st edition as described in MBC. Lectures on ethical topics.

1321. Maurice, Frederick Denison. *Theological Essays.* (Cambridge: Macmillan & Co., 1853). 449pp.

A791, B1135 (author, title, date), JS1495. 1st edition, as described in MBC, was published in June, 1853; a 2nd edition appeared in December 1853. The present book caused a controversy because in it Maurice asserts his belief that there is no eternal punishment in hell (Dodgson agreed).

1322. Maury, Matthew Fontaine (1806–73). *The Physical Geography of the Sea.* (London: Sampson, Low, Son, & Co., 1855). 274pp.

A332 (author, title), JS1496. Earliest edition in BL, which gives no publisher. Some entries in BL misattribute this title to the French scholar Louis Ferdinand Alfred Maury. M. F. Maury was a United States Navy Lieutenant considered by many the founder of the science of oceanography. This was the first textbook of oceanography and attempted to provide practical information for mariners. Maury strongly supported the link between science and religion, and this work is peppered with Biblical references. In an 1860 speech, he said "I have been blamed by men of science, both in this country and in England, for quoting the Bible in confirmation of the doctrines of physical geography. The Bible, they say, was not written for scientific purposes, and is therefore no authority in matters of science. I beg pardon! The Bible is authority for everything it touches."

1323. Mayhew, Augustus (1826–75). *Paved with Gold: or, the Romance and Reality of the London Streets. An Unfashionable Novel.* (London: Chapman & Hall, 1858). 408pp. With illustrations by Phiz (H. K. Browne).

A814 (title, illustrated), JS1497. 1st book edition of the only matching 19th-century title in BL. Mayhew was a journalist and brother of Henry Mayhew (see below). The preface states, "It has often struck me that if a truthful account were written of the miseries of criminal life, it would, by destroying the fancied romance of wickedness, have a quicker effect in checking juvenile depravity than any moral appeals that could be made to the understandings of the evil-disposed.... Of one thing I may humbly boast — the extreme truthfulness with which this book has been written. The descriptions of boy-life in the streets, the habits and customs of donkey-drivers, the peculiarities of tramp-dom and vagrancy, have all resulted from long and patient inquiries among the individuals themselves. They are actual records of the earnings and condition of these peculiar classes among the uncivilised of London. Indeed, some portions of this book ... were originally undertaken by me at the request of my brother, Mr. Henry Mayhew, and will, I believe, form part of his invaluable work on *London Labour and the Poor.*"

1324. Mayhew, Henry (1812–87). *London Labour and the London Poor: A Cyclopædia of the Condition and Earnings of Those that Will Work, those that Cannot Work, and those that Will not Work.* (London: Griffen, Bohn and Company, 1861–2). Vols. 2 & 3, plus Extra Volume (a.k.a. vol. 4). 512, 442, 504pp.

A573 (author, title, volumes), JS1498. Volumes 1–2 were first published in 1851. This appears to be the first uniform edition of all four volumes, but Dodgson may have owned earlier copies. His volume 1 may simply have gone missing. Mayhew was a founder of *Punch* and in 1849 took a job with the *Morning Chronicle* to document the conditions of London's poor. From this series of articles grew the present work, a monumental and important series on the life of the London poor. Vol. 1 includes information on various kinds of street-folk, including sellers of food, books, etc. Vol. 2 includes information on street sellers, scavengers, rubbish carters, chimney sweeps, sewage and drains, etc. Vol. 3 includes information on insects, street performers, laborers, vagrants, etc. The extra volume includes information on beggars and cheats, thieves and swindlers, prostitutes, etc. Mayhew wrote only a portion of this volume.

1325. Mayhew, Henry and Augustus Mayhew. *The Greatest Plague of Life; or the Adventures of a Lady in Search of a Good Servant. By One who has been "Almost Worried to Death."* (London: David Bogue, [1847]). 286pp. Edited by the Brothers Mayhew. Illustrated by George Cruikshank.

A652 (author, title, illustrator), JS1499. Earliest edition in BL. A comic novel about the "servant problem." The "problem" was that middle-class Victorians both depended upon and feared their servants. Servants are here portrayed as both players forced to take part in the drama of the Victorian household and lazy figures prone to crime.

1326. Mayne, Robert Gray (1808–68). *An Expository Lexicon of the Terms, Ancient and Modern, in Medical and General Science: Including a Complete Medico-legal Vocabulary.* (London: J. Churchill, 1860). 1506pp.

A315 (author, title), JS1500. Only edition published under this title. Dodgson also owned a later edition under a new title (see below). Mayne was a surgeon to the Leeds Lock Hospital. The *Association Medical Journal* said of this work, "We have great pleasure in expressing our high and unqualified admiration of the manner in which it is executed."

1327. Mayne, Robert Gray. *Medical Vocabulary; or, An Explanation of all Names,* *Synonyms, Terms, and Phrases Used in Medicine.* (London: Churchill, 1862). 2nd edition. 439pp.

B1136 (author, title), JS1501. See above for 1st edition. Earliest edition in BL or NUC under the present title.

1328. McCarthy, Justin (1830–1912). *A Fair Saxon. A Novel.* (London: Chatto and Windus, 1878).

Not in JS. In his diary for 26 July 1883, Dodgson lists this among several novels read during a recent illness and pronounces it "excellent." First published in 3 vols. in 1873, this is the edition in BL closest to Dodgson's diary mention. Justin McCarthy was an Irish politician, journalist, and author of novels and historical works.

1329. McCarthy, Justin. *A History of Our Own Times From Accession of Queen Victoria to The General Election of 1880.* (London: Chatto and Windus, 1881). 4 vols.

A384, D118 (author, title, 4 vols., city, date), JS1502. D118 specifies that this is a "Library Edition." This work was eventually updated to cover the period to the accession of Edward VII.

1330. McCarthy, Justin Huntly (1860–1936). *The Case for Home Rule.* (London: Chatto & Windus, 1887). 256pp.

A555 (author, title), JS1503. Only edition in BL or BOD. J. H. McCarthy should not be confused with his father Justin McCarthy (see above)—they are listed as one in JS. J. H. McCarthy was an Irishman who achieved fame as a novelist, playwright, and lyricist for musical dramas.

1331. McKinley, Carlyle (1847–1904). *An Appeal to Pharaoh. The Negro Problem and its Radical Solution.* (?London: 1890).

B946 (title, date), JS281 (Anon./Sociology). No 1890 edition traced. Originally published in New York by Fords & Co., 1889. McKinley fought for the South in the American Civil War and worked, beginning in 1875, on the staff of the *Charleston (SC) News and Courier*. He was known for his poetry lauding the "Lost Cause" of the American South. In this work because "it was a mistake to bring the Negro here in the first instance" and because "the Negro is not our equal in every respect," so that we only "give him half his rights as a man," the author advocates "gradual and induced emigration," and, if necessary, "the forcible removal of the whole black and colored population of the United States." See index under "Negro Problem" for similar works.

1332. Meadows, F. C. *New Italian and English Dictionary.* (London: Wm. Tegg and Co., 1852). 13th edition. 664pp.

B1137 (author, title, date), JS1504. Meadows was lexicographer and grammarian who also wrote a French-English dictionary.

1333. *Measles; Its Complications and Fatality Prevented by Homœopathy: Being Contributions from More than Twenty Medical Men.* (London: Homœopathic Publishing Company, 1875). 2nd edition. 22pp. 5th of a series of *Homœopathic Missionary Tracts.*

Not listed separately in JS (see JS163). Dodgson's copy is in HAC in a bound volume with 7 other tracts from this series and one additional Homœopathic pamphlet (see 970).

1334. Medhurst, Walter Henry (1798–1857). *Chinese Dialogues, Questions and Familiar Sentences Literally Rendered into English with a View to Promote Commercial Intercourse and to Assist Beginners in the Language.* (Shanghae: London Mission Press, 1863). 225pp. Revised by his son [Sir Walter Henry Medhurst (1822–85)].

D119 (author, title, city, date), JS1505. Medhurst was an English Congregationalist missionary to China.

1335. Meigs, Charles Delucena (1792–1869). *Females and Their Diseases; A Series of Letters to his Class.* (Philadelphia: Lea & Blanchard, 1848). 670pp.

Not in JS. In a letter to his illustrator A. B. Frost on 30 January 1879, Dodgson writes, "In my Medical studies I have met with 2 excellent books by Dr. Meigs, published by Lea and Blanchard, Philadelphia." He goes on to request that Frost locate some other medical books which he thinks are by Meigs (in fact, they are by Michael Ryan; there is no indication if Dodgson ever acquired them), saying "The two I do not want are called *Females and their Diseases* and *Obstetrics.*" Only edition in BL. Meigs was Professor of Midwifery and Diseases of Women and Children at Jefferson Medical College, Philadelphia. In his letter, Dodgson called him a "most genial and thoroughly *healthy* writer."

1336. Meigs, Charles Delucena. *Obstetrics: The Science and the Art.* (Philadelphia: Lea & Blanchard, 1849). 685pp.

Not in JS. See above for the reference in Dodgson's letters to this title. This is the earliest edition traced.

1337. Menken, Adah Isaacs [stage name of Ada C. McCord, afterwards Menken, afterwards Heenan, afterwards Newell, afterwards Barclay] (1835–1868). *Infelicia. Poems.* (London, Paris, New York: Privately Printed, 1868). 141pp. With a portrait, and with vignettes by Alfred Concanen.

A458 (author, title, edition, date), JS1506. A458 notes "first edition," presumably referring to this, which also appears to be the only 1868 British edition. Menken was an American actress who told so many stories about her own origins that even her original name is shrouded in mystery. Starting off with minor roles, she eventually achieved fame in both Europe and America and was one of the highest paid actresses of the mid-19th century. This book was published posthumously and dedicated to Charles Dickens. The work includes a facsimile of a letter from Dickens to Menken.

1338. Meredith, George (1828–1909). *Ballads and Poems of Tragic Life.* (London: Macmillan and Co., 1887). 160pp. 1st edition.

A864 (author, title, edition), JS1507. Meredith was an English poet and novelist and intimate of the Pre-Raphaelite group and their satellites. This was the follow-up to his first major successful volume, *Diana of the Crossways,* and contained the ode "France, December 1870."

1339. Meredith, George. *Modern Love and Poems of the English Roadside, with Poems and Ballads.* (London: Chapman & Hall, 1862). 542pp. 1st edition.

A840 (author, title, edition), JS1508. Fifty 16-line poems telling the story of a modern marriage and ending in the poisoning of the wife.

1340. Meredith, George. *Poems and Lyrics of the Joy of Earth.* (London: Macmillan and Co., 1883). 184pp. 1st edition.

A864 (author, title, edition), JS1509. Published in May 1883; another edition appeared in September.

1341. Meredith, George. *The Shaving of Shagpat. An Arabian Entertainment*. (London: Chapman and Hall, 1856). 384pp. 1st edition.

A840 (author, title, edition), JS1510. Meredith's first novel — a linked series of tales in the tradition of the Arabian Nights.

1342. Meredith, Owen [pseud. of Edward Robert Bulwer-Lytton] (1831–91). *Clytemnestra, The Earl's Return, the Artist, and other Poems*. (London: Chapman and Hall, 1855). 352pp. 1st edition.

A452, D121 (author, title, edition, date), JS1512. D121 notes Dodgson's signature and a note. Bulwer-Lytton was the son of the novelist, a poet, and a diplomat.

1343. Meredith, Owen [pseud. of Edward Robert Bulwer-Lytton]. *The Wanderer*. (London: Chapman and Hall, 1859). 436pp. 1st edition.

A451, D120 (author, title, edition, date), JS1511. D120 notes, "with autograph pencil note by Mr. Dodgson." A poem.

1344. Metcalfe, Frederick (1815–85). *The Oxonian in Iceland: or, Notes of Travel in that Island in the Summer of 1860, with Glances at Icelandic Folk-lore and Sagas*. (London: Longman, Green, Longman, and Roberts, 1861). 424pp. Illustrated. Folded plate.

A589 (author, title), JS1514. Earliest edition in BL. Metcalfe was a fellow of Lincoln College, Oxford from 1844 until his death and vicar of St. Michael's, Oxford from 1849 until his death. A Scandinavian scholar, he recorded his northern travels in this book and others (see below). Dodgson met Metcalfe while on a walk in Oxford on 30 November 1866.

1345. Metcalfe, Frederick. *The Oxonian in Norway: or, Notes of Excursions in that Country in 1854–1855*. (London: Hurst and Blackett, 1857). 387pp. 2nd edition.

A589 (author, title), JS1513. First published in 1856 in 2 vols. Earliest 1-volume edition traced. Since A589 does not specify 2 vols., this seems the most likely.

1346. [Middleton, Conyers] (1683–1750). *A Full and Impartial Account of All the Late Proceedings in the University of Cambridge Against Dr. Bentley, by A Member of that University*. (London: J. Bettenham, 1719). 44pp.

B962 ("Account of the Proceedings in the University of Cambridge Against Dr. Bentley, 1719"), JS1515. This is the only match in BL or BOD. A second part of Middleton's account was also published (London: Printed for J. Bettenham, 1719). The description in B962 does not specify a part, so it seems likely that Dodgson had only the first part, but he may have had both. His copy was bound together with Arthur Ashley's Sykes response to the pamphlet (see 1990). Richard Bentley (1662–1742) was a great classical scholar and friend of Isaac Newton. He was Master of Trinity College, Cambridge, and ruled that institution with such an iron hand that he was, according to OCEL "brought before the bishop and nominally, though not effectually, deprived of his mastership." Middleton was a fellow of Trinity and an opponent of Bentley.

1347. Mignet, François Auguste Marie (1796–1884). *The History of Mary Queen of Scots*. (London: R. Bentley, 1861). 466pp. Translated from the French by Andrew Richard Scoble.

A919 (author, title), JS1516. A London edition of 1851 was published by Richard Bentley in 2 vols., but A919 includes another item that specifies multiple volumes, while this item does not, so this earliest traced 1-volume edition seems more likely. Mignet was a French historian and journalist, best known for a history of the French Revolution.

1348. Mill, John Stuart (1806–73). *Autobiography*. (London: Longmans, Green, Reader, and Dyer, 1873). 313pp. Edited by Helen Taylor.

A919 ("Mills' Autobiography"), JS1517. BL lists only this title with the combination of an author named Mill or Mills and the word "Autobiography" appearing in the title. This is the 1st edition. A 2nd edition was published the same year. Published posthumously and edited by Mill's stepdaughter, who was his companion following the death of her mother.

1349. Mill, John Stuart. *An Examination of Sir William Hamilton's Philosophy*. (London: Longmans, Green, Reader and Dyer, 1872). 650pp. 4th edition.

A510, B1139 (author, title, date), JS1518. Besides his great *System of Logic*, below, Mill's only other work on general philosophy. Mill uses his attack on Hamilton (see 858) as a means to examine the rival philosophies of Intuitionism and Empiricism. He writes, "The difference between these two schools of philosophy, that of Intuition, and that of Experience and Association, is not a mere matter of abstract speculation; it is full of practical consequences, and lies at the foundation of all the greatest differences of practical opinion in an age of progress."

1350. Mill, John Stuart. *A System of Logic, Ratiocinative and Inductive, Being a Connected View of the Principles of Evidence and the Methods of Scientific Investigation.* (London: John W. Parker, 1851). 2 vols. 502, 527pp. 3rd edition.

A510, B1140 (author, title, 2 vols., date), JS1519. The most important work of this great English philosopher.

1351. Millais, John Everett (1829–96). *Millais's Illustrations. A Collection of Drawings on Wood.* (London: Alexander Strahan, 1866). Unpaginated. 80 plates.

A275 (illustrator, title), not in JS. Only edition in BL. Millais was a founding member of the Pre-Raphaelite Brotherhood in 1848 and worked closely with Ruskin. He had a successful career at the Royal Academy, but also, especially during the 1860s, as an illustrator, as exhibited by the present volume. This collection includes illustrations from Tennyson, Trollope, and various magazines. Dodgson writes frequently of Millais' paintings in his diary. On 7 April 1864 he met Millais (with a letter of introduction from Holman Hunt). He mentions at least three other meetings with Millais (including some with his children) in the published diaries.

1352. Miller, William Allen (1817–80). *Elements of Chemistry, Theoretical and Practical. Part I. Chemical Physics. Part 2. Inorganic Chemistry Part 3. Organic Chemistry.* (London: Parker, 1855–57). 3 vols.

A307 ("Miller's Chemistry, 3 vols."), JS1520. This is the only pre–1898 title matching the particulars of A307. Earliest edition in BL. Miller was Professor of Chemistry at King's College, London. Dodgson advertised for a copy of this book in his 1893 pamphlet *Second-Hand Books* (see Stern, x–xi).

1353. Miller, W[illiam] J[ohn Clarke] and D[aniel Biddle] editors. *Mathematical Questions with their Solutions. From the "Educational Times."* (London: The Educational Times, 1864–1897). Vols. 1–67 (vols. 1–66 edited by Miller; vol. 67 edited by Biddle). "With many papers ... not published in the 'Educational Times.'"

A956 (title, 67 vols.), A957 ("Mathematical Questions, 4 vols."), JS147 and JS150 (Anon./Mathematics). The A957 entry follows immediately on the A956 entry and surely refers to extra odd volumes (possibly including Dodgson's own contributions), as there are no other multi-volume works by that short title listed in BL. Volume 67 was for Jan.–June 1897, the last volume Dodgson could have been expected to purchase, as he died in Guildford in January 1898. Dodgson contributed several pieces to the *Educational Times*, some of which were reprinted in this semi-annual volume (see LCP).

1354. Milligan, William (1821–93). *The Resurrection of Our Lord.* (London: Macmillan and Co., 1881). 304pp.

A789 (author, title), JS1521. 1st edition as described in MBC. W. Milligan was Professor of Divinity and Biblical Criticism at the University of Aberdeen. Six lectures.

1355. Milman, Henry Hart (1791–1868). *The History of Christianity from the Birth of Christ to the Abolition of Paganism in the Roman Empire.* (London: John Murray, 1840). 3 vols.

A381 (author, title, 3 vols.), JS1522. Earliest edition in BL or BOD. Milman was Professor of Poetry at Oxford from 1821 to 1831 and became Dean of St. Paul's in 1849. He wrote poetry and dramas, but is best known for his historical works such as the present volume.

1356. Milman, Henry Hart. *The Poetical Works of the Rev. H. H. Milman.* (London: John Murray, 1839). 3 vols. With plates, including a portrait.

A857 ("Milman's Poems, 3 vols."), JS1523. Only 3-volume edition in BL or BOD.

1357. Milnes, Richard Monckton (1809–85). *The Life and Letters of John Keats.* (London: Edward Moxon, 1848). 2 vols.

A880 (author, title), not numbered in JS (listed after JS1524). Dodgson records that he began reading this book on 11 January 1855 and this is the only pre–1855 edition in BL. A880 lists another item for which it specifies multiple volumes so it is possible that Dodgson purchased the 1867 1-volume edition after his initial reading and that this is the version listed in A880. Milnes was friends with Tennyson, Hallam and Thackeray during his undergraduate years at Cambridge. He was a poet, politician, and, according to OCEL, "the first open champion of Keats as a poet of the first rank." Dodgson records that he began reading this book on 11 January 1855.

1358. Milnes, Richard Monckton. *The Poems of Richard Monckton Milnes. Volume 1. Poems of Many Years. Volume 2. Memorials of a Residence on the Continent.* (London: Edward Moxon, 1838). 2 vols.

A490 (author, title, date [given as 1828], 2 vols.), JS1524. Apparently a typographical error in A490, as BL, BOD, OCEL, and DEL all list no poetical works by Milnes prior to 1838 (he would have been 19 in 1828). Milnes' best known poems are "Strangers Yet," and "The Brookside."

1359. Milton, John (1608–74). *Milton's Poetical Works. With Life, Critical Dissertation, and Explanatory Notes, by the Rev. George Gilfillan.* (Edinburgh: J. Nichol, 1853). 2 vols. 333, 328pp. In the *Library Edition of the British Poets* series.

A392, D122, JS1525. Dodgson's copy is in HAC and includes an inscription on the front end-paper, "Charles Lutwidge Dodgson. Given to him by his affectionate Father on his 21st Birthday, 1853." Vol. II contains Dodgson's signature. Dodgson also owned a (presumably) one-volume collection of Milton's poetry, described in A356 as "Milton's Poetical Works, half morocco." See 776 for more on Gilfillan.

1360. Milton, John. *Paradise Lost.* (London: Pickering, 1835). 3 vols. In the *Pickering Diamond Classics* series.

A475 (author, title, date, series), JS1526 (not listed separately from facsimile edition below). For a full description of the *Pickering Diamond Classics*, see 153. The Pickering edition of 1828 was issued with an engraved title in 1835.

1361. Milton, John. *Paradise Lost, as Originally Published by John Milton. Being a Facsimile Reproduction of the First Edition.* (London: Elliot Stock, 1877). 170 leaves. With an introduction by David Masson.

A851, B1141 (author, full title, introducer, date), JS1526 (not listed separately from Pickering edition above).

1362. (Milton, John). *Concordance to Milton.* Details unknown.

A550 ("Concordance to Milton"), JS1527. Three possibilities in BL (in each case the earliest edition listed in BL is described):

Bradshaw, John. *A Concordance to the Poetical Works of John Milton.* (London: Swan Sonnenschein & Co., 1894). 412pp.

Cleveland, Charles Dexter. *A Complete Concordance to the Poetical Works of John Milton.* (London: Sampson Low, Son & Marston, 1867). 308pp.

Prendergast, Guy Lushington. *A Complete Concordance to the Poetical Works of Milton.* (Madras: Pharoah and Co., 1857). 416pp.

1363. Mingaud, Monsieur. *The Noble Game of Billiards, Wherein are Exhibited Extraordinary and Surprising Strokes which have Excited the Admiration of Most of the Sovereigns of Europe.* (London: John Thurstan, 1830). 7pp. + 40 plates. Translated by John Thurstan. Folding frontispiece.

D19 (author, title, translator, publisher, date), JS1528. D19 describes this as inscribed "C. L. Dodgson, Ch. Ch., January 1862." The book was offered at Sotheby's, London, in 1926 (DAA1087), and DAA dates the inscription 1869. Mingaud was a former captain in the French artillery. John Thurstan was a manufacturer of billiard tables. Dodgson's rules for his own version of Billiards, "Circular Billiards," were published in 1890 (see WMGC, 166–68).

1364. Minto, William (1845–93). *Logic. Inductive and Deductive.* (London: Murray, 1893). Part of W. A. Knight's *University Extension Manuals* series.

A506 (author, title), JS1529. Earliest edition listed in BL or BOD. An American edition of the same year had 373pp. Minto was educated at the University of Aberdeen. He worked for a time as a journalist (including work on the staff of the *Pall Mall Gazette*, to which Dodgson made many contributions, see LCP) before returning to Aberdeen in 1880 to take up the post of Professor of Logic. In addition to work on logic, he published books on English literature and at least one novel.

1365. Mitford, A[lgernon] B[ertram] [later Freeman] (b. 1837). *Tales of Old Japan.* (London: Macmillan and Co., 1874). 383pp. 2nd edition.

A917 (author, title), JS1530. A917 lists another item for which it specifies multiple volumes, thus this, the earliest 1-volume edition as described in MBC, seems most likely. The 1st edition was published by Macmillan in 2 volumes in 1871. Mitford was a civil servant who served as second secretary to the British legation in Japan. *Saturday Review* wrote of this book, "The most interesting of the stories collected by Mr. Mitford are undoubtedly the 'Fairy-Tales,' for in them the links become clearly visible which unite the folk-lore of Japan with that of the Indo-European nations." The same review also praised Mitford's work as a translator.

1366. Mitford, Mary Russell (1786–1855). *Recollections of a Literary Life, or, Books, Places, and People.* (London: Richard Bentley, 1852). 3 vols. 323, 302, 296pp.

A880 (Mitford's Notes of a Literary Life, 3 vols.), JS1531. This is the only 3-volume edition of the only matching title listed in BL. M. R. Mitford was a popular writer of poetry and prose known now mainly for her letters but in her own life for her stories of village life. DEL quotes Harriet Martineau as saying of Mitford, "She had a charming humour and her style was delightful.... She may be considered as the representative of household cheerfulness in the humbler range of the literature of fiction." Her recollections are peppered with quotes from her favorite authors and friends.

1367. Mivart, St. George (1827–1900). *On the Genesis of the Species.* (London: Macmillan and Co., 1871). 296pp. With numerous illustrations.

A910 (author, title), JS1532. The 1st edition, as described in MBC, was published in January 1871; a 2nd followed in August. Mivart converted to Catholicism as a young man. Though he studied under Thomas Huxley (noted supporter of Darwin) he became an opponent of Darwin's theories. In this, his most important work, he put forth an evolutionary theory opposed to Darwin's but reconciled with Catholicism. Darwin took Mivart's work seriously, and

addressed many of Mivart's objections in later editions of his *Origin of Species.* In his introductory remarks Mivart writes, "The general theory of evolution has indeed for some time past steadily gained ground, and it may be safely predicted that the number of facts which can be brought forward in its support will, in a few years, be vastly augmented. But the prevalence of this theory need alarm no one, for it is, without any doubt, perfectly consistent with strictest and most orthodox Christian theology. Moreover, it is not altogether without obscurities, and cannot yet be considered as fully demonstrated." In 1876, Mivart received an honorary doctorate from Pope Pius IX. Dodgson wrote of the book in his diary on 1 November 1874 that it showed "the insufficiency of 'Natural Selection' *alone* to account for the universe, and its perfect compatibility with the creative and guiding power of God." (See *Diary 6*).

1368. Moir, Erskine [pseud. of Felicia Mary Frances Skene] (1821–99). *Through the Shadows. A Test of the Truth.* (London: Elliot Stock, 1888). 232pp.

Uncertain. F163 (author, title, date), not numbered in JS. Identified as Dodgson's only by the gothic stamp. See 1855 for a note on Skene and her controversial novels.

1369. Molesworth, Mrs. [Mary Louisa] (1839–1921). *The Adventures of Herr Baby.* (London: Macmillan & Co., 1881). 171pp. Illustrated by Walter Crane.

A675 (title), JS36 (Anon./Children). Earliest edition in BL. Mrs. Molesworth (who began using her own name to sign her works in 1877) was one of the most popular and prolific of 19th-century children's authors; her novels for adults were less successful. See 808–809 for other works by her. A book about Mrs. Molesworth's youngest son and a trip to the south of France.

1370. Molesworth, Mrs. [Mary Louisa]. *Christmas Tree Land.* (London: Macmillan and Co., 1884). 223pp. Illustrated by Walter Crane.

A647 (author, title, illustrator), JS1534. 1st edition as described in MBC. A fantasy story for children.

1371. Molesworth, Mrs. [Mary Louisa]. *The Palace in the Garden.* (London: Hatchards, 1887). 298pp. Illustrated by Harriet M. Bennett.

A641 (author, title, illustrated), JS1535. Only 19th-century edition listed in BL. Novel for children.

1372. Molesworth, William Nassau (1816–90). *The History of England from the Year 1830–1874.* (London: Chapman and Hall, 1876). 3 vols. Library Edition.

A875, D124 (author, title, 3 vols. date, Library Edition), JS1536. Molesworth was educated at Pembroke College, Cambridge and served as perpetual curate of St. Andrew's, Manchester from 1842 to 1844 and then as vicar of St. Clement's, Spotland, Rochdale. Though *The Athenæum* chided the author for his lack of private knowledge of his subject, *The Spectator* wrote that the book was "indespensible to those who would have more than a general recollection of the events of their time."

1373. Molloy, Joseph Fitzgerald. *The Faiths of the Peoples.* (London: Ward and Downey, 1892). 2 vols.

A797 (author, title, 2 vols.), JS1537. Only edition in BL. Molloy was a miscellaneous writer with a special interest in London and the theatre. BL describes this title as "An account of the author's visits to various places of worship in London."

1374. Moncrieff, A. R. Hope, editor. *Where Shall We Go? A Guide to the Watering-places and Health Resorts of England, Scotland, Ireland, and Wales.* (London & Edinburgh: Adam & Charles Black, 1892). 348pp., plates, maps. 12th edition.

E352 ("Black's Where Shall We Go?"), JS347 (Anon./Topography). Earliest edition traced, but Dodgson probably owned an earlier edition. By 1892, he had decided where to go (to Eastbourne, where he spent all his long vacations from 1877 to 1897), but in the 1850s–70s he visited a number of "watering-places."

1375. Monro, Edward (1815–66). *The Revellers, the Midnight Sea, and the Wanderer. Three Allegories.* (London: J. Masters, 1849). 86pp.

A933 ("Munro's Allegories"), JS1572. Clearly a misprint in A933 ("Munro" for "Monro") as this is the only title in BL, BOD, or NUC that could possibly match. Only edition traced.

Monro was a prolific author of books for children. He founded the College of St. Andrews in Harrow Weald for boys from humble backgrounds.

1376. Monsell, John Samuel Bewley (1811–75). *Parish Musings: In Verse.* (London: 1855). 3rd edition.

Not in JS. In his diary for 20 August 1855 Dodgson notes, "Ordered Mansell's *Parish Musings.*" (See *Diary 1*). Despite the misspelling, this is the only possible match. This is the edition that would have been available when Dodgson placed his order. Monsell became rector of St. Nicholas, Guildford in 1870. He wrote many volumes of religious verse.

1377. Montaigne, Michel de (1533–92). *Essays.* Edition unknown.

A344 ("Montaigne's Essays in English, 3 vols."), JS1538. BL lists 3-volume editions ranging from 1685 to 1892. All but one of the editions listed in BL is either translated by Charles Cotton or based on Cotton's translation. The other is an edition of 1892 "Done into English by John Florio, anno 1615."

1378. Montgomery, Florence (1843–1923). *Misunderstood.* (London: Bentley & Son, 1874). New edition, with illustrations by George Du Maurier.

A678 (title, illustrator), JS1539. Only matching title in BL. Originally published in 1869; this is the 1st illustrated edition. A novel originally intended for adults, but widely read by children. It tells of two brothers, one largely neglected by his father. The father feels guilt and remorse when the neglected son dies in an accident. OCCL compares the relaxed attitude towards children's behavior in this book to that in *Holiday House* by Catherine Sinclair, a book Dodgson gave a copy of to Alice Liddell and her sisters. See 300 for a note on DuMaurier.

1379. [Montgomery, Florence]. *Thwarted; or, Ducks' Eggs in a Hen's Nest. A Story.* (London: Richard Bentley & Son, 1874). 255pp.

A643 (title), JS1540. Only edition in BL of the only matching title. A story for children.

1380. Montgomery, James (1771–1854). *The Poetical Works of James Montgomery.* (London: Longman, Rees, Orme, Brown, & Green, 1828). 4 vols.

Uncertain. A857 ("Montgomery's Poems, 4

Down knelt the two little brothers on the grass, baring their curly heads as they did so.

Illustration by George Du Maurier for Florence Montgomery's *Misunderstood* (item 1378).

vols."), JS1541 (listed under Robert Montgomery). Certainly the two English poets named Montgomery whose works Dodgson might have owned are Robert (1807–1855) and James (1771–1854). BL and BOD list no 4-volume editions of Robert's works and DEL states that his collected poems were published in six volumes. This is the earlier of two 4-volume editions of James's poems listed in BL, thus James seems the likely match. Montgomery was the son of a Moravian minister and was a newspaper editor for over 30 years. His religious verse was popular in its day, and his sentiments noble (for instance his condemnation of the slave trade).

1381. Moody, T. H. Croft. *A Complete Refutation of Astrology; Consisting Principally of a Series of Letters, which Appeared in "The Cheltenham Chronicle," in Reply to the Arguments of Lieut. Morrison and Others, in which its Principles are Proved to be Unphilosophical: with Additional Remarks, Notices of the Royal Nativities, and an Introduction: also Observations on the Weather Prophets, and Anecdotes of Several Astrologers.* (Cheltenham: W. Wight, 1838).

Not in JS. DAA1602 (author, title). Only edition in BL. Moody was a professor of mathematics. Dodgson's copy sold at Steven's Auction Rooms, London on 13 September 1932. It is described in DAA as "With marginal annotations throughout, entirely in the hand of Charles Lutwidge Dodgson. The title-page is signed by him, C. L. Dodgson, and opposite, in his own hand, he has written, 'The great objection to this work is that it assumes in part that Astrology is false, because unscriptural. But this last is a mere assertion, as Genesis "He made them for Signs."— With all rational inquirers this mode of attacking will be considered against Moody's Cause; and had he not given some excellent arguments besides, would have made his defeat.' On page 78, 'It is a mere trick in the Astrologer to say Fate can be arrested — if 'twere not fixed he could not calculate it...' On page 67, 'God the creator of evil and fatalism taught Amos to believe in Astrology...' With other observations throughout, relating to Kepler, Earthquakes, Earth an Animal, Moon an influence on the Weather, etc. Apparently these notes were written by Dodgson when quite a young man."

1382. Moon, George Washington (1823–1909). *The Revisers' English. With Photographs of the Revisers. A Series of Criticisms, Showing the Revisers' Violations of the Laws of the Language.* (London: Hatchards, 1882). 145pp.

B1142 (author, title, date [1892]), JS1542. Possible typographical error ("1892" for "1882") in B1142, as no 1892 edition is listed in NUC, BL, or BOD. This is the only UK edition in NUC, BOD, or BL (which lists this as 2 parts, the 2nd published in 1886). A work detailing the literary defects of the new Revised Standard Version of the Bible.

1383. Moore, Edward (1835–1916). Untitled paper on the proposed Proctorial Cycle. (Oxford: [October, 1885]).

Not in JS. Moore's response to Dodgson's paper on the same topic. Dodgson wrote a second paper on the controversy, responding to Moore's criticisms. See WMGC #178–80; *Oxford* #30–32. Moore was principal of St. Edmund Hall, Oxford.

1384. Moore, George (1803–80). *The Power of the Soul over the Body Considered in Relation to Health and Morals.* (London: Longman, Green and Co., 1868). 436pp. 6th edition.

B1143 (author, title, date), JS1544. Moore was a member of the Royal College of Surgeons. He wrote several books on health and disease as well as *The Use of the Body in Relation to the Mind*. Of the present book, the *Home Journal* wrote, "The science of the writer is skillfully popularized so as to be comprehensible and entertaining." Moore explains that by "soul" he means "that which is conscious of acting, thinking and willing." He explores issues of dreaming, memory, "The Positive Action of the Mind on the Body," and more, including a section on "Evils of Popular Phrenology."

1385. [Moore, J. B.] *Brown's Stranger's Handbook and Illustrated Guide to Salisbury Cathedral, etc.* (Salisbury: Brown and Co., 1867). 66pp.

E212 ("Salisbury Cathedral — Illustrated guide to, with 14 engravings"), JS368 (Anon./Topography). This is the only pre–1898 guide to the cathedral listed in BL. It was first printed in 1857, but this edition is listed as most closely matching the date of Dodgson's other Salisbury related guide, the guide to Old Sarum and Stonehenge (see 1755). Dodgson records a visit to Salisbury in 1872 to visit his dying uncle (and again a few days later when his uncle died) and this 1867 edition is also the last listed in BL before Dodgson's visits.

1386. Moore, J[oseph] S., editor. *The Pictorial Book of Ancient Ballad Poetry of Great Britain, Historical, Traditional, and Romantic. Together with a Selection of Modern Imitations and Translations.* (London: Bell, 1860). 872pp. "With Introductory Notices, Glossary, etc., a new edition."

A390, JS102. Dodgson's copy is in the collection of Jon Lindseth, Cleveland, OH. It is inscribed by Dodgson "Charles L. Dodgson from T. V. B. Ch. Ch. March 1860" and was a gift from his friend Thomas Vere Bayne. A collection of poetry from the 14th century, some anonymous, including works on Arthur and his knights and about 100 pages of poems on the Robin Hood legends.

1387. Moore, Thomas (1779–1852). *Lalla Rookh: An Oriental Romance.* (London: Longman, Green, Longman, & Roberts, 1861 [1860]). 381pp. With 69 illustrations from original drawings by John Tenniel, engraved on wood by the brothers Dalziel; and five ornamental pages of Persian design by T. Sulman, Jun. engraved on wood by H. N. Woods.

A873 (author, title, illustrator), JS1547. 1st Tenniel edition. Moore was an Irish poet and friend to Byron and Shelley. One of the largest published collections of book illustrations by John Tenniel, who was shortly to begin work on the illustrations for AAIW. The text is a series of poems relating tales of the far East, connected with prose sections.

1388. Moore, Thomas. *National Airs, and Other Songs, Now First Collected.* (London: Longman, Brown, Green, Longmans, and Roberts, 1858). 351pp. Includes music.

A825 ("Moore's National Airs with Music"), JS1546. This is the closest matching title in either BL or NUC and is the only British edition of this title listed in either catalogue.

1389. Moore, Thomas. *The Poetical Works of Thomas Moore.* (London: Longman, Brown, Green and Longmans, 1843). 691pp.

A546 ("Moore's Poetical Works"), JS1545. Earliest 1-volume edition listed in BL (A546 does not specify multiple volumes). Moore's poetical works were published in many editions throughout the 19th century.

1390. More, Hannah (1745–1833). *The Works of Hannah More, Including Several Pieces Never Before Published.* (London: Cadell, 1818–19). 19 vols.

A329 (author, title, 19 vols.), JS1548. Only 19-volume edition of More's works in BL. More was a prolific writer of children's books, primarily of a religious or moral nature. She also wrote for the stage, before giving it up due to her newfound Evangelistic objections. She began writing works of moral philosophy, attacking the behavior of the wealthy and the lack of religious education. She founded many Sunday Schools and oversaw the production of the famous series of *Cheap Repository Tracts* (many of which she also wrote), which provided religious instruction.

1391. Morel, Bénédict Auguste (1809–73). *Études Cliniques. Traité Théorique et Pratique des Maladies Mentales Considérées dans Leur Nature, Leur Traitment, et dans Leur Rapport avec la Médecine Légale des Aliénés.* (Nancy: Grimbolt et Veuve Raybois; Paris: J.–B. Baillière, 1852–53). 2 vols. 471, 600pp. 24 plates, folding tables.

B1144 (author, title, 2 vols., city, date), JS1549. Morel was a French doctor who later suggested Degeneracy Theory — the idea that physical, emotional, and moral maladies could all be traced to what he called "degeneration." The title of the present work translates: *Clinical Studies. Theoretical and Practical Treatise of Mental Maladies Considered in their Nature, their Treatment, and in their Relationship with the Legal Treatment of the Insane.*

1392. Morell, Charles [pseud. of James Ridley] (1736–65). *The Tales of the Genii: or, The Delightful Lesson of Horam the Son of Asmar.* (London: Henry G. Bohn, 1857). 420pp. 12 steel engravings. "Translated from the Persian by Charles Morrell." In the *Bohn's Illustrated Library* series.

E302 (author, title, series, date), JS1551, JS1735. A pastiche of the Arabian Nights tales originally published in the 18th century and frequently reprinted.

1393. Morell, John Daniel (1816–91). *An Introduction to Mental Philosophy, on the Inductive Method.* (London: Stewart Williams, [1884]). 389pp. In *Stewart's Educational Series.*

A882, B1145 (author, title, n.d.), JS1550. Only undated edition in BL, which also lists an 1862 edition. Morrell was educated at Glasgow University and in Bonn. He gave up the pastorship of a Congregationalist church to pursue philosophical matters. As inspector of schools he produced many books for educational use, but he also wrote several works on philosophy. The DNB writes, "Morrell's own position in metaphysical philosophy was that of an eclectic, with a decided leaning to idealism."

1394. Morell, J[ohn] R[eynell]. *Euclid Simplified, Compiled from the Most Important French Works, Approved by the University of Paris and the Minister of Public Instruction.* (London, Beccles [printed]: 1875).

Not in JS. Dodgson examines this book is his *Euclid and His Modern Rivals* (137–48). Morell was Inspector of Schools and author of several books, including travel books.

1395. Morgan, Henry Arthur (1830–1912). *A Collection of Problems and Examples in Mathematics, Selected from the Jesus College Examination Papers: with Answers.* (Cambridge: Macmillan, 1858). 190pp.

D125 (author, title, city, date), JS1553. D125 notes Dodgson's signature. Only edition in BL.

1396. Morgan, Lewis Henry (1818–81). *The American Beaver and his Works.* (Philadelphia: J. B. Lippincott, 1868). 330pp. 23 black and white plates, folding map, and appendices, including Samuel Hearne's article on the beaver.

A824 (author, title), JS1552. Only edition in BL or BOD. Morgan was a lawyer turned anthropologist. A classic ecological work regarded as one of the earliest modern studies of the behavior of a single species and the earliest American work of comparative psychology. "There is no animal, below man, in the entire range of the mammalia," Morgan writes, "which offers to our investigation such a series of works, or presents such remarkable materials for the study and illustration of animal psychology." Dodgson's epic nonsense poem *The Hunting of the Snark* includes a Beaver as a character. The

speculation as to the gender of that Beaver should perhaps be colored by Morgan's assertion that the mother is the most important member of the Beaver colony.

1397. Morley, Henry (1822–94). *The Chicken Market and Other Fairy Tales.* (London: Cassell, Petter and Galpin, [1877]). 362pp. New edition. Illustrated by C[harles] H. Bennett.

A646 (title), JS42 (Anon./Children). Earliest edition in BL, and it seems likely that the Bennett illustrations would have appealed to Dodgson as Bennett illustrated two of Dodgson's own poems in *The Train* (see LCP). Morley was Professor of English Literature at University College, London, and at one time assisted Dickens in editing *Household Words*. He wrote many biographies, an unfinished history of English literature (in 11 volumes) and other works. This is a collection of fanciful tales, one of which, "Adventures in Skitzland" might be considered an early *Alice* imitation. It concerns a man who digs a hole so deep in his garden that eventually "the ground broke beneath me in a hollow, and I fell a considerable distance." He arrives in a strange land in which he observes various animated but detached body parts and is eventually put on trial for murder. Convicted, he is fired out of a large cannon and passes through his hole back to his garden to discover that less than a day has passed. Dodgson was a friend of the Morley family, whom he first met on the Isle of Wight in 1874 (see *Letters*, 228).

1398. Morley, Henry. *The Dream of the Lilybell, Tales and Poems; with Translations of the "Hymns to Night" from the German of Novalis and Jean Paul's "Death of an Angel."* (London: Sherwood, Gilbert and Piper, 1845). 164pp.

A838 (author, title), JS1554. Only edition in BL or BOD. Novalis was the pseudonym of German writer Baron Friedrich Leopold von Hardenberg (1772–1801).

1399. Morley, Henry. *The Journal of a London Playgoer from 1851 to 1866.* (London: Routledge, 1866). 384pp.

A670 (title), JS291 (Anon./Theatre). Earliest edition of the only matching title in BL. Dodgson's theatre-going in London began in 1855, during the period covered by this journal. Morley was theatre critic for *The Examiner* from

Charles H. Bennett illustrates "Adventures in Skitzland" (item 1397).

1851 to 1866 and his book is an important source of information on Victorian theatre.

1400. Morris, Charles (1833–1922), editor. *Half-hours with the Best American Authors.* (Philadelphia: J. B. Lippincott Company, 1887). 4 vols.

A331 (title, 4 vols.), JS1382 (listed under Charles Knight). Only dated edition traced of the only matching title traced. The mistake in JS1382 comes from the assumption that Charles Knight, editor of *Half-hours with the Best Authors* (see 1167) also edited this collection of American writings. However, neither BL nor BOD list any such work. An undated London edition published by Frederick Warne may have preceded 1898 and thus be more likely than the more common Philadelphia edition. A collection of American writing.

1401. [Morris, Lewis] (1833–1907). *The Epic of Hades.* (London: Henry S. King & Co., 1876–77). 2 vols. 157; 76, 54pp.

A864 (title, edition, 2 vols.), JS1557. Vol. 1 contained what became Book 2 of the complete work, vol. 2, Books 1 and 3. Morris was a Welshman educated at Oxford and helped found the University of Wales. OCEL describes his poetry as popular though mediocre. This is a poem in blank verse in which Morris created monologues for characters from Greek mythology.

1402. [**Morris**, Lewis]. *Songs of Two Worlds.* (London: H. S. King & Co., 1871–75). 1st–3rd series.

A356 (title), JS390 (Anon./Unclassified). Three series were published between 1871 and 1875; volumes published in 1875 and 1878 state 3rd series, but may contain all 3. There is no indication which series Dodgson owned. Together with *The Epic of Hades* (see above) this was Morris' chief poetical work.

1403. Morris, Richard (1833–94). *Specimens of Early English Selected from the Chief English Authors A.D. 1250–A.D. 1400, with Grammatical Introduction, Notes, and Glossary.* (Oxford: Clarendon Press, 1867). 492pp. In the *Clarendon Press Series*.

A301, D127 (author, title, city, date), JS1558. Morris was an English philologist and editor. He published 12 books for the Early English Text Society, edited editions of Chaucer and Spenser, and wrote works on early English grammar.

1404. Morris, William (1834–96). *The Defence of Guenevere, and Other Poems.* (London: Bell & Daldy, 1858). 248pp. 1st edition.

A466 (author, title, edition, date), JS1559. Morris was a well-known writer, designer, and artist connected to nearly every facet of the world of Victorian arts and literature. He was inspired by Arthurian themes in much of his work, as here in his first volume of poetry.

1405. Morton, John Maddison (1811–1891). *Away with Melancholy; A Farce in One Act.* (London: Thomas Hailes Lacy, [1854]). 19pp.

Not in JS. Dodgson records several occasions in his diary when he read this play aloud as part of evening entertainments (see *Diary 1–3*). He first saw the play on 22 June 1855 as part of his first recorded visit to the London legitimate theatre. He purchased a copy on 24 March 1856. This is the traced edition closest in date to Dodgson's purchase. Morton was a prolific author of plays. This play was adapted from a French play by Delacour, de la Roûnat and Montjoye, entitled, "Un Homme entre deux Airs."

1406. Motherwell, William (1797–1835). *Minstrelsy Ancient and Modern, with an Historical Introduction and Notes.* (Glasgow: J. Wylie, 1827). 390pp. With an appendix containing the music of several ballads.

A479, D128 (author, title, city, date), JS1560. D128 notes Dodgson's initials. Motherwell was a Scottish newspaper editor. A collection of ballads.

1407. Motherwell, William. *The Poetical Works of William Motherwell, with Memoir, by J. M'Conechy.* (Glasgow: David Robertson, 1849). 318pp. 3rd edition, greatly enlarged of Motherwell's *Poems, Narrative and Lyrical.*

A838 (author, title, date), JS1561. Preface states that "The poems added to this edition have been selected by Mr. [William] Kennedy [1799–1871], and are published under his express authority." Originally issued in 1832, this collection of poems includes Motherwell's best known, "Jeanie Morrison."

1408. Moultrie, John (1799–1874). *The Dream of Life, Lays of the English Church, and Other Poems.* (London: Pickering, 1843). 368pp.

B1147 (author, title, publisher, date), JS1563. Moultrie, a London-born poet, became rector at Rugby in 1825 and held the living for the rest of his life. He would, therefore, have been rector during Dodgson's tenure at Rugby School in the 1840s.

1409. Moultrie, John. *Poems.* (London: William Pickering, 1838). 359pp. 2nd edition.

A359, B1146 (author, title, edition, publisher, date), JS1562.

1410. Mountford, William (1816–85). *Miracles, Past and Present.* (Boston: Fields, Osgood and Co., 1870). 512pp.

A900 (title), JS183 (Anon./Occult). Only edition in BL. The author is described in BL as a "Unitarian Minister." Covers issues of science and the supernatural, including miracles, spiritualism, signs, pneumatology, and the Church.

1411. Mozley, James Bowling (1813–78). *Eight Lectures on Miracles Preached Before the University of Oxford in the Year 1865, on* *the Foundation of the Late Rev. J. Bampton.* (London: Rivingtons, 1865). 390pp.

A803, B1148 (author, title, date), JS1565. Mozley was a fellow of Magdalen College, Oxford, and was active in the Oxford Movement, though he did not follow Newman and others to Rome. Unlike many High Churchmen, he agreed with the Gorham decision (see 1534), and resigned his editorship of *The Christian Remembrancer* in the wake of that decision. *Contemporary Review* wrote, "In the deeper qualities of scientific theology, the book is thoroughly worthy of the highest reputation." Dodgson met Mozley at least twice in 1873 (see *Diary* 6) and Mozley also served as a canon at Dodgson's college, Christ Church from 1871 to 1878. In 1873 Dodgson successfully lobbied Mozley to appoint his cousin, Arthur Wilcox, to a vacant curacy.

1412. Mozley, James Bowling. *Essays, Historical and Theological.* (London: Rivingtons, 1878). 2 vols. 442, 452pp.

A337 ("Mozley's Essays, 2 vols."), JS1564. Earliest edition in BL. This could, theoretically, be essays by Anne Mozley, (sister to James) published in two series in Edinburgh by Blackwood in 1864–65. However, Dodgson owned several other works by J. B. Mozley, and knew Mozley personally (see above). The present collection includes 12 long essays contributed to *British Critic* 1843, *Christian Remembrancer* 1844–54, and *Bentley's Quarterly* 1859.

1413. Mozley, James Bowling. *Sermons. Parochial and Occasional.* (London: Rivingtons, 1879). 355pp.

A757 (author, title), JS1566. Earliest edition listed in BL or BOD.

1414. Mozley, James Bowling. *Sermons Preached Before the University of Oxford and on Various Occasions.* (London: Rivingtons, 1876). 304pp. 2nd edition.

A799, D129 (author, title, date), JS1567, JS1568. D129 notes Dodgson's initials and describes this as a "Library Edition." This is the only 1876 edition in BL or BOD.

1415. Muir, William (1819–1905). *Mahomet and Islam.* (London: The Religious Tract Society, 1895). 256pp. 3rd edition.

B1149 (author, title, date), JS1569. In 1858, Muir published *Life of Mahomet and History of Islam To the Era of the Hegira. With Introductory Chapters on the Original Sources for the Bi-ography of Mahomet, and on the Pre-Islamite History of Arabia*; as early as 1883 the Religious Tract Society published his work as *Mahomet & Islam. A Sketch of the Prophet's Life from Original Sources, and a Brief Outline of his Religion*, an abridgement of his earlier work. This work is a reprint of the 1883 edition.

1416. Mulhall, Michael G. (1836–1900). *Mulhall's Dictionary of Statistics.* (London: G. Routledge and Sons, 1884 [1883]). 504pp.

A328 (author, title), JS1570. Earliest edition in BL. Mulhall was a member of the Royal Statistical Society. The first statistical dictionary in any language. A standard economic reference and, because it contains statistical information on a wide variety of areas (from cheese to disease, agriculture to prostitution), also provides an excellent window into 19th-century life.

1417. Munk, William (1816–98). *Euthanasia: or, Medical Treatment in Aid of an Easy Death.* (London: Longmans & Co., 1887). 105pp.

B1150 (author, title, date), JS1571. A book largely out of synch with the medical world of 1887, but surprisingly relevant today. Munk, an eminent physician, writes of death as a phenomenon, arguing that it need not be painful and frightening. His section on "symptoms and modes" helps identify the point at which curative care should be replaced by what today is called palliative care, and, in his concluding section on "management" he writes what must certainly be the first handbook of palliative care, addressing issues of appropriate drug use to manage symptoms as well as creating an appropriate environment for the terminally ill, etc.

1418. Munro, John Mackintosh Mackay. *Spiritual Dynamics.* (Paisley: A. Gardner, 1886.) 40pp.

A889 (title), JS331 (Anon./Theology). Only edition in BL or BOD of the only pre–1898 matching title.

1419. Mure, Reginald James (b. 1842), Henry Bull and Charles Brodrick Scott (1825–94), editors. *Lusus Alteri Westmonasterienses, Sive Prologi et Epilogi ad Fabulas in Sti. Petri Collegio Actas, qui Exstabant Collecti et Justa, Quoad Licuit,*

Annorum serie Ordinati. Quibus accedit Declamationum et Epigrammatum Delectus. (Oxford: J. Parker and Sons, 1863–67). 2 vols. Curantibus J. Mure H. Bull ... C. B. Scott.

B1288 (editors, title, date, city, 2 vols.), JS1574. Title translates *Other Westminster Amusements, or Prologues and Epilogues to Stories Done in St. Peter's College, which Appear Collected and In Due Order, As Far As Is Possible, Chronologically. To Which A Selection of Declamations and Epigrams is Added.*

1420. Murray, C[harles] [O]liver (1842–1924), illustrator. *Merry Elves; or, Little Adventures in Fairyland.* (London: Seeley, Jackson, & Halliday, 1874). 95pp. 24 illustrations by Murray.

A530 (title), JS65 (Anon./Children's). Only edition in BL. No other titles match precisely and other similar matches are all sheet music. A530 is a lot of illustrated books. Four fairy stories involving elves. Dodgson presented a copy of this book to Prince Charles, Duke of Albany (see *Letters*, 749).

1421. [Murray, Eustace Clare Grenville] (1824–81). *Six Months in the Ranks; or the Gentleman Private.* (London: Smith, Elder & Co., 1881). 363pp.

A596, B1218 (title, date), JS1575. An early and regular contributor to *Vanity Fair* and other well known periodicals, Murray established a reputation for candor mixed with humor and innuendo, a kind of yellow journalism, which cost him numerous lawsuits and finally exile to France. Murray was the author of many works, the majority of which were published anonymously or pseudonymously, including novels, travel literature, social satire and history. This work is an autobiographical account of Murray's experience as a nobleman compelled by circumstance to enlist in the ranks of the Royal Artillery.

1422. [Murray, Eustace Clare Grenville]. *Strange Tales. From "Vanity Fair." By Silly Billy.* (London: Vanity Fair Office, [1882]). 240pp. 1st edition.

A655, JS78 (Anon./Children). Earliest edition in BL. A collection of humorous social sketches. Dodgson contributed his word game "Doublets" to *Vanity Fair* from 1879 to 1881 and was friends with the founder and editor of *Vanity Fair*, Thomas Gibson Bowles (see 206).

1423. [Murray, John], publisher. *A Handbook of Travel-talk: Being a Collection of Questions, Phrases, and Vocabularies, in English, German, French, and Italian; Intended to Serve as Interpreter to English Travellers Abroad, or Foreigners Visiting England.* (London: John Murray, 1865). 358pp. 24th thousand, carefully revised. By the editors of the Handbooks.

E329 ("English–German–French–Italian Handbook of Travel-talk, Murray"), JS350 (Anon./Topography). This title was printed, under slightly varying names, from 1844 until 1927. This edition seems a likely guess as it is the closest edition listed in BL and BOD to Dodgson's one adventure in foreign travel, his trip to Russia (which included stops in Germany and France) in 1867.

1424. Murray, John Carrick. *Smoking: When Injurious, When Innocuous, When Beneficial. With Compendium of the Temperaments, Shewing how they are Influenced by Tobacco.* (Newcastle-upon-Tyne: 1876). 112pp. 3rd edition.

E193 (author, title, date), JS1576. The author was a physician who also wrote a book on snuff-taking.

1425. Napheys, George Henry (1842–76). *Physical Life of Women. Advice to the Maiden, Wife, and Mother.* (London: Homœopathic Publishing Co., [1895]). 320pp.

A570 (title), JS403 (Anon./Women). Only matching title in BL. Published in Philadelphia by H. C. Watts as early as 1878; this is the only London edition traced. Napheys was an American physician. Includes "The Dangers of Puberty," "Knowledge is Power," "Concerning Long Engagements," "How to Choose a Husband," "Signs of Fruitful Conjunction," "Shall Husband and Wife Occupy the Same Room and Bed?," "Pregnancy," "How to Preserve the Form After Child-Birth," "Nursing," "Wet-nursing by Virgins," "The Single Life," and more.

1426. Nasir al-Dîn, Shah of Persia (reigned 1848–96). *The Diary of H. M. the Shah of Persia During his Tour through Europe in and in the Year 1873. A Verbatim Translation.* Translated by J. W. Redhouse. (London: Murray, 1874). 427pp.

B1219 (title, translator), JS1723 (listed under Redhouse). Only edition in BL. The Shah traveled from Tehran to Astrakhan, through Russia, Germany, Belgium, England, France, Switzerland, Italy, Austria, Turkey and Georgia. In his diary he describes peoples, agriculture, industry, museums, natural environment, etc.

1427. Nesfield, John Collinson, editor. *The Anglo-Oriental Series of English Readers.* (London: Macmillan and Co., 1895).

E129 (editor, title, date), JS1578. Nesfield took his M.A. at Merton College, Oxford in 1862 and served as a civil servant in India. He was the author of works on English grammar. BOD lists this as "Part 5." In a letter to his publisher Macmillan (4 May 1895) discussing the look of his forthcoming *Curiosa Mathematica*, Dodgson wrote, "I like the look of your *Anglo-Oriental Reader* better than the Clarendon Shakespeare-plays: but the sides are not *stiff* enough for a book of 200 pages."

1428. Nevius, John Livingston (1829–93). *Demon Possession and Allied Themes. Being an Inductive Study of Phenomena of Our Own Times.* (London: G. Redway, 1897). 520pp. With an introduction by Rev. F. F. Ellinwood and an index: bibliographical, biblical, pathological and general.

A311 (title), JS181 (Anon./Occult). Only edition in BL. Nevius was a missionary who here presents his opinions on demon possession drawn largely from his experience in China but also with chapters on demon possession in India, Japan, and Christian countries.

1429. Newland, Henry Garrett (1804–60). *South Church Union Lectures. Lectures on Tractarianism, Delivered in the Town Hall, Brighton.* (London: Joseph Masters, 1852). 4 parts. 170pp.

E232 (author, title, date), JS1579. E232 notes that this has "a note at the end in Lewis Carroll's handwriting." Newland was rector and vicar of Westbourne and argues for High Church "Tractarian" (see 1431) reform in these three lectures.

1430. Newman, Francis William (1805–97). *The Difficulties of Elementary Geometry, Especially those which Concern the Straight Line, the Plane, and the Theory of Parallels.* (London: W. Ball and Co., 1841). 143pp.

E394 (author, title, date), JS1587. E394 notes that this has the autographs of "R[obinson] Duckworth and Lewis Carroll." Duckworth was Dodgson's friend who accompanied him on the famous 4 July 1862 river trip with the Liddell children. Newman was educated at Worcester College, Oxford, and resigned his fellowship at Balliol because he could not subscribe to the 39 Articles. From 1846–63 he served as Professor of Latin at University College, London. He wrote on a wide variety of topics, including mathematics and logic. MOT notes that this variety is "explained by the violent interruption in his original career, as detailed in his *Phases of Faith*." Dodgson published his own book on parallels, *Curiosa Mathematica Part I A New Theory of Parallels*, in 1888.

1431. Newman, [John Henry] (1801–90). *Apologia Pro Vita Sua Being A Reply to a Pamphlet Entitled "What, Then, Does Dr. Newman Mean?"* (London: Longman, Green, Longman, Roberts, and Green, 1864). 430pp. plus 127pp. appendix, notes, and postscriptum.

A780 (author, title), JS1580. 1st edition. As vicar of the University Church of St. Mary's Oxford, Newman was a guiding force behind the religious revival known as the Oxford Movement. He wrote many of the "Tracts for the Times," the series that earned the revivalists the name "Tractarians." He eventually left the English Church and converted to Roman Catholicism, rising to the rank of cardinal. Replying to a remark by Charles Kingsley in *Macmillan's Magazine*, Newman wrote this theological autobiography, probably his most famous and influential work. In it he discusses his early thoughts, especially with reference to the Oxford Movement. Dodgson almost met Newman in 1880 when arrangements were attempted for Dodgson to take a photograph of the cardinal, but the plans fell through. A letter from Newman to "Helen" commenting on Dodgson's *Snark* and the "Easter Greeting" contained therein is reprinted in *Letters* (250–51).

1432. Newman, John Henry. *Essay in Aid of a Grammar of Assent.* (London: Burn, Oates, & Co., 1870). 485pp.

A516 (author, title), JS1581. Earliest edition listed in BL or BOD. ODCC says of this work, "It is especially remarkable for its differentiation between real and notional assent, its analysis of the function of the conscience in our knowledge of God and of the role of 'illative sense', i.e. the faculty of judging from given facts by processes outside the limits of strict logic, in reaching religious certitude."

1433. Newman, John Henry. *Lectures on Certain Difficulties Felt by Anglicans in Submitting to the Catholic Church.* (London: Burns & Lambert, 1850). 325pp.

A794 ("Newman on Anglican Difficulties"), JS1583. Earliest edition in BL of the only possible match. In his preface to these lectures, intended to smooth the path from Anglicanism to Roman Catholicism for those who chose that route, Newman writes, "The very first objection which he [i.e. the author] took on starting [these lectures], the alleged connection of the Movement of 1833 with the National Church, has afforded matter for the greater part of the course; and, before he had well finished the discussion of it, it was getting time to think of concluding, and that, in any such way as would give a character of completeness to the whole. Else, after the seventh Lecture, it had been his intention to proceed to the consideration of the alleged claim of the National Church on the allegiance of its members; of the alleged duty of our remaining in the communion in which we were born; of the alleged danger of trusting to reason; of the alleged right of the National Church to forbid doubt about its own claims; of the alleged uncertainty which necessarily attends the claims of any religion whatever; of the tests of certainty; of the relation of faith to reason; of the legitimate force of objections; and of the matter of Catholic evidence."

1434. Newman, John Henry. *A Letter to the Rev. E. B. Pusey, D.D. on his Recent Eirenicon.* (London: Longmans, Green, Reader, & Dyer, 1866). 159pp.

C7 (author, title), JS1694 (not listed separately). Earliest edition in BL. One of 11 items by or related to Pusey bound together in a volume and described in C7 as "Eleven Sermons and Pamphlets, 1843–1878." For a complete list of items enumerated in C7 see 1591. Dodgson owned a copy of Pusey's *Eirenicon* (see 1434) in which Pusey makes a theological argument for the union of the English and Roman churches. Newman praises Pusey's intent but then goes on to enumerate theological differences between Catholics and Anglicans, particularly with regard to the Virgin Mary.

1435. Newman, John Henry. *Loss and Gain.* (London: James Burns, 1848). 386pp. 1st edition.

A870, B1151 (author, title, edition, date), JS1582. Later editions were titled *Loss and Gain, or, The Story of a Convert.* In this novel of conversion Newman wrote that his gain of Roman Catholicism would be accompanied by his loss of his beloved Oxford.

1436. Newman, John Henry. *Parochial Sermons.* (London: J. G. & F. Rivington, 1834–42). 6 vols.

A762 (author, title, 6 vols.), JS1584. Earliest edition in BL or BOD. These sermons, preached from the pulpit of St. Mary's Oxford, were widely influential and largely based on a careful study of the early church fathers as advocated by the Tractarians.

1437. Newman, John Henry. *Selection Adapted to the Seasons of the Ecclesiastical Year from the Parochial & Plain Sermons of John Henry Newman, B.D., Sometime Vicar of St. Mary's, Oxford.* (London: Rivingtons, 1878). 468pp. 1st edition.

A757 ("Newman's Sermons for the Seasons"), JS1585. Only pre–1898 edition of the only matching title in BL. A selection of Newman's St. Mary's sermons (see above).

1438. Newman, John Henry, E. B. Pusey, Frederick Oakeley (1802–80). *Tract 90: Tracts for the Times. Remarks On Certain Passages in the Thirty Nine Articles* with *A Letter Addressed to the Rev. J.W. Jelf in Explanation of No. 90 by the Author* with *The Articles Treated On in Tract 90 Reconsidered and Their Interpretation Vindicated in a Letter to Rev. R. W. Jelf* with *The Subject of Tract XC Historically Examined to which is Added, The Case of Bishop Montague in the Reign of King James I.* (Oxford: John Henry Parker, 1841). 4 tracts bound as 1. 84, 30, 217, 87pp.

Details uncertain. A794 ("Tract 90 with Letters"), JS1586. The first two items by Newman, the 2nd letter to Jelf by E. B. Pusey, and the last item by Oakeley. BOD lists a privately printed item under the heading "Letters and Tract 90," which, in its detailed description, lists only 1 letter and seems to be a collection of separately published items bound together. This particular combination of titles not listed in BL, but the present description is taken from a copy in the author's collection. It seems a likely match to A794. Tract 90 was the last of the "Tracts for the Times." In it Newman argues that nothing in the 39 Articles (the articles of Anglican faith) is contravened by Roman Catholicism. It was this tract, especially, that caused many to believe that the leaders of the Oxford Movement advocated a return to Rome. The tract was highly controversial and condemned by the Hebdomadal Board of Oxford University and the Bishop of Oxford. Dodgson certainly owned *Tract XC*; which letters he also owned is a matter of conjecture.

1439. Newton, Isaac (1642–1727). *Sir Isaac Newton's Enumeration of Lines of the Third Order, Generation of Curves by Shadows, Organic Description of Curves, and Construction of Equations by Curves.* (London: H. G. Bohn, 1860). 140pp. Originally printed as an appendix to the *Treatise on Optics.* Translated, with notes and examples, by Christopher Rice Mansel Talbot. With plates.

D132 (author, title, city, date), JS1588. D132 notes Dodgson's signature.

1440. Nichols, Thomas Low (1815–1901). *A Biography of the Brothers Davenport. With some Account of the Physical and Psychical Phenomena which have Occurred in their Presence, in America and Europe.* (London: Saunders, Otley and Co., 1864). 360pp.

B1024 (author, title, date), JS1589. Together with his wife, Mary Grove Nichols, Thomas was an influential American social reformer who dabbled in sexual liberation, women's rights, spiritualism, medical writing, and other areas. A biography of Ira Erastus Davenport (1839–1911) and William Henry Harrison Davenport (1841–1877), two of the most famous mediums of the 19th century. Their psychic stage show was both popular and controversial. Men as prominent as Harry Houdini dismissed their abilities as sleight of hand. Ira Davenport wrote to Houdini in 1909, "We never in public affirmed our belief in spiritualism, that we regarded as no business of the public, nor did we offer our entertainment as the results of sleight of hand, nor on the other hand as spiritualism, we let our friends and foes settle that as best they could between themselves." See also 1443.

1441. Nichols, Thomas Low. *How to Cook. The Principles and Practice of Scientific, Economic, Aygienic, and Æsthetic Gastronomy.* (London: 1872).

E198 (author, title, date), JS1590. E198 notes this has Dodgson's initials. An 1873 edition (139pp.) was published by Longmans Green, but no 1872 edition has been traced.

1442. Nichols, Thomas Low. *Human Physiology the Basis of Sanitary and Social Science.* (London: Trübner & Co., 1872). 480pp. Illustrated.

A551 ("Nickols' Human Physiology"), JS1591. Clearly a typographical error in A551 as no such title is listed in BL. The present title is certainly the one referred to. Also published in 1872 by William Reeves. These are the earliest editions traced.

1443. Nichols, Thomas Low, editor. *Supramundane Facts in the Life of Rev. Jesse Babcock Ferguson Including Twenty Years' Observation of Preternatural Phenomena.* (London: F. Pitman, 1865). 264pp. Edited by T. L. Nichols.

D181 (author, title, city, date), JS1592. Ferguson (1819–70) was a minister and orator who earned his reputation in the ante-bellum American South. Pastor at the Church of Christ in Nashville, TN, his conversion to Unitarianism forced him from his pulpit and his belief in spiritualism kept him from receiving other calls. He met the Davenport Brothers (see 1440) in New York and agreed to accompany them on a European tour during which he would deliver lectures on spiritualism before their act. He eventually came to believe that their act demeaned spiritualism. This biography was prepared by a group of English spiritualists in preparation for Ferguson's tour with the Davenports.

1444. [Nicolas, Nicholas Harris] (1799–1848), editor. *The Cynosure. Being Select Passages from the Most Distinguished Writers.* (London: William Pickering, 1837). 257pp.

Not in JS. DAA893 (title, city, publisher, date), DAA933, DAA2031. Dodgson's copy, with his signature, was offered at Anderson Auction Co., New York on 18–22 January 1915;

at Anderson Galleries, New York on 2–3 December 1918; and at City Book Auctions, New York on 1 January 1941. DAA933 notes that this copy included a note stating only 20 copies were issued. Harris was a barrister who spent much of his time as an antiquary and historian.

1445. [**Nister**, Ernest] (*fl.* 1891–1900), producer. *Changing Pictures. A Book of Transformation Pictures.* (London: E. Nister; New York: E. P. Dutton, [1894]). 16pp. 6 full-page changing chromolithographic illustrations. Produced in Nuremburg, Germany.

E38 (title, physical description of plates), JS41 (Anon./Children). Almost certainly the same as A542 (*Transformation Pictures*) which is listed separately as JS81 (Anon./Children's). Though generally dated 1894, a copy inscribed 1893 has been recorded. Dodgson's copy is in HAC and has the gothic stamp on the front paste-down. Nister was an influential producer of moveable books for children. This title is an example of one of his "venetian blind' production, in which colored pictures, by means of pulling on a tab, are transformed into different scenes. The illustrated cover includes a color illustration by Beatrix Potter of a rabbit peering around a door at a basket of carrots and turnips in the snow. Each picture is accompanied by a poem.

1446. Noel, Roden Berkeley Wriothesley (1834–94). *Beatrice and other Poems.* (London: Macmillan and Co., 1868). 324pp.

A839, B1152 (author, title, date), JS1593. Second volume of verse by the prolific but mediocre Noel who was a close friend of John Addington Symonds.

1447. Norris, John Pilkington (1823–91). *Easy Lessons Addressed to Candidates for Confirmation.* (London: Rivingtons, 1877). 108pp. With the text of the Order.

E186 (author, title, date), JS1595. Norris was a clergyman, educated at Trinity College, Cambridge, who rose to the rank of Archdeacon of Bristol.

1448. Norris, John Pilkington. *Rudiments of Theology. A First Book for Students.* (London: 1876).

A598 (author, title), JS1594. Earliest edition in BL.

1449. Northcote, James (1746–1831). *Fables Original and Selected.* (London: J.

Murray, 1833). 248pp. 2nd series. Edited by E. S. Rogers. Illustrated.

B1153 (author, title, series, date), JS1596. B1153 notes that this book is "illustrated by 280 engravings on wood." Northcote was an English portrait painter and student of Joshua Reynolds. A sometime writer, he assembled this collection in his old age, adding some of his own fables to more traditional ones, and adding his own moralizing. The chief attractions of the book are the illustrations, which are oddities—Northcote clipped details from his collection of prints (mostly of animals) and had William Hervey (1796–1866) adapt these drawings for woodcuts.

1450. Northcote, Stafford Henry (1818–87). *Lectures and Essays.* (Edinburgh: W. Blackwood & Sons, 1887). 465pp. Edited by Cecilia Frances Northcote.

A336, D133 (author, title, city, date), JS1597. Northcote was a Conservative M.P. who, on Disraeli's elevation to the House of Lords in 1876, became leader of the opposition in the Commons. He himself became a Lord in 1885. Dodgson sent him a copy of his *Principles of Parliamentary Representation* in 1884. This collection was edited by his wife in the year of his death.

1451. Norton, Caroline Elizabeth Sarah [née Sheridan, afterwards Lady Stirling-Maxwell] (1808–77). *The Lady of La Garaye.* (Cambridge: Macmillan, 1862 [1861]). 128pp.

D134 (author, "The Lady of Garaze," city, date), JS1598. Clearly a typographical error in D134. This is the only possible match in BL. 1st–4th editions published in 1862. A gifted writer, renowned for her beauty, Miss Sheridan published her first work at age 17. She wrote both poetry and prose, and the *Quarterly* called her "the Byron of her sex." Her first marriage, to George Norton (by all accounts a scoundrel) ended in a court case and a 40-year estrangement. Following Norton's death in 1875, she married her longtime friend, Sir William Stirling-Maxwell, but she lived only three months after her second wedding. Of this collection of verse, *The Athenæum* wrote, "The author has not lost the cunning of her hand for writing verse that moves in measured music with a stately flow."

1452. Nugent, Thomas (1700?–72). *Nugent's Pocket Dictionary of the French and English Languages.* (London: 1844).

D135 (author, title, date), JS1599. D135 notes, "With inscription: — 'Charles Lutwidge Dodgson, School House, Rugby.'" No exact match traced but the 24th edition of 1841 and the 27th edition of 1850 were both published by Longman. The 24th edition was "carefully revised and arranged" by John Charles Tarver. Nugent was born in Ireland and spent much of his career in the employ of London booksellers. He wrote and translated many works. This dictionary was first published in 1767 and was still held in high regard (and was still in print) as late as the 1850s.

1453. *Nursery Rhymes*. Details unknown.
A594 ("Nursery Rhymes"), JS69 (Anon./ Children's).

1454. Nuttall, Peter Austin. *Nuttall's Standard Dictionary of the English Language*. (London: F. Warne & Co., 1887). 816pp. New edition, extended by James Wood.
A326 ("Nuttall's Standard Dictionary"), JS1600. Earliest edition in BL under this title. Nuttall's work began as a re-editing of Johnson's dictionary.

1455. Oakley, Charles Edward (1832–65). *El Dorado, ein Unbekanntes Land. A Prize Poem, Recited in Rugby School, June 29, 1849*. (Rugby: Crossley and Billington, 1849). 10pp.
D60 (author, title, city, date), JS1602. The author went on from Rugby to a successful career at Pembroke and Magdalen Colleges, Oxford and eventually became rector of St. Paul's, Covent Garden, London. Dodgson was a student at Rugby School from 1846 through December of 1849 and so may have been acquainted with the author and probably was present at the recitation.

1456. Oedipus [pseud.]. *Three Problems by Oedipus*. (London: Harrison & Sons, 1895).
E102 (title, pseudo., date), F147, JS936. F147 describes this as "with initials, C. L. D. May 1896." A copy with Dodgson's initials and the date "May, 1895" was offered by Anderson Galleries, New York on 23–24 April 1923 (DAA1010). Undoubtedly this is the same as E102 and one reference has an error in transcribing the date. Mathematical problems on the cube and fifth root of 2, the circle and inscribed polygons, and the trisection of an angle. E102 attributes this

to Dodgson and it is listed as doubtful in WMGC (#364). Abeles states that "it is quite clear from the notation and terminology used that Dodgson is not its author" (*Math*, 117).

1457. Ogilby, John (1600–76) and John Owen. *Britannia Depicta, or, Ogilby Improv'd, a Correct Copy of Ogilby's Actual Survey of all Direct and Principal Crossroads in England and Wales, with a Full Description of all the Cities by J[ohn] Owen [and] Maps of all Ye Counties of South Britain*. (London: 1859). [Engraved] by E[manuel] Bowen.
B968 (engraver, title, date), JS540 (listed under Bowen). Cartographer John Ogilby saw his road map of England and Wales published in 1675. It was one of the first comprehensive road maps of Britain. Emanuel Bowen's (d. 1767) engravings appeared under the title *Britannia Depicta, or, Ogilby Improv'd* at least as early as 1720.

1458. Oldham, Charles Frederick (1832–1913). *What is Malaria? And Why is it Most Intense in Hot Climates? An Enquiry into the Nature and Cause of the So-called Marsh Poison, with Remarks on the Principles to be Observed for the Preservation of Health in Tropical Climates and Malarious Districts*. (London: Lewis, 1871). 186pp.
D136 (author, title, city, date), JS1603. Oldham was an army surgeon who served in India.

1459. Oliver, George (1841–1915). *Plain Facts on Vaccination*. (London: Simpkin Marshall, 1871). 74pp.
E165 (author, title, date), JS1604. Oliver was a member of the Royal College of Physicians. In 1877, Dodgson exchanged letters in *The Eastbourne Chronicle* with William Hume-Rothery on the subject of vaccination, Dodgson disputing Hume-Rothery's anti-vaccination arguments (LCP, #65–67).

1460. O'Neil, Henry Nelson (1817–80). *Two Thousand Years Hence*. (London: Chapman and Hall, [1867]). 351pp. Illustrated by J. Gilbert.
D137 (author, title, city, date), JS1601. A work of Utopian literature.

1461. [O'Reilly, Eleanor Grace]. *Daisy's Companions; or, Scenes from Child Life*.

(London: Bell & Daldy, [1869]). 332pp. "By the author of *Grandmother's Nest*."

A934 (title), JS54 (Anon./Children). Only edition in BL. O'Reilly was a prolific author of books for children.

1462. O'Reilly, Eleanor Grace. *Deborah's Drawer*. (London: Bell & Daldy, 1871 [1870]). With illustrations.

A934 (title, illustrated), JS55 (Anon./Children). Only edition in BL. Book for children.

1463. O'Reilly, Mrs. Robert [Eleanor Grace]. *Doll World; or, Play and Earnest*. (London: Bell & Daldy, 1872 [1871]). 324pp. With illustrations by C. A. Saltmarsh.

A934 (title, illustrated), JS56 (Anon./Children). Only British edition traced. A book for children about the world of dolls and childish imaginations. A pair of excerpts should show how the writing is possibly Carroll-inspired and how the subject relates to the *Alice* books: "My governess complained to me today of Rose's dreadful fits of passion; she threw the geography book in the fire because—because—let me see what *was* it? Oh! Because Miss Laurel said Rouen was in France, and Rosie insisted that it was not; and, when she was shown the place, declared it had got there since the last lesson, for it always used to be in Spain." "There *were* a great many more worlds than Miss Peters knew anything about. Doll world, for instance, with its mimic joys and sorrows, its cares and anxieties … its wonderful *reality* to childish imagination."

1464. O'Reilly, Eleanor Grace. *Giles's Minority; or, Scenes at the Red House*. (London: 1874 [1873]). With illustrations.

A934 (title), JS1068 (listed under Giles). Only edition in BL. Book for children.

1465. Orsini, [Teobaldus Orsus] F[elice] (1819–58). *The Austrian Dungeons in Italy. A Narrative of Fifteen Months' Imprisonment and Final Escape from the Fortress of S. Giorgio*. (London: George Routledge and Co., 1856). 79pp. Translated from the unpublished manuscript by J. M. White.

Not in JS. In his diary for 7 January 1857 Dodgson writes, "Today I also read Austrian Dungeons in Italy by Felice Orsini. If ever escape was providential, his seems to have been so. I know nothing of Austrian and Italian affairs, and must read some statement on the other side." The author was involved in a plot to assassinate Napolean III and the present book is an account of his 15-month imprisonment in Italy. He was eventually executed in Paris.

1466. Ossian. *The Poems of Ossian. Translated by James Macpherson. With Dissertations on the Era and Poems of Ossian; and Dr. Blair's Critical Dissertation*. (London, Glasgow: Printed for Scott, Webster & Geary, 1840). 428pp.

E306 (author, title, translator, date), JS1605. Ossian was a Gaelic writer probably of the 3rd century whose works are variations on Celtic legends and tell of the feats of his father (Fingal) and other warriors. Macpherson (1736–96) published these poems as romantic translations of Gaelic originals, but was not, when under investigation, able to produce originals, and it is widely believed that he fabricated much of the content, inserting it into loose translations of traditional Gaelic poems (see OCEL).

1467. [Ossoli, Margaret Fuller] (1810–50). *Memoirs of M. F. O.* (London: Richard Bentley, 1852). 3 vols. Consisting of the autobiography of Margaret Fuller Ossoli, and notices of her life by James Freeman Clarke, Ralph Waldo Emerson, and W. H. Channing.

A901 ("Memories of Margaret Fuller-Ossoli, 3 vols."), JS1040 (listed under Fuller-Ossoli). Sarah Margaret Fuller was an important New England feminist and Transcendentalist. She served for a time as editor of *The Dial*, the journal of the Transcendentalists. In 1844 she became, at the behest of Horace Greeley, the first woman reporter in America. She traveled in Europe, sending reports back to America. She met and married an Italian nobleman, but she, her husband, and their child perished in a shipwreck off the coast of New Jersey. Dodgson's diary for 10 May 1882 reads, in part, "[Called] on Mrs. Harcourt, to lend her sister Isabel vol. 1 of *Margaret Fuller*."

1468. Ossoli, Margaret Fuller. *Woman in the Nineteenth Century, and Kindred Papers Relating to the Sphere, Condition and Duties of Woman*. (Boston: John P. Jewett and Co., 1855). 428pp. Edited by her brother Arthur B. Fuller. With an introduction by Horace Greeley.

D234 (author, title, city, date), JS1041 (listed under Fuller-Ossoli). The title essay was first published in 1845, the remainder are printed here in book form for the first time, five years after the author's death. One of the most important tracts of 19th-century feminism, and sometimes called the first American book on woman's liberation, the volume includes the essays "Wrongs and Duties of American Women," "Woman's Influence over the Insane," "Woman in Poverty," and "Educate Men and Women as Souls."

1469. Otley, Jonathan (1766–1856). *A Concise Description of the English Lakes and Adjacent Mountains; with General Directions to Tourists, Notices of the Botany, Mineralogy, and Geology of the District, Observations on Meteorology, the Floating Island in Derwent Lake, and the Black-Lead Mine in Borrowdale.* (Keswick: The Author, 1830). 188pp. 4th edition.

E355 (author, title, date), JS1606. Otley was a watchmaker and surveyor living in Keswick, who guided many famous tourists (especially those of scientific bent) in the Lake District. This was the first tourist guide of the district, originally published in 1823.

1470. Owen, Frances Mary (1842–83). *John Keats. A Study.* (London: C. Kegan Paul & Co., 1880) 183pp.

A342, B1103 (author, title, date), JS1607.

1471. Owen, Robert Dale (1801–77). *The Debatable Land Between this World and the Next.* (London: Trübner and Co., 1874). 442pp. 2nd edition. With illustrative narrations.

A887, JS1608. Dodgson's copy is in the collection of Mark and Catherine Richards, London. It is signed "C. L. Dodgson, June 1876." Owen was an American who lobbied for emancipation during the Civil War. He was a member of the United States Congress and American Minister to Naples. He investigated spiritual phenomena that were spontaneous, rather than those that had been evoked. *The Nation* wrote of the present work, "Upon the question, On what basis of fact do the alleged spiritual manifestations rest? Mr. Owen has a better right to be patiently heard than many, even than most, other writers who have discussed it. A more dispassionate mind, a more laborious observation, has seldom been brought to the study of the question." Includes illustrations of "spirit writing."

1472. Owen, Robert Dale. *Footfalls on the Boundary of Another World.* (London: Trübner, 1860). 392pp. With narrative illustrations. From the 10th American edition, with emendations and additions by the author.

A887 (title), JS182 (Anon./Occult). Earliest British edition in BL. Deals with the physiological side of spiritualism and delves into psychology, sleep, hallucination, insanity, etc. Also examines specific manifestations and answers critics of spiritualism.

1473. Owen, Sidney James (b. 1828). *Occasional Notes on British-Indian Subjects.* (Oxford: Privately Printed, 1868). 191pp.

E196 (author, title, publisher, city, date), JS1609. E196 notes that this was a presentation copy to Dodgson. Owen served as Professor of History at Elphinstone College, Bombay before returning to England where he was reader in law and modern history and tutor at Christ Church, Oxford. Dodgson attended a party given by Owen on 16 November 1871 and had some correspondence with him (see *Letters*).

1474. Oxenham, Frank Nutcombe (b. 1840). *What is the Truth as to Everlasting Punishment? In Reply to Dr. Pusey's Treatise, "What is of Faith as to Everlasting Punishment?"* (London: Rivingtons, 1881–82). 2 parts.

A805 (author, title), JS1610. Only edition in BL. A805 does not specify number of volumes, but Dodgson likely had both parts (perhaps bound as one). Oxenham took his degree at Exeter College, Oxford in 1862 and became incumbent of St. Margaret's, Inellan in 1882. The work was in response to Edward Bouverie Pusey's *What is of Faith as to Everlasting Punishment?*, which itself was a reply to Frederic Farrar's *Eternal Hope.* Dodgson owned a copy of Farrar's book and Pusey's reply (see 697 and 1602). Oxenham, like Dodgson, opposed the doctrine of Eternal Punishment. The two parts of this work were: *Being a Critical Examination of Certain Arguments Urged in Support of the Popular Doctrine* and *Being an Historical Inquiry into the Witness and Weight of Certain Anti-Origenist Councils.*

1475. (Oxford). *Account of the Visit of the Prince Regent, the Emperor of Russia and King of Prussia to the University of Oxford in June 1814.* (Oxford: Clarendon Press, 1815). 77pp.

F145 (author, title, date), not numbered in JS. F145 describes this as "with signature on fly-leaf." The visit was part of a state visit by Alexander I of Russia and Frederick William III of Prussia. The Prince Regent at the time was the future George IV.

1476. *Oxford Essays, Contributed by Members of the University.* (London: J. W. Parker & Son, 1855–58). 4 vols.

A335, D138 (title, dates), JS199 (Anon./ Oxford). 1855 volume includes "National Education," by Frederick Temple. 1856 volume includes "Comparative Mythology," by Max Muller; "The Raphael Drawings in the University Galleries, Oxford," by Rev. George Butler; and "The Land System of Ireland," by William O'Connor. 1857 volume includes "The Study of the Evidences of Natural Theology," by Baden Powell. 1858 volume includes "The Ancient Stoics," by Alexander Grant; "Hymns and Hymn-Writers," by Charles Buchanan Pearson; "The Poetry of Pope," by John Conington; "Theories of Parliamentary Reform," by Robert Cecil, Marquis of Salisbury; and "Oxford University Reform," by Goldwin Smith.

1477. (Oxford Movement). *"Rome's Recruits:" A List of Protestants who have Become Catholics since the Tractarian Movement.* (London: Published at the office of "The Whitehall Review," 1878). 31pp. Reprinted, with additions and corrections from *The Whitehall Review* of September 28th, October 5th, 12th, and 19th, 1878.

C4 (title), not in JS. Earliest edition in BL. John Henry Newman was the most famous of the High Churchmen who converted to Roman Catholicism, but there were many others, including several in the family of Bishop of Oxford Samuel Wilberforce.

1478. (Oxford University Rifles). *Muster Roll of the Oxford University Rifles, 1859–1881.*

E35 (title), JS1555 (listed under Morrell). E35 states that this book is "with Lt. Col. G. H. Morrell's compliments," hence the listing in JS. Description taken from E35; no copy traced.

Morrell may have been the compiler, or he may have merely presented this copy.

1479. (Oxford University Statutes). *Parecbolæ, sive Excerpta è Corpore Statutorum Universitatis Oxoniensis. Accedent Articuli Religionis xxxix, Nec non Juramenta Fidelitatis & Suprematûs.* (Oxford: 1849).

B1158 (title, city, date), E145, F162, JS204 (Anon./Oxford). Earliest edition of the University Statutes Dodgson owned (presumably acquired about the time of his matriculation in 1850). It includes the 39 articles of religion to which all members of the University were compelled to subscribe. He also owned copies from 1856 (E145/JS204), 1872 (F162), and 1882 (by which time the title had been simplified to *Statuta Universitatis Oxoniensis*) (E91/F162). F162 notes the gothic stamp on the editions of 1872 and 1882.

1480. (Oxfordshire). *A Handbook for Travellers in Berks, Bucks, and Oxfordshire. Including a Particular Description of the University and City of Oxford.* (London: John Murray, 1860). 244pp. With a travelling map and plans.

E389 ("Murray's Berks, Bucks, and Oxfordshire, 1860"), JS362 (Anon./Topography). Dodgson's copy, with his autograph, was offered for sale by Maggs of London in 1911. According to E389 this includes the "autographs of J. L. Lamplugh-Raper and Lewis Carroll." John Lamplugh Lamplugh-Raper was (according to an 1847 reference) lord of the manor of Lamplugh at Merton, Cumberland.

1481. Page, H. A. [pseud. of Alexander Hay Japp] (1839–1905). *Thomas De Quincey; His Life and Writings. With Unpublished Correspondence.* (London: J. Hogg & Co., 1877). 2 vols.

A879 ("De Quincey's Life, 2 vols."), JS824 (listed under De Quincey). This is the only edition of the only pre–1898 life of De Quincey in 2 vols. listed in BL. Japp was a Scottish-born journalist who worked first for several Scottish papers and then in London where he edited *Sunday Magazine* and contributed widely to the periodical press. His many miscellaneous writings include several biographies. Of the present work, the *Nation* wrote, "Mr. Page errs only on the side of excess, as a good memoir should." See 564 for a note on De Quincey.

1482. Paget, James (1814–99). *Clinical Lectures and Essays.* (London: Longmans, Green and Co., 1875). 428pp. Edited by Howard Marsh.

Not in JS. Dodgson's diary for 8 August 1877 reads, in part "My talk with [Dr. Charles Hayman] led to my lending him Paget's *Clinical Lectures.*" This is the only pre–1877 edition in BL. Paget was Sergeant-Surgeon Extraordinary, Surgeon to the Prince of Wales, and Consulting Surgeon to St. Bartholomew's Hospital.

1483. Paley, William (1743–1805). *The Works of William Paley, D.D., Archdeacon of Carlisle. Containing his Life, Moral and Political Philosophy, Evidences of Christianity, Natural Theology, Tracts, Horæ Paulinæ, Clergyman's Companion, and Sermons. Printed Verbatim from the Original Editions.* (Edinburgh: P. Brown and T. Nelson, 1833). 712pp.

A751 ("Paley's Works"), JS1611. Earliest 1-volume edition traced (entries before and after A751 specify multiple-volume items). Dodgson's edition was probably published before 1849, when Dodgson received "Paley's *Works*" as a prize at Rugby School. Paley was a fellow of Christ College, Cambridge and an influential clergyman and Utilitarian philosopher. His *Evidences of Christianity* was required reading for incoming Cambridge students until the 20th century. *Natural Theology*, which argued that the existence of the world presupposes a creator, influenced Charles Darwin.

1484. Palgrave, Francis Turner (1824–97). *Lyrical Poems.* (London: Macmillan and Co., 1871). 264pp.

A832 ("Palgrave's Poems"), JS1612. Only edition in BL of the only book by Palgrave with the word "poems" in the title listed there. Palgrave was a civil servant who served from 1885 to 1895 as Professor of Poetry at Oxford. He greatest contribution to poetry was his editing of the influential anthology *The Golden Treasury of English Songs and Lyrics* (1861). He wrote some original verse, collected here, the best known of which was his *Visions of England* (1880–81).

1485. Palmer, Abram Smythe (b. 1844). *Folk-etymology, a Dictionary of Verbal Corruptions or Words Perverted in Form or Meaning, by False Derivation or Mistaken Analogy.* (London: G. Bell and Sons, 1882). 664pp.

A360 (author, title), JS1613. Only edition in BL. Palmer was educated at Trinity College, Dublin and served as curate (and later vicar) of Holy Trinity in that city. *Saturday Review* wrote, "Besides its bearing on mythology, Mr. Palmer's book is replete with casual matters of interest, odd and out-of-the-way quotations, and 'things not generally known'."

1486. Palmer, Abram Smythe. *A Misunderstood Miracle: An Essay in Favour of a New Interpretation of "The Sun Standing Still," in Joshua X. 12–14.* (London: Sonnenschein & Co., 1887). 119pp.

A784 (author, title), JS1614. Only edition in BL. The title is a reference to a passage in the book of Joshua, "The sun stayed in the midst of heaven, and did not hasten to go down for about a whole day. There has been no day like it before or since."

1487. Palmer, F[rancis] P[aul] (d. 1879). *Puss in Books.* (London: W. S. Orr & Co., 1844). Illustrated by Cham with 7 lithographic plates. In the *Comic Nursery Tales* series.

A483 (title, series, publisher), JS52 (Anon./Children). 1st edition. Children's picture book. See 123 for a note on Cham.

1488. Palmer, Roundell (1812–95), editor. *The Book of Praise From the Best English Hymn-Writers.* (London: Macmillan & Co., 1867). 512pp.

A844, E31 (title, editor, date), F166, JS103 (Anon./Literature), JS506 (listed under Bibles, Prayer and Hymn Books). F166 notes the gothic stamp. Roundell was educated at Rugby, Winchester, and Trinity College, Oxford. He served as an M.P. and became Attorney-General in 1864. In addition to political works, he also edited collections of hymns such as the present book.

1489. Palmer, Roundell. *A Defence of the Church of England Against Disestablishment. With an Introductory Letter Addressed to the Right Hon. W. E. Gladstone.* (London: Macmillan & Co., 1888). 381pp. 4th edition.

A772, B1215 (author, title, date), JS1615. The letter addressed to Gladstone concerns "passages relating to this subject contained in [his] Midlothian Address of September, 1885."

1490. Paludan-Müller, F[rederik] (1809–76). *The Fountain of Youth.* (London: Macmillan and Co., 1867 [1866]). 148pp. Translated from the Danish by Humphrey William Freeland. 18 wood engravings, including 10 full-page illustrations by J. D. Cooper after drawings by Walter Allen.

A642 (title), JS58 (Anon./Children's). Only edition in BL. The story is of a man who discovers the fountain of youth but, though he lives through two lives, he sacrifices what Cohen calls, "the essential harmony between inner and outer life" (*Letters*, 95). The book includes a full-page advertisement for AAIW. Dodgson gave a copy of this book to Lilia MacDonald, daughter of George MacDonald.

1491. Parallax [pseud. of Samuel Birley Rowbotham] (1816–84). *Zetetic Astronomy. Earth not a Globe! An Experimental Inquiry into the True Figure of the Earth Proving It a Plane, without Axial or Orbital Motion; and the Only Material World in The Universe!* (London: Simpkin, Marshall, and Co.; Bath: S. Hayward, 1865). 221pp.

D59 (title except first two words, city, date), JS269 (Anon./Science). Also issued with a printed slip pasted on the title page giving the publisher as J. Nisbet and Co. Rowbotham was the founder of modern Zetetic philosophy, which he defines as "making special experiments and collecting manifest and undeniable facts." The philosophy is closely related to Theosophy (which combines science, religion, and philosophy, looking for points of convergence). Rowbotham practiced medicine under the name "Dr. Birley." Photographs of the earth from outer space show that his conclusions in the present volume are not quite correct.

1492. (Paris). *A Handbook for Visitors to Paris; Containing a Description of the Most Remarkable Objects in Paris, General Advice and Information for English Travellers in the Metropolis, and on the Way to It. With a Notice of the Universal Exhibition of 1867, etc.* (London: John Murray, 1867). 267pp. 3rd edition, carefully revised. With a clue map and plans.

E367 ("Paris—Murray's Handbook, 1867"),

JS361 (Anon./Topography). Dodgson traveled to Paris in 1867 on his Russian journey with H. P. Liddon.

1493. Paris, John Ayrton (1785–1856). *Philosophy in Sport Made Science in Earnest; Being an Attempt to Illustrate the First Principles of Natural Philosophy by the Aid of Popular Toys and Sports.* (London: Longman, Rees, Orme, Brown, and Green, 1827). 3 vols. 316, 314, 207pp. With illustrations, some by George Cruikshank, the elder.

A649 (title, illustrator, 3 vols., date), JS1649. Paris was a successful physician and lecturer. While serving as physician in Penzance he helped found the Royal Geological Society of Cornwall. Returning to London in 1817 he became a lecturer on Materia Medica and eventually became chair of that subject at the College of Physicians. His lectures were well attended and though he wrote widely on medical and other subjects, it was probably through his teaching that he was most valuable to the next generation of physicians.

1494. Parkman, Francis (1823–93). *La Salle and the Discovery of the Great West.* (London: Macmillan and Co., 1885). 483pp. 12th edition, revised, with additions.

B1114 (author, title), JS1616. Earliest edition in BL with the title matching B1114. Earlier (American) editions bear the title *The Discovery of the Great West.* Parkman was Professor of Horticulture at the Agriculture School of Harvard University. *Saturday Review* wrote, "Mr. Parkman tells the story with great spirit and in an excellent style; his own experience amongst the savage descendants of La Salle's Indians enables him to add many characteristic sketches of scenery and manners."

1495. (Parliament). *The New House of Commons. July 1892. With Biographical Notices of its Members.* (London: Macmillan and Co., 1892). 328pp. Reprinted from the *Times.*

Uncertain. Not in JS. Listed in WS (title, date) only and identified by gothic stamp and property label only.

1496. Parry, John [Orlando] (1810–79). *John Parry's Manual of Musical Terms, and*

ALICE'S ADVENTURES IN WONDERLAND:

A Tale for Children.

By Lewis Carroll.   With Forty-Two Illustrations by John Tenniel, Engraved by Dalziel Brothers.   Crown 8vo. cloth, 7s. 6d.

SPECIMEN OF THE ILLUSTRATIONS.

" We beg your acceptance of this elegant Thimble."

OPINIONS OF THE PRESS.

"So graceful and so full of humour that one can hardly help reading it through.   The Illustrations are, if anything, still better than the story."—*Guardian*.

"A very elegant piece of fancy work wrought by a clear brain."—*Illus. London News*.

"A piece of downright hearty drollery and fanciful humour."—*London Review*.

"An excellent piece of nonsense . . . illustrated with extraordinary taste."—*Times*.

MACMILLAN & CO. LONDON.

Advertisement for *Alice's Adventures in Wonderland* in *The Fountain of Youth* (item 1490).

Various Other Subjects Connected with Musical Art. (London: T. McLean, [1863]). 11 plates.

A279, D66 (author, title, city, n.d.), JS1617. This is the only 19th-century edition in BL. Parry was a hugely successful comic singer (many of his songs were written by Albert Smith, see 1870) who took up drawing when poor health forced him into temporary retirement. This comic manual consists of a collection of musical terms, each illustrated by a witty drawing by Parry.

1497. Pascal, Blaise (1623–62). *Pensées de Pascal sur la Religion et sur Quelques Autres Sujets.* (Paris: Garnier, [1866]). 500pp. New edition.

A755, JS1619. Dodgson's copy is in the collection formed by Jeffrey Stern, now at Seitoku Gakuin College, Tokyo, Japan. Stern estimates the date at 1850 and notes that the volume has "C. L. Dodgson, Ch. Ch." inscribed on the front free endpaper. The famous work of Christian apologetics by the French mathematician and philosopher.

1498. Paterson, Hugh Sinclair (b. 1832). *Life, Function, Health. Studies for Young Men.* (London: Hodder & Stoughton, 1884). 209pp.

A511 (title), JS167 (Anon./Medical and not listed separately from other works). Only edition listed in BL of the only matching title. Paterson was a Scot who served as pastor of Trinity Presbyterian Church, Notting Hill, London beginning in 1880. The present collection of lectures was originally published in three parts: *Studies in Life, The Human Body and Its Functions,* and *Health Studies.*

1499. [Patmore, Coventry] (1823–96). *The Angel in the House. The Betrothal.* (London: John W. Parker & Son, 1854). 191pp. 1st edition of the 1st part of this 4-part poem.

A839 (title, edition), B1161 (author, title, subtitle, date), JS1621. Patmore worked in the book department of the British Museum and was a friend of Tennyson and the Pre-Raphaelites. The four parts of the poem are: *The Betrothal* (1854), *The Espousal* (1856), *Faithful Forever* (1860), and *The Victories of Love* (1862). The poem chronicles the courtship and marriage of Felix and Honoria and sets their pure love against the happenings of daily

life. On 1 August 1855, Dodgson wrote of this poem in his diary, "it contains much deep thought, much beautiful language, and is entirely original in style, which I think is its chief merit, its chief feature being quaintness; the verse occasionally degenerates into undeniable prose." Dodgson met Patmore on 4 October 1890 in Hastings, and gives a lengthy account of their visit in his diary. Four days later he met the rest of the Patmore family. He visited with Patmore again the following summer.

1500. Patmore, Coventry. *The Angel in the House.* (London: Cassell & Co., 1887). 192pp. 4th edition. *Cassell's National Library* no. 70.

E466 (author, title, publisher), JS1621 (not listed separately from above). Books 1 & 2 of the complete work. Uniform with the Cassell edition of *The Victories of Love* (1505) — together the two volumes contain the entire work. E466 notes that Dodgson's copy contained an "inscription to Lewis Carroll with Coventry Patmore's autograph and date." See above for more on this poem.

1501. Patmore, Coventry, editor. *The Children's Garland From the Best Poets.* (London: Macmillan, 1863). 344pp. Selected and arranged by Coventry Patmore. In the *Golden Treasury Series.*

A844, E50 (author, title, date [1864]), JS1622. The date 1864 in E50 is a typographical error — no edition of that date is listed in MBC. The book was first published by Macmillan in 1861 (dated 1862) and reprinted in various editions by that firm for many years. This edition is most likely as Dodgson acquired a copy by 1864 when he looked at its red cloth cover when considering binding colors for AAIW (see *Macmillan,* 35–6). The cloth color and cover design of this volume is similar in many respects to that of AAIW.

1502. Patmore, Coventry. *Faithful for Ever.* (London: John W. Parker, 1860). 238pp. Being the 3rd part of *The Angel in the House.* 1st edition.

A839 (author, title, edition), B1163 (author, title, date), JS1623. See 1499 for more on this poem.

1503. Patmore, Coventry. *Religio Poetæ Etc.* (London: George Bell & Sons, 1893). 229pp.

JS1624. Dodgson's copy was offered by Sotheby's, London, in 1981 (see DAA2849). It is now in the collection formed by Jeffrey Stern, now at Seitoku Gakuin College, Tokyo, Japan. Stern notes that this copy is inscribed "Rev. C. L. Dodgson from Coventry Patmore, January 1, 1894." A collection of essays reprinted from various periodicals.

1504. Patmore, Coventry. *Tamerton Church-tower and Other Poems.* (London: John Parker & Son, 1854). 219pp. According to BL a republication of the 1853 1st edition.

A839 (author, title, "first edition"), B1162 (author, title, date), JS1625. Most likely A839 and B1162 represent the same copy, though A839 styles itself "first edition." The 1854 edition was in fact, the second issue of the 1st edition, so both entries could be technically correct and refer to the same volume. The entire volume is a new edition (with additions) of Patmore's 1844 book, *Poems.*

1505. Patmore, Coventry. *The Victories of Love.* (London: Cassell & Co., 1888). 192pp. 4th edition. *Cassell's National Library,* no. 122.

E468 (author, title, publisher), JS1627. This is the only Cassell edition in BL. Books 3 & 4 of *The Angel in the House.* Uniform with the Cassell edition of *The Angel in the House* (1500) — together the two volumes contain the entire work. E468 notes that Dodgson's copy was inscribed to him by the author. See 1499 for more on this poem.

1506. Patmore, Coventry. *The Unknown Eros.* (London: George Bell & Sons, 1890). 131pp. 3rd edition.

E467 (author, title, publisher, date), JS1626. E467 notes that Dodgson's copy was inscribed to him by the author (he thanked Patmore for the book in a letter of 6 March 1890, see *Letters*). Contains a new preface by Patmore. The book was first published in 1877 with 31 odes; the 1890 edition included 42 odes, a Proem, and an additional section, "Amelia, etc." containing another 8 poems. This work was a departure from Patmore's earlier more domestic poems, containing odes on loftier themes.

1507. Paton, Joseph Noël (1821–1901). *Compositions from Shakespeare's Tempest. Fifteen Engravings in Outline. And Compo-*sitions from Shelley's Prometheus Unbound. Twelve Engravings in Outline.* (Edinburgh: W. P. Nimmo & Co., 1845). 2 parts. [32] leaves, [27] leaves. Engravings by Joseph Noël Paton.

A290 (titles, illustrator), not in JS. BL lists an [1844?] edition of the Shelley volume, but as A290 lists these two together, the 2-part 1845 edition seems more likely. Paton was a Scottish-born painter who studied at the Royal Academy and worked in a style similar to the Pre-Raphaelites. Dodgson particularly admired Paton's fairy paintings, and at various times approached Paton as a possible illustrator for *Phantasmagoria* and for *Through the Looking-Glass.* Dodgson met Paton on his trip to Scotland in 1871 and visited him there again in 1882. See index for other works illustrated by Paton.

1508. Paton, J[oseph] Noël (illustrator). *The Dowie Dens O'Yarrow.* ([Edinburgh]: Royal Association for the Promotion of the Fine Arts in Scotland, 1860). 5pp. 6 plates.

A291 (title, illustrator), not in JS. Only edition in BL.

1509. [Paton, Joseph Noël]. *Poems by A Painter.* (Edinburgh and London: William Blackwood and Sons, 1861). 159pp.

B1165 (author, title), JS1629. Only edition in BL. B1165 describes this as "Presentation copy, inscribed 'To Lewis Carroll, with the kindest regards of The Culprit, Nov. 1871.'" This copy sold for $2.00 at The Anderson Auction Co., New York, in 1908 (see DAA852).

1510. Paton, Joseph Noël. *Spindrift.* (Edinburgh and London: William Blackwood and Sons, 1867). 188pp.

B1164 (author, title, date), JS1628. The only edition published of this volume of verse. Dodgson's copy, with his initials on the endpaper, was sold at the Leicester Harmsworth sale at Sotheby's London, 26 March 1947 (DAA2191).

1511. Patterson, Robert (1802–72). *Letters on the Natural History of Insects Mentioned in Shakespeare's Plays. With Incidental Notices of the Entomology of Ireland.* (London: W. S. Orr and Co., 1838). 270pp.

A877 ("Insects Mentioned in Shakespeare"), JS122 (Anon./Literature). Earliest edition in BL of the only possible match. The author was a zoologist who served as secretary of the natural history section of the British Association and helped found the Natural History Society of Belfast.

1512. Pavy, Frederick William (1829–1911). *A Treatise on Food and Dietetics, Physiologically and Therapeutically Considered.* (London: J. & A. Churchill, 1874). 559pp.

A514 (author, title), JS1631. Earliest edition in BL. Pavy was a physician who practiced (and lectured) at Guy's Hospital.

1513. Pearson, John (1613–86). *An Exposition of the Creed.* (Oxford: University Press, 1847). 2 vols. 472, 350pp. 3rd edition. Revised and corrected by the Rev. E. Burton.

A778, D140 (author, title, city, date, 2 vols.), JS1632. Dodgson's copy was offered at Parke-Bernet Galleries in New York on 1 Dec. 1947 (DAA2223) and on 9–10 April 1963 (DAA2528). DAA2528 implies that this was bound uniformly with an 1855 copy of the *Book of Common Prayer*. Each volume was signed by Dodgson. Pearson was a royalist clergyman who became, after the Restoration, master of Jesus College, Cambridge; master of Trinity College, Cambridge; and Bishop of Chester. Burton was Oxford Professor of Divinity and a canon of Christ Church. This book was originally published in 1659. It was long a standard work on the creed as it is filled with Pearson's erudition and references to the church fathers.

1514. Pearson, Philippa. *Acrostic Dictionary; Containing More than Thirty Thousand Words with their Initials and Finals Alphabetically Arranged.* (London: Routledge & Sons, 1884). 256pp.

B1167 (author, title, date), JS1633. Dodgson was a fan of acrostics and wrote several of his own, including the dedicatory poems to *Snark* and *Sylvie and Bruno*, and the epilogue poem in TTLG.

1515. [Peart, Emily]. *A Book for Governesses. By one of them.* (Edinburgh: W. Oliphant & Co., [1868]). 213pp.

D22 (title, city), JS259 (Anon./Education). D22 notes Dodgson's initials. Only edition in BL. JS259 also gives A609 as a reference for this item, but A609 states "The Governess," and is clearly a different title (see 752). *The Athenæum* wrote that this book, "is a healthy, sensible, and invigorating work ... addressed not so much to

trained young women ... as to those who ... are thrown upon their own resources and elect to become governesses.... It is not often that good advice is so thoroughly applicable to the case in hand."

1516. Peck, William (1862–1925). *The Constellations, and How to Find Them.* (Edinburgh: Archibald & Peck, 1884). 2nd edition. 13 maps with explanations, etc.

A543 (title), JS266 (Anon./Science). Earliest edition in BL. Peck was an Edinburgh astronomer and maker of telescopes and other scientific instruments.

1517. Peirce, Benjamin (1809–80). *An Elementary Treatise on Plane and Solid Geometry.* (Boston: William H. Dennet, 1872). 150pp.

E142, JS1634, JS1650. Dodgson's copy is in HAC. It contains his monogram in purple on the front pastedown and minor annotations on pp. 6, 8–11 in purple ink. A lengthy list of numbers, correlating the present book with Euclid, is in Dodgson's hand in pencil on the rear pastedown. Peirce was Perkins Professor of Astronomy and Mathematics at Harvard University and among the foremost American mathematicians of his era. The book includes foldout plates of geometrical figures. Dodgson examines this book is his *Euclid and His Modern Rivals* (118–22) (ironically, he spells Peirce's name wrong). "However useful this Manual may be to an advanced student, it is *not* adapted to the wants of a beginner."

1518. [Peirce, Charles Santiago Sanders] (1839–1914), editor. *Studies in Logic. By Members of the Johns Hopkins University.* (Boston: Little Brown, and Co., 1883). 203pp.

B1245 (title), JS154 (Anon./Mathematics). Only edition in BL. B1245 states "MS references on fly-leaf by C. L. D." Peirce was an eminent American philosopher, logician and scientist, son of Benjamin Peirce (see above). He was educated at Harvard and taught there and at Johns Hopkins University, spending most of his life working outside the classroom. This book included contributions by Peirce and four of his students at Johns Hopkins.

1519. Pellico, Silvio (1789–1854). *My Imprisonments: Memoirs of Silvio Pellico Da Saluzzo.* (London: Whittaker, Treacher &

Arnot, 1833). 249pp. Translated from the Italian by Thomas Roscoe.

D170 (author, title, translator, date), JS1635. Pellico was an Italian dramatist and poet who was a political prisoner in Austria for eight years because of his involvement with the Carbonari, a secret society that advocated political freedom. See 1691 for a note on Roscoe.

1520. Pember, Edward Henry (1833–1911). *The Maid of Messene and Other Poems.* (London: Longman, Brown, Green, and Longmans, 1855). 236pp.

B1168 (author, title, date), JS1637. Like Dodgson, Pember matriculated at Christ Church, Oxford, in 1850, so the two may have known each other as undergraduates. Pember was a Student at Christ Church from 1854 to 1861 and went on to become a barrister at Lincoln's Inn. In addition to his career in the law, he also wrote verse. The title work is "a tragedy in three acts and in verse."

1521. Pember, Edward Henry. *The Tragedy of Lesbos.* (London: Macmillan, 1870). 147pp.

B1169 (author, title, date), JS1638.

1522. Pember, Edward Henry. *The Voyage of the Phocæans, and Other Poems. With the Prometheus Bound of Æschylus Done into English Verse.* (London: Chiswick Press, 1895). 177pp. Printed for private circulation. Limited to 250 copies.

A876 (author, title), JS1636. Only edition in BL. Pember published other volumes in private limited editions, often presenting these books to prominent Victorians.

1523. [Percy, Thomas] (1729–1811). *Bishop Percy's Folio Manuscript: Ballads and Romances.* (London: N. Trübner & Co., 1867–68). 3 vols. 536, 609, 595pp. Edited by John W. Hales and Frederick J. Furnivall, assisted by Prof. Child, W. Chappell, &c.

A396 ("Percy's Manuscripts, Ballads and Romances, 6 vols. ... 1868"), JS1639. This is surely the work referred to by A396; no other title in BL or BOD even comes close to matching. Apparently Dodgson had his 3-volume set bound in 6 volumes. Only edition in BL. A fourth volume of "Loose and Humourous Songs" was published separately, and its bawdy contents

were controversial at the time. It seems unlikely that Dodgson would have owned this latter volume. This was a reprinting of a folio in 17th-century hand from which Percy drew many of the poems included in his *Reliques* (see below). Percy was educated at Christ Church, Oxford and went on to serve as Bishop of Dromore.

1524. Percy, Thomas, editor. *Reliques of Ancient English Poetry: Consisting of Old Heroic Ballads, Songs, and Other Pieces of our Earlier Poets, Together with Some Few of a Later Date.* (London: J. Dodsley, 1765). 3 vols. 344, 384, 346pp. 1st edition.

A486 (author, title, edition, 3 vols., date), JS1640. A collection of "ancient" poetry (ranging in period from great antiquity to as recent as the time of Charles I) edited, and in some cases "restored" by Percy. This popular work did much to revive an interest in early English literature.

1525. Perrin, Jean Baptiste (fl. 1786). *The Elements of French Conversation.* (London: 1841).

E254 (author, title, date), JS1641. No exact match traced, but an 1842 edition was published in London by T. Allman, and many British editions were published by Longmans. The London edition of 1840 was the 28th. E254 notes: "Simply an old school book, but has the autograph of Lewis Carroll, and an amusing mock letter from a Rugby school-fellow to him, written across the whole title page, a trifle of sketching at the end." Perrin was born in Paris but came to Ireland where he taught French to the Irish gentry. This work was originally published in 1774.

1526. Petit, A. *La Gastronomie en Russie.* (Paris: L'auteur, 1860). 208pp.

B1170 (author, title, city, date), JS1642. BL describes the author as "Chef de cuisine du comte Panine." Dodgson traveled to Russia in 1867, hence, perhaps, his interest in Russian cuisine.

1527. Petrarch, Francesco (1304–74). *Le Rime del Petrarca.* (London: G. Pickering, 1822). 237pp. In the *Pickering Diamond Classics* series.

A476 (author, date, series, 3 vols.), JS1643. BL does not list this as a multi-volume edition; perhaps Dodgson had multiple copies. Petrarch was an Italian Humanist, scholar, and poet who contributed greatly to the lyric poetry and scholarly advancement of his age. See 153 for more on this series.

1528. P[hillips], E[dward] (1630?–96). *The New World of Words: or, A Universal English Dictionary: Containing the Proper Significations and Derivations of all Words from Other Languages ... as Now Made Use of in our English Tongue: Together with Definitions of all those Terms that Conduce to the Understanding of any of the Arts or Sciences... To which is Added the Interpretations of Proper Names ... and Likewise the Geographical Descriptions of the Chief Countries and Cities in the World.* (London: R. Bently, etc. 1696). 415pp. 5th edition, with large additions.

A740, B1298 (author, title, date), JS1644. Phillips was the son of John Milton's sister, Ann. His dictionary was first published in 1658, just two years after Thomas Blount's dictionary *Glossographia*. Blount felt that Phillips had borrowed a little too liberally from his own work and published a scathing attack on Phillips under the title *A World of Errors Discovered in a New World of Words*. The quarrel was the first of the "dictionary wars" that sprang up between rival lexicographers in the years to follow.

1529. Phillips, John (1800–74). *Illustrations of the Geology of Yorkshire; or a Description of the Strata and Organic Remains of the Yorkshire Coast Accompanied by a Geological Map, Sections, and Plates of the Fossil Plants and Animals.* (York: Printed for the Author, 1829). 192pp. 24 plates.

A571, D142 (author, title, city, date, 2 vols.), JS1646. This is part 1 of a 2-part work (thus the 2 vols.) See below for part 2. Phillips was an English geologist who was based for many years in York. Towards the end of his life he was appointed Reader in Geology at Oxford, and he was one of the prime movers of the project to erect a university museum of natural history. The present work was prepared during his many years at York.

1530. Phillips, John. *Illustrations of the Geology of Yorkshire: or, A Description of the Strata and Organic Remains: Accompanied by a Geological Map, Sections, and Diagrams, and Figures of the Fossils. Part 2,* *The Mountain Limestone District.* (London: J. Murray, 1836). 253pp. 24 plates.

A571, D142 (author, title, city, date, 2 vols.), JS1646. This is part 2 of a 2-part work (thus the 2 vols.) See above for part 1.

1531. Phillips, John. *Life on the Earth. Its Origin and Succession.* (Cambridge: Macmillan and Co., 1860). 224pp.

D144 (author, title, city, date), JS1647. Published just a year after Darwin's *Origin of Species*, this highly important book provided a better estimate of the age of earth than Darwin had been able to, and, more importantly, used the fossil record to show increasing biological diversity over time, something Darwin had said would be impossible to do. Yet Phillips was still ultimately in opposition to Darwin, partly on spiritual grounds. He did call evolution, "the unquestionable power of adaptation which living creatures possess, through exercise of the organs of life, by which *some change* is possible in structure and some change in function also, the new qualities being in *some degree* transmitted to the descendants," but he saw evolution only as a means of making minor changes in a pre-existing species.

1532. Phillips, John. *Vesuvius.* (Oxford: Clarendon Press, 1869). 355pp.

A343, D143 (author, title, city, date), JS1648. A history of the mountain and of its successive eruptions; with illustrations.

1533. [**Phillips**, Samuel] (1815–54). *Essays from "The Times"; Being a Selection from the Literary Papers which have Appeared in that Journal and A Second Series of Essays from "The Times."* (London: John Murray, 1852–54). 2 vols.

A561, JS214 (Anon./Periodicals). Dodgson's copy is in the collection of Jon Lindseth, Cleveland, OH. It is inscribed in Vol. 1 "C. L. Dodgson A Birthday Gift from F. & E. [i.e. his sisters Fanny and Elizabeth] 1854." Vol. 2 is signed on the endpaper "C. L. Dodgson Ch. Ch." Phillips was a journalist who wrote for several papers. He contributed literary reviews (published here) to the *Times* and political leaders for the *Morning Herald*. He was literary director of the Crystal Palace Company, and wrote a *Guide to the Crystal Palace and Park*.

1534. Phillpotts, Henry (1778–1869). *A Letter to the Archbishop of Canterbury. By the Bishop of Exeter.* (London: John Murray, 1850). 91pp. 20 March, 1850. On the judgment of the Privy Council in the Gorham Case.

C5 (title), not in JS. Only edition in BL. G. C. Gorham had been granted a living in the diocese of Exeter in 1847, but Phillpotts, Bishop of Exeter, refused to install him, on the grounds that Gorham's views on baptism were unorthodox. Gorham was an Evangelical; Phillpotts' views were more conservative. The Privy Council overturned Phillpotts' decision (attributing to Gorham a view on baptism that was not his), unleashing a huge protest among High Churchmen who opposed Gorham. Phillpotts still refused to install Gorham, and he was ultimately installed by Archbishop Sumner. The case resulted in a number of High Churchmen defecting to the Roman church. (See J. C. S. Nias, *Gorham and the Bishop of Exeter* [1951]).

1535. [**Philp**, Robert Kemp] (1819–82). *The Denominational Reason Why. Giving the Origin, History, and Tenets of the Christian Sects, with the Reasons Assigned by Themselves for their Specialities of Faith and Forms of Worship.* (London: Houlston & Wright, 1860). 360pp.

A555, B1031 (title, date), JS1651. Philp was a journalist who served as editor and sub-editor of several London papers. He published a large number of books, most of which were compilations of information, often on domestic matters.

1536. [**Philp**, Robert Kemp]. *Notices to Correspondents, Consisting of Ten Thousand Editorial Answers to Questions Selected from the Best Authorities, Supplying a Fund of Information which Cannot be Obtained from any Other Source.* (London: Houlston and Stoneman, [1856]). 320pp.

B1154 (title, n.d.), JS247 (Anon./Reference). Only edition in BL or BOD. A collection of questions from correspondents of various papers and journals and their answers from the editors of those publications. Dodgson bought this book on 23 February 1858 (see *Diary 3*).

1537. (**Photography**). *The ABC of Modern (Dry-plate) Photography.* (London: London Stereoscopic Company, 1886). 149pp. 22nd edition, revised.

E236 (title ["The ABC of Modern Dry-

plate"], publisher), JS225 (Anon./Photography). This description from a copy in the Harry Ransom Center, University of Texas at Austin (the only copy traced). It is unclear if this bears any relation to William Kinninmond Burton's *The ABC of Modern Photography* (published in 1882 with several subsequent editions). Dodgson used the wet-plate photographic process and gave up photography after 1880, about the time the dry-plate process was coming into wide use.

1538. (**Photography**). *Handbook of Photography.* Details unknown.

Title only given in A304/JS228. Dodgson gave up photography in 1880, so it is unlikely that he would have bought a handbook published after that time; nonetheless, he did own a book on dryplate that may have been published after 1880 (see above), so Ellerbeck's work has been included here as a possibility. The most likely candidate is Tissandier, but several possibilities are listed here:

Tissandier, Gaston, (1843–1899). *A History and Handbook of Photography.* (London: S. Low Marston, Searle, & Rivington, 1878). 2nd edition (earliest traced). Translated from the French by J. Thomson. With upwards of 70 illustrations and some specimens of permanent processes. With an appendix by the late Henry Fox Talbot.

Crookes, William. *A Handbook to the Waxed Paper Process in Photography.* (London: 1857).

Ellerbeck, J. H. T. *The Amateur's First Handbook of Modern Dry-plate Photography.* (Liverpool: D. N. Cussons & Co., 1883).

Sutton, Thomas. *The Calotype Process: A Handbook to Photography on Paper.* (London: Sampson Low, 1856). 2nd edition (earliest traced).

1539. Physician, A. *The Traveller's Medical Companion: Being a Guide to the Use of Remedies for Common Ailments.* (London: 1875).

E127 (title, date [1875]), JS176 (Anon./Medical). No 1875 edition traced, but BL lists the 1874 2nd edition as published in London by H. & T. Kirby & Co.

1540. Pick, Eduard [a.k.a. Edward Pick] (b. 1824). *An Etymological Dictionary of the French Language.* (London: J. Murray, 1869). 324pp.

E64 (author, title, date), F161, JS1652. F161

notes the gothic stamp. Pick was a linguist who specialized in mnemonics. Dodgson also had an interest in memory shortcuts and invented a "Memoria Technica" for remembering numbers (WMGC, 97–98).

1541. Picton, James Allanson (1832–1910). *The Mystery of Matter, and Other Essays.* (London: Macmillan and Co., 1873). 492pp.

A506 (author, title), JS1653. 1st edition as described in MBC. Picton was an M.P. and, from 1870 to 1879, a member of the London School Board. He wrote several works on history and on religion. The essays in the present collection include "The Philosophy of Ignorance," "The Antithesis of Faith and Light," "The Essential Nature of Religion," and "Christian Pantheism." The *New Englander and Yale Review* wrote of this book that it was, "written in a pleasant though somewhat diffuse style, with a thoroughly philosophical spirit and a competent knowledge of the new aspects of metaphysical philosophy."

1542. Pirie, George (1843–1904). *A Short Account of the Principal Geometrical Methods of Approximating to the Value of ⅔.* (London: Macmillan and Co., 1877). 24pp. For the Use of Colleges and Schools.

E423 (author, title), JS1654. E423 notes this has Dodgson's initials. Only edition in BL. Pirie was Professor of Mathematics at the University of Aberdeen.

1543. Plain, Peter [pseud. of Edward Harris Ruddock] (1822–75). *Fallacies and Claims: Being a Word to the World on Homœopathy.* (London: Homœopathic Publishing Company, 1875). 5th edition. 1st of a series of *Homœopathic Missionary Tracts.* 27pp.

Not listed separately in JS (see JS163). Dodgson's copy is in HAC in a volume with 7 other tracts from this series and one additional Homœopathic pamphlet (see 970). See 1717–20 for other works by Ruddock. The present tract addresses the "most common fallacies and objections prevalent in regard to Homœopathy."

1544. Platts, John Thompson (1830–1904) and A[lfred Wrigley] (1817–98). *A Companion to Wrigley's Collection of Examples and Problems, Being Illustrations of Mathematical Processes and Methods of Solution.* (Cambridge: Deighton, Bell and Co., 1861). 449pp.

D245 (authors, title, city, date), JS2225 (listed under Wrigley). D245 notes Dodgson's signature. The book to which this is a companion was first published as *A Collection of Examples in Pure and Mixed Mathematics, with Hints and Answers* by Wrigley and William H. Johnstone. Dodgson owned a copy of a later edition attributed to Wrigley only (see 2317).

1545. Plumtre, Edward Hayes (1821–91). *The Spirits in Prison and Other Studies on the Life after Death.* (London: Isbister, 1885). 416pp.

A804, D146 (author, title, date), JS1655. D146 notes Dodgson's signature. Plumtre was an English scholar and divine who held many church posts, culminating with the Deanship of Wells to which he was appointed in 1881. Plumtre argues that the state of the soul is not finally fixed at death, writing, "In every form; from the solemn liturgies which embodied the belief of her profoundest thinkers and truest worshippers, to the simple words of hope and love which were traced over the graves of the poor, her voice [the early Church] went up without a doubt or misgiving, in prayers for the souls of the departed."

1546. *Pocket Atlas*. Details unknown.

Title only given in A322/JS366 (Anon./Topography). Several possibilities traced, the most likely being one of the several editions of one of the following:

The Travellers Pocket Atlas Consisting of a Complete Set of County Maps, for England and Wales. (London: G. & W. B. Whittaker, 1823).

Bartholomew, John (1831–1893). *The Pocket Atlas of the World. A Comprehensive and Popular Series of Maps Illustrating Physical and Political Geography.* (London: John Walker, 1886). 2nd edition (earliest traced).

Bartholomew, John. *Tourist's Pocket Atlas of England and Wales, with Descriptive Gazetteer.* (London, Walker & Co., 1893).

1547. Pocock, William Willmer (1813–99). *Darwinism a Fallacy.* (London: C. H. Kelly, 1891). 160pp.

A909 (title), JS268 (Anon./Science). Only edition in BL of the only matching title listed.

1548. Poe, Edgar Allan (1809–49). *The Poetical Works of Edgar Allan Poe. With a Notice of his Life and Genius by James Hannay.* (London: Addey and Co., 1853). 144pp. With 20 illustrations.

A841, B1171 (author, title, editor, date), JS1657. Dodgson apparently owned other works by Poe, as A401 states "3 vols. of E. A. Poe" but gives no indication of what those 3 volumes might be. JS1656 lists this attribution as "Poems," presumably on the basis that other items in A401 are collections of poetry.

1549. Polano, Pietro Soave [pseud. of Paolo (formerly Pietro) Sarpi] (1552–1623). *The History of the Council of Trent. Containing Eight Books. Written in Italian by Pietro Soave Polano and Faithfully Translated into English by Sr. Nathanael Brent Whereunto is Added the Life of the Learned Author and the History of the Inquisition.* (London: Printed by J. Macock, for S. Mearne, J. Martyn, and H. Herringman, 1676). 889pp.

B1166 (title, date), JS1630 (listed under Father Paul, the author ascribed in B1166). The *Life of the Learned Author* was written by F. Micanzio and translated by "A Person of Quality"; the *History of the Inquisition* was translated by Robert Gentilis. Sarpi was a Venetian who, though ordained in the Catholic church, was a bitter enemy of the pope and of Rome. His work to pass anti-ecclesiastical laws in Venice was partly responsible for that region's being placed under an interdict in 1606. He supported the idea of Venice's becoming a Protestant republic. This work, his best known, was originally published in 1619 and is, according to the *Catholic Encyclopedia*, "a bitter invective against the popes." The work has been refuted by Catholic and even some Protestant authorities.

1550. Polidori, John William (1795–1821). *The Vampyre; A Tale.* (London: Printed for Sherwood, Neely, and Jones, 1819). 84pp.

A418 (author [incorrectly attributed to Byron], title), JS1659. Dodgson's copy is in the Lovett Collection, Winston-Salem, NC. It bears his monogrammed initials on the front endpaper. Polidori was educated at Edinburgh and became personal physician to Byron. He was present on the famous night when Byron and the Shelleys read horror stories and suggested that each attempt a story in the gothic genre. Mary Shelley wrote *Frankenstein* and Polidori wrote the present work, the first book length treatment of the vampire legend. For many years the anonymous book was attributed to Byron. Byron was, in fact, the model for Polidori's vampire, Lord Ruthven, who was the first aristocratic vampire (along the lines of Dracula) to appear in print.

1551. Pollok, Robert (1798–1827). *The Course of Time. A Poem in Ten Books.* (Edinburgh & London: William Blackwell & T. Cadell, 1829). 294pp. 8th edition.

A366, B1174 (author, title, date), JS1661. According to BL the 9th edition was also published in 1829. Pollok was a Scottish preacher whose career was cut short by pulmonary disease. A lengthy poem written in a style similar to Milton, it tells of the mortal and immortal destiny of man and ranges from the Creation to Armageddon. In 1857 it was issued in an illustrated edition which included pictures by John Tenniel.

1552. Pope, Alexander (1688–1744). *The Poetical Works of Alexander Pope.* (London: Macmillan and Co., 1869). 506pp. The Globe Edition. Edited with notes and an introductory memoir by Adolphus William Ward.

A368 (author, title, "Globe Edition"), JS1662. This is the first printing of the Globe Edition as listed in MBC. Ward (b. 1837) was the principal of Owens College, Manchester.

1553. *Possibilities of Creation, or What the World Might Have Been. A Book of Fancies.* (London: Simpkin, Marshall, 1863). 410pp.

A554 ("Possibilities of Creation"), JS274 (Anon./Science). Only edition in BL of the only matching title. A book of essays based on imagined differences in the world such as "What kind of world would an evil spirit have made?" "Suppose we had all been insane?" "Suppose there had been no differences of opinion" "Suppose we had walked on our heads?" *The Athenæum* called this "dull after twenty pages ... four hundred pages is beyond all reading."

1554. Potter, Richard (1799–1886). *An Elementary Treatise on Optics. Part I. Con-*

taining All the Requisite Propositions Carried to the First Approximations; With the Construction of Optical Instruments. (London: Taylor, Walton, and Maberly, 1851). 166pp. 2nd edition, revised.

E67 (author, title, date), JS1663. The title page of the 1st edition (1847) noted that this was "for the use of junior university students."

1555. Potts, Robert (1805–85). *Cambridge Scholarships and Examinations.* (London: Longmans and Co., 1883). 536pp.

D37 (author, title, city, date), JS1664. D37 notes Dodgson's initials. Potts was educated at Trinity College, Cambridge and though he married not long after receiving his degree he remained involved in University affairs for most of his life. He was an advocate for University reform and also worked as a private tutor. He wrote a number of works on mathematics and his edition of Euclid (see 679) was used as a text in many schools. Dodgson corresponded with Potts on the subject of teaching Euclid (see *Diary 4*, 49–52).

1556. Potts, Robert. *Elementary Algebra, with Brief Notices of its History.* (London: Longmans & Co., 1879–80). 12 parts in 1 volume.

E409 (author, title, dates), F139. Listed in JS without number following JS1664. F139 describes this as inscribed "To the Rev. C. L. Dodgson, M.A. with the Editor's kind regards, 1880."

1557. Powell, G[eorge] H[erbert] (1856–1924), editor. *Musa Jocosa: Choice Pieces of Comic Poetry.* (London: Bliss, Sands & Co., 1894). 192pp. Selected and with an introduction by G. H. Powell.

A843 (editor, title), JS1665. Dodgson's copy is in Berg. It bears the inscription "Presented to Lewis Carroll by the editor Nov. 20 1894 Geo H. Powell." The author was a member of the Inner Temple who also compiled collections of verse. This anthology of comic poetry includes "The Walrus and the Carpenter," "Father William," and "Jabberwocky," the first and last with annotations from Carroll's text. It also includes a Latin translation of "Jabberwocky" by Augustus Arthur Vansittart (identified only by his initials). Though the book states that this translation is here published for the first time, it had in fact been printed twice previously (1872 and 1881 both separate editions). Pow-

ell's introduction states, "Equal to the author of 'Fly Leaves' [i.e. C. S. Calverley] in fame, but diverse in his peculiar genius, stands the immortal 'Lewis Carroll,' the inventor of what may be called the modern domestic humour, the creator of that fascinating dreamland through which, veiled in a sunny mist of ethereal mirth, the daily round of life, its peaceful joys, its inanities, its fuss, friction, and augmentation pass before our eyes in admired disorder. 'Father William,' 'The Walrus and the Carpenter,' and 'Jabberwocky' would, it is needless to say, have been more remarkable by their absence from this collection than anything which could have taken their place. Moreover to the brief epic which goes by the latter title we have ventured to add for the benefit of classical readers a Latin version (published here for the first time) by a late distinguished fellow of Trinity College, Cambridge."

1558. Poynter, Edward John (1836–1919). *Ten Lectures on Art.* (London: Chapman & Hall, 1879). 283pp.

A595, E445 (author, title, date), F159, JS1666. F159 notes the gothic stamp. Poynter was born in Paris and educated in England. He was a member of the Royal Academy and served as Slade Professor of Art at University College, London. In addition to his successful career as a painter, he designed architectural and tile decorations for the grill room of the South Kensington Museum and made cartoons for the mosaic of St. George at Westminster Palace. The present lectures were for the instruction of art students. *Saturday Review* wrote of them, "It is only when he has to speak of the past that Mr. Poynter fairly casts aside the austere manners of the teacher; and it is here, therefore, that his capabilities as a critic are displayed to the best advantage."

1559. Praed, Winthrop Mackworth (1802–39). *The Poems of Winthrop Mackworth Praed.* (London: Edward Moxon, 1864). 2 vols. 397, 439pp. With a memoir by Derwent Coleridge.

A830, B1177 (author, title, publisher, date), JS1667. Dodgson's copy was offered for sale at Charles Hamilton, New York on 14 December 1965 (see DAA2571, which notes that this is a 2-volume work). Praed was an M.P. and eventually secretary to the Board of Control. He is best known for his humorous verse, his more serious poetry being less successful. Derwent

Coleridge was the grandson of Samuel Taylor Coleridge.

1560. Pratt, Anne [later Mrs. John Pearless] (1806–93). *The British Grasses and Sedges.* (London: Society for Promoting Christian Knowledge, [1859]). 136pp. Illustrated.

A823, B1178 (author, title, n.d.), JS1668. Earliest edition in BL or BOD. Pratt was a prolific writer and illustrator of botanical books. Her work on English plants was the standard in its field for many decades. She turned to botany at an early age due to ill health and her sister assisted her in collecting specimens. Her works were written in a popular style, but were nonetheless important contributions to her field.

1561. Pratt, Anne [later Mrs. John Pearless]. *The Ferns of Great Britain, and their Allies the Club Mosses, Pepperworts and Horsetails.* (London: Society for Promoting Christian Knowledge, [1855]). 164pp. Illustrated with 40 color plates.

A823, B1179 (author, title, n.d.), JS1669. Earliest edition in BL or BOD.

1562. Pratt, Anne [later Mrs. John Pearless]. *Wild Flowers.* (London: Society for Promoting Christian Knowledge, 1852–53). 2 vols. 192, 192pp. Illustrated with 96 colored plates.

A867 (author, title), JS1670. Although A867 does not specify multiple volumes (while another item in A867 does so specify), there is no 1-volume edition in BL or BOD. Earliest edition traced.

1563. Pratt, William. *A Physician's Sermon to Young Men.* (London: Balliere, Tindall, and Cox, [1872]). 47pp.

E366 (author, title), JS1671. Only edition in BL or BOD. Pratt was a fellow of the Royal College of Surgeons. The sermon, on 2 Tim. 2:22, concerns what Pratt calls the "appetite of sex" among young men. It commends early marriage, condemns masturbation and "illicit intercourse," and suggests, as means towards "self-control," cold bathing, hard beds, abundant work, plain food, careful selection of both reading material and companions, and religion.

1564. Prendergast, Thomas (1806–86). *The Mastery Series. French.* (London: Longmans, Green, and Co., 1868). 2nd edition. 107pp.

E110 (author, title, date), JS1673. Dodgson owned 2 copies, the second being listed in E185 (author, title, 1870, "with many corrections by Lewis Carroll in MS.")—this would be the 4th edition. A569/JS1672 lists "Prendergast's Mastery Series, 6 vol." Five of the volumes are the present two volumes and the next three listed. The 6th volume could be: *Mastery Series: Manual for Learning Spanish* (first published in London, 1869, at least some of the subsequent editions published by Longmans, etc.). Another possibility is *Handbook to the Mastery Series* (first published London, 1868). Dodgson presented a copy of this book to a Mrs. Egerton. That copy is now in the collection formed by Jeffrey Stern, now at Seitoku Gakuin College, Tokyo, Japan. Prendergast was a blind man who invented a means of learning languages. In his preface to *Hebrew* (see 1566) the author writes of his Mastery method, "Mastery is the highest degree of fluency and readiness in reproducing foreign sentences with the words in their idiomatic order of arrangement.... Mastery is an exact method, if beginners will be exact in learning its laws." Prendergast's method requires frequent study (at least six times a day in the first fortnight) of short lessons comprising sentences filled with typical grammatical constructions. "The exercises must be carried on so that one lesson shall never expel another from the memory." Prendergast developed his system as an official in the Indian Civil Service where he was required to learn the local languages. In a letter to Charlotte Yonge (19 July 1881), Dodgson wrote, "I have undertaken on behalf of Mr Prendergast, with whom I am acquainted as a correspondent, to recommend his system of learning languages to your favourable notice ... having tested his system by learning his French Handbook (I am now learning the German one) I can confidently recommend it to anyone wishing to acquire the art of conversing in a foreign language."

1565. Prendergast, Thomas. *The Mastery Series. German.* (?London: Longmans, Green, 1870).

E183 (author, title, date), JS1674. No 1870 British edition traced, but Longmans, Green, and Co. published a 2nd edition in London in 1868 and a 5th edition was published in London in 1871 (no publisher in BL). There was an 1870 American edition (New York: D. Appleton). See above for more on the *Mastery* series.

1566. Prendergast, Thomas. *The Mastery Series. Hebrew.* (London: Longmans, Green, 1871). 104pp.

E282 (author, title, date), JS1676. Dodgson's copy, with his initials and the gothic stamp, was offered for sale by Maggs of London in 1911. See 1564 for more on the *Mastery* series

1567. Prendergast, Thomas. *The Mastery Series. Latin.* (London: Longmans, Green and Co., 1872). 96pp.

E188 (author, title, date), JS1675. E188 notes this has Dodgson's initials. See 1564 for more on the *Mastery* series

1568. Prescott, William Hickling (1796–1859). *History of the Conquest of Mexico. With a Preliminary View of the Ancient Mexican Civilization and the Life of the Conqueror Hernando Cortes.* (London: Richard Bentley, 1850). 2 vols. 580, 580pp. 6th edition. Maps and portraits.

A907, B1182 (author, title, date, 2 vols.), JS1678. Only edition in BL matching the particulars of B1182 (the 5th edition of 1850 was published in 3 vols.). Prescott was an American historian, known as the first "scientific historian" of that country.

1569. Prescott, William Hickling. *History of the Conquest of Peru, with a Preliminary View of the Civilization of the Incas.* (London: R. Bentley, 1847). 2 vols. 480, 490pp. 1st edition.

A907, B1181 (author, title, 2 vols., date), JS1680.

1570. Prescott, William Hickling. *History of the Reign of Ferdinand and Isabella, The Catholic, of Spain.* (London: Bentley, 1846). 3 vols. 4th edition, revised.

A907, B1180 (author, title, 3 vols., publisher, date), JS1679.

1571. Price, Bartholomew (1818–98). *A Treatise on Infinitesimal Calculus; Containing Differential and Integral Calculus, Calculus of Variations, Applications to Algebra and Geometry, and Analytical Mechanics.* (Oxford: 1852–60). 4 vols.

A584 (author, title, 4 vols.), JS1681. Earliest edition in BL. Price was Master of Pembroke College and Sedleian Professor of Natural Philosophy at Oxford. He also served in many

other capacities, including tutor and mathematical lecturer. In the summer of 1854, Dodgson spent several weeks at Whitby reading mathematics with Price. He continued working with Price in 1855, the two remained friends, and Price continued to encourage Dodgson's mathematical career. In 1864 Dodgson photographed Price's children. The verses "Twinkle, twinkle, little bat," in AAIW are said to refer to Price, whose nickname was Bat. In his diary for 16 January 1855, Dodgson writes, "Today I observed in the cross-multiplication in Price's *Differential Calculus* that the three denominators are identical, and working one out does for all. I wonder if he has noticed it."

1572. Price, Bonamy (1807–88). *Chapters on Practical Political Economy; Being the Substance of Lectures Delivered in the University of Oxford.* (London: Kegan Paul & Co., 1882). 488pp. 2nd edition.

A305, D147 (author, title, city, date), JS1682. Price was an economist who served as mathematical master at Dodgson's school, Rugby, until 1850 when he became Professor of Political Economy at Oxford. Dodgson writes of meeting Price on 17 May 1856 and makes other minor mentions in his diary (including an 1881 dinner party that inspired Dodgson to write how much he wearied of such occasions).

1573. [Price, Edward David], editor. *Hazell's Annual Cyclopaedia 1886.* (London: Hazell, Watson and Viney, Ltd., 1886).

E311 (title, date), JS241 (Anon./Reference). This was the first year of publication for this annual which, under various names, continued publication until 1922.

1574. Price, George (d. 1887). *A Treatise on Fire and Thief-proof Depositories and Locks and Keys.* (London, Wolverhampton [printed]: Simpkin, Marshall and Hall, 1856). 916pp.

A639, D148 (author, title, city, date), JS1683. George Price worked at the Cleveland Safe Works, Wolverhampton. A comprehensive history of the technology of locks and safes which also provides a glimpse into the state of security technology in the 1850s. Some called the book the "Burglar's Bible" because of its diagrams of locks. Price also used the book to promote his own wares.

1575. [Privy Council]. *Strictures in the Recent Decisions of the Judicial Committee of the Privy Council.* ([London]: English Church Union, 1871). 28pp.

C4 (title), not in JS. Only edition in BL. When the Judicial Committee issued its judgment in the Purchas case (see 828) they also issued these strictures which were sent to every clergyman in the Church of England (Dodgson was a deacon in the Church). This final judgment overturned the previous judgment of the Arches Court, and the strictures were meant to explain the errors of that judgment.

1576. Procter, Adelaide Anne (1825–64). *A Chaplet of Verses.* (London: Longman, Green, Longman & Roberts, 1862). 126pp. 1st edition.

A843 (author, title, edition), JS1684. Catholic daughter of the poet Bryan Waller Procter ("Barry Cornwall"), Adelaide Anne Procter contributed most of her poems to Dickens' periodicals *All the Year Round* and *Household Words*. Procter was a tireless campaigner for those less fortunate, especially women, and this volume was "published for the benefit of the Providence Row Night Refuge for Homeless Women and Children," the first Catholic refuge in the U.K. Her poems dealt largely with simple themes of emotion. Dickens called her "a finely sympathetic woman with a great accordant heart and a sterling noble nature."

1577. Procter, Adelaide Anne. *Legends and Lyrics. A Book of Verses.* (London: Bell and Daldy, 1858–61). 2 vols.

A838 (author, title), JS1687 (listed under Richard Anthony Procter). The 1st edition is described here, since Dodgson owned a 1st edition of the companion volume, *A Chaplet of Verse.* No entries in A838 specify a number of volumes. Dodgson could have owned only the 1st volume (which went through 4 editions before volume 2 was published). He might also have owned the new edition of 1866 with an introduction by Charles Dickens and illustrations including some by John Tenniel. This collection of poems was hugely popular. According to the *Catholic Encyclopedia*, in 1877 only Tennyson exceeded Procter in British sales.

1578. Procter, Richard Anthony (1837–88). *Easy Star Lessons.* (London: Chatto & Windus, 1881). 239pp. With illustrations and maps.

A303 (author, title), JS1686. Only edition in BL. Proctor was a British astronomer whose early financial troubles caused him to seek a popular audience. His many works on astronomy gained just such a following, and he was largely responsible for introducing the wider public to the ideas of astronomy. This work is divided into 12 chapters, one for each month of the year. Replete with star maps, it offers a beginner's guide to the night sky.

1579. Proctor, R[ichard] A[nthony], editor. *Knowledge. An Illustrated Magazine of Science.* (London: ?1881–1885). 8 vols.

A734 (title, 8 vols.), JS270 (Anon./Science). A734 does not specify which volumes Dodgson owned, but it seems likely that he owned the first 8. Proctor founded this magazine of popular science, beginning publication on 4 Nov. 1881. It continued (with a change of title in 1904) until 1917 (later edited by Robert Baden-Powell). Proctor contributed articles on a variety of subjects, including whist and chess. The 1884 volume includes an exchange of letters between Dodgson and Proctor on Euclid's theory of parallels (Dodgson's letter appears on pp. 390–91). Another letter by Dodgson, on divisibility by seven, appears in the issue for 4 July 1884. See *Math.*

1580. Proctor, Richard Anthony. *The Moon: Her Motions, Aspect, Scenery, and Physical Condition.* (London: Longmans, Green & Co., 1873). 394pp. 24 plates. With 3 photographs by Rutherfurd.

A333 (author, title), JS1685 (not listed separately from *The Sun,* and *Other Worlds*). Earliest edition in BL.

1581. Proctor, Richard Anthony. *Other Worlds than Ours: The Plurality of Worlds Studied Under the Light of Recent Scientific Researches.* (London: Longmans, Green & Co., 1870). 324pp. 5 plates.

A333 (author, title), JS1685 (not listed separately from *The Sun* and *The Moon*). Earliest edition in BL. Proctor here presents his thesis that the larger planets are in fact subsidiary suns providing heat to their own satellites.

1582. Proctor, Richard Anthony. *A Star Atlas for the Library, the School, and the Observatory. Showing all the Stars Visible to the Naked Eye, and Fifteen Hundred Objects of Interest, in Twelve Circular Maps on* *the Equidistant Projection.* (London: Long-mans, Green & Co., 1870). 27pp. With two index plates.

A529, D149 (author, title, city, date), JS1688.

1583. Proctor, Richard Anthony. *The Sun. Ruler, Fire, Light and Life of the Planetary System.* (London: Longmans, Green & Co., 1871). 480pp. With plates and drawings.

A333 (author, title), JS1685 (not listed separately from *The Moon* and *Other Worlds*). Earliest edition in BL.

1584. Prout, William (1785–1850). *On the Nature and Treatment of Stomach and Urinary Diseases; Being an Inquiry into the Connexion of Diabetes, Calculus, and Other Affections of the Kidney and Bladder, with Indigestion.* (London: Churchill, 1840). 483pp. 3rd edition.

A587 ("Stomach and Urinary Diseases"), JS169 (Anon./Medical). Only edition of the only matching title in BL. The work was originally published in 1821 as *An Enquiry into the Nature and Treatment of Gravel, Calculus, and Other Diseases Connected with a Deranged Operations of the Urinary Organs.*

1585. [Pryde, James] (1802–79). *Mathematical Tables Consisting of Logarithmic, Nautical, and Other Tables.* (London & Edinburgh: W. & R. Chambers, 1869). 404pp. New edition. In the *Chamber's Educational Course* series.

E315 (title, date), JS1689. Dodgson's copy is in HAC. It is signed in purple ink on the title page "C. L. Dodgson." Includes logarithms of all numbers from 1 to 100,000.

1586. Psalmanazar, George [pseud.] (1679?–1763). *An Enquiry into the Objections Against George Psalmanaazaar of Formosa. In Which the Accounts of the People, and Language of Formosa by Candidius, and the Other European Authors, and the Letters from Geneva, and from Suffolk, about Psalmanaazaar are Proved not to Contradict his Accounts. With Accurate and Authentick Maps. To which is Added, George Psalmanaazaar's Answer to Mons. D'Amalvy of Sluice.* (London: Printed for Bernard Lintott, [1710?]). 78pp.

B1185 (author, title, n.d.), JS1692. Only edition in BL or BOD. The work to which Psalmanazar (spelling from BL) responds in this treatise is Isaac d'Amalvi's *Eclaircissemens, Nécessaires Pour Bien Entendre ce que le Sr N. F. D. B. R. Dit être Arrivé à l'Écluse en Flandres par Rapport à la Conversion de Mr. George Psalmanaazaar, Japonois, dans son Livre Intitulé, Description de l'Isle Formosa*, a work challenging the authenticity of Psalmanazar's account of Formosa (see below). See the following entry for information on the literary imposter known as George Psalmanazar.

1587. Psalmanazar, George [pseud.]. *An Historical and Geographical Description of Formosa, An Island Subject to the Emperor of Japan, Giving an Account of the Religion, Customs, Manners, &c. of the Inhabitants. Together with a Relation of What Happen'd to the Author in his Travels; Particularly his Conferences with the Jesuits, and Others. Also the History and Reasons of his Conversion to Christianity. To which is Prefix'd a Preface in Vindication of Himself from the Reflections of a Jesuit Lately Come from China.* (London: Printed for Mat. Wotton, Abel Roper and B. Lintott, etc., 1705). 2nd edition, corrected. Illustrated with several cuts. To which are added, a map, and the figure of an idol not in the former edition.

A320, B1183 (author, title, date), JS1690. Psalmanazar was the pseudonym of an English literary fraud, whose real name remains a mystery. He presented himself as a native of Formosa and in 1704 produced the present work, in which he even invented a Formosan language. He was exposed in 1706, but went on to work as a hack writer and to pen his memoirs (see below).

1588. Psalmanazar, George [pseud.]. *Memoirs of ****, Commonly Known by the Name of George Psalmanazar, a Reputed Native of Formosa, Written by Himself, in Order to be Published after his Death.* (London: Printed for the Executrix. Sold by R. Davis, J. Newbery, L. Davis, and C. Reymers, 1764). 364pp.

B1184 (author, title, date), JS1691. Psalmanazar herein describes his various deceptions.

1589. *Punch's Almanacks.* 1st and 2nd series, 1842–1880. (London: Punch Office, [1861], [1880]). Bound in one volume.

A371 ("Punch's Almanacs, 1842–1880 in 1 vol."), JS211 (Anon./Periodicals). 1st series is 1842–1861; 2nd series is 1862–1880. Each issue consists of 12 pages, replete with wood engravings, cartoons, etc., published by the humor magazine *Punch*.

1590. Purchas, J[ohn] (1823–72) and Frederick George Lee (1832–1902), editors. *Directorium Anglicanum; Being a Manual of Directions for the Right Celebration of the Holy Communion ... and for the Performance of Other Rites and Ceremonies ... According to Ancient Uses of the Church of England.* (London: Thomas Bosworth, 1865). 306pp. 2nd edition, revised.

A752 (title, date), JS312 (Anon./Theology). Purchas held several curacies and eventually became an incumbent at Brighton. This High Church ritualistic guide to worship was first published by Purchas in 1858. The edition Dodgson owned was revised by Lee, an Anglo-Catholic who crossed over to Rome late in life. See 828 and 1575 for more on Purchas.

1591. Pusey, Edward Bouverie (1800–82). *All Faith the Gift of God. Real Faith Entire. Two Sermons, Preached before the University of Oxford, on the Twenty-third and Twenty-fourth Sundays after Trinity, 1855.* (Oxford: John Henry Parker, 1855). 94pp.

C7 (author, title), JS1694 (not listed separately). Only edition in BL. Pusey took his degree at Christ Church, Oxford in 1822 and was elected fellow of Oriel College in 1823. In 1828 he became a canon of Christ Church and Regius Professor of Hebrew. He was closely connected with the Oxford Tractarians, and following Newman's move to the Roman Church, Pusey became the de facto leader of the Oxford Movement and the chief spokesman of the High Church party. He nominated Dodgson for his Studentship at Christ Church. The present booklet is one of 11 items by or related to Pusey bound together in a volume and described in C7 as "Eleven Sermons and Pamphlets, 1843–1878." 8 of the items are enumerated in C7, the present pamphlet plus: *Everlasting Punishment, Holy Eucharist, Miracles of Prayer, Responsibility of Intellect,* and *Un-science not Science* (all by Pusey); and Maskell's

Letter to Pusey and Newman's *Letter on Eirenicon.* These two sermons on faith argue that all faith comes as a gift from God and include a deep theological and historical analysis of faith concluding that difficulties of faith "disappear upon complete submission to God." The publication includes notes on "Professor [Benjamin] Jowett on the Doctrine of the Atonement" and "Professor [Baden] Powell [d. 1860] on Miracles." Both Powell and Jowett contributed essays to the controversial 1860 collection *Essays and Reviews* (see 2075).

1592. Pusey, Edward Bouverie. *The Church of England, a Portion of Christ's One Holy Catholic Church, and a Means of Restoring Visible Unity: An Eirenicon, in a Letter to the Author of "The Christian Year."* (London: Rivington, 1865). 409pp. Part 1 only of the 3-part work *An Eirenicon.*

E106 (author, title, date), F163, JS1693. F163 notes the gothic stamp. Also published in the same year by Parker of Oxford. The author of *The Christian Year* was John Keble (see 1111). Part 2 of this work was *First Letter to J[ohn] H[enry] Newman in Explanation Chiefly in Regard to the Reverential Love Due to the Ever-blessed Theotokos, and the Doctrine of her Immaculate Conception; with an Analysis of Cardinal de Turrecremata's Work on the Immaculate Conception;* part 3 was *Is Healthful Reunion Impossible? A Second Letter to J[ohn] H[enry] Newman.* In this work, Pusey attempted to show that there was a theological basis for union between the English Church and the Roman Catholic Church, based on the Council of Trent. Dodgson also owned Newman's response (see 1434).

1593. Pusey, Edward Bouverie. *Daniel the Prophet. Nine Lectures, Delivered in the Divinity School of the University of Oxford, with Copious Notes.* (Oxford and London: John Henry & James Parker, 1864). 628pp.

A796 (author, title), JS1695. Earliest edition in BL or BOD. Pusey's learned study of Daniel dealt with radical views (especially those of German theologians) as infidel.

1594. Pusey, Edward Bouverie. *The Holy Eucharist, a Comfort to the Penitent. A Sermon Preached before the University, in the Cathedral Church of Christ, in Oxford, on the Fourth Sunday after Easter.* (Oxford: John Henry Parker, 1843). 93pp.

C7 (author, "Holy Eucharist"), JS1694 (not listed separately). Only British edition in BL. One of 11 items by or related to Pusey bound together in a volume and described in C7 as "Eleven Sermons and Pamphlets, 1843–1878." For a complete list of items enumerated in C7 see 1591, *All Faith*. Pusey published other sermons on the Eucharist, but this is the only one dated 1843, and none of the other items listed in C7 are as early as 1843, hence this seems the most likely match. This is a sermon on Matt. 26:28. Includes: "Extracts from some writers in our later English Church on the doctrine of the Holy Eucharist." Pusey here argues for the doctrine of Real Presence of Christ in the Eucharist. As a result of this teaching (a doctrine that many saw as Roman Catholic), Pusey was suspended from preaching for three years.

1595. **Pusey**, Edward Bouverie. *Everlasting Punishment. A Sermon Preached before the University in the Cathedral Church of Christ, in Oxford, on the Twenty-first Sunday after Trinity.* (Oxford: John Henry and James Parker, 1864). 31pp.

C7 (author, title), JS1694 (not listed separately). Earliest edition in BL. One of 11 items by or related to Pusey bound together in a volume and described in C7 as "Eleven Sermons and Pamphlets, 1843–1878." For a complete list of items enumerated in C7 see 1591. A sermon on Matt. 25:46, in which Pusey defends the orthodox doctrine of Everlasting Punishment for the wicked (a doctrine to which Dodgson did not subscribe).

1596. Pusey, Edward Bouverie. *A Letter on the "Essays and Reviews."* [Oxford: The Guardian, 1861]. 4pp.

C5 (author, title), not in JS. Only edition traced. For an account of the controversial volume *Essays and Reviews* (1860) see 2075. Pusey condemned the volume in this letter to *The Guardian* on 6 March 1861.

1597. Pusey, Edward Bouverie. *The Miracles of Prayer. A Sermon Preached before the University, in the Cathedral Church of Christ, in Oxford, on Septuagesima Sunday, 1866.* (Oxford: John Henry and James Parker; London: Rivingtons, 1866). 35pp.

C7 (author, title), JS1694 (not listed separately). Only edition in BL. One of 11 items by or related to Pusey bound together in a volume and described in C7 as "Eleven Sermons and

Pamphlets, 1843–1878." For a complete list of items enumerated in C7 see 1591.

1598. Pusey, Edward Bouverie. *Parochial Sermons Preached and Printed on Various Occasions, Now Collected into One Volume.* (Oxford and London: J. H. and J. Parker, 1865). 423pp.

C6 (author, title, date), JS1696. The present sermons were for the season from Advent to Whitsuntide. Two more volumes of Pusey's Parochial Sermons were subsequently published.

1599. Pusey, Edward Bouverie. *The Responsibility of Intellect in Matters of Faith: A Sermon Preached on Advent Sunday, 1872. With an Appendix on Bishop Moberly's Strictures on the Warning Clauses of the Athanasian Creed.* (Oxford: J. Parker & Co.; London: Rivingtons, 1873). 84pp.

C7 (author, title), JS1694 (not listed separately). Earliest edition in BL. This work is one of 11 items by or related to Pusey bound together in a volume and described in C7 as "Eleven Sermons and Pamphlets, 1843–1878." For a complete list of items enumerated in C7 see 1591. A sermon on John 12:48. The work to which Pusey responds herein is Bishop of Salisbury George Moberly's *"He that believeth and is baptized shall be saved; but he that believeth not shall be condemned." A Sermon [on Mark xvi. 15, 16]. With an Appendix on the Athanasian Creed.* Pusey here writes, "Ask any tolerably instructed Christian person... 'Will any soul be lost, heathen, idolater, heretic, or in any form of hereditary unbelief or misbelief, if in good faith he was what he was, living up to the light he had, whencesoever it came, and repenting him when he did amiss?' All Christendom would answer you, God forbid! He would not be 'saved by that law which he professeth,' but he would be saved in it, by the one love of God the Father who made him, and of God the Son who redeemed him, and God the Holy Ghost who drew, and in a measure sanctified him."

1600. Pusey, Edward Bouverie. *Sermons.* Details unknown.

A764 (Pusey's Sermons, 4 vols.), JS1697. Pusey published scores of sermons in his lifetime, some separately and some in collections, but no 4-volume collection has been traced. In all likelihood this was a collection of separately published sermons which Dodgson had bound into 4 volumes. C7 lists a single volume with 11 separate sermons and pamphlets by or related to Pusey bound together (see 1591), but whether this is one of the 4 volumes referred to in A764 is not known.

1601. Pusey, Edward Bouverie. *Un-Science, not Science, Adverse to Faith. A Sermon Preached before the University of Oxford on the Twentieth Sunday after Trinity, 1878.* (Oxford: James Parker; London: Rivingtons, 1878). 56pp.

C7 (author, title), JS1694 (not listed separately). Only edition in BL. A sermon on John 1:27. One of 11 items by or related to Pusey bound together in a volume and described in C7 as "Eleven Sermons and Pamphlets, 1843–1878." For a complete list of items enumerated in C7 see 1591. Pusey here asks the question, "Why is the study of the physical sciences at this time so often adverse to the faith in God, and His Son, Jesus Christ Our Lord? There is no doubt alas! That it is so: the long list of eminent scientific men of old, of unimpaired faith, shews that it need not be so. To consider why of late it has been so, may, by God's blessing, save individuals from being borne away into the whirlpool."

1602. Pusey, Edward Bouverie. *What is of Faith as to Everlasting Punishment?: In Reply to Dr. Farrar's Challenge in his Eternal Hope, 1879.* (Oxford: James Parker; London: Rivingtons, 1880). 284pp.

A804 (author, title), JS1698. Earliest edition in BL or BOD. Dodgson also owned a copy of the book to which the present work responds (see 697). H. N. Oxenham wrote in the *Academy*, "His book should at least convince all unprejudiced readers, whether they are willing to accept the doctrine or not, that it was in fact held and taught from the first in the Christian Church, as an integral portion of the revealed deposit of faith." Pusey also here argues that man has free will. Dodgson did not believe in the doctrine of Eternal Punishment.

1603. Pycroft, James (1813–95). *Oxford Memories, a Retrospect after Fifty Years.* (London: Bentley & Son, 1886). 2 vols.

A572 (author, title, 2 vols.), JS1699. Only edition in BL. Pycroft took a B.A. at Trinity College, Oxford in 1836 and served as incumbent at St. Mary's Barnstaple from 1845 to 1856. *Saturday Review* wrote of this work, "Though

these volumes record too many reminiscences of a wholly unprofitable sort, too many silly stories of silly lads and their rowdy doings, they also contain some matter of interest." *The Spectator* wrote, "The bulk of the book consists of cricket reminiscences."

1604. Pym, T. [pseud of Clara Creed]. *Pretty Pictures for Little Paint Brushes. With Descriptive Stories.* (London: J. F. Shaw & Co., [1885]). Outline pictures by T. Pym.

E63, JS1700. Dodgson's copy is in HAC and has the gothic stamp on the illustrated front cover. 29 scenes printed in brown ink on heavy paper, each accompanied by a brief story on the opposite page. Includes a brief introduction that gives suggestions to children for painting the outline pictures.

1605. Quain, Richard (1816–98), editor. *A Dictionary of Medicine, Including General Pathology, General Therapeutics, Hygiene, and the Diseases Peculiar to Women and Children, By Various Writers.* (London: 1885). 2 vols.

A383 (2 vols.), A536 (2 vols.), B1186 (author, title, date, 2 vols.), JS1701. No 1885 2-volume edition has been traced, but Longmans, Green published the 1883 2-volume edition and a 1-volume edition in 1886, and no other British publisher is listed in NUC. Dodgson owned at least 2 copies. Quain was a fellow of the Royal College of Physicians. He served as physician to the hospital for consumption at Brompton from 1855 to 1875. *The Spectator* wrote of this work, "To those who know something of the enormous bulk of even current medical literature, the comprehensive survey of the 'mystery' afforded by this volume will appear a marvel of informed and patient industry."

1606. (Quakers). *What is My Faith?* (Carlisle: Hudson Scott, 1888). 15pp. By a member of the Society of Friends.

E231 (title, authorial attribution, date), JS336 (Anon./Theology).

1607. Quarles, Francis (1592–1644). *Emblems*. Edition unknown.

A896 (author, title), JS1702. First published in 1635 and widely published in the 18th and 19th centuries, often under the title *Emblems, Divine and Moral*. A book of devotional poetry and the best-known work of the author.

1608. R. *The Man in the Moon and Other Tales.* (Glasgow: Hamilton, 1872).

A643 ("The Man in the Moon and Other Tales"), JS (not numbered but listed under Anon./Children). Only edition in BL of the only precisely matching title. BOD describes this as being by "various authors."

1609. Radcliffe, Ann [née Ward] (1764–1823). *Gaston de Blondeville, or the Court of Henry III. Keeping Festival in Ardenne, a Romance. St. Alban's Abbey, a Metrical Tale; with some Poetical Pieces. To which is Prefixed a Memoir of the Author, with Extracts from her Journals.* (London: Henry Colburn, 1826). 4 vols. 132, 186; 399; 375; 333pp.

A826, B1189 (author, title, 4 vols., date), JS1703. Vols. 3 and 4 have a half-title stating: "The Posthumous Works of Mrs. Radcliffe." Radcliffe was a leading exponent of the gothic novel and one of the most popular writers of her day. Many of her novels presented an apparently supernatural situation then gave a natural explanation. This is the 1st edition of her final novel, published posthumously with other works.

1610. Radcliffe, Ann. *The Italian, or, The Confessional of the Black Penitents.* (London: T. Cadell and W. Davies, 1797). 3 vols. 380, 360, 444pp. 2nd edition.

A826, B1188 (author, title, date, 3 vols.), JS1704. Walter Scott commented that Radcliffe, in this novel, "selected the new and powerful machinery afforded by the Popish religion, when established in its paramount superiority, and thereby had at her disposal monks, spies, dungeons, the mute obedience of the bigot, and the dark and domineering spirit of the crafty priest."

1611. Radcliffe, Ann. *The Mysteries of Udolpho, a Romance.* (London: G. G. & J. Robinson, 1795). 4 vols. 3rd edition.

A826, B1187 (author, title, date, 4 vols.), JS1705. A gothic novel in which the heroine is held captive in a mysterious castle by her guardian aunt before escaping to be reunited with her love.

1612. Radcliffe, Ann. *The Romance of the Forest.* (London: A. K. Newman, 1827). 3 vols.

B1190 (author, title, 3 vols., date), JS1706.

This novel established Radcliffe's reputation as a gothic novelist.

1613. Radcliffe, Charles Bland (1822–89). *Behind the Tides.* (London: Macmillan & Co., 1888). 65pp.

E65 (author, title, date), F161, JS1707. F161 notes the gothic stamp. Radcliffe was assistant physician to the Westminster Hospital. E65 describes this work as "arguments against the generally received opinion as to solar and lunar gravitation."

1614. (Radcliffe Library). *Catalogue of Books Added to the Radcliffe Library, Oxford University Museum.* (Oxford: Printed for the Radcliffe Trustees, 1874–76). 3 volumes.

E112 (title, dates), JS202 (Anon./Oxford). These annual volumes were published as early as 1871 and through at least 1926. The present volumes cover acquisitions from 1873 to 1875.

1615. Ragg, Frederick William (b. 1845). *Sonnets and other Poems.* (London: Rivington, Percival & Co., 1895). 103pp.

A841, B1191 (author, title, date), JS1708.

1616. Ralston, William (d. 1911) and C. W. Cole. *Tippoo: A Tale of a Tiger.* (London: G. Routledge & Sons, [1886]). 27pp.

E26 (authors, title), JS1709. E26 notes that Dodgson's copy was inscribed on the title, "To C. L. Dodgson from Kate Ralston, Nov. 6th 1886." William Ralston was a photographer and cartoonist who contributed to *Punch*. A comic tale (which is really no more than an excuse for the accompanying comic illustrations) of a tiger brought back from "foreign parts" by a doctor and the ensuing havoc caused by a wild animal in domestic surroundings. Dodgson might especially have enjoyed the scene in which Tippoo sits for a photographic portrait.

1617. Ralston, William Ralston Shedden (1828–89). *Early Russian History: Four Lectures Delivered at Oxford, in the Taylor Institution, According to the Terms of Lord Ilchester's Bequest to the University.* (London: S. Low, Marston, Low, & Searle, 1874). 236pp.

A526, B1192 (author, title, date), JS87, JS1710. Ralston was a Russian scholar and folklorist and an assistant librarian at the British Museum. Dodgson first met Ralston at the

Tippoo at the photographer (item 1616).

home of George MacDonald. On 16 November 1871, he heard Ralston tell some Russian stories to a group of children and noted in his diary, "Two of them … will do, with some modification, for telling to children."

1618. Ralston, William Ralston Shedden. *Russian Folk-tales.* (London: Smith, Elder, & Co, 1873). 383pp.

A891 (author, title), JS1712. Only edition in BL or BOD. "A few of the ghost stories appeared in the *Cornhill Magazine* for August, 1872, and an account of some of the 'legends' was given in the *Fortnightly Review* for April 1, 1868."

1619. Ralston, William Ralston Shedden. *The Songs of the Russian People: as Illustrative of Slavonic Mythology and Russian Social Life.* (London: Ellis & Green, 1872). 439pp.

A874 (author, title), JS1713. Earliest edition in BL or BOD.

1620. Ramachandra, Y. (1820–81). *Treatise on Problems of Maxima and Minima Solved by Algebra (Calcutta, 1850). Reprinted in Acknowledgment of the Merit of the Author, and in Testimony of the Sense Entertained of the Importance of Indepen-*dent *Speculation as an Instrument of National Progress in India, Under the Superintendence of A[ugustus] De Morgan.* (London: Wm. H. Allen, 1859). 185pp.

E404 (author, title, date), JS1714. E404 describes this copy as having Dodgson's initials and as "presented by Sec. of State for India to R. C. Carrington, Esq." Ramachandra was an Indian polymath, a self taught mathematician and an important figure in Indian education. He translated much important scientific work into Urdu, and believed that Indians were best taught in their own language. In this text, which De Morgan (see 551) did much to popularize in Europe, he tries to revive an Indian spirit of algebra. In his preface, De Morgan writes, "Ramachandra's problem — I think it ought to go by that name, for I cannot find it was ever current as an exercise of ingenuity in Europe — is to find the maximum or minimum without introducing the concept of differentiation."

1621. Ramsay, Arthur. *The Catechiser's Manual: or, the Church Catechism Illustrated and Explained. For the Use of Clergymen, Schoolmasters, and Teachers.* (Cambridge: Macmillan & Co., 1854). 204pp.

E164 (author, title, date), F141, JS1715. F141 describes this as inscribed "Charles Lutwidge Dodgson, from his most affec. Aunt, Lucy Lutwidge." E164 notes that it "bears evidence of [Dodgson's] critical examination." Allibone describes Ramsay as "of Trinity College, Cambridge."

1622. [Rands, William Brighty] (1823–89). *Lilliput Levee.* (London: Alexander Strahan, 1864). 111pp. With illustrations by J[ohn] E[verett] Millais and George John Pinwell.

A935 (title), JS1716. Earliest edition of the only matching title in BL. A 2nd edition of 1867, under the title *Lilliput Levee. Poems of Childhood, Child-fancy, and Child-like Moods* added new poems and additional illustrations by C. Green and B. Bradley. Rands was known as the "laureate of the nursery" for his children's poetry and fairy tales. He also worked as a reporter in the House of Commons. See 254 for another work by this author. See 1351 for a note on Millais. Pinwell (1842–75) was a successful water-colorist and book illustrator whose work appeared in many periodicals.

G. J. Pinwell's frontispiece for W. B. Rands's *Lilliput Levee* **(item 1622) (note the Alice-like figure in the lower right corner).**

These were his first book illustrations. *Saturday Review* said of this collection of nursery rhymes, "One of the most sparkling, whimsical, yet withal wholesome outpourings of fun and frolic that have ever issued from our modern press." In 1897 Dodgson suggested to his publisher, Macmillan, that they compile a collection of pieces to be read by small children during the "unmitigated boredom" of Sunday sermons. He suggested the poem "Little Cristel" from this collection as a piece that ought to be included. The poem tells of a little girl who hears a sermon's call that "Even the youngest, humblest child/Something may do to please the Lord." Without fully understanding what she can do, she performs a series of kindnesses. At the end of the poem she wakes to find it all a dream. Macmillan did not take up the idea.

1623. Ranjitsinhji, [Kumar Shri] (1872–1933). *The Jubilee Book of Cricket.* (Edinburgh & London: W. Blackwood & Sons, 1897). 474pp. With plates, including portraits.

A310 (author, title), JS1717. Published in Queen Victoria's Golden Jubilee year, this book ran through several editions by year's end. Ranjitsinhji (a.k.a. Ranji) was an extremely successful Indian-born cricketer who played for Cambridge University and later for Sussex and London County, as well as for England. The book describes the game and gives a history of cricket at Public Schools, Oxford and Cambridge, and at the county level. It makes mention of the transformation of part of the Oxford University Parks to a cricket pitch, something that Dodgson opposed in his squib, *The Deserted Parks.*

1624. Ranke, Leopold von (1795–1886). *The Ecclesiastical and Political History of the Popes of Rome During the Sixteenth and Seventeenth Centuries.* Translated from the German by Sarah Austin. (London: John Murray, 1840). 3 vols. 528, 596, 416pp.

A632 (author, title, 3 vols.), JS1718. Earliest edition in BL. Dodgson received this book as a prize at Rugby School for "1st class in Mathematics, 1st class in History and Divinity, 2nd class in Classics" at Christmas 1848. Ranke was a highly influential German historian and professor (from 1825 to 1871) at the University of Berlin. He insisted that historical recreations of the past not be colored by present day ideas and emphasized working only from primary source material.

1625. Rankine, William John Macquorn (1820–72). *Songs and Fables.* (Glasgow: J. Maclehose, 1874). 95pp. With illustrations by J[ane] B[lackburn] (a.k.a. Mrs. Hugh Blackburn).

A841, B1193 (author, title, illustrator), JS1719. 1st edition. A 2nd edition was published in the same year by J. Maclehose and Macmillan. Rankine was an engineer who served as Professor of Civil Engineering and Mechanics at Glasgow, held numerous posts in various scientific societies, and wrote works on mechanics and civil engineering. This appears to be his only non-scientific work.

1626. Raymond, Walter (1852–1931). *Tryphena in Love.* (London: J. M. Dent, 1895). 176pp. Illustrated by I. Walter West.

A867 (author, title, 2 vols.), JS1721. Apparently an error in A867 as there is no 2-volume edition of this work (the 1st edition is listed here). Perhaps Dodgson owned 2 copies. Raymond was best known for his novels, of which this was one, set in the West Country.

1627. Reach, Angus B[ethune]. *The Natural History of Humbugs.* (London: D. Bogue, 1847). 126pp.

A472 (title, date), JS1902 (listed with 2 other titles under Smith). Dodgson's copy was bound together with two other titles from the same series, the natural histories of *The Flirt* (by Albert Richard Smith, see 1872) and *Tuft-Hunters* (by Theodore Alois William Buckley, see 283). Reach was co-editor (with Albert Smith) of the short-lived (1847–49) periodical *The Man in the Moon* and also contributed to *Punch.* His chief work, however, was not as a humorist but as a serious journalist. He was parliamentary reporter for the *Morning Chronicle* and his picturesque style of reporting influenced a generation of journalists. This work is of a humorous nature.

1628. Reade, Charles (1814–84). *Christie Johnstone. A Novel.* (London: Richard Bentley, 1853). 334pp.

A814 (author, title), JS1722. Earliest edition in BL. Reade was a fellow of Magdalen College and prolific novelist and dramatist whose most famous work was *The Cloister and the Hearth.* The present romance was among his earliest works. A later novel, *The Wandering Heir*, was inspired by the Tichborne case (see 416). Dodgson saw a dramatized version of *The Wandering Heir* on 15 January 1874, just a few months before he began work on *The Hunting of the Snark* (said by some to be influenced by the Tichborne case). Dodgson saw at least three other plays written by or adapted from Reade. On 19 October 1856, he records that James Barmby (also of Magdalen) advised him to read Reade's novel in favor of prison reform, *It's Never Too Late to Mend: A Matter of Fact Romance.* Dodgson does not record whether or not he took this advice.

1629. Reeve, Isaac. *An Essay on the Comparative Intellect of Woman, and her Little Recognised but Resistless Influence on the Moral, Religious, and Political Prosperity of a Nation.* (Hounslow: J. Gotelee; London: C. H. Law, 1849). 119pp. 2nd edition.

D237 (author, title, city, date), JS1724. Only edition traced. BL describes Reeve as a schoolmaster.

1630. Rehberg, Friedrich (1758–1835). *Drawings Faithfully Copied from Nature at Naples; and with Permission Dedicated to the Right Honourable Sir William Hamilton. His Britannic Majesty's Envoy Extraordinary and Plenipotentiary at the Court of Naples. By his most Humble Servant Frederick Rehberg. Historical Painter in His Prussian Majesty's Service at Rome.* ([London]: S. W. Fores, 1794). 2pp. 24 plates. With the cover title: *Lady Hamilton's Attitudes.*

A272 ("Lady Hamilton's Attitudes, 1794"), not in JS. Two 1794 editions are listed in BOD, one published in Rome and the present, apparently not actually issued until 1797, but bearing the date 1794 on the engraved title-page. The London edition seems more likely. Rehberg was a German artist. These sketches of Hamilton's second wife, Emma, showed her in various classical poses and were a popular attraction in Naples. Emma was subsequently involved in a ménage a trois with Horatio Nelson and bore him a daughter.

1631. Reichel, Charles Parsons (1816–94). *The History and Claims of the Confessional. A Sermon Preached before the University of Cambridge on the Third Sunday after Trin-*

ity 1883. With an Appendix Containing the Chief Authorities. (London: Longmans and Co., 1884). 79pp.

D150 (author, title, city, date), JS1725. D150 notes Dodgson's initials. Reichel was Bishop of Meath. He also served as Professor of Latin at Queen's University, Dublin. A sermon on Ps. 22:5.

1632. Renshaw, S. A. *The Cone and Its Sections Treated Geometrically.* (London: Hamilton, Adams & Co., 1875). 148pp.

E392 (author, title, date), F179, JS1726. F179 notes the gothic stamp.

1633. Reynolds, Edward Morris. *Modern Methods in Elementary Geometry.* (London: Macmillan and Co., 1868). 112pp.

Not in JS. Dodgson examines this book is his *Euclid and His Modern Rivals* (149–50). Reynolds was mathematical master at Clifton College, Modern Side.

1634. [Reynolds, Joseph William] (1821–99). *The Mystery of Miracles.* (London: Kegan Paul, 1879). 261pp.

A784 (title), JS321 (Anon./Theology). Earliest edition of the only matching title in BL. A 2nd edition was published in 1881 (London: C. Kegan Paul & Co.) under the title *The Mystery of Miracles; a Scientific and Philosophical Investigation.* Reynolds was principal of the Operative Jewish Converts' Institution and a writer on miracles.

1635. [Reynolds, Joseph William]. *The Supernatural in Nature. A Verification by Free Use of Science.* (London: Kegan Paul, 1878). 484pp.

A906 (title), JS187 (Anon./Occult). Earliest edition in BL. This book examines the universe in the light of scientific progress all the while looking for the influence of a supreme being.

1636. Ribot, Théodule Armand (1839–1916). *Diseases of Memory, an Essay in the Positive Psychology.* Translated by William Huntington Smith. (London: Kegan Paul, Trench, 1882). 209pp. In the *International Scientific Series.*

A311 (title), JS160 (Anon./Medical). Earliest English language edition in BL. Ribot was a French psychologist whose influential early work on memory used observations of clinical cases to attempt to infer psychological princi-

ples. Among his conclusions were that the most recent memories are the first lost.

1637. Ricardo, David, the elder (1772–1823). *The Works of David Ricardo. With a Notice of the Life and Writings of the Author by J. R. McCulloch.* (London: John Murray, 1852). 584pp.

A317 ("Ricardo's Works"), JS1727. Only matching title in BL. First published in 1846; this is the edition closest to Dodgson's date of purchase (23 February 1858, see *Diary 3*). Ricardo was a successful businessman and member of the London stock exchange with an interest in literature and science. He is best remembered as a writer on economics, his most important work being *Principles of Political Economy and Taxation* (1817). This 1st edition of his collected works was limited to 500 copies, and Dodgson may have owned a later reprint. According to the book's "Advertisement," "The high esteem in which Mr Ricardo's works are held, and their increasing scarcity, have occasioned their being collected, and published in this volume. It contains, in addition to the *Principles of Political Economy and Taxation,* and his detached Tracts, his Essays on the Funding System and on Parliamentary Reform, and his Speech on the Ballot, originally published in the Supplement to the *Encyclopaedia Britannica* and in the *Scotsman.*" Dodgson had a strong interest in Parliamentary reform (see *Political*).

1638. Richard, Léopold. *Sténarithmie-Richard, ou l'art de Calculer Aussi Vite que la Pensée, etc.* (Paris: L'Auteur, 1886). 86pp.

Not in JS. Dodgson's 1897 paper on *Abridged Long Division* (WMGC, 151; *Math,* #36) refers to and quotes from this work, which Dodgson writes he "had not previously met with." The sub-title translates, "the art of calculating as quick as thinking." Earliest edition in BNF.

1639. Richards, Anna M. *A New Alice in the Old Wonderland.* (Philadelphia: J. B. Lippincott Company, 1895). 309pp. 67 illustrations by the author.

A724 (title, city, date), JS1728. An imitation of AAIW, with illustrations in the style of Tenniel. Even the binding is in the style of the "red cloth" editions of the *Alice* books. Before even seeing this volume Dodgson wrote to Macmillan (4 May 1895) on the subject of whether they should undertake its publication in England

Anna Richards' imitation of Tenniel in her imitation of Dodgson, *A New Alice in the Old Wonderland* (item 1639).

and expressed his "absolute disapproval." "I entirely agree with you in thinking such a publication impudent and offensive," he wrote. (See *Macmillan* 315).

1640. Richards, John (b. 1834). *Mechanical Humour. A Collection of Original Anecdotes Connected with Engineering and Mechanics.* (London: G. Richards, [1874]). 150pp.

B1196 (author, title, n.d.), JS1729. Only edition in BL and BOD. Richards was a mechanical engineer who wrote several works on woodworking machinery and related topics.

1641. Richards, Thomas (1710–1790). *Antiquæ Linguæ Britannicæ Thesaurus. A Welsh and English Dictionary: Wherein the Welsh Words are often Exemplified by Select Quotations from Celebrated Ancient Authors; and many of them Etymologized, and Compared with the Oriental and other Languages. It is also Adorned with many Valuable British Antiquities, to Elucidate the Meaning of Obscure Words. To which are Annexed, a Welsh and English Botanology; and a Large Collection of Welsh Proverbs; and to the Whole is Prefixed, a Compendious Welsh Grammar, with the Rules in English.* (Treriw: I. Davies, 1815). 463pp. 2nd edition. MS. notes by S. Smallbroke.

Uncertain. E191 ("Welsh-English Dictionary, 8vo, 1815"), JS257 (Anon./Reference). This is one of three Welsh-English dictionaries in BL published in 1815, but seems the most likely. Two editions of this title are listed in BL for 1815 (this and the 3rd published in Dolgelley).

An English-Welsh Dictionary, etc. by John Waters was published in 2 vols. (E191 makes no mention of multiple volumes and E entries seem always to note multi-volume items). *A Welsh-English Dictionary* by Titus Lewis is described only perfunctorily in BL and the format is not noted; the format of the title described above is 8vo, matching E191.

1642. Richardson, Benjamin Ward (1828–76). *On Alcohol: A Course of Six Cantor Lectures Delivered before the Society of Arts.* (London: Macmillan and Co., 1878). 122pp.

E215 (author, title, publisher, date), JS1732. A reprint, with slight alterations, of the edition of 1875. Richardson was a fellow of the Royal College of Physicians. The author summarizes his work thus: "This chemical substance, alcohol, an artificial product devised by man for his purposes, and in many things that lie outside his organism a useful substance, is neither a food nor a drink suitable for his natural demands. Its application as an agent that shall enter the living organization is properly limited by the learning and skill possessed by the physician, a learning that itself admits of being recast and revised in many important details, and perhaps in principles. If this agent do really for the moment cheer the weary, and impart a flush of transient pleasure to the unwearied who crave for mirth, its influence (doubtful even in these modest and moderate degrees) is an infinitesimal advantage, by the side of an infinity of evil for which there is no compensation, and no human cure."

1643. Richardson, Charles (1775–1865). *A New Dictionary of the English Language, Combining Explanation with Etymology To which is Prefixed a Grammatical and Etymological Examination Adapted to the Dictionary.* (London: Bell and Daldy, 1856). 2 vols. 2221pp. New edition.

A596, B1197 (author, title, 2 vols. date), JS251 (Anon./Reference), JS1730. Richardson was an important English lexicographer who introduced the principle of historical illustration in his dictionary first published in 1836–37. Despite his groundbreaking work, the Philological Society did not accept this principle until much later. Volume 1 of Dodgson's copy was offered for sale at Sotheby's New York in April, 1999 (DAA3168). This volume includes the inscription "C. L. Dodgson Ch. Ch. 1857."

1644. Richardson, Charlotte Caroline (1775–1850?). *Poems Written on Different Occasions. To Which is Prefixed Some Account of the Author, Together with the Reasons which have Led to their Publication by the Editor Catharine Cappe.* (York: Wilson and Spence, J. Todd, and J. Wolstenholme; London: J. Johnson, J. Hatchard, J. Mawman, etc., 1806). 127pp.

B1198 (author, title, date), JS1731. Richardson was born in York and was a domestic servant until her marriage in 1802. When her husband died two years later, she was left with no income and a small child. She opened a school, but it soon failed. Her poems were published by subscription with assistance from Mrs. Newton Cappe.

1645. Rickman, Thomas (1776–1841). *An Attempt to Discriminate the Styles of English Architecture, from the Conquest to the Reformation; Preceded by a Sketch of the Grecian and Roman Orders.* (London: Longman, Hurst, Rees, Orme, & Brown, [1817?]). 146pp.

A876 (author, "Gothic Architecture"), JS1733. Earliest edition in BL. The 4th edition (1848) added "very considerable additions and new plates." A likely candidate for Dodgson is the 6th edition (Oxford and London: John Henry and James Parker, 1862), the latest edition before Dodgson's writings about architecture (7th edition was 1881). This edition (but possibly also others) used the cover title *Gothic Architecture*, which matches the title in A876. Rickman went through several careers before settling on architecture and he had a particular passion for the gothic. Among his designs were the buildings of St. John's College, Cambridge. This work was influential in the Victorian gothic revival.

1646. Ridgeway, Charles John. *How to Prepare for Confirmation. Eight Plain Addresses with Questions for Candidates.* (London: Skeffington & Son, 1889). 103pp.

E190 (author, title, date), JS1734. A 2nd edition was also published in 1889. Ridgeway was educated at Trinity College, Cambridge and served as vicar of Christ Church, Paddington from 1884. He eventually became Bishop of Chichester.

1647. Ritchie, Anne Isabella [Thackeray] (1837–1919). *Bluebeard's Keys and Other Stories.* (London: Smith, Elder, 1876). 412pp. Volume V of *The Works of Miss Thackeray.*

A606 (author, title), JS2048. First published in 1874. Ritchie's Works were published in a 10-volume edition from 1875 to 1890, and E353 lists volumes I, III, VI, and VIII of this set. The other Ritchie titles listed in A600, A601, and A606 (with the exception of *Records of Tennyson, etc.* and *Book of Sybils*) fill out the missing volumes. Thus it seems that Dodgson owned the complete set. JS lists all Ritchie's works except *Records of Tennyson, etc.* under her maiden name, Thackeray. She was the eldest daughter of William Makepeace Thackeray and the aunt of Virginia Woolf. She achieved success as a novelist and author of stories. *The Spectator* said of her, "By very delicate instinct she is able to discern, and by very subtle art to realize and make apparent, the interest which lies in the neglected corners of common life." Dodgson was acquainted with Thackeray and had some correspondence with her (see *Letters*, 170). See also 1655 for a note on *From this Island.*

1648. Ritchie, Anne Isabella [Thackeray]. *A Book of Sybils: Mrs. Barbauld, Miss Edgeworth, Mrs. Opie, Miss Austen.* (London: Smith, Elder, 1883). 229pp.

A606 (author, title), JS2049. A collection of essays on woman writers including George Eliot, Currer Bell, and Margaret Oliphant.

1649. [Ritchie, Anne Isabella Thackeray]. *Five Old Friends, and A Young Prince.* (London: Smith, Elder, 1868). 402pp.

A600? (author, title), JS2051, JS2062. A copy of this edition with Dodgson's signature inside the front cover and his initials on the title page was offered for sale by Maggs of London in 1920, at Anderson Galleries, New York on 28–29 April, 1929, and at Parke-Bernet Galleries, New York on 27–28 October 1953 (DAA2372). Dodgson also owned a later edition: Ritchie, Anne Isabella [Thackeray]. *Five Old Friends, and A Young Prince.* (London: Smith, Elder, 1876). 419pp. Volume III of *The Works of Miss Thackeray,* as described in E353 (author, series, volume number, title), JS2051, JS2062. A600 more likely refers to this edition. Contains: "Five Old Friends," "The Sleeping Beauty in the Wood," "Cinderella," "Beauty and the Beast," "Little Red Riding Hood," "Jack the Giant-Killer," and "A Young Prince." In a letter to the author (24 October 1887) Dodgson mentions having read this book (see *Letters*, 686).

1650. Ritchie, Anne Isabella [Thackeray]. *Miss Angel and Fulham Lawn.* (London: Smith, Elder, 1876). 380pp. Volume VIII of *The Works of Miss Thackeray.*

A600, E353 (author, series, volume number, title), JS2055, JS2053. The *Athenæum* wrote of *Miss Angel*, "Miss Thackeray has given in the guise of a story a most interesting picture of that Georgian time which her father appreciated so well."

1651. Ritchie, Anne Isabella [Thackeray]. *Miss Williamson's Divagations.* (London: Smith, Elder, 1882). 419pp. Volume IX of *The Works of Miss Thackeray.*

A633, B1254 (author, title, date), JS2054. Novel.

1652. Ritchie, Anne Isabella [Thackeray]. *Mrs. Dymond.* (London: Smith, Elder, 1890). 516pp. Volume X of *The Works of Miss Thackeray.*

A606 (author, title), JS2056. First published in 1885. Dodgson apparently owned the 10-volume set of Ritchie's works published between 1875 and 1890 (see 1647) which included this title. Novel.

1653. Ritchie, Anne Isabella [Thackeray]. *Old Kensington.* (London: Smith, Elder, 1875). 502pp. Volume I of *The Works of Miss Thackeray.*

A600, E353 (author, series, volume number, title), JS2057. The *Athenæum* wrote of this novel, "A calm reflective story of very real and rather dull life, full of touches of art, but a little laboured in its very simplicity." Dodgson read this during an illness in July 1883 (see *Diaries*).

1654. Ritchie, Anne Isabella [Thackeray]. *Records of Tennyson, Ruskin and Browning.* (London: Macmillan and Co., 1892). 245pp.

A409 (author, title), JS1736. Earliest edition in BL. Includes information on both Robert and Elizabeth Barrett Browning. Ritchie wrote of these eminent Victorians from personal experience.

1655. Ritchie, Anne Isabella [Thackeray]. *The Story of Elizabeth, Two Hours, and From an Island.* (London: Smith, Elder, 1876). 502pp. Volume VI of *The Works of Miss Thackeray.*

A600, E353 (author, series, volume number, title), JS2058, JS2060, JS2052. *The Story of Elizabeth* is a novel about a foolish heroine who learns wisdom through her own folly. In her article "'Lewis Carroll' as Romantic Hero," (*The Carrollian*, no. 13, Autumn 2003), Karoline Leach suggests that Dodgson may have been a model for one of the characters in *From an Island*, a novel based on personalities on the Isle of Wight.

1656. Ritchie, Anne Isabella [Thackeray]. *To Esther, and Other Sketches.* (London: Smith, Elder, 1876). 394pp. Volume IV of *The Works of Miss Thackeray.*

A601 (author, title), JS2050. First published in 1869. Dodgson apparently owned the 10-volume set of Ritchie's works published between 1875 and 1890 (see 1647) which included this title. Includes: "To Esther," "Out of the World," "Merry Making," "Sola," and "Moretti's Campanula."

1657. Ritchie, Anne Isabella [Thackeray]. *Toilers and Spinsters, and Other Essays.* (London: Smith, Elder, 1876). 389pp. Volume VII of *The Works of Miss Thackeray.*

A601 (author, title), JS2059. First published in 1869. Dodgson apparently owned the 10-volume set of Ritchie's works published between 1875 and 1890 (see 1647) which included this title. *The Athenæum* wrote, "The greater number [of these essays] have reference to various charitable works, and those who conduct them … while there are two or three about authoresses."

1658. Ritchie, Anne Isabella [Thackeray]. *The Village on the Cliff.* (London: Smith, Elder, ca. 1875). 399pp. Volume II of *The Works of Miss Thackeray.*

A601 (author, title), JS2061. First published in 1867. Dodgson apparently owned the 10-volume set of Ritchie's works published between 1875 and 1890 (see 1647) which included this title. The author's second novel and her most popular work.

1659. Ritchie, James Ewing (1820–98). *The Night Side of London.* (London: Tinsley, 1869). 284pp. New edition, revised and enlarged.

D110 (author, title, date), JS1737. Originally published in 1857. Ritchie was a journalist with a particular interest in the less glamorous side of life in Victorian London. Chapters include "Seeing a Man Hanged," "The Cyder Cellars," "Judge and Jury Clubs," "The Police-Court," and "The Lunatic Asylum."

1660. Roach, Thomas. *Elementary Trigonometry.* (Oxford: Clarendon Press, 1887). 265pp. In the *Clarendon Press Series.*

A583 (author, title), JS1738. Only edition in BL.

1661. Robert-Houdin, Jean Eugène (1805–71). *The Sharper Detected and Exposed.* (London: Chapman & Hall, 1863). 268pp.

B1080 (author, title, date), JS1739. Robert-Houdin was a French clockmaker turned performer widely regarded as the father of modern magic. Ehrich Weiss paid tribute to Robert-Houdin by choosing the stage name Harry Houdini. Robert-Houdin wrote this and at least one other book on exposing card sharps.

1662. Roberts, Robert Henry (1838–1900). *The Witness of the Bible to the Kingdom of Heaven upon Earth: An Address from the Chair of the Baptist Union of Great Britain and Ireland, at the Autumn Assembly in London, October 3rd, 1892.* (London: E. Marlborough & Co., 1892). 22pp.

A598 ("The Witness of the Bible"), JS340 (Anon./Theology). Only edition in BL of the only matching title traced. Roberts was a Baptist minister whose other posts included principal of Baptist College, Regent's Park, London from 1892 to 1896.

1663. Robertson, Eric Sutherland, editor. *The Children of the Poets. An Anthology from English and American Writers of Three Centuries. Edited, with an Introduction, by Eric S. Robertson.* ([London]: Walter Scott, [1886]). 273pp. In *The Canterbury Poets* series.

E296 (editor, title, date, series, publisher), JS1740. Robertson was Professor of English at Lahore. In the introduction to this anthology he writes, "I must express a warm sense of gratitude for the favours extended to me by almost every author from Lord Tennyson to the youngest."

1664. Robertson, Frederick William (1816–53). *Analysis of Mr. Tennyson's "In Memoriam."* (London: Smith, Elder & Co., 1862). [56]pp.

B1253 (author, title), JS1741. Earliest edition in BL. Robertson was a remarkable and dynamic liberal churchman. He resigned his curacy at Cheltenham amidst doubts during the height of the Oxford Movement and studied metaphysics and theology for several months in Germany. Returning, he took the helm of Trinity Chapel in Brighton for the last six years of his short life, during which time he preached the sermons which, as MOR states "became afterward the text-book of liberal churchmen." He was adept at appealing to the working classes through both his sermons and lectures, the latter delivered at a working men's institute which he established. Though few of his works were published during his lifetime, his sermons and other work were frequently reprinted during the second half of the 19th century. Dodgson supervised the preparation of an index to Tennyson's *In Memoriam*, also published in 1862.

1665. Robertson, Frederick William. *Expository Lectures on St. Paul's Epistles to the Corinthians.* (London: Smith, Elder and Co., 1859). 513pp.

A759 (author, title), JS1743. Earliest edition in BL.

1666. Robertson, Frederick William. *Lectures and Addresses on Literary and Social Topics.* (London: Smith, Elder, 1858). 308pp.

D152 (author, title, city, date), JS1742. This collection includes two of Robertson's most famous pieces, "Two Lectures on the Influence of Poetry on the Working Classes," and a "Lecture on Wordsworth."

1667. Robertson, Frederick William. *Notes on Genesis.* (London: Henry S. King, 1877). 211pp. Edited, with a preface, by Charles Boyd Robertson.

A759 (author, title), JS1745. Earliest edition in BL. Published posthumously from notes on his lectures (not covering all chapters of Genesis) edited by Robertson's son.

1668. Robertson, Frederick William. *Sermons Preached at Trinity Chapel, Brighton.*

(London: Smith, Elder & Co., 1855–63). 4 series in 4 vols. Edited, with a preface, by Struan E. Robertson.

A759 (author, title, 4 vols.), JS1746. Earliest edition in BL.

1669. Robertson, James Craigie (1813–82). *How Shall We "Conform to the Liturgy of the Church of England?"* (London: William Pickering, 1843). 187pp.

A757 ("Robertson on the Liturgy"), JS1744 (listed under Frederick William Robertson). This is the only book traced by a Robertson containing the word "Liturgy" in the title. Certainly Frederick W. Robertson wrote no such book. Earliest edition in BL. Pickering issued a revised and expanded edition in 1844 and a 3rd edition of 1869 added "two articles on ultra-ritualism." Robertson was educated at Trinity College, Cambridge and served as vicar of Bekesbourne near Canterbury from 1846 to 1859 before becoming a canon of Canterbury Cathedral. This controversial book was written to reaffirm the authority of the Church of Scotland at the time of the 1843 separation when Scottish Evangelicals formed the Free Church of Scotland.

1670. Robinson, Edward (1794–1863). *A Greek and English Lexicon of the New Testament.* (London: Longman, Orme, Brown, Green and Longmans, 1837). 926pp. New edition revised and corrected, with additions, by S. T. Bloomfield.

A326 (author, title), JS1748. Earliest British edition in BL. Originally published in Andover, MA, in 1825 as *A Greek and English Lexicon of the New Testament, from the "Clavis Philologica" of C[hristian] A[braham] W[ahl].* A522 states simply "Greek and English Lexicon" and could refer to another copy of this item. Robinson was an American philologist and Professor of Biblical Literature (first at Andover and later at Union Theological Seminary). He was the founder of the American Biblical Repository.

1671. Robinson, Horatio Nelson (1806–67). *New University Algebra. A Theoretical and Practical Treatise, Containing Many New and Original Methods and Applications for Colleges and High Schools.* (New York: Ivison, Blakeman and Company, 1872). 420pp. In *Robinson's Mathematical Series.*

E256 (author, title, city, date), JS1749. E256

notes this has the autograph of C. E. Cross. Robinson was an American who showed a natural aptitude for mathematics at an early age. He taught mathematics in the Navy beginning at the age of 19, and later taught elsewhere, but in 1844 he gave up teaching and began work on a series of mathematical texts which proved most successful.

1672. Robinson, M[ary] E[lizabeth] (ca. 1775–1818). *The Wild Wreath*. ([London]: Richard Phillips, 1804). 228pp. "Tales, etc. in verse; written by herself and others, edited by Miss M. E. Robinson."

A525 ("Wild Wreath"), JS395 (Anon./Unclassified). Only edition of the only matching title in BL. Robinson was an English Romantic poet. This is an anthology of poems mostly by Robinson, but including "A War Poem" by Southey, "The Mad Monk" by Coleridge and several pieces by M. G. Lewis.

1673. Robinson, Philip S[tewart] (b. 1849). *The Poets' Beasts: A Sequel to "The Poets' Birds."* (London: Chatto & Windus, 1885). 356pp.

A511 ("The Poet's Beasts"), JS383 (Anon./Unclassified). Only edition of the only matching title in BL. Robinson was a newspaper editor and journalist who was born and spent much of his career in India. He also served as a correspondent in the United States and in the Afghan and Egyptian wars.

1674. Robinson, Tom (d. 1916). *The Diagnosis and Treatment of Eczema*. (London: J. & A. Churchill, 1887). 136pp.

E360 (author, title, date), JS1750. Robinson was a physician to St. John's Hospital for Diseases of the Skin, London.

1675. Robson, J[ohn] H[enry]. *Geometrical Drawing; Comprising the Uses of Scales and Practical Geometry, with Numerous Examples, Selected Chiefly from Army Examination Papers*. (London: Relfe Bros., 1886). 2nd edition, revised and enlarged. With fold-out diagrams and drawings.

E343 (author, title, date), F139, JS1751. E343 and F139 describe this as a presentation copy. Robson was educated at Downing College, Cambridge and served as chaplain to the Surrey County Hospital from 1866 to 1876. The last chapter consists of examination questions for admission to Sandhurst.

1676. [Roger (a.k.a. Royer), Clerk of the Treasury]. *East-Bourn, Being a Descriptive Account of that Village in the County of Sussex, and its Environs*. (London: Hookham, 1799). 152pp. 2nd edition with additions and alterations. Plates, map.

B1046 (title, date), JS349 (Anon./Topography). Dodgson spent summers from 1877 to 1897 in Eastbourne on the south coast of England.

1677. Rogers, James E[dwin] Thorold (1823–90). *Education in Oxford: Its Method, its Aids, and its Rewards*. (London: Smith, Elder, and Co., 1861). 266pp.

A572 (title), JS190 (Anon./Oxford). Only edition in BL of the only matching title. Rogers was educated at Magdalen Hall, Oxford. He became Drummond Professor of Political Economy in 1862. He later became an M.P. He and Dodgson were close friends.

1678. Rogers, James Edwin Thorold. *A Manual of Political Economy for Schools and Colleges*. (Oxford: University Press, 1876). 331pp. 3rd edition. In the *Clarendon Press Series*.

A302, D153 (author, title, city, date), JS1752.

1679. Rogers, Samuel (1763–1855). *Human Life, a Poem*. (John Murray: London, 1820). 108pp.

Uncertain. F168 (author, title, date), not numbered in JS. Identified as Dodgson's only by the gothic stamp. Rogers began publishing poetry in 1792 and in 1850 was offered (and declined) the post of poet laureate. Hazlitt called him "an elegant but feeble writer [who] wraps up obvious thoughts in a glittering cover of fine words."

1680. Rogers, Samuel. *Poems*. (London: T. Cadell & E. Moxon, 1834). 296pp. With vignettes after Turner & Stothard.

A419, B1199, E20 (author, title, illustrators, date), F137 (notes 1st edition), JS1753, JS1754. E20 notes that Dodgson's copy is "presented to Lewis Carroll in Memoriam of a member of the family of the late Dean Liddell," and F137 notes the following inscription: "Charles Lutwidge Dodgson, In Memoriam, Nov. 30, 1869." In a letter to Gertrude Thomson of 2 June 1893, Dodgson alludes to illustrations of Rogers; on 25 June he writes, "Thanks for 'Rogers'"; and on 12 August he writes, "Those lovely vignettes of Stothard's do not, in any way, *illustrate* Roger's Poems, but their poetry and grace *harmonise* with them." The original reference may be to this volume. The book received from Thomson may have been another copy of this title, or could be Rogers' *Italy* (1830), also illustrated by Stothard.

1681. Rogers, Samuel. *The Poetical Works of Samuel Rogers.* (London: Edward Moxon, 1848). 377pp.

A366 (author, title), JS1755. Earliest edition in BL.

1682. Rohde, Robert Turner. *A Practical Decimal System for Great Britain and Her Colonies.* (London: Effingham Wilson, 1885). 17pp.

E400 ("A Practicable Decimal System for Gt. Britain and her Colonies by R. T. Ronde"), JS1762. Despite the errors in both the title and the author in E400, this is clearly the book referred to. Only edition in BL. See 687 for another work on metric measurement.

1683. Rolleston, Frances (1781–1864). *Notes on the Apocalypse as Explained by the Hebrew Scriptures: The Place in Prophecy of America and Australia Being Pointed Out.* (London: Rivingtons, 1859). 150pp.

B1156 (title, date), JS323 (Anon./Theology). Rolleston was a passionate interpreter of the scriptures with a special interest in stars and constellations, which she saw as visual records of holy prophecies. Her best known work, in which she propounded these theories was *Mazzaroth* (1862–65).

1684. Rolleston, George (1829–81). *Forms of Animal Life. Being Outlines of Zoological Classification Based upon Anatomical Investigation.* (Oxford: Clarendon Press, 1870). 268pp.

A921 (author, title), JS1757. Earliest edition in BL. Rolleston was Professor of Anatomy and Physiology at Oxford. Dodgson was apparently acquainted with Rolleston as he wrote in his diary on 24 February 1863 that he called at the University Museum, "with a note for Dr. Rolleston."

1685. Rolleston, George. *The Harveian Oration 1873.* (London: Macmillan, 1873). 90pp.

E189 (title, date, author, contents), F138, JS1758. According to E189, this includes: "I.— Advances in Knowledge of Circulatory Organs; II.— The Warrenex M.S." E189 further notes that Dodgson's copy was a presentation copy to "Lewis Carroll" from Dr. Rolleston. The Harveian Oration is delivered annually before the Royal College of Physicians.

1686. Romanes, George J[ohn] (1848–94). *Animal Intelligence.* (London: Kegan Paul, Trench, 1882). 520pp. 2nd edition. No. 41 in *The International Scientific Series.*

A852 (author, title), JS1759. First published as an article in *The Nineteenth Century* in 1878 and separately published that year as *Animal Intelligence an Evening Lecture.* This expanded edition is the first under this title. Dodgson owned other items in this series (see index), and it seems more likely that he would have owned this book-length study than the earlier proto-version of this important work. Romanes was a close friend and associate of Darwin and did much to popularize Darwinism. His work on animal psychology tended towards the anthropomorphic and was quickly superseded.

1687. Romanes, George John. *Thoughts on Religion.* (London: Longmans & Co., 1895). 184pp. Edited by Charles Gore.

A792 (author, title), JS1760. Earliest edition in BL. See 797 for a note on Charles Gore. Romanes, though a scientist, came to embrace Christianity. This book, created by Gore out of notes Romanes left at the time of his death, deals largely with the relationship of religion and science. The two parts are "The Influence of Science upon Religion" and "Notes for a Work on a Candid Examination of Religion." In his concluding note, Gore writes, "The intellectual attitude towards Christianity expressed in these notes may be described as—(1) 'pure agnosticism' in the region of the scientific 'reason,' coupled with (2) a vivid recognition of the spiritual necessity of faith and of the legitimacy and value of its institutions; (3) a perception of the positive strength of the historical and spiritual evidences of Christianity."

1688. Romilly, Henry (1805–84). *The Punishment of Death, to which is Appended his Treatise on Public Responsibility and Vote by Ballot.* (London: John Murray, 1886). 337pp. Edited by Frederick Romilly.

A343, D154 (author, title, city, date), JS1761.

1689. R[orison], G[ilbert] (1821–69). *The Three Barriers: Notes on Mr. Darwin's "Origin of Species."* (Edinburgh and London: Blackwood's, 1861). 180pp.

A909 ("The Three Barriers"), JS278 (Anon./Science). Only edition of only matching title in BL. A909 also includes *Darwinism A Fallacy* (see 1547). Rorison was a clergyman in the Scottish Episcopal Church who served as curate of St. John's Episcopal Church, Edinburgh, 1844–5; curate of St. James's, Leith, 1845–6; and incumbent of St. Peter's, Peterhead, 1846–69. He was also a hymn writer. He unsuccessfully brought charges against a fellow clergyman whom he accused of preaching the Real Presence at the Eucharist, an indication of Rorison's opposition to sympathy with the Oxford Movement in the Scottish church. This work is an attack on Darwin's theories.

1690. R[orison], G[ilbert]. *What is Truth?* (London: 1854).

Uncertain. A909 ("What is Truth?"), JS280 (Anon./Science). There are many 19th-century works with this or a similar title. BL and BOD both attribute this only to G. R. A909 lists, immediately after this title, *The Three Barriers*, which is also signed G. R. and attributed to Rorison in BL and BOD. As like books are often lotted together, it seems most likely that this book is also by Rorison, similarly signed, and shelved next to another book by the same author.

1691. Roscoe, Thomas (1791–1871), editor. *The Juvenile Keepsake.* (London: 1829).

E262 (editor, title, date), JS1763. Roscoe was the son of William Roscoe and a writer and translator who wrote widely on literature, edited a series of English novels with illustrations by Cruikshank, and wrote original works of literature. This volume is a periodical for children (also published in 1830).

1692. Roscoe, William (1753–1831). *The Life of Lorenzo de'Medici, Called the Magnificent.* (London: Scott, Webster, and Geary, 1836). 370pp. A new edition with a memoir of the author by his son, Thomas Roscoe.

A632 (author, title), JS1764. Earliest 1-volume edition in BL or NUC. Other items in A632 specify multiple volumes. First published in 1795 in 2 vols. This book was a prize received by Dodgson at Rugby School on 3 December

1847 for 1st prize of the division in Mathematics for the work of the half. Roscoe was an English historian who fought against slavery as an M.P. This was his principal work.

1693. Ross, Alexander (1699–1784). *Helenore; or, The Fortunate Shepherdess. A Poem, in the Broad Scotch Dialect to which are Added Songs by the Same Author, and a Glossary.* (Aberdeen: Lewis Smith, 1842). 100pp.

E330 (author, title, city, date), JS1765. BL describes the author as a schoolmaster at Lochlee.

1694. [Ross, Christian Kunkel]. *Charley Ross: The Story of his Abduction and the Incidents of the Search for his Recovery.* (London: Hodder & Stoughton, 1877 [1876]). 431pp. With an introduction by C[harles] P[orterfield] Krauth. With portraits, illustrations, etc.

E318 (title, date), JS108 (Anon./Literature). E318 gives an extended title including "with other cases of children lost and found (including a child recovered from Cuba)." The present title is from BL. The book is written by the father of Charley Ross, America's first victim kidnapped for ransom. Four-year-old Charley was kidnapped on 1 July 1874 in Philadelphia. A ransom of $20,000 was demanded. Despite months of investigations and some negotiations, the boy could not be found. In December 1874 a bungled burglary led to the mortal shooting of two men, one of whom confessed that they were the kidnappers. Unfortunately, the man who knew Charley's whereabouts had already died when the confession came, and Charley was never found.

1695. Ross, Frederick Augustus (1796–1883). *Slavery Ordained of God.* (Philadelphia: J. B. Lippincott & Co., 1857). 186pp.

A526, B1200 (author, title, city, date), JS1766. Ross was pastor of the Presbyterian Church in Huntsville, Alabama. See index for similar views on slavery.

1696. Rosser, W[illiam] H[enry]. *The Bijou Gazetteer of the World: Briefly Describing, as Regards Position, Area, and Population, Every Country and State, their Subdivision, Provinces, Counties, Principal Towns, Villages, Mountains, Rivers, Lakes, Capes, etc.* (London: Frederick Warne and

Co.; New York: Scribner, Welford, and Co., [1871]). 636pp.

D18 (author, title), JS1767. D18 notes Dodgson's initials. Earliest edition in BL. A miniature book. Rosser wrote several reference books related to navigation.

1697. Rossetti, Christina [Georgina] (1830–94). *Goblin Market and Other Poems.* (Cambridge and London: Macmillan & Co., 1862). 192pp. With 2 designs by Dante Gabriel Rossetti.

A428 (author, title, "first edition," date [listed as 1866]), JS1768. The 1st edition of this work was 1862, not 1866. MBC lists no 1866 edition and the only 1866 edition listed in BL was published in Boston. The date in A428 must be a typographical error, possibly confused for the date of the 1st edition of *The Prince's Progress*, listed as the next item in A429. Rossetti was the sister of Dante Gabriel Rossetti. She contributed poems to the Pre-Raphaelite journal *The Germ* (see 1709) and in 1862 published this, her first publicly issued volume of poetry. With her fame established, she began to write stories and poems primarily for children. On 12 May 1862, Dodgson wrote in his diary, "I have been reading in these last few days Miss Rossetti's *Goblin Market*, etc., and admire them very much." He first met Christina on 6 October 1863 at her brother's, where he photographed her. He called on her in London several times subsequently. The two exchanged letters (see *Letters*), and Dodgson presented Rossetti with a copy of AAIW. When discussing the design of *Phantasmagoria* (1869) with his publisher, Dodgson wrote, "I fancy *Goblin Market* would be a good model in every way." (See *Macmillan*, 60).

1698. [Rossetti, Christina.] "Hero, a Metamorphosis." In *The Argosy A Magazine of Tales, Travels, Essays and Poems*, vol. I, no ii (London: January, 1866).

Uncertain. JS206 (Anon./Periodicals). The JS entry is based on the presence of a copy of this periodical in HAC. Livingston, p. 175 states, "A letter from D. G. Rossetti to Lewis Carroll, dated Feb. 2, 1866, states 'Let me suggest that you should get No. II of *The Argosy* for January which contains a capital fairy tale by my sister which I am sure would please you.'" However, the Houghton Library contains only bound volumes of The Argosy, and these have no markings that indicate ownership by Dodg-

son. In all likelihood, Mr. Amory purchased these copies as a result of the letter quoted by Livingston, but whether Dodgson took Rossetti's advice is not known.

1699. Rossetti, Christina Georgina. *Maude: A Story for Girls.* (London: J. Bowden, 1897). 81pp. With an introduction by W[illiam] M[ichael] Rossetti.

Uncertain. A868 ("Maude"), JS855 (listed under Dill). Only edition in BL. There seem to be only two possibilities for the book *Maude*, listed in A868: the present volume and Augusta Dill's *Maude, or The Anglican Sister of Mercy* (London: Harrison, 1869). There are several reasons to opt for Rossetti. The title matches A868 more closely and Dodgson did not own any other books by either Dill or Elizabeth Jane Whately, editor of Dill's volume. Most compelling is that Dodgson was a friend of Rossetti and owned at least nine other books by her. He photographed her and her famous brothers, and seems to have followed her career fairly closely. This work, a verse and prose story about a teenage girl and her moral character, was written by Rossetti when she was 19 but published by her brother William after her death.

1700. Rossetti, Christina G[eorgina]. *A Pageant and Other Poems.* (London: Macmillan and Co., 1881). 198pp. 1st edition.

A431 (author, title, edition, date), JS1769. Dodgson's copy is in a private collection, Delaware, USA. A431 notes the inscription "Rev. C. L. Dodgson from his obliged friend Christina G. Rossetti." *The Athenæum* wrote, "The principal poem in this volume is a personification of the months…. Unlike her other allegories, however, this poem seeks to inculcate no distinct moral lesson."

1701. Rossetti, Christina [Georgina]. *The Prince's Progress and Other Poems.* (London: Macmillan and Co., 1866 [1865]). 216pp. 1st edition.

A429 (author, title, edition, date), JS1770. Rossetti's second publicly issued book of verse. When writing to his publisher about the cover design for *Phantasmagoria* (1869), Dodgson wrote, "We might try a cover of the same kind as that of *The Prince's Progress*." (See *Macmillan*, 61).

1702. Rossetti, Christina G[eorgina]. *Seek and Find; A Double Series of Short Studies* *of the Benedicite*. (London: Society for Promoting Christian Knowledge; New York: Pott, Young, & Co. [1879]). 327pp.

B1201 (author, title), JS1772. Only edition in BL. 1st series is "Creation," 2nd series is "Redemption." A theological work in prose.

1703. Rossetti, Christina G[eorgina]. *Singsong: A Nursery Rhyme Book*. (London: G. Routledge, 1872). 130pp. With 120 illustrations by Arthur Hughes, engraved by the brothers Dalziel.

A840 (author, title), JS1771. 1st edition. Dodgson's copy, with his initials twice inside the front cover, was offered for sale by Maggs of London in 1927. A book of short poetry for children. Not up to the standard of *Goblin Market*, but Hughes' illustrations are superb.

1704. Rossetti, Christina [Georgina]. *Speaking Likenesses*. (London: Macmillan and Co., 1874). 96pp. With pictures by Arthur Hughes. 1st edition.

A430 (author, title, illustrator, date), JS1773. A story for children, somewhat in the style of AAIW. In a letter to her brother, Dante Gabriel, Rossetti wrote of this book, "The story is really a Christmas trifle, would-be in the Alice style with an eye to the market."

1705. Rossetti, Christina G[eorgina]. *Time Flies: A Reading Diary*. (London: Society for Promoting Christian Knowledge, 1885). 280pp.

C8 (author, title, date), JS1774. Dodgson's copy is in the collection of Jon Lindseth, Cleveland, OH. C8 notes that this copy has "an autograph inscription inserted, 'The Rev. C. L. Dodgson from C. G. R.'" That inscription is now pasted inside the front cover. A collection of poems and thoughts for each day.

1706. Rossetti, Christina G[eorgina]. *Verses*. (London: Privately Printed at G. Polidori's, 1847). 66pp. "Dedicated to her mother."

A427 (author, title, "Privately printed," date), F135, JS1775. According to F135, Dodgson's copy was inscribed "The Rev. C. L. Dodgson, from his old acquaintance, the author, 1894." A collection of verse written by Rossetti as a teenager and privately printed by her maternal grandfather when the author was only 17.

1707. Rossetti, Christina G[eorgina]. *Verses*. (London: Society for Promoting Christian Knowledge; New York: E. & J. B. Young & Co., 1894). 236pp. 6th edition. Published under the direction of the Tract Committee.

A433, E436 (author, title, date), F135, JS1776. A433 notes that this copy has an "inscription on flyleaf, 'Rev. C. L. Dodgson, from his old acquaintance the Author, 1894.'" Reprinted from *Called to be Saints*, *Time Flies*, and *The Face of the Deep*.

1708. Rossetti, D[ante] G[abriel] (1828–82). *Pictures, Drawings, Designs and Studies by the Late D. G. Rossetti*. (London: Burlington Fine Arts Club, 1883). 56pp. A catalogue, with a preface by H. Virtue Tebbs, Member of the Burlington Fine Arts Club.

E61 (author, title, publisher, date), JS1777. Dante Gabriel Rossetti was brother to Christina and William Michael. He was a poet and painter and helped found the Pre-Raphaelite Brotherhood. He was among the most influential English artists of the Victorian era. Dodgson was acquainted with Rossetti and photographed him and his family, visited the Rossetti home in Cheyne Walk, Chelsea, and made frequent reference to Rossetti in his diaries.

1709. [**Rossetti**, William Michael] (1829–1919), editor. *The Germ: Thoughts Towards Nature in Poetry, Literature, and Art*, Nos. 1–2 (Jan.–Feb., 1850) and *Art and Poetry: Being Thoughts Towards Nature*, Nos. 3–4 (March–Apr. 1850). (London: Aylott and Jones, 1850). Illustrated.

A417 (title, illustrator [Holman Hunt]), JS1677. The brother of Dante Gabriel and Christina Rossetti, William Michael was an art critic for *The Spectator* and helped support his artistic family through his career with Inland Revenue. He was a member of the original Pre-Raphaelite Brotherhood. He was also a man of letters and literary critic in his own right. All four issues published of this journal, intended to be a mouthpiece for the Pre-Raphaelite movement. The title was changed after the publication of the first 2 numbers. The journal includes: "original Poems, Stories to develop thought and principle, essays concerning Art and other subjects, and analytic Reviews of current Literature — particularly Poetry. Each number will also contain an Etching; the subject to be taken from the opening article of the month."

1710. Rossetti, William Michael. *Swinburne's Poems and Ballads. A Criticism.* (London: John Camden Hotten, 1866). 80pp.

A456, B1202 (author, title, date), JS1778.

1711. Rowell, George Augustus (1804–92). *On the Storm in the Isle of Wight, Sept. 28, 1876, and on the Cause of Storms.* (Oxford: The Author, 1876). 44pp.

E181 (author, title, date), JS1779. Dodgson was on the Isle of Wight for his long vacation at the time of this storm, but he does not record it. He does record a rough passage to the mainland and back several days later on October 2. On the morning of September 29, *The Times* carried the following notice under the dateline "West Cowes, Isle of Wight, Sept. 28": "This morning, about 7 o'clock, one of the most fearful whirlwinds passed over a part of this town, causing immense loss to property.... There is scarcely a house on the west side that has not received some damage ... many persons have been seriously injured by the falling in of the roofs and floorings. Business is nearly wholly suspended, and also all communication by rail and telegraph cut off." West Cowes is on the north coast of the Isle of Wight. In 1876, Dodgson stayed in Sandown, on the southeastern coast of the island.

1712. Rowley, Henry. *The Story of the Universities' Mission to Central Africa, from its Commencement, under Bishop Mackenzie, to its Withdrawal from the Zambesi.* (London: Saunders, Otley, and Co., 1866). 493pp. Portraits, maps, and illustrations.

A639, D123 (author, title, city, date), JS1780. D123 notes Dodgson's initials. An account of the short-lived attempt by Oxford and Cambridge Universities to establish a Christian missionary base in the Zambesi. The work followed a call from Dr. David Livingstone following his expeditions in the African interior. Rowley was a part of the 1862 mission, which withdrew after only 2 years, following the deaths of many members, including Bishop Charles Mackenzie. Dodgson's brother Edwin was involved in a later mission to central Africa in 1879.

1713. (Royal Academy). *[Catalogues of the] Exhibition of the Royal Academy of Arts. 1851–1890.* (London: 1851–73 and 1874–90). Bound in 3+2 vols.

A389, A951, D155 (title, dates), JS30, JS31 (Anon./Art). D155 notes Dodgson's initials. Describing the 83rd–122nd Exhibitions of the Royal Academy. Dodgson frequently attended the annual Royal Academy exhibitions, and often recorded his favorite paintings in his diary.

1714. (Royal Academy). *Royal Academy Pictures. 1888–1895. Royal Academy Supplement of "The Magazine Of Art."* (London: Cassell & Company, 1888–95). 8 parts bound in 2 vols.

A271, D156 (title, dates), JS32 (Anon./Art). D156 notes Dodgson's signature. Imprints may vary, but 1892–94 published by Cassell. Illustrating the 120th–127th exhibitions of the Royal Academy.

1715. (Royal Academy). *Pictures. 1896. Illustrating 128th exhibition of the Royal Academy. Royal Academy Supplement of The Magazine of Art.* (London: Cassell, [1896]).

A276 (title, date), not in JS.

1716. (Royal College of Physicians). *The Nomenclature of Diseases.* (London: Issued By the Authority of the Director-General of the Medical Department of the Army, 1869). 327pp. Drawn up by a joint Committee appointed by the Royal College of Physicians.

E211 (title, date), JS170 (Anon./Medical).

1717. Ruddock, E[dward] H[arris] (1822–75). *The Clinical Directory, Chapter on Poisons, etc.: Being Parts V. and VI. of the "Text Book of Modern Medicine and Surgery on Homœopathic Principles."* (London: Homœopathic Pub. Co., 1875). 99pp.

E184 (author, title, date), JS1782. Ruddock was a physician and the author of several works on Homœopathy. See 1543 for another work by him.

1718. Ruddock, Edward Harris. *The Diseases of Infants & Children, and Their Homœopathic Treatment.* (London: 1878). 3rd edition, revised by G. Lade.

E161 (author, title, date), JS1781. Probably published by The Homœopathic Publishing Company (as were editions of 1874 [246pp.] and 1882 [230pp.]). A reviewer for the *U.S. Medical and Surgical Journal* wrote, "This is another of Dr. Ruddock's popular works for domestic use. Its pages are full of familiar notes on disease, and of simple remedies and expedients therefore. It is written in a popular and pleasing style, and its arrangement is creditable and convenient. An improvement over other works of its kind will be found in its excellent remarks on the differential diagnosis between diseases which are so nearly alike as not only to puzzle the lay practitioner, but oftentimes the doctor also."

1719. Ruddock, [Edward Harris]. *Principles, Practice, and Progress of Homœopathy.* (London: Homœopathic Publishing Company, 1875). 4th edition. 27pp. 3rd of a series of *Homœopathic Missionary Tracts.*

Not listed separately in JS (see JS163). Dodgson's copy is in HAC in a bound volume with 7 other tracts from this series and one additional Homœopathic pamphlet (see 970). Ruddock begins with a simple definition: "Homœopathy is a system of curing all curable diseases by means of small doses of those medicines which, administered in large doses to healthy persons, produce in them symptoms *similar* to those produced by the diseases in unhealthy persons. The law is expressed by the *formula — similia similibus curantur*; that is, *like is cured by like.*"

1720. Ruddock, Edward Harris. *A Stepping-Stone to Homœopathy and Health.* (London: 1874).

E414 (title, date), JS173 (Anon./Medical). E414 notes this has Dodgson's autograph. Probably the 9th edition as the 8th edition was published by Jarrold and Sons in 1872. By 1880 the work was being published by the Homœopathic Publishing Company, London.

1721. (Rugby School). *The Rugbæan.* Nos. 1–5, 7, 10–13, 19. (Rugby: Rugby School, 1850–52).

D157 (title, numbers), JS260 (Anon./School Books). A literary magazine of Rugby School. No. 1 was published 14 November 1850 and the magazine was issued weekly in term time. Dodgson attended Rugby from 1846 to 1849.

1722. Rushton, William Lowes (1825?–1909). *Shakespeare's Euphuism.* (London: Longmans, Green and Co., 1871). 107pp. Containing illustrations of Shakespeare from the "Euphues" of John Lyly.

B1226 (author, title, date), JS1783. Rushton was the author of several books on Shakespeare and grammar. Lyly (1553 or 54–1606) was an English dramatist.

1723. Ruskin, John (1819–1900). *Ariadne Florentina. Six Lectures on Wood and Metal Engraving. Given before the University of Oxford, in Michaelmas Term, 1872.* (Keston, Kent: G. Allen, 1873–75).

B1205 (author, title, date), JS1784. Originally published in 6 parts, however B1205 lists only 4 parts (most likely the first 4). Ruskin was the pre-eminent critic of the Victorian era and a writer in many fields (as shown by Dodgson's collection of at least 25 Ruskin titles). He was a great defender of the Pre-Raphaelites, whom Dodgson also admired. An artist himself, he also wrote poetry. His writings pervaded nearly every field of Victorian endeavor. He was Slade Professor of Fine Art at Oxford University. The present collection of lectures includes techniques of metal and wood engraving with reference to the German and Florentine schools. Dodgson writes of first meeting Ruskin on 27 October 1857 at breakfast in the Christ Church Common Room. He records several other meetings with Ruskin in his diary — he asked Ruskin's opinion of Henry Holiday as an illustrator for *The Hunting of the Snark* (1876) and discussed illustrations for *Phantasmagoria* (1869), he photographed Ruskin, dined with Ruskin and several friends, and arranged for Ruskin to see artwork by Gertrude Thomson prior to Ruskin's giving a lecture on illustrating fairyland. Dodgson also wrote to Dean Liddell to suggest that if Ruskin were appointed Slade Professor of Art (he was) that he be offered rooms in Christ Church. In a letter to Gertrude Thomson in 1879, Dodgson wrote of Ruskin, "I have the pleasure of numbering him among my friends." Ruskin was a drawing tutor for Alice Liddell and is said to be the model of the "drawling master" in AAIW. His opinion of Dodgson's own draughtsmanship was not enthusiastic.

1724. Ruskin, John. *The Art of England: Lectures Given in Oxford by John Ruskin During his Second Tenure of the Slade Pro-*

fessorship. (Sunnyside, Orpington, Kent: George Allen, 1884). 292pp.

A406, B1208 (author, title, date), JS1785. Contents include: "Realistic Schools of Painting: D. G. Rossetti and W. Holman Hunt," "Mythic Schools of Painting: E. Burne-Jones and G. F. Watts," "Classic Schools of Painting: Sir F. Leighton and Alma Tadema," "Fairy Land: Mrs. Allingham and Kate Greenaway," "The Fireside: John Leech and John Tenniel," "The Hillside: George Robson and Copley Fielding."

1725. Ruskin, John. *The Crown of Wild Olive: Three Lectures on Work, Traffic, and War.* (London: Smith, Elder, 1866). 219pp. 1st edition.

A410, E443 (author, title, date), F157 (specifies 1st), JS1786. F157 notes the gothic stamp. Critics widely disapproved of these lectures. The first is a demand for justice among working men, the second a pronouncement on *laissez-faire* economics, in the third he argues that all art has been produced by war.

1726. Ruskin, John. *The Elements of Drawing: In Three Letters to Beginners.* (London: Smith, Elder, & Co., 1857). 350pp. With illustrations drawn by the author.

A409, E53 (author, title, edition, date), F153, JS1787. E53 specifies 2nd edition, 1st year; this is the only description of an 1857 edition in BL. The E53 copy has the autograph of R. H. Inglis Synnot [matriculated Christ Church, Oxford 1856; died 1872] with "Ch. Ch." added in Dodgson's hand. Dodgson presented a copy of this same edition to his sister, Mary. That copy is in WWC and is inscribed "Mary C. Dodgson from her affte. brother, Charles. July. 1857." F153 notes only the gothic stamp and may be a different copy. This is Ruskin's principal educational book in the field of art. Ruskin taught drawing for a time at the Working Men's College, and this work is designed for such students. Dodgson valued Ruskin's opinion of his own work—an opinion that was not high. In addition to drawing illustrations for AAUG, Dodgson took pleasure in sketching throughout his life.

1727. Ruskin, John. *The Elements of Perspective: Arranged for the Use of Schools and Intended to be Read in Connexion with the First Three Books of Euclid.* (London: Smith, Elder, & Co., 1859). 144pp. 1st edition.

A408 (author, title, edition), JS1788. Another educational book for art students.

1728. Ruskin, John. *The Ethics of the Dust: Ten Lectures to Little Housewives on the Elements of Crystallisation.* (London: Smith, Elder, 1866). 244pp. 1st edition.

A408 (author, title, edition), JS1789. A series of lectures first given at a girls' school on the subject of mineralogy but more broadly intended to awake intellectual curiosity. Contents include "The Valley of Diamonds, "The Pyramid Builders," "The Crystal Life," "The Crystal Orders," "Crystal Virtues," "Crystal Quarrels," "Home Virtues," "Crystal Caprice," "Crystal Sorrows," and "The Crystal Rest."

1729. Ruskin, John. *Fors Clavigera. Letters to the Workmen and Labourers of Great Britain.* (Orpington, Kent: G. Allen, 1871–1884). 8 vols. 1st and 2nd series. Illustrated by the author.

A411 (author, title, 8 vols.), JS1790. Earliest edition traced. Originally published as 96 monthly letters (of 20–24pp. each) and collected into 8 vols. of 12 letters each. Vol. 8 has 7 illustrations by Kate Greenaway (see 819). One of the most controversial of Ruskin's works, these letters were on a wide variety of subjects. The DNB calls this, "one of the curiosities of literature. Its discursiveness, its garrulity, its petulance are amazing ... [it] is full of passionate intensity; it abounds in forcible writing, and the ingenuity with which innumerable threads are knit together to enforce the author's economic principles is remarkable." OCEL states that Ruskin's "underlying theme" here is "the redress of poverty and misery."

1730. Ruskin, John. *The King of the Golden River, or, The Black Brothers: A Legend of Stiria.* (London: Smith, Elder, & Co., 1867). 64pp. 6th edition. Illustrated by Richard Doyle.

A410, E446 (author, title, illustrator, edition), JS1791. Dodgson may have owned 2 or more copies of this title. F143 lists an undated copy with Dodgson's initials and the gothic stamp; F156 lists a copy dated 1851, which would correspond to the 2nd edition, published in London by Smith, Elder, & Co. E446 notes that Dodgson's copy "has initials of Lewis Carroll inside cover." F143 notes both initials and the gothic stamp while F156 notes only the gothic stamp. A fantasy story of three brothers, two cruel and one noble.

1731. Ruskin, John. *Lectures on Art Delivered before the University of Oxford in Hilary Term, 1870.* (Oxford: Clarendon Press, 1870). 189pp. 1st edition.

A591, D158 (author, title, city, date, edition), JS1792. D158 notes Dodgson's signature. Contents include, "The Relation of Art to Religion," "The Relation of Art to Morals," "Line," "Light," and "Colour." These lectures were so popular that they had to be moved to a larger hall to accommodate the throngs who wished to attend. Ruskin here defends his belief that art is connected to all aspects of life.

1732. [Ruskin, John]. *Modern Painters by a Graduate of Oxford.* (London: Smith, Elder and Co., 1848–60). 5 vols. 423, 217?, 348, 412, 384pp. Vol. 1, 5th edition, 1851; Vol. 2, 2nd edition, 1848; Vols. 3–5, 1st editions, 1856, 1856, 1860.

A403 (author, title, editions), JS1793. Contains: "Of General Principles and of Truth," "Of the Imaginative and Theoretic Faculties," "Of Many Things," "Of Mountain Beauty," "Of Leaf Beauty," "Of Cloud Beauty," and "Of Ideas of Relation." This monument of Victorian art criticism began with a defense of the "truth" of Turner's depiction of nature. It goes on to consider, in great detail, Turner's "truth" of tone, color, space, skies, earth, water, and vegetation. The work on *Modern Painters* occupied Ruskin from 1843 to 1860.

1733. Ruskin, John. *Notes on the Construction of Sheepfolds.* (London: Smith, Elder and Co., 1851). 50pp. 1st edition.

B1203 (author, title, date, edition), JS1795. An essay addressing the relationship of the clergy to the laity.

1734. [Ruskin, John]. *Notes on Some of the Principal Pictures Exhibited in the Rooms of the Royal Academy (and the Society of Painters in Water Colours).* (London: Smith, Elder & Co., 1855–59). Nos. I–V. 30, 51, 60, 64, 56pp.

A407, B1204 (author, title, dates), JS1800. Bound together with 2 other Ruskin pamphlets—*Notes on the Turner Gallery* and *Pre-Raphaelitism* (see 1736 and 1740). Ruskin issued a total of 6 series of reviews of London art

exhibits in the present series—the five included here, and one for the 1875 season (see below).

1735. Ruskin, John. *Notes on Some of the Principal Pictures Exhibited in the Rooms of the Royal Academy: 1875.* ([London]: Ellis & White; Orpington: George Allen, 1875). 59pp.

B1206 (author, title, date), JS1794. This work went through at least 3 editions in 1875.

1736. Ruskin, John. *Notes on the Turner Gallery at Marlborough House: 1856.* (London: Smith, Elder, 1857). 88pp.

A407, B1204 (author, title, date), JS1800 (not listed separately). Bound together with other Ruskin pamphlets (see 1734).

1737. Ruskin, John. *Poems.* (New York: J. Wiley & Sons, 1882). 233pp. Collected and edited by James Osborne Wright.

A409 (author, title), E439 (author, title, editor), F155 (author, title, editor, date), JS1796, JS1797. It seems likely that all three citations refer to the same book (this is the earliest edition traced). F155 notes the gothic stamp (this copy sold at the Leicester Harmsworth Sale, Sotheby's London, 26 March 1947 (DAA2191). There was an edition of Ruskin's poems edited by W. G. Collingwood (Orpington and London: G. Allen, 1891), but this was a 2-volume edition and A409 does not specify multiple volumes. On 5 February 1883, Dodgson writes in his diary, "Received, from Howell, the copy I had sent for of *Ruskin's Poems*, marked as very scarce, at 25/-. A copy of the original book sold, about two years ago, for £40. I find this is a reprint, edited by James Osborne Wright, and with no printer's name. I wrote to tell Ruskin about it, and to urge him to counter-plot, by announcing a genuine new edition." (See *Diary 7* for this and Ruskin's reply).

1738. Ruskin, John. *The Political Economy of Art: Being the Substance (with Additions) of Two Lectures Delivered at Manchester, July 10th and 13th, 1857.* (London: Smith, Elder, 1857). 248pp.

A410, E297 (author, title, publisher, date), F157, F158, JS1798, WS. Dodgson apparently owned 2 copies. One copy is in WWC. It has the gothic stamp and has the property label on the cover. The other copy sold at Sotheby's, London on 10–11 Dec. 1993 and is in the collection of Jon Lindseth, Cleveland, OH. It has the gothic stamp on the front endpaper. A fascinating series of arguments on art and economy, centered around the question of how the labor of the artist should be valued by society. Later reprinted as *A Joy Forever*.

1739. Ruskin, John. *Praeterita: Outlines of Scenes and Thoughts Perhaps Worthy of Memory in my Past Life*. (Orpington, Kent: George Allen, 1886–87). 2 vols. 432, 442pp.

A405 (author, title), JS1799. Originally issued in parts. 1st book edition. Dodgson's copy, with his signature on the titles, was sold at the Leicester Harmsworth sale at Sotheby's London, 26 March 1947 (DAA2194) and is now in the Ruskin Library, University of Lancaster. An unfinished autobiography tracing some of Ruskin's influences. It includes some of his reminiscences about Alice Liddell and her sisters.

1740. Ruskin, John. *Pre-Raphaelitism*. (London: Smith and Elder, 1851?). 68pp.

A407, B1204 (author, title, date [1855]), JS1800. The 1st edition of this title was published in 1851 and the 2nd in 1862. No 1855 edition has been traced. Probably a misprint ("1855" for "1851") in B1204. Ruskin was a great defender of the Pre-Raphaelite Brotherhood and their artwork, and largely through his influence they came to be accepted.

1741. Ruskin, John. *The Queen of the Air: Being a Study of the Greek Myths of Cloud and Storm*. (London: Smith, Elder, 1869). 199pp. 2nd edition.

A409, E23 (author, title, date, edition), F154, JS1801. F154 notes the gothic stamp. The Queen referred to in the title of Ruskin's study of ancient Greek myths is Athena. The study contains three lectures, in which Ruskin tries to recapture heroic ideals: "Athena in the Heavens," "Athena in the Earth," "Athena in the Heart."

1742. Ruskin, John. *Salsette and Elephanta: A Prize Poem. Recited in the Theatre, Oxford, June 12th, 1839*. (Sunnyside, Orpington, Kent: George Allen, 1879). 16pp. New edition.

B1207 (author, title, date), JS1802. As an undergraduate at Christ Church, Ruskin won the Newdigate Prize with this poem.

1743. Ruskin, John. *Sesame and Lilies: Two Lectures Delivered at Manchester in 1864*. (London: Smith, Elder & Co., 1865). 196pp.

A410, E25 (author, title, date), F144, JS1803. F144 notes Dodgson's signature. The two lectures are "Of Kings' Treasuries," and "Of Queens' Gardens." The first refers to collections of books and is a lecture on reading and the author's desire to see the private libraries of the realm flung open. The second is on the education and responsibilities of women of privilege.

1744. Ruskin, John. *The Seven Lamps of Architecture*. (London: Smith, Elder, 1849). 205pp. 1st edition. With illustrations, drawn and etched by the author.

A404 (author, title, edition), JS1804. Dodgson's copy, with his signature on the title, was sold at the Leicester Harmsworth sale at Sotheby's London, 26 March 1947 (DAA2193). Ruskin's seven principals of architecture are: Sacrifice, Truth, Power, Beauty, Life, Memory, and Obedience. Ruskin here defends Gothic architecture, which underwent a major revival in the 19th century, as the most noble style.

1745. Ruskin, John. *The Stones of Venice*. (London: Smith, Elder, and Co., 1851–53). 3 vols. 413, 394, 362pp. 1st edition. With illustrations drawn by the author.

A402 (author, title, edition), JS1805. The 3 volumes are "The Foundations," "The Sea-stories," and "The Fall." On 1 August 1855 Dodgson wrote in his diary, "At present I am engaged on Ruskin's *Stones of Venice*." As in *The Seven Lamps of Architecture*, Ruskin here defends Gothic architecture, but here he does it more through a casting down of Renaissance principals. These he attacks with specific reference to Venice, where he also finds examples of the Gothic to praise. Dodgson quotes this work at length in his *Objections, Submitted to the Governing Body of Christ Church, Oxford, Against Certain Proposed Alterations in the Great Quadrangle* (WMGC, #95; *Oxford*, 101).

1746. Ruskin, John. *Time and Tide, by Weare and Tyne. Twenty-five Letters to a Working Man of Sunderland on the Laws of Work*. (London: Smith, Elder and Co., 1868). 199pp. 2nd edition.

A410, E442 (author, title, date), JS1806. E442 notes Dodgson's autograph on the title. The letters are to Thomas Dixon and are social essays that reveal Ruskin's ideal of a society without luxury or poverty.

1747. Ruskin, John. *"Unto this Last": Four Essays on the First Principles of Political Economy.* (London: Smith, Elder, 1862). 174pp.

A410, E444 (author, title, date), F158, JS1807. F158 notes the gothic stamp. Publication of these essays began in the *Cornhill Magazine*, but Thackeray, the editor, cancelled the series after a public outcry against them. Ruskin discusses wages (the possibility that they could be fixed, in what way they can be made just, etc.), and calls for "not greater wealth, but simpler pleasure.... Care in no wise to make more of money, but care to make much of it; remembering always the great, palpable, inevitable fact — that what one person has, another cannot have."

1748. Russell, John (1792–1878). *An Essay on the History of the English Government and Constitution, from the Reign of Henry VII to the Present Time.* (London: Longman, Hurst, Rees, Orme, and Brown, 1821). 320pp.

A553 ("Russell on the English Government"), JS1808. 1st edition of the only matching title in BL. Russell was prime minister from 1846 to 1852 and from 1865 to 1866. A history of the English constitution, reprinted in the 20th century because of interest in the influence of the English constitution on that of other countries.

1749. Russell, John Scott (1808–82). *Geometry in Modern Life, Being the Substance of Two Lectures on Useful Geometry Given before the Literary Society at Eton.* (Eton: Williams and Son; London: Simpkin, Marshall, and Co., 1878). 197pp.

E396 (author, title, date), JS1826 (listed under Scott), WS. Dodgson's copy is in WWC. It is inscribed with Dodgson's monogram. Russell was an important civil engineer and shipbuilder who created the "Wave System" of ship construction. He was vice-president of the Institutions of Civil Engineers and Naval Architects and a frequent lecturer.

1750. Ryder, Dudley, Earl of Harrowby (1798–1882), preface by. *Credentials of Christianity: A Course of Lectures Delivered at the Request of the Christian Evidence Society.* (London: Hodder and Stoughton, 1875). 282pp. With a preface by the Earl of Harrowby.

D47 (title, "Christian Evidence Lectures"), JS309 (Anon./Theology). D47 notes Dodgson's initials. Ryder was an M.P. for over 25 years before ascending to his father's seat in the House of Lords. Includes: [Goodwin, Harvey], "The Evidences for the Inspiration of Holy Scripture"; Alexander, William L., "The Evidence to the Truth of Christianity Supplied by Prophecy"; Row, Charles, "The Positive Evidence in Proof of the Historical Truth of the Miracles of the New Testament"; Barry, Alfred, "The Adaptation of Christianity to the Requirements of Human Society"; Lorimer, Peter, "The Evidence to Christianity Arising from its Adaptation to all Deeper Wants of the Human Heart"; and [Ellicott, Charles J.], "The Adequacy of the Christian Answer to All Deeper Questions."

1751. S., H. *The History of the Davenport Family in which is Displayed a Striking Contrast Between Haughty Indolence and Healthful Activity, in the Characters of the Young Davenports, and their Cousins Interspersed with Moral Reflections.* (London: E. Newbery, [1791]). 120pp. Embellished with cuts.

A935 (title, "Embellished with cuts," "2 vols. in 1" publisher), JS60 (Anon./Children's). Only edition traced matching all the particulars in A935. See below for the 2nd volume. BL also includes a 180pp. 1798 edition, which does not specify "Embellished with cuts" in the listing. A moral tale for children.

1752. S., H. *The History of the Davenport Family: Exhibiting the Characters of the Young Davenports and Their Cousins Sophia and Amelia Easy. Vol. II.* (London: Printed for E. Newbery [ca. 1795]). 134pp.

A935 (title, "Embellished with cuts," "2 vols. in 1" publisher), JS60 (Anon./Children's). Only edition traced matching all the particulars in A935. See above for the 1st volume. Dodgson had both titles bound in a single volume. A moral tale.

1753. Sadler, John. *An Explanation of the Terms Used in Chemistry.* (London: From the Press of the Royal Institution of Great Britain, 1804). 22pp.

D50 (author, title, date), JS1809. Bound with Davy's *Outlines of a Course of Lectures on Chemistry* (see 538).

1754. Sala, George Augustus Henry (1828–95). *A Journey Due North; Being Notes of a Residence in Russia in the Summer of 1856.* (London: Richard Bentley, 1858). 311pp.

D159 (author, title, city, date), JS1810. Sala, a prolific English journalist with close connections to Charles Dickens and Edmund Yates, traveled to Russia in 1856 as a correspondent for Dickens' periodical *Household Words.*

1755. (Salisbury). *The Illustrated Guide to Old Sarum and Stonehenge.* (Salisbury: Brown & Co., 1868). 52pp. With engravings.

E240 ("Old Sarum and Stonehenge — Guide to, with woodcuts, 1868"), JS364 (Anon./Topography). Only title in BL matching the particulars in E240. Dodgson traveled to Salisbury twice in 1873 to visit his sick uncle Skeffington, and to attend that uncle's funeral.

1756. Sallustius Crispus, Caius (86–34 B.C.E.). *C. Crispi Sallustii Quæ Supersunt Opera.* (Cupri in Fifa: Typis R. Tulis, 1807). 252pp. Edited by John Hunter.

B1209 (author, title, date, editor), JS1814. Sallustius was a Roman historian known for his literary style.

1757. Sallustius Crispus, Caius. *C. Sallustii Crispi De Catilinae Conjuratione Deque Bello Jugurthino, Libri; Recensuit Atque Adnotationibus Illustravit H[enry] E[llis] Allen.* (London: 1832).

Uncertain. E399 (author, date), JS1815. This is one of only 4 books by Sallustius published in 1832 traced. Of the other 3 one was published in Basel, another in Philadelphia, and the other is a specific work in English. This seems far and away the most likely match to the rather cryptic entry in E399 ("Sallust — 16mo., shabby calf, 1832"), especially as BL lists this title as 12mo. E399 goes on to say "Another of Lewis Carroll's Rugby school-books with his autograph (1845) and some portrait sketches in pencil; with MS notes."

1758. Salmon, George (1819–1904*).* *A Treatise on the Analytic Geometry of Three Dimensions.* (Dublin: Hodges, 1862). 465pp.

JS1812. Dodgson's copy is in the collection formed by Jeffrey Stern, now at Seitoku Gakuin College, Tokyo, Japan, and is signed "C. L.

Dodgson" on the title and inside front cover. It also includes some minor corrections and markings in Dodgson's hand, though most of the pages are unopened. Salmon was an Irishman who took his degree in mathematics at Trinity College, Dublin in 1838 and became a fellow there in 1841. He wrote four textbooks on mathematics (two of which we know Dodgson owned) and took a special interest in the algebraic approach to geometry.

1759. Salmon, George. *A Treatise on Conic Sections, Containing an Account of Some of the Most Important Modern Algebraic and Geometric Methods.* (London: Longman, Brown, Green, Longman, and Roberts, 1863). 362pp. 4th edition.

D160, JS1813. Dodgson's copy is in HAC and has his signature in brown ink on the brown front paste-down. It is similarly signed in brown ink on the title page. Many of the pages are uncut.

1760. Salverte, Anne Joseph Eusèbe [i.e. Eusèbe Bacconnière-Salverte] (1771–1839). *The Occult Sciences. The Philosophy of Magic, Prodigies and Apparent Miracles.* (London: Richard Bentley, 1846). 2 vols. Translated, with notes illustrative, explanatory and critical by Anthony Todd Thomson (1778–1849).

A892, D183 (translator, title, author, city, date), JS443. Salverte was a lawyer prior to the French Revolution; afterwards, he expressed his liberal thoughts in the Ministry of Foreign Affairs. He saw nature as a delicate balance disturbed by man.

1761. Sampson, Edward Frank (b. 1848). *Christ Church Sermons; with an Introductory Essay.* (London: Longmans & Co., 1896). 292pp.

A768 (author, title), JS1816. Only edition in BL. Sampson was one of Dodgson's fellow Senior Students at Christ Church and also served as a mathematical tutor there. The two were close friends throughout Dodgson's nearly 50-year residence at Christ Church. They took frequent journeys together to Guildford and the seaside, and even traveled to Dublin and the Channel Islands together. They met in London on many occasions, and Sampson sometimes joined Dodgson at Eastbourne for a sojourn.

1762. Sand, George [pseudonym of Armandine Aurore Lucile Dupin] (1804–76). *La Petite Fadette*. (Paris: Michel Lévy Frères, 1869). 287pp.

B1210 (author, title, date), JS1817. Sand was a French novelist. This is one of her last novels, which OCEL calls a "charming rustic idyll." On 24 July 1881, Dodgson wrote in his diary of his desire to translate some of this book (see *Diary 7*).

1763. Sanday, William (1843–1920). *Inspiration. Eight Lectures on the Early History and Origin of the Doctrine of Biblical Inspiration, being the Bampton Lectures for 1893*. (London: Longmans Green, 1893). 464pp.

A803 ("Sandy's Bampton Lectures"), JS1819. Clearly the name "Sandy" was a typographical error as no such Bampton lecturer existed. Earliest edition in BL. Sanday was Lady Margaret Professor of Divinity at Oxford and a canon at Christ Church. Dodgson met him on at least one occasion, on 12 May 1897. Sanday preached a sermon at Christ Church (after Dodgson's death on 14 January 1898) in which he referred to Dodgson (see *In Memoriam*).

1764. Sanday, William. *The Oracles of God: Nine Lectures on the Nature and Extent of Biblical Inspiration and on the Special Significance of the Old Testament Scriptures at the Present Time*. (London: Longmans, Green 1892). 156pp. 4th edition.

A793, C9, D161 (author, title, date), JS1818. D161 notes Dodgson's initials. A presentation copy from Dodgson to his brother Edwin (inscription dates 3/14/93) was offered for sale by Maggs of London in 1918.

1765. Sandford, Mrs. John. *Female Improvement*. (London: Longman, Orme, Brown, Green, and Longmans, and J. Hatchard and Son, 1839). 344pp. 2nd edition.

Not in JS. Dodgson's copy was sold by Marchpane Booksellers, London. It had the gothic stamp and his monogram in black ink on the title page. According to Kenneth Fuller, of Marchpane, "The authoress was the wife of the Reverend John Sandford, an Oxford cleric, Bampton Lecturer and author of many religious/historical works. She wrote a number of books on the domestic role of Women in the Victorian household, as well as a biography of Lady Jane Grey. This work contains 'the Authoress's fuller and more matured opinions upon some points touched upon in her previous publication: — they also embrace many new and important topics…' such as religion, the employment of time, study, temper, taste, benevolence, marriage, the young wife, and the young mother."

1766. Sannazaro, Jacopo (1458–1530). *Arcadia*. (1566).

Uncertain. F191 (author, title, date), not numbered in JS. Identified only by gothic stamp. Sannazaro was an Italian poet. The present pastoral idyll, in prose and verse, was the first of many on Arcadia.

1767. Saulcy, Louis Félicien Joseph Caignart de (1807–80). *Narrative of a Journey Round the Dead Sea, and in the Bible Lands, in 1850 and 1851*. (London: R. Bentley, 1854). 2 vols. 560, 604pp. 2nd edition. Edited by Count Edward de Warren.

A590, B1032 (author, title, date), JS348 (Anon./Topography), JS825 (listed under De Saulcy). The author was a numismatist, archeologist, museum keeper and Egyptologist. This work includes an account of the discovery of the sites of Soddom and Gomorrah.

1768. [Savage, Marmion W.] (1803–72). *The Bachelor of the Albany*. (London: Chapman & Hall, 1854). 311pp.

Not in JS. Dodgson records reading this novel and writes a long review of it in his diary on 28 April 1855. He writes, "I like very little in it." (See *Diary 1*). First published in 1848; this is the edition in BL closest to Dodgson's diary mention. Marmion was an Irish novelist.

1769. Sawyer, John. *Automatic Arithmetic: A New System for Multiplication and Division without Mental Labour and Without the Use of Logarithms*. (London: G. Bell and Sons, [1878]). 17pp.

E66 (title, author), JS1820. Earliest edition in BL or BOD. E66 describes this as having "tables of decimals of a £ and an ingenious arrangement of automatic calculating tables." It notes the stamp of Lewis Carroll (possibly the gothic stamp) inside cover. Sawyer was a fellow of the Institute of Accountants. Dodgson had an interest in mathematical shortcuts and published some in *Nature* (see LCP).

1770. Scheffler, Hermann (1820–1903?). *Die Magischen Figuren. Allgemeine Lösung und Erweiterung eines aus dem Alterthume Stammenden Problems.* (Leipzig Teubner, 1882). 112pp. Plates.

E331 (author, title, city, date), JS1821. Title translates: *The Magic Figures. General Solution and Extension of a Problem Originating with Alterthume.*

1771. Scheller, Immanuel Johann Gerhard (1735–1803). *Lexicon Totius Latinitatis. A Dictionary of the Latin Language.* (Oxford: University Press, 1835). [1469]pp. Originally compiled with explanations in German. Revised and translated into English by Joseph Esmond Riddle (d. 1859).

A937, D162 (author, title, translator, city, date), JS1822. Educated in Leipzig, Scheller eventually became rector and professor of the Royal High School in Breig, where he served from 1771 until his death. Riddle was educated at St. Edmund Hall, Oxford, where he received his M.A. in 1831. He was Bampton lecturer in 1852 and incumbent of St. Philip and St. James, Leckhampton from 1840 until his death.

1772. Schiller, Johann Christoph Friedrich von (1759–1805). *The Dragon of the Isle of Rhodes, Sixteen Etchings from Retsch: To which is Annexed a Literal Translation of Schiller's Der Kampf mit dem Drachen.* (London: Ackermann, 1829 [1830]). 16pp.

A255 (title, illustrator), not in JS. Only edition in BL. An edition published by Boosey in 1825 bore the title *Sixteen Outlines by M. Retsch to Schiller's Fight with the Dragon.* Schiller was a German philosopher and poet. The poem title translates "The Fight with the Dragon." Friedrich August Moritz Retzsch (1779–1857) was a German artist and engraver whose outline style influenced many English artists, including Rossetti and Ford Madox Brown.

1773. Schofield, Alfred Taylor (1846–1929). *Another World; or, the Fourth Dimension.* (London: Sonnenschein & Co., 1888). 92pp.

B1211 (author, title, date), JS1823. Schofield was a division surgeon to the Metropolitan Police and a member of the Royal College of Physicians. In an attempt to help readers understand a world with four dimensions, he takes them to worlds with fewer than three dimensions. Similar to the important 1884 work *Flatland* by Edwin Abbott (see 1).

1774. Scholefield, James (1789–1853), ed. *The Greek and English Testament.* (London: Parker, 1850).

Not in JS. DAA2541. Dodgson's copy was offered at Park-Bernet Galleries, New York on 12 May 1964. It is Dodgson's father's copy, and is "inscribed on front fly-leaf 'Charles Dodgson/A birthday Gift/from his afte. Children/1855.'" This copy is also inscribed in Oct. 1898 by Edward G. Phillimore of Keble College with a note saying "N.B. This book came from the library of the late Rev. Charles Lutwidge Dodgson (Lewis Carroll)." Scholefield was a classical scholar and clergyman whose works included *Hints for an Improved Translation of the New Testament.*

1775. Schroen, Heinrich Ludwig Friedrich (1799–1875). *Seven-figure Logarithms of Numbers from 1 to 108000 and of Sines, Cosines, Tangents, Cotangents, to Every 10 Seconds of the Quadrant, with a Table of Proportional Parts.* (London: Williams and Norgate, 1865). 474, 76pp. 5th edition corrected. With a description of the tables added by A[ugustus] De Morgan.

A387, E101 (title, author, city, date), F147, JS816 (listed under De Morgan), JS1824. E101 notes this has Dodgson's initials. F147 further notes the gothic stamp. See 551 for a note on De Morgan.

1776. Scott, C[lement], editor (1841–1904). *Drawing-room Plays and Parlour Pantomimes.* (London: Stanley Rivers and Co., 1870). 360pp. Frontispiece by Alfred Thompson.

Uncertain. A671 ("Drawing-room Plays"), JS287 (Anon./Theatre). This is the most likely of 3 possibilities. Henry Dalton's *The Book of Drawing-Room Plays and Evening Amusements* (1861) does not exactly match the short title. Adelaide Cadogan's *Drawing-room Plays, Selected and Adapted from the French* (1888) is possible, but Dodgson knew Scott, wrote two articles specifically for *The Theatre* (a journal edited by Scott, see 1778) and had another work by Scott in his library. Thus Scott seems the right choice. Scott was the dramatic critic for the *Daily Telegraph* and an influential figure in the London theatre scene. This volume includes: "An Induction," by E. L. Blanchard;

"Two Gentlemen at Mivart's," by J. Palgrave Simpson; "A Medical Man," by W. S. Gilbert; "Harlequin Little Red Riding-Hood; or the Wicked Wolf and the Wirtuous Woodcutter," by Tom Hood; "Fireside Diplomacy," by Charles Smith Cheltnam; "Ingomar; or the Noble Savage," by R. Reece; "Money Makes the Man," by Arthur Sketchley; "The Happy Dispatch," by Alfred Thompson; "An Eligible Situation," by Thomas Archer and J. C. Brough; "The Pet-Lamb," by Clement Scott; "The Last Lily," by Clement Scott; "The Three Temptations," by E. L. Blanchard; "Katherine and Petruchio, of the Shaming of the True," by J. Ashby Sterry; "His First Brief," by Sidney Daryl; and "The Girls of the Period," by A. B.

1777. Scott, Clement. *Lays of a Londoner.* (London: Carson & Comerford, 1886). 93pp.

D164, E30 (author, title, date), JS1825. E30 describes this as containing "poems for recitation." Dodgson wrote Scott correcting his grammar in one line of poetry in this collection (See *Letters*, 674).

1778. Scott, Clement, Bernard Capes, Charles Eglington, and Addison Bright, editors. *The Theatre: A Monthly Review and Magazine.* (London: Wyman and Sons, August 1878–79), new series vols. 1–3; continued as *The Theatre: A Monthly Review of the Drama, Music, and the Fine Arts* (London: David Bogue [and perhaps others], 1880–June 1897), news series vols. 1–6 and 1–29.

A636, B1255 (states new series vols. 1–38), JS298 (Anon./Theatre). Also A679 ("Odd Numbers of the Theatre, &c.") listed separately as JS299 (Anon./Theatre) and E395 ("The Theatre, September 1889"), listed separately as JS300 (under Anon./Theatre). This last item includes a reprint of Dodgson's letter on "Stage Children" (see citation below) and "notes on the same and a MS note supplying an omission in it; initialed on cover by Lewis Carroll." The numbering of this monthly theatrical periodical was anything but standard. Certainly 38 volumes were published from August 1878–June 1897, however the numbering of the "new series" which began in 1878, began again in 1880 and again in 1883. Each volume covered six months. The editors were as follows: Jan. 1880–Dec. 1889, Clement Scott; Jan.–June 1890, Bernard Capes; July 1890–June 1892, Bernard

Capes, Charles Eglington; July 1892–June 1893, Charles Eglington; July 1893–June 1894, Addison Bright. This was the principal theatrical monthly of the Victorian period and included a photographic plate in each issue. Dodgson contributed two original essays to *The Theatre* ("Alice on Stage," accompanied by a photograph of the 1886 Savile Clarke production of *Alice in Wonderland*, and "The Stage and the Spirit of Reverence") and had one piece reprinted there (see LCP, #249, #258, #264).

1779. [Scott, Walter] (1771–1832). *The Antiquary.* (Edinburgh: Printed by J. Ballantyne and Co. for A. Constable and Co., etc., 1816). 3 vols. 336, 348, 372pp. 1st edition.

A819 (author, title, edition, 3 vols., date), JS1827. A novel in which Major Neville pursues Isabella Wardour. The title character, Jonathan Oldbuck was based on a friend of Scott.

1780. Scott, Walter. *The Lady of the Lake: A Poem.* (Edinburgh: John Ballantyne and Co.; London: Longman, Hurst, Rees, and Orme, and William Miller, 1810). 290pp. 1st edition

A378 (author, title, edition, date), JS1834. A poem of Scotland in which Ellen Douglas is courted by various Scots. Dodgson wrote a parody of this poem called "The Lady of the Ladle" (see LCP, #4).

1781. Scott, Walter. *Minstrelsy of the Scottish Border: Consisting of Historical and Romantic Ballads, Collected in the Southern Counties of Scotland; with a Few of Modern Date, Founded upon Local Tradition.* (Kelso: Printed by James Ballantyne, for T. Cadell Jun. and W. Davies [vol. 3: Edinburgh: Longman and Rees], 1802–03). 3 vols. 1st edition.

A390, JS127, JS1828. Dodgson's copy is in the collection of Jon Lindseth, Cleveland, OH. The first two volumes were issued together, the third, which contains material by Scott, John Leyden, C. K. Sharpe and others, followed the next year. Dodgson wrote parodies of Scottish ballads, including "The Lady of the Ladle" (see LCP, #4).

1782. Scott, Walter. *Novels and Poetry.* (1830). 49 vols.

A380 (author, title, 49 vols., date), JS1829, JS1833. No collected edition of 1830 nor any collected edition in 49 volumes of Scott's works has been traced. Possibly a collection of different editions of works by Scott.

1783. [**Scott, Walter**]. *Paul's Letters to his Kinsfolk.* (Edinburgh: A. Constable, 1816). 519pp. 3rd edition.

D163 (author, title, edition, date), JS1830. An account of the battle of Waterloo is given in the context of a series of letters from the author recounting a trip to Brussels, Waterloo, and Paris shortly after the battle.

1784. Scott, Walter. *The Poetical Works of Walter Scott.* 12 vols. Details unknown.

A364 (author, title, 12 vols.), JS1832. Three different 12-volume editions have been traced: (Edinburgh: A. Constable, 1820), (Edinburgh: Robert Cadell, 1833), and (Edinburgh: Adam and Charles Black, 1851–57). Dodgson also owned another (presumably 1-volume) edition of Scott's *Poetical Works* (A356).

1785. Scott, Walter. *Waverley; or, 'Tis Sixty Years Since.* (Edinburgh: Archibald Constable & Co.; London: Longman, Hurst, Rees, Orme, & Brown, 1814). 3 vols. 3rd edition.

A819 (author, title, edition, 3 vols., date), JS1835. The first of Scott's Waverly novels.

1786. Scott, William Bell (1811–90). *Poems by William Bell Scott. Ballads, Studies from Nature, Sonnets.* (London: 1875). 271pp. Illustrated by 17 etchings by the author and Lawrence Alma Tadema.

A851, B1212 (author, title, illustrator, date), JS1831 (listed under Walter Scott), JS1837. Scott was a poet and artist who was friends with Swinburne and Rossetti. Tadema (1836–1912) was a Dutch-born artist. He came to England in 1869 and spent most of his career there, painting in the Classicist style.

1787. Scudder, Horace Elisha (1838–1902). *Childhood in Literature and Art; with Some Observations on Literature for Children. A Study.* (Boston and New York: Houghton and Mifflin, 1894). 253pp.

D165 (author, title, city, date), JS1838. Scudder was an American and editor of the *Riverside Magazine for Young People*. He became editor of *Atlantic Monthly* (succeeding Thomas Bailey Aldrich) in 1890. One of his earliest publications was *The Game of Croquet; Its Ap-*

pointments and Laws (New York: Hurd and Houghton, 1868), which included an uncredited reprint of Dodgson's "Castle Croquet for Four Players" (WMGC, 38). He wrote a wide variety of works. The present study began as a series of articles in *Atlantic Monthly* in 1885. It includes no references to Dodgson or his books for children.

1788. Seafield, Frank [pseud. of Alexander Henley Grant]. *The Literature and Curiosities of Dreams: A Commonplace Book of Speculations Concerning the Mystery of Dreams and Visions, Record of Curious and Well-Authenticated Dreams, and Notes on The Various Modes of Interpretation Adopted in Ancient and Modern Times.* (London: Chapman & Hall, 1865). 360, 394pp.

A899, D55 (author, title, city, date, 2 vols.), JS1404 (listed under Leafield), JS1839. 1st edition. Published after Dodgson had written AAIW, perhaps the most famous dream book ever written. Dodgson's fascination with the dream state continued in TTLG (1872) and in the 2 volumes of *Sylvie and Bruno* (1889, 1893). The preface states, "The great object of these volumes has been to select, from all sources, whatever is most characteristic of the opinions which have been held on the subject of Dreams, and of the examples upon which these opinions have been founded." The *London Reader* wrote, "An immense mass of diligent compilation, and no attempt to reduce it either to system or order."

1789. (Seaside). *Cassell's Handy Guide to the Sea-side. A Description of All the Principal English Sea Watering-places.* (London: Cassell and Co., [1865]). 2nd edition. Illustrated.

E377 ["The Sea-side, Cassell's Handy Guide to (principal English watering-places)"], JS369 (Anon./Topography). Earliest edition in BL. E377 states "with note by Lewis Carroll as to 'No pier at Hastings!'" Dodgson often visited his two maiden aunts who lived in Hastings (see LCE, 79), especially during his summers at nearby Eastbourne (1877–1897), but as early as 1860. The Hastings Pier was begun in 1869 and completed in 1872; the description in E377 makes it unclear whether Dodgson is commenting on the lack of a pier at Hastings, or commenting on the antiquity of the guide as not reflecting the presence of a pier.

1790. [Seeley, John Robert] (1834–95). *Ecce Homo, A Survey of the Life and Work of Jesus Christ.* (London: Macmillan, 1866 [1865]). 330pp.

A797 (title), JS313 (Anon./Theology). 1st edition. Seeley was a British essayist and historian and Professor of Latin at University College, London. A highly popular and influential book in Victorian theology, Seeley's anonymously published life of Christ presented a historical Jesus without mention of much Christian doctrine. Though it sold in great numbers, moving through multiple editions in its first year, it also drew a storm of response from figures such as John Henry Newman and Arthur Penrhyn Stanley who found it unorthodox. Dodgson also owned a critique of the work by W. E. Gladstone (see 777). In a letter to Tom Taylor dated 25 January 1866, he wrote "I have not read *Ecce Homo*, but I have heard it spoken of as a remarkable book." The Latin title translates "Behold the Man."

1791. Seeley, John Robert. *The Expansion of England. Two Courses of Lectures.* (London: Macmillan and Co., 1883). 309pp.

A305, D166 (author, title, city, date), JS1840. D166 notes Dodgson's initials. A work on the creation of the British Empire and, to many, a convincing defense of that empire.

1792. Ségur, Comtesse de [previously Sophaletta Feodorovna Rostopchine] (1799–1874). *Les Malheurs de Sophie.* (Paris: Librairie de L. Hachette, 1869). 251pp. 7th edition. 48 illustrations by Horace Castelli.

E97 (author, title, number of illustrations, date), JS1841. The author was born and raised in Russia but moved to France after the 1812 invasion. The mother of 8 children she was, in later life, an invalid, who passed her days by telling stories to children and grandchildren. This story is of a young girl, Sophie, whose bad behavior offers ample opportunity for moralizing by the author. In his diary on 31 October 1882, Dodgson wrote, "Began translating *Les Malheurs de Sophie*. I hope to shortly get into a regular system of work." Whether he hoped to translate the book merely for his own linguistic education or towards some idea of publication is not known. In either case, he seems not to have completed the project.

1793. Serret, Joseph-Alfred. *Cours d'Algèbre Supérieure.* (Paris: Gauthier-Villars, 1866). 2 vols. 3rd edition.

A586 (author, title, 2 vols.), JS1843. Earliest 2-volume edition in BNF. Serret was a French mathematician. The title translates, *Advanced Course of Algebra*.

1794. Settle, Elkanah (1648–1724). *Pastor Fido: or, The Faithful Shepherd. A Pastoral.* (London: 1677). Founded on the poem of Giovanni Battista Guarini.

Uncertain. F185 (author, title, date), not numbered in JS. Identified only by gothic stamp. Settle was an English poet and dramatist. Guarini (1537–1612) was an Italian poet. A five-act verse drama.

1795. Severance, Frank H[ayward] (1856–1931). *Niagara in London A Brief Study from Many Standpoints.* (Buffalo, NY: Matthews Northrup & Co., n.d.). Illustrated.

JS1844. Dodgson's copy is in HAC, and is identified only by the gothic stamp on the illustrated front cover. The book is an illustrated history of the falls. In the back are descriptions of the artists Paul Philippoteaux "whose latest and greatest work is the most ambitious of Niagara ever attempted," and of Adrien Shulz, who "did much of the excellent work on the picture of Niagara." The Harvard catalogue dates this item as 189?, though it may be as early as 1888, as it almost certainly refers to the panorama of Niagara Falls that Dodgson visited with his child friend Isa Bowman on 11 July 1888. In the diary he wrote for Isa of her visit with him he describes the panorama thus: "You seemed to be on the top of a tower, with miles and miles of country all round you ... near the foot of the Falls, there was a steam-packet crossing the river, which showed what a tremendous height the Falls must be." The canvas of Niagara was "four hundred feet in circumference and fifty feet high ... and [was] on exhibit in York Street, Westminster."

1796. Sewell, Elizabeth Missing (1815–1906). *Sewell's Works.* (London: Longmans, Green, [1858–62]). 10 vols.

Details uncertain. A323 ("Sewell's Works, 20 vols."), JS1845. No 20-volume edition of works by any author named Sewell traced. This is certainly a reference to the works of British novelist E. M. Sewell, a prolific writer of High

Church fiction, and the only Sewell to have written enough works to fill even 10 volumes. Probably a misprint ("20" for "10") in A323, unless Dodgson had his set specially bound, which seems unlikely. Contains: *Amy Herbert; Cleve Hall; The Earl's Daughter; The Experience of Life; Gertrude; Ivors, or the Two Cousins; Katharine Ashton; Laneton Parsonage, A Tale for Children; Margaret Percival*; and *Ursula, A Tale of Country Life*. This could also be a reference to a collection of 20 separate volumes of Sewell's works— MOT lists well over twenty titles including novels as well as church history and theology for young people. In a letter to his sister of 4 May 1849, Dodgson writes "There is a 3rd part of *Laneton Pasonage [A Tale for Children on the Practical Use of a Portion of the Church Catechism]* come out, have you seen it?" It is unclear if Dodgson had read this or merely noted its existence.

1797. Seymour, Michael Hobart (1800–74). *The Confessional: An Appeal to the Primitive and Catholic Forms of Absolution, in the East and in the West*. (London: Seeley, Jackson, & Halliday, 1870 [1869]). 212pp.

B1214 (author, title, date), E73, JS1847. E73 notes this has Dodgson's initials. Seymour was educated at Trinity College, Dublin and served as a priest in Ireland, where his attacks on Roman dogma made him unpopular. He moved to England and was admitted to Oxford University in 1836. He served as lecturer at several churches in greater London. His book *A Pilgrimage to Rome* was on the Vatican's banned book list.

1798. Seymour, Michael Hobart. *Evenings with Romanists; with an Introductory Chapter on the Moral Results of the Romish System*. (London: Seeleys, 1854). 524pp.

B1213 (author, title, date), JS1846. The advertisement at the front of the 1855 American edition reads, in part, "The author, in refuting errors of Romanism, takes occasion to state the evangelical doctrines of which these errors are but corruptions."

1799. Seymour, Robert (ca. 1800–1836). *Sketches*. (London: G. S. Tregear, [1835–36]). 5 vols.

A504 ("Seymour's Sketches, 5 parts in 2 vols., 134 humourous plates"), JS1848. Earliest edition traced of the only 5 part collection of plates by Seymour. Each of the 5 parts included an illustrated title page plus 36 plates, so either Dodgson was missing some plates or there is an error in A504. Seymour was a painter who turned to the more lucrative business of illustration and created this series of comic sketches based on his "cockney sportsman." He was commissioned by Edward Chapman to produce a series of plates which young Charles Dickens would provide text for, but Dickens insisted that the plates follow the text, not the other way around. Seymour committed suicide after illustrating two installments of *The Pickwick Papers*.

1800. Shairp, J[ohn] C[ampbell] (1819–85). *Culture and Religion in Some of Their Relations*. (Edinburgh: Edmonston & Douglas, 1875). 147pp. 5th edition.

A599, D167 (author ["J. C. Sharp"], title, edition, city, date), JS1862. Clearly a typographical error ("Sharp" for "Shairp" in D167). Shairp was Professor of Humanity at the University of St. Andrews and was, in 1877, appointed Professor of Poetry at Oxford. *Saturday Review* writes of this work, "He is ... quite in accord with Mr. Arnold in his rejection of the utilitarian view of education, and in making the perfection of our nature consist in the harmonious development of all its capacities. But he quarrels with him for advocating a culture which must become practically 'a principle of exclusion and isolation,' unattainable by the many, and for assigning to religion a secondary place."

1801. Shakespeare, William (1564–1616) (edited by Samuel Brandram [1824–92]). *Certain Selected Plays, Abridged for the Use of the Young*. (London: Smith, Elder & Co., 1881). 381pp. 9 plays abridged by Samuel Brandram.

A878, B1224 (author, title, editor, date), JS1850, JS1858. In his diary for 15 March 1882, Dodgson writes, in part, "received Brandram's Selections from Shakespeare—I had fancied it would make my idea, of a 'Girl's own Shakespeare' superfluous—but it does not do so. He has not expurgated nearly as much as I should wish." Dodgson hoped to publish an edition of Shakespeare appropriate for young girls, but he never did so.

1802. Shakespeare, William. *Cymbeline*. (London: Macmillan and Co., 1889).

223pp. With an introduction and notes by Kenneth Deighton. In the *English Classics* series.

Not in JS. In a letter to his publisher, Macmillan (30 September 1896), Dodgson writes, "Thanks for 2 copies of *Cymbeline*." This was the only separately published edition of *Cymbeline* that Macmillan had in print at the time. Deighton was Inspector of Schools for Bareilly, Principal of Agra College and edited many of Shakespeare's plays.

1803. Shakespeare, William. *A Midsummer-Night's Dream*. (London: Longmans, Green & Co., 1868). 88pp. Illustrated with 24 silhouettes by Paul Konewka.

A286 (title, illustrator), not in JS. Only British edition listed in BL. See 1171 for a note on Konewka.

1804. Shakespeare, William. *A Midsummer Night's Dream*. Illustrated. Edition unknown.

A544 (title, illustrated), JS1854.

1805. Shakespeare, William (edited by Alexander Chalmers [1759–1834]). *The Plays of William Shakspeare, Accurately Printed from the Text of the Corrected Copies Left by the Late George Stevens and Edmund Malone Esq., with Mr Malone's Various Readings, a Selection of Explanatory and Historical Notes from the Most Eminent Commentators; a History of the Stage, and a Life of Shakespeare*. (London: F. C. and J. Rivington et al., 1823). New edition.

A395 ("Shakespeare's Works by Chalmers, 8 vols."), JS1851. Earliest 8-volume edition of Chalmers' Shakespeare in BL or BOD. Chalmers also edited works of many other English writers. Edmund Malone (1741–1812) wrote works on Shakespeare (especially on questions of authenticity of various pieces) and edited his works.

1806. Shakespeare, William. *Shakespeare as Put Forth in 1623. A Reprint of Mr. William Shakespeare's Comedies, Histories, & Tragedies. Published According to the True Originall Copies*. (London: Reprinted for Lionel Booth, 1864). 3 parts.

A732, B1221 (author, title, publisher, date), JS1852, JS1861. A reduced-size facsimile of the First Folio, reproducing all the illustrations of the original. A732 gives the date as 1884 (hence the separate listing in JS1861), but BL lists no facsimile edition of that date—certainly this must be a typographical error for 1864 and A732 and B1221 are the same book.

1807. Shakespeare, William (edited by Charles John Kean [1811–68]). *Shakespeare's Comedy of Much Ado about Nothing. Arranged for Representation at the Princess's Theatre, with Explanatory Notes by Charles Kean, and Revived on Saturday, November 20th, 1858*. (London: J. K. Chapman & Co., [1858]). 68pp.

A878, B1223 (editor, title, dates), JS1855 (not listed separately). This was one of 9 acting editions of Shakespeare edited by Kean that Dodgson owned. All were bound in a single volume and are described individually below. B1223 gives the dates for these plays as 1853–59 and notes that Dodgson's volume included a "MS index on fly leaf by C. L. D." Charles Kean was one of the most respected actors of his day and the son of the great actor Edmund Kean. He was especially known for his portrayal of Shakespearean heroes. Dodgson's first recorded night at the legitimate theatre was to see Kean in Henry VIII in 1855. He immediately became an admirer and saw at least three other Shakespeare productions starring Kean.

1808. Shakespeare, William (edited by Charles John Kean). *Shakespeare's Historical Play of King Henry the Eighth; Arranged for Representation at the Princess's Theatre by Charles Kean. First Performed on Wednesday, 16th May, 1855*. (London: J. K. Chapman & Co., [1855]). 91pp.

A878, B1223 (editor, title, date), JS1855 (not listed separately). See 1807 concerning Dodgson's collection of Kean's acting editions of Shakespeare. Dodgson saw this production on 22 June 1855 (his first recorded trip to the legitimate theatre) and raved about it in his diary.

1809. Shakespeare, William (edited by Charles John Kean). *Shakespeare's Play of King Henry the Fifth, Arranged for Representation at the Princess's Theatre, with Historical and Explanatory Notes, by Charles Kean. As First Performed on Monday,*

March 28th, 1859. (London: J. K. Chapman & Co., [1859]). 96pp.

A878, B1223 (editor, title, date), JS1855 (not listed separately). See 1807 concerning Dodgson's collection of Kean's acting editions of Shakespeare.

1810. Shakespeare, William (edited by Charles John Kean). *Shakespeare's Play of King Richard II, Arranged for Representation at the Princess's Theatre, with Historical and Explanatory Notes by Charles Kean. As First Performed on Thursday, March 12, 1857.* (London: J. K. Chapman & Co., [1857]). 88pp.

A878, B1223 (editor, title, date), JS1855 (not listed separately). See 1807 concerning Dodgson's collection of Kean's acting editions of Shakespeare.

1811. Shakespeare, William (edited by Charles John Kean). *Shakespeare's Play of A Midsummer Night's Dream; Arranged for Representation at the Princess's Theatre; With Historical and Explanatory Notes, by Charles Kean: as First Performed on Wednesday, October 15th 1856.* (London: J. K. Chapman & Co., [1856]). 60pp.

A878, B1223 (editor, title, date), JS1855 (not listed separately). See 1807 concerning Dodgson's collection of Kean's acting editions of Shakespeare.

1812. Shakespeare, William (edited by Charles John Kean). *Shakespeare's Play of The Tempest. Arranged for Representation at the Princess's Theatre. With Historical and Explanatory Notes, by Charles Kean. As First Performed on Wednesday, July 1, 1857.* (London: J. K. Chapman & Co., [1857]). 74pp.

A878, B1223 (editor, title, date), JS1855 (not listed separately). See 1807 concerning Dodgson's collection of Kean's acting editions of Shakespeare. Dodgson twice saw Kean play Prosepro in *The Tempest*, on 3 July 1857 and again on 28 November 1857. He especially admired the scenic effects.

1813. Shakespeare, William (edited by Charles John Kean). *Shakespeare's Play of The Winter's Tale. Arranged for Representation at the Princess's Theatre, with His-*torical and Explanatory Notes, by Charles Kean. As First Performed on Monday, April 28th, 1856.* (London: J. K. Chapman & Co., [1856]). 105pp.

A878, B1223 (editor, title, date), JS1855 (not listed separately). See 1807 concerning Dodgson's collection of Kean's acting editions of Shakespeare. Dodgson saw this production (starring Kean as Leontes and featuring Ellen Terry in her stage debut at age eight) on 16 June 1856.

1814. Shakespeare, William (edited by Charles John Kean). *Shakespeare's Tragedy of King Lear Arranged for Representation at the Princess's Theatre, with Historical and Explanatory Notes, by Charles Kean. As First Performed on Saturday, April 17, 1858.* (London: J. K. Chapman & Co., [1858]). 90pp.

A878, B1223 (editor, title, date), JS1855 (not listed separately). See 1807 concerning Dodgson's collection of Kean's acting editions of Shakespeare.

1815. Shakespeare, William (edited by Charles John Kean). *Shakespeare's Tragedy of Macbeth, with Locke's Music; Arranged for Representation at the Princess's Theatre, with Historical and Explanatory Notes, by Charles Kean. As First Performed on Monday, February 14th, 1853.* (London: J. K. Chapman & Co., [1853]). 92pp.

A878, B1223 (editor, title, date), JS1855 (not listed separately). See 1807 concerning Dodgson's collection of Kean's acting editions of Shakespeare.

1816. Shakespeare, William (edited by William Henry Davenport Adams). *Shakspeare's Dramatic Works. With 370 Illustrations by the Late F. Howard, R.A., and with Explanatory Notes, Parallel Passages, Historical and Critical Illustrations, a Copious Glossary, Biographical Sketch, and Indexes.* (London: T. Nelson & Sons, 1876). 1421pp. *The Howard Shakspeare.*

A878, B1220 (author, title, illustrator, date), JS1853. The half-title calls this edition *The Annotated Household Shakspeare.* See 14 for a note on Adams. Frank Howard was the son of the artist Henry Howard. This work was originally published (1827–33) in 5 vols. with 491 illustrations.

1817. Shakespeare, William. *Shakspeare's Songs and Sonnets.* (London: Sampson Low, Son & Co., 1862). [43]pp. Illustrated by John Gilbert, with colored plates.

A567 (author, title), JS1859. Earliest edition of the only precisely matching title in BL. Gilbert (1817–97) was a leading British artist and illustrator and president of the Society of Painters in Water-Colours. He drew for the *Illustrated London News* from that journal's inception and illustrated many British classics.

1818. Shakespeare, William. *Twelve Plays of Shakespeare.* (Oxford: Clarendon Press). Details unknown.

So listed in A877/JS1849, but no edition of Shakespeare limited to only 12 plays and published by the Clarendon Press has been traced. Possibly Dodgson owned 12 of the 14 volumes of Shakespeare published by the press as part of the *Clarendon Press Series of English Classics* (1868–86). Each volume contained a single play. Vols. 1–4 were edited by W. C. Clark and W. A. Wright (see below), the remainder by Wright alone.

1819. Shakespeare, William (edited by William George Clark and William Aldis Wright). *The Works of William Shakespeare.* (Cambridge and London: Macmillan and Co., 1864). 1079pp. The Globe Edition.

A368 (author, title, Globe Edition), JS1860 (listed together with other Shakespeare omnibuses). This is the 1st printing of the Globe Edition as described in MBC. Clark was a fellow of Trinity College, Cambridge who served as vice-master and as public orator of the university. Wright also served as vice-master of Trinity College, Cambridge.

1820. Shakespeare. *Works*. Dodgson owned several editions of Shakespeare's works for which insufficient evidence exists to specifically identify.

A356/JS1860 ("Shakespeare's Works"); A369/JS1860 ("Shakespeare's Works"); A556/JS1860 ("Shakespeare's Works, 12 vols. in case") (there were many 12-volume editions in the 18th and 19th centuries, including several printings of the edition edited by Charles Knight); B1222/JS1857 ("A Portable selection of 19 Plays with the Poems and Glossary from the Globe Edition")— no matching title has been traced, (see above for the Globe Edition); and A564/JS1857 (Pocket Shakespeare in Case)— two possibilities are: *The Illustrated Pocket Shakespeare. Complete with Glossary*, edited by J. Talfourd Blair (Glasgow: D. Bryce & Son, [1886]), or *Mansell's Pocket Shakespeare* ([London]: G. Mansell, [1835?]).

1821. Shaw, Edward B. L. *The Medical Remembrancer, or, Book of Emergencies.* (London: 1867). 5th edition, rewritten and much enlarged by Jonathan Hutchinson, etc.

E147 (author, title, re-writer, date), JS1277 (listed under Hutchinson). E147 notes this has Dodgson's autograph. A guide to first aid. An 1837 edition published by Churchill was titled: *The Medical Remembrancer, or Practical Pocket Guide, in which is Concisely Pointed out the Treatment to be Adopted in the First Moments of Danger from Poisoning, Drowning, Apoplexy, Burns, & Other Accidents. To which are Added Various Useful Tables and Memoranda.* The *British and Foreign Medical Review* wrote of the 5th edition, "The plan is well conceived and the execution corresponds thereunto."

1822. Shaw, S. Parsons. *Odontalgia, Commonly Called Toothache; Its Causes, Prevention, and Cure.* (London: Palmer & Howe, 1868 [1867]). 258pp.

B1228 (author, title, date), JS1863. Shaw was a dentist.

1823. Shaw, Thomas George. *Wine, the Vine, and the Cellar.* (London: Longman, Green, Longman, Roberts & Green, 1864). 540pp. 2nd edition.

A920, D228 (author, title, date), JS399 (Anon./Wine), JS1864. A920 states the title as "Wine and the Wine Cellar," but no such title has been traced and the appearance of the above title in D228 clearly indicates the transcription error in A920. Shaw was a wine merchant. In his book *Wine into Words A History and Bibliography of Wine Books in the English Language* (1985), James Gabler writes, "Seventy years ago, André Simon [in his 1913 work *Bibliotheca Vinaria*] called [Shaw's book] 'one of the most interesting books we have on the subject', and it still is. Shaw's wit, sense of humour and love of wine pervades every page. Although there is much historical data, of real interest in the book are Shaw's reminiscences and anecdotes of his forty-two years in the wine trade." During his 12 years as curator of the Senior Common Room at Christ Church, Dodgson was responsible for keeping the wine cellar. He had correspondence with wine merchants and printed a number of leaflets relating to wine and the Common Room (See *Oxford*).

1824. Sheldon, Frederick. *The Minstrelsy of the English Border. Being a Collection of Ballads, Ancient, Remodelled and Original, Founded on Well Known Border Legends. With Illustrative Notes.* (London: Longman, Brown, Green and Longmans, 1847). 432pp.

A480, D168 (author, title, city, date), JS1865. Sheldon was also the author of a history of Berwick-upon-Tweed. The *London Examiner* wrote that "The Illustrative Notes are full of information and interest."

1825. Shelley, Mary Wollstonecraft (1797–1851). *Frankenstein: or, The Modern Prometheus.* (London: G. & W. B. Whittaker, 1823). 2 vols. 249, 280pp. New edition.

A450 ("Frankenstein by Mrs. Shelley, 2 vols., 12mo, half-bound, 1823"), JS1870. Extremely scarce 2nd edition of Shelley's classic. Dodgson also owned copies of the 1st editions of the 1st books in English on vampires (see 1550) and werewolves (see 125).

1826. [**Shelley**, Mary Wollstonecraft]. *The Last Man.* (London: H. Colburn, 1826). 3 vols. 235, 218, 232pp. 1st edition.

A609 (title, edition, 3 vols.), JS1871. Only title in BL matching the particulars in A609. A story about the destruction, by disease, of all humankind but for one man.

1827. Shelley, Percy Bysshe (1792–1822). *The Dæmon of the World. By P. B. Shelley. The First Part, as Published in 1816 with Alastor; The Second Part, Deciphered and Now First Printed from his Own Manuscript Revision and Interpolations in the Newly Discovered Copy of Queen Mab.* (London: Privately Printed by H. B. Forman, 1876). 38pp. Edited by H. Buxton Forman. Only 50 copies printed.

A567 (author, title), JS1866. Only edition traced. The editor calls this "a retrenchment of Queen Mab."

2828. Shelley, [Percy Bysshe]. *Poems from Shelley.* (London: Macmillan and Co., 1882). 340pp. Selected and arranged by Stopford A. Brooke. In the *Golden Treasury Series*.

Not in JS. In May 1883, Dodgson corresponded with Macmillan on the subject of books containing "selections" of work from the great poets (see *Macmillan*, 163). Macmillan specifically mentioned the *Golden Treasury* edition of Byron and sent Dodgson works of Wordsworth (which Dodgson acknowledged as being from this series, see 2310), Byron, and Shelley. The *Golden Treasury Series* are the only editions in which Macmillan published "selected" poetry from all three of these poets. This volume was originally published in 1880; this is the closest printing to Dodgson's date of acquisition. See 243 for a note on the editor, Brooke.

1829. Shelley, Percy Bysshe. *The Poetical Works of Percy Bysshe Shelley.* Edited by Mrs. [Mary] Shelley. (London: Edward Moxon, 1839). 4 vols. 380, 347, 314, 361pp. 1st collected edition. Engraved frontispiece portrait by Finden.

A353 (author, title, 4 vols.), JS1867. Dodgson's copy sold at Christie's, New York on 9 June 1992 (DAA3029) and is in the collection of John Lindseth, Cleveland, OH, and includes an inscription from the editor: "For John George Perry Esq. from M. W. Shelley." It has Dodgson's monogram on the front free endpaper of vol. 1.

1830. Shelley, Percy Bysshe. *Works.* Edition unknown.

A399 (author, title), JS1869.

1831. Shelton, Edward. *The Historical Finger-Post: A Handy Book of Terms, Phrases, Epithets, Cognomens, Allusions ... in Connection with Universal History, etc.* (London: Lockwood & Co., 1861). 380pp.

B1229 (author, title, date), JS1872. Shelton was assistant editor of *The Dictionary of Daily Wants.* This work was, according to Allibone, commended by at least 12 authorities.

1832. Shenstone, William (1714–63). *The Poetical Works of William Shenstone. With Life, Critical Dissertation, and Explanatory Notes by Rev. George Gilfillan.* (Edinburgh: Nicol, 1854). 284pp.

A401, JS1873. Dodgson's copy is in the collection of Jon Lindseth, Cleveland, OH. It is signed "C. L. Dodgson. Ch: Ch:" on the front pastedown. Shenstone was an English poet. Hazlitt called his poems "indifferent and tasteless, except his 'Pastoral Ballad,' his 'Lines on Jenny Dawson,' and his 'Schoolmistress,' which last is a perfect piece of writing." See 776 for more on Gilfillan.

1833. Shepherd, Richard Herne (1842–95), compiler. *Tennysoniana. Notes Bibliographical and Critical on Early Poems of Alfred and Charles Tennyson. Opinions of Contemporary Writers. In Memoriam; Various Readings, with Parallel Passages in Shakespeare's Sonnets. Various Readings in Later Poems (1842–1865). Patriotic and Minor Poems. Allusions to Scripture and to Classic Authors. The Tennyson Portraits. Bibliographical List of Tennyson's Volumes and his Contributions to Periodical Publications.* (London: B. M. Pickering, 1866). 170pp.

A468 (title, date), JS1874. Shepherd was known primarily as an editor of poetry. *The Lover's Tale; a Supplementary Chapter to Tennysoniana* was issued in an edition of 50 copies in 1875, but A468 lists only 1866 for the date and does not mention multiple volumes. Dodgson supervised the compilation of an index to Tennyson's *In Memoriam* (see WMGC, #31).

1834. Sheridan, Richard Brinsley (1751–1816). *Dramatic Works.* Edition unknown.

A670 ("Sheridan's Dramatic Works"), JS1875.

1835. Sheridan, Richard Brinsley. *Here's to the Maiden of Bashful Fifteen.* (London: Hildesheimer & Faulkner; New York: Geo. C. Whitney, [1892]). 12pp. Illustrated wrappers. Illustrated by Alice Havers and Ernest Wilson.

E57 (author, title, illustrators), F184, JS1147, JS1876. Dodgson's copy is in HAC, and includes the gothic stamp on the inside of the front cover. See 880 for a note on Havers. Dodgson wrote a parody of this poem in his 1873 pamphlet *The Vision of the Three T's.*

1836. Sherlock, Thomas (1678–1761). *The Tryal of the Witnesses of the Resurrection of Jesus.* (London: Printed for John Whiston

and Benjamin White, 1765). 112pp. 14th edition.

B1265 (title, date), JS1877. Sherlock was an English divine who was serving as Bishop of Bangor when the 1st edition of this book was published in 1729. He later became Bishop of Salisbury and then of London. According to a note in the book, "Not only Mr. Woolston's objections, in his Sixth discourse on our Saviour's miracles, but those also … published in other books, are here considered." Thomas Woolston (1669–1773) was a deist whose attacks on the Bible were met with vitriolic opposition. In his *Sixth Discourse on the Miracles of Our Saviour* (1728–29) he called Jesus, as portrayed in the Gospels, a "deceiver, imposter, and malefactor," and called the apostles' story of the resurrection "the most bare-fac'd Imposture that ever was put upon the World."

1837. Shortfellow, Harry Wandsworth [pseud. of Mary Victoria Cowden Clarke] (1809–98). *The Song of Drop o' Wather — A London Legend.* (London: G. Routledge & Co., 1856). 120pp. "A Companion to Longfellow's 'Hiawatha'."

E28 (title, pseudonym, date), JS701. Mary was the wife of Charles Cowden Clarke, a friend of Keats and a lecturer, particularly on Shakespeare. A parody of Henry Wadsworth Longfellow's poem "The Song of Hiawatha." Dodgson's own parody of "Hiawatha," "Hiawatha Photographing," was published in December of the following year. Perhaps the present work suggested the idea of a parody to Dodgson.

1838. Shuldham, E[dward] B[arton] (1837?–92). *Chronic Sore Throat, or, Follicular Disease of the Pharynx: Its Local and Constitutional Treatment. With a Special Chapter on Hygiene of the Voice.* (London: E. Gould & Son, 1881). 90pp.

E124 (author, title, date), JS1878. E124 notes this has a presentation from the author. Shuldham was editor of *The Homœopathic World.* This is the 2nd edition of *Clergyman's Sore Throat* (see below). In addition to altering the title, Shuldham removed the chapter on Elocution, "because better chapters on this subject have been written by … C. J. Plumtre and the Rev. C. A. D'Orsey."

1839. Shuldham, E[dward] B[arton]. *Clergyman's Sore Throat, or, Follicular Dis-*

ease of the Pharynx: Its Local, Constitutional and Elocutionary Treatment. With a Special Chapter on Hygiene of the Voice. (London: The Homœopathic Publishing Company, E. Gould & Son, 1878). 92pp.

E160 (author, title, date), JS1879. E160 notes this is a presentation copy from the author. A treatise not just for Clergy, but for all who make extensive use of their voices. Shuldham writes of chronic sore throat, "Bad management of the voice I conceive to be its most fruitful cause; the reader's art must therefore form the basis of its most rational treatment. This treatment, unlike most forms of therapeutics, is truly preventative.... For this reason I have dwelt on the importance of elocutionary treatment, and added the chapter on the Art of Breathing." A 2nd edition was published under the title *Chronic Sore Throat* (see above).

1840. Shuldham, E[dward] B[arton]. *Coughs and Their Cure: With Special Chapters on Consumption and Change of Climate.* (London: The Homœopathic Publishing Company, 1878). 244pp.

E155 (author, title, date), JS1880.

1841. Shuldham, E[dward] B[arton]. *Headaches: Their Causes and Treatments.* (London: The Homœopathic Publishing Company, 1879?).

E174 (author, title, date), JS1881. No 1879 edition traced. Possibly this was a misprint for 1876 (the date of the 2nd edition, 77pp.). All traced editions published by The Homœopathic Publishing Company. A reviewer for the *Sussex Daily News* wrote, "There are sufferers from other things besides headaches who would be glad of such cheap and skilful advice as that of Dr. Shuldham. It is the most readable of medical treatises, and yet betokens a thorough acquaintance with the subject."

1842. Shute, E[dith] L[etitia] [i.e. Mrs. Richard Shute, née Hutchinson] (1854?–1952). *Jappie-Chappie, and How he Loved a Dollie.* (London: Frederick Warne & Co., [1887]). [16pp.] + wrappers. Told and illustrated by E. L. Shute.

A545, E2 (author, title), JS1883. Only edition traced. Walter Spencer (see preface) catalogued a copy of this book inscribed by Dodgson, "Edith from C. L. D." Mrs. Shute was the widow of a Christ Church tutor (see 1844) and

a friend of Dodgson (see also 2259). A picture book telling the story, in verse, of a Japanese youth who falls in love with a fair English maiden. She rejects him on a wholly racist basis, but when he rescues her from a monster, her eyes are opened and she agrees to marry him. The illustrations show the characters as dolls. Dodgson visited Shute's London studio and was fond of giving away copies of this book. He wrote to her on 26 December 1887: "I keep ordering batches of the *Jappie* book: and they flow out, in the direction of young (and sometimes old) friends, nearly as fast as they come in ... when the final smash comes, it is to be hoped that the Report, of the proceedings in the Bankruptcy Court, will end like this... 'It is understood that an illustrated book, such as he was likely to buy in large quantities, had been most *artfully* prepared by a *designing* friend, and that the enormous outlay, into which he was thus drawn, was the chief cause of the catastrophe.'" In an unpublished letter of 1889 to a lady-in-waiting to the young Duke and Duchess of Albany, whom he had recently met, Dodgson called the book "suitable for *very* young children, and appropriate for *one* to five." In 1889, Dodgson published a nursery version of AAIW for children "from naught to five."

1843. Shute, E[dith] L[etitia] [i.e. Mrs. Richard Shute, née Hutchinson]. *Over the Hills.* (London: F. Warne & Co., [1888]). 47pp. Illustrated by Jessie Watkins.

A543 (author, title, illustrator), JS1882. Only edition in BL. Verse.

1844. Shute, Richard (1849–86). *A Discourse on Truth.* (London: H. S. King, 1877). 299pp.

D169 (author, title, city, date), JS1884. D169 notes Dodgson's initials. Shute was educated at Cambridge and at New Inn Hall, Oxford. He was a tutor at Christ Church, whose widow was befriended by Dodgson (see 1842). Shute and Dodgson seem to have been friends—Dodgson mentions several meetings in his diaries, including one when the two discussed "getting a better form of drama encouraged in Oxford."

1845. Sidgwick, Alfred (1850–1943). *Fallacies. A View of Logic from the Practical Side.* (London: K. Paul, Trench, 1883). 375pp. Volume 48 in *The International Scientific Series.*

A516 (author, title), JS1885. Earliest edition

Jappie Chappie rescues his beloved dollie. Illustration by E. L. Shute for her book *Jappie-Chappie* (item 1842).

in BL or BOD. Sidgewick took his B.A. at Lincoln College, Oxford in 1869 and became a fellow of Owen's College of Victoria University, Manchester in 1882. A largely forgotten figure in logic and philosophy, he attempted to create a new theory of logic based on fallacies, but his work was not ultimately successful.

1846. Sikes, William Wirt (1836–83). *British Goblins: Welsh Folk-lore, Fairy Mythology, Legends and Traditions.* (London: S. Low, Marston, Searle & Rivington, 1880 [1879]). 412pp. With illustrations.
 A891 (author, "British Goblins"), JS179 (Anon./Occult), JS396 (author's name as if a title under Anon./Unclassified). Earliest edition in BL. Sikes was the U.S. consul at Cardiff from 1876 until his death. He writes, "In a certain sense, Wales may be spoken of as the cra-

dle of fairy legend. It is not now disputed that from the Welsh were borrowed many of the first subjects of composition in the literature of all the cultivated peoples of Europe."

1847. Sim, Adelaide C. Gordon. *Phœbe's Shakespeare Arranged for Children.* (London: Bickers & Son, 1894). 146pp.
 B1225 (author, title, date), JS1856 (listed under Shakespeare). Stories from Shakespeare's plays. Dodgson considered producing an edited edition of Shakespeare suitable for young girls, but the project never came to fruition.

1848. Simpson, Martin (1798–1892). *Guide to the Geology of the Yorkshire Coast; Illustrated with Sections.* (Whitby: S. Reed, 1859). 32pp. 3rd edition.
 E195 (author, title, date), JS1886.

1849. Sims, George Robert (1847–1922). *Ballads and Poems*. (London: J. P. Fuller, [1883]). 3 parts. With a portrait.

A840 (author, title), JS1887. Only edition in BL. Sims was a dramatist and author of *Lights of London* (a play Dodgson attended). He also wrote widely for the periodical press, and wrote a series of letters on the London poor to the *London Daily News* which helped lead to the formation of a Royal Commission.

1850. Sims, Thomas. *Ministers and Medicine: An Appeal to Christian Ministers and Others on the Subject of Homœopathy.* (London: Homœopathic Publishing Company, 1877). 28pp. 4th edition, revised. 2nd of a series of *Homœopathic Missionary Tracts*.

Not listed separately in JS (see JS163). Dodgson's copy is in HAC in a bound volume with 7 other tracts from this series and one additional Homœopathic pamphlet (see 970). The author was former rector of St. Swithin's-upon-Kingsgate, Winchester. "Having often witnessed [Homœopathy's] beneficial effects, the writer trusts it will not be deemed presumptuous to submit with respectful deference, for the consideration of Christian ministers, a few of the many reasons that may be adduced why their earnest attention should be directed to the proofs that exist in favour of Homœopathy."

1851. Sinclair, William Macdonald (1850–1917). *Christ and Our Times*. (London: Isbister and Company, Limited, 1893). 320pp.

B1216 (author, title, date [1894]), JS1888. Only edition in BL, BOD, or NUC. Perhaps a misprint in B1216 or perhaps Dodgson owned an unrecorded reprint of 1894. Sinclair was educated at Balliol College, Oxford where he took his degree in 1873. He served as vicar of St. Stephen's, Westminster from 1880 and later rose to the rank of archdeacon of London and canon of St. Paul's. This volume is a collection of sermons which, "form an attempt to express, from within the national Church of England … the reasonable grounds of belief in the Christian faith, and its application to some of the needs and inquiries of the age." Includes sermons on "Christ and Modern Scepticism," "The Voice of Secularism," "Christ and the Atonement," "Christ and the Day of Rest," "Christ and the National Sin of Intemperance" and others.

1852. Sinnett, Alfred Percy (1840–1921). *Esoteric Buddhism*. (London: Chapman and Hall, 1885). 239pp. 5th edition.

B1217 (author, title, edition, date), JS1889. Sinnett was an English journalist who worked in both Hong Kong and India. In the latter location, he became a member of the Theosophical Society in 1879, and when he returned to London in 1882 he became president of the London lodge of that society. Of the present work, *Saturday Review* wrote, "To ourselves, 'Esoteric Buddhism' seems to be a blending of old Brahmanic ideas of Kalpas and 'austrity' with the speculations of American 'Spiritualists' and a dash of scientific terminology. But … it is certain that Mr. Sinnett delivers his gospel with much clearness and obvious good faith."

1853. Sinnett, Alfred Percy. *The Occult World*. (London: Trübner & Co., 1881). 172pp.

A887 (title), JS184 (Anon./Occult). Earliest edition in BL of the only matching title. *Saturday Review* wrote, "The averment is that there is a school of philosophy still in existence of which modern culture has lost sight; and that, while modern metaphysics and modern physical science 'have been groping for centuries after knowledge,' occult philosophy has enjoyed it in full measure all the while."

1854. Skeat, Walter William (1835–1912). *A Concise Etymological Dictionary of the English Language*. (Oxford: Clarendon Press, 1882). 616pp. In the *Clarendon Press Series*.

A326, A376, B1230 (author, title, date), JS1890 and JS1891. Dodgson owned 2 copies. A326 is described only as "Skeat's English Dictionary," but this is the only English dictionary compiled by Skeat (*A Dictionary of Middle English* compiled with Andrew Mayhew seems an unlikely match with A326). Skeat was Professor of Anglo-Saxon at Cambridge, founder of the English Dialect Society, the author of several textbooks, and editor of several important editions of Early English literature. The present dictionary, according to OCEL, "was begun with the object of collecting and sifting material for the [Oxford] English Dictionary."

1855. [Skene, Felicia Mary Frances] (1821–99). *Hidden Depths*. (Edinburgh: Edmonston & Douglas, 1866). 2 vols.

A610 (title, 2 vols.), JS1892. Only title in BL

matching the particulars of A610; only 2-volume edition in BL. Skene was a novelist who lived abroad (for several years in Athens) before settling in Oxford where, as a High Churchwoman, she also campaigned for social reform and wrote controversial novels. The present novel tells of the heroine's attempt to save a woman from prostitution. The novel includes graphic depictions of London brothels and insane asylums. See 1368 for another novel by Skene.

1856. Skene, William Forbes (1881–92). *The Gospel History for the Young, Being Lessons on the Life of Christ, etc.* (Edinburgh: D. Douglas, 1883–84). 3 vols.

A766 (title, 3 vols.), JS2229 (listed under C. M. Yonge). Only 3-volume edition of the only matching title in BL. The error in JS stems from the listing in A766 which states "Yonge's Scripture Readings, with Comments, 5 vols., Gospel History for the Young, 3 vols. and 2 others." Yonge wrote no such book; clearly the author's name in this entry was not meant to be inclusive. Skene was a Scot, educated in Germany, Edinburgh, and at St. Andrews. In 1881 he became Historiographer for Scotland, and he wrote several works on Scottish history.

1857. Skrine, John Huntley (1848–1923). *Songs of the Maid, and Other Ballads and Lyrics.* (London: Constable & Co., 1896). 143pp.

A513 (title), JS77 (Anon./Children). Only edition in BL of the only matching title. Skrine was educated at Merton College, Oxford and was a fellow there from 1871 to 1879. He was assistant master at Uppingham School from 1873 to 1888 and subsequently Warden of Trinity College, Glenalmond.

1858. (Slang). *Slang Dictionary.* Details unknown.

Title ("Slang Dictionary") only given in A324/JS252 (Anon./Reference). Several possibilities in BL, the most likely being Hotten, which was published in many editions throughout the 19th century, and which is altogether the type of book that would have interested Dodgson. The primary candidates in BL (earliest editions listed are described) are:

Andrewes, George. *A Dictionary of the Slang and Cant Languages: Ancient and Modern, as Used by Every Class of Offenders.* (London: G. Smeeton, [1809]).

Bee, John [pseud. of John Badcock]. *Slang. A*

Dictionary of the Turf, the Ring, the Chase, the Pit, of Bon-ton, and the Varieties of Life, Forming the Completest and Most Authentic Lexicon Balatronicum of the Sporting World. (London: T. Hughes, 1823).

[Hotten, John Camden]. *A Dictionary of Modern Slang, Cant, and Vulgar Words, Used at the Present Day in the Streets of London; the Universities of Oxford and Cambridge; the Houses of Parliament; the Dens of St. Giles; and the Palaces of St. James. Preceded by a History of Cant and Vulgar Language from the Time of Henry VIII. With Glossaries of Two Secret Languages, Spoken by the Wandering Tribes of London, the Costermongers and the Patterers.* (London: John Camden Hotten, 1859).

1859. Slatter, John (b. 1816?). *The Essential Connexion Existing between the Old and New Testaments, Followed by Some Remarks on Mr. Gore's Paper on Inspiration, Contained in "Lux Mundi."* (London: Parker & Co., 1890). 39pp.

Not in JS. Listed in WS (author, title, date) only and described there as having Dodgson's autograph initials. Slatter was educated at Lincoln College, Oxford and served as vicar of Streatley, Berkshire, from 1861 to 1880. He became a canon of Christ Church in 1876 and rector of Whitchurch in 1880. Dodgson met him on 10 February 1865 and mentions him in his diaries. See 797 and 799 for notes on Gore and *Lux Mundi.*

1860. Slatter, John. *Some Notes of the History of the Parish of Whitchurch, Oxon.* (London: E. Stock, 1895). 150pp.

JS1894. Dodgson's copy is the collection of Edward Wakeling and is inscribed "C. L. Dodgson with kindest regards from JS."

1861. Slatter, John. *The Student's Gospel Harmony, Being the Four Gospels in the Original Greek, Arranged in Parallel Columns Together with a Preface and Various Analytical Tables.* (London: W. Wells Gardner, 1878). 499pp.

B1231 (author, title, date), JS1893.

1862. Smalley, George Robarts. *A Compendium of Facts and Formulæ in Pure Mathematics and Natural Philosophy.* (London: 1862).

E52 (author, title ["Mathematical Facts and

Formulae ... an Appendix of Tables, in Interest, etc., and in Natural Philosophy, etc."], date), JS1895. Though the title in E52 is a paraphrase of the actual title, the matching subject, author, and date and the absence of any other possible match in BL all point to this being the book described. Smalley was Lecturer on Natural Philosophy at King's College, London and also served as head mathematical master at King's College School.

1863. Smart, Bath Charles and Henry Thomas Crofton (b. 1848). *The Dialect of the English Gypsies.* (London: Asher and Co., 1875). 302pp. 2nd edition, enlarged.

D81 (author, title, city, date, edition), JS1896. Smart was a Manchester physician.

1864. Smedley, Edward (ca. 1789–1836). *Erin. A Geographical and Descriptive Poem.* (London: Printed by Hamblin and Seyfang, for the author; sold by W. Ginger, 1810). 63pp. Illustrations, colored map.

E325 (title, date), JS1898. F180 lists "Smed-

Illustration (signed W. J. W. and engraved by the Dalziels) from "Prince Fie-for-Shame; or, Self-Control," in *Child-World* (item 1866).

ley (E.) Erin: a Poem, part 1, 1814." No such edition appears in BL or BOD, but Dodgson may have owned 2 copies. F180 notes the gothic stamp. Smedley was a clergyman and poet who served for 40 years as usher at Westminster School. Not to be confused with the novelist (and Dodgson's distant cousin) Francis Edward Smedley (1819–64).

1865. Smedley, Edward (1809–36). *Poems, by the Late Rev. Edward Smedley, A.M., with a Selection from his Correspondence, and a Memoir of his Life.* (London: Baldwin & Cradock, 1837). 457pp.

A920, D171 (author, title, city, date), JS1897. Smedley was the son of the Edward Smedley listed above. He was educated at Trinity College, Cambridge and served as precentor of Lincoln. *The London Athenæum* wrote of the volume, "Mr. Smedley's poems are easy and graceful, rather than energetic ... the great charm of the volume lies in the letters." The memoir of his life was by his widow.

1866. [Smedley, Menella Bute (1820–77) and Elizabeth Anna Hart (1822–90?)]. *Child-World.* (London: Strahan & Co., 1869). 263pp. Illustrated.

A567 (title), JS43 (Anon./Children). Only edition in BL. A567 states simply, "Child World," but undoubtedly refers to this volume co-authored by Dodgson's cousin, the poet Menella Bute Smedley. Other candidates by James Whitcomb Riley and Gail Hamilton [i.e. Mary Abigail Dodge] seem far less likely. Smedley lived in the coastal town of Tenby and wrote verse both on her own and together with her younger sister Elizabeth Hart. She also helped Dodgson in the early days of his own literary career (see *Diaries*, 55–8; 86–7). The text is 37 ballads and poems, many about fairies. A footnote in the poem "Prince Fie-for-Shame" reads, "It is evident that the Queen has profited — as who has not? — by the study of Alice's Adventures in Wonderland."

1867. [Smedley, Menella Bute and Elizabeth Anna Hart]. *Poems Written for a Child. By Two Friends..* (London: Strahan & Co., 1868). 307pp. Illustrated.

Not in JS. The collection formed by Jeffrey Stern, now at Seitoku Gakuin College, Tokyo, Japan, includes a copy inscribed from Dodgson to Ada Grace Sant. WMGC (p. 308) notes, "Dodgson certainly read all that Menella published, and records giving copies of *Poems Writ-ten for a Child*, 1868, to child friends."

1868. S[medley], M[enella] Bute. *The Story of Queen Isabel and Other Verses.* (London: Bell & Daldy, 1863). 111pp.

JS1899. Dodgson's copy is in the collection of Mark & Catherine Richards, London, and has the signature "C. L. Dodgson" on the flyleaf.

1869. **Smee**, Alfred (1818–77). *Instinct and Reason: Deduced from Electro-biology.* (London: Reeve and Benham, 1850). 320pp. Illustrated.

D172 (author, title, city, date), JS1900. Smee was a fellow of the Royal College of Surgeons and surgeon to the Bank of England. He invented a type of voltaic battery and lectured on electro-metallurgy at the Bank of England. This work is the second (and more popular) that Smee wrote on the subject. The previous year he published *Elements of Electro-Biology*, which DNB calls "a pioneer excursion into the territory of electrical physiology."

1870. **Smith**, Albert Richard (1816–60). *The Adventures of Mr. Ledbury, and his Friend Jack Johnson.* (London: R. Bentley, 1847). 499pp. No. 108 in the *Standard Novels* series.

A806, F174, WS, JS1901. Dodgson's copy is in WWC and has the gothic stamp and property label on the cover. Smith was a popular entertainer and humorist who contributed regularly to *Punch* and *Bentley's Miscellany*. He adapted some of Dickens' stories for the theatre and founded and edited a short-lived magazine, *The Man in the Moon*. This novel was his most successful.

1871. **Smith**, Albert [Richard]. *Beauty and the Beast.* (London: Wm. S. Orr and Co., [1844]). 51pp. + plates. Illustrated by Alfred Crowquill. In the *Comic Nursery Tales* series.

A483 (title, series, publisher), JS46 (Anon./Children's). A530/JS39 also lists this title (described only as "Beauty and the Beast"). This could be another copy of the same edition, or it could be another edition altogether. See 505 for a note on Crowquill.

1872. **Smith**, Albert Richard. *The Natural History of the Flirt.* (London: D. Bogue, 1848). 107pp. Illustrated by Paul Gavarni, Gilbert and Henning.

A472 (title, date), JS1902 (listed with 2 other titles). Dodgson's copy was bound together with two other titles from the same series, the natural histories of *Tuft-Hunters* (by Theodore Alois William Buckley, see 283) and *Humbugs* (by Angus Bethune Reach, see 1627). One of several humorous "Natural Histories" published by Smith and reprinted in various collections (see 1874–75). Paul Gavarni (1804–66) was a Frenchman known for his satirical prints in journals and fashion magazines (he drew over 4000 of them).

1873. **Smith**, Albert [Richard]. *The Pottleton Legacy: A Story of Town and Country Life.* (London: G. Routledge, 1852). 472pp. Illustrated by Halbot K. Browne.

A616 (author, title, illustrator, date), JS1903. A novel in 40 interconnected episodes.

1874. **Smith**, Albert [Richard]. *Sketches of the Day (1st Series) in Three Parts.* (London: Ward Lock, [ca. 1859]). 107, 119, 112pp. Illustrated by Gavarni, Henning & Gilbert.

A472 (author, title, illustrators, "3 series in 1 volume"), JS1904. Reprint of Smith's sketches. There were two series published by Ward Lock under the title *Sketches of the Day*. Probably A472 uses the word series incorrectly and refers to the fact that this volume consisted of three parts. The second series also consisted of three parts, and is another possible candidate. First series includes: "The Flirt," "The Natural History of Evening Parties," and "The Natural History of Stuck-Up People." Second series includes: "The Natural History of the Gent," "The Natural History of the Ballet-Girl," and "The Idler Upon Town."

1875. **Smith**, Albert [Richard], editor. *Sketches of London Life & Characters.* (London: Dean & Son, [1859?]). 188pp. Illustrations by [Paul] Gavarni. With illustrative essays by popular writers.

A467 (author, title, illustrator, publisher, n.d.), JS1905. Only edition traced. The conjectural date is from the Yale University Library catalogue. The London sketches of the French illustrator Gavarni (see 1872) are accompanied by prose sketches by Albert Smith, Shirley Brooks, John Oxenford, Charles Kenney, Thomas Miller, James Hannay, Horace Mayhew, Angus B. Reach, Joseph Stirling Coyne, Robert B. Brough and others. Among the subjects are the opera, a street beggar, a drawing-room, thieves, a barmaid, the parks, and the lounger in Regent Street.

1876. Smith, Albert [Richard]. *The Story of Mont Blanc.* (London: D. Bogue, 1854). 299pp. 2nd edition, enlarged.

A914, B1232 (author, title, date), JS1906. A later (ca. 1860) edition of the book included a memoir of the author by Edmund Yates, the editor who helped choose Charles Dodgson's pen name (see 2321). After his 1851 ascent of Mont Blanc, Smith presented a popular entertainment about the journey at the Egyptian Hall in London (on which occasion the present piece was published). He managed the Egyptian Hall from 1852 to 1860.

1877. Smith, Albert Richard. *The Struggles and Adventures of Christopher Tadpole at Home and Abroad.* (London: R. Bentley, 1848). 512pp. Illustrated by [John] Leech.

A626 (title, illustrator), JS110 (Anon./Literature). Earliest edition in BL or BOD. A comic novel originally published in monthly parts by Bentley; in publication and conception it is reminiscent of *The Pickwick Papers.*

1878. Smith, Albert [Richard]. *To China and Back: Being a Diary Kept, Out and Home.* ([London]: Published for the Author, [1859]). 72pp. Cover title reads "Handbook to Mr. Albert Smith's Entertainment."

A471 (author, title, date), JS1907. A471 lists 2 copies. Like *Mont Blanc* (1876), this was published in conjunction with Smith's popular entertainment at the Egyptian Hall. In this book he described his trip to China.

1879. Smith, Alexander (1830–67). *City Poems.* (Cambridge: Macmillan and Co., 1857). 190pp.

A865 (author, title), JS1908. 1st edition as described in MBC. No other pre–1898 edition in MBC or BL. A Glaswegian lace-pattern designer, Smith established a reputation as a poet and essayist. His best-known work, "Glasgow" is in the present collection. DEL quotes a letter from Miss Mitford, "Alfred Tennyson says that Alexander Smith's poems show fancy, but not imagination; and on my repeating this to Mrs. Browning, she said it was exactly her impression."

1880. Smith, Alexander. *Dreamthorp: A Book of Essays Written in the Country.* (London: Strahan & Co., 1863). 296pp.

Uncertain. F175 (author, title, date), JS1909. Identified as Dodgson's only by the gothic stamp. *The Daily News* wrote of this work, "Mr. Alexander Smith is remarkable for his love of nature, and for the pleasing language in which he describes the beauties of the common earth."

1881. Smith, Alexander. *Edwin of Diera.* (Cambridge: Macmillan & Co., 1861). 186pp.

A865 (author, title), JS1910. This is the July 1861 1st edition as described in MBC.

1882. Smith, Alexander. *Poems.* (London: David Bogue, 1853). 238pp.

A865 (author, title), JS1911. 1st edition as described in MBC.

1883. Smith, Charles (1844–1916). *An Elementary Treatise on Conic Sections.* (London: Macmillan and Co., 1882). 339pp.

A583 ("Smith's Conic Selections"), JS1912. Clearly a typographical error in A583. There is no such title in BL; the present title is the only possible match. This is the 1st edition as described in MBC. Charles Smith was Master of Sidney Sussex College, Cambridge. In his preface he writes, "In the following work I have investigated the more elementary properties of the Ellipse, Parabola, and Hyperbola ... before considering the General Equation of the Second Degree.... The examples at the end of each chapter ... include very many of those which have been set in the recent University and College examinations." He also cites the works of Salmon, Ferrers, and C. Taylor as more in-depth studies of the subject. Dodgson owned Salmon's book on the topic (1759).

1884. Smith, Charles John (1818–72). *Common Words with Curious Derivations.* (London: Bell and Daldy, 1865). 112pp.

E368 (author, title, date), JS1914. Smith matriculated at Christ Church, Oxford in 1838. He was Archdeacon of Jamaica from 1848 to 1852, and vicar of Erith, Kent from 1852 until his death.

1885. Smith, Charles John. *Synonyms Discriminated. A Complete Catalogue of Synonymous Words in the English Language, with Descriptions of their Various Shades of Meaning. Illustrated by Quotations from Standard Writers.* (London: Bell & Daldy, 1871). 610pp.

A361, D173 (author, title, city, date), JS1913.

1886. Smith, George (1831–95). *Gipsy Life: Being an Account of our Gipsies and their Children, with Suggestions for their Improvement.* (London: Haughton & Co., 1880). 296pp. With illustrations.

A914, B1233 (author, title, date), JS1915. Smith was known as the Children's Friend. His efforts to liberate poor children from industrial "slavery" led to legislation which took children out of factories and sent them to school.

1887. Smith, Goldwin (1823–1910). *The Elections to the Hebdomadal Council: A Letter to the Rev. C. W. Sandford, M.A., Senior Censor of Christ Church.* (Oxford: James Parker and Co., 1866). 20pp.

Not in JS. Dodgson responds to this letter in his own pamphlet *Elections to the Hebdomadal Council* (WMGC, #51). He acquired a copy on 3 November 1866 (see *Diary 5*). Smith was educated at Oxford and served on both the first and second commissions for the university. He served as Regius Professor of Modern History at Oxford from 1858 to 1866 and was an advocate for political reform. In 1868 he accepted a professorship at Cornell University. See *Oxford* for a full account of this Oxford controversy.

1888. Smith, Goldwin. *Irish History and Irish Character.* (Oxford: J. H. and J. Parker, 1872?). 197pp.

D174 (author, title, date [1882]), JS1917. No 1882 edition traced, but the 1872 2nd edition (described above) corresponds in all other particulars. Probably a typographical error in D174 (1882 for 1872). This work is an expansion of a lecture delivered before the Oxford Architectural and Historical Society in June 1861.

1889. Smith, Goldwin. *Lectures and Essays.* (New York: Macmillan & Company, 1881). 336pp.

A336 (author, title), JS1916. Apparently not published in Britain, this collection first appeared in a privately printed edition published in Toronto. The present edition seems more likely and is the only other edition traced. This volume reprints pieces from various periodicals, including *Canadian Monthly*, *Macmillan's Magazine*, *Toronto Mail*, and *New York Nation* on topics such as "The Greatness of England," "The Ascent of Man," "What is Culpable Luxury?," "The Early Years of Abraham Lincoln," and "Coleridge's Life of Keble."

1890. Smith, Horatio (1779–1849) and James Smith (1775–1839). *Rejected Addresses: or, the New Theatrum Poetarum.* (London: John Miller, 1812). 126pp.

A321 (title), A460 (title, date), B1234 (author, title, date), JS1918. The 1st edition is described above; the work went through many editions in 1812. Dodgson owned 2 copies. He bought one on 23 January 1855. Horatio (or Horace) Smith was a novelist, poet, and miscellaneous writer. James was his brother, who collaborated with him on two collections. This work is primarily a collection of parodies of famous authors of the day, such as Wordsworth, Byron, Scott and Southey. The book was taken from concept to publication in just six weeks to coincide with the opening of the new Drury Lane Theatre.

1891. Smith, James (1805–72). *The British Association in Jeopardy and Professor De Morgan in the Pillory without Hope of Escape.* (London: Simpkin, Marshall & Co., 1866). 94pp.

E398 (title), JS265 (Anon./Science). Only edition traced. The present description is from NUC. E398 gives a longer title, adding: *A Curious Record of Points in Dispute Among Mathematicians.* NUC describes this as a "Controversial letter on the quadrature of the circle and other geometrical puzzles." Smith was a mathematician who claimed to have solved the problem of squaring the circle and to have proved that pi=25/8. See 551 for a note on De Morgan, whom he attacks here. Dodgson attacked circle-squarers in his own incomplete work on the subject (see *Math*, 144).

1892. Smith, James Elimalet (1801–57). *Legends and Miracles, and Other Curious and Marvellous Stories of Human Nature, Collected from Scarce Books and Ancient Records. No. 1–12.* (London: Printed and published by B. D. Cousins, 1837). Published every Saturday. Each issue illustrated with a woodcut.

D175 (author, title, date), JS1919. Smith was a popular educator and eccentric preacher known as "Shepherd Smith" who also wrote leaders for the cheap periodical the *Family Herald*.

1893. Smith, John. *Irish Diamonds; or, a Theory of Irish Wit and Blunders, Combined* *with Other Kindred Subjects.* (London: Chapman and Hall, 1847). 175pp. With illustrations by Phiz (H. K. Browne).

A493 (author, title, illustrator, date), JS1920. The title page describes Smith, as "one of the editors of *The Liverpool Mercury*, late lecturer on education and geographical science."

1894. Smith, Thomas (fl. 1830–42). *Evolution: or the Power and Operation of Numbers, in the Statement, the Calculation, the Distribution, and the Arrangement of Quantities, Linear Superficial and Solid.* (London: Longman, Rees, Orme, Brown, Green and Longman, 1835). 160pp.

E267 (author, title, date), JS1921. Smith was a Liverpool accountant.

1895. Smith, William (1813–93), editor. *A Dictionary of the Bible, Comprising Its Antiquities, Biography, Geography and Natural History.* (London: John Murray, 1860–63). 3 vols. 1176, 1088, 1862pp.

A775, A782, A798 (author, title, 3 vols.), JS1923. Earliest edition in BL. Dodgson owned 3 copies. Both A775 and A798 specify 3 vols., A782 lists author and title only. Smith was educated at the University of London and for many years served as classical examiner there. He abandoned plans for a legal career to pursue a career in classical literature and was the author or editor of many works relating to that field, including many texts for students.

1896. Smith, William, editor. *A Dictionary of Greek and Roman Antiquities.* (London: Printed for Taylor and Walton, 1842). 1121pp. Illustrated.

A313 (author, title), JS1922. Earliest edition in BL.

1897. Smith, William. *A Latin-English Dictionary. Based upon the Works of Forcellini and Freund.* (London: Murray, 1855). 1212pp.

A326 ("Smith's Latin Dictionary"), JS1924. This title, and its later abridgements, are the only possible matches in BL. Earliest edition in BL.

1898. Smyth, John Paterson (1852–1932). *How God Inspired the Bible. Thoughts for the Present Disquiet.* (Dublin: Eason and Son, 1893). 222pp. 2nd edition.

A791, B1236 (author, title, date), JS1927. Smyth was educated at Trinity College, Dublin and was a clergyman who later went on to become Archdeacon of Montreal. "The burning question of the day," writes Smyth, "in the so-called 'religious world,' and indeed in an increasingly large circle without it as well, is that of the true position of the Bible. Many men are everywhere asking, though perhaps not always asking aloud: What of the claims of the Bible, what of its inspiration? How far is it human in its origin? How far is it Divine? How far is it infallible? Is it merely the word of 'holy men of old,' or is its every utterance literally 'the Word of God'?"

1899. Smyth, John Paterson. *How We Got Our Bible: An Answer to Questions Suggested by the New Revision.* (London: Bagster and Sons, [1885]). 127pp.

B1237 (author, title, n.d.), JS1928. Earliest edition in BL. The Revised Version of the Bible was commissioned by the Church of England and published from 1881 to 1884. It was the first major revision of the English language Bible since the publication of the King James version over 250 years earlier.

1900. Smyth, John Paterson. *The Old Documents and the New Bible. An Easy Lesson for the People in Biblical Criticism.* (London: Bagster & Sons, 1890). 216pp.

B1235 (author, title), JS1926. This is the only pre–1898 edition in BL.

1901. Smyth, William (1765–1849). *Lectures on Modern History from the Irruption of the Northern Nations to the Close of the American Revolution.* (London: William Pickering, 1840). 2 vols.

A633, B1238 (author, title, 2 vols., date), JS1925 (listed under J. Paterson Smyth). A 2nd edition was also published in 1840 in 2 vols. Smyth was, for 42 years, Professor of Modern History at Cambridge. This work is composed of many of his lectures in that capacity.

1902. Snowball, John Charles (d. 1855). *The Elements of Plane and Spherical Trigonometry; With the Construction and Use of Tables of Logarithms, Both of Numbers, and for Angles.* (Cambridge: Macmillan & Co., 1852). 140, 72pp. 7th edition.

E141 (author, title, date), F149, JS1929. 1st Macmillan edition, as described in MBC. BL gives 1852 for the date of the 8th edition, but MBC lists only this 1852 edition, the next not following until 1857. F149 describes Dodgson's copy as having his signature and the gothic stamp. Snowball was a Fellow of St. John's College, Cambridge.

1903. Society for Psychical Research. *Journal.* Vols. 1–7. (London: 1884–97). 7 vols.

A890 (title, 7 vols.), JS186 (Anon./Occult). Certainly vol. I (1884/85) through vol. 7 (1896/97). The *Journal* was to inform members of Society business, described fully in the Proceedings (see below), and to briefly describe the work of the Society's committees. The title pages states "for the private circulation among members only." Dodgson was a charter member of the society.

1904. Society for Psychical Research. *Proceedings.* Vols. 1–11 (London: 1882–95).

A890 (title, 11 vols.), JS186 (Anon./Occult). Almost certainly vol. 1 (1882/83) through vol. 11 (1895) (Volume 12 was for 1896/97). The *Proceedings* were the official public record of the Society, filled with scholarly articles. Dodgson was a charter member of the society.

1905. Somerset, Edward (1601–77). *The Century of Inventions of the Marquis of Worcester, with Historical and Explanatory Notes and a Biographical Memoir by C[harles] F[rederic] Partington.* (London: J. Murray, 1825). 138pp.

D139 (author, editor, title, city, date), JS1618 (listed under Partington). Somerset was the 2nd Marquis of Worcester. His work was originally published in 1663 under the title *A Century of the Names and Scantlings of Such Inventions, as at Present I can Call to Mind to Have Tried and Perfected, which (my Former Notes Being Lost) I have, at the Instance of a Powerful Friend, Endeavoured Now in the Year 1655 to Set these Down in such a Way as May Sufficiently Instruct me to Put any of Them in Practice.* The book included inventions such as calculating machines, time bombs, a mechanical flying bird, a flying machine for a man (which he claims to have tested successfully on a child), and a device for raising water using steam, which has been used as a claim for Somerset as the inventor of the steam engine.

1906. Sophocles (496–406 B.C. E.). *Tragoediae.* Edition unknown.

A929 (author, title), JS1930.

1907. [**Soulsby**, Lucy Helen Muriel]. *Stray Thoughts for Teachers.* (Oxford & London: J. Parker & Co., 1893). 178pp.

A567 ("Stray Thoughts for Teachers"), JS262 (Anon./Education). Only edition in BL. The preface to the 1897 expanded edition (published as *Stray Thoughts for Mothers and Teachers*) states: "Most teachers are now so well trained that such obvious suggestions as are here given will be useless to them. There may, however, still be some untaught elder sisters, and some untrained teachers, who may be interested in papers by one able from experience to sympathize with their difficulties."

1908. South, John Flint (1797–1882). *Household Surgery; or, Hints on Emergencies with an Additional Chapter on Poisons.* (London: G. Cox, 1853). 370pp. 4th edition.

Uncertain. Not in JS. In his diary for 4 March 1856, Dodgson writes, "Ordered *Hints for Emergencies.*" This is the only possible match in BL for a book published prior to 1856, but the incorrect title leaves some doubt. This could also refer to one of the two other books on emergencies Dodgson owned (see 1821 and 1983), but the present title seems most likely. Published as early as 1847; this is the traced edition closest in date to Dodgson's purchase. South was a surgeon who entered St. Thomas's Hospital, London in 1814 and wrote several medical texts. This book is a comprehensive first aid manual for home use.

1909. Southey, Robert (1774–1843). *The Poetical Works of Robert Southey: Complete in One Volume.* (London: Longman, Brown, Green, and Longmans, 1844). 800pp.

A314 (author, title), JS1931. This appears to be the 1st British 1-volume edition. Earlier editions (except for an 1829 Paris edition) were published in 10 volumes. It seems unlikely that A314 would neglect to mention such a large set. Southey was a prolific English poet and prose writer and friend of Coleridge (the two men married sisters). He also did much work as a translator and was a talented and prolific letter writer.

1910. Southey, Robert. *Southey's Common-Place Book. 1st series, Choice Passages Collections for English Manners and Literature; 2nd series: Special Collections; 3rd series: Analytical Readings; 4th series: Origi-*

nal Memorandum. (London: Longman, Brown, Green and Longmans, 1849–51). 4 vols. 596, 693, 841, 748pp. Edited by John Wood Warter (Southey's son-in-law).

A815 (author, title, 4 vols.), JS1932. Earliest edition in BL.

1911. Souvestre, Émile (1806–54). *Pleasures of Old Age.* (London: G. Routledge and Sons, 1868 [1867]). 344pp. Translated from the French work, *Souvenirs d'un Vieillard.*

D176 (author, title, city, date), JS1933. Souvestre was born in Brittany and from an early age showed an interest in the tales and stories of local peasants and in creating his own fairy tales. The editor's preface to this, his final work, describes his life as one of self-devotion and self-sacrifice. He had a successful literary career, an unsuccessful run for the national assembly in 1848, and retired to Switzerland in 1853. This collection of anecdotes and short pieces of memoir includes his "final thoughts."

1912. Sowerby, George Brettingham (the younger) (1812–84). *Companion to Mr. Kingsley's Glaucus Containing Colored Illustrations of the Objects Mentioned in the Work, Accompanied by Descriptions.* (Cambridge: Macmillan & Co., 1858). 48pp. With 12 hand-colored plates of seaweeds, starfish, shellfish and aquatic organisms.

D100 (title, author, city, date), not in JS. D100 describes Dodgson's copy as "with MS Index to the plates in Mr. Dodgson's autograph." Sowerby was one of a family of well-known botanical illustrators (grandson of James Sowerby). According to MBC, Sowerby's illustrations were "added to the edition of *Glaucus* printed in 1859." Dodgson also owned a copy of *Glaucus,* a book about the natural history of the beach (see 1133).

1913. Sowerby, James (1757–1822). *English Botany; or, Coloured Figures of British Plants, with their Essential Characters, Synonyms, and Places of Growth.: To which will be Added, Occasional Remarks.* (London: Printed for the Author by J. Davis, 1814). 36 vols.

Not in JS. In a letter to Harry Furniss dated 21 September 1889, Dodgson includes a sketch of some flowers meant to show Furniss what he

wants by way of an illustration. "The above is copied from Sowerby's *Botany,*" he writes. It is unlikely that Dodgson owned this, the first edition, and in all likelihood he consulted an edition at one of Oxford's libraries. The 1st edition is in libraries at All Souls and Magdalen as well as in the Radcliffe Science Library. Sowerby was a prolific natural history artist who trained at the Royal Academy. This was his largest work.

1914. Spalding, Thomas Alfred (b. 1850). *The House of Lords: A Retrospect and a Forecast.* (London: T. F. Unwin, 1894 [1893]). 281pp.

A347 ("Spalding's House of Lords"), JS1936. Only edition in BL. BL also lists the following 40pp. article in the 1895 annual volume of *The Eighty Club*: Spalding, Thomas Alfred. "The House of Lords. 'An Anomaly and a Danger,'" but the above description seems more likely for A347 as being a separate publication. Spalding was a lawyer and Shakespeare enthusiast.

1915. Spelman, Henry (1562–1641). *The History and Fate of Sacrilege; Edited, in Part from Two Mss., Rev. and Corr., with a Continuation, Large Additions, and an Introductory Essay, by Two Priests of the Church of England.* (London: J. Masters, 1853). 371pp. 2nd edition, with further additions.

A799, C10 (author, title, edition, date), JS1937. Includes an added title page with the imprint "London, J. Hartley, 1698," the imprint of the original edition. Spelman was educated at Trinity College, Cambridge and served as High Sheriff of Norfolk. He was knighted by King James and settled in London in 1612 to pursue scholarly research. Though written in 1632, this title was not published until 1698. It argues that those who have committed acts of sacrilege have subsequently suffered misfortune as a result.

1916. Spencer, Herbert (1820–1903). *The Data of Ethics.* (London: Williams & Norgate, 1879). 288pp.

A345 (author, title), JS1938. 1st edition in BL. Spencer was an important 19th-century philosopher and the founder of Evolutionary Philosophy — a philosophical theory based on the theory of evolution. This was the first part of Spencer's work *Principles of Ethics* (1879–93), one of several volumes which elaborated on his 1860 work *Programme of a System of Synthetic Philosophy* (see also 1919).

1917. Spencer, Herbert. *Education: Intellectual, Moral, and Physical.* (London: G. Manwaring, 1861). 190pp.

A345 (author, title), JS1939 (listed as Education and Essays). Earliest edition in BL. The entry in A345 is somewhat confusing. Listing several items under Spencer, it concludes with "Education and Essays (3 vols.)." Despite the lack of a comma, this must indicate that Dodgson owned the present volume, Spencer's famous work titled *Education* (in which he condemns the humanities and argues that science should be the basis of all education), and 3 volumes of Spencer's essays (see below).

1918. Spencer, Herbert. *Essays: Scientific, Political, and Speculative.* (London: Williams and Norgate, 1868–74). 3 vols. Reprinted, chiefly from the quarterly reviews.

A345 (author, title), JS1939 (listed as Education and Essays). See above for a note on the entry in A345. Spencer published two works under the title "Essays" during Dodgson's lifetime, but the present work is the only one recorded in BL in 3 volumes. Originally published in 2 series in 1858–63, it was issued in several 3-volume editions; this is the earliest in BL.

1919. Spencer, Herbert. *First Principles.* (London, Williams and Norgate, 1862). 503pp.

A345 (author, title), JS1940. Earliest edition in BL. The first volume of Spencer's elaboration on his 1860 work *Programme of a System of Synthetic Philosophy* (see also 1916).

1920. Spencer, Herbert. *The Principles of Psychology.* (London: Longman, Brown, Green and Longmans, 1855). 620 pp.

A345 (author, title), JS1941. Earliest edition in BL. A recasting of some of Spencer's earlier works.

1921. Spencer, Herbert. *The Study of Sociology.* (London: Henry S. King and Co., 1873). 423pp. Volume 5 in *The International Scientific Series.*

A306 (author, title), JS1942. Earliest edition in BL. Includes sections on "Nature of The Social Science," "Objective Difficulties," and "The Theological Bias."

1922. Spenser, Edmund (1552?–99). *Fairie Queene.* Edition unknown.

A865 (author, title), JS1943.

1923. Spicer, Henry (d. 1891). *Sights and Sounds: The Mystery of the Day: Comprising an Entire History of the American Spirit Manifestations.* (London: T. Bosworth, 1853). 480pp.

A886, B1242 (author, title, date), JS1944. Spicer was the author of several plays as well as poetry and other works. This work was followed by a sequel, *Facts and Fantasies.*

1924. Spielmann, M[arion] H[arry Alexander] (1858–48), editor. *European Pictures of the Year: Being the Foreign Art Supplement to the "Magazine of Art."* (London: Cassell & Co., 1892–1894). 3 vols. 96, 120, 95pp. Each volume with an introduction by M. H. Spielmann.

A276 (title, dates, 3 vols.), not in JS. Includes reproductions (in black and white) of paintings and sculpture from France; Belgium and Holland; Italy; Spain; Norway, Sweden and Denmark; Germany and Austro-Hungary; Russia; Switzerland; and a section of American Art in the Salons.

1925. Spiers, A[lexander] (1807–1869). *Dictionnaire Général Anglais-Français, Nouvellement Redigé d'après Johnson, Webster, Richardson, etc., les Dictionnaires Français de l'Académie, de Laveaux, de Boiste, etc.* (Paris: Baudry, Librairie Européenne, 1846–49). 2 vols.

A374 ("Spiers French and English Dictionary, 2 vols."), JS1945. Earliest edition traced. Editions, listed in BL and elsewhere, with English titles, published in London, seem to all be single volumes. The only exception, and thus a possibility, is: *School Dictionary of the French and English Languages, (French-English and English-French,) Abridged from the Author's General French and English Dictionary* (London: 1851), which is described as published in 2 parts. It seems more likely that Dodgson would have owned a complete edition, though it is somewhat perplexing that A374 gives the short title in English. Spiers, an Englishman, was a Professor of English at the Imperial College of Bonaparte, Paris.

1926. Splene, Megathym [pseud. of John Cockburn Thomson] (1834–60). *Almæ Matres. Dedicated, Without Permission, to the Freshmen and Dons of Oxford.* (London: J. Hogg and Sons, [1859]). 308pp.

A318 (title), JS2071 (listed under Thomson). Only pre–1898 edition in BL. Thomson matriculated at Trinity College, Oxford in 1852 and received his B.A. from St. Mary Hall in 1857. *The Athenæum* wrote that the author wrote, "mostly about by-gone things. According to his account of Oxford, the tutors are fast-drinking imbeciles; the students either very fast or very slow ... the representation, as applied to the whole University, is an absurdity."

1927. Spratt, Mrs. George. *The Language of Birds, Containing Poetic and Prose Illustrations of the Most Favourite Cage-Birds.* (London: 1837). With plates.

E92 ("The Language of Birds, with illustrations beautifully colored by hand; 18mo, incomplete, commencing at p. 13 of the Introduction"), JS271 (Anon./Science). This is the only edition of the only matching title in BL.

1928. [**Spruner**, Karl von] (1803–92). *Dr. Karl von Spruner's Historico-geographical Hand Atlas.* (London: Trübner and Co., 1861). 8pp. + 26 maps.

A523 ("Spruner's Hand-Atlas"), JS371 (Anon./Topography). Several German language editions are listed in BL and BOD. The earliest English edition traced (listed in BOD only), was translated, with additions, and published in 1853 by Edward Gover under the title *The Historic Geographical Atlas of the Middle and Modern Ages*, but this is the only English-language edition that comes close to matching the short title in A523, and so seems the most likely. The 1853 German edition was titled *Historisch-Geographischer Hand-Atlas zur Geschichte Asiens, Africa's, America's und Australiens.* Spruner was influential in pioneering the technique of depicting the development of the relationships between states in his Atlas.

1929. Stahl, P. J. [pseud. of Pierre Jules Hetzel] (1814–86). *La Journée de Mademoiselle Lili.* (Paris: J. Hetzel, n.d. [ca. 1862]). 20pp. "Vignettes par [Lorenz] Fröhlich, texte par un papa."

E58 (title), JS1034 (listed under Frolich). Only edition traced. One of a series of French children's books written by Hetzel and illustrated by Lorenz Frölich. E58 described the illustrations as "quaint woodcuts strongly appealing to young children." Hetzel was a friend of Jules Verne and godfather to Frölich's daughter. See 733 for a note on Frölich.

1930. Stahl, P. J. [pseud. of Pierre Jules Hetzel]. *Little Rosy's Travels: or, Country Scenes in the South of France.* (London: Seeley, 1867). Illustrated by L[orenz] Frölich.

A645 ("Little Rosy's Travels"), JS63 (Anon./Children's). Only British edition in BL of the only possible match. JS speculates that A645 and A678 (*Little Rory's Voyage of Discovery*) may both refer to *Little Rosy's Voyage* by P. J. Stahl. This seems unlikely as the present volume matches A645. A book for children.

1931. Stahl, P. J. [pseud. of Pierre Jules Hetzel]. *Little Rosy's Voyage of Discovery Undertaken in Company with Her Cousin Charley.* (London: Seeley, 1868). 95pp. + 48 plates by L[orenz] Frölich.

A678 ("Little Rory's Voyage of Discovery"), JS63 (Anon./Children), WS. Only edition in BL (clearly a typographical error in A678). See above concerning the incorrect speculation concerning this title made in JS. A book for children. The Walter Spencer copy was "inscribed on the inside of the front fly leaf "Ethel Rivers. From Lewis Carroll Jan. 1874." This

Rosy and her cousin Charley. Frontispiece by Lorenz Frölich for *Little Rosy's Voyage of Discovery* (item 1931).

copy is in the collection formed by Jeffrey Stern, now at Seitoku Gakuin College, Tokyo, Japan.

1932. Stanford, John Frederick (1815–1880) and Charles August Maude Fennell (d. 1916). *The Stanford Dictionary of Anglicised Words and Phrases*. (Cambridge: University Press, 1892). 826pp. Edited for the syndics of the University Press by C. A. M. Fennell; based on notes and collections made by J. F. Stanford.

A377 ("Stanford's English Dictionary"), JS254 (Anon./Reference). No precisely matching title traced, but this is the only close match and seems likely. This is the only pre–1898 edition.

1933. Stannus, Hugh H[utton] (1840–1908). *A History of the Origin of the Doctrine of the Trinity in the Christian Church*. (London: Christian Life Publishing Co., Williams & Norgate, 1883). 104pp. 40th thousand. With an introduction and appendix by R. Spears.

E248 (author, title, date), JS1947. Stannus was best known as an architect and designer, but he also wrote on other topics.

1934. Stapleton, Joseph Whitaker. *The Great Crime of 1860: Being a Summary of the Facts Relating to the Murder Committed at Road; A Critical Review of its Social and Scientific Aspects; and an Authorised Account of the Family*. (London: E. Marlborough and Co., 1861). 379pp. With a preface by Rowland Rodway.

A637, D186 (author, title, city, date), JS1948. A book about the murder of the child Saville Kent, taken from his bed in the Kent home near Frome in the night — a crime that caused a sensation in Victorian England. Kent's body was found in an abandoned privy nearby, his throat slit. Initial inquiries placed suspicion on his older sister, Constance, but the lack of evidence led to her being discharged into her father's care, though not formally acquitted. Four years after the publication of the present volume (written by the family doctor), Constance confessed publicly to the crime. She served 20 years in prison and then disappeared from public view, though there are many stories of what happened to her in circulation. In spite of her confession, mystery still surrounds the crime. And some historians claim her innocence.

1935. *The Stars and the Angels: or, the Natural History of the Universe and its Inhabitants*. (London: Hamilton, Adams, 1858). 376pp.

A522, B1243 (title, date), JS277 (Anon./Science).

1936. Staunton, Howard (1810–74). *The Chess-player's Companion. Comprising a New Treatise on Odds, and a Collection of Games Contested by the Author with Various Distinguished Players during the Last Ten Years; Including the Great French Match with Mons. St. Amant; to which are Added a Selection of New and Instructive Problems*. (London: Bohn, 1849). 510pp. In *Bohn's Scientific Library*.

A895 (author, title), JS1949. Earliest edition in BL. Howard was a scholar of Elizabethan drama, but was primarily known as a chess player. In 1843 he challenged and defeated the European champion M. St. Amand at a match in Paris. He was editor, for many years, of the chess column in the *Illustrated London News*. Dodgson's book TTLG is largely based on the game of chess.

1937. Staunton, Howard. *The Chess Tournament. A Collection of the Games Played at this Celebrated Assemblage*. (London: Bohn, 1852). 377pp. In *Bohn's Scientific Library*.

A895 (author, title), JS1950. Only pre–1898 edition in BL. A report of the London chess tournament of 1851.

1938. Steere, Edward (1828–82), translator. *Swahili Tales, as Told by Natives of Zanzibar*. (London: Bell & Daldy, 1870). 503pp. Swahili original with an English translation.

A339 (title, translator), JS1951. Earliest edition in BL. Steere was a missionary bishop in Central Africa. In addition to the present collection of African tales, he was author of handbooks of the Swahili and Shambella languages as well as Christian works.

1939. Stenhouse, Mrs. Fanny (b. 1829). *An Englishwoman in Utah: The Story of a Life's Experience in Mormonism. An Autobiography*. (London: Sampson Low & Co., 1880). 404pp. With an introductory preface by Mrs. Harriet Beecher Stowe. Illustrated.

A904 (author, title), JS1953 (listed under T. B. H. Stenhouse). Earliest edition traced under this title. Also published as *"Tell it all:" The Story of a Life's Experience in Mormonism. An Autobiography* and as *The Tyranny of Mormonism, or, An Englishwoman in Utah*. The author was the wife of T. B. H. Stenhouse (see below), for twenty-five years a Mormon missionary and church elder. She here tells her personal story, complete with a glimpse into the Utah of Brigham Young with its sexual mores and social customs.

1940. Stenhouse, T[homas] B. H. (1825–82). *The Rocky Mountain Saints: A Full and Complete History of the Mormons, from the First Vision of Joseph Smith to the Last Courtship of Brigham Young and the Development of the Great Mineral Wealth of the Territory of Utah*. (London: Ward, Lock, and Tyler, [1874]). 761pp. Illustrated with 24 full-page engravings, a steel plate frontispiece, an autographic letter of Brigham Young, and numerous woodcuts.

A637, D126 (title, author, city), JS1952. A reissue with a new title page of the 1874 American edition published by D. Appleton, N.Y. This is the only London edition in BL. Stenhouse was a Mormon elder and missionary for 25 years, and was editor of the *Salt Lake Daily Telegraph*. He claimed to have, "daily intercourse" with Brigham Young for 12 years. A part of the 1869 rebellion within the church, Stenhouse left the church (with his wife, see above) and returned east. An unsigned preface to this exposé is fiercely anti–Mormon, and addressed to the possibility that Utah could become a state of the United States. In his introduction, Stenhouse states, "The author has no pet theories to advance, no revelations to announce, no personal animosity to satisfy. He has simply outgrown the past, and utterly disbelieves Brigham Young's recent claim to the possession of a 'Priesthood that is Infallible,' and the assumption that the Mormon Church is the exclusive and only true Church of Christ upon the earth." See 692 for another book on Mormons.

1941. [**Stephen**, George] (b. 1794). *Adventures of an Attorney in Search of Practice*. (London: Saunders & Otley, 1839). 407pp.

A650, D2 (title, city, date), JS1954. Stephen was a lawyer and Deputy-Lieutenant for Buckinghamshire. Like his father, he was a vocal opponent of slavery. He wrote several novels and a number of works on the law and on slavery. The present book is a novel for lawyers.

1942. Sterne, Laurence (1713–68). *The Works of Laurence Sterne. With a Life of the Author, Written by Himself*. (London: J. Rivington & Sons, etc., 1788). 10 vols. Illustrated.

A658, B1244 (author, title, date, 10 vols.), JS1955.

1943. Stevenson, Robert Louis (1850–94). *Across the Plains With Other Memories and Essays*. (London: Chatto & Windus, 1892). 317pp. 1st edition.

A621 (author, title, edition), JS1956. A collection of essays that includes: "Across the Plains," "The Old Pacific Capital," "Fontainebleau," "Epilogue to 'An Island Voyage'," "Random Memories," "Random Memories Continued," "The Lantern-bearers," "A Chapter on Dreams," "Beggars," "Letter to a Young Gentleman," "Pulvis et Umbra," and "A Christmas Sermon." In a letter to Gertrude Thomson (5 December 1895) Dodgson writes, "Some while ago I rashly gave a general order to my bookseller, to get me Robert Louis Stevenson's Works" (see *Illustrators*, 304).

1944. Stevenson, Robert Louis. *The Black Arrow: A Tale of Two Roses*. (London: Cassell, 1888). 324pp. 1st edition.

A622 (author, title, edition), JS1957. A novel set in England in the late stages of the War of the Roses. Originally serialized in *Young Folks* magazine.

1945. Stevenson, Robert Louis. *Catriona. A Sequel to "Kidnapped". Being Memoirs of the Further Adventures of David Balfour at Home and Abroad*. (London: Cassell and Company, 1893). 371pp.

A618 (author, title,) JS1958. 1st edition. In which David Balfour, in love with a woman named Catronia, escapes a plot against his life.

1946. Stevenson, Robert Louis. *Familiar Studies of Men and Books*. (London: Chatto & Windus, 1882). 397pp.

A617 (author, title), JS1961. 1st edition. A collection of essays that includes: "Victor

Hugo's Romances," "Some Aspects of Robert Burns," "Walt Whitman," "Henry David Thoreau," "François Villon," "Charles of Orleans," and "John Knox and Women."

1947. Stevenson, Robert Louis. *Father Damien: An Open Letter to the Reverend Doctor Hyde of Honolulu from Robert Louis Stevenson.* (London: Chatto & Windus, July 1890). 30pp.

A619 (author, title), JS1962. This, the 1st trade edition, is the only public pre–1898 British edition in BL. Two privately printed editions (of 25 and 300 copies each) preceded this one, but Dodgson likely owned the trade edition. The letter is Stevenson's vehement answer to Dr. Hyde's criticism of Roman Catholic missionary Joseph Damien who died of leprosy after many years of working in a leper colony in the Sandwich Isles. Hyde, when asked to comment on Damien's life, wrote a private letter in which he called Damien "a coarse, dirty man, headstrong and bigoted," and claimed that he spent little time at the leper colony prior to his own infection. The letter was made public, eliciting this response from Stevenson, who was living in the islands at that time.

1948. Stevenson, Robert Louis. *An Inland Voyage.* (London: C. Kegan Paul, 1878). 237pp.

A619 (author, title), JS1963. 1st edition. An account of the author's trip through France and Belgium by canoe.

1949. Stevenson, Robert Louis. *Kidnapped: Being Memoirs of the Adventures of David Balfour in the Year 1751.* (London: Cassell, 1886). 311pp. Folding map.

A617 (author, title), JS1964. 1st edition.

1950. Stevenson, Robert Louis. *The Master of Ballantrae: A Winter's Tale.* (London: Cassell, 1889). 332pp. 1st edition.

A620 (author, title, edition), JS1965. A novel set in Scotland after the 1745 Rebellion. Based on the true story of the Marquis of Tullibardine.

1951. Stevenson, Robert Louis. *Memories and Portraits.* (London: Chatto & Windus, November 1887). 299pp. 1st edition.

A621 (author, title, edition), JS1966. A collection of essays that includes: "The Foreigner at Home," "Some College Memories," "Old Mortality," "A College Magazine," "An Old Scotch Gardener," "Pastoral," "The Manse," "Memoirs of an Islet," "Thomas Stevenson," "Talk and Talkers," "The Character of Dogs," "'A Penny Plain and Twopence Coloured'," "A Gossip on a Novel of Dumas's," "A Gossip on Romance," and "A Humble Remonstrance."

1952. Stevenson, Robert Louis. *The Merry Men and Other Tales and Fables.* (London: Chatto & Windus, 1887). 296pp.

A618 (author, title), JS1967. This, the 1st edition, is the only pre–1898 British edition in BL. A collection of stories.

1953. Stevenson, Robert Louis. *New Arabian Nights.* (London: Chatto & Windus, 1889). 328pp.

A618 (author, title), JS1968. First 1-volume edition (A618 does not specify multiple volumes) Originally published in 2 vols. in 1882. A collection of stories that includes: "The Suicide Club," "The Rajah's Diamond," "The Pavilion on the Links," "A Lodging for the Night," "The Sire de Maletroit's Door," and "Providence and the Guitar."

1954. Stevenson, Robert Louis. *Prince Otto. A Romance.* (London: Chatto & Windus, 1885). 300pp.

A619 (author, title), JS1969. 1st edition. A novel.

1955. Stevenson, Robert Louis. *The Silverado Squatters.* (London: Chatto & Windus, 1884). 254pp. 1st edition.

A622 (author, title, edition), JS1970. A record of the author's stay in California during his years in America (1879–83).

1956. Stevenson, Robert Louis. *Songs of Travel and other Verses.* (London: Chatto & Windus, 1896). 85pp. 1st edition.

A861 (author, title, edition), JS1971. Verses published in *The Pall Mall Gazette, The New Review, The Scots Observer, The Court and Society Review, The Antipodean, Longman's Magazine*, and *Scribner's Magazine*, July 1890–Jan. 1895.

1957. Stevenson, Robert Louis. *Strange Case of Dr Jekyll and Mr Hyde.* (London: Longmans, Green and Co., 1886). 141pp.

A619 (author, title), JS1959. 1st edition.

1958. Stevenson, Robert Louis. *Travels with a Donkey in the Cévennes.* (London: Kegan Paul, 1879). 227pp.

A619 (author, title), JS1973. 1st edition. Another of Stevenson's travel memoirs.

1959. Stevenson, Robert Louis. *Treasure Island*. (London: Cassell, 1883). 292pp.
A619 (author, title), JS1972. 1st edition.

1960. Stevenson, Robert Louis. *Underwoods*. (London: Chatto & Windus, 1887). 137pp. 1st edition.
A861 (author, title, edition), JS1974. Poems previously published in *Travels with a Donkey in the Cévennes* (1879) and in *The Magazine of Art*, *Alma Mater's Mirror*, *The Century Magazine*, *The Cornhill Magazine*, *Atlantic Monthly*, *The Scottish Church*, and *Fraser's Magazine* October 1880–April 1887.

1961. Stevenson, Robert Louis. *Virginibus Puerisque and other Papers*. (London: C. Kegan Paul, 1881). 296pp.
A617 (author, title), JS1975. 1st edition. A collection of essays that includes: "Virginibus Puerisque," "Crabbed Age and Youth," "An Apology of Idlers," "Ordered South," "Æs Triplex," "El Dorado," "The English Admirals," "Child's Play," "Walking Tours," "Pan's Pipes," and "A Plea for Gas Lamps."

1962. Stevenson, Robert Louis and Fanny van de Grift Stevenson. *More New Arabian Nights: The Dynamiter*. (London: Longmans, Green, 1885). 207pp. 1st edition.
A620 (author, title, edition), JS1960. Dodgson's copy, with his monogram, was offered for sale by Swann Galleries, New York on 9 January 1975 (DAA2725). Fanny was the wife of Robert Louis Stevenson. Most of the stories in this collection were written by Fanny Stevenson and improved by Robert. Only "Zero's Tale of The Explosive Bomb" was written entirely by Robert and gave the collection its subtitle (the story, in Stevenson's words, was "designed to make dynamite ridiculous if he could not make it horrible.") Two stories were entirely written by Fanny.

1963. Stewart, Dugald (1753–1828). *Elements of the Philosophy of the Human Mind*. (London: Printed by A. Strahan and T. Cadell, 1792). 566pp.
A575 (author, title), JS1976. Earliest edition in BL. Stewart was a Scottish philosopher who held the chair of Moral Philosophy at Edinburgh University from 1785. This was his most important work, in which he espoused the

"philosophy of common sense" as set forth by his teacher Thomas Reid.

1964. [Stirling, Walter], editor. *The Prose Moralist, Consisting of Selections and Extracts from the Most Eminent Authors: For the Use of Young Persons*. (Winchester: James Robbins; London: James Wallis, 1814). 180pp.
Uncertain. Not in JS. Listed in WS only and identified by gothic stamp and property label only. Dodgson's copy is in WWC and bears the gothic stamp and property label.

1965. Stokes, Edward (1823–63). *Poems*. ([London?]: Printed for Private Circulation, [1861?]). 173pp.
D188 (author, title, Private Circulation, n.d.), JS1977. Only edition of the only matching title in BL. Stokes matriculated at Christ Church, Oxford in 1840 and was a Student there from 1842 to 1860. He must certainly have been known to Dodgson.

1966. [Stokes, Francis Griffin] (b. ca. 1853?), editor. *The Shotover Papers, or, Echoes from Oxford*. Vol. 1, nos. 1–13. (Oxford: J. Vincent, 1874–75). 208pp.
A572 (title), JS203 (Anon./Oxford). Numbers not specified, but this periodical only lasted through its 1st 13 issues. Stokes was an undergraduate at Merton College, Oxford, having matriculated in 1872. This work is a short-lived comic magazine. In no. 3, (April 14, 1874), in an article titled "Convocation: A Farce," the following lines appear: "Next, is a book by cunning D. C. L., | 'Alice in Wonderland,' we know it well, | Of course we do, we don't like 'Cakeless' though | His forte is lying and his form is low." "Cakeless" was a comic squib which made fun of Dodgson (among other college figures) and which caused Dean Liddell to send down its author, John Howe Jenkins. No. VI (May 30, 1874), contains an article titled "Answers to Our Riddle." The "Riddle" was "Who is the editor of the Shotover Papers?" Eleven answers are given, with the men in question receiving between 1 and 17 votes. Number 5 on the list is "Rev. C. L. Dodgson" with 7 votes. In an undated manuscript list of Lewis Carroll items offered for sale by Walter Spencer of London (probably ca. 1932, collection of the author) the following unpublished item is described: "Autograph letter 2 pages, 8vo to F. G. Stokes 'Ch. Ch May 8/75' with regard to a din-

ner given by the editors of the Shotover Papers and saying 'As a private individual I have no connection with the book to which you allude in such complimentary terms. It was published anonymously — though of course the name of the writer is accidentally known to many private individuals, it is at present my wish that it should continue to be as far as possible an anonymous publication'."

1967. Stokes, William. *Stokes's Rapid Arithmetic for Rapidly Teaching to Calculate, and for Teaching to Calculate Rapidly.* (London: Houlston & Sons, 1879). 124pp. 3rd edition.

E344 (author, title, date), JS1978. BL describes the author as a "Teacher of Memory." NUC lists him as "of the Royal Polytechnic Institute." Dodgson was also interested in memory and invented a "Memoria Technica" to help remember numbers (see WMGC, 97–98). He also invented his own mathematical shortcuts, published in *Nature* (see LCP).

1968. [Stone, Mrs. Elizabeth] (fl. 1840–60). *The Art of Needle-Work, from the Earliest Ages; Including some Notices of the Ancient Historical Tapestries.* (London: Henry Colburn, 1844). 405pp. New edition. Edited by the Right Honourable the Countess of Wilton (Mary Margaret Egerton).

Uncertain. F162 (author, title, date), not in JS. Identified as Dodgson's only by the gothic stamp. A history of the art from biblical times to the 19th century, including tapestries, book decoration, costume work, etc.

1969. [Stout, George Frederick] (1860–1944), editor. *Mind: A Quarterly Review of Psychology and Philosophy*, new series vol. 3 (London: April 1894).

E422 (title, date), JS223 (Anon./Philosophy). Dodgson contributed two pieces to *Mind,* one in July 1894 and one in April 1895.

1970. Stowe, Harriet Beecher (1811–96). *Dred: A Tale of the Great Dismal Swamp.* (London: S. Low, Son & Co., 1856). 2 vols. in 1. 524pp.

Not in JS. In his diary for 1 September 1856, Dodgson writes, "Bought *Dred.*" This is the edition in BL dated closest to Dodgson's date of purchase. The author's second (after *Uncle Tom's Cabin*), and less well-known, novel of America slavery.

1971. Stowe, Harriet Beecher. *Uncle Tom's Cabin.* (London: John Cassell, 1852). 391pp. 27 illustrations by George Cruikshank.

A893 (author, title, illustrated), JS1979. 1st English edition (originally published in 13 parts) and the 1st illustrated edition. There were many other British editions in the 19th century, including one illustrated by George H. Thomas in 1890.

1972. Strahan, Alexander (1834?–1918), publisher. *Touches of Nature by Eminent Artists and Authors.* (London: Alexander Strahan, 1867). 98pp.

A281 (title), not in JS. Only edition in BL. A collection, in poetry and art of "much of the richest fruit of Strahan and Company's magazines." Includes writing by George MacDonald, Maria Craik, Christina Rossetti, Jean Ingelow, Charles Kingsley, William Gilbert, M. B. Smedley, and many others. Illustrations by J. E. Millais, Holman Hunt, George DuMaurier, John Tenniel, and many others.

Illustration by John Tenniel for "The Way in the Wood" by Isa Craig, in *Touches of Nature* (item 1972).

1973. Strivelyne, Elsie [pseud. of Mrs. MacCallum]. *The Princess of Silverland, and Other Tales.* (London: Printed at Crystal Palace, [1874]). With a frontispiece by Sir [Joseph] N[oel] Paton.

A641 (title), JS73 (Anon./Children). Only edition of the only matching title in BL. See 1507 for a note on Paton. This is the only title by this Scottish author traced. Dodgson wrote to Macmillan in 1874 asking for the author's identity, but no reply from the publisher survives (see *Macmillan*, 104).

1974. Strong, Thomas Banks (1861–1944). *Christian Ethics. Eight Lectures Preached before the University of Oxford in the Year 1895 on the Foundation of the Late Rev. John Bampton.* (London: Longmans, Green, and Co., 1896). 380pp.

A803 (author, "Bampton Lectures"), not in JS. Earliest edition in BL. Strong was a Student at Christ Church, and thus a colleague of Dodgson. He succeeded Dodgson as curator of the Senior Common Room in 1892. He served as Bishop of Oxford from 1935 to 1937.

1975. Strutt, Joseph (1749–1802). *The Sports and Pastimes of the People of England Including the Rural and Domestic Recreations, May Games, Mummeries, Shows, Processions, Pageants, and Pompous Spectacles, from the Earliest Period to the Present Time.* (London: T. T. & J. Tegg, 1833). 420pp. A new edition edited by William Hone. With 140 engravings in the text.

A895, D187 (author, title, editor, city, date), JS1980. D187 notes Dodgson's initials. Strutt was an engraver and antiquarian writer who wrote works of history, social history and some novels. The introduction calls this work, "A General Arrangement of the Popular Sports, Pastimes, and Military Games, Together with the Various Spectacles of Mirth and Splendour, Exhibited Publicly or Privately, for the Sake of Amusement, at Different Periods, in England." Includes sections on tumbling, jugglers and performing animals.

1976. Sturges, Octavius (1833–94). *Chorea and Whooping-Cough. Five Lectures.* (London: Smith Elder & Co., 1877). 149pp.

B1246 (author, title, date), JS1981. The introduction states, "It is part of the design of the following pages to place chorea and whooping cough in the category of functional derangements."

1977. Suckling, John (1609–41). *The Works of Sir John Suckling. Containing his Poems,*

Letters and Plays. (London: Jacob Tonson, 1709). 376pp.

A491 (author, title, date), JS1982. Suckling was a poet and dramatist. Hallam writes of him that he "is acknowledged to have left far behind him all former writers of song in gaiety and ease; it is not equally clear that he has ever since been surpassed."

1978. Sulivan, George Lydiard (b. 1832). *Dhow Chasing in Zanzibar Waters and on the Eastern Coast of Africa: Narrative of Five Years' Experiences in the Suppression of the Slave Trade.* (London: S. Low, Marston, Low & Searle, 1873). 453pp. With map and illustrations from photographs and sketches taken on the spot by the author.

A518 (author, title), JS1983. Only pre-1898 edition in BL. Sullivan was a rear admiral. *The Spectator* writes of this book, "It tells the horrid truth so plainly and so simply that it is sure to inflame the 'old fever' of anti-slavery, as the Bishop of Winchester [Samuel Wilberforce] calls it."

1979. Sullivan, James Frank (1853–1936). *The British Working Man by One who Does not Believe in Him, and Other Sketches.* (London: "Fun" Office, 1878). 103pp. of illustrations. Engraved by Dalziel Brothers.

A532 ("The British Workman by J. F. Sullivan"), JS1984. Earliest edition traced of the only possible match. Sullivan was a British illustrator and author who served as resident illustrator for *Fun* for 24 years. His character "The British Working-Man" appeared regularly the pages of that humorous journal.

1980. Sully, James (1842–1923). *Illusions. A Psychological Study.* (London: Kegan Paul & Co., 1881). 372pp. Vol. 34 in the *International Scientific Series.*

A900 (author, title), JS1985. Earliest edition in BL. Sully was a contributor to many journals, including *Mind*, and to the *Encyclopaedia Britannica*. He lectured on psychology, logic, and pedagogics in London, Cambridge, and elsewhere. Of the present work, *Saturday Review* wrote, "Mr. Sully's analysis of the whole subject leaves us at the close impressed, on the one hand, with the ability of the writer's treatment; on the other, with the force of his practical conclusion that our intuitions or perceptions of things are more relatively than absolutely true, and that ... the true standard of reality, as opposed to illusion, is a stable consensus of general belief."

1981. Summerly, Felix [pseud. of Henry Cole] (1808–82), editor. Bound volume of five fairy story books from the *Home Treasury* series. (London: Joseph Cundall, 1846).

A487 ("Home Treasury. Five Fairy Story Books, with illustrations in the original ornamental cover, 1846."), JS82 (Anon./Children). Cole was the first director of the South Kensington Museum (later the Victoria and Albert Museum) and the man who, in 1843, commissioned the first Christmas card. He began his *Home Treasury* series with Joseph Cundall in 1840 when he found a dearth of appropriate material to read to his children. He published classic fairy tales, Bible stories, and other similar fare, in illustrated editions, which were available colored or uncolored. The most likely candidates for this collection of "Fairy Story Books" are *Jack the Giant Killer, Jack and the Beanstalk, The Sleeping Beauty, Little Red Riding Hood, Cinderella*, and *Beauty and the Beast*. The books were printed by Charles Whittingham at the distinguished Chiswick Press.

1982. S[utton], T[homas] (1818–75). *A Dictionary of Photography. The Chemical Articles of A, B, C, by J[ohn] Worden*. (London: S. Low, Son, and Co., 1858). 423pp. Illustrated with diagrams.

Uncertain. A553 ("Dictionary of Photography"), JS226 (Anon./Photography). Earliest edition in BL and corresponds to Dodgson's early years of photographing. A similar title by John Wall was not published until 1889, several years after Dodgson gave up photography, thus the Sutton book is the best candidate for this item. Sutton was editor of *Photographic Notes* and author of several books on photography. *The London Athenæum* wrote of this work, "We do not know a better book to put in the hands of either the learner or the successful photographer." Dodgson bought his first camera in 1856.

1983. Swain, William Paul (b. 1837). *Surgical Emergencies; Together with the Emergencies Attendant on Parturition and the Treatment of Poisoning. A Manual for the Use of General Practitioners*. (London: 1874). 220pp. 1st edition.

A563 (title), JS174 (Anon./Medical). Earliest edition traced. The 3rd, 4th, and 5th editions (1880, 87, & 96) were all published by J. & A. Churchill. Swain was a fellow of the Royal College of Surgeons and surgeon to the South Devon and East Cornwall Hospital in Devonport.

1984. Swete, Henry Barclay (1835–1917), editor. *The Akhmîm Fragment of the Apocryphal Gospel of St. Peter*. (London: Macmillan & Co., 1893). 34pp. Edited with an introduction, notes and indices by H. B. Swete.

D6 (editor, title, date), JS1986. D6 notes Dodgson's initials. Text in Greek and English; notes, etc. in English. Not to be confused with: *The Apocryphal Gospel of St. Peter: The Greek Text of the Newly Discovered Fragment* (London: Macmillan, 1892), which was published in a 6pp. revised edition in 1893. Swete was Rector of Ashdon, Essex from 1877, examining chaplain to the Bishop of St. Albans from 1881, and Professor of Pastoral Theology at King's College, London, from 1882. In the winter of 1866-67 this fragment of the Gospel of Peter (a book previously known only through mention) was discovered in the tomb of a monk at Akhmîm in Upper Egypt.

1985. Swinbourne, Alfred James (1846–1915). *Picture Logic; or, the Grave Made Gay*. (London: Longmans, 1875, [1874]). 166pp. With illustrations from drawings by the author engraved by G[eorge] Pearson.

A516 (title), JS71 (Anon./Children). Earliest edition in BL. Swinbourne was educated at Lincoln College, Oxford and was a scholar of Queen's College from 1866 to 1871. He became inspector of schools in 1876. The subtitle for the 3rd edition of 1877 reads: *An Attempt to Popularise the Science of Reasoning by the Combination of Humorous Pictures with Examples of Reasoning Taken from Daily Life*. A witty attempt to popularize the study of logic.

1986. Swinburne, Algernon Charles (1837–1909). *Chastelard; A Tragedy*. (London: Edward Moxon & Co., 1865). 219pp. 1st edition.

A455 (author, title, date, edition), JS1987. The first play of a trilogy on the subject of Mary, Queen of Scots. Dodgson's copy, with his signature, was offered at Parke-Bernet Galleries, New York on 22 January 1969 (DAA2621).

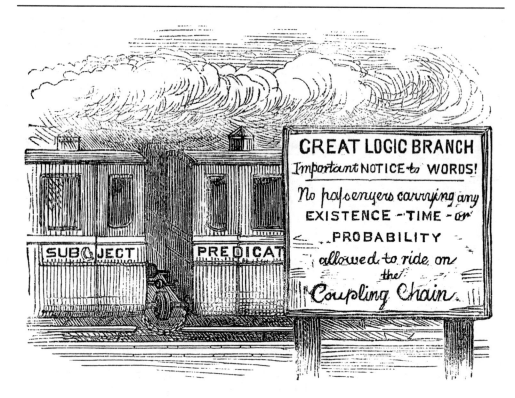

"The Great Logic Branch" from Alfred James Swinbourne's *Picture Logic* (item 1985).

1987. Swinburne, Algernon Charles. *Notes on Poems and Reviews.* (London: John Camden Hotten, 1866). 23pp. 1st edition.

D190 (author, title, date, edition), JS1988. Swinburne's defense of his own poems against charges of blasphemy and indecency.

1988. Swinburne, Algernon Charles. *Poems and Ballads.* (London: Edward Moxon & Co., 1866). 344pp. 1st edition.

B1247 (author, title, publisher, date, edition), JS1989. This is the rare first issue of Swinburne's most important book. A second issue was published by J. C. Hotten in the same year.

1989. Swinburne, Algernon Charles. *The Queen-Mother and Rosamund.* (London: Basil Montague Pickering, 1860). 217pp. 1st edition.

A454 (author, title, date, edition), JS1990. Swinburne's 1st published book. The 1st edition is a bibliographical complexity, being suppressed and reissued in the same year by E. Moxon. It is likely that Dodgson owned the 2nd

(Moxon) issue of the 1st edition, but A454 is not specific. Certainly the Pickering issue is quite rare. Two plays.

1990. [**Sykes**, Arthur Ashley] (1683 or 4– 1756). *The Case of Dr. Bentley Regius Professor of Divinity Truly Stated. Wherein Two Late Pamphlets, Entitled The Proceedings of the Vice-Chancellor and the University, &c. And A Full and Impartial Account of the Late Proceedings, &c. Are Examined.* (London: Printed for James Roberts, 1719). 40pp. 4 letters reprinted from the *St. James's Post.*

B962 ("The Case of Dr. Bentley Truly Stated, 1719"), not listed separately in JS. Only matching title in BL or BOD. The pamphlets referred to in the title are by Thomas Sherlock and Conyers Middleton respectively (see 1836 and 1346). Dodgson's copy was bound together with a copy of the Middleton pamphlet (see 1346 for Middleton's pamphlet and a note on Bentley and the case against him). Sykes held posts at Salisbury Cathedral beginning in 1723 and became assistant preacher at St. James's Westminster in 1725. He later held posts at St. Burien, Cornwall and Winchester.

1991. Symonds, John Addington (1807–71). *The Principles of Beauty.* (London: Bell and Daldy, 1857). 72pp. With illustrations.

A592 (author, title), JS1991. Only edition in BL. Symonds was a fellow of the Royal College of Physicians and father of the famous Renaissance scholar of the same name. In the present work he considers beauty through sensation, intellect, morality, emotion and art.

1992. [Synge, William Webb Follett] (1826–91). *Bumblebee Bogo's Budget.* (London: Macmillan & Co., 1887). 152pp. With 11 illustrations by Alice Havers. "By a Retired Judge."

A557, A558, A559, A560 (all giving only the title); E464 (title, illustrator, date), JS1992. April 1887 edition as described in MBC. A "People's Edition" was printed in December 1887. Dodgson owned at least 4 copies. He also owned the original drawings by Alice Havers for most of the illustrations as well as proof copies of the woodcuts of all but one of the illustrations (E117). See 880 for a note on Alice Havers. Synge was a diplomat and a contributor to the periodical press (including *Punch*).

"The Truants," illustration by Alice Havers from *Bumblebee Bogo's Budget* (item 1992).

This book of verses was published at Dodgson's instigation. Synge was a neighbor of the Dodgson family in Guildford and the two men were friends there and in Eastbourne. Dodgson's own privately published *Guildford Gazette Extraordinary* (1870) comprised mostly pieces by Synge. Dodgson sent the present verses to Macmillan in 1886, and Macmillan agreed to publish them only because Dodgson asked them to. Dodgson shepherded the book through the press as he would one of his own (see *Macmillan*). Macmillan did not believe the book would sell well, but the first edition of 500 seems to have sold out and Dodgson directed them to publish a People's Edition (along the lines of the recently published People's Editions of the *Alice* books) in an edition of 1000 copies (by January of 1888, 500 copies had sold). In 1947 Sotheby's, London offered a copy inscribed by Dodgson to Dorothy Furniss (daughter of Harry Furniss, the illustrator of the *Sylvie and Bruno* Books) (DAA2144).

1993. Synge, William Webb Follett. *Tom Singleton. Dragoon and Dramatist.* (London, Sydenham [printed]: Chapman & Hall, 1879). 3 vols.

A610 (title, 3 vols.), JS393 (Anon./Unclassified). Only 3-volume edition of the only matching title in BL. Novel.

1994. Tainsh, Edward Campbell (1834–1919). *A Study of the Works of Alfred Tennyson, D.C.L., Poet Laureate.* (London: Chapman and Hall, 1868). 256pp.

A367 (author, title), JS1993. Earliest edition in BL or BOD. Tainsh was the author of at least three novels in addition to this study of the poet laureate.

1995. Tait, Archibald Campbell (1811–82). *Four Sermons Connected with Confirmation, Preached in the Chapel of Rugby School.* (1847).

E321 (author, title, date), JS1995. E321 notes that this has autograph and markings by Dodgson. No copy traced. Tait was headmaster of Rugby School when Dodgson attended there in the 1840s. He was also Dodgson's housemaster. He later became Bishop of London and Archbishop of Canterbury.

1996. [Tait, Lawson?] (1845–99). *Proceedings of the Birmingham Philosophical Society.* Vol. 3, pt. 1. (Birmingham, 1882). Covering the 1881–82 session.

E346 (title, volume, part, date), JS222 (Anon./Philosophy). Dodgson may have owned this issue because it may describe or reprint an anti-vivisection speech given by Lawson Tait (sometimes called the "father of surgery") before the Society on 20 April 1882 in which he said, "I dismiss at once the employment of experiments on living animals for the purpose of instruction as absolutely necessary, and to be put an end to by legislation without any reservation whatsoever." Dodgson's own article opposing vivisection, "Some Popular Fallacies About Vivisection," was published in *Fortnightly Review* in 1875 (LCP, #62).

1997. Tait, Peter Guthrie (1831–1901). *An Elementary Treatise on Quaternions.* (Oxford: Clarendon Press, 1867). 320pp. In the *Clarendon Press Series.*

A585 ("Tait's Quaternions"), JS1994. Tait, a Professor of Mathematics at Edinburgh University, was co-author, with P. Kelland, of *Introduction to Quaternions, with Numerous Examples* (1873). The concept of Quaternions, which have been described as "hyper-complex numbers" was introduced by the British mathematician William Rowan Hamilton (1805–65) in 1843.

1998. Talbot, E. S. and others. *Oxford House Papers. A Series for Working Men, Written by Members of the University.* (London: Rivingtons, 1886–97). 22 parts in 3 series.

A769 (title, 2 vols.), JS192 (Anon./Oxford). Earliest edition in BL. No indication of which 2 vols. Dodgson owned. The 1st series included "Difficulties about Christianity no Reason for Disbelieving It," by E. S. Talbot; "Can Man Know God," by T. B. Strong; "Free Thinking; What the First Christians Thought about Christ," by W. Sanday; and "Why do We Call the Bible Inspired," by W. Lock. The 3rd series, also published in a volume by Longmans, Green, London in 1897, included contributions by Charles Gore, H. O. Wakeman, H. Hensley Henson, Walter Lock, W. Sanday, and G. W. Gent. Mainly, but not exclusively, papers with a High Church bias.

1999. Talfourd, T[homas] N[oon] (1795–1854). *Ion: a Tragedy, in Five Acts.* (London: Printed for Private Circulation, [1835]). 204pp.

A874 (title), JS123. Earliest edition in BL. An equally likely candidate is the 4th edition "to which are added sonnets" (London: Moxon, 1837). Talfourd was a judge and M.P. who made his first and biggest literary splash with this play. The story is of the sacrifice of King Ion of Argos in response to the prediction of the oracle at Delphi. The play was produced at Covent Garden in 1836 and also in America.

2000. Talmage, T[homas] De Witt (1832–1902). *The Abominations of Modern Society.* (New York: Adams, Victor & Co., 1872). 290 pp.

D192 (author, title, city, date), E43 (bound together with *Sports that Kill* [see below]), JS1996. Dodgson may have owned 2 copies, one separate and one bound with *Sports that Kill.* Talmage was a popular American Presbyterian minister who edited several Christian publications and made lecture tours in both America and England. Talmage warns of the dangers of dancing, drink, and many other "evils." An entertainment offered by Harry Furniss (see 742) in 1896 included a parody of Talmage, and brought scorn from Dodgson who did not believe that one should make fun of holy things, in which category he included, if not the somewhat sensational Talmage, certainly the subjects of his sermons (see *Illustrators,* 225ff).

2001. Talmage, T[homas] De Witt. *Sports that Kill.* (New York: Harper, 1875). 241pp. "Phonographically reported and revised."

A310, E43 (author, title), JS1997. Earliest edition in BL. Dodgson may have owned 2 copies, one separate and one bound with *The Abominations of Modern Society.* Dodgson may have owned the [1879] London edition, but the fact that he owned the New York edition of *The Abominations of Modern Society* suggests a stronger possibility for the New York edition of this title. This work is the evangelist's "diatribe against the irreligious effects of the theatre." Dodgson was an enthusiastic theatregoer, but both his father and his bishop, Samuel Wilberforce, agreed with Talmage that the theatre was not a place for a good Christian. Dodgson wrote a defense of the theatre as wholesome in "The Stage and the Spirit of Reverence" (see LCP, #258).

2002. (Tangrams). *The Fashionable Chinese Puzzle.* (Sidmouth: J. & E. Wallis, ca. 1815).

Not in JS. In his book *Amusements in Mathematics* (1917), Henry Ernest Dudeney writes,

"A few years ago a little book came into my possession, from the library of the late Lewis Carroll, entitled *The Fashionable Chinese Puzzle*. In contains three hundred and twenty-three Tangram designs, mostly nondescript geometrical figures, to be constructed from the seven pieces.... There is no date, but the following note fixes the time of publication pretty closely: 'This ingenious contrivance has for some time past been the favourite amusement of the ex-Emperor Napolean, who, now being in a debilitated state and living very retired, passes many hours a day in thus exercising his patience and ingenuity.'" Only British edition traced. An American edition of 32pp. (expanded to 355 tangrams) was published in 1818. Tangrams were a Chinese puzzle form in which shapes are formed by seven pieces.

2003. Tarver, John Charles (1791–1851). *The Royal Phraseological English-French, French-English Dictionary.* (London: 1845–50). 2 vols.

A349 (author, title, 2 vols.), JS1998. Earliest edition in BL or BOD. The 3rd edition was published in London by Dulau & Co. (1854–58).

2004. Tasso, Torquato (1544–95). *La Gerusalemme Liberata.* (London: G. Pickering, 1822). 2 vols. In the *Pickering Diamond Classics* series.

A476 ("Pickering Diamond Classics, Tasso, 2 vols. in 1, 1822"), JS2000. This is the only Pickering edition of a Tasso title published in 1822 in BL. Dodgson's 2 volumes were apparently bound as one. Tasso was an Italian poet and *Jerusalem Delivered*, his epic glorification of the first Crusade, was his most important work. In his diary for 18 April 1855, Dodgson writes, "This evening I began reading Tasso instead of Dante; I think I shall like it much better. Though I have only been learning Italian for three days, I can already make out the author tolerably well." See 153 for more on this series.

2005. Tasso, Torquato *La Gerusalemme Liberata di Torquato Tasso.* (Milano: Per Nicolo Bettoni, 1824). 2 vols.

A394 ("Tasso in Italian, 2 vols., vellum, gilt"), JS1999 (described as "Works"). Dodgson's copy offered for sale at Sotheby's, London on 18 April 1985 (DAA2909). The description of that volume gives the date (1824) and place of publication (Milan) and notes that it was

signed by Dodgson on the front endleaves. This is the only 2-volume edition of this title published in 1824 in Milan listed in the Italian National Library catalogue.

2006. Tate, James (1801–63). *First Classical Maps, with Chronological Tables of Grecian and Roman History.* (London: George Bell; Richmond [Yorkshire]: T. and A. Bowman and M. Bell, 1845). [14pp.] plus 4 fold out maps (printed in color).

E83, JS2001. Dodgson's copy is in HAC. It is inscribed in brown ink on the front endpaper "Charles Lutwidge Dodgson. Richmond School Yorkshire. XI. Cal: Nov: 1845," and has annotations in brown ink and pencil on many pages, though these may not be in Dodgson's hand. Tate was the headmaster of Richmond Grammar School and Dodgson's housemaster when Dodgson attended the school in the 1840s. Tate writes, "It is the particular object of the following maps prominently to exhibit those places, and those only, which possess a leading interest in the Ancient History of Greece and Rome."

2007. Tate, William (1781?–1848). *The Modern Cambist: Forming a Manual of Foreign Exchanges, in the Different Operations of Bills of Exchange and Bullion; According to the Practice of All Trading Nations: with Tables of Foreign Weights and Measures, and their Equivalents in English and French. With Extensive Alterations and Additions, Brought down to the Present Time and Tables of the New French Tariff Rates of Gold and Silver.* (London: E. Wilson, 1863). 262pp. 12th edition.

Not in JS. Listed in WS (author, title, date) only and described there as having the autograph of Dodgson. Possibly Dodgson purchased this in preparation for his one foreign trip — to Russia in 1867.

2008. Taylor, Henry (1800–86). *Autobiography of Henry Taylor. 1800–1875.* (London: Longmans, Green and Co., 1885). 2 vols. 375, 345pp.

A893 (author, title, 2 vols.), JS2002. Only edition in BL. Taylor was the author of many verse dramas (most of which were not produced) and a civil servant. In a prefatory note the author states that the book was originally intended for posthumous publication but that "publication in the 85th year of a man's life comes rather near to posthumous publication." Dodgson was friends with Taylor and his family.

2009. Taylor, Henry. *Edwin the Fair. An Historical Drama; together with Isaac Conmenus; A Play and The Eve of the Conquest and Other Poems.* (London: Edward Moxon, 1852). 416pp. 3rd edition.

A866 (title), D194 (author, title, city, date), JS2003. A866 gives the title only as "Edwin the Fair," and this could refer to the separate edition of this work published in 1842. Verse historical drama.

2010. Taylor, Henry. *Notes from Books. In Four Essays.* (London: J. Murray, 1849). 295pp.

B1250 (author, title, date), JS2004. Most of this book is devoted to two essays on Wordsworth.

2011. Taylor, Henry. *Notes from Life in Six Essays.* (London: J. Murray, 1847). 192pp.

B1249 (author, title, date), JS2005. Contains "Money," "Humility and Independence," "Choice in Marriage," "Wisdom," "Children," and "The Life Poetic."

2012. Taylor, Henry. *Philip van Artevelde; A Dramatic Romance. In Two Parts.* (London: Edward Moxon, 1852). 431pp. 6th edition.

A866, D195, JS2006. Dodgson's copy is in HAC and has his monogram on the front endpaper in purple ink. This was Taylor's most successful drama. After reading the story of Artevelde, the medieval governor of Ghent, Taylor wrote of the play he hoped to compose, "The first part should conduct him from obscurity to his conquest of Bruges ... the second part might bring him from the splendour of his first achievement through the consequent moral changes to his death."

2013. Taylor, Henry. *St. Clement's Eve. A Play.* (London: Chapman and Hall, 1862). 182pp. 1st edition.

A866, D196 (author, title, date, edition), JS2007. Historical verse drama.

2014. Taylor, Henry. *The Virgin Widow. A Play.* (London: Longman, Brown, Green, and Longmans, 1850). 192pp.

D193 (author, title, city, edition, date), JS2008. D193 notes the inscription "C. L. Dodgson from H. Taylor." A verse drama in which, Taylor wrote, he "wished to revive the Elizabethan comedy of romance."

2015. [Taylor, Isaac] (1787–1865). *Natural History of Enthusiasm.* (London: Holdsworth and Ball, 1829). 311pp.

A575 (title), JS2009. Earliest edition in BL or BOD. Taylor was an artist, author, inventor, and brother of the children's poets, Ann and Jane Taylor (see below). This book dealt with current religious and political problems with particular regard to the Oxford Movement. "Enthusiasm" is here used in its meaning "Possession by a god, supernatural inspiration, prophetic or poetic ecstasy."

2016. Taylor, Jane (1783–1824). *The Contributions of Q. Q. to a Periodical Work: With Some Pieces not before Published.* (London: Holdsworth and Ball, 1831). 2 vols. 302, 286pp. 6th edition.

A320, B1251 (author, title, 2 vols. date), JS2010. With her sister Ann, Jane Taylor was author of some of the best-known 19th-century children's poetry, including "Twinkle, Twinkle, Little Star" (of which Dodgson wrote a parody in AAIW). The periodical mentioned in the title is *The Youth's Magazine.* Volume I contains religious and didactic pieces, volume II miscellaneous pieces. Originally published in 1824 under the editorship of the author's brother, Isaac Taylor (see above).

2017. Taylor, Jeremy (1613–67). *Ductor Dubitantium: or, The Rule of Conscience in All her General Measures; Serving as a Great Instrument for the Determination of Cases of Conscience, in Four Books.* (London: Printed by R. Norton for R. Royston, 1671). 819pp. 2nd edition.

A743 (author, title), JS2011. 1st published in 2-volumes in 1660. This is the earliest 1-volume edition in BL (A743 makes no mention of multiple volumes). The latest pre–20th century edition in BL is a 2-volume edition of 1725. Taylor was an English devotional writer who served as chaplain to Charles I and was made bishop at the Restoration. This work was a Christian manual of ethics and casuistry.

2018. Taylor, John Ellor (1837–95). *Half hours at the Sea-side; or, Recreations with*

Marine Objects. (London: R. Hardwicke, 1872). 260pp.

A562 ("Half-hours at the Seaside"), JS380 (Anon./Unclassified). Earliest edition of the only matching title in BL or BOD. The 3rd edition was published in London by Hardwicke and Bogue in 1876, and BL gives the title as a more precise match to A562, "*Half-hours at the Seaside.*" Taylor was editor of the *Norwich People's Journal*, a lecturer on science, the curator of the Ipswich Museum and a founder of the Norwich Geological Society. This work is a popular guide to marine biology.

2019. Taylor, John Ellor. *The Sagacity and Morality of Plants. A Sketch of the Life and Conduct of the Vegetable Kingdom.* (London: Chatto & Windus, 1884). 311pp. With illustrations.

A554 (title), JS275 (Anon./Science). Earliest edition of the only matching title in BL. This work is an attempt to make complex issues of botany accessible to the layman. Includes stories that illustrate heredity, natural selection, and adaptation.

2020. Taylor, Lucy. *Fairy Phœbe; or Facing the Footlights.* (London: Shaw and Co., [1887]). 222pp.

A673 (title), JS288 (Anon./Theatre). Only edition in BL of the only matching title.

2021. Temple, Frederick (1821–1902). *The Relations Between Religion and Science. Eight Lectures Preached before the University of Oxford in the Year 1884 on the Foundation of the Late Rev. John Bampton.* (London: Macmillan and Co., 1884). 252pp.

A803, B1252 (author, title, date), JS2012. 1st edition as described in MBC. Temple was educated at Balliol College, Oxford and served as headmaster of Dodgson's old school, Rugby, from 1857 to 1869. He was a contributor to the controversial collection *Essays and Reviews* (see 2075) and though his own essay was fairly orthodox, its presence in the volume caused trouble when he was nominated to the bishopric of Exeter and he agreed to withdraw it from future editions. He later became Bishop of London and Archbishop of Canterbury (1897). He was interested in the Tractarians when he was at Oxford, but eventually adopted liberal principles. ODCC calls his Bampton Lectures "impressive." In this volume he addresses the "apparent conflict between religion and the doctrine of evolution" and concludes that the conflict is "not real."

2022. Tenniel, John (1820–1914). *Cartoons from Punch.* Details unknown.

A293 (author, title). There were at least 4 volumes published under this title during Dodgson's lifetime. Series 1 and 2, representing cartoons from 1864 to 1870 were published (in 2 vols.) in London in 1870. Bradbury, Agnew & Co. of London published a 2-volume edition in 1895 covering cartoons from 1871 to 1881 and 1882 to 1891. A293 does not specify multiple volumes, so Dodgson probably owned one of these four volumes. Tenniel was a cartoonist for *Punch* for the entire second half of the 19th century. He illustrated Dodgson's *Alice* books.

2023. [Tenniel, John and John Leech]. *The Rt. Hon. W. E. Gladstone. Cartoons from the Collection of "Mr. Punch."* (London: Punch, 1878). 46 plates.

A293 (title), not in JS. Although another collection of cartoons of Gladstone was published by the comic periodical *Judy*, this is the obvious match, not only because of Dodgson's connection with Tenniel, but also because the other item in A293 is Tenniel's *Cartoons from Punch*.

2024. Tennyson, Alfred (1809–92). "Attempts at Classical Metres in Quantity." *The Cornhill Magazine*, No. 48 (December, 1863). 707–709.

D204 (author, title, publication citation), JS2013. According to D204, the publication information was written on this item in Dodgson's hand. Apparently his copy was excised from the magazine in which it was published. Translations of Homer and Milton. Dodgson sought out Tennyson first in the Lake District and later at the poet's home on the Isle of Wight. His acquaintance with the poet laureate has been well documented in his biographies (see for instance Cohen, 260ff).

2025. Tennyson, Alfred. *Ballads and Other Poems.* (London: C. Kegan Paul and Co., 1880). 184pp. 1st edition.

A352 (author, title, edition), JS2014. Includes "The Defence of Lucknow," "To Victor Hugo," and other poems.

2026. Tennyson, Alfred. *The Death of Œnone, Akbar's Dream, and Other Poems.*

(London: Macmillan and Co., 1892). 113pp.

A352, F144, JS2016. Dodgson's copy is in HAC and has his monogram on the title page. Tennyson's final volume of poetry.

2027. Tennyson, Alfred. *Enoch Arden, etc.* (London: Edward Moxon & Co., 1864). 178pp.

A351 (author, title), JS2017. 1st edition. Though A351 does not specify an edition, by 1864 it seems likely that Dodgson would be buying Tennyson's works as they were published. A precursor to the film *Castaway*, this poem tells of a shipwrecked sailor who returns home to find his wife married to another man.

2028. Tennyson, Alfred. *The Foresters: Robin Hood and Maid Marian.* (London: Macmillan and Co., 1892). 155pp. 1st edition.

A352 (author, title, edition), JS2018. One of Tennyson's dramas, this work was first formally staged at Daly's Theatre in New York in March, 1892.

2029. Tennyson, Alfred. *Gareth and Lynette etc.* (London: Strahan & Co., 1872). 136pp. 1st edition.

A352 (author, title, edition), JS2019. The completion of Tennyson's twelve book sequence of Arthurian poems. Contains "Gareth and Lynette," and "The Last Tournament." The title poem is about a young man who comes to Camelot for his education.

2030. Tennyson, Alfred. *Gedichte.* (Dessau: Gebrüder Katz, 1853). 369pp. Translated by Wilhelm Adolf Boguslaw Hertzberg (1813–79).

D206 (author, title, translator, publisher, date), JS2020. D206 notes Dodgson's initials. The 1st edition of the German translation of Tennyson's 1842 *Poems.*

2031. Tennyson, Alfred. *The Holy Grail; and Other Poems.* (London: Strahan & Co., 1870 [1869]). 222pp. 1st edition.

A352 (author, title, edition), JS2021. An expansion of Tennyson's Arthurian poems, this collection includes four previously published poems and four new ones, including "The Coming of Arthur," "The Holy Grail," and "Pelleas and Ettarre."

2032. Tennyson, Alfred. *Idylls of the King.* (London: E. Moxon, 1859). 261pp.

A425, E435 (author, title, date), F136, F164, JS2022. According to F136 Dodgson's was a presentation copy from Tennyson and also had the gothic stamp. F164 is a second, uninscribed, copy. This copy, identified by the gothic stamp, was offered for sale by Maggs of London in 1911. One of Tennyson's volumes of poetry inspired by Arthurian legend. Contains "Enid," "Vivien," "Elaine," and "Guinevere."

2033. Tennyson, Alfred. *In Memoriam.* (London: Henry S. King and Co., 1875). 212pp.

A351, F164, JS2024. Dodgson's copy is in HAC and has the gothic stamp on the verso of the front endpaper. In his lifetime, this elegy to his friend Arthur Hallam was Tennyson's most famous poem. It is also a meditation on issues ranging from science to religion to the place of the individual. Dodgson supervised the compilation of an index to *In Memoriam* that was published by Moxon in 1862 (see WMGC, #31). He had 13 copies of the index in his library at the time of his death, but it has not been listed here as it is more properly an item in Dodgson's bibliography.

2034. Tennyson, Alfred. *In Memoriam Aus dem Englischen nach der Fünften Auflage.* (Braunschweig: 1854).

D207 (author, title, city, date), JS2023. D207 notes Dodgson's initials. German translation of *In Memoriam.*

2035. Tennyson, Alfred. *The Lady of Shalott.* (Nottingham: Printed by R. and M. H. Allen, 1852). 14 leaves, 12 plates. Reprinted by permission of the author and illustrated by a lady for the benefit of the Midland Institute for the Blind.

A282 (title, author, "reprint, by permission of the author"), not in JS. Only edition traced matching the particulars in A282. The poem, first published in 1832 and revised for the 1842 collection of *Poems*, was among Tennyson's first Arthurian compositions. The title character lives a life of isolation and observes life through a mirror. She dies when she deigns to gaze directly at a passing Launcelot.

2036. Tennyson, Alfred. *The Lover's Tale.* (London: C. Kegan Paul & Co., 1879). 95pp.

A351 (author, title), JS2025. This is the 1st, and only, trade edition of this title in BL. Dodgson owned a privately printed version of this poem as well (see below). Tennyson authorized the present edition of his early poem, which he had left out of his 1832 collection, in order to counteract the pirated editions then on the market.

2037. Tennyson, Alfred. *The Lover's Tale and Other Poems Now First Collected*. (London: Printed for private circulation, 1875). 64pp. Edited by Richard Herne Shepherd. Limited to 50 copies.

A425 (author, title, "50 copies for private circulation," date), JS2026. Dodgson had written to Tennyson some time earlier about a pirated edition of this poem, but this apparently was a later, but still unauthorized, edition (see *Letters*, 150–53). See 1833 for a note on Shepherd.

2038. Tennyson, Alfred. *Maud, and Other Poems*. (London: Edward Moxon, 1855). 154pp.

A425 (author, title), JS2027. 1st edition. Now widely considered Tennyson's finest poem. It is about a disillusioned Victorian man who loves a woman named Maud and decides to enlist in the military during the Crimean War. Dodgson reviewed this volume in his diary on 14 August 1855 (see *Diary, 1*).

2039. Tennyson, Alfred. *Ode on the Death of the Duke of Wellington*. (London: Edward Moxon, 1852). 16pp.

D202 (author, title, city, date, edition), JS2028. The Duke of Wellington, who had also been chancellor of Oxford University since 1832, died on 14 September 1852 and his funeral, perhaps the largest public event held in London to that time, took place in St. Paul's Cathedral on 18 November 1852. 10,000 copies of Tennyson's tribute (a poem in 9 short sections) were printed 2 days before the funeral and sold to the crowds in the streets. Dodgson was probably in Oxford during the funeral; shortly afterwards he was recommended for a Studentship at Christ Church by E. B. Pusey and a few days later on 9 December, wrote to his sister that he had just earned a First Class in Mathematics. In that same letter, he notes that the censor of Christ Church (Osborne Gordon) "gave me a copy of [his] speech … it is mostly about the Duke [of Wellington]" (see 796).

2040. Tennyson, Alfred. *Poems*. (London: E. Moxon, 1833 [1832]). 163pp.

A424 (author, title, date), JS2030. This was Tennyson's first volume published by Moxon (his regular publishers for the next forty years). It was supervised by his friend Arthur Hallam and included "The Lady of Shalott," "Œnone," "The Palace of Art," and "The Lotos-Eaters."

2041. Tennyson, Alfred. *Poems*. (London: E. Moxon, 1851). 375pp. 7th edition of Tennyson's 1842 collection.

E435 (author, title, date), F144, JS2033. Dodgson's copy is in the library of Yale University. It was offered at The Walpole Galleries, New York, 1 May 1917 and at Anderson Galleries, New York, on 4 Nov. 1920 (DAA962). It includes Dodgson's signature and the gothic stamp. DAA also notes of this copy, "Throughout the volume Dodgson has written the variations in reading in this edition as compared with the original publication in 1830 or 1833, and in addition has written the whole of such poems as were suppressed. These notes and additions are on many pages." The book was composed of both earlier work (such as "The Lady of Shalott" and "The Lotos-Eaters") and work newly published in 1842 (such as "Locksley Hall" and "Ulysses").

2042. Tennyson, Alfred. *Poems, Chiefly Lyrical*. (London: Effingham Wilson, 1830). 154pp.

A424 (author, title, date), JS2031. 1st edition. Tennyson's first solo collection of verse. It includes poems such as "Mariana," "Ode to Memory," and "The Dying Swan." On 13 May 1864, Dodgson writes in his diary, "Received from Pickering the 1st edition of Tennyson's Poems (of 1830) for which I have to pay 38 shillings! The only consolation being that it will always fetch as much if sold" (see *Diary 4*).

2043. Tennyson, Alfred. *The Princess A Medley*. (London: Henry S. King, 1874). 183pp.

F164, JS2035. Dodgson's copy is in HAC and is identified by the gothic stamp only. A copy in the collection of Mark Burstein has Dodgson's initials, is inscribed "Miss Thomson. In Mem. Jan. 14, 1898," and includes an autographed letter from Elizabeth Lucy Dodgson to E. Gertrude Thomson. Apparently it was presented to Thomson from the Dodgson family at the time of Charles L. Dodgson's death. A poem partly inspired by the opening of a college for women in London. In it, a prince and two of his friends sneak into a women's college disguised as women. It inspired Gilbert and Sullivan's *Princess Ida*.

2044. Tennyson, Alfred. *Queen Mary. A Drama.* (London: H. S. King, 1875). 278pp.

Uncertain. F164 (author, title, date), JS2036. Identified as Dodgson's only by the gothic stamp. This copy was offered for sale by Maggs of London in 1911. Drama based on the life of Mary Tudor.

2045. Tennyson, A[lfred]. *Timbuctoo: A Poem, which Obtained the Chancellor's Medal at the Cambridge Commencement, M.DCCC.XXIX.* (Cambridge: Printed by J. Smith, 1829). 13pp.

A425 (author, full title), JS2037. Only separate edition in BL. The topic, "Timbuctoo," was assigned for the competition. Tennyson's poem was in blank verse, unlike all other previous winners which had been in heroic couplets.

2046. Tennyson, Alfred. *Tiresias, and Other Poems.* (London: Macmillan and Co., 1885). 203pp.

Uncertain. F164 (author, title, date), JS2038. Identified as Dodgson's only by the gothic stamp. This copy was offered for sale by Maggs of London in 1911. The title poem is a dramatic monologue based on the legend of a Theban soothsayer.

2047. Tennyson, Alfred. *A Welcome. To Her Royal Highness the Princess of Wales From the Poet Laureate.* (London: Edward Moxon and Co, 1863). 4pp.

D203 (author, title, publisher, city, date), JS2039. There were two issues of this, the 1st edition. A single sheet, once folded containing a poem of 25 lines welcoming the Danish Princess (and future Princess of Wales) Alexandra to England on her arrival in March 1863 to marry Queen Victoria's son and heir Prince Albert Edward. Part of Tennyson's official work as poet laureate.

2048. Tennyson, Alfred. *The Works of Alfred Tennyson.* (London: C. Kegan Paul & Co., 1881 [1880]). 665pp. With portrait and illustrations.

A367, A837, D205 (author, title, date), JS2034, JS2032. Dodgson owned 2, 2-volume sets of Tennyson's poems. Copy 1) D205 notes

that this was "bound in 2 vols." The wording here is important — noting that it was bound, rather than merely stating 2 vols. implies that Dodgson had a 1-volume edition specially bound. No 2-volume edition of 1881 has been traced. The only 1881 edition traced is here described. D205 also offers a possible explanation for Dodgson's binding the book in a more manageable manner — "It was apparently Mr. Dodgson's intention to annotate this copy, giving parallel passages, etc., as it contains 3 entries in his autograph." Surely this indicates that D205 is the same book as A837 which is described "Tennyson's Poems, interleaved, 2 vols., morocco." D205 is described as bound in "full olive green morocco." Copy 2) A367 is described as "Tennyson's Poetical Works, 2 vols., half morocco." Possibly Dodgson had 2 copies of the same edition prepared, or perhaps this represents another edition. BL lists no English 2-volume editions of Tennyson under the title *Poetical Works*, only the various editions of his *Poems* (for which see 2040–41).

2049. Tennyson, Alfred and Charles Tennyson. *Poems, by Two Brothers.* (London: W. Simpkin and R. Marshall, 1827). 228pp.

A351 (author, title), JS2029. Earliest edition in BL; the only other edition listed (1893) includes poems by Frederick Tennyson also. See below for a note on Charles. The preface states, "The following poems were written from ages fifteen to eighteen, not conjointly, but individually.... [N]o doubt, if submitted to the microscopical eye of periodical Criticism, a long list of inaccuracies and imitations would result from the investigation. But so it is; we have passed the Rubicon, and we leave the rest to fate."

2050. Tennyson, Charles (later Charles Tennyson Turner) (1808–79). *Sonnets and Fugitive Pieces.* (Cambridge: B. Bridges, 1830). 83pp.

A424 (author, title, date), JS2040. The brother of the poet laureate, Charles Tennyson struggled with opium addiction early in his career. He served as vicar of Grasby in North Lincolnshire and published, in addition to the present collection, three more volumes of sonnets.

2051. Tennyson, Frederick (1807–98). *Days and Hours.* (London: John W. Parker and Son, 1854). 346pp.

A425 (author, title), JS2015 (listed under Alfred Tennyson). JS also lists this item as F136 and F164, but it appears in neither entry. Frederick was the brother of Alfred Lord Tennyson, and a minor poet in his own right. This work is a collection of lyrics.

2052. Terentius, Publius [a.k.a. Terence] (190–159 B.C.E.). *P. Terentii Comoediae Sex ex Recensione Heinsiana*. (Amstelaedami: Apud Henri Wetstenium, [1700?]).

E320 (author, city, publisher), JS2041. The conjectural date is provided by BL. E320 describes this as "scarce." Terentius was a Roman poet and author of six surviving comedies.

2053. Terentius, Publius [a.k.a. Terence]. *Publius Terentius Afer*. (London: G. Pickering, 1823). 220pp. Portrait. In the *Pickering Diamond Classics* series.

A477 (author, publisher, series), JS2042. See 153 for more on this series of miniature books.

2054. [Tergolina, Anna Carolina Eugenia, Contessa di]. *Sketches and Stories of Life in Italy, by an Italian Countess*. (London: Religious Tract Society, [1871]). 320pp.

A589 ("Sketches of Italian Life"), JS370 (Anon./Topography). There are no precisely matching titles in either BL or BOD; this is the closest match among pre–1898 titles and the only edition listed in either source. The only other title that even comes close is *North Italian Folk. Sketches of Town and Country Life*, illustrated by Randolph Caldecott, but this book is listed as A482 (see 357). The author was the wife of a Venetian count. A collection of black and white sketches and stories based on the author's residence in Italy.

2055. The Terrific Register; or, Record of Crimes, Judgments, Providences and Calamities. Vol. 1, nos. 1–52 (London: 1825).

D197 (title, vol. 1), JS256 (Anon./Reference). This periodical was published for 104 weekly issues in two volumes.

2056. Thackeray, William Makepeace (1811–63). *Christmas Books: Mrs. Perkins's Ball; Our Street; Dr. Birch*. (London: Chapman & Hall, 1857). 49, 54, 49pp. With illustrations by the author. New edition in one volume.

A660 (author, "Christmas Books"), JS2043. Earliest edition in BL under the title *Christmas*

Books. A collection of Thackeray's annual Christmas books, beginning with his first, *Mrs. Perkins's Ball*, published in 1846. See 2086 for another work by Thackeray. Dodgson met Thackeray on 9 May 1857 and recorded his impressions in his diary (see *Diary 3*).

2057. Thackeray, William Makepeace. *The Four Georges: Sketches of Manners, Moral, Court and Town Life*. (London: Smith, Elder, and Co., 1866). 226pp.

A464 (author, title, "first edition," date), JS2044. Clearly a mistake in A464 as the 1st (English) edition was 1861 not 1866. That edition was also published by Smith, Elder. The four Georges of the title are George I–George IV, the kings of England.

2058. Thackeray, William Makepeace. *Miscellanies: Prose and Verse*. (London: Bradbury & Evans, 1854–57). 4 vols.

A659 (author, title, 4 vols.), JS2045. Earliest 4-volume edition in BL. Includes: Vol. I, "Ballads," "The Book of Snobs," "The Tremendous Adventures of Major Gahagan," "The Fatal Boots," "Cox's Diary"; Vol. II, "Memoirs of Mr. C. J. Yellowplush," "Diary of C. Jeames De La Pluche, Esq.," "Sketches and Travels in London," "Novels by Eminent Hands," "Character Sketches"; Vol. III, "The Memoirs of Barry Lyndon," "A Legend of the Rhine," "Rebecca and Rowena," "A Little Dinner at Timmins's," "The Bedford-Row Conspiracy"; Vol. IV, "The Fitz-Boodle Papers," "Men's Wives," "A Shabby Genteel Story," "The History of Samuel Titmarsh and the Great Hoggarty Diamond."

2059. [Thackeray, William Makepeace]. *The Newcomes. Memoirs of a Most Respectable Family. Edited by Arthur Pendennis, Esq*. (London: Bradbury and Evans, 1854–55). 2 vols. With illustrations by Richard Doyle.

Uncertain. Not in JS. Listed in WS (author, title, date, volume 2 only) and identified with the property label only. Not in WWC. This is the 1st edition in book form (previously published in monthly parts). Novel about Clive Newcome, his family, and his unhappy marriage.

2060. Thackeray, William Makepeace. *Roundabout Papers*. (London: Smith Elder, 1863). 352pp. 1st edition. Reprinted from *The Cornhill Magazine*. With illustrations.

A660, JS2047. Dodgson's copy, with his signature on the front endpaper, sold at Sotheby Parke Bernet, Los Angeles on 8–10 May 1975 and is now in the collection of Jon Lindseth, Cleveland, OH. A series of discursive essays contributed to the magazine of which Thackeray was a founder.

2061. Thackeray, William Makepeace. *Vanity Fair: a Novel without a Hero* (London: Bradbury & Evans, 1848). 625pp.

Not in JS. Dodgson's copy is in the collection of Mark Burstein, California. It includes Dodgson's signature on the front endpaper and a penciled note in his handwriting regarding the Marquis of Steyne.

2062. (Theatre). *The London Stage. A Collection of the Most Reputed Tragedies, Comedies, Operas, Melo-dramas, Farces and Interludes. Accurately Printed from Acting Copies as Performed at the Theatres Royal, and Carefully Collated and Revised.* (London: Sherwood, 1824–25). Vol. 1–2 (of 4) only. Each play individually paginated.

A949, E104 (title, 2 vols., date), F165, JS294. This title was published in 4 volumes from 1824 to 1827. Dodgson's copy is in WWC. It has the gothic stamp and has the property label on the front cover. Vol. 2 is inscribed "T[homas] Vere Bayne." Perhaps these volumes were on loan from Dodgson's friend. The first two volumes contain nearly 100 plays, from those whose titles have long been forgotten in obscurity to well-known titles such as *She Stoops to Conquer* and *The Rivals*.

2063. (Theatre). *The Pulpit and the Stage.* Details unknown.

Title only given in A657/JS384. 2 possibilities in BL:
Dixon, James Matthias. *The Pulpit and the Stage.* (London: E. W. Allen, [1879]).
Ham, James Panton. *The Pulpit and the Stage. Four Lectures.* (London: [1878]). With illustrative notes by F. Whymper.

Dodgson defended the theatre as a wholesome recreation in his article "The Stage and the Spirit of Reverence" (see LCP, #258).

2064. Theocritus (ca. 310–250 B.C.E.). *Theocritus Translated into English Verse.* (London: Bell & Sons, 1883). 184pp. 2nd edition, revised. Translated by Charles Stuart Calverley.

A858, B993 (author, title, translator, date), JS2063. Theocritus was a Greek pastoral poet. See 336 for a note on Calverley.

2065. Thickins, John. *Prescience; or, the Foreknowledge of God, Consistent with the Free-Agency of Man.* (Coventry: 1822).

E172 (author, title, date), JS2064. E172 notes this has a "MS note by Lewis Carroll." An attempt to reconcile divine omnipotence with free will.

2066. Thierry, Augustin (1795–1856). *History of the Conquest of England by the Normans; Its Causes, and its Consequences, in England, Scotland, Ireland, & on the Continent.* (London: D. Bogue, 1847). 2 vols. Translated from the 7th Paris edition by William Hazlitt.

Not in JS. In a letter of 25 June 1847 to her sister Lucy Lutwidge, Dodgson's mother wrote of prizes gained by Dodgson at Rugby: "the other is Thierry's *Norman Conquest* just *now* gained for having been the best in Composition (Latin & English verse)." Earliest English edition traced and a logical match, being published in the year the award was made. Thierry was a French historian more remembered for his popularity than for his accuracy.

2067. Thirlwall, Connop (1797–1875). *Primitiæ; or, Essays and Poems on Various Subjects, Religious, Moral and Entertaining. By Connop Thirlwall, Eleven Years of Age.* (London: Printed for the Author by T. Plummer, 1809). 230pp. With a preface by Thomas Thirlwall, father of the author.

B1256 (author [misspelled as "Thirwall"], title, date), JS2065. Thirlwall became Bishop of St. David's, and was a Greek historian, but this collection of devotional essays and verses was written when the author was between 8 and 11 years old and collected by his father.

2068. [Thomas, Richard W.] *Directions, Remarks, etc., on the Use of Thomas's Negative Collodion.* (1861).

E333 (title, date), JS227 (Anon./Photography). No copy traced but the University of Texas at Austin records a copy of a 4pp. pamphlet: *Directions for Using Thomas's Negative Collodion, Prepared Solely by Richard W. Thomas, Chemist, etc.* (London: n.d.). Thomas was a London photographer and author of *The Modern Practice of Photography* (1866). Dodgson used the collodion wet plate process in his photography.

2069. Thompson, Edward P[ett]. *The Passions of Animals.* (London: Chapman and Hall, 1851). 414pp.

A852 (author, title), JS2066. Only edition in BL. Thompson was a creationist naturalist who served as mayor of Dover and donated his collection of specimens to the museum there. An "encyclopaedia" of comparative psychology in 64 topics, including, for instance, "playfulness" defined as "exuberance of animal spirits" in which the animal "abandons itself" to "the performance of some one of its passions, whether of joy or mischief, defiance or fear."

2070. Thompson, Henry (1820–1904), et al. *Moderate Drinking: Opinions of Sir Henry Thompson, Dr. Richardson, Cannon Farrar, E. Baines, Esq., Admiral Sullivan, and Dr. Patterson.* (London: National Temperance Publication Depôt, [1877]). 31pp. In the *Standard Temperance Tracts* series.

E158 (authors, title, n.d.), JS2067. Published in the same year in an undated edition by S. W. Partridge (these are the only editions in BL). Thompson was a fellow of the Royal College of Surgeons and served at various times as a professor of Clinical Surgery, Surgery, and Pathology. Report of a meeting of the National Temperance League, held in Exeter Hall, Feb. 7, 1877.

2071. Thompson, T[homas] Perronet (1783–1869). *Geometry Without Axioms. Or The First Book of Euclid's Elements.* (London: Robert Heward, 1834). 156pp. 5th edition.

Not in JS. Dodgson's copy sold at Sotheby's, London on 18 December 1995 (DAA3095), is in the collection of John Lindseth, Cleveland, OH, and has "C. L. Dodgson" signed on the front pastedown in purple ink and autograph corrections by Dodgson in black ink on p. 96. Thompson was a member of the University of Cambridge who wrote on Euclid and on political issues. The full title of the 4th edition added: *With Alterations and … Notes; and an Intercalary Book in which the Straight Line and Plane are Derived from Properties of the Sphere … To which is Added an Appendix Containing Notices of Methods at Different Times Proposed for Getting over the Difficulty in the Twelfth Axiom of Euclid.*

2072. [**Thoms**, William John] (1803–85), et al., editors. *Notes and Queries: A Medium of Inter-Communication for Literary Men, Artists, Antiquaries, Genealogists, etc.* (London: George Bell, Bell & Daldy, or John C. Francis, November 1849–June 1897). 1st–8th series, 102 volumes (including 7 index volumes).

A348, JS210 (Anon./Periodicals). In 2003, Dodgson's copy was offered for sale by Justin Schiller, who noted that the set had passed through the collection of Peter and Iona Opie. Several volumes of Dodgson's set have ownership signatures or monograms. There are also, according to Schiller, "at least nine manuscript notations by Dodgson (all written on the rear pastedowns)." Schiller writes "*Notes and Queries* was founded in 1849 by William John Thoms as a threepenny weekly for bookish amateurs to ask and answer each other's questions, a means for the interchange or sharing of thought and information among those interested in literature, art and science. It expanded upon a regular column in the pages of *The Athenæum* by Thoms devoted to recording surviving rural legends, cures, proverbs, manners, and ballads, a subject for which he coined a term — 'Folk-Lore' — that would quickly assume the status of a household word. Devoted principally to English language and literature, lexicography, history, and scholarly antiquarianism, *N&Q* emphasized the factual rather than the speculative." Thoms retired from *Notes & Queries* in October 1873.

2073. Thomson, James. *Poetical Works.* Details unknown.

A946/JS2068 states only "Thomson's Poetical Works." This could refer to a collection by James Thomson (1700–48) author of "Liberty" or by James Thomson (1834–82), author of "The City of the Dreadful Night."

2074. Thomson, John (fl. 1761–1809). *Tables of Interest, at 3, 4, 4-1/2, and 5 per cent: From 1 to 10,000, and from 1 to 365 Days. In a Regular Progression of Single Days; which is an Advantage not to be Found in any Other Book of the Kind: Also, Tables, at all the Above Rates, from 1 to 12 Months, and from 1 to 10 Years. And Tables, Shewing the Exchange on Bills, or Commission on Goods, &c. from ⅛ to 3 per cent. To which is Pre-*

fixed, a Table of Discount on Bills at a Certain Number of Days or Months. (Edinburgh: W. Creech and C. Elliot, etc.; London: C. Elliot, T. Kay, and Co., etc., 1888). 531pp. 5th edition.

WS, not in JS. Dodgson's copy is in WWC and has his autograph initials and the property label. It lacks pp. i–ii. Thomson was an 18th-century Edinburgh accountant.

2075. Thomson, W[illiam] (1819–90), editor. *Aids to Faith; a Series of Theological Essays By Several Writers Being a Reply to "Essays and Reviews."* (London: John Murray, 1861) 469pp.

A796 ("Aids to Faith"), JS301 (Anon./Theology). Earliest edition of the only matching title in BL (and clearly a book Dodgson would have owned). Thomson matriculated at Queen's College, Oxford in 1836, was a fellow there from 1840 to 1855, and was successively Bishop of Gloucester and Bristol and Archbishop of York. *Essays and Reviews* was published in 1860 by seven authors who, according to the ODCC "believed in the necessity of free inquiry." The book was eventually condemned first by Bishop of Oxford Samuel Wilberforce and eventually by the archbishop of Canterbury. One of the contributors to *Essays and Reviews*, Benjamin Jowett, came under especially close scrutiny in Oxford. His orthodoxy was challenged during the debate over whether or not the endowment of the Greek Professorship (to which Jowett would be elected) should be increased. Dodgson weighed in on this debate with a humorous broadside "The Endowment of the Greek Professorship" (See WMGC, #29). Dodgson met Thomson at Henry Acland's home in Oxford on 15 February 1858, when Thomson was Provost of Queen's College.

2076. Thomson, William. *An Outline of the Necessary Laws of Thought; A Treatise on Pure and Applied Logic.* (London: Pickering, 1849). 392pp. 2nd edition, much enlarged.

A505 ("Laws of Thought"), B1257 (author, title, publisher, date), JS532 (listed under Boole), JS2069. JS suggests that A505 may refer to Boole's *An Investigation of the Laws of Thought*, but it seems most likely that A505 and B1257 are the same book. However, Dodgson owned several replies to Boole's book (see index) and so may have owned a copy of it as well. The present work is an influential treatise on logic.

2077. Thomson, William [Baron Kelvin] (1824–1907) and Peter Guthrie Tait. *Treatise on Natural Philosophy.* (Oxford: Clarendon Press, 1867). Volume 1.

Not in JS. Dodgson's copy was offered for sale at City Book Auction, New York on 29 January 1944 (DAA2073). It included his signature (partially erased) and "the whole of the extensive errata transferred to the text in Carroll's hand.... Containing several hundred or more words in his neat hand added to the body of the work." DAA2073 describes the work: "Thomson and Tait established the concept of the conservation of energy and effected a revolution in the development of scientific thought."

2078. Thornely, Thomas (b. 1855). *The Ethical and Social Aspect of Habitual Confession to a Priest.* (London: Macmillan and Co., 1880). 120pp. The Burney Prize Essay.

A870, B1259.a (author, title, date), JS2072. There are 2 entries numbered 1259 in B. Thornely was a fellow of Trinity Hall, Cambridge. *The Spectator* wrote of this work, "Though it is ... a thoroughgoing attack on the practice of habitual confession, it is one based upon principles clearly set down, and entirely free from the buncombe which one generally expects to read on such a subject when treated by Protestants."

2079. Thornton, Lewis. *Opposites. A Series of Essays on the Unpopular Sides of Popular Questions.* (Edinburgh and London: Blackwood, 1890). 380pp.

A797, D201, JS2073. Dodgson's copy is in HAC and has his monogram on the title page in brown ink. The essays are: "Forwards or Backwards," in which the author argues that perhaps the world is not constantly improving; "Philosophy, Religious Thought, and the Bible"; "Intellect and Morals"; "Evolution"; "Atheistic Christianity"; "Spiritualism"; "The Ancient Religions of the Future," a discussion of "new supernatural religions" such as Theosophy; "Gods and Women"; "Politics"; "Theology"; and "The Christ of Scripture."

2080. Thucydides (ca. 471–400 B. C. E.). *The History of the Peloponnesian War by Thucydides; The Text According to Bekker's*

Edition, with Some Alterations; With Notes, Chiefly Historical and Geographical by Thomas Arnold. (Oxford: J. Parker, [1830?]—1835). 3 vols. 674, 468, 518pp.

A382 (author, editor, 3 vols.), JS2075. 1st edition of Arnold's edition. The conjectural date of 1830 for the first volume is from the Harvard University Library catalogue. See 57 for a note on Thomas Arnold. E338/JS2074 may refer to this item or to another edition of Thucydides. The entry reads "Thucydides—Vol. I, with 'Dodgson' stamped on title [possibly the gothic stamp], marked throughout, Errata, and problem at the end, in his hand." This could be an additional copy of Volume I of the present set, the set may have been separated for some reason following the auction, or this could be a different edition altogether.

2081. Timbs, John (1801–75). *English Eccentrics and Eccentricities.* (London: Chatto and Windus, 1875 [1874]). 578pp. Color frontispiece, illustrations.

A894 (author [given incorrectly as Tomb], title), JS2081 (listed under Tomb). Earliest edition in BL is a 2-volume edition of 1866; this is the earliest single-volume edition in BL. Surrounding entries (e.g. A892, A893, and A896) mention multiple volume works. Timbs was a popular author of about 150 volumes. He began his career writing for Richard Phillips' *Monthly Magazine* and subsequently wrote for and edited several publications. He writes, "This book trys [sic] to show that with oddity of character may co-exist much goodness of heart; and your strange fellow, though, according to the lexicographer, he be out-landish, odd, queer and eccentric, may possess claims to our notice which the man who is ever studying the fitness of things would not readily present. It is hoped that this book will convey a fair idea of the number and variety of characters and incidents to be found in this gallery of [largely Victorian] English Eccentrics."

2082. (*The Times*). *The Times. no. 55, 567. Thursday, May 1, 1962.* (London: [1862]).

D198, JS215 (Anon./Periodicals). Described in D198 as "*The Times.* Every Day, 1962. A Bogus Number filled with imaginary advertisements and news." Described in BL as "A burlesque edition of *The Times,*" and "Newspaper as it may be in 1962."

2083. (*The Times*). *The Times, Wednesday October 3, 1798.* (London: 1862).

D199 (title with date, "Reprint, 1862"), JS216 (Anon./Periodicals). Reprint of the original edition containing the account of Nelson's Victory of the Nile.

2084. Tinling, James Forbes Bisset. *Hidden Lessons from the Verbal Repetitions and Varieties of the New Testament.* (London: Bagster, 1876).

A598 ("Hidden Lessons from the New Testament"), JS316 (Anon./Theology). Only edition of the only matching title in BL or BOD. Tinling is described by Allibone as "of St. John's College, Cambridge."

2085. Tipper, John (d. 1713), et al, editors. *The Ladies Diary: or, The Women's Almanack, for the Year of Our Lord…* ([London]: Printed by J. Wilde, for the Company of Stationers, 1704–1840). Issues unknown.

A566 (title), JS402 and JS405 (Anon./Women). A566 describes this as a "bundle of old ones." This annual was published [under varying imprints] from 1704 to 1840 with the following compilers: 1704–1713, John Tipper; 1714–1743, Henry Beighton; 1744–1753, Robert Heath; 1754–1760, Thomas Simpson; 1760?–1773?, Edward Rollinson; 1773–1818, Charles Hutton; 1819–1840, O. G. Gregory. The present imprint description is from the Harvard University Library catalogue.

2086. Titmarsh, M. A. [pseud. of William Makepeace Thackeray]. *The Rose and the Ring; or, the History of Prince Giglio and Prince Bulbo. A Fire-side Pantomime for Great and Small Children.* (London: Smith, Elder and Co., 1855). 128pp. With illustrations by the author.

A660 (author, title), JS2046. This is the 1st edition; the work was frequently reprinted. The last and most successful of Thackeray's Christmas stories. See 2056–61 for other works by Thackeray.

2087. Todd, R[obert] B[entley] (1809–60), editor. *The Cyclopædia of Anatomy and Physiology.* (London: Longman, 1836–59). 5 vol.

A924 (title, 6 vols.), JS159 (Anon./Medical). BL only lists this title in 5 volumes (other listings in BL are for excerpts). Perhaps Dodgson's was 5 volumes bound as 6, or 6 volumes was a miscount. Todd was a physician and Professor of Physiology and of General and Morbid Anatomy at King's College, London. He helped found King's College Hospital. The *Med.-Chir. Review* called this "A work indispensable to the Physiologist, and scarcely less so for the Physician."

2088. Todhunter, Isaac (1820–84). *The Conflict of Studies, and Other Essays on Subjects Connected with Education.* (London: Macmillan and Co., 1873). 242pp.

A308 (author, title), JS2076. Only edition in BL or MBC. Todhunter began his career as a mathematical school master before entering St. John's College, Cambridge, where he later became a fellow, lecturer and tutor. He was a fellow of the Royal Society and a member of the Mathematical Society of London. *Saturday Review* wrote, "We have here the statements and opinions of an eminent Cambridge teacher on various important points of the Cambridge system which are peculiarly within his own knowledge." See 1092 for a review of this book. Dodgson reprints a long excerpt from Todhunter's essay "Elementary Geometry" in his book *Euclid and his Modern Rivals* (1879).

2089. Todhunter, I[saac]. *An Elementary Treatise on the Theory of Equations, with a Collection of Examples.* (London: Macmillan and Co., 1875). 382pp. 3rd edition.

E169 (author, title, date), JS2079. "The examples have been selected from the College and University exam papers."

2090. Todhunter, I[saac]. *Examples of Analytical Geometry of Three Dimensions.* (Cambridge: Macmillan and Co., 1864). 84pp. 2nd edition, revised.

E157, JS2077. Dodgson's copy is in HAC and has his signature on the front free endpaper in brown ink. Consists of 438 "examples" in the form of problems in analytical geometry, along with solutions. "These examples have been principally obtained from University and College Examinations, but many of them are original."

2091. Todhunter, I[saac]. *A History of the Mathematical Theory of Probability from the Time of Pascal to that of Laplace.* (Cambridge: Macmillan and Co., 1865). 624pp.

A585 (author, title), JS2078. Only edition in BL or MBC.

2092. Todhunter, Isaac. *On the Differential and Integral Calculus.* (Cambridge:

Macmillan and Co., 1855). 403pp. 2nd edition, revised with additional examples.

Uncertain. F169 (author, title, date), not numbered in JS. Identified as Dodgson's only by the gothic stamp.

2093. Toland, Mary B[ertha] M[cKenzie] (1825?–95). *Ægle and the Elf.* (Philadelphia: J. B. Lippincott Company, 1887). 55pp.

A278, E115 (author, title, illustrators), F182 (author, title, date), JS2080. F182 notes the gothic stamp. Illustrated with photogravures of original drawings by Harper, Mowbray, Church, Gibson, Van Schaick, Jessie Shepherd, and Quelin, and a modeled relief by Baur. E115 notes, "The fantasy describes and pictures illustrate how a woodland fairy was attracted by one of a company of water nymphs."

2094. Tolstoy, Leo (1828–1910). *What Men Live By.* (New York and Boston: Thomas Y. Crowell, [c.1888]). 51pp.

Not in JS. In a letter to Edith Rix (31 December 1889) Dodgson writes, "What a good girl you are to have sent me *What Men Live By*." This is the only pre–1889 edition traced. Cohen describes this tale by the Russian novelist as "about the angel Michael who, for disobeying God's command, must live among men until he learns how God wishes them to live. He finally sees that men do not live by self-love but by love for one another."

2095. [Tom Thumb Drawing Society]. Pink printed folder bearing the legend "Tom Thumb Drawing Society" and containing a broadsheet titled "Rules for the Tom-Thumb Drawing Society" and 12 black and white prints of various subjects.

JS33. Dodgson's copy was offered at The Anderson Auction Co., New York on 30–31 January 1908 and is in HAC. It is inscribed in brown ink inside the front cover "Lewis Carroll From the Secretary of the Tom Thumb Society." The "Rules" sheet states that the secretary of the Society is Miss E. Ergles and the treasurers are the Misses Pratt. The rules state that each member was to make a drawing of identical size each month. Includes a drawing with a fairy that might have appealed to Dodgson. "E. Ergles" is clearly a misprint for Dodgson's friend Edith Argles. On 29 April 1868 he writes to her, "I have tried my hand at a picture for you, but I have not much time for drawing, so it is but a simple affair." In December of that year he writes to Edith's sister, Agnes, "Please tell [Edith] I'm afraid it's no use keeping me on in the Tom Thumb Society. I really haven't time to do any drawings at all." Whether Dodgson's drawing sent to Edith was issued by the society is not known.

2096. Tooke, John Horne (1736–1812). *Diversions of Purley*. (London: Thomas Tegg, 1840). 739pp. New edition with numerous additions.

Not in JS. In his diary for 5 January 1855, Dodgson wrote, "read some of *Diversions of Purley*." The edition listed here is the one in BL closest to the date when Dodgson read the book. This book was originally published in 1786 with a second volume following in 1805. Tooke was a philologist and radical politician who was imprisoned at one time for aiding Americans on the battlefields of Lexington and Concord. An important book detailing Tooke's influential theories of grammar and syntax in the social context. The work was originally prepared as Tooke undertook his own defense on the charge of slander.

2097. Töpffer, Rodolphe (1799–1846). *The Adventures of Mr. Obadiah Oldbuck. Wherein are Duly Set Forth the Crosses, Chagrins, Calamities, Checks, Chills, Changes, and Circumgirations by which his Courtship was Attended. Showing also, the Issue of his Suit and his Espousal to his Ladye-love.* (London: Tilt and Bogue, [1841?]). 84 illustrated plates. Printed by Bradbury and Evans.

A531 ("Adventures of Mr. Oldbuck"), JS37 (Anon./Children). Earliest English edition traced (and the only edition in BL). Töpffer was a Swiss cartoonist. This work tells, in pictures with captions, the story of the hero's attempts to woe his "ladye-love." It is considered by some to be the first comic book, and is certainly an important precursor to that form. It was first published in Europe in 1837.

2098. Townsend, Geo[rge] Fyler (1814–1900). *The Arabian Nights' Entertainments.* (London: F. Warne & Co., 1866). 632pp. A new edition, revised, with notes, by the Rev. Geo. Fyler Townsend. With illustrations by [Arthur Boyd] Houghton, [Thomas Bolton Gilchrist Septimus] Dalziel, etc.

A730 ("Arabian Nights with Dalziel's illus-trations"), JS101 (Anon./Literature). Only edition illustrated by Dalziel in BL. Townsend was educated at Trinity College, Cambridge and served as incumbent of St. Michael's, Burleigh St., London. The Dalziel brothers engraved the illustrations for AAIW and other works by Dodgson.

2099. Townshend, Chauncy Hare (1798–1868). *Facts in Mesmerism, with Reasons for a Dispassionate Inquiry into It.* (London: Hippolyte Bailliere, 1844). 390pp. 2nd edition, revised and enlarged.

A892, D184 (author, title, edition, city, date), JS2082. Townshend was educated at Trinity College, Cambridge where he won the poetry prize. He owned a luxurious home in London, but spent most of his later years in Lausanne. He bequeathed a sum of money and some manuscript material to Charles Dickens who published his *Religious Opinions* as directed by Townshend's will. This work argues the validity of mesmerism.

2100. Traill, H[enry] D[uff] (1842–1900). *Recaptured Rhymes: Being a Batch of Political and Other Fugitives Arrested and Brought to Book.* (Edinburgh: William Blackwood and Sons, 1882). 162pp.

A866, D211 (author, title, edition, city, date [given as 1872]), JS2083. 1st edition. The date in D276 is a misprint (1882 was the 1st). Traill was a critic, poet, playwright, and miscellaneous writer. He wrote works on Coleridge, Dodgson's friend the Marquis of Salisbury, and other 19th-century figures.

2101. Tree, Herbert Beerbohm (1853–1917). *Some Interesting Fallacies of the Modern Stage. An Address Delivered to the Playgoers' Club, etc.* (London: W. Heinemann, 1892). 36pp.

JS474 (listed under Beerbohm), Dodgson's copy, inscribed to him from the author, is in the collection of Selwyn Goodacre. Derbyshire, England. Tree was among the most successful actor-managers of the late 19th century. He was especially known for his productions of Shakespeare at the Haymarket Theatre, which he managed from 1887 to 1897. Dodgson saw Tree on stage multiple times (including as Hamlet in 1892), and met the actor at least twice, once on 8 June 1892 when he called on Tree and his family and found them "very friendly," and again on 14 December 1895 when he visited with Tree while the latter wore his Svengali makeup for *Trilby*.

2102. Trench, Mrs. Melesina [Chenevix St. George] (1768–1827). *Laura's Dream; or, the Moonlanders*. (London: J. Hatchard, 1816). 47pp.

B1116 (title, date), JS2084. Mrs. Trench, who married Richard Trench after being widowed by an army colonel, spent much of her time on the continent. Her diaries and letters were published to acclaim. BL describes this work as "A poem, with notes."

2103. Trench, Richard Chenevix (1807– 86). *Lectures on Medieval Church History. Being the Substance of Lectures Delivered at Queen's College, London*. (London: Kegan Paul Trench & Co., 1886). 453pp. 2nd edition, revised and improved.

A800, B1260 (author, title, date), JS2085. As a young clergyman, Trench made a reputation as a poet. He became a curate for Samuel Wilberforce in 1841 and was examining chaplain for Wilberforce when the latter was Bishop of Oxford. Trench became Dean of Canterbury and in 1864 Archbishop of Dublin. Dodgson heard Trench preach at St. Mary's, Oxford on 11 May 1857 and wrote, "it seemed a good sermon, but his delivery is bad and I lost the greater part of it." Dodgson ordered this book from Macmillan on 25 April 1887 (see *Macmillan*, 229).

2104. Trench, Richard Chenevix, editor. *Sacred Latin Poetry, Chiefly Lyrical, Selected and Arranged for Use; With Notes and Introduction*. (London: John W. Parker, 1849). 316pp.

A869 (author, title), JS2086. Earliest edition in BL.

2105. Trench, William Steuart (1808–72). *Realities of Irish Life*. (London: Longmans, Green and Co., 1868). 407pp. With illustrations by the author's son, John Townsend Trench.

A917 (author, title), JS2087. 1st edition. Trench, a land agent in Ireland to Marquis of Lansdowne, Marquis of Bath and Lord Digby, writes in his preface that the true incidents related from experience in his book are designed "to give the English public some idea of the difficulties which occasionally beset the path of an Irish landlord or agent who is desirous to improve the district in which he is interested and to relate the fact that Ireland — notwithstanding the many difficulties which may beset the path of those who earnestly desire to improve her condition — is nevertheless not altogether unmanageable." He concludes, "it has been my lot to live surrounded by a kind of poetic turbulence and almost romantic violence, which I believe could scarcely belong to real life in any other country in the world."

2106. (Trent, Council of). *The Canons and Decrees of the Council of Trent. With a Supplement, Containing the Condemnations of the Early Reformers, and Other Matters Relating to the Council*. Literally translated by T[heodore] A[lois William] Buckley. (London: George Routledge and Co., 1851). 399pp.

B995 (title, date, translator), JS2089. The Council of Trent (1545–63) was a direct response by the Roman church to the spread of Protestantism and expressed the ideals of the Counter-Reformation.

2107. (Trent, Council of). *The Catechism of the Council of Trent, Translated into English, with Notes*. (London: George Routledge and Co., 1852). 591pp. Translated by Theodore Alois William Buckley.

A794 (title), JS2088. The edition described here is sheer conjecture, but as Dodgson owned Buckley's translation of the *Canons and Decrees of the Council of Trent* (see above), this seems a likely candidate. The only other possibility in BL is the translation by Jeremiah Donovan first published in Dublin in 1829 and reprinted several times.

2108. [Trevelyan, George Otto] (1838– 1928). *The Bear; A University Magazine*. No. 1 (Cambridge, 1862). 3rd edition.

D15 (title, edition, city, date), JS207 (Anon./ Periodicals). Originally published in October 1858. This was the only "issue" of this "satirical imitation of *The Lion*." *The Lion: University Magazine* was published by J. Palmer, Cambridge, 1858. Only issues 1–3 are listed in BL. Trevelyan was an undergraduate at Trinity College, Cambridge. He went on to become an M.P. and served briefly as Civil Lord of the Admiralty.

2109. Trevelyan, G[eorge] O[tto]. *The Ladies in Parliament and Other Pieces. Re-*

published with Additions and Annotations. (Cambridge: Deighton, Bell, and Co., etc., 1869). 196pp.

A594 (author, title), JS2090. Earliest edition in BL.

2110. [**Trevenen**, Emily]. *Little Derwent's Breakfast.* (London: Smith, Elder & Co., 1839). 84pp. Poems written for Derwent Moultrie Coleridge. Illustrated by engravings.

A460 (title, date), JS712 (listed under Coleridge). Derwent was the grandson of Samuel Taylor Coleridge. Trevenen, a friend of Wordsworth and of Charles and Mary Lamb, uses the ordinary items at a breakfast table (sugar, coffee, etc.) to exhort Derwent to good behavior and to teach him about larger issues of society — trade, class, etc.

2111. Trevigra [pseud.]. *The Reaction of Gravity in Motion; or, The Third Motion of the Earth.* (London: London Literary Society, [1887]). 40pp.

E369 (title, author), JS279 (Anon./Science). Only edition in BL. E369 notes "with the dated autograph initials of Lewis Carroll."

2112. Trimmer, Mrs. [Sarah] (1741–1810). *Fabulous Histories, or, The History of the Robins: Designed for the Instruction of Children, Respecting their Treatment of Animals.* (London: Printed for N. Hailes, Juvenile Library, 1818). 164pp. 12th edition. Illustrations possibly by Thomas Bewick.

B1264 (author, title), JS2091. Originally published in 1786 under the title *Fabulous Histories: Designed for the Instruction of Children, Respecting their Treatment of Animals.* This is the earliest edition traced with title quoted in B1264. Clearly a different edition from below (A640), which specifies the illustrator and has a different title. The Weir edition was also 8vo and B1264 describes this as 12mo. Mrs. Trimmer was an author and reviewer of children's literature who wielded significant influence in the field. This work is a didactic story about a family of robins, and Mrs. Trimmer's best known work for children.

2113. Trimmer, Sarah. *The History of the Robins: For the Instruction of Children on their Treatment of Animals.* (London: Griffith and Farran, 1869). 141pp. 24 illustration by Harrison Weir.

A640 (title, illustrator), JS2091. See above for a note on this title.

2114. Tristram, Henry Baker (1822–1906). *The Land of Moab; Travels and Discoveries on the East Side of the Dead Sea and the Jordan. With a Chapter on the Persian Palace of Mashita by J[ames] Fergusson.* (London: J. Murray, 1873). 408pp. With map, and illustrations by Charles Louis Buxton and R. C. Johnson. Includes an Appendix, "On the Flora of Moab," by William Amherst Hayne.

B1261 (author, title, illustrators, date), JS2092. Tristram was master of Greatham Hospital and vicar of Greatham, Stockton-on-Tees. He wrote several books about biblical lands. A reviewer for *The Athenæum* wrote of this work, "Pleasantly written and well illustrated, the narrative sustains its interest throughout, and gives a vivid picture of the present condition of the country."

2115. Trojan, Johannes (1837–1915). *Der Schwarze Peter. Ein Bilderbuch für Artige Kinder. Mit Reimen von J. Trojan Holzschnitte von A. Closs Nach Silhouetten von P[aul] Konewka.* (Stuttgart: Julius Hoffman R. Heinemann's Verlag, [1870]). 20pp.

E27 (author, title, illustrator), JS2093. E27 notes, "with the stamped name and initials of Lewis Carroll." Only edition in BL. German children's book with verse by Trojan and silhouettes by Konewka (see 1171). Trojan was a German author of humorous verse and satire.

2116. Trollope, Mrs. [Frances] (1780–1863). *Domestic Manners of the Americans.* (London: Whittaker, Treacher & Co., 1832). 2 vols. 304, 303pp. Illustrated.

A596 (author, title, 2 vols.), B1262 (author, title, date), JS2094. The 1st, 2nd, and 3rd editions were published in 2-volume sets by Whittaker, Treacher & Co. in 1832. Frances Trollope was the mother of the famous novelist. She traveled to America in 1827 with two children hoping to live a utopian life among emancipated slaves. She found a society of spitters and braggarts where "the dreary coldness and want of enthusiasm in American manners is one of

Silhouette by Paul Konewka from *Der Schwarze Peter* (item 2115).

their greatest defects." She returned to England and wrote this tremendously popular book, seen by many as a satire of travel writing and others as a comic indictment of Americans. She went on to write similar books on other countries.

2117. Trommius, Abraham (1633–1719). *Abrahami Trommii Concordantiae Graecae Versionis Vulgo Dictae LXX Interpretum: Cujus Voces Secundum Ordinem Elementorum Sermonis Graeci Digestae Recensentur, Contra Atque in Opere Kircheriano Factum Fuerat: Leguntur hic Praeterea Voces Graecae pro Hebraicis Redditae ab Antiquis Omnibus Veteris Testamenti Interpretibus, Quorum Nonnisi Fragmenta Extant, Aquila, Symmacho, Theodotione & Aliis. Quorum Maximam Partem Nuper in Lucem Edidit Domnus Bernardus de Montfaucon.* (Amstelodami et Trajecti ad Rhenum: Sumptibus Societatis, 1718). 2 vols. 1008; 713, 134, 70pp. Index Hebræus et Chaldæus.- Duplex Additamentum ad Præcedentes Concordantias Græcas, Quorum Prius Continet Lexicon Græcum ad Hexapla Origenis A Dmno B. de Montfaucon, Posterius D. Lamberti Bos, Succintam Collationem Daurum Editionum Francofurtensis et Vaticanæ.

A742 ("*Trommii* Concordantiae Graecae, 2 vols."), JS335 (Anon./Theology). Only edition in BL. Trommius was a minister at Groningen. His Greek/Latin Concordance to the Septuagint has not yet been entirely superceded. He incorporated the reading from Auila, Theodotion, and Symmachus. Trommius' work was wholly unmatched for 175 years until Hatch and Redpath published their concordance.

2118. Tuck, Robert (1836–1911). *A Handbook of Biblical Difficulties; or, Reasonable Solutions of Perplexing Things in Sacred Scripture.* (E. Stock: London, 1886). 568pp.
A793 (author, title), JS2095. Only edition in BL. A second series was published in 1890 under the title *A Handbook of Scientific and Literary Bible Difficulties.* Tuck was a clergyman.

2119. Tucker, Henry Saint George (1771–1851). *The Sphinx.* ([London]: Cox & Wyman, [1850]). [81]pp.
A470 (author, title, n.d.), JS2096. Only edition in BL or BOD. Tucker was Accountant-General of Bengal. A collection of riddles in verse.

2120. Tuke, Daniel Hack (1827–95). *Illustrations of the Influence of the Mind upon the Body in Health and Disease, Designed to Elucidate the Action of the Imagination.* (London: J. & A. Churchill, 1872). 444pp.
A921 (author, title), JS1097. 1st edition. Tuke was a fellow of the Royal College of Physicians and editor of the *Journal of Mental Science.* This work explores, among other ramifications of its subject, the use of the power of the mind as a "practical remedy" for disease. Dodgson quoted at length from the present work in his letter to the *St. James's Gazette,* "Hydrophobia Curable" (see LCP, #244). The excerpt argued that Hydrophobia is not curable.

2121. Tuke, Daniel Hack. *Sleep-Walking and Hypnotism.* (London: J. & A. Churchill, 1884). 119pp.
D185 (author, title, city, date), JS2098.

2122. Tupper, Martin Farquhar (1810–89). *Ballads for the Times, Now First Collected. Geraldine, A Modern Pyramid, Hactenus, A Thousand Lines, and Other Poems.* (London: Arthur Hall, Virtue & Co., [1850]). 440pp.
A857 ("Tupper's Ballads and Poems"),

JS2099. Earliest edition in BL of the only possible match among Tupper's works. Tupper was educated at Christ Church, Oxford and published several works of poetry and drama.

2123. [**Tupper**, Martin Farquhar]. *Probabilities; an Aid to Faith*. (London: 1854). 3rd edition.

E261 (author, title, date), JS2100.

2124. Tupper, Martin Farquhar. *Proverbial Philosophy: A Book of Thoughts and Arguments, Originally Treated*. (London: J. Rickerby, 1838). 224pp. 1st edition of the 1st series.

A856 (title only), B1266 (author, title, date), JS2101. D212 lists the same author and title with a date of 1848, but no British edition of 1848 has been traced. This may refer to an American edition (there were several that year), or it could be a misprint ("1848" for "1838"). If Dodgson did own an 1848 edition, it likely included the 1st and 2nd series, the latter of which was first published in 1842. This immensely popular work consisted of moralistic writing presented in blank verse.

2125. Turgenev, Ivan Sergeevich (1818–83). *Liza*. Translated from the Russian by William Ralston Shedden Ralston (London: Chapman and Hall, 1869). 2 vols. 245, 231pp. 1st edition of this translation.

A807 (translator, title, date, edition, 2 vols.), JS1711 (listed under Ralston). Turgenev was a Russian novelist, poet and playwright. A translation of *Dvorianskoe Gnezdo*, the author's second novel, which has also been translated under the title *A House of Gentlefolk*. See 1617 for a note on Ralston.

2126. Turner, Ethel Sybil [afterwards Curlewis] (1870–1958). *Seven Little Australians, etc.* (London: Ward & Lock, [1894]). 236pp. Illustrated by A. J. Johnson.

A554 (title), JS75 (Anon./Children). Earliest edition traced. Turner was an Australian writer of children's stories. This children's story begins, "If you imagine that you are going to read of model children, with perhaps a naughtily-inclined one to point a moral, you had best lay down the book immediately and betake yourself to 'Sandford and Merton,' or similar standard juvenile works. Not one of the seven is really good, for the very excellent reason that Australian children never are."

2127. *The Twelve Churches, or, Tracings along the Watling Street*. (London: Rivingtons, 1860). 56pp. By the authoress of "The Red Rose". Illustrated by H. H. T.

Not in JS. Listed in WS (title, date) only and described there as having Dodgson's autograph. *The Athenæum* wrote of this book that "It conducts the reader in a very agreeable manner along the road from London by Hyde Park Corner to St. Albans, gossiping cheerfully the whole way, setting up stations, or halting places, whereat to indulge in historic and antiquarian reminiscences."

2128. [**Twycross**, John] (1795–1868). *The Commentary Wholly Biblical: an Exposition of the Old and New Testaments, in the Very Words of Scripture*. (London: S. Bagster & Sons, [1856–59]). 3 vols. 857; 762; 643, 85pp. With the [biblical] text, and with maps.

A750 ("Commentary — Wholly Biblical, 3 vols."), JS307 (Anon./Theology). Only edition of the only matching title in BL or BOD. Twycross was educated at Trinity College, Dublin and was curate of St. Olave's, Southwark and later of St. Peter-le-Poor, London. He edited the works of Burke and other works.

2129. [**Tyas**, Robert] (1811–79). *Woodland Gleanings*. (London: 1837). 188pp. With 32 engravings of trees.

D243 (title, city, date), JS397 (Anon./Unclassified). No 1837 edition traced, but the 1838 edition was published by Robert Tyas. Includes "a popular and concise description of each tree, with an account of its origin and history, interspersed with select allusions from the Poets."

2130. Tyndall, John (1820–93). *Heat Considered as a Mode of Motion: Being a Course of Twelve Lectures Delivered at the Royal Institution of Great Britain in 1862*. (London: Longmans, Green and Co., 1865). 532pp. 2nd edition, with additions and illustrations.

A343, D213 (author, title, city, date), JS2102. D213 notes Dodgson's signature. Tyndall was a British physicist, born in Ireland. In 1853 he became Professor of Natural Philosophy at the Royal Institution and succeeded the famous Michael Faraday as superintendent of that institution. He was especially known for his scientific writings for laymen.

2131. Tyrwhitt, Richard Saint John (1827–95). *An Amateur Art-Book. Lectures. With some Notes on the Oxford Educational Collection of Casts.* (Oxford: I. Vincent, 1886). 111pp.

E289 (author, title), JS2103. Only edition in BL. Tyrwhitt took his degree from Christ Church, Oxford in 1849, just missing being an undergraduate with Dodgson, who arrived in 1850. Tyrwhitt was a High Churchman, a Student of Christ Church from 1845 to 1859 (during some of which time he served as a tutor) and vicar of St. Mary Magdalen, Oxford from 1858 to 1872. In 1884 he was elected honorary fellow of King's College, London. He was best known for his writings on art. Dodgson first mentions Tyrwhitt in his diary on 23 December 1856, when he saw some of his colleague's poetry. Dodgson mentions four other meetings with Tyrwhitt all between 1856 and 1863. The two shared an interest in photography.

2132. Tyrwhitt, Richard Saint John. *Battle and After. Concerning Sergeant Thomas Atkins, Grenadier Guards, with Other Verses.* (London: Macmillan and Co., 1889). 95pp.

D216 (author, title, city, date), JS2104.

2133. Tyrwhitt, Richard Saint John. *Free Field: Lyrics Chiefly Descriptive.* (London: Macmillan & Co., 1888). 114pp.

D215 (author, title, city, date), JS2105.

2134. Tyrwhitt, Richard Saint John. *A Handbook of Pictorial Art.* (Oxford: Clarendon Press, 1868). 480pp. With a Chapter on Perspective by A. Macdonald. In the *Clarendon Press Series*.

A591, D214 (author, title, city, date), JS2106. D214 notes Dodgson's initials.

2135. Tyrwhitt, R[ichard] Saint John. *Hugh Heron, Ch. Ch., An Oxford Novel.* (London: Strahan and Company Limited, [1880]). 474pp.

A931, JS2107. Dodgson's copy is in the collection of Selwyn Goodacre, Derbyshire. A largely autobiographical novel. Dodgson quotes this briefly in his 1886 pamphlet *Three Years in a Curatorship* (see *Oxford*, 229).

2136. Tyrwhitt, Richard Saint John. *The Natural Theology of Natural Beauty.* (London: Society for the Promotion of Christian Knowledge, [1882]). 176pp.

E336 (author, title), JS2108. Only edition in BL.

2137. Tytler, Sarah [pseud. of Henrietta Keddie] (1827–1914). *Papers for Thoughtful Girls, with Illustrative Sketches of Some Girls' Lives.* (Edinburgh: Alexander Strahan, 1862). 357pp.

D238 (author, title, city, date), JS2109. The 3rd edition of 1862 was the first to include 4 illustrations by J. E. Millais, and is almost certainly that owned by Dodgson. Tytler was a novelist and biographer of Jane Austen and Queen Victoria. *The Scotsman* wrote of this work, "Here we have one of the best books that ever was written for a purpose. There has recently been no lack of books on the whole duty of women; but in none of them has there been so catholic a spirit, so just an appreciation of all the adornments of the feminine character."

2138. Uhland, Johann Ludwig (1787–1862). *The Songs and Ballads of Uhland.* (London: Williams and Norgate, Ltd., 1864). 455pp. Translated from the German by W. W. Skeat.

D217 (author, title, translator, city, date), JS2110. Uhland was a German poet and liberal politician with a penchant for medieval themes.

2139. [University Extension College, Reading]. *Calendar and General Directory 1894–1895.* (Reading: University Extension College, 1894).

E319 (title, date), JS250 (Anon./Reference). University Extension College was a precursor to Reading University. The college was founded as part of the Oxford University Extension program — a program gaining popularity at the time and which brought lectures to thousands of people across the country. Dodgson does not record any involvement with the extension program in his published diaries.

2140. Upton, Charles Barnes (1831–1920). *Lectures on the Bases of Religious Belief.* (London: Williams & Norgate, 1894). 364pp. The Hibbert Lectures, 1893.

A790 ("Upton's Hibbert Lectures, 1893"), JS2111. Only edition listed in BL. Upton was Professor of Philosophy at Manchester College and served from 1867 to 1875 as minister of Toxteth Park Chapel, Liverpool.

Illustration by J. E. Millais for Sarah Tytler's *Papers for Thoughtful Girls* (item 2137).

2141. Urling, George F. *Vocal Gymnastics; or a Guide for Stammerers and for Public Speakers and Others*. (London: 1857).

E182 (author, title, date), JS2112. The book was commended by the *London Medical Times* and the *London Gazette*. Dodgson and several family members suffered from a slight hesitation of speech.

2142. Valters, J. C., compiler. *The Oxford Post-Office Directory: 1887*. (Oxford: J. C. Valters, 1887).

JS2113. Dodgson's copy was offered for sale by Maggs of London in 1911 and is now in HAC. The gothic stamp appears on the front pastedown; Dodgson's monogram is in purple ink on the title page. On p. 264, under Rag, Bone & Metal dealers, he has added, in purple ink, "Warburton, T. 17 Bridge St., S. Ebbe's." On p. 173, he has added, in the alphabetical list of residents, "Legge, Prof. J. 3 Keble Road." On p. 210 he has changed the address of J. Barclay Thompson to 39 St. Margaret's Road from 11 Banbury Rd. On p. 157 he has altered the address of H. Hassall to 8 St. Aldates from 2 Keble Rd. Other small corrections throughout. Dodgson is listed among the resident graduate members of the University on p. 294.

2143. Vanbrugh, John (1664–1726). *Plays, Written by Sir John Vanbrugh*. (London: Printed for W. Feales, R. Wellington, etc., 1735). 2 vols. Each play has separate title page, frontispiece, and pagination.

A672, B1267 (author, title, date, 2 vols.), JS2114. Vanbrugh was an architect and playwright. Includes: *The Relapse; or, Virtue in Danger, The Provok'd Wife, La Maison Rustique: or, The Country House, The Confederacy, The False Friend, The Mistake, A Journey to London,* and *The Provok'd Husband; or, A Journey to London.*

2144. Vase, Gillan [pseud. of Elizabeth Newton]. *A Great Mystery Solved: Being a Sequel to "The Mystery of Edwin Drood."* (London: Remington and Co., 1878). 3 vols.

A603 (title, 3 vols.), JS839. This is the only 3-volume edition of the only matching title in BL. See 586 for description of *The Mystery of Edwin Drood*, the unfinished novel this book completes. The present title is a scarce book in which Drood escapes the attack by Jaspar, Jaspar commits suicide and Drood marries Rosa.

2145. Vaughan, Charles John (1816–97). *Counsels to Young Students; Three Sermons Preached before the University of Cambridge, at the Opening of the Academical Year 1870–71*. (London: Macmillan and Co., 1870). 95pp.

B1269 (author, title, date), JS2115. Educated at Trinity College, Cambridge, Vaughan served as headmaster of Harrow for 15 years, bringing a great improvement to that school. He was Dean of Llandaff and helped found University College at Cardiff. Sympathetic with the nonconformists, and a conservative who opposed much contemporary Biblical criticism, he was a powerful preacher.

2146. Vaughan, Charles John. *Lectures on St. Paul's Epistle to the Philippians*. (London & Cambridge: Macmillan & Co., 1862). 342pp.

A774 (author, title), JS2116. 1st edition as described in MBC.

2147. Vaughan, Charles John. *Twelve Discourses on Subjects Connected with the Liturgy and Worship of the Church of England*. (London and Cambridge: Macmillan and Co., 1867). 396pp.

B1268 (author, title, date), JS2117.

2148. Vaughan, Charles John. *The Two Great Temptations. The Temptation of Man, and the Temptation of Christ. Lectures Delivered in the Temple Church, Lent 1872*. (London: Macmillan and Co., 1872). 178pp.

A758, B1270 (author, title, date), JS2118.

2149. Vaughan, Henry (1622–95). *Silex Scintillans: Sacred Poems and Private Ejaculations*. (London: Pickering, 1847). 231pp. With a biographical sketch of the author by Henry Francis Lyte.

A869 (author, title, date), JS2119. Vaughan was an English poet, who studied for a time at Jesus College, Oxford. After undergoing a spiritual transformation, he wrote this collection of spiritual poems, his best known work. It was originally published in two parts (1650 and 1655).

2150. Vaughan, Robert (1795–1868). *Ritualism in the English Church, in its Relation to Scripture, Piety, and Law*. (London: Jackson, 1866).

B1271 (author, title, date), JS2120. Vaughan was a non-conformist divine who served congregations in Worcester and Kensington. He was Professor of Ancient and Modern History at the University of London and later President of Lancashire Independent College. He was also founder and editor of *British Quarterly Review*.

2151. Velleius, Paterculus Caius (20 B.C.E.–after 30 C.E.). *Caii Velleii Paterculi Historiae Romanae. Libri Duo. Accurante Steph. And. Philippi.* (Lutetiae Parisiorun: Typis Josephi Barbuo, 1754). 238pp. Plate engraved by Étienne Fessard after Jacques de Sève; engraved head- and tail-pieces.

B1160 (author, title, publisher, city, date), JS1620 (listed under Paterculus). A Roman history written by a Roman officer.

2152. Venn, John (1834–1923). *The Logic of Chance; An Essay on the Foundations and Province of the Theory of Probability, with Especial Reference to its Application to Moral and Social Science.* (London: Macmillan and Co., 1876). 488pp. 2nd edition, re-written and enlarged.

A517, B1272 (author, title, edition), JS2121. Venn was educated at Gonvill and Caius College, Cambridge and wrote a history of that college and the first three volumes of a history of the University. He is best known, however, for introducing the Venn diagram in 1880. The diagrams were a visual representation of logical and mathematical classes.

2153. Venn, John. *On Some Characteristics of Belief, Scientific and Religious.* (London: Macmillan and Co., 1870). 126pp. The Hulsean Lectures for 1869.

Not in JS. In a letter to his publisher Macmillan (14 June 1895), Dodgson writes about a book he has "been long working at" that will be 'an attempt to treat some of the religious difficulties of the day from a logical point of view.... Venn's Hulsean lectures, which I have just met with, called *Characteristics of Belief*, is very much on those lines, but deals with only *one* such difficulty." (See *Macmillan*, 319).

2154. Venn, John. *Symbolic Logic.* (London: Macmillan & Co., 1894). 540pp. 2nd edition, revised and rewritten.

A517, B1273 (author, title, edition, date), listed in JS but not numbered. The original edi-

tion was the first book to include Venn diagrams. It was an attempt to elaborate on Boolean algebra. According to the preface, this revised edition added nearly 100 pages. Dodgson's own work on *Symbolic Logic* was left incomplete at the time of his death; only the first part of a projected three-part work was published. In that work, Dodgson makes reference to Venn and prints (on p. 179 of the 1st edition, 1896) a Venn diagram and a "Solution by Venn's Method of Diagrams." He writes that the solution "has been kindly provided to me by Mr. Venn himself," so Dodgson must have had some correspondence or meeting with Venn, though Venn is not mentioned in *Letters* or *Diaries*.

2155. Verdad, Don Pedro [pseud. of Walter MacGee]. *From Vineyard to Decanter. A Book About Sherry.* (London: E. Stanford, 1876). 118pp. 3rd edition, revised. Preface signed W. M. G. (i.e. Walter MacGee).

Not in JS. Dodgson quotes from this book at some length in his 1884 pamphlet *Twelve Months in a Curatorship* (WMGC, 3163; see *Oxford*, 158–59), calling it, "'From Vineyards to Decanter,' a little book about Sherry published in 1876." First published in 1875.

2156. Vere, Langton George (1844–1924), compiler. *The Catholic Hymn Book.* (1894).

E146 (compiler, title, date), JS2122. No 1894 edition traced. BL and BOD list only a London edition of 1877.

2157. Viardot, Louis (1800–83). *Wonders of Sculpture.* (London: Sampson Low, Marston, Low & Searle, 1872). 360pp. Illustrated with 62 engravings. Translated from the French by Nancy D'Anvers [pseud. of Nancy R. E. Meugens, later Bell].

A595, E274 (author, title), F159 (author, title, date [1862]), JS2123. Apparently a misprint in F159 (1862 for 1872), as the earliest edition of the original French work in the BNF is 1869. Earliest edition in BL of the English translation. F159 notes the gothic stamp. Viardot wrote several works popularizing fine art.

2158. Viger, François (1590–1647). *De Præcipuis Græcæ Dictionis Idiotismis.* (London: Excudebat J. D. impensis Guilielmi Adderton, apud quem væneunt ad insigne Trium Deauratorum Falconum in vico vulgò vocato Duck-Lane, 1647). 408pp. Decima editio prioribus nitidior.

E310 (author, title, "in vico vulgo-vocato, Duck-lane, 1647"), JS2125 (incorrectly identifies this as the Cambridge edition of the same year). E310 notes that "This volume is rendered of great interest from its possessing the very rare eighteenth century Book Plate of Exeter College, Oxford." A Dictionary of Greek idioms first published in 1632.

2159. Viger, François. *De Praecipuis Graecae Dicitionis Idiotismis Liber; Cum Animadversionibus Henrici Hoogeveeni et Joannis Caroli Zeunii. Edidit et Andotationes addidit Godofredus Hermannus.* (Glasguae: Excudebat A. Duncan, [etc.], 1813). 733pp.

B1274 (author, title "De Praecipuis Graecae Dicitionis Idiotismis Liber," date), JS2124. The listing in JS gives the city of publication as Oxford, but no such indication is given in B1274, and this is the only 1813 edition traced. B1274 notes, "Prize to C. D. [i.e. Lewis Carroll's father], May, 1817, with inscription."

2160. Vines, Charles. *The Dictionary Appendix and Orthographer, Containing Upwards of Seven Thousand Words not Found in the Dictionary.* (London: J. F. Shaw, 1857). 109pp. 9th edition.

E205 (author, title, date), JS2126. E205 notes that this has "'Thos. W. Lenty' on title; 'very scarce' in Lewis Carroll's hand."

2161. Virgil (70–19 B.C.E.). *The Æneid of Virgil Translated into English Verse, by John Conington.* (London: Longmans, Green, and Co., 1879). 455pp. 3rd edition.

A837 (title, translator), D219 (author, title, translator, date), JS2127, JS2128. Conington (1825–69) was an English classicist and primarily a Latin scholar. This was his most famous work, a fine translation into the octosyllabic metre of Scott.

2162. Virgil. *Publius Virgilius Maro.* (London: Pickering, 1821). 283pp. In the *Pickering Diamond Classics* series.

A477 (author, series), JS2129 (not listed separately). See 153 for a note on this series of miniature books.

2163. Virgil. *Works.* (Oxford: Printed by I. Shrimpton, 1845). 420pp.

JS2129, E337. Dodgson's copy is in HAC. It lacks the title page (no complete copy has been traced). It is signed in brown ink as follows: "Dodgson/School House" on the front endpaper, "Dodgson" at the head of the preface, "Dodgson" on the rear pastedown. Dodgson has added numbers to many of the entries in the table of contents and there is some minor underlining and marginal marking throughout, all in brown ink. Other markings in pencil may not be in Dodgson's hand (signatures on p. 318 and 319 appear to be spelled without the "g" in Dodgson.) The preface states, "This volume contains the entire works of Virgil after the text of Heyne, except in some half-a-dozen places where the alterations are made on MS. authority, adopted by Wagner and other learned editors ... its object is ... solely to serve as a Hand-book for the Lecture room at College; for the school-boy when 'up at Class'..."

2164. Vores, Thomas (1804–75). *Loving Counsels; Being Recollections of Sermons Preached by T. V. By a Member of the Congregation.* (London: Wertheim, Macintosh & Hung, 1858). 1st (of 4) series only.

B1275 (author, title, date), JS2130. Vores was educated at Wadham College, Oxford and was vicar of St. Mary-in-the-Castle, Hastings from 1841 until his death. Dodgson visited Hastings many times during his 20 years of vacationing in nearby Eastbourne, and he had two aunts who lived there.

2165. [Voysey, Charles] (1828–1912). *An Examination of Canon Liddon's Bampton Lectures. By a Clergyman of the Church of England, etc.* (London: Trübner & Co., 1871). 343pp.

B1121 (title, date), not in JS. Voysey was a controversial clergyman who preached Theism and who held a number of curacies (including one from which he was ejected after preaching against Everlasting Punishment). As vicar of Healaugh, Yorkshire, he preached more controversial sermons, questioning the strict truth of some statements in the Bible. He was eventually tried on charges of having made statements at variance with the 39 Articles and Holy Scripture and was convicted and deprived of his living in 1871. He refused to recant, and continued to preach with the support of a number of wealthy patrons. He later founded the Theistic Church. Dodgson owned a copy of Liddon's *Bampton Lectures* (see 1230).

2166. Wace, Henry (1836–1924). *Christianity and Agnosticism. Reviews of Some Recent Attacks on the Christian Faith.* (Edinburgh: W. Blackwood & Sons, 1895). 339pp.

A790 (author, title), JS2131. This is the only pre-1898 edition in BL. Wace was educated at Brasenose College, Oxford. He served in several ecclesiastical positions, eventually becoming Dean of Canterbury in 1903. He was a strong Evangelical, opposed to High Church attempts at prayer book reform. The "attacks" mentioned in the present title were by Professor Thomas Huxley (1825–95), best known for his support of Darwinism. An 1889 a book titled *Christianity and Agnosticism; A Controversy* contained articles by Wace, Huxley, and others. The book focused on "the recent controversy between the Rev. Dr. Henry Wace, Principal of King's College, London, and Prof. Huxley, over the question of the true significance of agnosticism, and incidentally of the limits of natural knowledge." This work is a continuation of that controversy.

2167. Wace, Henry. *Christianity and Morality, or the Correspondence of the Gospel with the Moral Nature of Man. The Boyle Lectures for 1874 and 1875.* (London and Aylesbury: Basil Montagu Pickering, 1876). 320pp.

A758, A790, B1278 (author, title), JS2132. Earliest edition in BL. Dodgson owned 2 copies.

2168. Wace, Henry. *The Foundations of Faith Considered in Eight Sermons Preached before the University of Oxford in the Year M.DCCC.LXXIX at the Lecture Founded by John Bampton.* (London: Pickering & Co., 1880). 399pp.

A803, B1276 (author, title, date), JS2133.

2169. Wace, Henry. *The Gospel and its Witnesses. Some of the Chief Facts in the Life of our Lord and the Authority of the Evangelical Narratives Considered in Lectures Chiefly Preached at St. James's Westminster.* (London: John Murray, 1884). 211pp. 2nd edition.

A758, B1277 (author, title, date), JS2134.

2170. Wace, Henry. *Some Central Points of our Lord's Ministry.* (London: Hodder and Stoughton, 1890). 352pp.

A768 (author, title), JS2135. Only edition in BL. According to the preface, "Most of these expositions … were originally printed in the *Clergyman's Magazine.*" A collection of 18 expositions under titles such as "Our Lord's Motive," "Our Lord's Education, "The First Temptation," "Our Lord's Manifestation of Himself," etc.

2171. Wade, John (1788–1875). *Women, Past and Present: Exhibiting their Social Vicissitudes; Single and Matrimonial Relations; Rights, Privileges, and Wrongs.* (London: Charles J. Skeet, 1859). 364pp.

A588, D239 (author, title, city, date), JS2136. Wade traces the history of women and their status in Asia, Greece, and Rome and through 18th-century Europe. He discusses equality of the sexes, love and passion, marriage, celibacy, divorce and women's rights and privileges. A supplementary chapter on harlotry and concubinage was published separately.

2172. Wainwright, Samuel. *Scientific Sophisms. A Review of Current Theories Concerning Atoms, Apes, and Men.* (London: Hodder & Stoughton, 1881). 310pp.

A909 (author, title), JS2137. Only edition in BL. Wainwright was vicar of Holy Trinity, York. This book explores current theories, including Darwin's theory of evolution and related work by Huxley, in great detail. The author divides theories of evolution into three categories (Theistic, Atheistic, and Agnostic) and concludes that Darwin's theory is "strongly Theistic" and "not antagonistic to Christianity."

2173. Walford, Edward (1823–97), editor. *Men of the Time. Biographical Sketches of Eminent Living Characters, also Biographical Sketches of the Celebrated Women of the Time.* (London: W. Kent & Co., 1859). 895pp.

A324 (title), JS244 (Anon./Reference). The edition above is pure speculation (it appears to be the 1st published without reference to a year in the title). This biographical dictionary was originally issued anonymously as *Men of the Time in 1852.* It went through many editions as the century wore on, later versions being edited by Thomas Cooper. It was uniform with *Men of the Reign* (see 2195).

2174. Walker, Alexander (1779–1852). *Beauty: Illustrated Chiefly by an Analysis and Classification of Beauty in Woman. Preceded by a Critical View of the General Hypotheses Respecting Beauty by Hume, Hogarth, Burke, etc., and Followed by a Similar View of the Hypotheses of Beauty in Sculpture and Painting by Leonardo da Vinci, Winckelmann, Mengs, Bossi, etc.* (London: H. G. Bohn, 1846). 395pp. 2nd edition. Illustrated by drawings from life, by H. Howard, etc.

A537, D240 (author, title, city, edition, date), JS2138. Walker was the author of books on physiology, pathology, and related topics.

2175. Walker, Alexander. *Physiognomy Founded on Physiology, and Applied to Various Countries, Professions and Individuals: with an Appendix on the Bones at Hythe, the Sculls of the Ancient Inhabitants of Britain and its Invaders.* (London: Smith, Elder & Co., 1834). 286pp. Illustrated.

B1279 (author, title, date), JS2139. Physiognomy is the "science" of deducing personality characteristics through the study of facial structure. (See also 1193.)

2176. Walker, Alexander. *Woman Physiologically Considered as to Mind, Morals, Marriage, Matrimonial Slavery, Infidelity, and Divorce.* (London: A. H. Bailey, 1840). 404pp. 2nd edition.

E356 (author, title, date), JS2140. An important attempt to gauge the difference between the sexes based on physiology rather than on social history. According to the jacket copy of a 20th century reprint, "Alexander Walker has attempted to discuss philosophically the moral relations between man and woman on physiological principles. He has shown that nature, for the preservation of the human species, has conferred on woman a sacred character and given her prompt and infallible instinct as a guide in all her gentle thoughts, her charming words and her beneficent actions, while man has only slow and often erring reason to guide his cold and calculated conduct. The author has thoroughly analyzed the thinking process in woman and made a few important discoveries regarding their head and heart. He has shown that woman sometimes more quickly understands many reasoned statements than man does. He has also proved that the superiority of instinct in woman is connected with the greater development of her vital system and this superiority of instinct affects all her mental operations. The author has gone deep into the causes of many a social evils like polygamy, infidelity, concubinage, prostitution, etc."

2177. Walker, George (1734–1807). *A Treatise on Conic Sections in Five Books. Book I. On the General Properties of the Conic Sections: or the Properties which are Common to Them All.* (London: Printed for Charles Dilly, 1794). 218pp. Plates.

E351 (author, title, date), JS2141. Only Book I was ever published. Walker was a pastor to dissenters and served as a mathematical tutor at Warrington from 1772 to 1796 and a tutor in theology, mathematics, and classics at Manchester beginning in 1796.

2178. Walker, George. *On Chess.* Details unknown.

A895 ("Walker on Chess"), JS2142, but no further details given. Walker is almost certainly George Walker, a stockbroker who wrote widely on the subject of chess. Walker has no fewer than 6 titles (some in several editions), listed in BL, including (with earliest listed dates): *A New Treatise on Chess: Containing the Rudiments of the Science* (1832); *A Selection of Games at Chess, Actually Played by Philidor and His Contemporaries* (1835); *Chess Made Easy; Being a New Introduction to the Rudiments of that Scientific and Popular Game* (1836); *Chess Studies: Comprising One Thousand Games Actually Played during the Last Half Century* (1844); and *Chess and Chess Players: Consisting of Original Stories and Sketches* (1850). The most likely of these is the first. Not only was it the most frequently reprinted, but the wording "On Chess," more closely corresponds with this title.

2179. Walker, James Edward (1850–1911). *The Blessed Dead in Paradise. With Some Reply to Canon Luckock's 'After Death.'* (London: Elliot Stock, 1891). 305pp.

A805 (author, title), JS2146. Only edition in BL. Walker was educated at Corpus Christi College, Oxford and was sometime vicar of Cheltenham and afterward minister to the Scottish Church in Cheltenham. The book to which the author responds is Herbert Mortimer

Luckock's *After Death*, of which Dodgson owned a copy (see 1265).

2180. Walker, John (1732–1807). *The Rhyming Dictionary of the English Language in Which the Whole Language is Arranged According to its Terminations.* (London: George Routledge & Sons, [1879?]). 549pp. Revised and enlarged by J. Longmuir.

A325, B1280 (author, title, "revised and enlarged by J. Longmuir," date [1879]), JS2143. No matches for B1280 traced, however, Routledge published the edition revised and edited by Longmuir — an undated edition and an edition of 1888 have been traced. Walker was a lexicographer and author of a 1775 *Dictionary of the English Language* and other related works.

2181. [Walker, John] (1770–1831). *Oxoniana.* (London: Printed for Richard Phillips, [1809]). 4 vols. 238, 256, 248, 275pp.

A318 (author, title, 4 vols.), JS2144. Walker was a fellow of New College, Oxford from 1797 to 1820. He was a proprietor of the *Oxford Herald* and editor of *Selections from the Gentleman's Magazine.* The preface to volume I states that "The first volume will be found to contain historical and antiquarian articles relative to Oxford University in general, while the second is confined to those different colleges. The third and fourth volumes, after having noticed some of the public establishments, such as the Bodleian Library, the Picture Gallery, the Theatre, &c. contain letters from eminent men, curious articles of biography, miscellaneous anecdotes, and a collection of historical memoranda."

2182. Walker, Thomas (1784–1836). *The Original.* (London: H. Renshaw, 1836). 444pp. 2nd edition.

A312, D220 (author, title, edition, city, date), JS2145. D220 notes Dodgson's initials on the cover and title. Walker was a magistrate, principally known for the present work. A collection of the 29 numbers of Walker's weekly periodical which originally appeared between 20 May and 2 December 1835 (Walker died in January 1836). The purpose of the periodical was "to treat, as forcibly, perspicuously, and concisely as each subject and my own ability will allow, of whatever is most interesting and important in Religion and Politics, in Morals and Manners, and in our Habits and Customs."

2183. Walker, William Sydney (1795–1846), editor. *Corpus Poetarum Latinorum.* (London: J. Duncan, 1828). 1209pp.

A382 ("Corpus Poetarum"), JS112 (Anon./Literature). Earliest edition of the only matching title in BL or BOD. The book was reprinted several times. Walker was a poet and editor. This work is an anthology, in Latin, of the ancient Latin poets.

2184. [Walkingame, Francis] (fl. 1751–85). *The Tutor's Assistant; Being a Compendium of Arithmetic and a Complete Question-book.* (York: T. Wilson & Sons, 1842.) 199pp. Crosby's new edition, with considerable additions.

D221 (author, city, date), JS2147. Dodgson's copy is in HAC. Livingston notes that this copy has "annotations in pencil on pp. 55, 111, 129, 139." These are minor, but the most interesting is that on p. 129 where Dodgson notes, next to question 11, "Not a fair question in decimals." The brown ink inscription on the front endpaper, including five lines of Latin, elaborate scrolling, Dodgson's name and age (13), and the date (March 3, 1845) is reproduced on p. 166 of Livingston. On the rear pastedown is a rough draft of what became the first two lines of the Latin inscription. Dodgson's Latinizing of his own name in the inscription is significant in its foreshadowing of his choosing a pen name based on his own name Latinized. Walkingame was the author of two school books in arithmetic, both of which were revised and reprinted many times. This is a mathematics book designed for the use of school children (a schoolmaster's key was also available). It contains: Arithmetic in Whole Numbers, Vulgar Fractions, Decimals, Duodecimals, or Multiplication, The Mensuration of Circles, and "A Collection of Questions, set down promiscuously, for the greater Trial of the foregoing Rules."

2185. Wallace, Alfred Russell (1823–1913). *On Miracles and Modern Spiritualism. Three Essays.* (London: James Burns, 1875). 236pp.

A889 (author, title), JS2148. Earliest edition in BL. Russell was one of the great unsung scientists of the 19th century. Through his observations in the Malay archipelago he developed a theory of evolution similar to that being developed at the same time by Darwin. He was a believer in spiritualism. In the present work, according to a review in the *Academy*, the author "by no means confines himself to the spiritualistic phenomena which have occurred under his own observation or in our own time, but stretches his hypothesis in a most elastic fashion to all the occurrences in ancient and mediaeval history which have ever been reputed to be supernatural."

2186. Wallace, Robert. *The Practical Mathematician's Pocket Guide; A Set of Tables on Logarithms of Numbers.* (Glasgow: M'Phun, 1847?). One of McPhun's series of pocket guides.

D222 (author, title, city, n.d.), JS2149. D222 notes Dodgson's signature. No undated edition traced; the above is the earliest edition traced.

2187. Walton, Izaak (1593–1683). *The Lives of Donne, Wotton, Hooker, Herbert and Sanderson.* (London: W. Pickering, 1827). 442pp. *Pickering Diamond Classics* series.

A475 (author, title, date, series), JS2151. See 153 for more on this series of miniature books.

2188. Walton, Izaak and Charles Cotton (1630–87). *The Complete Angler. Two Parts. The First by Isaak Walton. The Second by Charles Cotton.* (London: William Pickering, 1826). 325pp. In the *Pickering Diamond Classics* series.

A475 (author, title, date, series), JS2150. A340 lists another edition of this title, but as it lists only author and title it is impossible to say what edition. See 153 for more on this series of miniature books.

2189. Walton, William (1813–1901). *A Collection of Problems in Illustration of the Principles of Theoretical Mechanics.* (Cambridge: W. P. Grant, 1842). 450pp.

E408 (author, title, date), F148, JS2152. E408 and F148 describe this as having Dodgson's signature.

2190. Wanley, Nathanial (1634–80). *The Wonders of the Little World: or, a General History of Man, Displaying the Various Faculties, Capacities, Powers and Defects of the Human Body and Mind.* (London: W. J. and J. Richardson, etc., 1806). 2 vols. 403, 543pp. New edition, with the addition of much new and curious matter, and the whole revised and corrected by William Johnston.

A850, B1284 (author, title, reviser, date), JS2153. First published in 1678, this compilation is, according to an old catalogue description found pasted into this 1806 edition, "A general history of man, recounting all the most memorable facts, inventions, etc. in art, science, politics, philosophy, it is chiefly remarkable as a concise memorial (in the words of contemporaries or eye-witnesses) of all such record-breaking feats of crime, cruelty, virtue, heroism, genius, eccentricity, etc., etc., as serve to display 'the faculties, powers and defects of the human body and mind.' Here may the reader sup full of horrors. The most savage barbarities of remote antiquity, the inhuman orgies of ancient and mediaeval tyranny, national sufferings and calamities, private wrongs, revenges, tortures, wholesale executions, and other nameless atrocities of the dark ages are here retailed side by side with every singularity of morals and manners."

2191. Ward, Artemus [pseud. of Charles Farrar Browne] (1834–67). *Artemus Ward's Lecture. (As Delivered at the Egyptian Hall, London.).* (London: John Camden Hotten; New York: G. W. Carleton & Co., 1869). 213pp. Edited by his executors, T. W. Robertson and E. P. Hingston. With 22 engraved plates.

A848 ("Artemus Ward's Lectures, 1869"), JS580. This is the only possible match traced as Ward did not publish a collection of lectures; this, however, matches all particulars except the plural of "lectures." Ward was a popular American humorist whose pseudonym was the name of a character he invented. He was successful as a traveling lecturer and author of many comic pieces. Subtitled *Artemus Ward Among the Mormons*, this is a send-up of the "illustrated lecture in the Egyptian Hall" genre. (For an example of this genre, see 1876).

2192. Ward, Artemus [pseud. of Charles Farrar Browne]. *The Complete Works of Charles F. Browne, Better Known as "Artemus Ward."* (London: John Camden Hotten, 1870). 518pp. With portrait by Geflowski the sculptor.

A911 (author, title), JS581. Earliest edition traced.

2193. Ward, Mary Augusta [née Arnold] (1851–1920). *Milly and Olly; or, a Holiday among the Mountains.* (London: Macmillan & Co., 1881). 224pp. Illustrated by Mrs. Alma Tadema.

A644 ("Milly and Olly by Mrs. T. Howard"), JS1259 (listed under Howard). Only 19th-century edition in BL and the only printing in MBC. Clearly a misprint in A644 — there is no other book in BL by this or any similar title. Also, Dodgson was good friends with the family of the author and even wrote her a letter (as Mary Arnold) shortly before her marriage to novelist Humphrey Ward. He was a friend of the Ward family as well. Mary Arnold Ward was the granddaughter of Rugby headmaster Thomas Arnold and niece of poet Matthew Arnold. Her younger sisters, Julia and Ethel, were among Dodgson's close child friends. This children's book was the first book by Mrs. Ward, who went on to write many novels for adults.

2194. Ward, Robert (d. 1883). *The Fallacies of Teetotalism; or, the Duty of the Legislature in Dealing with Personal Freedom, and an Elucidation of the Dietetic and Medicinal Virtues of Alcoholic Liquors.* (London: Simpkin, Marshall & Co., 1872).

B1282 (author, title, date), JS2154. An 1874 edition had 415pp. and added to the title: *Comprehending an Exposure of the False Doctrines of the United Kingdom Alliance, and of the Detestable Tyrrany of the Maine Law, or Permissive Bill.* The United Kingdom Alliance was a temperance organization originally dedicated to prohibition of alcohol. It still exists today as an educational and support group under the name Alliance House Foundation. The "Maine Law" was an 1846 statute prohibiting the sale of liquor in Maine.

2195. Ward, Thomas Humphry (1845–1926). *Men of the Reign: A Biographical Dictionary of Eminent Persons of British and Colonial Birth who have Died during the Reign of Queen Victoria.* (London: G. Routledge, 1885). 1028pp. With addenda.

A324 (title), JS245 (Anon./Reference). BL lists an 1883 edition, but this is almost certainly an error as the preface to the 1885 edition is dated 1885 and makes no mention of an earlier edition. This volume was uniform with the current edition of *Men of the Time* (see 2173). Ward was art critic for *The Times*.

Milly Tries the Stepping Stones. Illustration by Alma Tadema for Mary Ward's *Milly and Olly* (item 2193).

2196. Ward, William George (1812–82). *The Ideal of a Christian Church Considered in Comparison with Existing Practice; Containing a Defence of Certain Articles in the British Critic in Reply to Remarks on them in Mr. Palmer's "Narrative."* (London: J. Toovey, 1844).

A796 (author, title), JS2155. 1st edition (a 2nd followed in the same year and had 601pp.) The book referred to in the title is William Palmer's 1843 work *A Narrative of Events Connected with the Publication of the Tracts for the Times, with Reflections on Existing Tendencies to Romanism, and on the Present Duties and Prospects of Members of the Church.* Ward was educated at Christ Church, Oxford and was a fellow and mathematical tutor at Balliol. Shortly after the publication of this book, he was accepted into the Roman Catholic church. This work was a strong endorsement of the Roman church.

2197. Warden, Florence [pseud. of Mrs. Florence Alice James, née Price] (1857–1929). *The House on the Marsh.* (London: William Stevens, n.d. [1877?]). 210pp.

Not in JS. In his diary for 20 April 1885 Dodgson records, "I have lately read ... *The House on the Marsh* (a rather weak imitation of *Jane Eyre*)." The book was a neo-gothic melodrama, typical of its author's work. Only edition traced. Conjectural date from Yale.

2198. Waring, Edward (1734–1798). *Meditationes Algebraicæ*. (Cambridge: Typis Academicis Excudebat J. Archdeacon, 1770). 219pp.

Not in JS. Dodgson took this book out of the Christ Church Library on 5 March 1855 and returned it on 28 March. In his diary he wrote that he had "not succeeded in getting any information out of it, as I have not had time to do more than dip into it." (See *Diary, 1*). This is the earliest edition in the Bodleian (no Christ Church copies listed in BOD). Waring was an English physician and mathematician who held the Lucasian Chair at Cambridge. He was one of the most important English analysts of his time.

2199. Waring, Edward (1734–98). *Meditationes Analyticæ*. (Cambridge: University Press, 1785). Editio secunda. Cum nonnullis additionibus.

A938, D223 (author, title, city, date), JS2156. A massive work on the calculus.

2200. Warner, Anna Bartlett (1827–1915). *Tired Christians*. (London: Nisbet & Co., 1881). 77pp.

E234 (author, title, date), JS2157. Warner was an American novelist and writer of children's books. Her sister Susan was the author of the novel *Queechy*. A charming book on how Christians can enjoy theatre, music, dancing and similar amusements in an appropriate way. Dodgson was an enthusiastic theatergoer in a time when both his father and his bishop disapproved. He wrote an article, "The Stage and the Spirit of Reverence" defending the morality of some theatrical productions (see LCP, #258).

2201. Warren, Samuel (1807–77). *The Intellectual and Moral Development of the Present Age*. (Edinburgh: W. Blackwood and Sons, 1853). 127pp.

D224 (author, title, city, date), JS2158. A 2nd edition was published in the same year. Warren was a medical student, a barrister, and an M.P., but he achieved greatest success as the author

of many works, including legal texts and novels. This work is a pessimistic treatment of its subject.

2202. Warren, Samuel. *Miscellanies, Critical, Imaginative, and Juridical: Contributed to Blackwood's Magazine*. (Edinburgh: W. Blackwood and Sons, 1855). 501pp.

A650 (author, title), JS2159. Also published by Blackwood the same year in a 2-vol. edition; these are the only editions traced. It is possible that Dodgson owned only one of the two volumes. Includes, in vol. I: "The Bracelets," "My First Circuit," "Sir William Follett," "Memoir of John William Smith," "Who is the Murderer?," "The Duke of Marlborough," "The Paradise in the Pacific," "Uncle Tom's Cabin," "Calais," "Pegsworth"; and in vol. II: "The Mystery of Murder, and its Defence," "Modern State Trials," "The Martyr Patriots," "Speculators among the Stars," "A Few Personal Recollections of Christopher North."

2203. Warren, Samuel. *Now and Then*. (Edinburgh: W. Blackwood and Sons, 1848). 527pp. 1st edition.

A806, E340 (author, title, edition, date), F174, JS2161. F174 notes the gothic stamp. A follow-up to his popular novel *Ten Thousand A-Year*, this book was not a wide success.

2204. Warren, Samuel. *Passages from the Diary of a Late Physician*. (London: 1832–38). 3 vols. With notes and illustrations by the editor.

A651 (author, title, 3 vols.), JS2160. Earliest edition in BL. A popular collection of realistic, and at times somewhat morbid, short stories.

2205. Warren, Samuel. *Ten Thousand A-Year*. (Edinburgh: William Blackwood & Sons 1853). 3 vols. New edition, carefully revised, with notes & illustrations.

A806, E349 (author, title, 3 vols., date), JS2162. The author's most popular work, this novel tells of Miss Tittlebat Titmouse who inherits a fortune through a set of forged documents only to be blackmailed by the lawyers who helped her to her high station.

2206. Warton, John [pseud. of William Wood] (1770–1841). *Death-bed Scenes and Pastoral Conversations*. (London: John Murray, 1827–28). 3 vols. Edited by Wood's sons.

A754 ("Death-bed Scenes, 3 vols."), JS1079 (listed under Golburn). This is the only 3-volume work with a matching title in BL. Earliest 3-vol. edition in BL. JS lists this as "Personal Religional Death-bed Scenes" by Golburn because "Goldburn's Personal Religional" is listed immediately before this title in A754, but there is no work by Goldburn that includes the phrase "Death-bed Scenes" or any similar phrase in its title. Clearly the comma after "Religional" in A754 indicates the start of a new work by a new author. This work consists of pastoral conversations of a clergyman (originally published in 1826 in Philadelphia).

2207. Waters, John Henry. *Fits. Diagnosis and Immediate Treatment of Cases of Insensibility and Convulsions.* (London: J. and A. Churchill, 1879). 138pp.

E202 (author, title, date), JS2163. Waters was a surgeon to the Metropolitan Police and to Westminster Hospital.

2208. Watson, George Bott Churchill. *Hints for Pedestrians Practical and Medical.* (London: Bell and Daldy, 1862). 3rd edition, revised. 116pp.

B1283 (author, title, date), JS2165. A guide to walking. Includes "Introductory Observations" on the benefits of exercise, "pure air," and sections on seasonal preparations for walking, training, care of the feet, corns and bunions, nail care, dressing the feet prepatory to walking, swelling of the feet, boots and shoes, stockings and socks, coats and caps for walking, shooting jackets, velveteen and other types of jackets, waterproof coats, pantaloons and gaiters, shirts, caps and hats, walking sticks, gloves, allotment of the first exercise, early rising, breakfast, benefits of singing and loud talking, thirst and methods of relief, drinking of fermented liquors, cautions of sleeping after meals, conduct in storms, trees bad for shelter, and "Extracts for directing, encouraging, and cautioning Pedestrians on sundry matters." Dodgson enjoyed long walks, and late in his life often took walks of 15–20 miles in the Oxford area.

2209. Watson, John Selby (1804–84). *The Reasoning Power in Animals.* (London: Reeve & Co., 1867). 471pp.

A852 (author, title), JS2164. Only edition in BL. Watson was educated at Trinity College, Dublin and served as headmaster of the Proprietary Grammar School, Stockwell, Surrey. He edited many volumes of classical writings

for *Bohn's Classical Library.* Preface states, "This book has one object, which is to show that the inferior animals, or many of them, have a portion of that reason which is possessed by man."

2210. Watson, Richard (1781–1833). *Conversations for the Young: Designed to Promote the Profitable Reading of the Holy Scriptures.* (London: 1873).

E334 (author, title, date), JS2166. No edition of 1873 traced. The 10th edition (1861) was published in London by John Mason. Watson was a Wesleyan Minister. E334 notes that Dodgson's copy contains the "autograph of Lewis Carroll and the initials, by him, 'E. L. L.'"

2211. Watson, Thomas (1792–1882). *Lectures on the Principles and Practice of Physic.* (London: 1843). 2 vols.

A535 (author, title, 2 vols.), A587 (2 vols. in 4), JS2167. 1st book edition. Dodgson owned 2 copies. Watson was a prominent physician who held a number of important posts. He was Professor of Physic at King's College and Physician Extraordinary to the Queen. He was among those who attended Prince Albert in his final illness. First published in the *Medical Times,* 1840–42, this famous series of medical lectures was the first to suggest the use of rubber gloves.

2212. Watts, Alaric Alexander (1797–1854). *Poetical Sketches: The Profession, The Broken Heart, etc. With Stanzas for Music and Other Poems.* (London: Hurst, Robinson & Co., 1824). 189pp. 3rd edition, with additional poems. Illustrated with engravings.

D225 (author, title, city, date), JS2168. Dodgson's copy was bound with Hervey's *Australia* (see 934). Watts was a popular poet and journalist. This was his first book of poetry, originally published in 1822.

2213. W[atts], I[saac] (1674–1748). *Philosophical Essays on Various Subjects, viz. Space, Substance, Body, Spirit ... With some Remarks on Mr. Locke's Essay on the Human Understanding. To which is Subjoined a Brief Scheme of Ontology, or the Science of Being in General with its Affections.* (London: Richard Ford, Richard Hett, 1733). 402pp.

Not in JS. In his diary for 19 March 1855, Dodgson writes, "I spent most of the time [at the Christ Church library] however over Watt's *Philosophical Essays*: the part on 'Space' is very interesting, I do not think conclusive." (See *Diary 1*). This is the 1st edition (no Christ Church copies listed in BOD). Watts was a non-conformist pastor best known for his prolific hymn writing.

2214. Weatherly, Frederick E[dward] (1848–1929). *Elsie's Expedition*. (London: Frederick Warne and Co.; New York: Scribner, Welford and Armstrong, [1874]). 144pp. Illustrated by H. Cross.

Not in JS. In his diary for 11 September 1891, Dodgson included this title in his list of "books of the *Alice* type" he had collected. Weatherly was educated at Brasnose College, Oxford, and called to the bar in 1887. He was a prolific writer of illustrated books for children and provided text for a number of early mechanical books.

2215. Weatherly, F[rederick] E[dward]. *There's Many a Slip, Twixt Cup and Lip. And Other Proverbs in Verse*. (London: Hildesheimer & Faulkner, [1884]). 21pp. Illustrations by W. J. Hodgson.

Uncertain. F184 (author, title, n.d., illustrator), not numbered in JS. Only edition in BL. Identified as Dodgson's only by the gothic stamp.

2216. [Webb, Jane, later Loudon] (1807–58). *The Mummy! A Tale of the Twenty Second Century*. (London: Henry Colburn, 1827). 3 vols.

A820 (title, 3 vols.), JS2169. This is the only 3-volume edition of the only matching title in BL. Webb attracted the attention of her future husband John Claudius Loudon (1783–1843) through the publication of this novel. She later assisted him in his work as a botanist and edited many of his works following his death. *The Mummy* is a futuristic novel set in the year 2126 in which a Catholic priest and the Mummy of Cheops try to control the choice of the next Queen of England. Includes inventions such as mobile housing, controllable weather, and mechanical farming.

2217. [Webster, David], editor. *A Collection of Rare and Curious Tracts on Witchcraft and the Second Sight: with an Original Essay on Witchcraft*. (Edinburgh: D. Webster, 1820). 183pp.

B1296 (title, city, date), JS2171. Includes "News from Scotland Declaring the Damnable Life of Doctor Fian a Notable Sorcerer who was Burned at Edinburgh 1591," "Extracts from King James's Daemononologie Concerning Sorcery and Witchcraft," "An Answer of a Letter from an Gentleman in Fife to a Nobleman Containing a Brief Account of the Barbarous Treatment these Poor Women Accused of Witchcraft Met," and other tracts relating to witchcraft and second sight.

2218. Webster, Noah (1758–1843). *A Dictionary of the English Language: Intended to Exhibit 1. The Origin and Affinities of Every English Word, as Far as They have been Ascertained, with its Primary Signification, as Now Generally Established; 2. The Orthography and the Pronunciation of Words, as Sanctioned by Reputable Usage, and Where this Usage is Divided, as Determinable by a Reference to the Principle of Analogy; 3. Accurate and Discriminating Definitions of Technical and Scientific Terms, with Numerous Authorities and Illustrations: To which are Prefixed an Introductory Dissertation on the Origin, History, and Connection of the Languages of Western Asia and of Europe, and a Concise Grammar, Philosophical and Practical, of the English Language*. (London: Printed for Black, Young, and Young, 1830). 12 parts.

A388 ("Webster's Dictionary"), JS2170. This is the 1st English edition of Webster's most famous dictionary, originally published in 1828 as *An American Dictionary of the English Language*, a book reprinted and revised many times during the 19th century. It seems less likely that Dodgson would have owned either of Webster's earlier works, the 1807 *A Compendious Dictionary of the English Language*, or the 1807 *A Dictionary of the English Language, Compiled for the Use Of Common Schools in the United States*. A388 does not specify multiple volumes. Though copies as described above exist bound in 1 volume, the collected edition was published by Black, Young, and Young in 1832 in 2 volumes. In all likelihood, Dodgson owned one of the many later editions.

2219. Weigall, Charles Harvey (1794–1877). *The Art of Figure Drawing: Containing Practical Instructions for a Course of Study in this Branch of Art.* (London: Winsor & Newton, 1856). 53pp. With 17 illustrations drawn on wood by the author. 7th edition?

E317 (author, title, publisher [given as Windsor & Newton], date), JS2172. E317 notes that this has "photographic formulæ in Lewis Carroll's hand inside cover." Though no edition of 1856 has been traced, the 6th edition was published in 1855 by Windsor and Newton and the book had reached a 26th edition by 1881. Weigall was an artist.

2220. Welby, Horace, [pseud. of John Timbs] (1801–75). *Mysteries of Life, Death, and Futurity.* (London: Kent & Co., 1861). 276pp. "Illustrated from the best and latest authorities."

A883 ("Mysteries of Life, Death and Futurility"), JS310 ("Death and Futurility" in Anon./Theology) and JS320 ("Mysteries of Life" in Anonymous/Theology). Though listed as two titles in JS and with a misspelled word in A883, Timbs' book is clearly what is described. Earliest edition in BL. Timbs was a British antiquary who served as editor of the *Mirror of Literature, Harlequin, Literary World*, and as sub-editor of the *Illustrated London News.* He founded and edited the *Year-Book of Science and Art* and wrote scores of volumes, several of them collections of odd bits of information.

2221. Weld, Charles Richard (1813–69). *Last Winter in Rome.* (London: Longmans, Green, 1865). 589pp. With frontispiece lithographed by Hanhart and 4 woodcut plates.

A589 (title), JS357 (Anon./Topography). Only edition of the only matching title in BL or BOD. The following two titles (in A590) are both by Weld (see below). Weld was educated in Dublin and called to the bar in 1842. He was for many years assistant secretary to the Royal Society, and in 1847 published a history of that society. He wrote a number of works related to his travels including this title and the next two. His brother-in-law was Alfred, Lord Tennyson. Dodgson met Mrs. Weld in August 1857, and it was his photograph of Weld's daughter Agnes Grace as Little Red Riding Hood which helped secure Dodgson an introduction to Tennyson. Dodgson dined with Weld at least once, on 15 August 1864.

2222. Weld, Charles Richard. *The Pyrenees, West and East.* (London: Longman, Brown, Green, Longmans, & Roberts, 1859). 410pp.

A590 ("The Pyrenees East and West"), JS373 (Anon./Topography). Only edition in BL. Despite the difference in title, this is clearly the book referred to in A590. There are no other close matches in BL, and the books immediately preceding (A589) and following (in A590) are also by Weld.

2223. Weld, Charles Richard. *Two Months in the Highlands, Orcadia, and Skye.* (London: Longman, Green, Longman, and Roberts, 1860). 404pp. With coloured lithographed views.

A590 ("Two Months in the Highlands"), JS374. Only edition in BL and the closest match to A590. The two books preceding this (A589 and A590) are also by Weld (see above).

2224. Weld, Charles Richard. *Statistical Companion to the Pocket Book.* (London: 1844).

E250 (author, title, date), JS2173. An annual publication, this was the first issue. Probably a companion to *The Pocket-book Almanack*, an annual published by the Religious Tract Society beginning in 1843. BL lists that publication under the heading Ephemerides, meaning a list of locations of heavenly bodies computed in advance.

2225. Welldon, James Edward Cowell (1854–1937). *The Spiritual Life, and Other Sermons.* (London: Macmillan & Co., 1888). 259pp.

B1285 (author, title, date), JS2174. Welldon served as headmaster of various Public Schools before taking up the post of Bishop of Calcutta.

2226. [Welsman, M. S.]. *A Guide to the Unprotected in Everyday Matters Relating to Property and Income.* (London: Macmillan & Co., 1867). 164pp. 3rd edition.

E271 (title and date), JS92 (Anon./Law).

2227. Welton, James (b. 1864). *A Manual of Logic.* (London: W. B. Clive, 1891–96). 2 vols.

A517, B1286 (author, title, date, Vol. I), B1287 (author, title, date, Vol. II), JS2175. Welton wrote several works on logic and on education. Dodgson also owned Holman's companion to this book (see 953).

2228. Westcott, Brooke Foss (1825–1901). *The Gospel of the Resurrection: Thoughts on its Relation to Reason and History.* (London and Cambridge: Macmillan and Co., 1866). 216pp.

A788 (author, title), JS2177. This is the 1st edition as described in MBC. Westcott was for 20 years Professor of Divinity at Cambridge. In 1890 he became Bishop of Durham. He was known for his Biblical commentaries, his work with missionaries, and his social work in the Diocese of Durham.

2229. Westcott, Brooke Foss. *The Historic Faith. Lectures on the Apostles' Creed.* (London: Macmillan, 1883). 261pp.

A786 (author, title), JS2176. 1st edition as described in MBC.

2230. Westminster Divines. *The Shorter Catechism, Presented by the Assembly of Divines at Westminster to both Houses of Parliament.* (1810).

E373 (title, date), JS328 (Anon./Theology). No copy of this edition traced; details taken from E373. The meeting of church leaders at Westminster in 1643 was convened by Parliament to reform the Church in England. One result was the writing of two catechisms (Larger and Shorter), approved by Parliament in 1648. The Shorter Catechism, probably largely written by A. Tuckney and John Wallis, has become an important document for the Presbyterian Church.

2231. Whately, Richard (1787–1863). *Logic.* (London: Griffin, 1849). 112pp. In the series titled: *Encyclopædia Metropolitana; or, System of Universal Knowledge: On a Methodical Plan Projected by Samuel Taylor Coleridge.* 2nd edition, revised. *First Division. Pure Sciences.*

B1289 ("Whately, R. Logic, from the Encyclopaedia Metropolitana ... 1849"), JS2178. Only edition of Whately's *Logic* dated 1849 traced. Another possibility is of a misprint in B1289, since the standard edition of Whately's work entered its 9th edition in 1848 and was reprinted several times (including 1850 and 1859). That work was as follows: *Elements of Logic: Comprising the Substance of the Article in the Encyclopædia Metropolitana: With Additions.* (London: J. W. Parker, 1848). 402pp. 9th edition. On the other hand, the use of the title "*Logic*" rather than "*Elements of Logic*" in B1289 would seem to favor the entry above. Whately was a fellow and tutor at Oriel College, Oxford and in 1831 became Archbishop of Dublin. This popular work on Logic brought great interest to the subject in Great Britain.

2232. Wheeler, Mrs. Charlotte Bickersteth. *Memoir of John Lang Bickersteth, Late of Rugby School.* (London: Religious Tract Society, [1850]). 103pp. With a preface by the Rev. J[ohn] Bickersteth. With a view of Rugby.

E179 (title, date [c. 1847]), JS509 (listed under Bickersteth). J. L. Bickersteth, son of Henry Bickersteth of the Cape of Good Hope, entered Rugby School on 23 April 1846 at the age of 14. He died on 28 January 1847. Dodgson entered Rugby on 27 January 1846, and almost certainly would have known Bickersteth. The book, which quotes from Bickersteth's letters and journal, gives a view of life at Rugby during Dodgson's tenure. The text does not mention boys by name, so it is not known if any of the boys described is Dodgson.

2233. Whewell, William (1794–1866). *History of the Inductive Sciences, From the Earliest to the Present Times.* (London: J. W. Parker, 1837). 3 vols. 438, 524, 624pp.

A385 (author, title, 3 vols.), JS2179. Earliest edition in BL. Whewell was Master of Trinity College, Cambridge and later Vice-Chancellor of that University, and did much to introduce the study of natural sciences. A highly influential polymath, he was a founder of the British Association for the Advancement of Science. A major work that looks at a wide range of "sciences" from Greek philosophy to the history of astronomy; from mineralogy, botany and anatomy to modern sciences such as acoustics and optics.

2234. Whewell, William. *The Mechanical Euclid, Containing the Elements of Mechanics and Hydrostatics Demonstrated after the Manner of the Elements of Geometry.* (Cambridge: J. & J. J. Deighton, 1843). 136pp. The 4th edition carefully adapted to the ordinary examination for the degree of B.A.

E239 (author, title, date), JS2180.

2235. Whewell, William. *The Philosophy of the Inductive Sciences, Founded upon their History*. (London: J. W. Parker, 1840). 2 vols. 523, 586pp.

A385 (author, title, 2 vols.), JS2181. Earliest edition in BL. Whewell here presents his theory of induction, which he says is based on Bacon.

2236. [Whitaker, Joseph] (1820–95). *An Almanack for the Year of Our Lord 1888*. (London: J. Whitaker, 1888).

E44 ("Whitaker's Almanack, 1888"), JS220 (Anon./Periodicals). *Whitaker's Almanack* began publication in 1869, and continues today. The 1889 edition described itself as "Containing an account of the astronomical and other phenomena, a large amount of information respecting the government finances, population, commerce, and general statistics of the British empire throughout the world with some notice of other countries, &c., &c."

2237. White, Gilbert (1720–93). *The Natural History and Antiquities of Selborne, in the County of Southampton: with Engravings and an Appendix*. (London: B. White and Son, 1789). 468pp. 1st edition.

A494 (author, title, edition, date), JS2182. White was born and died at Selborne. He was a fellow of Oriel College Oxford for 50 years, and for a time served as Dean. In a series of letters to Thomas Pennant and Daines Barrington (see 112), White details his twenty years (1767–87) of observations of the natural history of Selborne. His literary style and meticulous observations make this a classic of both literature and natural history. CHEAL calls this book "the solitary classic of natural history." Dodgson also owned a book which contained excerpts from this work (see 1070).

2238. White, James (ca. 1820–1862). *Landmarks of the History of England*. (London: 1855).

Not in JS. In his diary for 1 August 1855 Dodgson notes, "At present I am engaged on Ruskin's *Stones of Venice* and White's *Landmarks of English History*." (*See Diary, 1*). This is the only edition in BL of the only possible matching title. White was a historical and miscellaneous writer educated at Pembroke College, Oxford. He served as vicar of Loxley, Warwickshire and died at Bonchurch, Isle of Wight.

2239. Whitelaw, Thomas (1840–1917). *How Is the Divinity of Jesus Depicted in the Gospels and Epistles?* (London: Hodder and Stoughton, 1883). 271pp.

A792 (author, title), JS2183. Only edition in BL. Whitelaw was a Presbyterian minister who traveled widely doing work for the Scottish church.

2240. Whiter, Walter (1758–1832). *Etymologicon Magnum, or Universal Etymological Dictionary, on a New Plan. With Illustrations Drawn from Various Languages*. (Cambridge: Printed by F. Hodson, for the author, 1800). 507pp. Part the first (no more published).

A940, B1290 (author, title, date), JS2184 (not listed separately from *Etymologicon Universale* [see below], which is not a continuation of this work).

2241. Whiter, Walter. *Etymologicon Universale; or, Universal Etymological Dictionary. On a New Plan. In which is it is Shewn, that Consonants are Alone to be Regarded in Discovering the Affinities of Words, and that the Vowels are to be Wholly Rejected ... With Illustrations Drawn from Various Languages*. (Cambridge: Printed at the University Press, 1811–25). 3 vols.

A940, B1291 (author, title, date [1811], 3 vols.), JS2184 (not listed separately from *Etymologicon Magnum* [see above], of which the present work is not a continuation).

2242. Whitmore, C[harles] A[lgernon] (1851–1908). *Six Years of Unionist Government, 1886–1892*. (London: Edward Arnold, 1892). 88pp.

E204 (author, title, date), JS2185. Whitmore was a Conservative M.P. for Chelsea. An assessment of the progress at home and abroad (with special reference to Ireland) of the government of Lord Salisbury (a friend of Dodgson) from 1886 through 1892. The "Unionist" government was made possible by the defection of some liberals from Gladstone following his support of Irish Home Rule. They joined the conservative Salisbury, giving him a majority. This work concludes, "We, who have been glad to support Unionist principles through six years of unscrupulous opposition and incessant depreciation, ought to take every opportunity at the conclusion of this parliament to record our sense of the good practical work which has been done in every quarter of the Empire, and in every department of affairs, by the Government of Lord Salisbury."

2243. Whittock, Nathaniel (1791–1860). *The Microcosm of Oxford, Containing a Series of Views of the Churches, Colleges, Halls and Other Public Buildings of the University and City of Oxford.* (Oxford: Whittock, [1828]). 40pp. 37 plates.

Uncertain. F181 (author, title, city, n.d.), not numbered in JS. Identified as Dodgson's only by the gothic stamp. Earliest undated edition in BL or BOD. Whittock was a lithographer and printer at Oxford who removed his business to London in 1828.

2244. Whitworth, William Allen (1840–1905). *Choice and Chance: Two Chapters of Arithmetic. With an Appendix Containing the Algebraical Treatment of Permutations and Combinations Newly Set Forth.* (Cambridge: Deighton, Bell and Co.; London: Bell and Daldy, 1867). 160pp.

D226, JS2186. Dodgson's copy is in HAC, and has his signature in brown ink on the front endpaper. A brown ink inscription on the title page ("With the author's compts.") is marked through in brown ink. Includes, as examples, two of Dodgson's interests—in the "Choice" section, elections and in the "Chance" section, games.

2245. Whitworth, W[illiam] A[llen] and others, editors. *The Messenger of Mathematics.* (London & Cambridge: 1872–77?). 6 vols.

A586 (title, 6 vols.), JS151. This periodical continued until 1929; A586 does not specify which 6 volumes Dodgson owned. This is a continuation of *The Oxford, Cambridge, and Dublin Messenger of Mathematics, a Journal Supported by Junior Mathematical Students, and Conducted by a Board of Editors, Composed of Members of the Three Universities*, published in 5 volumes from 1862 to 1871. Since only five volumes were published before the name change, and since A586 specifies only "Messenger of Mathematics" it seems likely that Dodgson's volumes were from the latter incarnation. The first six volumes are described here.

2246. *Who Wrote It? A Dictionary of Common Poetical Quotations in the English Language*. (London: George Bell & Sons, 1878). 159pp.

B1292 (title, date), JS258 (Anon./Reference). Probably the same as A358 ("Dictionary of Poetical Quotations"), which is listed together with another item in JS233 (Anon./Reference). Originally published in 1855 as *Where is It? A Dictionary of Common Poetical Quotations in the English Language.*

2247. *Why Did God Create Man*. (Brighton: 1850).

E225 (title, city, date), JS339 (Anon./Theology). No copy traced; description taken from E225.

2248. *Why Evil was Permitted and Kindred Topics*. (Pittsburgh: 1881). With "Chart of the Ages."

E214 (title, city, date), JS338. No copy traced; description taken from E214. E214 notes this was "marked in Lewis Carroll's hand as scarce."

2249. Wiclif, John [a.k.a. John Wyclif] (ca. 1330–84), translator. *A Smaller Biblia Pauperum. Conteynynge Thyrtie and Eyghte Wodecuttes Illustratynge the Lyfe, Parablis, and Miraclis off oure Blessid Lord & Savioure Jhesus Crist. With the Propre Descrypcions Theroff Extracted from the Original Texte off Iohn Wiclif, Somtyme Rector of Lutterworth.* (London: Unwin Brothers, 1884). Preface by the late Verie Rev. A. P. Stanley, Dean of Westminster.

A769 (title, date), JS492. A reduced-size reproduction of a book first published in 1877 as part of the celebration of England's first printer, William Caxton. The printer's note reads, in part: "The text has been selected from Wiclif's translation of the New Testament.... The borders and ornaments which embellish the letterpress pages are exact fac-similes of those used in a Book of Hours.... The paper has been specially made by hand in Holland, by precisely the ancient method.... The binding is in accordance with the style of the period." Wyclif was an English reformer who taught at Oxford and held several church livings before being condemned as a heretic. He preached in the vernacular and oversaw this, the first translation of the Vulgate Bible into English. Stanley was a fellow of University College, Oxford and for a time Regius Professor of Ecclesiastical History. He was a Broad Churchman and a vocal advocate for university reform as well as a highly influential preacher.

2250. Wigram, G[eorge] V[icesimus] (1805–79), editor. *The Hebraist's Vade Mecum; A First Attempt at a Complete Verbal Index to the Contents of the Hebrew and Chaldee Scriptures. Arranged According to Grammar, etc.* (London: Groombridge & Sons, 1867). 582pp.

A581, B1074 (title, date), JS1061 (listed under Gesenius). This is the only matching title in BL. A581 lists two books by Gesenius plus this item, hence the error in JS. Wigram was a prominent and active member of the Plymouth Brethren. He organized the creation of two concordances designed to assist the understanding of the scriptures by non-scholars. He also provided much of the financing for the project.

2251. Wigram, Joseph C[otton] (1798–1867). *The Geography of the Holy Land: with References which Serve as a Key to the Map of Palestine; also, a Copious Index; and the Following Illustrations, a Small Map of Palestine, a Plan of Jerusalem and its Environs, and a Plan of the Temple and its Courts.* (London: Roake and Varty, 1836). 91pp. 2nd edition.

E242 (author, title), JS2187. E242 notes that this has "early autograph of Lewis Carroll twice repeated with date." Earliest edition traced. Wigram was Bishop of Rochester and brother of G. V. Wigram (see above).

2252. Wilberforce, Samuel (1805–73). *Addresses to the Candidates for Ordination, on the Questions in the Ordination Service.* (Oxford and London: J. H. and Jas. Parker, 1860). 258pp.

B1293 (author, title, date), JS2188. Wilberforce became Bishop of Oxford in 1845, and thus was Dodgson's bishop from Dodgson's arrival at Oxford in 1850 until Wilberforce's translation to Winchester in 1869. He founded the Cuddesdon Theological College near Oxford in 1854 (Dodgson's High Church friend H. P. Liddon served as first vice-principal of Cuddesdon). Wilberforce's stance against clergy attending the theatre may have been one reason why Dodgson chose to remain a deacon and

not take priest's orders. Many members of Wilberforce's family defected to Rome in the aftermath of the Oxford Movement, but Samuel (son of the anti-slave reformer William Wilberforce) remained in the Church of England until his 1873 death in a riding accident. He argued the side of creationists in the famous debate against the Darwinist Thomas Huxley at the Oxford University Museum in 1861. Dodgson was ordained deacon by Wilberforce in that same year, and it seems likely that he used the present work in preparation for his ordination. In his preface, Wilberforce writes that the purpose of the essays is to, "explain the meaning of our Ordinal, to stir up the devout and religious affections of those who were about to seek the great and blessed, but, at the same time, perilous office of Ministers of Christ." The titles and topics of the addresses are taken from the Ordination Offices (for priests and deacons).

2253. Wilberforce, Samuel. *Essays Contributed to the "Quarterly Review."* (London: J. Murray, 1874). 2 vols.

A347 ("Wilberforce's Essays, 2 vols."), JS2189. Only edition of the only matching title in BL. *The Spectator* wrote, "Our advice to those who wish heartily to enjoy the late Bishop of Winchester's writing is to read the essays in the first volume [containing articles on natural history and similar subjects] ... and leave his polemical disquisitions to the oblivion we think he would himself have desired for them." Among the important essays reprinted here is Wilberforce's review of Darwin's *Origin of Species*.

2254. Wilberforce, Samuel. *Words of Counsel on Some of the Chief Difficulties of the Day: Bequeathed to the Church in the Writings of Samuel Wilberforce, Late Lord Bishop of Winchester.* (Oxford: J. Parker, 1875). 437pp. Collected and arranged by Thomas Vincent Fosbery.

A774 (author, title), JS2190. Only edition in BL. A collection of pieces by Wilberforce. Fosbery (1807–75) was chaplain to Wilberforce.

2255. Wilberforce, William (1759–1833). *Le Christianisme des Gens du Monde, Mis en Opposition avec le Véritable Christianisme.* (Montauban: Imprimerie de Philippe Crosilhes, 1821). Vol. 2 (of 2) only. Traduit sur la onzième édition par M. Frossard.

Uncertain. Not in JS. Listed in WS (author,

Frontispiece from E. G. Wilcox's *Evie; or, The Visit to Orchard Farm* (item 2256). Dodgson suggested rewriting the text to fit this picture.

title, date, vol. 2 only) and identified by gothic stamp and property label only. Not in WWC. Wilberforce was a highly influential Evangelical politician who campaigned for the abolition of the slave trade and for many other social reforms. A translation into French of Wilberforce's most frequently reprinted work, *A Practical View of the Prevailing Religious System of Professed Christians, in the Higher and Middle Classes of this Country, Contrasted with Real Christianity*.

2256. Wilcox, E[lizabeth] G[eorgina] [later Mrs. E. G. Allen] (1848–1934). *Evie; or, The Visit to Orchard Farm*. (London: Wells Gardner & Co., 1889). 124pp.

A557, A558, A560, E290, JS2191. The listing in E290 specifies n.d. Other entries list author and title or title only. Only edition. The author was Dodgson's cousin, and Dodgson served as her literary advisor. In May of 1888 he wrote to Macmillan, enquiring where his cousin's story might find publication. Though neither of the publishers recommended by Macmillan were Wells Gardner, Dodgson seems to have been instrumental in getting the book published. In a letter to Wilcox on 8 October 1889, Dodgson wrote, "I found it very refreshing, when jaded with my own work at *Sylvie and Bruno*, to lie down on the sofa and read a chapter of *Evie*. I like it very much: and am glad to have helped bring it out. I would have been a real loss to the Children of England, if you had burned the MS, as you once thought of doing." (See *Letters*, 758 and *Macmillan*, 244). The book is the story of a sick girl who discovers the delights of the country.

2257. [**Wilcox**, Elizabeth Georgina] [later Mrs. E. G. Allen]. *Little Humphrey's Adventure.* (London: Society for the Promotion of Christian Knowledge, [1877]).

Not in JS. Dodgson refers to this, his cousin's first book for children, in his introduction to *The Lost Plum-Cake*, in a way that makes it clear he had read it. Only edition in BL.

2258. Wilcox, E[lizabeth] G[eorgina] [Mrs. E. G. Allen]. *The Lost Plum-Cake A Tale for Tiny Boys.* ([Oxford]: Privately printed, 1896).

Not in JS. Dodgson's copy was sold at Marchpane Booksellers, London. It had his autographed monogram. See below for a description of this title and its publication.

2259. Wilcox, E[lizabeth] G[eorgina] [Mrs. E. G. Allen]. *The Lost Plum-Cake A Tale for Tiny Boys.* (London: Macmillan and Co., Limited, 1897). 101pp. With 9 illustrations by E. L. Shute. Introduction by Lewis Carroll. Cover design by Gertrude Thomson.

Not in JS. Dodgson oversaw the publication of a private edition of this title (see above) and then helped it to be published in an expanded version by Macmillan. He recruited the illustrator and cover designer and convinced Macmillan to publish the book on the condition that he write a preface. This introductory piece was the last work of Dodgson's to appear in print in his lifetime. Whether he saw the published book before his death on 14 January 1898 is not known, but he certainly read the text. See *Illustrators* for Dodgson's correspondence with Gertrude Thomson concerning her lettering for the front cover and *Macmillan* for his correspondence with the publisher. See also WMGC, 201. The story, for very young children to read themselves, is composed in words of no more than four letters each.

2260. Wilcox, W[illiam] E[dward] (1835–76). *Spa Sketches, etc.* (London: 1876).

D227 (author, title, city, date), JS2192. Copies in BL and BOD catalogued as above; no other copies traced. Wilcox was Dodgson's cousin and a good friend. Dodgson visited the Wilcoxes in Whitburn and entertained William and his wife in Oxford.

2261. Wilde, John. *Constipation: Its Origin and Homœopathic Treatment; and the Use of Enemata.* (London: Homœopathic Publishing Company, 1877). 2nd edition, 10th thousand. 28pp. 7th of a series of *Homœopathic Missionary Tracts*.

Not listed separately in JS (see JS163). Dodgson's copy is in HAC in a bound volume with

Frontispiece by E. L. Shute for E. G. Wilcox's *The Lost Plum-Cake* (item 2259).

7 other tracts from this series and one additional Homœopathic pamphlet (see 970). Wilde, a member of the Royal College of Surgeons and licentiate of the Royal College of Physicians is described in the preface of the pamphlet below as one who "practised as an Allopath [i.e. traditional physician] for twelve [years] and has been a Homœopath for the last fourteen years," and has had "ample opportunities for comparing the results of the two systems." Wilde favors use of enema, which he describes as widespread in Europe but shunned in England.

2262. Wilde, John. *Homœopathy Explained: A Word to the Medical Profession.* (London: Homœopathic Publishing Company, 1877). 2nd edition, 10th thousand. 29pp. 6th of a series of *Homœopathic Missionary Tracts.*

Not listed separately in JS (see JS163). Dodgson's copy is in HAC in a bound volume with 7 other tracts from this series and one additional Homœopathic pamphlet (see 970). Wilde's conclusion here is that Homœopathy works and is superior to traditional medicine.

2263. [Wiljalba, Frikell] (1818–1903). *The Book of 500 Curious Puzzles: Containing a Large Collection of Entertaining Paradoxes, Perplexing Deceptions in Numbers, and Amusing Tricks in Geometry.* (New York: Dick & Fitzgerald, [1859]). 116pp.

A897 ("Curious Puzzles"), JS146 (Anon./ Mathematics). Only edition of the only closely matching title traced. Some sources give the author as George Arnold. Possibly Arnold translated and edited the work in much the same way that Wiljalba's work *The Secret Out* was translated and edited by W. H. Cremer. Dodgson's own interest in puzzles and related amusements would have made this book appeal to him.

2264. Wilkes, Anna. *Ireland: Ur of the Chaldees.* (London: Trübner, 1873). 207pp.

Uncertain. F163 (author, title, date), JS2193. Identified as Dodgson's only by the gothic stamp. The book states "Ireland had preserved to the present time more distinct marks of the ancient Ur than can be pointed to in any other country, whether of Asia or Europe."

2265. [Wilkins, John] (1614–72). *The Discovery of a World in the Moone. Or, A Discourse Tending to Prove, that it is Probable*

there May be Another Habitable World in that Planet. (London: Printed by E. G. for Michael Sparke and Edward Forrest, 1638). 209pp.

A465 (author, title, date), JS2194. Master of Trinity College, Cambridge and eventually Bishop of Chester, Wilkins promoted the view of the universe developed by Copernicus, Kepler, and Galileo. In addition to arguing that the moon was a three dimensional body with an earth-like landscape, he claimed that it was habitable and that travel from the earth to the moon would one day be possible. This work, along with his 1640 volume *A Discourse Concerning a New Planet*, was aimed at the general reader, not the scientist. He also addressed theological issues concerning life on the moon. Many of Wilkins' propositions were correct; others were not.

2266. Wilkinson, George Howard (1833–1907). *Some Laws in God's Spiritual Kingdom.* (London: Wells Gardner & Co., [1886]). 184pp.

A771 (title), JS329 (Anon./Theology). Only pre–1898 edition in BL. Wilkinson was an undergraduate at Oxford at the same time as Dodgson and was later successively Bishop of Truro and of St. Andrew's, Dunkeld and Dunblane. Dodgson heard him preach on 14 January 1872 and called him a "marvellous preacher."

2267. Wilkinson, James John G. (1812–99). *The Human Body and its Connexion with Man, Illustrated by the Principal Organs.* (London: Chapman and Hall, 1851). 491pp.

A514 (title), JS165 (Anon./Medical). Earliest edition of the only matching title in BL or BOD. The author was a member of the Royal College of Surgeons and wrote several medical books. Emerson wrote of him, "Wilkinson, the editor of Swedenborg, the annotator of Fourier, and the champion of Hahnemann, has brought to metaphysics and to physiology a native vigour, with a catholic perception of relations, equal to the highest attempt, and a rhetoric like the armoury, of the invincible knights of old." In his preface the author argues for universal education and calls this work on human physiology one designed for the "great outlying population [i.e. the masses]."

2268. Wilkinson, John Bourdieu (?1832–85). *Instructions on the "Parables of our*

Lord and Saviour Jesus Christ." (London and New York: [1870]). With a preface by T[homas] T[hellusson] Carter.

B1294 (author, title, author of preface), JS2195. Only edition in BL with a preface by Carter. Wilkinson was educated at St. Peter's, Cambridge, and served as perpetual curate at Lavender Hill, Battersea. See 362 for a note on Carter.

2269. Williams, Frederic Condé (1844– 1917). *Journalistic Jumbles; or, Trippings in Type, etc.* ([London]: Leadenhalle Presse: 1884). 80pp. In *Ye Leadenhalle Presse Oblong Shilling-Series.*

E105 (title), JS242 (Anon./Reference). Only edition in BL. A note in E105 states "Lewis Carroll searched the book for an error and found it — in the last sentence."

2270. Williams, Henry Willard (1821–95). *Our Eyes, and How to Take Care of Them.* (London: William Tegg, 1871). [32]pp.

E378 (author, title, date), JS2197. Dodgson's copy, with his signature on the title page, is in the collection of David Lansley, Lincolnshire. The author was a Massachusetts ophthalmologist. Originally published in *Atlantic Monthly,* Jan.–May, 1871. A sourcebook of ophthalmology.

2271. Williams, Howard (1837–1931). *The Superstitions of Witchcraft.* (London: Longmans, Green and Co., 1865). 278pp.

A903 (author, title), JS2196. Only edition in BL. Explains witchcraft, its history and persecutions, and looks at the effect of witchcraft on faith.

2272. Williams, Isaac (1802–65). *The Cathedral, or the Catholic and Apostolic Church in England.* (Oxford: J. H. & J. Parker, 1857). 296pp.

Not in JS. In his diary for 17 May 1855 Dodgson writes, "I got Williams' *Cathedral* the other day, and was much disappointed in it. I hardly know why I expected it to be better than his *Thoughts in Past Years*— if there is any difference, I should say that the *Cathedral* was decidedly inferior to the other, in point of Poetry." The edition described above was published closest (of those listed in BL) to the date when Dodgson read the book. Williams was an Oxford tutor, theologian and Tractarian poet. He was a fellow (and later Vice-president) of

Trinity College, and the author of three of the "Tracts for the Times." The present book is a collection of religious poems, each associated with an architectural element of a cathedral.

2273. Williams, Issac. *Thoughts in Past Years.* (Oxford: Parker, 1852). 405pp. 6th edition.

Not in JS. In his diary for 7 January 1855, Dodgson wrote, "I read some of *Thoughts in Past Years* ... they seem to be neither poetical nor reverential: affectation and mannerism throughout." The edition described above was published closest (of those listed in BL) to the date when Dodgson read the book. A book of poetry originally published in 1838.

2274. [Williams, W.] *The Art of Landscape Painting in Oil Colours.* (London: Winsor & Newton, 1863). 63pp.

E316 (title, date, publisher), JS28 (Anon./ Art). An instruction manual for painters. Dodgson dabbled in painting, using colored paint to decorate the title page of his manuscript AAUG, and painting a small watercolor of Alice Liddell and her sisters (see LCA, frontispiece).

2275. Willis, Nathaniel Parker (1806–67). *The Poems: Sacred, Passionate, and Humorous: of Nathaniel Parker Willis.* (New York: Clark, Austin & Smith, 1854). 352pp. Complete edition, revised and enlarged.

Not in JS. In a letter of 23 August 1854, Dodgson notes that he had recently "bought 3 other American poets in the cheap editions, Lowell, Willis, and Holmes." This seems the most likely title, as it was frequently reprinted after its initial publication in 1844. The present edition is the closest traced to the date of Dodgson's diary entry. Willis was an American poet and editor of the *New York Mirror* and other publications.

2276. Willock, William Alexander. *The Elementary Geometry of the Right Line and Circle. With Exercises.* (London: 1875).

Not in JS. Dodgson examines this book is his *Euclid and His Modern Rivals* (123–31). Willock was a Fellow of Trinity College, Dublin.

2277. Wills, William Henry (1810–80). *Old Leaves: Gathered from Household Words.* (London: Chapman & Hall, 1860). 437pp.

A320, B1295 (author, title, date), JS2198.

Household Words was a journal produced by Charles Dickens. Wills served as business manager and editor for the journal, and also wrote several stories (including some he co-wrote with Dickens) which are published in this collection. The book also includes pieces by Dickens.

2278. Wills, William Henry, editor. *Poets' Wit and Humour Selected by W. H. Wills.* (London: Bell and Daldy, 1861 [1860]). 283pp. Illustrated with 100 engravings from drawings by Charles Bennett and George H. Thomas.

A872 (title), JS1234 (listed under Hood). The preceding title in A872 is by Hood, hence the confusion in JS1234. This is earliest edition of the only matching title in BL or BOD. A collection of humorous English verse (none by Dodgson) including works by Chaucer, Pope, Swift, Goldsmith, Burns, Southey, Coleridge, Hood, Mark Lemon, the editor himself and many others.

2279. Wilson, Andrew (1852–1912). *Leisure-Time Studies, Chiefly Biological. A Series of Essays and Lectures.* (London: Chatto and Windus, 1879 [1878]). 381pp. 2nd edition. With illustrations.

A552 (author, title), JS2199. Earliest edition traced. Wilson was a lecturer on Zoology at Edinburgh. Lectures primarily on Zoology, Comparative Anatomy, and Physiology. *Saturday Review* wrote, "Dr. Wilson's pages teem with matter stimulating to a healthy love of science and a reverence for the truths of nature."

2280. Wilson, Daniel (1816–1892). *Caliban. The Missing Link.* (London: Macmillan, 1873). 274pp. With a commentary on *The Tempest* and *A Midsummer Night's Dream.*

A906 (author, title), J2200. Only edition in BL. Wilson was born in Edinburgh but eventually moved to Toronto to take up a professorship in History and English Literature. He argues that Shakespeare anticipated Darwin's theory of evolution and that Caliban represents the missing link between modern man and his simian ancestors.

2281. Wilson, James [pseud. of Andrew Park] (1807–63). *Silent Love. A Poem.* (Paisley [Strathclyde]: Murray & Stewart, 1845). 58pp. 4th edition. Illustrated with

engravings in outline by Joseph Noël Paton.

A471 (author, title, illustrator, date), JS2201. Park was a Scottish poet. See 1507 for a note on Paton.

2282. Wilson, James M[aurice] (1836–1931). *Elementary Geometry, Books I. II. III.: Angles, Parallels, Triangles, Equivalent Figures, the Circle, and Proportion.* (London: Macmillan, 1869). 184pp. 2nd edition, revised.

Not in JS. Dodgson's copy is in WWC. It is inscribed "C. L. Dodgson Feb. 1872," and is interleaved with manuscript notes throughout. Wilson was a fellow at St. John's College, Cambridge, and, from 1859 to 1868 an assistant master at Dodgson's old school, Rugby. In 1879 he became headmaster of Clifton School. This was one of the books Dodgson examined in his *Euclid and His Modern Rivals* (70–115). He also reprints there a review of this book by Augustus De Morgan (see 551) reprinted from *The Athenæum* of 18 July 1868. See below for a much revised edition.

2283. Wilson, James Maurice. *Elementary Geometry. Books I–V. Containing the Subjects of Euclid's First Six Books: Following the Syllabus of Geometry Prepared by the Geometrical Association.* (London: Macmillan and Co., 1878). 4th edition.

Not in JS. Dodgson acquired a copy of the 1878 edition in advance of its publication from Macmillan. Dodgson was working on his *Euclid and His Modern Rivals* (1879), and wrote to Macmillan, on 31 October 1878, "If there is a new edition of Wilson's *Geometry* since 1869, with any material alterations, please send me a copy." Macmillan sent the forthcoming edition in sheets and Dodgson wrote of it, "it is almost entirely different from his former book, and will require to be reviewed separately in my treatise — thus perhaps causing further delay." (See *Macmillan.*) He treats this work at length in *Euclid and His Modern Rivals* (155–182). See 66 for the book probably referred to in the title of this work as "Syllabus Prepared by the Geometrical Association."

2284. Wilson, John Mackay (1804–35), editor and principal contributor. *Wilson's Tales of the Borders and of Scotland.* 3 vols. Edition unknown.

A727 ("Wilson's Tales of the Borders, 3 vols., 4to"), JS2202. Many 3-volume editions have been traced. Wilson was a painter turned writer. The work includes tales by many authors. In the preface to an 1857 edition, Alexander Leighton (one of the original contributors who later revised the work) wrote of Wilson's intent for this collection that "the contributions should be genuine stories, not the ordinary mixture of narrative, didactic essay, and fanciful prolusion, but tales in the proper every-day sense, with such an objectiveness as would portray, graphically and naturally, the men and women of the times, acting on the stage where they were destined to perform their strange parts, and would exclude all false colourings of a sentimental fiction, belonging to mere subjective moods of the writer's fancy or feeling. The greatest care was also taken with the moral aspect of the Tales, with the view that parents and guardians might feel a confidence that, in committing them into the hands of their children and wards, they would be imparting the means of instruction, and at the same time securing a guarantee for the growth of moral convictions."

2285. Wilson, Thomas (1663–1755). *The Sacra Privata, or, Private Meditations and Prayers of Bishop Wilson.* (Bath: R. Cruttwell, 1786). 248pp.

A755 (author, title), JS2203. Earliest edition in BL and apparently the earliest separate publication. Many new editions appeared throughout the 19th century. A likely candidate is the first Oxford edition in BL (J. H. Parker, 1838) or Parker's edition of 1840. Wilson served as Bishop to the Isle of Man for 58 years, beginning in 1697, and his *Sacra Privata* is an important work of Anglican devotion.

2286. Winn, James Michell (1808–1900). *The Collapse of Scientific Atheism.* (London: D. Bogue, 1880). 36pp. Originally published in the *Journal of Psychological Medicine.*

E123 (author, title, date), JS2204. Educated in Glasgow, Winn was a consulting physician to St. George's and St. James's Dispensary, London and practiced medicine at various times in Truro, Hampshire, and Sussex.

2287. Winslow, Forbes [Benigus] (1810–74). *On Obscure Diseases of the Brain and Disorders of the Mind; Their Incipient*

Symptoms, Pathology, etc. (London: John Churchill, 1860). 721pp. 1st edition.

JS1025 (listed under Forbes). This book was part of lot 83 at the sale of the Thomas Erwin Lewis Carroll Collection (New York, Ritter-Hopson Galleries, 15 December 1932, DAA1669). It is described in the catalogue for that sale as "with the autograph signature 'C L Dodgson Ch Ch' on the half-title." It sold again at Christie's, New York on 29 October 1998 and is now in the library of David Lansley, Lincolnshire. Winslow founded *The Journal of Psychological Medicine and Mental Pathology*, the first British psychological journal, and was one of the leading experts on psychological medicine in Victorian England. This early psychiatric study (some claim it as the first written in English) covers symptoms of insanity and introduces a number of new ideas, including diagnostic testing for psychiatric ailments. Winslow recommends the use of several drugs (including opium, morphia, and Indian hemp) to treat insanity and depression. He also repeats a common Victorian misconception — that women, at the mercy of their emotions, must have an emotional outlet to avoid mental instability.

2288. Winslow, Lyttleton Stewart Forbes (1844–1913). *On Uncontrollable Drunkenness, Considered as a Form of Mental Disorder, with the Only Possible Means of Legally Dealing with Such Cases.* (London: Henderson & Spalding, 1892). 64pp.

E137 (author, title, date), JS1024 (listed under Forbes). Winslow was the son of Winslow B. Forbes (see above) and a physician and psychologist who served as editor of the *Journal of Psychological Medicine and Medical Pathology*. He spent much of his career arguing that crime and alcoholism were caused by mental instability.

2289. Winter, William (1836–1917). *My Witness: A Book of Verse.* (Boston: James R. Osgood and Company, 1871). 128pp.

D229 (author, title, city, date), JS2205. Possibly the book CLD refers to in his diary (17 Dec. 1881), when he writes "received as a present from Mrs. Gifford ... Winter's *Poems.*" Winter was a graduate of Harvard Law School who turned to journalism and served as dramatic critic for the *New York Tribune*.

2290. Winthrop, A. T. *Wilfred. A Story with a Happy Ending.* (New York: A. D. F. Randolph & Company, 1880). 298pp.

A627, E300 (author, title, city, date), F145, JS1105 (incorrectly listed under Greenwood), JS2206. E300 and F145 note this has Dodgson's initials. Macmillan ordered this book for Dodgson in October 1889 (see *Macmillan*, 267).

2291. Wolstenholme, Joseph (1829–91). *A Book of Mathematical Problems, on Subjects Included in the Cambridge Course.* (London: Macmillan, 1867). 344pp.

E159 (author, title, date), JS2207. E159 notes "with the initials of Lewis Carroll." Wolstenholme was educated at Cambridge and was a fellow at Christ's College, Cambridge and sometime mathematical examiner.

2292. *Wonderful Invention. The Past, Present, and Future Almanack. A Permanent Calendar, etc.* (London: [1865]).

E415 (title), JS248 (Anon./Reference). E415 describes this as being in "Triptych form, cloth; with the autograph of Lewis Carroll and Ch. Ch. Oxford."

2293. *The Wonderful Magazine*. Details unknown.

Title only listed in A876/JS221 (Anon./Periodicals). Multiple volumes are not mentioned in A876, so Dodgson probably owned an odd volume of one of the following (these are the closest matches of many possibilities):

The Wonderful Magazine, and Marvellous Chronicle; or, New Repository of Wonders. (London, C. Johnson [etc., 1793–1794]). 5 volumes published.

The Wonderful Magazine of All that is Singular, Curious and Rare in Nature and Art. (London: G. Smeeton, began in 1830).

2294. Wood, Edward J. [a.k.a. Edward George Wood] (1811–96). *Curiosities of Clocks and Watches from the Earliest Times.* (London: Richard Bentley, 1866). 443pp.

A580 ("Curiosities of Clocks and Watches"), JS267 (Anon./Science). Only edition of the only matching title in BL. Edward Wood was a maker of scientific instruments and miscellaneous writer.

2295. [Wood, Henry]. *Change for the American Notes: in Letters from London to New York. By an American Lady.* (London: Wiley & Putnam, 1843). 392pp.

A667 (title, "by an American Lady"), JS834. Earliest English edition. Written in the style of a series of letters from an American lady visit-

ing England, this work is Wood's witty rebuttal to Dickens' 1842 work *American Notes* (see 573), parts of which painted America in a less than flattering light.

2296. Wood, James (1760–1839). *The Elements of Algebra: Designed for the Use of Students in the University.* (Cambridge: J. Deighton, etc., 1790).

A957 (author, title, 3 vols.), JS2209. No 3-volume edition of this work has been traced (this is the 1st edition). However, this was originally volume 1 in the larger 4-volume work *The Principles of Mathematics and Natural Philosophy* (Cambridge: Deighton, 1790–99). Perhaps Dodgson owned 3 of the 4 volumes. The other volumes were: Vol. 2, *The Principles of Fluxions* (by S. Vince); Vol. 3 *The Principles of Mechanics* (by Wood) and *The Principles of Hydrostatics* (by Vince); Vol. 4 *The Elements of Optics* (by Wood) and *Principles of Astronomy* (by Vince). See 2363 for the companion to this work.

2297. Wood, John. *Bible Anticipations of Modern Science.* (London: S. W. Partridge & Co., [1880]). 41pp.

E149 (author, title), JS2212. 1st edition. E149 states that this book is "after Dr. Gaussen," possible referring to *The Canon of the Holy Scriptures from the Double Point of View of Science and Faith*, translated from the French of Samuel Robert Louis Gaussen (1862). Wood was a writer of works primarily on finance and economics.

2298. Wood, John George (1827–89). *The Common Objects of the Sea Shore; Including Hints for an Aquarium.* (London: G. Routledge & Co., 1857). 204pp. With coloured illustrations.

Not in JS. In a letter of 14 February 1882, Dodgson wrote that he left his copy of this book at Eastbourne (*Letters*, 455). Earliest edition in BL. Wood was educated at Merton College, Oxford, and worked with Henry Acland at the Anatomical Museum. He was, for a time, a curate in Oxford. He was the author of many popular books of natural history, and toured widely lecturing on the subject.

2299. Wood, John George. *Insects at Home. Being a Popular Account of British Insects, their Structure, Habits, and Transformations.* (London: Longmans & Co.,

1872). 670pp. With upwards of 700 figures by E. A. Smith and J. B. Zwecker.

A824 (author, title), JS2210 (not listed separately from *Nature's Teachings*, see 2301). Earliest edition in BL or BOD. In his preface, Wood calls the present book "a tolerably comprehensive account of the insects which inhabit England, together with the principal details of their structure, and the most interesting incidents of their mode of life."

2300. Wood, John George. *Man and Beast Here and Hereafter. Illustrated by More than Three Hundred Original Anecdotes.* (London: David Bogue, [1882]).

A852 (author, title), JS2211. Earliest edition traced was a 2-volume edition of 1874. This is the earliest 1-volume edition traced (A852 does not specify 2 volumes). Includes accounts meant to prove that animals have afterlives, language, reason, love, and other emotional and rational traits of human beings.

2301. Wood, John George. *Nature's Teachings: Human Invention Anticipated by Nature.* (London: Daldy, Isbister & Co., 1877 [1876]). 533pp. Profusely illustrated.

A824 (author, title), JS2210 (not listed separately from *Insects at Home*, see 2299). This is the only pre–1898 edition in BL or BOD.

2302. Wood, William Spicer (1817 or 18–1902). *Problems in the New Testament. Critical Essays.* (London: Rivingtons, 1890 [1889]). 164pp.

D242 (author, title, date), JS2213. D242 notes Dodgson's initials. Wood was educated at St. John's College, Cambridge, ordained in 1874, and served as rector of Ufford.

2303. Woods, Mary A., compiler. *A First School Poetry Book.* (London: Macmillan and Co., 1886). 267pp.

E303 (editor, title, date), JS2214. Includes Dodgson's poems "The Walrus and the Carpenter," and "Ye Carpette Knyghte" reprinted with the author's permission. The compiler was headmistress of the Clifton High School for Girls.

2304. Worcester, Joseph Emerson (1784–1865). *Dictionary of the English Language.* (Boston: Brewer and Tileston, 1867). 1786pp.

Uncertain. Not in JS. In his diary for 4 April

1867, Dodgson writes, "Received from Dr. Bosworth [Joseph Bosworth (1798–1876), Professor of Anglo-Saxon at Oxford] his magnificent present *Worcester's English Dictionary*" (see *Diary 5*). Worcester published several dictionaries in his career, but this seems most likely, as it was his most successful, was published closest to the date of the gift, and, a large illustrated quarto volume, it could rightly be called magnificent. First published in 1860, this is the edition closest to Dodgson's receipt of the gift. No British editions traced. Two of Worcester's dictionaries were published in pre–1867 British editions, and these are possibilities, though less likely: *A Pronouncing, Explanatory, and Synonymous Dictionary of the English Language* (London: 1856); and *An Elementary Dictionary of the English Language* (London: [1860]). Worcester was an American lexicographer who rivaled Webster. He introduced the use of synonyms in definitions.

2305. Wordsworth, Charles (1806–92). *On Shakespeare's Knowledge and Use of the Bible.* (London: Smith, Elder, 1864). 365pp. 2nd edition.

B1227 (author, title, date), JS2221. Only edition in BL. Charles Wordsworth was nephew of the poet William Wordsworth. He was a Scottish bishop with a deep interest in reuniting the English and Scottish churches. This work is in two parts, the first discussing forms of speech and words common to Shakespeare and the Bible (in his preface, Wordsworth notes that little new is written here), and the second, the bulk of the book, dealing with Biblical allusions and religious sentiments and principles in Shakespeare.

2306. Wordsworth, Christopher (1807–85). *Is the Church of Rome the Babylon of the Book of Revelation? An Essay, Partly Derived from the Author's Lectures on the Apocalypse, etc.* (London: F. & J. Rivington, 1850). 108pp.

B1297 (author, title, date), JS2222 (listed under Charles Wordsworth). 1st edition. Christopher was the nephew of poet William Wordsworth and a conservative High Churchman. He was, at times, a vicar, headmaster, Bishop of Lincoln, hymn writer, and Greek scholar. Wordsworth answers the title question with an emphatic "yes." This essay was opposed to union with Rome. A prefatory note to a later editions states, "the writer, an High Churchman of the old school, intensely loyal to the Church of England, writes from the standpoint of sound churchmanship, intimate knowledge of ecclesiastical history and classical antiquity, and devout loyalty to the Word of God." Dodgson heard Wordsworth preach at St. Mary's Oxford on 19 March 1858.

2307. Wordsworth, Chr[istopher], editor. *The New Testament in the Original Greek: With Notes and Introductions by Chr[istopher] Wordsworth*. (London: Rivingtons, 1872–75). 4 vols. New edition.

A746 (author, title, 4 vols.), JS501 (listed under Bibles), JS2220 (listed under Charles Wordsworth). This is the only 4-volume edition in BL. Christopher's brother Charles wrote a Greek grammar, but it was Christopher who edited this Greek New Testament.

2308. Wordsworth, William (1770–1850). *Peter Bell: A Tale in Verse*. (London: Longman, Hurst, Rees, Orme, and Brown, 1819). 88pp. 1st edition.

A469 (author, title, date, editions), JS2217. According to A469, Dodgson owned 2 copies of this work, one of the 1st edition and one of the 3rd edition, also published in 1819. Poem about a potter who steals the ass of a drowned man and has spiritual experiences on the ride to tell the widow of her husband's death.

2309. Wordsworth, William. *Poems, in Two Volumes*. (London: Longman, Hurst, Rees, and Orme, 1807). 2 vols. 158, 170pp.

A450 (author, title, 2 vols., date), A495, JS2216. 1st edition. Dodgson may have owned 2 copies of this; A945 lists the same author and title in 2 volumes, but gives no date. Dodgson also owned yet another edition of Wordsworth's Poems (A369, "Wordsworth's Poems"), likely a 1-volume edition (possibly 2310, but possibly another copy of this edition). Dodgson wrote a parody of Wordsworth's poem "Resolution and Independence," called "Upon the Lonely Moor," which was published in *The Train* in 1856 and later revised into the White Knight's song in TTLG.

2310. Wordsworth [William]. *Poems of Wordsworth*. (London: Macmillan and Co., 1882). 317pp. Chosen and edited by Matthew Arnold. In the *Golden Treasury Series*.

Not in JS. Macmillan sent Dodgson a copy of this book in May 1883. On 9 October 1895 he wrote to Macmillan asking for a copy of Selections from Wordsworth, presumably the same volume (see *Macmillan* 163, 204). Originally published in 1889, this printing is the closest to the date Dodgson received his first copy. It was reprinted as late as 1888.

2311. Wordsworth, William. *The Poetical Works of William Wordsworth*. (London: George Bell & Sons, 1892–93). 7 vols. Edited with memoir by Edward Dowden. *The Aldine Edition of the British Poets*.

A365 (author, title, 7 vols.), JS2215. This is the only British 7-volume edition in BL. BL also lists a 7-volume Boston edition published by Little, Brown and Co. in 1854. Dodgson owned at least one other copy of Wordsworth's *Poetical Works*, as detailed in A547/JS2218. This entry lists only author and title, so it is not likely to be a multi-volume edition. There are many possibilities, one of the more likely being the edition edited by John Morley (London: Macmillan and Co., 1888).

2312. Wordsworth, William. *The White Doe of Rylstone, or, The Fate of the Nortons: A Poem*. (London: Longman, Hurst, Rees, Orme, and Brown, 1815). 162pp. 1st edition.

A731 (author, title, date), D244 (author, title, date, edition), JS2219. Poem about a woman who is the only survivor of a family of Catholic rebels living in the time of Queen Elizabeth. She is comforted by the appearance of a white doe whom she had raised in what was, to her, a happier time. Dodgson read the poem on 30 January 1858 and wrote in his diary "it is a pretty piece of description, not much point or interest."

2313. [**Wright**, Lucy P., afterwards Hobart-Hampden]. *The Changed Cross, and Other Religious Poems*. (London: 1870).

Not in JS. DAA987 (title, city, date), DAA2008. Dodgson's copy, with his monogram on the title page, was offered at Anderson Galleries, New York on 25–26 October 1922 and at Park-Bernet Galleries, New York on 29 November 1939. No 1870 edition traced; 1871 "New edition" published by Sampson Low, Son, and Marston, 338pp. Published in the U.S. as early as 1863.

2314. Wright, Richard Pears. *The Elements of Plane Geometry*. (London: 1871). 2nd edition.

Not in JS. Dodgson examines this book in his *Euclid and His Modern Rivals* (151–54). Wright was a teacher of mathematics at University College School, London.

2315. Wright, Thomas (1810–77). *Narratives of Sorcery and Magic, From the Most Authentic Sources.* (London: Richard Bentley, 1851). 2 vols. 349, 342pp.

A886, B1299 (author, title, date, 2 vols.), JS2223. Wright was an English writer chiefly remembered as an editor of works from the middle ages. This work is a history of magic from the 12th–17th centuries. Includes chapters on magical processes, treasure hunting, the trial and execution of witches, Matthew Hopkins, the poetry of witchcraft, Friar Bacon and Dr. Faustus, alchemy, John Dee, Lancashire witches, and witchcraft in Sweden and America.

2316. Wright, Thomas. *Womankind in Western Europe from the Earliest Times to the Seventeenth Century.* (London: Groombridge & Sons, 1869). 340pp. Illustrated with color plates and in black and white.

A580 (title), JS2224. Only edition of the only matching title in BL. In his preface, Wright writes "I have endeavoured to trace from sources which are not commonly known, and many of which are not very approachable, the history of Womankind in Western Europe, and to describe the condition, character, and manners of the sex through the various revolutions of Western society. My desire has been to give, as far as possible, a true picture of female life in each particular period." Covers the periods from the Celtic and Roman age through the beginning of the reign of Charles I.

2317. Wrigley, Alfred (1817–98). *A Collection of Examples and Problems in Pure and Mixed Mathematics, with Answers and Occasional Hints.* (London: Longman, 1859). 309pp. 5th edition.

Not in JS. Dodgson's copy with his signature on the front pastedown is in the collection of David Lansley, Lincolnshire. Wrigley was Professor of Mathematics at the Royal Military College, Addiscombe, Surrey from 1841 to 1861. See 1544 for a companion to this volume.

2318. Wu Han-ch'ên (13th century). *Laou-Seng-Urh, or, "An Heir in his Old Age." A Chinese Drama.* (London: John Murray, 1817). 115pp. Translated by Sir John F[rancis] Davis.

A320, B1113 (title, first word spelled "Laon"), JS293 (Anon./Theatre). Only edition in BL. The first translation of a Chinese drama into English. The play is a domestic drama from a 1616 collection called *Yuen-jin-pe-tchung.* The book also includes: "A brief view of the Chinese Drama, and of their Theatrical Exhibitions." Davis was a writer who lived in Canton.

2319. Xenophon (ca. 444–357 B.C.E.). *Xenophontis Oeconomicus, Apologia Socratis, Convivium Hiero, Agesilaus.* (Lipsiae: Sumtibus et Typis Caroli Tauchnitii, 1829). 208pp. Volume 5 of the works of Xenophon. Stereotype edition.

E375, JS2226. Dodgson's copy is in HAC. On the front pastedown, in brown ink is written "C. L. Dodgson, School House, Rugby. Nov. 13, 1846." On the front endpaper, Dodgson has written several versions of his name in pencil. On the verso of the front endpaper are a list of days and a sketch (perhaps of a schoolmaster) all in pencil, presumably by Dodgson. Another pencil sketch of a man, with additional faces scribbled nearby, is on the rear pastedown. All the sketches are quite crude. On the front pastedown are the words, "Dodgson is a muff," in pencil, the "Dodgson" possibly in Dodgson's hand, the rest clearly not. Following his name on the ink inscription are also the words "is a muff" in the same hand. Xenophon was a Greek author and student of Socrates. Text in Greek.

2320. Y., N. [pseud. of John Fry] (1792–1822), editor. *Pieces of Ancient Poetry, From Unpublished Manuscripts and Scarce Books.* (Bristol: Printed by J. Evans and Co., 1814). 95pp. With notes and a glossary.

A479, D145 (title, city, date, editor), JS1039 (listed under Fry). D145 notes Dodgson's initials. This edition was limited to 102 copies for subscribers. Includes poems from 17th-century manuscripts, including one by Donne, and "A Christmas Carol" from a 15th-century manuscript. Fry was a bookseller in Bristol.

2321. Yates, Edmund Hodgson (1831–94). *My Haunts and their Frequenters.* (London: David Bogue, 1854). 109pp.

Not in JS. According to his diary, Dodgson bought this book on 8 April 1856. Edmund Yates was a friend of Dickens, magazine editor, and poet, who chose the pseudonym "Lewis

Carroll" from a short list suggested by Dodgson when the latter was a contributor to *The Train* (see below). *The Athenæum* wrote, "There is more bone in this contribution to shilling light literature than we usually recognize. Some of the sketches are amusing and neatly finished off, although others read like filling up. The German practical joke is well told."

2322. Yates, Edmund [Hodgson], editor. *The Train: A First Class Magazine.* (London: Groombridge and Sons, 1856). Vols. 1–2.

A312 (title, 2 vols.), A578 (title, vol. 1), JS2227. *The Train* was published in 2 volumes per year, from January 1856 to June 1858. Dodgson made several contributions to this journal during its first two years (see LCP), and it seems likely that, as he owned only 2 volumes, they would be the first two volumes where all but two of his contributions appeared.

2323. Yonge, Charlotte Mary (1823–1901). *Heartsease; or, the Brother's Wife.* (London: John W. Parker and Son, 1855). 2 vols. 362, 379pp.

Not in JS. In his diary for 27 March 1856 Dodgson writes, "Finished *Heartsease*: the characters of Theodora and Percy are well conceived, and Violet is also clever, but the story generally wants form and incident. The fire and falling in of the coal-pit are about as much connected with the story as the accidents in a newspaper are with the leaders." Only pre–1856 edition in BL. Yonge was the author of numerous works for children and of the novel *The Heir of Redclyffe*. She edited *The Monthly Packet*, a Church of England magazine for girls to which Dodgson made many contributions (see LCP). The present book is a novel in which an officer, Arthur Martindale, first keeps his marriage to a sixteen-year-old secret from his family, then sends her into their world of aristocracy without assistance.

2324. Yonge, Charlotte Mary. *Scripture Readings for Schools and Families. With Comments.* (London & New York: Macmillan & Co., 1871–79). 5 vols.

A766 (author, title, 5 vols.), JS2228. Earliest 5-volume edition in BL.

2325. Yonge, Charlotte Mary. *The Victorian Half Century a Jubilee Book.* (London:

Macmillan, 1887). 114pp. With a portrait of the Queen.

Not in JS. In a letter to Macmillan on 25 April 1887, Dodgson writes, "Please send me, at Christ Church, Trench's *Medieval Church History* [see 2103] and *The Victorian Half-Century.*" The book was first published in 1886, but the February 1887 printing would have been the one available at the date of Dodgson's query. This celebrated Victoria's Golden Jubilee.

2326. Yonge, Frances Mary (1795–1868), compiler. *The Child's Christian Year: Hymns for Every Sunday and Holy-days, Compiled for the Use of Parochial Schools.* (Oxford & London: J. G. F. & J. Rivington, 1844). 198pp. 3rd edition. With contributions by the compiler, John Keble (who contributed the preface) and Joseph Anstice.

D43 (date, city, year), JS44 (Anon./Children's). D43 notes Dodgson's initials. This is the only title in BL that matches the particulars in D43. Frances was the mother of the children's author Charlotte M. Yonge (see 2323). John Keble became vicar of the family's parish at Hursley in 1835. He was a strong influence on the family, and his presence probably explains Frances' interest in the present project, a children's answer to Keble's popular work *The Christian Year* (see 1111).

2327. Yonge, Norman B[ond] (1829–72). *The Shadow of the Yew and Other Poems.* (London: Saunders & Otley, 1856). 208pp.

Uncertain. F168 (author, title, date), not numbered in JS. Identified as Dodgson's only by the gothic stamp. Yonge matriculated at Queen's College, Oxford in 1847.

2328. Yorke, Sydney. *The Ways of Women. A Study of their Virtues and Vices, and their Charms and Caprices.* (London: J. & R. Maxwell, [1885]). 317pp.

A588, D241 (author, title), JS2230. Only edition in BL.

2329. Yorke-Davies, Nathaniel Edward (b. 1844). *Foods for the Fat. A Treatise on Corpulency, with Dietary for Its Cure.* (London: 1890). 138pp.

E103 (title, author, date [1890]), JS796 (listed under Davies). 1890 edition not traced. BL and

BOD list only the Chatto and Windus edition of 1889. Davies was a physician and dietician.

2330. Young, Edward (1800–1890). *Pre-Raffaelitism, or A Popular Enquiry into Some Newly Asserted Principles Connected with the Philosophy, Poetry, Religion, and Revolution of Art.* (London: Longman, Brown, Green, Longmans, and Roberts, 1857). 317pp.

Not in JS. Dodgson received this book from "Miss Barnes" on 2 April 1857. On 7 April he wrote of Young in his diary, "He makes a strong case against Ruskin here and there, and proves contradictions in his writings, but I can detect neither definite aim nor method in the book. He is perpetually shifting the question, and keeps the reader in a constant state of transition, without the satisfaction of feeling that any of the questions raised have been properly settled." In dismissing the Pre-Raphaelite movement, Young wrote, "Had Pre-Raffaelitism appeared either as a peculiarity or a preference; had it been simply said that the Old Masters were good and great in their way, but times are changed, and men with not a tythe of Salvator's endowments would blush for inadvertencies everywhere traceable in his finest works; had, I say, anything like this been the drift of Mr. Ruskin's writings, we had been spared a heap of uncomfortable adjectives." Young was a member of Trinity College, Cambridge and, to quote Allibone, "leader of the anti–Ruskin party."

2331. *The Youth's Companion, or, Every Day Stories: Book for Boys with Fine Engravings.* (London: E. Lacey, [1844?]). 4 vols. in 1. 72, 72, 72, 71pp. 10 leaves of plates. Engraved title page.

E93 (title, publisher, 4 vols. in 1), JS34. Conjectural date from the catalogue of the Baldwin Collection, University of Florida. E93 describes this as "a curious, shabby, decrepit little volume … one of the "fine engravings" is after Bigg, others are either nice or quaint." Contains: "What Trade Shall I Be?," "The New Almanack," "Filial Affection," "Dialogues on Dogs," "The Wounded Sailor," "Dangers of Dutchland," "Benevolence Rewarded," "False Impressions," and "The Triumph of Innocence." Possibly one of Dodgson's childhood books.

2332. Zeta [pseud. of James Anthony Froude] (1818–94). *Shadows of the Clouds.* (London: J. Ollivier, 1847). 287pp. 1st edition.

A473 (author, title, date), JS1037. A volume of religious stories that signaled the beginning of Froude's dissatisfaction with the High Church party. For more on Froude see other works above under his name. On 14 May 1855, Dodgson wrote in his diary, "I finished reading *Shadows of the Clouds* by Froude, which I have lately had bound, after cutting out the objectionable parts of the book. Its chief fascination lies, I think, in style — the writer seems to write exactly as he thought, without even pausing to consider how to express himself."

2333. Zöllner, Johann Carl Friedrich, (1834–82). *Transcendental Physics, an Account of Experimental Investigations: From the Scientific Treatises.* (London: W. H. Harrison, 1880). 266pp. Translated by C[harles] C[arleton] Massey.

B1300 (author, title, translator, date), JS2231. Zöllner was a Professor of Physics and Astronomy at the University of Leipzig. This work is a defense of spiritualism based on "scientific" experiments. Dodgson refers to this book in a letter of 4 December 1882 (see *Letters*, 471).

MYSTERY TITLES

2334. *American Poets.* 2 vols. Details unknown.

A945 (title, 2 vols.), JS100. No 2-volume work with "American Poets" in the title has been traced. There are many such single-volume works— perhaps Dodgson owned 2 copies of one of these, or owned 2 different anthologies. Among the more likely titles are:

Hows, John W. S., editor. *Golden Leaves from the American Poets.* (London: 1866). With an introductory essay by Alexander Smith. (Dodgson definitely owned one copy of this— see 1016 and A843— but A945 could refer to another copy).

Linton, W. J., editor. *Poetry of America. Selections from one Hundred American Poets from 1776 to 1876.* (London: Bell, 1878).

Specimens of the American Poets. (London: T. & J. Allman, 1822).

Tyas, Robert, editor. *Gems from American Poets.* (London: R. Tyas, 1838). Dodgson owned another book by Tyas (see 2129)

2335. Church. *Newman's Life.*

So cited in A786/JS691, but no work matching these particulars has been traced. Possibly a reference to one or more of several articles by Richard William Church (1815–90) all of which were printed in *Occasional Papers, Selected from The Guardian, The Times, and The Saturday Review, 1846–1890.* (London: Macmillan and Co., 1897). Vol. 2 of this 2-volume work includes "Newman's 'Apologia'," "Dr. Newman on the 'Eirenicon'," "Newman's Parochial Sermons," "Cardinal Newman," "Cardinal Newman's Course," and "Cardinal Newman's Naturalness."

2336. Degrees for Women.

D232/JS400 (Anon./Women) reads: "Degrees for Women. A collection of over 40 Leaflets and Pamphlets issued during the agitation at Oxford in February and March 1896, on the above subject, with the pages from the Gazette, containing the text of the Resolutions submitted to Congregation. Mr. Dodgson's own copies, many docketed in his handwriting, in a packet labeled by him, 'Degrees, &c., for Women, March 1896.'" Dodgson contributed his pamphlet *Resident Women Students* (WMGC, #281; *Oxford*, #66) to this debate. He mentions an argument put forth by J. L. Strachan-Davidson, member of Balliol College, but no copy of a pamphlet by that author has been traced.

2337. The Descendants of Conan of Glenochie and Tartans.

So stated in A524/JS86 (Anon./History). The exact spelling is not certain, since this is a handwritten entry. No such title, nor any similar title has been traced.

2338. Domestic Economy.

So listed in A309/JS234 (Anon./Reference), but no further details given. There are scores of possibilities in various sources. While most deal with the art of homemaking, an intriguing possibility is: Lemon, Mark. *Domestic Economy: A Farce.* (London). No date traced for this 14pp. pamphlet. Lemon was one of the founders of *Punch*.

2339. Dudgeon, Robert Ellis. Rational Medicine. (1878).

So listed in E132/JS958, but no work fitting this description has been located. Possibly an unrecorded pamphlet (E132 describes the binding as paper). Dudgeon translated Samuel Hahnemann's work *Organon der Rationellen Heilkunde* as early as 1849, and that work was usually published (in its many editions) as *Organon of Medicine*, but it could be translated *Organon of Rational Medicine* (a 1913 edition gives the title as *Organon of Rational Healing*). If E132 is not a pamphlet, it could be a copy of this translation with the cover title "Rational Medicine."

2340. Fashion Book, with colored plates. 2 vols.

So listed in A576/JS29. No matching title traced. Possible a reference to a Victorian fashion periodical (this seems especially likely as the other item in A576 is a collection of pieces from 2 other periodicals). A likely candidate is *The Ladies' Book of Fashion* (nos. 1–6, 1858–59 listed in BL).

2341. Folk-Lore.

In a letter to Arthur Frost (16 June 1884) Dodgson writes, "The book on Folk-Lore, which you said you would send, has not yet appeared." On 5 August, he wrote that the book had arrived safely. Dodgson owned several books on folk-lore (see index), but there is no indication if this is one of those catalogued above or another title (see *Illustrators*, 86, 89). Cohen and Wakeling suggest *Folk-Lore* by Michael Aislabie Denham (1858) (Denham actually published two works under that general title that year).

2342. Great Plague of London.

So listed in A319/JS88. No precisely matching titles traced. The best match is Boghurst, William. *Loimographia. An Account of the Great Plague of London in the Year 1665. Now First Printed from the British Museum Sloane MS. 349.* (London: Epidemiological Society of London, 1894). Edited by Joseph Frank Payne. Another possibility is that this is a copy of Daniel DeFoe's *Journal of the Plague Year*, which was frequently published in the 19th century under the title *The History of the Great Plague in London, in the Year 1665.*

2343. Greek Concordance.

A747. The entry in A747 is rather cryptic. In its entirety it reads "Grimm's Lexicon, Novi Testamenti and Greek Concordance." It is unclear whether this refers to a single item (see 833) or two items (the first two titles paraphrase the title of 833, which is not a concordance but a lexicon). If these are 2 separate items, the most likely candidates for the 2nd are (earliest BL editions listed):

Bullinger, Ethelbert. *A Critical Lexicon and Concordance to the English and Greek New Testament, together with an Index of Greek*

Words and Several Appendices. (London: Longmans & Co., 1877).

Hudson, Charles F. *A Critical Greek and English Concordance of the New Testament.* (London: S. Bagster & Sons, 1882). 2nd edition.

Wigram, George, assisted by William Burgh. *The Englishman's Greek Concordance of the New Testament.* (London: Central Tract Depôt, 1839).

Williams, John. *A Concordance to the Greek Testament: with the English Version to each Word, the Principal Hebrew Roots Corresponding to the Greek Words of the Septuagint.* (London: The Author, 1767).

Young, Robert. *Twofold Concordance to the New Testament. Concordance to the Greek New Testament together with a Concordance and Dictionary of Bible Words and Synonyms.* (Edinburgh: G. A. Young & Co., 1884).

2344. Hazlitt. *Fairy Mythology of Shakespeare.*

So listed in A877/JS1169, but no such book has been traced. Certainly the essayist William Hazlitt wrote no book or essay with this title. The closest work by that author is the 1875 book *Fairy Tales, Legends and Romances, Illustrating Shakespeare and Other Early English Writers.* The only work in BL or BOD that matches the title in A877 is by Alfred Trübner Nutt, but was not published until 1900.

2345. Hogarth. *On the Will.*

So listed in A555 (JS1211), but no work of this or any similar title by a Hogarth has been located.

2346. Howitt, Mary Botham (1799–1888). *Sketches of a Literary Life.*

Not in JS. Dodgson's diary for 12 January 1856 notes, "I met with a curious anecdote in Mary Howitt's *Sketches of a Literary Life*" and goes on to describe a story about Longfellow seeing the ghost of George Washington (see *Diary 2*). No book or essay by Howitt by this title has been traced. Howitt was a prolific author and translator known especially for her poems and stories for children (including the poem "Will you Walk into my Parlour," parodied in AAIW).

2347. Jameson. *Bible Glossary.*

So listed in A771/JS1296, but no such book has been traced by either Jameson or Jamieson. The closest matches found are:

Jamieson, Robert and E. H. Bickersteth. *The Holy Bible; With a Devotional and Practical Commentary.* (London and New York: James S. Virtue, 1861–65). 3 vols.

Booker, John. *A Scripture & Prayer Book Glossary; Being an Explanation of Obsolete Words and Phrases.* (Dublin: Hodges, Smith & Co., 1856).

Lumby, Joseph Rawson. *A Glossary of Difficult, Ambiguous, or Obsolete Bible Words, Illustrated from English Writers Contemporary with the Authorised Version.* (London: Christian Knowledge Society, [1880]).

Mayhew, Anthony Lawson. *A Select Glossary of Bible Words: Also a Glossary of Important Words and Phrases in the Prayer Book.* (London: Eyre & Spottiswoode, [1891]).

2348. Jones, T. Percy [pseud. of William Edmondstone Aytoun]. *Poems.* (1854). 1st edition.

So listed in A460/JS1322, but no such book has been traced. Aytoun published no book in the 19th century under the title *Poems*, nor does CBEL or any other standard source list an 1854 edition of any work by him with the word "Poems" in the title. His most popular book, and the most likely match, was *Lays of the Scottish Cavaliers and Other Poems* (see 82). Blackwood published editions in 1853 and 1856.

2349. *Marriage Rights.*

So listed in A319/JS94 (Anon./Law), but no book by this title has been located. Possibly a reference to Hamilton, Lady Augusta: *Marriage Rites, Customs, and Ceremonies, or All Nations of the Universe.* (London: Printed for Chapple and Son, etc.; Bath: E. Barrett, 1822).

2350. *Medical Essays.*

So listed in A513/JS168, but no additional information given. BL, together with other major sources, offers dozens of possibilities. Narrowing the field to even a few is impossible without further information.

2351. Morris, Lewis. *The Place and Function of Poetry in Education.* [1881].

So listed in E167/JS1556, where it is described as "a very scarce booklet." This is certainly true as no copy is listed in BL, BOD, or NUC or any of the libraries of the University of Wales, of which Morris was active in the establishment. This title also not listed in CBEL. E167 describes Dodgson's copy as "presentation to Mrs. Margaret Seward from E. Nicholson."

2352. *Original Nature and Use of Wine.*

So listed in A920/JS398 (Anon./Wine), but no such title has been traced. Quite likely this refers to: Ellis, Charles, of Richmond. *The Origin, Nature, and History of Wine: Its Use as a Beverage, Lawful and Needful to Civilized Man: A Lecture.* (London: F. S. Ellis; Richmond: J. Hiscoke and J. Darnill, 1861). 56pp. This is the only similar title traced.

2353. Rathmann, Hermann. *Medulla Patrum, hoc est Consensus Harmoniacus Patrum a M. Hermanno Rathmanno.* (1555).

So described in B1138/JS1720, but no copy of this book has been traced and there are clearly errors in the description. Hermann Rathmann lived from 1585 to 1628, so clearly the date 1555 is incorrect (the fact that the book sold for only 3 shillings also argues against its being 16th-century). The only closely matching title traced is Abraham Scultetus' *Medulla Theologiae Patrum* (earliest edition recorded in NUC is 1598), but no edition of the book matching any of the particulars in B1138 has been located.

2354. *Schundii Concordantiae*.

So stated in A952/JS386 (Anon./Unclassified), but no such title traced. This could refer to one of the several editions of this work (this is the earliest citation in BL):

Schmidii, Erasmi. *Novi Testamenti Jesu Christi Græci hoc est Originalis Linguæ ... Aliis Concordantiæ ita Concinnatum, ut et Loca Reperiendi, et Vocum Veras Significationes et Significationum Diversitates per Collationem Investigandi, Ducis Instar esse Possit.* (Gothæ & Lipsiæ: 1717).

2355. *Secret Society*. 2 vols.

So stated in A304/JS387 (Anon./Unclassified), but no 2-volume work containing the phrase "Secret Society" in its title has been traced. Sophia Elizabeth De Morgan wrote a book for children called *The Secret Society* which was first published in a collection and then by Cassell in 1866 in a volume with a story by Jacob Abbott. Other titles with the phrase "Secret Society" published before 1898 include:

A Glimpse of the Great Secret Society (London: William Macintosh, 1872), a book about Jesuits.

Pott, Constance Mary Fearon. *Francis Bacon and his Secret Society* (London: S. Low, Marston & Company, Limited, 1891).

2356. *Selection from Fortnightly and Contemporary*.

So listed in A576/JS134, but no matching book has been traced. Probably a bound volume of selections from the *Fortnightly* and *Contemporary Reviews*. Dodgson's article "Some Popular Fallacies about Vivisection" appeared in *The Fortnightly Review* on 1 June 1875 (see WMGC, #105a).

2357. *Sermons and Charges*. 8 vols.

So listed in A760/JS327 (Anon./Theology). No 8-volume work by this title has been located. The entry in A760, which states "8 vols., bound," implies that this is a collection of sermons and charges by various authors.

2358. *The Shining Waif and Other Tales*.

So listed in A653/JS137 (Anon./Literature), but no book by this or any similar title has been traced.

2359. *Songs of Faith*.

So listed in A869/JS330 (Anon./Theology). The only matching title traced is *Songs of Faith* (Cleveland: Brainard, 1876), which seems unlikely. The only other possibility in BL, which also seems unlikely because of its non-matching title, is Chapman, Lavinia Elizabeth. *Songs of Faith, Hope, and Joy. Founded on the Prophecies, Given from 1792, by Joanna Southcott.* [1835].

2360. *Supernatural Illustrations*.

So stated in A904/JS188 (Anon./Occult), but no such title traced. The only reasonable possibility traced is: Begbie, Peter James (d. 1864). *Supernatural Illusions.* (London: T. C. Newby, 1851). 2 vols. A904 does not specify 2 vols. but this may be an oversight, or, if this is the correct item, perhaps Dodgson had only 1 of the 2 volumes in his library at the time of his death.

2361. *The White Lady of Rose Mount*.

So listed in A626/JS2208, but no book by this title has been traced. The most likely match among traced books is: [Woltmann, Karoline] (1782–1847). *The White Lady: A Romance.* (London: J. Burns, 1845). Translated by James D. Haas. Might someone transcribing a list of book have heard "of Rose Mount" for "A Romance"? Another edition of Woltmann's story was published under the title *The White Lady and Undine, Tales from the German* [the latter title by F. H. C. La Motté Fouqué]. (London: Pickering, 1844). Translated by Caroline Lavinia Lyttleton. A less likely candidate is B[eaumont], T[homas] W[entworth]. *The White Lady. A Legend of Artagh.* (London: Manning & Smithson, 1837).

ADDENDA

2362. [**Keble**, John]. *Lyra Innocentium: Thoughts in Verse on Christian Children, Their Ways, and Their Privileges.* (Oxford: J. H. Parker, 1846). 353pp.

Not in JS. DAA2059 (title, city, date). Dodgson's copy was offered at G. A. Baker & Co., New York on 5 May 1942. It was described thus: "Lewis Carroll's copy with his initials on the fly leaf. After his death it was left to a member of his family whose signature is also present on the fly leaf, with the date of Carroll's death."

2363. Lund, Thomas (1805–77). *Companion to Wood's Algebra.* (London: 1852). 2nd edition.

Not in JS. DAA1132 (author, title, city, date). Dodgson's copy was offered at Sotheby's London on 25–26 April 1927. It had his signature on the front cover. Also on the cover was the name "M. Dodgson, 1898," perhaps indicating that it passed to another member of the family after his death in January, 1898. Lund was a fellow and Sadlerian Lecturer of St. John's College, Cambridge. Published in 1848 by J. & J. J. Deighton, Macmillan, etc. as *A Companion to Wood's Algebra, Containing Solutions of Various Questions and Problems in Algebra, and Forming a Key to the Chief Difficulties Found in the Collection of Examples Appended to Wood's Algebra, 12th Edition.* See 2296 for the book to which this was a companion.

2364. [**More**, Hannah]. *The Story of Sinful Sally. The Hampshire Tragedy. The Bad Bargain, and Robert and Richard.* (London: J. Evans & Son, Printers to the Cheap Repository for Moral and Religious Thought, [n.d., ca. 1800]). 16pp.

Not in JS. A copy in Berg has Dodgson's monogram at the head of the title page in purple ink. The property label is on p. 3. Two of the stories are described thus: "Shewing how from being Sally of the Green she was first led to become Sinful Sally, and afterwards Drunken Sal, and how at last she came to a most melancholy and almost hopeless end, being therein a warning to all young women both in Town and Country"; and "Shewing how a servant maid first robbed her master, and was afterwards struck dead for telling a lie. A True story."

2365. [**Primrose**, Archibald Philip], Lord Rosebery. (1847–1929). *Pitt.* (London: Macmillan, 1891). 297pp. In the *Twelve English Statesmen* series.

Not in JS. Dodgson's copy survives in a private collection and is inscribed, "To C. L. Dodgson from the Author's second daughter. August 1894." The daughter was Lady Margaret "Peggy" Etrenne Hannah Primrose (1881–1967). The author was the 5th Earl of Rosebery. He was educated at Christ Church, where he matriculated in 1866, but was sent down in 1868 because he insisted on keeping a racing stud. He was active in political affairs, serving as foreign secretary in Gladstone's government and eventually serving briefly as prime minister (he was, in fact, the only sitting prime minister ever to win the Derby). A biography of William Pitt (1759–1806) a distant relative of the author. Dodgson knew Lord Roseberry, for he wrote to him in 1893 (*Letters*, 998) presenting books to him and his daughters. He visited Lord Roseberry in June 1894 and finally met, "my hitherto unseen friends, Sybil and Peggy," the Earl's daughters.

Name Index

References are to entry numbers

357

SUBJECT INDEX

References are to entry numbers

Absolution 368
Acoustics 2233
Acrostic 1514
Actors and acting 166, 596, 1216
Aesthetics 541
Africa 1712, 1978
Alcohol 820, 1642, 1851, 2000, 2070, 2194, 2288
Alexandrian manuscript 84
Algebra 181, 666, 1556, 1571, 1620, 1671, 1759, 1793, 2198, 2296, 2363
Alice books: advertisements for 1490; allusions to 55; binding 1501, 1137; birthday book 1196; dramatizations 402, 524, 729–30, 888; excerpts from 780, 792, 918, 1557, 2303; imitations of 83, 253, 383, 951, 982, 1031, 1049, 1397, 1463, 1639, 1704, 2214; influences on 1280, 1284; mentions of 709, 1186, 1866
Allegories 10, 940, 1375
Allusions 234
Almanacs 369, 552, 972–74, 1573, 2224, 2236, 2292
Alphabets 720
America 573, 890, 2116, 2295
Americas, native population 363
Anatomy 127, 135, 703, 815, 1169, 2087, 2233
Angling 539, 1069, 2188
Animal stories 251, 322
Animals 40, 529, 757, 853, 879, 1144, 1149, 1616, 2300; minds of 1235, 1686, 2069, 2209; see also zoology and individual species
Aphorisms 446, 764
Arabic 536, 1105
Architecture 541, 1645, 1744–45
Army 200, 1421
Art 608, 860, 1010, 1053–56, 1169, 1207, 1351, 1476, 1507–1508, 1557, 1630, 1708–1709, 1723–27,

1731–32, 1734–36, 1738, 1787, 1972, 2095, 2131, 2134, 2219, 2330; see also painting; sculpture, etc.
Art and antique agency catalogue 4–8
Aryan civilization 109
Assent 1432
Astrology 1234, 2233
Astronomy 236, 561, 641, 749, 1083, 1246, 1381, 1491, 1516, 1578, 1580–83, 1935, 2265
Atlases 69, 1085, 1224, 1457, 1546, 1928
Australia 737
Austria 482

Baptism 10, 609
Bath 119
Bathing-machines 742
Beauty 541, 1991, 2136, 2174
Beaver 1396
Belgium 1948
Bible 151–52, 154, 159, 2249, annotated 184; apocryphal books 339, 971, 1192, 1984; authority of 1289; chronology 702; coincidences in 187; commentary 297, 518, 998, 1098, 1162, 1290, 2118, 2128, 2303 (see also individual books); concordance 506, 2117, 2354; criticism 1900; dictionary of 334, 1895; diseases of 142; for all people 672; glossary 194, 2347; Greek 26–27, 84, 117, 153, 155, 1240, 1774, 1861, 2307; guide to 39, 110, 628, 1002; Hebrew 156; history of 158; language of 535; lessons from 2084, 2324; and modern thought 161; moral difficulties 936; Polyglot 157; Revised Version 292, 518, 1382, 1899; and science 276; sources and inspiration 158, 193, 424,

698, 1763–64, 1859, 1898–99, 1998; witness of 1662
Billiards 1363
Biographical dictionaries 13, 722–24, 898, 950, 2173, 2195
Birds 9
Blackwell catalogue 3
Blindness 1165
Book of Common Prayer 394, 449; Annotated 185; glossary 194; history of 522; in Latin 450
Book register 8
Bookkeeping 856
Books 1186
Botany 95, 544, 762, 836–37, 1078, 1159, 1258, 1559–62, 1913, 3019, 2233; see also trees
Bounty, H.M.S. 183
Boyhood 404, 1013
Bristol 119
Brooks catalogue 3, 8–9
Buddhism 475; Esoteric 1852

Calculus 195, 554, 1175, 1571, 2092, 2199
California 1955
Cambridge 97, 339–40, 631, 746, 1346, 1555, 2088, 2108
Canterbury 344
Cards, playing 990, 1017, 1661
Carpentry 81
Cartoons 3, 2022–23, 2097
Casuistry 1319, 2017
Catachisms 1621, 2230
Cats 372
Cévennes 1958
Charities 341
Chastity 941, 1563
Cheltenham 119
Chemistry 178, 538, 695, 1089, 1352, 1753
Chess 251, 673, 1936–37, 2178
Children: conversion of 859; in literature and art 1787; portraits of 693

371